Good Manufacturing Practices for Pharmaceuticals

DRUGS AND THE PHARMACEUTICAL SCIENCES
A Series of Textbooks and Monographs

Series Executive Editor
James Swarbrick
PharmaceuTech, Inc.
Pinehurst, North Carolina

Recent Titles in Series

Pharmaceutical Extrusion Technology, Second Edition, Isaac Ghebre-Sellassie, Charles E. Martin, Feng Zhang, and James Dinunzio

Biosimilar Drug Product Development, Laszlo Endrenyi, Paul Declerck, and Shein-Chung Chow

High Throughput Screening in Drug Discovery, Amancio Carnero

Generic Drug Product Development: International Regulatory Requirements for Bioequivalence, Second Edition, Isadore Kanfer and Leon Shargel

Aqueous Polymeric Coatings for Pharmaceutical Dosage Forms, Fourth Edition, Linda A. Felton

Good Design Practices for GMP Pharmaceutical Facilities, Second Edition, Terry Jacobs and Andrew A. Signore

Handbook of Bioequivalence Testing, Second Edition, Sarfaraz K. Niazi

Generic Drug Product Development: Solid Oral Dosage Forms, Second Edition, edited by Leon Shargel and Isadore Kanfer

Drug Stereochemistry: Analytical Methods and Pharmacology, Third Edition, edited by Krzysztof Jozwiak, W. J. Lough, and Irving W. Wainer

Pharmaceutical Powder Compaction Technology, Second Edition, edited by Metin Çelik

Pharmaceutical Stress Testing: Predicting Drug Degradation, Second Edition, edited by Steven W. Baertschi, Karen M. Alsante, and Robert A. Reed

Pharmaceutical Process Scale-Up, Third Edition, edited by Michael Levin

Sterile Drug Products: Formulation, Packaging, Manufacturing and Quality, Michael J. Akers

Freeze-Drying/Lyophilization of Pharmaceutical and Biological Products, Third Edition, edited by Louis Rey and Joan C. May

Good Manufacturing Practices for Pharmaceuticals

Seventh Edition

Edited by

Graham P. Bunn

CRC Press
Taylor & Francis Group
Boca Raton London New York

CRC Press is an imprint of the
Taylor & Francis Group, an **informa** business

CRC Press
Taylor & Francis Group
6000 Broken Sound Parkway NW, Suite 300
Boca Raton, FL 33487-2742

First issued in paperback 2021

© 2019 by Taylor & Francis Group, LLC
CRC Press is an imprint of Taylor & Francis Group, an Informa business

No claim to original U.S. Government works

ISBN-13: 978-1-4987-3206-2 (hbk)
ISBN-13: 978-1-03-217838-7 (pbk)
DOI: 10.1201/9781315120669

Publisher's Note

The publisher has gone to great lengths to ensure the quality of this reprint but points out that some imperfections in the original copies may be apparent.

Library of Congress Cataloging-in-Publication Data

Names: Bunn, Graham P., editor.
Title: Good manufacturing practices for pharmaceuticals / [edited by] Graham P. Bunn.
Description: Seventh edition. | Boca Raton, Florida : CRC Press, 2019. | Includes bibliographical references and index.
Identifiers: LCCN 2018042994| ISBN 9781498732062 (hardback : alk. paper) | ISBN 9781315120669 (ebook)
Subjects: LCSH: Pharmaceutical industry--Quality control. | Drugs--Standards--United States.
Classification: LCC RS189 .W57 2019 | DDC 338.4/76151--dc23
LC record available at https://lccn.loc.gov/2018042994

Visit the Taylor & Francis Web site at
http://www.taylorandfrancis.com

and the CRC Press Web site at
http://www.crcpress.com

Contents

Preface

This book is dedicated to my dad, Roy Bernard Bunn, of Wymondham, Norfolk, England. Without his encouragement to "Do what you love and love what you do," I would not be writing chapters in this book today. Pharmacy, medicines, quality, and most of all patient focus have been my entire career, and I would not change anything.

There have been many changes in the world of pharmacy since I started making medicinal products in the Norfolk and Norwich hospital pharmacy during the early 1970s. The changes include advances in pharmacology, discovery of new treatments, and changes in manufacturing processes technologies, with significant increase supporting documentation requirements.

Building on the vast information and reputation of original authors and further developed in the 6th edition edited by Joe Nally, I have taken the opportunity to reorganize this 7th edition to collate the related regulation parts. In addition to the core regulatory chapters, I have added new related chapters (Chapters 3, 19, 23, and 24) to provide readers with additional insight and supporting information. These new chapters include the current regulatory focus for Management Responsibility and Control, Microbiological Aspects of Pharmaceutical Aseptic Processing in the Compounding Pharmacy, Worldwide Good Manufacturing Practices, and Data Integrity and Fundamental Responsibilities. In addition, FDA regulatory inspections and enforcements have been refocused into three new chapters by the contributions from Alson and Bird LLP, Washington Attorneys.

I am privileged to have worked with many distinguished colleagues with outstanding expertise and experience in pharmaceuticals, quality, and regulatory compliance. My special thanks goes to the authors for their time and contributions to this book from over 360 years of experience and making this an exceptional 7th edition. Thank you; I am forever in your debt.

From the FDA website:

A drug is defined as:

- A substance recognized by an official pharmacopoeia or formulary.
- A substance intended for use in the diagnosis, cure, mitigation, treatment, or prevention of disease.
- A substance (other than food) intended to affect the structure or any function of the body.
- A substance intended for use as a component of a medicine but not a device or a component, part or accessory of a device.
- Biological products are included within this definition and are generally covered by the same laws and regulations, but differences exist regarding their manufacturing processes (chemical process versus biological process).

And as noted in Sec. 210.1, "Status of current good manufacturing practice regulations":

(a) The regulations set forth in this part and in parts 211, 225, and 226 of this chapter contain the minimum current good manufacturing practice for methods to be used in, and the facilities or controls to be used for, the manufacture, processing, packing, or holding of a drug to assure that such drug meets the requirements of the act as to *safety*, and has the *identity* and *strength* and meets the *quality* and *purity* characteristics that it purports or is represented to possess.
(b) The failure to comply with any regulation set forth in this part and in parts 211, 225, and 226 of this chapter in the manufacture, processing, packing, or holding of a drug shall render such drug to be adulterated under section 501(a)(2)(B) of the act and such drug, as well as the person who is responsible for the failure to comply, shall be subject to regulatory action.

Objectives of the pharmaceutical business include producing drugs for patients and use by health-care professionals meeting broad requirements in a global competitive market place while keeping up with regulatory requirements and interpretations. The consequences for not being in adequate compliance can be far-reaching regulatory actions.

This business is challenging from a science and technology approach, and compliance with ever-evolving regulations adds additional complexity. No one has ever said that this business had an easy job to comply with requirements, but then that's what continuously challenges us every day.

As mentioned in the 6th edition of this book by Joe Nally (editor), and again here, pharmaceutical current good manufacturing practice (CGMP) compliance will never slow up its pace of evolution, as there are always external influences to challenge the industry. The FDA continues to evolve and develop its approach to regulating manufacturers, regulatory requirements and global harmonization of quality standards. Technological advancements do not wait for the industry but as a supporting business continue to provide new opportunities for the enhancement of regulatory compliance. The FDA evaluates these advancements for compliance with regulatory requirements and periodically issues further clarification through "Guidance for Industry" documents. Readers are encouraged to register for updates to existing and new documents from the FDA website. As noted in "Guidance for Industry 'Emerging Technology Applications for Pharmaceutical Innovation and Modernization' September 2017": "FDA continues to support flexible approaches in the manufacturing of quality pharmaceutical products. While the implementation of emerging technology is critical to advancing product design, modernizing pharmaceutical manufacturing, and improving quality, FDA also recognizes that the adoption of innovative approaches may represent challenges to industry and the Agency."

Changes in the sourcing of materials, especially active pharmaceutical ingredients and finished products to overseas companies and/or subsidiaries in other countries continues to increase the need for FDA inspections worldwide. The Government Accountability Agency noted in the December 2016 report to the Committee on Energy and Commerce, "Drug Safety: FDA Has Improved Its Foreign Drug Inspection Program, but Needs to Assess the Effectiveness and Staffing of Its Foreign Offices":

a. Globalization has complicated FDA's oversight of drugs marketed in the United States. FDA reports that more than 40% of finished drugs and 80% of active pharmaceutical ingredients are produced overseas. FDA inspects drug manufacturing establishments to ensure that the safety and quality of drugs are not jeopardized by poor manufacturing practices. Beginning in 2008, FDA established foreign offices to obtain better information on products coming from overseas and perform inspections, among other things.

b. The number of foreign inspections has consistently increased each year since fiscal year 2009. Beginning in fiscal year 2015, FDA conducted more foreign than domestic inspections. FDA has also improved the accuracy and completeness of information on its catalog of drug establishments subject to inspection. It has also reduced its catalog of drug establishments with no inspection history to 33% of foreign establishments, compared to 64% in 2010. However, the number of such establishments remains large, at almost 1,000 of the approximately 3,000 foreign establishments. FDA plans to inspect all of these establishments over the next 3 years.

On August 23, 2017, a milestone agreement was reached between the FDA, European Commission, and European Medicines Agency as noted below from the EMA website:

The European Commission (EC), the United States (US) Food and Drug Administration (FDA), and the European Medicines Agency (EMA) have signed a new confidentiality commitment that allows the US regulator to share non-public and commercially confidential information, including trade secret information relating to medicine inspections with EU regulators. This confidentiality commitment is a milestone in the ongoing implementation of the mutual recognition of inspections of medicine manufacturers, and it aims to strengthen the EU-US relationship. Ultimately it will contribute to a more efficient use of inspection resources by regulators for the protection of human and animal health.

The EU and the US have had confidentiality arrangements in place since 2003, allowing for the exchange of confidential information as part of their regulatory and scientific processes. However, complete exchange of information was not possible under these arrangements.

The new confidentiality commitment formally recognises that FDA's EU counterparts have the authority and demonstrated ability to protect the relevant information. This step now allows the sharing of full inspection reports, allowing regulators to make decisions based on findings in each other's inspection reports and to make better use of their inspection resources to focus on manufacturing sites of higher risk.

The most significant FDA regulatory action focus areas since the last edition of this book have been in data integrity, aseptic technique, and those relating to compounding pharmacies. Data integrity is covered in a new chapter (Chapter 24, "Data Integrity and Fundamental Responsibilities") with unique perspectives contributed by two leading experts. The other two focus areas are linked, but consistent compliance requirements for aseptic technique continues to be a significant challenge for pharmaceutical companies and major pharma and relates to the significant reliance on operators (see Chapter 4, "Organization and Personnel"). A new chapter (Chapter 19, "Microbiological Aspects of Pharmaceutical Aseptic Processing in the Compounding Pharmacy") was identified and contributed by a leading microbiologist with extensive experience in this area and in the remediation of these regulatory actions.

Data integrity is not new, the basis of which are in the daily-use standard operating procedure (SOP) of every regulated business submitting data and information to FDA for application approval. Advances in technology created a need for the regulations defined in 21 CFR 211, Electronic Records; Electronic Signatures, initially made official March 20, 1997. The FDA and other regulatory agencies detected further data integrity issues leading to the issuance of the draft Guidance for Industry, "Data Integrity and Compliance with CGMP" in April 2016 and together with worldwide regulatory agencies have continued to develop the regulatory requirements and expectations through ongoing assessments.

With reference to compounding pharmacies: FDA reported on its website that "In October 2012, the United States faced the most serious outbreak associated with contaminated compounded drugs in recent history. A pharmacy in Massachusetts shipped compounded drugs that were contaminated with a fungus throughout the country, and these drugs were injected into patients' spines and joints. More than 750 people in 20 states developed fungal infections, and more than 60 people died. Approximately 14,000 patients received injections from the lots of contaminated drug product." See 2012 "Fungal Meningitis Outbreak: Persons with Fungal Infections Linked to Steroid Injections, by State, Centers for Disease Control and Prevention" for more information. As a result, on November 27, 2013, the Drug Quality and Security Act (DQSA) was signed into law. Title 1 of the new law, the Compounding Quality Act, requires compliance of compounding pharmacies with CGMPs, Section 501(a)(2)(B).

I have retained with due reference some of the wording used in the 6th edition of this book by Joe Nally because it still holds true today 40 years after its inception:

...since 1978 the discussions, arguments and debates continue over mainly the intent and "how to" of GMP compliance. This all goes back to the original 1978 regulations and the intent of Congress. They intended that the agency (FDA) determine what constitutes current or the "C" in CGMP, based on their experience. The Congress also interpreted current as not necessarily widely prevalent. They did not require that a majority of manufacturers had to be following a practice before it was accepted as current. If a practice was shown to be feasible and valuable in assuring drug quality it could be considered current. This is what makes life in Pharmaceutical operations and CGMP compliance interesting.

For those professionals considering pharmaceuticals as a career, take a good look because it offers countless opportunities to develop and apply your creative thoughts, skills, and expertise. When you think you know it all, there is always more to do and learn as science combines with evolving regulatory compliance requirements. You will be challenged by "What if...?" and "How do you know...?" and that's what is on many minds at the end of the day and drives us getting up each morning, as each day has more challenges and problems to be solved.

The industry will continue to need people, good people, those who are passionate about what they do and want to contribute to the health and wellbeing of the patient. Remember someone, somewhere at 1:50 a.m. needs the product that you manufactured, your colleague tested, another QA-reviewed the batch record, materials management shipped with a label that I approved, and we all, with many others, ensured it met its safety, quality, identity, potency, and strength.

It's a reality when a patient says, "Without my medications I would not be able to carry out my typical day-to-day routines; I would have to rely on more assistance from others." — Maria Elsey, Registered General Nurse.

Graham P. Bunn

Editor

Graham P. Bunn is the president of GB Consulting LLC, in Pennsylvania, a company providing regulatory compliance, quality systems, regulatory action remediation, training and technical consulting services for pharmaceutical, biotechnology and other FDA and European Medicines Agency (EMA)-related industries. Before founding GB Consulting LLC, Graham gained broad good manufacturing practices (GMP) and FDA inspection experience through his work in the pharmaceutical industry, including working for SmithKline Beecham PLC (GlaxoSmithKline PLC), Wyeth Pharmaceuticals (Pfizer), and Astra Merck Inc. (AstraZeneca PLC). His career experience includes management positions and responsibilities as a corporate quality auditor and in quality assurance, validation, and clinical trials manufacturing and packaging. He has developed and facilitated numerous highly interactive learning and training workshops worldwide. Graham is also the author of several book chapters and journal articles. A member of the Regulatory Affairs Professional Society (RAPS). Graham received a BSc in pharmacy from Brighton University, England, and an MSc in quality assurance and regulatory affairs from Temple University, in Philadelphia.

Contributors

Andrew Acker
AQAC, Inc.
Wake Forest, North Carolina

Graham P. Bunn
GB Consulting LLC
Berwyn, Pennsylvania

Cathy L. Burgess
Alston & Bird LLC
Washington, District of Columbia

Joseph T. Busfield
Pharmaceutical Technical Services
Warrington, Pennsylvania

Robert Del Ciello
Northshire Associates
Martinsville, New Jersey

Joanna B. Gallant
JGTA, LLC
Hollis, New Hampshire

Randy Hightower
Hightower Consulting Services Inc.
Acworth, Georgia

Alex M. Hoinowski
Hoinowski Consulting, LLC
Annandale, New Jersey

Daniel G. Jarcho
Alston & Bird LLC
Washington, District of Columbia

Justin Mann
Alston & Bird LLC
Washington, District of Columbia

Dawn McIver
MicroWorks, Inc.
Crown Point, Indiana

Joseph C. Near
J Charles Consulting LLC
Apex, North Carolina

Seth Olson
Alston & Bird LLC
Washington, District of Columbia

Dominic Parry
Inspired Pharma Training Ltd.
Berkshire, United Kingdom

Michele Pruett
MLP Gxp Solutions LLC, Inc.
Durham, North Carolina

Irwin Silverstein
IBS Consulting in Quality LLC
Piscataway, New Jersey

John E. Snyder
John Snyder & Company Inc.
Denton, Texas

David Stephon
David Stephon Consulting
Reinholds, Pennsylvania

Jocelyn A. Zephrani
Quality Initiatives Inc.
Ontario, Canada

1 Status and Applicability of U.S. Regulations *CGMP*

Graham P. Bunn

CONTENTS

The Food and Drug Administration (FDA) is responsible for ensuring the quality of drug products by carefully monitoring drug manufacturers' compliance with Current Good Manufacturing Practice (CGMP) regulations. The CGMP regulations for drugs contain minimum requirements for the methods, facilities, and controls used in manufacturing, processing, and packing of a drug product. The regulations make sure that a product is safe for use, and that it has the ingredients and strength it claims to have. FDA's portion of the *CFR* is in Title 21, which interprets the *Federal Food, Drug and Cosmetic Act* (FD&C Act) and related statutes, including the Public Health Service Act.

The regulations discussed are primarily in Title 21 of the Code of Federal Regulations, which consists of nine volumes. The parts in these volumes are arranged in the following order: Parts 1–99, 100–169, 170–199, 200–299 (containing the bulk of the current good manufacturing practices [CGMPs], 300–499 (containing the bulk of the investigational new drug [IND] application, new drug application [NDA], and abbreviated new drug application [ANDA] materials), 500–599, 600–799, 800–1299, and 1300–end. This last volume addresses matters subject to the Drug Enforcement Administration (DEA), the Department of Justice (DOJ), and the Office of National Drug Control Policy.

The CGMP regulations (21 CFR 210–226) are promulgated by the Commissioner of the FDA under Section 701 (a) of the FD&C Act (21 USC 371 [a]) in furtherance of the requirement of Section 501(a)(2)(B) of the FD&C Act (21 USC 351[a][2][B]), which specifies that a drug is deemed adulterated "if the methods used in, or the facilities or the controls used for, its manufacture, processing, packing, or holding do not conform to or are not operated or administered in conformity with current good manufacturing practice." The purpose of Section 501(a)(2)(B) is to assure that such drug meets the requirements of the act as to safety and has the identity and strength and meets the quality and purity characteristics that it purports or is represented to possess. The FDA is, of course, committed to various programs and systems designed to assure the quality of all drug products by careful monitoring of drug manufacturer's compliance with CGMP regulations. In order to identify their regulatees, Section 510(b) and (c) of the FD&C Act requires the registration of all producers of drugs and devices. Congressional language that accompanied this amendment stated it was "necessary to provide for the registration and inspection of all establishments in which drugs were manufactured, prepared, propagated, compounded, or processed" since these products were likely to enter interstate commerce. Section 510(h) requires that each registrant be inspected for compliance every two years.

FD&C Act Section Number	Title
Sec. 501	Sec. 351—Adulterated drugs and devices
Sec. 502	Sec. 352—Misbranded drugs and devices
Sec. 503	Sec. 353—Exemptions and consideration for certain drugs, devices, and biological products
Sec. 503A	Sec. 353a—Pharmacy compounding
Sec. 503A-1	Sec. 353a-1—Enhanced Communication
Sec. 503B	Sec. 353b—Outsourcing facilities
Sec. 505	Sec. 355—New drugs
	Sec. 355-1—Risk evaluation and mitigation strategies
Sec. 505D	Sec. 355e—Pharmaceutical security
Sec. 506A	Sec. 356a—Manufacturing changes
Sec. 510	Sec. 360—Registration of producers of drugs or devices
Sec. 511	Sec. 360a—Clinical trial guidance for antibiotic drugs
	Sec. 360a-1—Clinical trials

In recent years, the FDA has assumed additional roles for assurance to vendees through programs like the Government-Wide Quality Assurance Programs for drug purchase contracts by the Department of Defense and Veterans Affairs and the MAC program (Maximum Allowable Cost), a program that became seminal to the manufacture of generics. Their policy is outlined in the ORA (Office of Regulatory Affairs) Compliance Document Sec. 400.200 Consistent Application of CGMP Determinations (CPG 7132.12).[1]

Decisions regarding compliance with CGMP regulations are based on inspection of the facilities, sample analysis, and compliance history of the firm. These data are summarized in profiles that represent several years of history of the firms.

The CGMP deficiencies supporting regulatory action by the FDA also support decisions regarding nonapproval of NDA Supplements, as well as the purchasing contracts and candidacy for MAC; hence, some FDA expanded action is likely. Therefore, issuance of a "warning" letter or other regulatory action based on discovery of CGMP deficiencies must be accompanied by disapproval of any pending NDA, ANDA, or Supplement, or any government contract produced under the same deficiencies.

The FD&C Act applies to drugs introduced into interstate commerce in the United States, including drugs exported to or imported from other countries. Manufacturers in other countries who export to the United States are inspected either by the FDA or under reciprocal inspection agreements as part of the NDA approval process and antibiotic drug certification. Individual drug products are subjected to extensive examination, including laboratory testing, before being allowed into the United States.

On 1 November 2017, further aspects of the mutual recognition agreement between the European Union (EU) and the United States (US) was initiated to recognize inspections of manufacturing sites for human medicines conducted in their respective territories. This agreement, which updates the agreement from 1998, allows for recognition of each other's inspection outcomes and hence for better use of inspection expertise and resources. In June 2017, the European Commission confirmed that the US FDA had the capability, capacity, and procedures in place to carry out good manufacturing practice (GMP) inspections at a level equivalent to the EU. The FDA confirmed the capability of eight EU Member States (Austria, Croatia, France, Italy, Malta, Spain, Sweden, and United Kingdom). The remaining inspectorates will continue to be assessed until 15 July 2019.

The following was published on the FDA website in June 2018[2]:

The Mutual Recognition Agreement (MRA) between FDA and European Union allows drug inspectors to rely upon information from drug inspections conducted within each other's borders. Under the Food and Drug Administration Safety and Innovation Act, enacted in 2012, FDA has the authority to enter into agreements to recognize drug inspections conducted by foreign regulatory authorities if the FDA determined those authorities are capable of conducting inspections that met US requirements. FDA and the EU have collaborated since May 2014 to evaluate the way they each inspect drug manufacturers and assess the risk and benefits of mutual recognition of drug inspections.

MRA

- Yields greater efficiencies for US and EU regulatory systems by avoiding duplication of inspections
- Enables reallocation of resources towards inspection of drug manufacturing facilities with potentially higher public health risks across the globe

FDA will continue to perform some inspections in EU countries with capable inspectorates, such as product manufacturing assessment inspections to support marketing approval decisions. However, FDA expects to perform fewer routine surveillance inspections in EU countries with a capable inspectorate.

The FDA has the authority to deny entry to any drug if there is a question regarding its safety, identity, strength, quality, or purity. This authority is exercised unless factory inspection is permitted or inspection information is available concerning nondomestic firms, in lieu of conducting foreign inspections. Although this authority is exercised more rarely and tempered by Chapter 8 of the Act, the FDA also has the authority to deny exit to questionable drugs.

Since the inception of the GMPs, the FDA strived to ensure that the regulated industries comply with a total control of product quality concept through its factory inspection programs and through participation in voluntary CGMP compliance seminars and workshops sponsored jointly with the industries or with educational institutions. As part of the FDA's Pharmaceutical CGMPs for the 21st Century Initiative, they have introduced quality systems and risk management approaches into existing programs. Regardless of the approaches used, the FDA wants the industry to prevent a drug product from being deemed adulterated under Section 501(a)(2)(B) and violative of Section 301(b) of the Food, Drug, and Cosmetic Act as is indicated by 21 CFR 211, Current Good Manufacturing Practice for Finished Pharmaceuticals.

§ 210.1 STATUS OF CURRENT GOOD MANUFACTURING PRACTICE REGULATIONS

a. *The regulations set forth in this part and in parts 211, 225, and 226 of this chapter contain the minimum current good manufacturing practice for methods to be used in, and the facilities or controls to be used for, the manufacture, processing, packing, or holding of a drug to assure that such drug meets the requirements of the act as to safety, and has the identity and strength and meets the quality and purity characteristics that it purports or is represented to possess.*

b. *The failure to comply with any regulation set forth in this part and in parts 211, 225, and 226 of this chapter in the manufacture, processing, packing, or holding of a drug shall render such drug to be adulterated under section 501(a)(2)(B) of the act and such drug, as well as the person who is responsible for the failure to comply, shall be subject to regulatory action.*

c. *Owners and operators of establishments engaged in the recovery, donor screening, testing (including donor testing), processing, storage, labeling, packaging, or distribution of human cells, tissues, and cellular and tissue-based products (HCT/Ps), as defined in §1271.3(d) of this chapter, that are drugs (subject to review under an application submitted under section 505 of the act or under a biological product license application under section 351 of the Public Health Service Act), are subject to the donor-eligibility and applicable current good tissue practice procedures set forth in part 1271 subparts C and D of this chapter, in addition to the regulations in this part and in parts 211, 225, and 226 of this chapter. Failure to comply with any applicable regulation set forth in this part, in parts 211, 225, and 226 of this chapter, in part 1271 subpart C of this chapter, or in part 1271 subpart D of this chapter with respect to the manufacture, processing, packing, or holding of a drug, renders an HCT/P adulterated under section 501(a)(2)(B) of the act. Such HCT/P, as well as the person who is responsible for the failure to comply, is subject to regulatory action.*

[43 FR 45076, Sept. 29, 1978, as amended at 69 FR 29828, May 25, 2004; 74 FR 65431, Dec. 10, 2009]

§ 210.2 APPLICABILITY OF CURRENT GOOD MANUFACTURING PRACTICE REGULATIONS

a. *The regulations in this part and in parts 211, 225, and 226 of this chapter as they may pertain to a drug; in parts 600 through 680 of this chapter as they may pertain to a biological product for human use; and in part 1271 of this chapter as they are applicable to a human cell, tissue, or cellular or tissue-based product (HCT/P) that is a drug (subject to review under an application submitted under section 505 of the act or under a biological product license application under section 351 of the Public Health Service Act) shall be considered to supplement, not supersede, each other, unless the regulations explicitly provide otherwise. In the event of a conflict between applicable regulations in this part and in other parts of this chapter, the regulation specifically applicable to the drug product in question shall supersede the more general.*

b. *If a person engages in only some operations subject to the regulations in this part, in parts 211, 225, and 226 of this chapter, in parts 600 through 680 of this chapter, and in part 1271 of this chapter, and not in others, that person need only comply with those regulations applicable to the operations in which he or she is engaged.*

c. *An investigational drug for use in a phase 1 study, as described in 312.21(a) of this chapter, is subject to the statutory requirements set forth in 21 USC 351(a)(2)(B). The production of such drug is exempt from compliance with the regulations in part 211 of this chapter. However, this exemption does not apply to an investigational drug for use in a phase 1 study once the investigational drug has been made available for use by or for the sponsor in a phase 2 or phase 3 study, as described in 312.21(b) and (c) of this chapter, or the drug has been lawfully marketed. If the investigational drug has been made available in a phase 2 or phase 3 study or the drug has been lawfully marketed, the drug for use in the phase 1 study must comply with part 211.*

[69 FR 29828, May 25, 2004, as amended at 73 FR 40462, July 15, 2008; 74 FR 65431, Dec. 10, 2009]

§ 210.3 DEFINITIONS

a. *The definitions and interpretations contained in section 201 of the act shall be applicable to such terms when used in this part and in parts 211 through 226 of this chapter.*
b. *The following definitions of terms apply to this part and to parts 211 through 226 of this chapter.*
   1. *Act means the Federal Food, Drug, and Cosmetic Act, as amended (21 USC 301 et seq.).*
   2. *Batch means a specific quantity of a drug or other material that is intended to have uniform character and quality, within specified limits, and is produced according to a single manufacturing order during the same cycle of manufacture.*
   3. *Component means any ingredient intended for use in the manufacture of a drug product, including those that may not appear in such drug product.*
   4. *Drug product means a finished dosage form, for example, tablet, capsule, solution, etc., that contains an active drug ingredient generally, but not necessarily, in association with inactive ingredients. The term also includes a finished dosage form that does not contain an active ingredient but is intended to be used as a placebo.*
   5. *Fiber means any particulate contaminant with a length at least three times greater than its width.*
   6. *Nonfiber releasing filter means any filter, which after appropriate pretreatment such as washing or flushing, will not release fibers into the component or drug product that is being filtered.*
   7. *Active ingredient means any component that is intended to furnish pharmacological activity or other direct effect in the diagnosis, cure, mitigation, treatment, or prevention of disease, or to affect the structure or any function of the body of man or other animals. The term includes those components that may undergo chemical change in the manufacture of the drug product and be present in the drug product in a modified form intended to furnish the specified activity or effect.*
   8. *Inactive ingredient means any component other than an active ingredient.*
   9. *In-process material means any material fabricated, compounded, blended, or derived by chemical reaction that is produced for, and used in, the preparation of the drug product.*
   10. *Lot means a batch, or a specific identified portion of a batch, having uniform character and quality within specified limits, or, in the case of a drug product produced by continuous process, it is a specific identified amount produced in a unit of time or quantity in a manner that assures its having uniform character and quality within specified limits.*

11. *Lot number, control number, or batch number means any distinctive combination of letters, numbers, or symbols, or any combination of them, from which the complete history of the manufacture, processing, packing, holding, and distribution of a batch or lot of drug product or other material can be determined.*

12. *Manufacture, processing, packing, or holding of a drug product includes packaging and labeling operations, testing, and quality control of drug products.*

13. *The term medicated feed means any Type B or Type C medicated feed as defined in § 558.3 of this chapter. The feed contains one or more drugs as defined in section 201(g) of the act. The manufacture of medicated feeds is subject to the requirements of part 225 of this chapter.*

14. *The term medicated premix means a Type A medicated article as defined in § 558.3 of this chapter. The article contains one or more drugs as defined in section 201(g) of the act. The manufacture of medicated premixes is subject to the requirements of part 226 of this chapter.*

15. *Quality control unit means any person or organizational element designated by the firm to be responsible for the duties relating to quality control.*

16. *Strength means:*
     i.   *The concentration of the drug substance (for example, weight/weight, weight/volume, or unit dose/volume basis), and/or*
     ii. *The potency, that is, the therapeutic activity of the drug product as indicated by appropriate laboratory tests or by adequately developed and controlled clinical data (expressed, for example, in terms of units by reference to a standard).*

17. *Theoretical yield means the quantity that would be produced at any appropriate phase of manufacture, processing, or packing of a particular drug product, based upon the quantity of components to be used, in the absence of any loss or error in actual production.*

18. *Actual yield means the quantity that is actually produced at any appropriate phase of manufacture, processing, or packing of a particular drug product.*

19. *Percentage of theoretical yield means the ratio of the actual yield (at any appropriate phase of manufacture, processing, or packing of a particular drug product) to the theoretical yield (at the same phase), stated as a percentage.*

20. *Acceptance criteria means the product specifications and acceptance/rejection criteria, such as acceptable quality level and unacceptable quality level, with an associated sampling plan, that are necessary for making a decision to accept or reject a lot or batch (or any other convenient subgroups of manufactured units).*

21. *Representative sample means a sample that consists of a number of units that are drawn based on rational criteria, such as random sampling, and intended to assure that the sample accurately portrays the material being sampled.*

22. *Gang-printed labeling means labeling derived from a sheet of material on which more than one item of labeling is printed.*

[43 FR 45076, Sept. 29, 1978, as amended at 51 FR 7389, Mar. 3, 1986; 58 FR 41353, Aug. 3, 1993; 73 FR 51931, Sept. 8, 2008]

As described on the FDA Web page[1] at the time of writing:

FDA ensures the quality of drug products by carefully monitoring drug manufacturers' compliance with its Current Good Manufacturing Practice (CGMP) regulations. The CGMP regulations for drugs contain minimum requirements for the methods, facilities, and controls used in manufacturing, processing, and packing of a drug product. The regulations make sure that a product is safe for use, and that it has the ingredients and strength it claims to have.

The approval process for new and generic drug marketing applications includes a review of the manufacturer's compliance with the CGMPs. FDA assessors and inspectors determine whether the firm has the necessary facilities, equipment, and ability to manufacture the drug it intends to market.

Code of Federal Regulations (CFR). FDA's portion of the CFR is in Title 21, which interprets the Federal Food, Drug and Cosmetic Act and related statutes, including the Public Health Service Act. The pharmaceutical or drug quality-related regulations appear in several parts of Title 21, including sections in parts 1–99, 200–299, 300–499, 600–799, and 800–1299.

The regulations enable a common understanding of the regulatory process by describing the requirements to be followed by drug manufacturers, applicants, and FDA.

- 21 CFR Part 314 and Part 600. Application and licensing submission requirements for new and generic drug applicants.
- 21 CFR Part 210. Current Good Manufacturing Practice in Manufacturing Processing, packing, or Holding of Drugs.
- 21 CFR Part 211. Current Good Manufacturing Practice for Finished Pharmaceuticals.

The first paragraph, and repeated many other times on the FDA website, includes the identifiable phrase "…contain the minimum requirements for…" which are known to some recipients of warning letters, for example: "Your firm's planned corrections do not meet the minimum requirements of 21 CFR Parts 210 and 211, and there is no assurance that the drug products produced by your firm conform to the basic quality standards that ensure safety, identity, strength, quality, and purity."

FDA provides a brief introduction to the GMPs on the website[3] through a series of questions and answers:

Pharmaceutical Quality affects every American. The Food and Drug Administration (FDA) regulates the quality of pharmaceuticals very carefully. The main regulatory standard for ensuring pharmaceutical quality is the Current Good Manufacturing Practice (CGMPs) regulation for human pharmaceuticals. Consumers expect that each batch of medicines they take will meet quality standards so that they will be safe and effective. Most people, however, are not aware of CGMPs, or how FDA assures that drug manufacturing processes meet these basic objectives. Recently, FDA has announced a number of regulatory actions taken against drug manufacturers based on the lack of CGMPs. This paper discusses some facts that may be helpful in understanding how CGMPs establish the foundation for drug product quality.

WHAT ARE CGMPs?

CGMP refers to the Current Good Manufacturing Practice regulations enforced by the FDA. CGMPs provide for systems that assure proper design, monitoring, and control of manufacturing processes and facilities. Adherence to the CGMP regulations assures the identity, strength, quality, and purity of drug products by requiring that manufacturers of medications adequately control manufacturing operations. This includes establishing strong quality management systems, obtaining appropriate quality raw materials, establishing robust operating procedures, detecting and investigating product quality deviations, and maintaining reliable testing laboratories. This formal system of controls at a pharmaceutical company, if adequately put into practice, helps to prevent instances of contamination, mix-ups, deviations, failures, and errors. This assures that drug products meet their quality standards.

The CGMP requirements were established to be flexible in order to allow each manufacturer to decide individually how to best implement the necessary controls by using scientifically sound design, processing methods, and testing procedures. The flexibility in these regulations allows companies to use modern technologies and innovative approaches to achieve higher quality through continual improvement. Accordingly, the "C" in CGMP stands for "current," requiring companies to use technologies and systems that are up-to-date in order to comply with the regulations. Systems and equipment that may have been "top-of-the-line" to prevent contamination, mix-ups, and errors 10 or 20 years ago may be less than adequate by today's standards.

It is important to note that CGMPs are minimum requirements. Many pharmaceutical manufacturers are already implementing comprehensive, modern quality systems and risk management approaches that exceed these minimum standards.

WHY ARE CGMPs SO IMPORTANT?

A consumer usually cannot detect (through smell, touch, or sight) that a drug product is safe or if it will work. While CGMPs require testing, testing alone is not adequate to ensure quality. In most instances testing is done on a small sample of a batch (for example, a drug manufacturer may test 100 tablets from a batch that contains 2 million tablets), so that most of the batch can be used for patients rather than destroyed by testing. Therefore, it is important that drugs are manufactured under conditions and practices required by the CGMP regulations to assure that quality is built into the design and manufacturing process at every step. Facilities that are in good condition, equipment that is properly maintained and calibrated, employees who are qualified and fully trained, and processes that are reliable and reproducible, are a few examples of how CGMP requirements help to assure the safety and efficacy of drug products.

HOW DOES FDA DETERMINE IF A COMPANY IS COMPLYING WITH CGMP REGULATIONS?

FDA inspects pharmaceutical manufacturing facilities worldwide, including facilities that manufacture active ingredients and the finished product. Inspections follow a standard approach and are conducted by highly trained FDA staff. FDA also relies upon reports of potentially defective drug products from the public and the industry. FDA will often use these reports to identify sites for which an inspection or investigation is needed. Most companies that are inspected are found to be fully compliant with the CGMP regulations.

IF A MANUFACTURER IS NOT FOLLOWING CGMPs, ARE DRUG PRODUCTS SAFE FOR USE?

If a company is not complying with CGMP regulations, any drug it makes is considered "adulterated" under the law. This kind of adulteration means that the drug was not manufactured under conditions that comply with CGMP. It does not mean that there is necessarily something wrong with the drug.

For consumers currently taking medicines from a company that was not following CGMPs, FDA usually advises these consumers not to interrupt their drug therapy, which could have serious implications for their health. Consumers should seek advice from their health care professionals before stopping or changing medications. Regulatory actions against companies with poor CGMPs are often intended to prevent the possibility of unsafe and/or ineffective drugs. In rare cases, FDA regulatory action is intended to stop the distribution or manufacturing of violative product. The impact of CGMP violations depends on the nature of those violations and on the specific drugs involved. A drug manufactured in violation of CGMP may still meet its labeled specifications, and the risk that the drug is unsafe or ineffective could be minimal. Thus, FDA's advice will be specific to the circumstances, and health care professionals are best able to balance risks and benefits and make the right decision for their patients.

WHAT CAN FDA DO TO PROTECT THE PUBLIC WHEN THERE ARE CGMP VIOLATIONS?

If the failure to meet CGMPs results in the distribution of a drug that does not offer the benefit as labeled because, for example, it has too little active ingredient, the company may subsequently recall that product. This protects the public from further harm by removing these drugs from the market. While FDA cannot force a company to recall a drug, companies usually will recall voluntarily or at FDA's request. If a company refuses to recall a drug, FDA can warn the public and can seize the drug.

FDA can also bring a seizure or injunction case in court to address CGMP violations even where there is no direct evidence of a defect affecting the drug's performance. When FDA brings a seizure case, the agency asks the court for an order that allows federal officials to take possession of "adulterated" drugs. When FDA brings an injunction case, FDA asks the court to order a company to stop violating CGMPs. Both seizure and injunction cases often lead to court orders that require companies to take many steps to correct CGMP violations, which may include repairing facilities and equipment, improving sanitation and cleanliness, performing additional testing to verify quality, and improving employee training. FDA can also bring criminal cases because of CGMP violations, seeking fines and jail time.

HOW WOULD A NEW DRUG COMPANY LEARN ABOUT CGMPs AND ABOUT FDA'S EXPECTATIONS ON COMPLYING WITH THEM?

FDA publishes regulations and guidance documents for industry in the *Federal Register*. This is how the federal government notifies the public of what we are doing and why. FDA's website, www.fda.gov also contains links to the CGMP regulations, guidance documents, and various resources to help drug companies comply with the law. FDA also conducts extensive public outreach through presentations at national and international meetings and conferences, to discuss and explain the CGMP requirements and the latest policy documents.

The CGMP requirements were intentionally written with some vague terminology because as FDA points out they needed to be "...flexible in order to allow each manufacturer to decide individually how to best implement the necessary controls by using scientifically sound design, processing methods, and testing procedures." Companies are expected to use advances in technologies as they become available to enhance approaches to quality through continual improvement. The "C" in CGMP stands for "current," which requires companies to use technologies and systems to comply with the regulations that are current industry standards today but might be replaced or superseded in the future.

As described in the *Federal Register*[4], this general introduction to what is projected as a series of GMP regulations for all human drug products, as well as specific products or specific processes, is "intended to be general enough to be suitable for essentially all drug products, flexible enough to allow the use of sound judgment and permit innovation, and explicit enough to provide a clear understanding of what is required."

This approach places a large burden on pharmaceutical manufacturers, as adherence to the explicit regulations is a required minimum, but just by its use it is not adequate to ensure that a manufacturer is in compliance with the requirements. Additionally, manufacturers must be using current methods with current controls, thus setting as a requirement that which is overall current or generally accepted in the drug industry in relation to equipment, methodology, controls, and records. Thinking or allowing yourself as a manufacturer to be "average" in aspects and requirements, compared with the other manufacturers, still does not ensure compliance because the standard is not only that practices be "current" but that they also be "good." The introduction of a new practice, equipment, or acceptable standard/methodology that is "good" and enhances controls resets the industry standards.

Therefore, being in compliance with GMP is not a static situation but requires manufacturers to be aware not only of what is current in the industry but also to be aware of innovations that may be "good." FDA is conscious of these continuous changes within the industry and may reflect them in the "current" GMP interpretations.

Pharmaceutical manufacturers are expected to have processes in place to remain current with the changing regulatory environment in the countries/markets that their products are marketed by evaluating the changes and determining if, what, and when they need to make changes. Some changes may not require any actions because they may already be accommodated or not apply.

THE MEANING OF "CURRENT"

The most unique and interesting part of the GMP regulations is determining exactly what is "current" for GMPs.

Congress intended that the phrase itself (current good manufacturing practice) have a unique meaning. The FDA determines what constitutes "current good manufacturing practice" based upon its experience with the manufacture of drugs through inspectional and compliance activities. Although the practices must be "current" in the industry, they need not be widely prevalent. FDA notes[5]

> CGMP refers to the Current Good Manufacturing Practice regulations enforced by the FDA. CGMPs provide for systems that assure proper design, monitoring, and control of manufacturing processes and facilities. Adherence to the CGMP regulations assures the identity, strength, quality, and purity of drug products by requiring that manufacturers of medications adequately control manufacturing operations. This includes establishing strong quality management systems, obtaining appropriate quality raw materials, establishing robust operating procedures, detecting and investigating product quality deviations, and maintaining reliable testing laboratories. This formal system of controls at a pharmaceutical company, if adequately put into practice, helps to prevent instances of contamination, mix-ups, deviations, failures, and errors. This assures that drug products meet their quality standards.
>
> The CGMP requirements were established to be flexible in order to allow each manufacturer to decide individually how to best implement the necessary controls by using scientifically sound design, processing methods, and testing procedures. The flexibility in these regulations allows companies to use modern technologies and innovative approaches to achieve higher quality through continual improvement. Accordingly, the "C" in CGMP stands for "current," requiring companies to use technologies and systems that are up-to-date in order to comply with the regulations. Systems and equipment that may have been "top-of-the-line" to prevent contamination, mix-ups, and errors 10 or 20 years ago may be less than adequate by today's standards.
>
> It is important to note that CGMPs are minimum requirements. Many pharmaceutical manufacturers are already implementing comprehensive, modern quality systems and risk management approaches that exceed these minimum standards.

The FDA also notes that, although it does not manufacture drugs, it has the unique ability to determine CGMPs for drugs, since it alone has access to the facilities and records of every manufacturer of pharmaceuticals in the United States and the drug regulatory filings for all products sold in the United States. Given the fact that many processes and controls are considered by manufacturers to be trade secrets, their competitors are not likely to discover what nonpublic practices are current.

Even if current practices were available, the FDA holds that it has special technical and scientific expertise to determine which of the current practices are also "good." This expertise is inherent in reviews of production and control techniques in NDAs and ANDAs, supplemental applications, antibiotic certification forms, biological establishment and product licenses, new animal drug applications, and proposed and final compendial standards. Additional experience is based on establishment inspection reports filed by FDA investigators and the monitoring of drug recalls.

A current, although not necessarily predominant, practice is considered "good" if:

1. It is feasible for manufacturers to implement.
2. It contributes to ensuring the safety, quality, or purity of the drug product.
3. The value of the contributions or added assurance exceeds the cost in money or other burdens of implementing or continuing the practice.

It is worthwhile remembering, as all of us working in the industry are also consumers sometime during our life.

FDA publishes regulations and guidance documents for industry in the *Federal Register*. This is how the federal government notifies the public of what they are doing and why.

ROLE AND IMPORTANCE OF THE UNITED STATES PHARMOCOPEIA

The *United States Pharmacopeia* (USP) is a pharmacopeia published annually by the United States Pharmacopeial Convention and is published in a combined volume with the *National Formulary* as the USP–NF. A drug ingredient or drug product having an applicable USP quality standard monograph must conform in order to use the designation "USP" or "NF." The USP–NF standards also have a role in US federal law; a drug or drug ingredient recognized in USP–NF is considered adulterated if it does not satisfy compendial standards for strength, quality, or purity.

The role of the USP is of course not limited to the United States. This was true even prior to the time it became incorporated within the FD&C Act for its ultimate importance in dealing with such portions of that law that recite prohibited acts.

About the USP: The US Pharmacopeial Convention is an independent, nonprofit organization that safeguards the public's health by developing quality standards for medicines, dietary supplements, and food ingredients.

USP–FDA Shared History and Mission: The USP–FDA relationship dates back to the 1906 Pure Food and Drug Act, which deemed the *United States Pharmacopeia* and the *National Formulary* official compendia under federal law.

How USP and FDA Work Together: USP and FDA maintain official contact through a number of established channels:

- Five FDA centers and the Office of the Commissioner have established delegates at USP's Convention, the top leadership body of our organization.
- USP staff maintain executive-level contacts with FDA leadership and routine contacts with FDA's Compendial Operations and Standards Branch through quarterly meetings.
- More than 100 FDA staff participate as government liaisons on USP's Expert Committees and Expert Panels, the scientific bodies that develop and revise USP's written and physical standards.

Government liaisons represent FDA opinions and viewpoints (as opposed to other USP volunteers, who represent their own opinions rather than their employers') at public USP meetings such as the Expert Committee Meetings, Expert Panels, and Stakeholder Forums.

The Importance of USP–FDA Collaboration: FDA-USP collaboration is essential to ensure appropriate quality standards and, where applicable, standards that reflect FDA-approved product quality standards.

The FDA Office of Regulatory Affairs/USP Cooperative Research and Development Agreements enable USP and FDA to collaborate on protocols and work plans that impact the effective development of up-to-date monographs and nomenclature.

FDA and USP work together to identify areas for monograph or general chapter development where there is a need for quality issues to be addressed. Our interactions lead to a more efficient standards development process.

USP's Role Under the Federal Food, Drug, and Cosmetic Act: USP standards are an integral part of the patient safety framework:

- The Federal Food, Drug, and Cosmetic Act (Act) expressly recognizes USP quality standards for medicines.
- Under the "Act," USP standards are binding for dietary supplement manufacturers that label their products as compliant with USP specifications.
- FDA has issued more than 200 regulations for food substances that incorporate USP's *Food Chemicals Codex* specifications by reference.

Compendial standards remain connected to FDA provisions in the Act and other consumer protection laws, regulations and guidance that have been part of the important safeguards that make medicines, dietary supplements and food ingredients in the U.S. among the safest in the world.[6]

Key milestones in USP history:[7] Established in 1820 "to ensure that consumers receive medicines of the highest possible quality, strength, and purity in the United States," it was destined to reflect medical and pharmaceutical advances from the major European laboratories and academia from the first. In 1900, USP incorporates and sets up a Board of Trustees. This establishes USP as a sustainable, nonprofit organization with the goal of protecting public health. Then in 1906 the Food and Drugs Act mandates that drugs meet the standards of strength, quality, and purity stipulated in the USP and NF. The year 1941 saw the USP develop an insulin Reference Standard, which ensures continued production and access. By 1969, the USP is recognized in 27 countries and serves as the sole standard in Costa Rica, El Salvador, and Panama. In 1994, the Dietary Supplements Health and Education Act (DSHEA) names USP and NF as official compendia for dietary supplements. Products that suppliers represent as confirming to USP standards may be deemed misbranded if they fail to conform. In 2001, USP launches its Dietary Supplement Verification Program, followed by the Dietary Ingredient Verification Program (2004), and the Pharmaceutical Ingredient Verification Program (2006). These assure customers that the dietary and pharmaceutical ingredients are of the highest quality. A significant event in 2007 resulted in the USP working with regulators and industry to control potential impurities by revising monograph methods and introducing new Reference Standards to help thwart adulteration of the global heparin supply. The year 2013 sees the USP create the Herbal Medicines Compendium, a freely available, online resource that provides standards for herbal ingredients used in herbal medicines. Then in 2017, USP and USAID celebrate 25 years of collaborating to help developing countries address critical issues related to medicines information and quality.

Located nearby the FDA in Rockville, Maryland, USA, they can be reached at 301-998-6821 or at: http://www.usp.org.

USP develops and publishes standards for drug substances, drug products, excipients, and dietary supplements in the United States Pharmacopeia–National Formulary (USP–NF). These standards have been recognized in the Federal Food, Drug and Cosmetic (FD&C) Act since it was first enacted in 1938. The FD&C Act defines the term "official compendium" as the official USP, the official NF, the official Homeopathic Pharmacopeia of the United States, or any Supplement to them. USP–NF standards play a role in the adulteration and misbranding provisions of the FD&C Act (which apply as well to biologics, a subset of drugs, under the Public Health Service Act). USP has no role in enforcement of these or other provisions that recognize USP–NF standards, which is the responsibility of FDA and other government authorities in the United States and elsewhere. Manufacturers and potentially affected parties are encouraged to contact FDA with questions about the specific applicability of USP standards to their products.

All proposed revisions to USP–NF standards are published for review and comment in a USP publication, *Pharmacopeia Forum*.

SPECIFIC DRUG CATEGORIES AND TOPICS

- **Drugs:** USP's goal is to have substance and preparation (product) monographs in USP–NF for all FDA-approved drugs, including biologics and their ingredients. USP also develops monographs for therapeutic products not approved by FDA, for example, pre-1938 drugs, dietary supplements, and compounded preparations. Although submission of information needed to develop a monograph by the Council of Experts is voluntary, compliance with a USP–NF monograph, if available, is mandatory in the following respects:
- **Nonproprietary Name:** Under the relevant FD&C Act provisions, a drug will be deemed misbranded unless its label bears to the exclusion of any other nonproprietary name the "established" name, which ordinarily is the compendial name (see discussion of nomenclature below).
- **Identity:** A drug with a name recognized in USP–NF must comply with the identity/identification requirements of its monograph, or be deemed adulterated, misbranded, or both.
- **Strength, Quality, Purity:** Drugs also must comply with compendial standards for strength, quality, and purity (tests for assay and impurities), unless labeled to show all respects in which the drugs differ. FDA requires that names for articles that are not official must be clearly distinguishing and differentiating from any name recognized in an official compendium.
- **Packaging, Labeling:** Drugs with a name recognized in USP–NF also will be considered misbranded unless they meet compendial standards for packaging and labeling.

The USP Reference Standards are highly characterized specimens of drug substances, major impurities, degradation products, and performance calibrators for use in testing drugs and nutritional supplements. They are used to perform official methods of analysis in pharmaceutical testing. The manufacturer may use other than the official method of analysis, but the substance used and the product manufactured must meet the official specifications contained in the USP–NF, following the official method of analysis. USP Material Safety Data Sheets are available to purchasers of standards. The USP also tests and distributes other authenticated substances not currently included in the USP–NF that are still in sufficient demand; FCC Reference Standards specified in the latest edition of the Food Chemicals Codex; and highly purified samples of chemicals, including drugs of abuse. The USP website http://www.usp.org has links to Reference Standards, USP–NF, Patient Safety, and USP-Verified and other topics.

Continuous update acquisition of official and unofficial compendia is necessary to remain current with CGMPs, and the law requires that products meet the requirements of the USP–NF for the monographs applicable to their products as labeled. It is typical for many revisions to occur in USP–NF Supplements and Editions. However, it is the responsibility of the drug manufacturer to keep ahead of the proposed changes, assess potential impacts, and take appropriate actions.

On the FDA website[8] there is a response to the question relating to the relationship between the USP and FDA guidance:

Are USP general chapters above <999> considered equivalent to FDA guidance? What is their purpose and how should manufacturers use these informational chapters?

"No, FDA is the only source of policy on pharmaceutical CGMPs and quality. CGMP requirements are found in statutes and regulations, and FDA's current thinking on these requirements is explained in the Agency's guidance documents.

The US Pharmacopeial Convention is a private, nongovernmental organization that publishes the United States Pharmacopeia (USP) and the National Formulary (NF) as official compendia of the United States. Although much of the USP and NF is legally enforceable, the USP general chapters numbered above <999> (general information chapters) are informational and generally do not contain any mandatory requirements (see USP General Notices 2.10). General information chapters might include some recommendations that may help a firm meet CGMPs."

RECENT FOOD AND DRUG ADMINISTRATION DRUG-RELATED MILESTONES

This section has been revised and includes those specifically for compounded drug products. A history of regulations can be found on the FDA website www.FDA.gov

2000

The US Supreme Court, upholding an earlier decision in *Food and Drug Administration v. Brown Williamson Tobacco Corp. et al.,* ruled 5–4 that FDA does not have authority to regulate tobacco as a drug. Within weeks of this ruling, FDA revoked its final rule, issued in 1996, that restricted the sale and distribution of cigarettes and smokeless tobacco products to children and adolescents, and that determined that cigarettes and smokeless tobacco products are combination products consisting of a drug (nicotine) and device components intended to deliver nicotine to the body.

Federal agencies are required to issue guidelines to maximize the quality, objectivity, utility, and integrity of the information they generate, and to provide a mechanism whereby those affected can secure correction of information that does not meet these guidelines, under the Data Quality Act.

Publication of a rule on dietary supplements defines the type of statement that can be labeled regarding the effect of supplements on the structure or function of the body.

2002

The Best Pharmaceuticals for Children Act improves safety and efficacy of patented and off-patent medicines for children. It continues the exclusivity provisions for pediatric drugs as mandated under the Food and Drug Administration Modernization Act of 1997, in which market exclusivity of a drug is extended by six months, and in exchange the manufacturer carries out studies of the effects of drugs when taken by children. The provisions both clarify aspects of the exclusivity period and amend procedures for generic drug approval in cases when pediatric guidelines are added to the labeling.

In the wake of the events of September 11, 2001, the Public Health Security and Bioterrorism Preparedness and Response Act of 2002 is designed to improve the country's ability to prevent and respond to public health emergencies, and provisions include a requirement that FDA issue regulations to enhance controls over imported and domestically produced commodities it regulates.

Under the Medical Device User Fee and Modernization Act, *fees are assessed to sponsors of* medical device applications for evaluation, provisions are established for device establishment inspections by accredited third-parties, and new requirements emerge for reprocessed single-use devices.

The Office of Combination Products is formed within the Office of the Commissioner, as mandated under the Medical Device User Fee and Modernization Act, to oversee review of products that fall into multiple jurisdictions within the FDA.

An effort to enhance and update the regulation of manufacturing processes and end-product quality of animal and human drugs and biological medicines is announced: the CGMP initiative. The goals of the initiative are to focus on the greatest risks to public health in manufacturing procedures, to ensure that process and product quality standards do not impede innovation, and to apply a consistent approach to these issues across the FDA.

2003

The Medicare Prescription Drug Improvement and Modernization Act requires, among other elements, that a study be made of how current and emerging technologies can be utilized to make essential information about prescription drugs available to the blind and visually impaired.

The Animal Drug User Fee Act permits the FDA to collect subsidies for the review of certain animal drug applications from sponsors, analogous to laws passed for the evaluation of other products the FDA regulates, ensuring the safety and effectiveness of drugs for animals and the safety of animals used as foodstuffs.

The FDA is given clear authority under the Pediatric Research Equity Act to require that sponsors conduct clinical research into pediatric applications for new drugs and biological products.

2004

Project BioShield Act of 2004 authorizes the FDA to expedite its review procedures to enable rapid distribution of treatments as countermeasures to chemical, biological, and nuclear agents that may be used in a terrorist attack against the United States, among other provisions.

A ban on over-the-counter steroid precursors, increased penalties for making, selling, or possessing illegal steroids precursors, and funds for preventive education to children are features of the Anabolic Steroid Control Act of 2004.

The FDA publishes "Innovation or Stagnation?—Challenge and Opportunity on the Critical Path to New Medical Products," which examines the critical path needed to bring therapeutic products to fruition, and how the FDA can collaborate in the process, from laboratory to production to end use, to make medical breakthroughs available to those in need as quickly as possible.

On the basis of recent results from controlled clinical studies indicating that Cox-2 selective agents may be connected to an elevated risk of serious cardiovascular events, including heart attack and stroke, the FDA issues a public health advisory urging health professionals to limit the use of these drugs.

To provide for the treatment of animal species other than cattle, horses, swine, chickens, turkeys, dogs, and cats, as well as other species that may be added at a later time, the Minor Use and Minor Species Animal Health Act is passed to encourage the development of treatments for species that would otherwise attract little interest in the development of veterinary therapies.

Deeming such products to present an unreasonable risk of harm, the FDA bans dietary supplements containing ephedrine alkaloids based on an increasing number of adverse events linked to these products and the known pharmacology of these alkaloids.

2005

Formation of the Drug Safety Board is announced, consisting of FDA staff and representatives from the National Institutes of Health and the Veterans Administration. The Board will advise the director, Center for Drug Evaluation and Research, and the FDA on drug safety issues and work with the agency in communicating safety information to health professionals and patients.

2006

FDA approves final rule, Requirements on Content and Format of Labeling for Human Prescription Drug and Biological Products.

New content and format requirements make it easier for health-care professionals to access, read, and use information in FDA-approved labeling.

2009

President Obama signs the Family Smoking Prevention and Tobacco Control Act into law. The Tobacco Control Act gives FDA authority to regulate the manufacture, distribution, and marketing of tobacco products to protect public health.

FDA Center for Tobacco Products established.
FDA announced a ban on cigarettes with flavors characterizing fruit, candy, or clove.

2012

Food and Drug Administration Safety and Innovation Act (FDASIA). Expands FDA authorities to collect user fees from industry to fund reviews of innovator drugs, medical devices, generic drugs, and biosimilar biological products; promotes innovation to speed patient access to safe and effective products; increases stakeholder involvement in FDA processes; and enhances the safety of the drug supply chain.

Medical Device User Fee and Modernization Act (MDUFMA III). As part of FDASIA, reauthorizes user fees from industry to fund reviews of medical devices in exchange for FDA to meet certain performance goals.

In 2012, an outbreak of fungal meningitis linked to a contaminated compounded drug product resulted in the loss of 64 lives and caused more than 751 illnesses. In response, Congress enacted the 2013 Drug Quality and Security Act (DQSA) that insures greater regulatory oversight of facilities creating compounded drugs. Among other provisions it outlines steps for an electronic and interoperable system to identify and trace certain prescription drugs throughout the United States.

2013

Pandemic and All-Hazards Preparedness Reauthorization Act (PAHPRA). Establishes and reauthorizes certain programs under the Public Health Service Act and the Food, Drug, and Cosmetic Act with respect to public health security and all-hazards preparedness and response.

OBTAINING FOOD AND DRUG ADMINISTRATION REGULATIONS

The FDA's regulations are printed in Title 21, Code of Federal Regulations (21 CFR). In addition, the FDA and other government agencies publish new regulations and proposals in the *Federal Register* throughout the year. Readers may purchase the books in 21 CFR from the US Government Printing Office.

THE *FEDERAL REGISTER*

The *Federal Register* is published Monday through Friday by the US Government Printing Office in paper and microfiche editions, and as a database on Internet.

REFERENCES

1. CPG Sec. 400.200 Consistent Application of CGMP Determinations (CPG 7132.12). Available at http://www.fda.gov/ora/compliance_ref/cpg/cpgdrg/cpg400-200.html.
2. https://www.fda.gov/internationalprograms/agreements/ucm598735.htm.
3. https://www.fda.gov/drugs/developmentapprovalprocess/manufacturing/ucm169105.htm.
4. Federal Register, Vol. 43, No. 190 - Friday, September 29, 1978: Chapter I-Food and Drug Administration Department of Health, Education, and Welfare Subchapter C-Drugs: General [Docket No. 75n-0339] Human and Veterinary Drugs Current Good Manufacturing Practice in Manufacture, Processing, Packing, or Holding.
5. Facts About the Current Good Manufacturing Practices (cGMPs): Available at https://www.fda.gov/Drugs/DevelopmentApprovalProcess/Manufacturing/ucm169105.htm.
6. www.USP.org.

7. http://www.usp.org/about/usp-timeline.
8. Questions and Answers on Current Good Manufacturing Practices–General Provisions. Available at https://www.fda.gov/Drugs/GuidanceComplianceRegulatoryInformation/Guidances/ucm124747.htm.

SUGGESTED READINGS

- FDA Guidance for Industry: Quality Systems Approach to Pharmaceutical CGMP Regulations, Rockville, MD, US Dept. of Health and Human Services, Food and Drug Administration, Center for Drug Evaluation and Research, 2006, www.FDA.gov
- Core Guideline Draft: Q12 Technical and Regulatory Considerations for Pharmaceutical Product Lifecycle Management, 2017, www.FDA.gov
- FDA Guidance for Industry: Advancement of Emerging Technology Applications for Pharmaceutical Innovation and Modernization, September 2017, www.FDA.gov
- FDA Guidance for Industry and FDA Staff: Current Good Manufacturing Practice Requirements for Combination Products, January 2017, www.FDA.gov
- FDA Draft Guidance for Industry: Request for Quality Metrics, June 2016, www.FDA.gov.
- 21 CFR Part 111 entitled 'Current Good Manufacturing Practice (CGMP) In Manufacturing, Packaging, Labeling, Or Holding Operations For Dietary Supplements' (72 FR 34752).
- FDA Draft Guidance for Industry: Current Good Manufacturing Practice—Interim Guidance for Human Drug Compounding Outsourcing Facilities Under Section 503B of the FD&C Act, July 2014, www.FDA.gov
- FDA Guidance for Industry: Contract Manufacturing Arrangements for Drugs: Quality Agreements, November 2016, www.FDA.gov

2 Quality Management Systems and Risk Management

Joseph C. Near

CONTENTS

This chapter will cover Quality Management Systems (QMS) and the use of Risk Management methodologies in pharmaceutical manufacturing, and is based upon guidance described in two Food and Drug Administration (FDA) Guidance Documents on Quality Systems Approaches: *Quality Systems Approach to Pharmaceutical Current Good Manufacturing Practice Regulations, September 2006, and Compliance Program Guidance Manual for FDA Staff: Drug Manufacturing Inspections Program 7356.002.* These documents provide insight into the FDA's current thinking and change in approach since the introduction of their *Pharmaceutical Current Good Manufacturing Practices (CGMPs) for the 21st Century Initiative.*

The introduction to FDA's *Quality Systems Approach to Pharmaceutical Current Good Manufacturing Practice Regulations* reads:

> This guidance is intended to help manufacturers that are implementing modern quality systems and risk management approaches to meet the requirements of the current good manufacturing practice (CGMP) regulations (21 CFR parts 210 and 211). The guidance describes a *comprehensive quality systems (QS) model*, highlighting the model's consistency with the CGMP regulatory requirements for manufacturing human and veterinary drugs, including biological drug products. The guidance also explains how manufacturers implementing such quality systems can be in full compliance with parts 210 and 211. This guidance is not intended to place new expectations on manufacturers or to replace the CGMP requirements. Readers are advised to always refer to parts 210 and 211 to ensure full compliance with the regulations.

The last two sentences are very important. The FDA is clearly saying that quality systems are not additional expectations or requirements and do not establish legally enforceable responsibilities. The quality system approach/model does not replace the GMP regulations. However, the document does allow for more operational flexibility and use of modern quality concepts and business practices to meet GMP requirements. In FDA's *Pharmaceutical CGMPs for the 21st Century Initiative*, the Agency expressed its intent to integrate *quality systems* and *risk management* approaches into existing programs with the goal of encouraging the adoption of modern and innovative manufacturing technologies. An important linkage between CGMP and robust, modern quality systems is the Quality by Design (QBD) principle and the fact that testing alone cannot be relied upon to ensure product quality.

The Agency also recognized the need to harmonize the CGMPs and other non-US pharmaceutical and regulatory systems (ISO 9000, Device Quality Systems Regulations, Drug Manufacturing Inspections Program, etc.) as well as FDA's own medical device quality system regulations 21 CFR 820. This harmonization brings into practice the science of process, systems, and quality management principles and allows for needed flexibility in applied GMP practices.

FDA QUALITY SYSTEM GUIDANCE

…a comprehensive quality systems model, which, if implemented, will allow manufacturers to operate robust, modern quality systems that are fully compliant with CGMP regulations. The guidance demonstrates how and where the requirements of the CGMP regulations fit within this comprehensive model. The inherent flexibility of the CGMP regulations should enable manufacturers to implement a quality system in a form that is appropriate for their specific operations.

The FDA is quite clear that this guidance is primarily based on sustainable GMP compliance and how that fits into modern quality systems approaches of running a business.

As with all guidance documents, there are fundamental concepts and principles. There are seven in this document.

1. Quality
2. Quality by Design (QBD) and Product Development
3. Risk Assessment and Management
4. Corrective and Preventive Action (CAPA)
5. Change Control
6. The Quality Unit
7. Six Quality System Inspection Approach (Figure 2.1)

FIGURE 2.1   Six Quality System Inspection Approach.

The six quality systems are organized into four sections:

Management Responsibilities
- Leadership
- Structure and organization
- Build/design quality systems to meet requirements
- Establish policies, objectives, and plans
- Review the system

Resources
- General arrangements (adequate resources)
- Develop personnel
- Facilities and equipment
- Control outsourcing operations

Manufacturing Operations
- Design and develop product and processes
- Monitor packaging and labeling processes
- Examine inputs
- Perform and monitor operations
- Address nonconformities

Evaluation Activities
- Analyze data for trends
- Conduct internal audits
- Risk assessment
- Corrective action
- Promote improvement

While still focused on product quality, the guidance brings in additional elements found in ISO and other quality standards.

In addition, the model and the section requirements go beyond the basic GMP/CFR requirements in some areas:

- Leadership
- General arrangements or providing adequate resources
- Internal audits (other than data)
- Preventive action
- Promote improvement

Failures in these specific areas will not show up in FDA inspection observations, but they are necessary parts of quality management and continuous improvement.

BASIC QUALITY SYSTEMS

A system is defined as a collection of components organized to accomplish a specific function or set of functions. A single process or collection of processes can make up a system.

A QMS is typically defined as a structured and documented management system describing the policies, objectives, principles, organizational authority, responsibilities, accountability, and implementation plan of an organization for ensuring quality in its work processes, products (items), and services. The quality system provides the framework for planning, implementing, and assessing the work performed by an organization and for carrying out required Quality Assurance (QA) and Quality Control (QC) activities (1). Elements of a QMS typically include:

1. Quality policy
2. Quality objectives
3. Quality manual
4. Organizational structures and responsibilities
5. Data management
6. Processes
7. Product quality
8. Continuous improvement

The following table lists the six FDA quality systems and the typical GMP quality systems in a pharmaceutical manufacturing business. (Table 2.1)

TABLE 2.1

FDA Quality Systems and the Typical GMP Quality Systems

FDA Quality System	Typical GMP Quality Systems

Facilities/ Equipment	• Facilities and equipment management
	  • Master planning
	  • Commissioning, qualification, and validation
	  • Drawings and document control
	• Facilities cleaning
	• Equipment maintenance
	• Corrective and preventive maintenance systems for utilities and production equipment
	• Equipment calibration—programs/systems for GMP and other equipment
	• Facility environmental monitoring

Production	• Manufacturing operations
	  • Batch record execution and review
	  • Document control
	  • Product sampling
	• Equipment operation and clearance
	• Equipment cleaning
	• Process validation
	• Contract manufacturing (management)
	• Technology transfer
	• Reprocessing and rework

Packaging/ Labeling	• Packaging operations
	  • Batch record execution and review
	  • Document control
	  • Product sampling
	  • Equipment operation and clearance
	• Labeling control systems
	  • Receipt, inspection, release, issuance, control reconciliation, and storage

Materials	• Raw material and components • Receipt, sampling, test, release, and storage • Warehousing and distribution • Returns and salvage

(Continued)

TABLE 2.1 (*Continued*)

FDA Quality Systems and the Typical GMP Quality Systems

FDA Quality System	Typical GMP Quality Systems

Laboratory Controls	• Laboratory control systems
	  • Sample management
	  • Test methods and specifications
	  • Method validation
	  • Instrument qualification, calibration, and maintenance
	  • Reference standards
	  • Reagents, solutions
	  • Data analysis and reporting
	  • Failure investigations
	  • Glassware control
	  • Contract laboratories management

Quality	• Policies and standards: creation and issuance • Documentation control: Standard Operating Procedures (SOPs), protocols, records and reports, forms, and log books • Regulatory reporting: new drug application (NDA), abbreviated new drug application (ANDA) • Training: GMP and job • Change control: document, equipment, labeling, process, and computer systems • Annual product review • Audit program: internal, contractors, regulatory • Complaint handling • Failure investigations (other than laboratory) • Batch record review and product release • Management notification • Product stability program management and reporting • Computer system validation • Recalls

There are a number of subsystems possible in any of the GMP Quality Systems identified above. For example, computer system validation has a number of subsystems that manage and control the computer system life cycle: validation master planning; Design/Installation/Operation/Process Qualification (DQ/IQ/OQ/PQ) protocols, execution; reporting; periodic revalidation; change control; data center management and control; disaster recovery; and so on.

It is worthwhile to note that the vast majority of operational and quality systems are multi- or cross-functional and involve more than one department for input, execution, and output. This is a reason why having standard operating procedures (SOPs) only defined by department usually results in disconnects and incomplete system design and deviations/observations in performance. Policies, "umbrella" (overarching) SOPs, multifunctional SOPs, or mapped and connected individual SOPs are needed to bridge those gaps and provide the communication links for a robust and sustainable system.

There are also system interdependencies that must be recognized. For example, the QA batch record reviews and product release process depends not only on a completed batch record but also on batch-related information from other control systems: laboratory out-of-specification investigations, process deviation or failure investigations, pending batch-related change controls, regulatory commitments, environmental monitoring and water testing results, product testing results, and so on.

To have effective, robust, and sustainable systems requires that the fundamental process elements are in place, are linked where needed, and sound process management and control is consistently being practiced.

The typical elements of a QMS and the GMP quality systems listed above are also in broad alignment with the essential elements that a quality system shall embody for medical device design, production, and distribution as promulgated in 21 CFR 820 (see below):

1. Personnel training and qualification
2. Product design control
3. Documentation control
4. Purchasing control
5. Product identification and traceability (at all stages of production)
6. Production and process definition and control
7. Process validation
8. Product acceptance
9. Controlling nonconforming product
10. Corrective and preventive actions
11. Labeling and packaging controls
12. Handling, storage, and distribution
13. Records
14. Servicing
15. Statistical techniques

KEY PROCESS/SYSTEMS ELEMENTS

The following elements are key to a robust, effective, and efficient QMS:

- *Process/system inputs are well defined, controlled, and monitored.* In most pharmaceutical systems, the input is documented information; for example, a change control system input is a detailed change request. Information must be complete, accurate, and timely. The input quality can and should be measured where needed. In the change control example, a change request can be right at the first time or sent back for more information. That success rate can be measured and fed back to the suppliers.
- *Process/system ownership, responsibility, and accountability are defined and accepted.* This involves job role and responsibility definition in procedures, job descriptions, and role profiles. It also involves management leadership, planning, resource allocation levels, support organization levels, and process oversight and follow-up. The ownership, responsibility, and accountability must be consistently practiced.
- *Process/system design is adequate for use.* Simple designs by work processes are best but need to include/identify input information, activities, decision criteria, decision outputs, timeliness requirements, document requirements, and how to handle exceptions or deviations and fail-safe or stop criteria where needed.
- *Level of process/system definition is adequate for use.* Having the proper balance of enough information in SOPs, instructions, documents, and forms to achieve consistent execution by different people on different days is the goal. Refer to Chapter 6 Production and Process Controls, for details on SOP content. SOPs should be concise, to the point, user friendly, and written for a trained operator. However, there must be enough "how to" detail to assure consistent execution. Operational SOPs are often good on what is supposed to be done but short on details of how it is done, which leads to varying approaches and unacceptable variation. Quality and consistency of systems relies on minimizing variation, ambiguity, and providing clarity.

- *Consistency in execution.* If the previous elements are in place, consistent execution should follow. Audits and process metrics can be the measurement tools.
- *Process performance and output should be monitored, measured, controlled, and reported where needed.* Process performance and output can be measured by metrics. Metrics can be diagnostic or performance-related. In the change control system, for example, the performance metrics could be on time and right at the first-time completion/approval of change control requests, change authorizations, and change close out. The ultimate performance metric is no adverse impact in product quality or compliance as a result of the change. Diagnostic measures of change control process performance may be types of changes submitted, departmental breakdowns, overall cycle times, and so on.

QUALITY SYSTEM INSPECTIONS

FDA's *Compliance Program Guidance Manual for FDA Staff: Drug Manufacturing Inspections Program 7356.002* closely follows the approaches of risk management and quality systems laid out in FDA's *Quality Systems Approach to Pharmaceutical CGMP Regulations Guide* and FDA's *21st Century Initiative.*

The background section states that the guidance is structured to provide for efficient use of resources devoted to routine surveillance coverage, recognizing that in-depth coverage is not feasible for all firms on a biennial basis. Inspections are defined as audit coverage of two or more systems, with mandatory coverage of the quality system, and coverage of a system should be sufficiently detailed so that the system inspection outcome reflects the state of control. The guidance further lists subsystems and compliance requirements/expectations in each of the six quality systems.

Inspectional observations support the new approach. They are listed in quality systems buckets but are written up in traditional GMP context.

To have an effective internal audit program to evaluate conditions and level of risk and most importantly to gain prompt corrective action, internal audit programs need to be designed to address the system deficiencies, root causes, or lasting improvement, and not just fixing the observation or symptom. Warning letters available on FDA's website show a pattern of comments from the FDA continually citing firms for inadequate response to inspectional observations because they are applying patches to procedures to fix observations and not addressing the root cause. Additionally, FDA will verify if the same or similar observations are made at multiple site inspections of the same company. Identification of quality system failures across sites indicates inadequate corporate quality oversite, lack of executive management visibility to quality issues, and/or lack of any or some corrective actions in a timely manner. Forward-thinking executive management, not just quality, will analyze site observations and determine if they could be the same on other company sites and if so they will promptly respond as needed. They may not have completed all the actions unless there is a significant compliance or product quality issue, but a plan with justifiable timelines to be shared with FDA investigators will be expected.

Performing process audits can provide for better identification of system deficiencies, root causes, and a more effective level of corrective actions.[1] However, this approach requires a different knowledge/skills base for a typical compliance auditor.

The following example is presented to illustrate the difference in approach. An analytical laboratory was audited, and after the first day, there was an observation that the secondary reference standard storage unit had expired reference standard vials co-mingled with in-date vials. The auditor was ready to write the observation as is. The likely action taken to that observation would have been to go through the incubator and remove the expired standards. This would have done little to fix the problem from recurring. By comparison, a system review of the total reference standard program might include a challenge of the following system elements:

- Quality of reference standard system inputs (compendial and other standards)
- Primary and secondary reference standard program ownership, responsibility, and accountability
- Overall system design
- Level of definition and detail in the SOPs
- Consistency in practice
- Training
- Management oversight of the process

This approach might find that the system failure was not an isolated incident, but that it has been happening for some time. The failure may be due primarily to the fact that a SOP requires one person to be in charge of primary standards and another person to be in charge of secondary standards, and in practice no backups were designated or assigned. In this situation, staff on leave would result in a significant gap in coverage. The overall cause would include a questionable system design and poor system oversight and resource allocation.

The resulting observation would cite the deficiencies in design, oversight, and resource allocation. A CAPA to this type of observation would need to address those system deficiencies instead of fixing only the symptom (outdated standards).

A systems audit approach is designed to challenge high-risk or value-adding systems with the fundamental system elements that should be in place rather than just looking for nonconformances (see Key Process/Systems Elements). However, this approach will require a different skill set level for the auditor, different sets of questions being asked, and, most importantly, management support of the concept.

QUALITY RISK MANAGEMENT

Risks are commonly defined as uncertain future events—both positive (opportunity) and negative (risks) that have the potential to affect the achievement of a company's goals and objectives. One of the elements that can help a company achieve their goals and objectives is an effectively functioning risk management and internal control framework. Risk management can be implemented at several different levels within an organization, including setting an organization's strategy, a unit's objectives, or running daily operations. Risks can also be categorized or classified in several different risk frameworks including Strategic Risks, Operational Risks, Financial Risks, and Hazard Risks (e.g., natural disasters). The following discussion of risk management methodologies will focus primarily on their application to pharmaceutical manufacturing operations.

Risk management methodologies have been used for a number of years and applied in many different areas including investment, finance, safety, and medicine. Quality risk management in the pharmaceutical industry is a relatively new concept but was utilized within the FDA in August 2002, when they announced their new major initiative for drug quality regulations on *Pharmaceutical CGMPs for the 21st Century: A Risk Based Approach*.

The FDA uses a risk management approach and methodology in the prioritization of CGMP inspections of pharmaceutical manufacturing sites. In the initial concept paper issued on the initiative, the FDA identified "a risk-based orientation" as one of the guiding principles that would drive the initiative. The concept paper stated that "resource limitations prevent uniformly intensive coverage of all pharmaceutical products and production" and that "to provide the most effective public health protection, the FDA must match its level of effort against the magnitude of the risk."[2] From the basis of this analysis, the FDA determined the top three priorities for their inspection program:

- Firms that produce sterile products
- Firms that produce prescription drugs
- Firms that have not been inspected previously

Applying risk management approaches to pharmaceutical manufacturing operations and decisions makes good business sense and benefits the company and the patient. The importance of quality systems has now been recognized in the pharmaceutical industry and quality risk management is a valuable component of an effective quality system. Risk management can be used in a number of different aspects of pharmaceutical manufacturing including: vendor assessments/audits; process and equipment risk assessments; and sampling/testing criteria.

The ICH Q9 Consensus Guideline on Quality Risk Management describes the general quality risk management process, tools, and application in pharmaceutical operations. Two additional sources of guidance on the elements of a risk management and internal control framework are the Australia/New Zealand Standard on Risk Management (AS/NZS 4360) and the Enterprise Risk Management Conceptual Framework. The COSO Framework identifies eight interrelated components:

1. Internal Environment
2. Objective Setting
3. Event Identification
4. Risk Assessment
5. Risk Response
6. Control Activities
7. Information and Communication
8. Monitoring

The COSO Framework and ICH Q9 are very similar in overall structure; however, for the purposes of this discussion, the ICH Q9 framework will be used. There are two very important cautions to consider before embarking on a quality risk management program:

1. The time, effort, formality, and documentation of the quality risk management process should be commensurate with the level of risk. One can spend more time on the process than mitigating the risk. Although a systematic approach and use of tools are preferred, informal processes can be acceptable, especially for more obvious risks.
2. The quality risk management process should not be used as an excuse to delay or avoid compliance gaps/issues.

Figure 2.2 is an overview of the risk management process described in ICH Q9.

The primary principle of risk management is that the evaluation of risk to quality is based on the risk to the patient. From a manufacturing perspective, anything that has a high impact or is very close to the product will be high risk. For example, weighing of active ingredients in pharmaceutical production operations is a high-risk process worthy of compliance monitoring.

In the world of GMP compliance, there are at least three types of risks to consider:

1. *Patient and Product-related.* These are obviously the highest risk and must always be considered.
2. *Collective Risk*: One can have a series of risks or failures identified that individually may not appear serious or have direct product impact but collectively could have direct

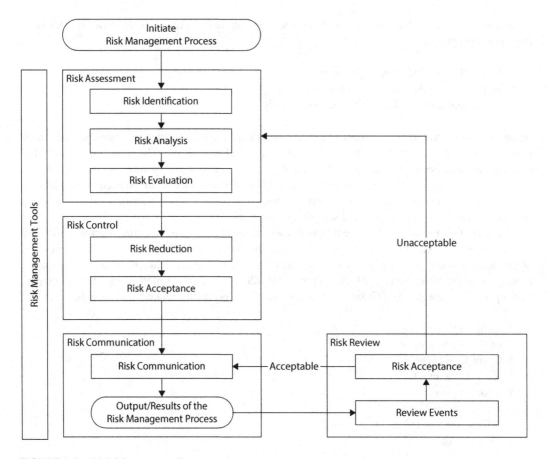

FIGURE 2.2 Risk Management Process.

product impact. An example would be a weak or incomplete change evaluation process, coupled with an inconsistent periodic revalidation process and incomplete historical product records and data. In combination, these deficiencies could lead to product failure. During the risk assessment phase, in addition to ranking individual risks, it is sometimes important to look at the collective risk, especially when systems and interdependencies are involved.

3. *Compliance Failures*: Patterns of failure in GMP compliance, regardless of individual severity, may have an adverse impact on the business if a regulatory agency perceives that the systems are still not in control.

Initiating a quality risk management process usually involves establishing a multidisciplinary team dedicated to the task. Key leaders and decision-makers need to assure risk management has cross-functional participation.

The process described below is based on the eight elements of the COSO Framework; however, they more closely follow ICH Q9 risk management process in order to focus on aspects most relevant to pharmaceutical manufacturing at an operational level.

The process begins by identifying a team leader, establishing project timelines and deliverables, and agreeing the process to be followed.

The first phase of the process is *Risk Assessment,* which includes risk identification, analysis, and evaluation. It is very important that the process starts with a well-defined problem description or risk question. This will help facilitate the gathering of information and data and to choose the correct tools for analysis.

Risk Identification typically involves asking three questions:

1. What might or could go wrong?
2. What is the probability or likelihood it will go wrong?
3. What is the severity or consequence if the event happens?

There are a number of tools that can be used to identify risks, including (1) internal interviews, discussions; (2) brainstorming sessions; (3) external sources (e.g., benchmarking, discussion with peers, comparison to other organizations); and (4) tools, diagnostics, and processes (e.g., checklists, scenario analysis, process mapping).

Risk Analysis involves focusing on the last two questions above and estimating the associated risk and ability to detect.

Risk Evaluation can involve a qualitative (high to low) or quantitative (numerical probability) approach evaluating the impact (significance) and likelihood (chance or probability of risk occurring) for each risk. The identified and analyzed risk is evaluated against the defined criteria. At this stage of the process, it's critical that the criteria are documented and well understood by individuals performing the evaluation. Criteria commonly used in the pharmaceutical industry are a five-by-five model:

Probability of Occurrence (Ratings): Improbable, Remote, Occasional, Probable, Frequent

Severity Levels (Ratings): Negligible, Insignificant, Serious, Critical, Catastrophic

The output of the risk assessment phase is an estimate of risk for a quantitative approach or a range of risk for a qualitative approach. At this stage, you may produce what is commonly referred to as a Risk Map. Two different styles of Risk Maps are shown in Figure 2.3a and b. A Risk Map is

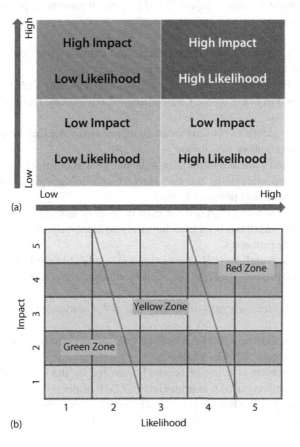

FIGURE 2.3 (a) Impact vs Likelihood and (b) Impact vs Likelihood.

a good tool to visualize the relative likelihood and impact of different risks and provide guidance in prioritizing risks for various mitigation activities.

The second phase is *Risk Control* where the goal is to eliminate or reduce the risk to an acceptable level. Risk control focuses on four questions:

1. Is the risk above an acceptable level?
2. What can be done to reduce, control, or eliminate the risk?
3. What is the correct balance between risk, benefits, and resources?
4. Are new risks introduced as a result of these efforts?

Risk control involves risk reduction (actions taken to mitigate or avoid the risk) and the risk acceptance decision. In some cases, it may not be possible to eliminate the risk altogether, but short-term remedial actions may reduce it to an acceptable level or make sure it is detected.

Risk Communication is the third phase. If a team has been working together on the problem, there should have already been communication between the decision-makers and stakeholders. However, there may be a need for a more formal process of notification for other parties involved in or impacted by the decisions and changes.

Risk Review is the final phase. The output of the risk management process should be documented, especially when a formal process is used. The output and results should be reviewed for new knowledge and lessons learned. The changes and results should be monitored, and if needed, the risk management process can be re-engaged to handle planned or unplanned events. Risk management should be an ongoing quality management process.

Similar to failure investigations (Chapter 7) and process improvement projects, a number of useful tools and techniques can be used including:

- Flowcharts, process mapping, check sheets, and cause-and-effect diagrams can help organize information and facilitate decision-making.
- Failure mode effects (and criticality) analyses (FMEA and FMECA) and evaluates potential failures and likely effect. Can be used for equipment, facilities, manufacturing, and system analysis.
- Fault tree analysis identifies root causes of an assumed failure. Can be used in failure and complaint investigations or deviations.
- Hazard analysis and critical control points (HACCP) was developed in the food industry and is a seven-step systematic and preventive methodology that is used primarily for chemical, biological, and physical hazards.
- Hazard operability analysis (HAZOP) is used in cases of suspected deviation from design or operating intentions. It has been used for safety concerns regarding facilities, equipment, and manufacturing processes.
- Preliminary hazard analysis (PHA) uses past knowledge to help identify future failures. Can be used for product, process, or facility design, especially when information is scarce.
- Risk ranking and filtering breaks down the basic risk question into its components.

Throughout the process, statistical tools can be used to gather and analyze data; for example, control charts and process capability (Cp, Cpk) analysis.

Quality Risk Management is being increasingly adopted by the FDA and the pharmaceutical industry. The FDA has actively used it in prioritizing CGMP inspections as a result of the increasing demand for inspections and the finite level of staff to cover them, and pharmaceutical companies recognize this as a powerful management tool, and as good business practice.

REFERENCES

1. Nally J, Kieffer R, Stoker J. From audits to process assessment—The more effective approach. *Pharm Technol* 1995, 19 (9): 128.
2. Dills DR. Risk-based method for prioritizing CGMP inspections of pharmaceutical manufacturing sites—A pilot risk ranking model. *J GXP Compliance* 2006, 10 (2): 75.

SUGGESTED READINGS

- Quality Systems Approach to Pharmaceutical Current Good Manufacturing Practice Regulations, September 2006.
- Compliance Program Guidance Manual for FDA Staff: Drug Manufacturing Inspections Program, 7356.002.
- Pharmaceutical Current Good Manufacturing Practices (CGMPs) for the 21st Century Initiative, 2004.
- FDA Guidance for Industry: Q9 Quality Risk Management, June 2006.
- Bhatt V. GMP Compliance, Productivity and Quality. *Interpharm*, 1998.
- Field P. *Modern Risk Management A History*. Risk Books, 2003.
- Vesper JL. *Risk Assessment and Risk Management in the Pharmaceutical Industry: Clear and Simple*. Bethesda, MD, Parenteral Drug Association. July 2006.
- Bhote KR. *The Power of Ultimate Six Sigma*. New York, Amacom, 2003.
- Russell JP. *The Process Auditing Techniques Guide*. Milwaukee, WI, ASQ, 2006.
- Kausek J. *The Management System Auditor's Handbook*. Milwaukee, WI, ASQ, 2006.
- Cobb CG. *Enterprise Process Mapping*, Milwaukee, WI, ASQ, 2005.
- Imler K. *Get It Right*. Milwaukee, WI, ASQ, 2006.
- PIC/S Guide to Good Distribution Practices for Medicinal Products, 2014.
- Kolisnyk YPORT. A new method for risk assessment of pharmaceutical excipients. *Pharmaceutical Technology* 2018, 42 (3): 38–44.
- Nally J, Kieffer R, Stoker J. From audits to process assessment—The more effective approach. *Pharmaceutical Technology* 1995, 19 (9): 128.
- Australia/New Zealand Standard on Risk Management (AS/NZS 4360)
- Enterprise Risk Management Conceptual Framework, published by the Committee of Sponsoring Organizations of the Treadway Commission (COSO).

3 Management Responsibility and Control

John E. Snyder

CONTENTS

Management responsibility is fundamentally no different in the pharmaceutical industry than any other business. The quote "The buck stops here" made famous by the sign on the former U.S. President Harry S. Truman's desk applies to anyone who holds the top job in any industry. The top job is where the ultimate accountability resides for the company strategies and decisions to achieve the intended outcomes of the enterprise. For pharmaceuticals, management is individually responsible for ensuring that systems to comply with current good manufacturing practice (CGMP) regulations are effectively implemented in order to establish and maintain a state of control for drug manufacturing, holding, and distribution.

CGMPs and state of control are inextricably connected. Lack of control leading to a Field Alert and Recall due to the potential of product being materially affected will be cited as violations of CGMPs. The converse is also true. A pattern of CGMP violations observed during a Food and Drug Administration (FDA) inspection will also be viewed as lack of control, whether or not the product is materially affected. Either way, the associated product will be deemed adulterated within the meaning of the Federal Food, Drug and Cosmetic Act (FDCA).

The implication of the impact of CGMP noncompliance on the business is not theoretical. There are ample examples in the pharmaceutical industry where ineffective implementation of CGMP systems resulted in loss of control that materially affected product quality, which, in turn, affected inventory and patient supply. Establishing a Pharmaceutical Quality System (PQS) that effectively implements the CGMPs is the means for maintaining a state of control—the fundamental intent of these regulations.

Management does not assume positions of responsibility with the intent of neglecting CGMP compliance. However, management may not enter the top position fully equipped to assume responsibility for CGMPs in a practical way. Management may delegate all CGMP matters to the Quality Department and take a hands-off approach and rely on this function to bring matters to its attention at their discretion. Such passivity leads to hearing only the bad news when it is far too late to contain and resolve the problem in the most cost-effective way with least risk to public safety.

Likewise, some Quality Departments may not be adequately equipped to bridge the space between top management and daily operations with effective structures and processes that enable management to exercise its responsibility for CGMP oversight. Too often, the default position is to rely upon the outcome of regulatory inspections. But as one might expect, a good outcome can give a false sense of security, and a poor outcome can be viewed as the exhaustive list of problems. As in any area of the business where risks must be managed, there is no better approach than having an intentional management system in place that provides actionable data to know internally where your daily operation stands at any given moment.

This chapter provides a model for structuring a practical and effective management system to fulfill this expectation. But first, it is useful to understand the background for the FDA requirement for management to exercise its responsibility for oversight and control.

THE REGULATORY BASIS FOR MANAGEMENT RESPONSIBILITY

Historically, the FDA has cited the Supreme Court decisions of United States v. Dotterweich (1943)[1] and United States v. Park (1975)[2] as FDCA legal cases that establish that the manager of a corporation can be prosecuted under the Federal FDCA, even if there is no affirmation of wrong doing of the corporation manager individually.

In the Dotterweich case, the jury found Dotterweich, the president and general manager of a drug repackaging company, guilty on two counts for shipping misbranded drugs in interstate commerce, and a third for shipping an adulterated drug. One dissenting judge of the Circuit Court of Appeals reversed the decision on the grounds that only the corporation was the "person" subject to prosecution, thus protecting the president personally. But the Supreme Court reversed the decision, thus holding Dotterweich individually responsible, not just the manufacturer. Justice Frankfurter delivered the opinion of the Court, "…under § 301 a corporation may commit an offense and all persons who aid and abet its commission are equally guilty…."

In the Park case, the chief executive officer was found guilty on all counts involving food held in a building accessible to rodents and being exposed to contamination by rodents, resulting in the adulteration of the food within the meaning of the FDCA. Park's defense was that he had an organizational structure responsible for certain functions to handle such matters. However, evidence from inspections of multiple locations indicated the same problems and inadequate system for which he had overall responsibility. Chief Justice Burger delivered the opinion of the Court, "…by reason of his position in the corporation, responsibility and authority either to prevent in the first instance, or promptly to correct, the violation complained of, and that he failed to do so…the imposition of this duty, and the scope of the duty, provide the measure of culpability…"

More recently, Public Law 112–144 (July 9, 2012) called the Food and Drug Administration Safety and Innovation Act (FDASIA) added to the definition of CGMP in the FDCA (Section 501, 21 USC 351) to explicitly include management oversight of manufacturing to ensure quality. Section 711 of FDASIA states:

> For the purpose of paragraph (a)(2)(B), the term "current good manufacturing practice" includes the implementation of oversight and controls over the manufacturing of drugs to ensure quality, including managing the risk of and establishing the safety of raw materials, materials used in the manufacturing of drugs, and finished drug products.

The addition of oversight and controls to the definition of CGMP has strengthened the FDA position with specific language for management's responsibility for oversight and control as a requirement in the Act. The question remains how to practically and operationally to perform this responsibility. The following model describes essential elements of a CGMP Management System for oversight and control.

THE QUALITY MANAGEMENT TRIAD MODEL

Three elements form the framework of this model for designing and implementing structures and processes that enable management to exercise responsibility for oversight and control of CGMP compliance: Governance, the Pharmaceutical Quality System, and Quality System Ownership. These elements are interdependent, and the effectiveness of the model depends upon how well they are designed to work together. The following sections discuss the key attributes of each element of the Quality Management Triad model (Figure 3.1).

THE GOVERNANCE ELEMENT

The governance body is comprised of the top leadership where the ultimate direction is given and decisions are made with respect to aligning resources, including those associated with CGMP compliance. Governance is the standard-bearer for what it endorses, enables, and oversees. To the watching organization, what management says, funds, and pays attention to, are the visible expressions of their values and the cultural setting for CGMP compliance.

Endorse

The governance body endorses a Quality Policy that declares the importance of CGMP compliance to the business by ensuring a continuous of supply of quality product to its patients. This policy provides the foundation for creating a set of Quality Standards that interprets and applies the CGMP regulations and current industry practice to its operations. Quality Standards are cross-functionally endorsed to demonstrate agreement with the minimum, irreducible requirements. Although Quality

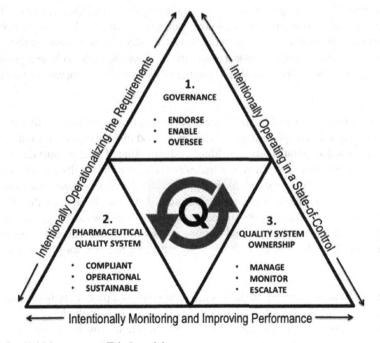

FIGURE 3.1 Quality Management Triad model.

Standards establish the "What," there is latitude for designing processes for "How" requirements are met. Thus, CGMP processes are opportune targets for continuous improvement. The "How" described in standard operating procedures (SOP) is open to creative approaches for designing processes as efficiently as possible that also comply with the Quality Standards, and thus CGMP.

Enable

The governance body enables CGMP compliance by providing the organization structure and resources to implement and support processes described in SOPs. While it is reasonable for management to question whether a process is designed as efficiently as possible, it is not reasonable to withhold resources that affect the ability to comply with Quality Standard requirements. Governance also establishes and partners with an independent Quality Unit that has the product knowledge, technical experience, and CGMP background to perform its unique regulatory responsibilities. The Quality Unit has the responsibility to objectively measure and report on the effectiveness of the PQS, and management has the responsibility for oversight and control.

Oversee

The governance body establishes the Quality Management Review (QMR) process to oversee the ongoing performance of the PQS and to give visibility to problems and risks as a means of understanding the state of control. The QMR process is a data-driven and action-oriented process to ensure that unacceptable risks and trends are quickly identified and verifiably resolved. The Quality Unit is best positioned to administer the QMR process to ensure objective reporting, proper risk assessment, and verification that the intended results of QMR decisions have been achieved. Normal business processes, such as planning and budget cycles, and operational goals and performance objectives, serve also to prioritize and focus company attention where significant change or effort is necessary to improve CGMP compliance.

THE PHARMACEUTICAL QUALITY SYSTEM ELEMENT

The PQS is the interpretation and application of CGMP regulations to the operation. It is an integrated library of documents of increasing specificity from the Quality Policy and Quality Standards down to the SOP, and other executable work instructions. Like a balanced outline, the PQS has an overall structure with each topic taking its position as part of an intentional architecture. SOPs must be fit-for-purpose and remain relevant within a dynamic operational environment. Thus, the PQS is a living system that reflects the requirements, but it also is operational and sustainable the moment its documents become effective.

Compliant

Procedures and the records created by following procedures provide the legal history that affirms that the work was performed in compliance with requirements and that the expected results were obtained. There is no work related to manufacturing, holding, or distributing of drug product that is not described in an approved, written procedure. There is a traceable path from the results entered onto a record up through procedures and directly to standards and policies. It cannot be underestimated the importance to CGMP compliance of having clearly written procedures that logically describe the process steps, the persons who perform them, where results are recorded, and who reviews and interprets. Writing simply and clearly, along with communication and training are special skills required to establish effective procedures so that CGMP requirements are faithfully translated to those doing the work.

Operational

The PQS is intended to work in the actual operation as soon as a procedure is approved and implemented through training. Process flow diagrams are a useful tool in the hands of the user groups to visualize the real-world steps of a process. They facilitate discovery of the supplier of inputs, customers of outputs, and dependent linkages to other processes that may need to be developed or aligned for the overall process to be effective. When and who makes decisions, as well as the conditions or situations in which the Quality Unit is notified are also part of SOP content for the daily operation. For the PQS to be operational, the user groups must actively participate to identify the obstacles to getting work accomplished and having meaningful procedures.

Sustainable

The PQS must be sustainable by providing a supporting organization structure, adequate number of skilled personnel, and an operating budget that are balanced with the demands on the system. Significant operational changes such as acquisitions, facility repurposing, production volume, portfolio complexity, and workforce levels invariably impact the effectiveness of PQS and present a compliance risk if not anticipated and addressed. Performance metrics are the primary tools to continually monitor the performance of the PQS and to provide the operational capability to self-detect and self-correct problems. This capability is essential since continual performance feedback is fundamental for sustaining performance and operating in a state of control.

THE QUALITY SYSTEM OWNERSHIP ELEMENT

The PQS lives in a dynamic business and regulatory environment. Thus, the PQS must be continually reevaluated to ensure its purpose is served. The Head of Quality has functional responsibility for the overall PQS, and management has the overall responsibility for oversight and control. But knowledgeable and skilled Quality System Owners (QSO) at the operational level are needed to take responsibility for ensuring that their respective processes and procedures are continuously relevant, compliant, and integrated. Each QSO has the responsibility for managing their part of the PQS, monitoring performance, and escalating significant issues to management.

Manage

The QSO is responsible for the resilience of their respective parts of the PQS amidst the business changes around them. The QSO has the knowledge and skills to ensure that his/her processes continue to meet compliance requirements, are relevant to the operation, fit-for-purpose, and perform effectively and efficiently. This requires being up to date with CGMP regulations and developing industry awareness to remain current with industry best practices. The QSO is the champion for their respective processes and leads the adoption of significant changes, as well as ongoing continuous improvement. The QSO is the subject-matter-expert and the face of their respective PQS processes.

Monitor

Data-driven information in the hands of a responsible and empowered QSO is essential to the ongoing management of the system and maintaining a state of control. Each QSO has carefully selected metrics that provide ongoing and objective feedback about their respective part of the PQS. There may be key performance metrics adopted by the company or a site operation. There may also be popular ideas about metrics and what they should or should not be. There may even be rules of thumb to limit the number of key performance metrics. However, these should not be confused with whatever performance metrics are personally needed by each QSO to have the data necessary to take responsibility for the daily management and problem detection. In the end, the QSO must be able to answer two questions at any moment: How well is the system operating? What problems or potential problems is the system detecting? The QSO is in the best position to decide on the performance metrics for the systems for which they are responsible.

Escalate

The QSO must have directed a path to management to escalate problems or potential problems that represent unacceptable or unmanageable risk to the patient, the business, or CGMP compliance. The Quality Management Review is the regularly occurring forum where QSOs have the opportunity to report on the state of their system. But there are instances where the degree of risk must permit a direct and unfiltered alert to management. Some problems or potential problems rise to the level where either the cost of the permanent solution or the cross-functional impact requires making the case directly and expeditiously to higher levels of management.

THE ROLE OF QUALITY

Everyone owns "CGMP compliance" much like everyone owns safety. Everyone has personal responsibility for having general CGMP knowledge and awareness, and also having and following specific procedures relevant to their areas of responsibility. However, the Quality Unit ensures that a strategy, such as this Quality Management Triad model, is in place procedurally, in use behaviorally, and has the capability to objectively measure and report on the state of control.

CONCLUSION

Management has the legal responsibility for implementing the CGMP regulations and overseeing and ensuring the operational state of control. To operate in a state of control does not mean perfection. It does mean, however, the capability of a firm to self-detect and self-correct potential problems. And whenever a problem does emerge, the firm is capable of taking action to understand the underlying causes the problem or unacceptable trend, and make decisions that favorably effect the trend, or that prevent recurrence of the problem. The model described here provides the framework for developing and implementing a practical and integrated system for management to have the means to exercise responsibility and have data-driven knowledge of the state of control.

REFERENCES

1. United States v. Dotterweich, 320 U.S. 277 (1943)
2. United States v. Park, 421 U.S. 658 (1975)

SUGGESTED READINGS

- J. Snyder, "Management Oversight of the Pharmaceutical Quality System: Obstacles and Opportunities." *Journal of GXP Compliance* 17 (2), 2013, available at: http://www.ivtnetwork.com/management-oversight.
- J. Snyder, "Management Responsibility for the Quality System: A Practical Understanding for the CEO in FDA-Regulated Industries." *Journal of cGMP Compliance* **3** (3), 55–59, 1999.
- J. Snyder, "Good Manufacturing Practices: Steps to Improve Quality," invited author for chapter in *Pharmaceutical Sciences Encyclopedia: Drug Discovery, Development, and Manufacturing.* Ed. Shayne Gad. New York, John Wiley & Sons, 2010, Published online doi:10.1002/9780470571224.pse406.
- J. Snyder, "Mindful Compliance: Where Knowledge and Regulations Meet." *BioPharm International Supplement, Guide to Good Manufacturing Practices*, 26–34, 2004.

4 Organization and Personnel

Graham P. Bunn and Joanna B. Gallant

CONTENTS

§211.22 RESPONSIBILITIES OF QUALITY CONTROL UNIT

Graham P. Bunn

a. *There shall be a quality control unit (QCU) that shall have the responsibility and authority to approve or reject all components, drug product containers, closures, in-process materials, packaging materials, labeling, and drug products and the authority to review production records to assure that no errors have occurred, or, if errors have occurred, that they have been fully investigated. The QCU shall be responsible for approving or rejecting drug products manufactured, processed, packed, or held under contract by another company.*

b. *Adequate laboratory facilities for the testing and approval (or rejection) of components, drug product containers, closures, packaging materials, in-process materials, and drug products shall be available to the QCU.*

c. *The QCU shall have the responsibility for approving or rejecting all procedures or specifications impacting on the identity, strength, quality, and purity of the drug product.*

d. *The responsibilities and procedures applicable to the QCU shall be in writing; such written procedures shall be followed.*

The QCU is an essential support function for the manufacturing process and the responsibilities are broad despite being based only on the four regulatory requirements above.

The preamble[1] to the regulations contains background information behind the original intent of the 21 CFR 210 and 211 good manufacturing practice (GMP) regulations when they were effective in 1978. A response from the Commissioner was "The quality control unit will still have the duty to assure that appropriate actions were implemented and completed satisfactorily. The Commissioner used the word 'unit' because it is a term broadly applicable to any group within a manufacturing establishment charged with the responsibility of quality control. The Commissioner is not concerned about the name given by a firm to its own unit that is responsible for quality control functions."

Also noted is "...the quality control unit have final responsibility for certain actions in the manufacturing process." Requirements (a) and (c) above are associated in the industry with the Quality Assurance function, requirement (b) with the Quality Control function responsible for testing, and requirement (d) with both functions. The §211.22 regulations do not specifically mention a Quality Assurance function, although it is clearly shown on most company organizational charts. Additionally, during regulatory inspections and customer audits, the ratio of QCU personnel to manufacturing personnel is often requested. This is to ensure that management had assigned adequate resources to cover all the responsibilities of the QCU function(s).

Although the pharmaceutical regulations have not changed with respect to quality since they were initially introduced, there has been a shift reflected in other regulations issued after them. The initial approach was to test the product during manufacturing and the finished product to "confirm" that it met specifications and therefore was a "quality product." Changes to the approach have resulted in building quality into the design (Quality by Design) and process of producing the product, which then uses finished product testing and documentation review as a confirmation step.

The FDA issued "Guidance for Industry, Quality Systems Approach to Pharmaceutical Current Good Manufacturing Practice Regulations".[2] The guidance noted that current industry practice generally divides responsibilities of the QCU between quality control (QC) and quality assurance (QA) functions.

The QC function responsibilities usually involve:

- Assessing the suitability of incoming components, containers, closures, labeling, in-process materials, and the finished products
- Evaluating the performance of the manufacturing process to ensure adherence to specifications and limits
- Determining the acceptability of each batch for release through testing

- Additionally, the microbiology department (same for sterile and non-sterile departments) is responsible for monitoring/testing the materials, environment, personnel, and products against predefined criteria

The QA responsibilities primarily involve:

- Review and approval of all procedures
- Review of associated records
- Auditing and performing/evaluating trend analyses

Procedure approval and review of associated documentation includes all the documents relating to GMP operations; some but not all are mentioned in the regulations, for example: standard operating procedures (SOPs), protocols, out of specification investigations, manufacturing investigations, analytical methods and specifications, protocols, change controls, master batch records, executed batch records, and all support documentation for determining batch disposition. Document approval includes all labeling.

The 21 CFR 211 regulations specifically assign the QCU the authority to create, monitor, and implement a quality system. This authority does not substitute for, or preclude, the daily responsibility of manufacturing personnel to build quality into the product. For a manufacturer to meet their responsibility to produce quality products, both manufacturing personnel and the QCU must be involved in quality decisions.

There does, however, need to be a clear separation between the manufacturing and quality function responsibilities. This prevents the interpretation or ability for any conflict of interest relating to quality decisions. There may be exceptional situations where manufacturing and quality functions are more closely aligned, but there still needs to be approved procedures defining responsibilities and management prepared to explain/justify any differences as needed. Another qualified individual, not involved in the production operation, can still conduct an additional, periodic review of QCU activities.

Equally, QA provides the independent confirmation that operations (manufacturing, testing, engineering, etc.) have been performed according to procedural requirements and predetermined specifications are met or other actions are taken. Ensuring compliance to requirements and reporting the results to management are also required. Quality improvement aspects of the overall organization are also assessed, managed, and presented to senior management by the Quality organization. The Quality organization is expected to not just monitor/assess and report but also to be proactive in all quality aspects, including those not directly originating from the code of federal regulations, for example, ISO and other worldwide guidelines.

When a product is also marketed in different countries, the QCU needs to be aware and ensure that the current good manufacturing practice (CGMP) regulations for that country are also met. There may be specific requirements relating to the Quality organization responsibilities and documentation requirements, for example in the European Union and the requirements of the Qualified Person (see Chapter 23). Other documents approved by the QCU include training related to CGMPs and quality aspects. Annual GMP training is often presented by the Quality organization, although this is not a regulatory requirement (see next section of this chapter). Quality, as it relates to the product and all the supporting aspects, is the responsibility of all personnel that contribute to the product. The Quality organization has the responsibility for providing quality information to the entire organization and ensuring that it is clearly understood. Executive management has specific defined quality-related responsibilities, which they are accountable for implementing, monitoring, and adequately responding to as necessary.

The responsibility for auditing in some organizations is assigned to a separate function of QA and often referred to as the compliance function, although it is still under the overarching QA responsibilities. This covers the internal audit program of all GMP activities on the site, including QA and also includes vendors/contractor/suppliers (companies/individuals providing components and services). Quality is responsible for approving suppliers, contractors, and vendors and also assigning their status (approved, restricted, disqualified) on a vendor list. The purchasing department is only permitted to obtain CGMP-related materials, components, and services from approved or restricted "suppliers." See also Chapter 9, "Contracting and Outsourcing".

Warning letters are notifications to executive management of violations that have regulatory significance, which include the severity of the violations (see Chapter 20, "CGMP Enforcement Alternatives in the United States"). As the QCU has the overarching responsibility for quality and related decisions in addition to keeping management informed of potential impacts to product quality, they are in a key position with all Regulatory Authorities. As such, the citing of the QCU is a significant regulatory observation and needs to be managed in an expeditious and comprehensive way. The fact that the QCU either did not detect the deviations, failed to act completely, or ignored the information/deviations, results in Regulatory Authorities concluding that quality operations are not in a state of control. As a result of these observations, executive management will be held accountable by the company and may respond with internal actions in addition to the announcement in the warning letter posted on the FDA website.

Quality culture has been discussed in relation to GMP operations and also reflects on the QCU,[4] even though all employees should be aware that everyone is responsible for quality. See also Chapter 3, "Management Responsibility and Control".

There must be adequate laboratory facilities available to the QCU in order to perform their responsibilities effectively. It is interesting that this is under the quality authority section and not the general laboratory testing section. This can be interpreted as permitting use of outside contract laboratories where necessary due to capacity or expertise, but these must be comprehensively evaluated according to procedures and approved before use.

Use of contract testing laboratories or any other function (manufacturing, packaging, calibration,) does not absolve the QCU of their responsibilities, and executive management is also held responsible for violations. This is clearly defined by the FDA in the following warning letters, which have been categorized, and the more significant wording underlined to stress the points that the FDA is making:

WARNING LETTER CITATIONS SPECIFICALLY FOR THE QCU

QUALITY OVERSIGHT

In addition to the issues discussed above, you should note that CGMP requires the implementation of quality oversight and controls over the manufacture of drugs, including the safety of raw materials, materials used in drug manufacturing, and finished drug products. *See* Section 501 of the FDCA, as amended by the Food and Drug Administration Safety and Innovation Act (Pub. L. 112-144, Title VII, section 711). If you choose to contract with a laboratory to perform some functions required by CGMP, it is essential that you select a qualified contractor and that you maintain sufficient oversight of the contractor's operations to ensure that it is fully CGMP compliant. Regardless of whether you rely on a contract facility, you are responsible for assuring that drugs you introduce into interstate commerce are neither adulterated nor misbranded. (*See* 21 CFR 210.1[b], 21 CFR 200.10[b].) (https://www.fda.gov/iceci/enforcementactions/warningletters/2016/ucm537064.htm)

QUALITY UNIT AUTHORITY

Significant findings in this letter indicate that your quality unit is not fully exercising its authority and/or responsibilities. Your firm must provide the quality unit with appropriate authority, sufficient resources, and staff to carry out its responsibilities and consistently ensure drug quality.

RESPONSIBILITIES AS A CONTRACTOR

Drugs must be manufactured in conformance with CGMP. FDA is aware that many drug manufacturers use independent contractors, such as production facilities, testing laboratories, packagers, and labelers. FDA regards contractors as extensions of the manufacturer.

You and your customer, (b)(4), have a quality agreement for the manufacture of (b)(4) drug products. You are responsible for the quality of drugs you produce as a contract facility, regardless of agreements in place with product owners. You are required to ensure that drugs are made in accordance with section 501(a)(2)(B) of the FD&C Act for safety, identity, strength, quality, and purity. The FDA issued a guidance document for using CGMP contractors and also contractor responsibilities.[3]

FAILURE TO ESTABLISH QUALITY CONTROL UNIT

Your firm failed to establish a quality control unit and procedures applicable to the quality control unit with the responsibility and authority to approve or reject all components, drug product containers, closures, in-process materials, packaging materials, labeling, and drug products, including drug products manufactured, processed, packed, or held under contract by another company. Your firm failed to establish adequate written responsibilities and procedures applicable to the quality control unit. (21 CFR 211.22[a] and [d]) (https://www.fda.gov/iceci/enforcementactions/warningletters/2017/ucm591826.htm).

You failed to establish written procedures for numerous functions. For example, there were no procedures addressing the quality control unit, deviations, investigations, stability studies, quality review of incoming materials, finished product batch release, and various other basic drug manufacturing operations (https://www.fda.gov/iceci/enforcementactions/warningletters/2017/ucm590011.htm).

Further, your quality control unit lacked documentation to demonstrate acceptability of batch manufacturing and quality. For instance, you lacked records relating to:

- Annual product reviews
- Full batch record review to evaluate if instructions were followed, and to assure that any errors or anomalies were fully investigated
- Approval or rejection of your drug products

During the inspection, our investigator determined that your production manager conducts the final batch review and releases the finished drug product, which is a quality control unit responsibility. Firms acting as contract manufacturers for various aspects of drug manufacturing must comply with CGMP (https://www.fda.gov/iceci/enforcementactions/warningletters/2017/ucm589455.htm).

CGMP CONSULTANT RECOMMENDED

Based upon the nature of the violations we identified at your firm, we strongly recommend engaging a consultant, qualified as set forth in 21 CFR 211.34, to assist your firm in meeting CGMP requirements. Your use of a consultant does not relieve your firm's obligation to comply with CGMP. Your firm's executive management remains responsible for fully resolving all deficiencies and ensuring ongoing CGMP compliance (https://www.fda.gov/iceci/enforcementactions/warningletters/2017/ucm577650.htm).

The FDA investigator requested records related to your QCU to review during the inspection. Your general manager was unfamiliar with QCU terminology. After the investigator explained QCU terminology, the general manager stated that he is "probably" the QCU. We note that essential functions of the QCU were not carried out, including the review of all information related to each batch prior to arriving at a batch disposition decision. For example, there was no secondary/QCU review of the batch production records with questionable data as detailed above. See Section 211.34 below for additional information relating to use of consultants.

PERSONNEL QUALIFICATIONS AND RESPONSIBILITIES

§211.25 PERSONNEL QUALIFICATIONS

Joanna B. Gallant

   a. *Each person engaged in the manufacturing, processing, packing, or holding of a drug product shall have education, training, and experience, or any combination thereof, to enable that person to perform the assigned functions. Training shall be in the particular operations that the individual performs and in CGMP (including the CGMP regulations in this chapter and written procedures required by these requirements), as they relate to the individual's functions. Training in CGMP shall be conducted by qualified individuals on a continuing basis and with sufficient frequency to assure that individuals remain familiar with CGMP requirements applicable to them.*
   b. *Each person responsible for supervising the manufacture, processing, packing, or holding of a drug product shall have the education, training, and experience, or any combination thereof, to perform assigned functions in such a manner as to provide assurance that drug product has the safety, identity, strength, quality, and purity that it purports or is represented to possess.*
   c. *There shall be an adequate number of qualified personnel to perform and supervise the manufacture, processing, packing, or holding of each drug product.*

§211.28 PERSONNEL RESPONSIBILITIES

   a. *Personnel engaged in the manufacture, processing, packing, or holding of a drug product shall wear clean clothing appropriate for the duties they perform. Protective apparel, such as head, face, hand, and arm coverings, shall be worn as necessary to protect drug products from contamination.*
   b. *Personnel shall practice good sanitation and health habits.*
   c. *Only personnel authorized by supervisory personnel shall enter those areas of the buildings and facilities designated as limited-access areas.*
   d. *Any person shown at any time (either by medical examination or supervisory observation) to have an apparent illness or open lesions that may adversely affect the safety or quality of drug products shall be excluded from direct contact with components, drug product containers, closures, in-process materials, and drug products until the condition is corrected or determined by competent medical personnel not to jeopardize the safety or quality of drug products. All personnel shall be instructed to report to supervisory personnel any health conditions that may have an adverse effect on drug products.*

§211.34 CONSULTANTS

Consultants advising on the manufacture, processing, packing, or holding of drug products shall have sufficient education, training, and experience, or any combination thereof, to advise on the subject for which they are retained. Records shall be maintained stating the name, address, and qualifications of any consultants and the type of service they provide.

EXPECTATIONS FOR TRAINING AND TRAINING SYSTEMS IN A GMP ENVIRONMENT

At the center of our operations are people—people who have the appropriate knowledge, skills, and abilities to perform tasks as expected in a GMP environment. The personnel qualification and responsibilities sections of the GMPs address this need, which also tells us that we must provide training that enables the proper performance of tasks.

The actual regulations give us precious little to go on in terms of what "qualified personnel" actually means and what it takes to get there. We can take from the GMPs that:

- Continued training must be provided on GMP and job skill topics.
- Additional expectations are placed on those supervising other personnel.
- Only qualified personnel (including contractors and consultants) perform GMP-related tasks.
- Behaviors, which include some specifically defined responsibilities, of those working in GMP environments are important to achieve compliance.

The FDA Guidance "*Quality Systems Approach to Pharmaceutical Current Good Manufacturing Practice Regulations*"[2] ("the QS Guidance") provides further detail on expectations relating to training:

> In a quality system, personnel should be qualified to do the operations that are assigned to them in accordance with the nature of, and potential risk of, their operational activities. Under a quality system, managers should define appropriate qualifications for each position to help ensure that individuals are assigned appropriate responsibilities. Personnel should also understand the effect of their activities on the product and the customer. Although QU personnel should not take on the responsibilities of other units of the organization, these personnel should be selected based on their scientific and technical understanding, product knowledge, process knowledge and/or risk assessment abilities to appropriately execute certain quality functions (this quality systems feature is also found in the CGMP regulations, which identify specific qualifications, such as education, training, and experience or any combination thereof (see § 211.25(a) and (b)).
>
> Under a quality system, continued training is critical to ensure that the employees remain proficient in their operational functions and in their understanding of CGMP regulations. Typical quality systems training should address the policies, processes, procedures, and written instructions related to operational activities, the product/service, the quality system, and the desired work culture (e.g., team building, communication, change, behavior). Under a quality system (and the CGMP regulations), training should focus on both the employees' specific job functions and the related CGMP regulatory requirements.
>
> Under a quality system, managers are expected to establish training programs that include the following:
>
> - Evaluation of training needs
> - Provision of training to satisfy these needs
> - Evaluation of effectiveness of training
> - Documentation of training and/or re-training
>
> When operating in a robust quality system environment, it is important that managers verify that skills gained from training are implemented in day-to-day performance.

But how do we meet these requirements and expectations? We do so by having an effective GMP training system in place and functioning.

Regulators expect the GMP training system to be focused on the correct performance of tasks and to provide the company the ability to recognize where task performance is not meeting the desired standard. Reference this 2012 warning letter observation to a company regarding their GMP training process:

> Your firm failed to ensure that each person engaged in the manufacture, processing, packing, or holding of a drug product has the education, training, and experience, or any combination thereof, to enable that person to perform his or her assigned functions (21 CFR 211.25(a)). For example, an employee examining (redacted) plates was unable to read and accurately record microbial counts. Additionally, our investigator observed employees functioning in roles supporting your sterile filling operations that were not following the procedures that govern their activities, such as glove change frequency, the handling of dropped objects, personnel monitoring, and sample acquisition.

Your responses indicate that the employees observed during the inspection had been trained in their respective job functions and that they have now been re-trained on these procedures, several of which were made more specific. Your response did not provide an explanation for <u>why your system was unable to recognize, identify and mitigate these performance lapses.</u>[5]

COMPONENTS OF AN EFFECTIVE TRAINING SYSTEM[6]

Let's explore the components of an effective GMP training system (Figure 4.1), describing what each component includes/requires, and how they function together to help us comply with the personnel requirements and expectations defined in the CGMPs. (21 CFR 211.25 & 211.34 are the only sections of the GMPs that address the personnel process, so elements of personnel processes are also discussed in relation to the training system—one can't function without the other.)

Job Descriptions

In order to provide training, first we need to know who is responsible for performing which roles and what baseline knowledge, experience, and skills they require to do so. This information is commonly found in a job description (JD), which is the starting point of our training system.

A JD should exist for each position in the company and define the role and tasks performed, along with describing the level of performance required. Defining these expectations enables the remaining elements of the training system. JDs also allow us to assess an individual's knowledge, skills, and experience against defined criteria, which helps avoid placing someone into a position they're not prepared to perform. For GMP-critical roles, a review by the QCU of the defined experience and educational requirements for the position should be considered. JDs should be approved by area management and the QCU as appropriate.

Organizational charts then should visually structure these positions to show reporting relationships, for purposes of determining accountability for functions and operations. Since neither of

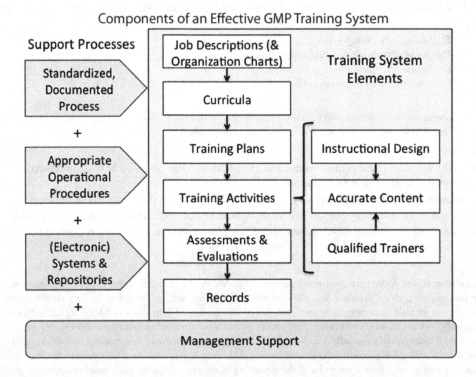

FIGURE 4.1   Components of an Effective GMP Training System. (From JGTA, LLC, Hollis, NH.)

these are currently GMP requirements in the US, we often consider them a non-GMP function—but both are often requested during FDA inspections. In contrast, the EU GMPs require both JDs and organizational charts.

Regulators expect that all positions have an approved job description defining the role, the tasks performed, and an appropriate background of education and experience to enable the individual in the position to perform the role to the expected level, with input from the QCU when appropriate. They also expect organizational charts to depict how the organization is structured, which parties in the organization are responsible for decision-making, and that the Quality organization is independent from the Manufacturing organization. Both JDs and organizational charts should be periodically reviewed for accuracy and completeness and updated as necessary. These are used by the regulators to assess whether the defined training requirements and curricula for the role appropriately align to the defined job tasks. The responsibility for defining required roles and background falls to the area management[2] and is often accomplished with assistance from Human Resources (HR) and/or Training department personnel.

Citings Issued by the FDA in This Area Include

- "Failure to have sufficient personnel with the necessary education, background, training, & experience to assure all activities are correctly performed. For example:
  - The Director of Quality Systems job description requires a Bachelor degree in Science/ Technical/or Engineering disciplines. The person holding the position has a Business Administration degree.
  - The Regulatory Affairs Manager lacks the minimum 5 years of regulatory experience required in the job description.
  - The Quality Control Supervisor lacks the required Bachelor degree in science or the alternative 5-8 years' experience in Quality Control defined in the job description.
  - The Calibration Coordinator lacks the required Bachelor degree and the 4 years of relevant experience."[7]
- "The job description for Sterility Test Technician requires a high school diploma or equivalent ad 1-5 years of related experience. The job description form is silent on minimal requirements for education and experience to interpret microbial contamination in sterility test samples and media fill units."[8]
- "There is no written procedure for quality unit review and approval of job position qualification and job descriptions for personnel to ensure personnel will have the education and experience required to successfully perform GMP operations."[8]
- "The organizational structure has not been adequately established and maintained.... Specifically, ...your firm had no written quality organization...your employee began to draw an organizational chart for me."[9]
- "Individuals responsible for supervising...lack the education, training and experience to perform their functions.... Specifically, the owner acts as the owner, supervisor, and quality control manager who approves and releases all drug products. The owner has no prior experience or training for conducting a supervisory or quality control role."[10]
- "Employees performing the Microbiological testing of finished products and process water used to manufacture products and clean equipment do not have an education in Microbiology."[11]
- "There is no one currently employed that has the education in the engineering field to design equipment for the production of pharmaceutical products."[11]

Curricula

For training to be effective, we must first know what training is needed. In the simplest terms, curricula define task-based groups of training requirements for personnel in a specific position to enable them to meet the expectations of the position (or role).

Training requirements for specific tasks and roles should be relatively standard and expressed as role-based curricula for *all* personnel, including senior management and contract personnel (including temporary employees, contractors, and consultants).

And curricula should define at least three different sets of training requirements—corporate, site, and functional area requirements. These should include whatever combination of items (procedural or policy documents, instructor-led training, classroom courses, self-study, or computer-based training courses) is defined as required for the topic/task, as defined by the area management or process/system owner, and include management/QCU approval as appropriate.

- Corporate requirements are those global items required for anyone working for the company, such as code of conduct, appropriate legal requirements, and Information Technology (IT) and HR policies.
- Site requirements encompass those items required for everyone working at a specific plant site, including plant-specific safety policies and Environmental Health & Safety (EHS) training, local HR/IT/legal requirements, and other requirements applicable to all personnel working on that site.
- Functional area requirements are the task-specific procedures, on-the-job training (OJT), and other task-related training needed for personnel to correctly perform specific job-related tasks, including requalification for tasks as appropriate. (At a minimum, requalification should be considered for tasks where technique or behavior is critical and a periodic verification of correctness is needed, for tasks that are difficult or prone to error, and for tasks that are not performed frequently.)
  - These should also include specific initial and ongoing GMP and other regulatory requirements, along with task-specific safety training—even though these may not be managed by the functional area.
  - In addition, a variety of industry standards reflect expectations for training on specific items that should be included in curricula. Beyond the expectations defined in 21 CFR 211.28's "*Personnel Requirements*" and the QS Guidance shown earlier:
    - Other FDA guidance documents also reflect training requirements and expectations. As examples, "*Sterile Drug Products Produced by Aseptic Processing: Current Good Manufacturing Practice*" lists training topics and an expectation for personnel who work in aseptic processing environments to regularly participate in media fills to demonstrate their qualification; "*Process Validation: General Principles & Practices*" expects that a process performance qualification (PPQ) is performed by personnel who are qualified to run the process.
    - Other industry standards spell out training expectations, such as USP <1116> "*Microbiological Control and Monitoring of Aseptic Processing Environments*," which defines training requirements and expected educational backgrounds (in some cases) for personnel performing processing tasks, monitoring, supervising, testing, or auditing these environments.
    - Other regulatory agencies may also provide guidance on training requirements for specific functions through their regulations and guidance documents. For example, Annex 8 of the European GMPs, "*Sampling of Starting and Packaging Materials*" defines an expected list of items personnel performing sampling are expected to be trained on, while Annex 16, "*Certification by a Qualified Person and Batch Release*" requires specific background and training for Qualified Persons (which in the US aligns to those personnel performing the review and release of batches to the market).
  - Also, curricula should include professional development requirements appropriate for specific positions or levels (such as leadership development training for management, or specific certifications required for IT, engineering, and project management positions).

Regulators expect to see each person assigned role-based curricula reflective of their job description and assigned job tasks, which is periodically reviewed for accuracy and updated as needed. These role-based curricula should also reflect differences in levels of positions (i.e., the difference between an Analyst II and an Analyst III—see *Training Plans*).

The responsibility for defining appropriate training curricula for each position falls to the area management responsible for the tasks or systems.[2] These individuals also hold the responsibility for periodically reviewing and updating curricula when appropriate.

Citings Issued by the FDA in This Area Include

- "You did not train contract employees in CGMP or in job-specific procedures....Your contract employees conducted critical CGMP operations for your finished drug products such as visual inspection of filled capsules, sealing, 100% verification of sealed bottles, final label quality inspection, outsert pasting on bottle caps, and the final packing in boxes."[12]
- "Manufacturing operators did not have specific training on corresponding manufacturing batch records and validation protocols before executing job functions. For example, ...an operator executed compression manufacturing activities without receiving training in the corresponding MBR. As a result of the current inspection, your Quality unit initiated a deviation to report the event. The investigation found other employees executed manufacturing operations for other lots without receiving training in the applicable MBRs. The investigation identified that the MBRs are not included as part of the training provided, and they are not reflected as missing in the Missing Report provided by the Training Department."[13]
- "Employees are not given training in written procedures required by cGMP. Specifically, the Record of Training checklist does not ensure that employees complete annual refresher training on all applicable written procedures.... For example, the Manufacturing Supervisor's 2014 procedure training did not include all his responsibilities such as equipment calibration, housekeeping and recordkeeping."[14]
- "Employees engaged in the manufacturing...of a drug product lack the training required to perform their assigned functions... Six of nine QA Inspectors assigned to this job function never had training in the QA inspection of (redacted) syringe safety guards or plunger rods."[15]
- "Procedures of training and identifying training needs have not been adequately established. Specifically, review of training records for two assembly employees revealed your firm has not identified the training needs for these two employees to ensure they adequately perform their assigned responsibilities."[16]
- "You designated X employees as members of the QCU, giving them the responsibility to approve or reject all components, containers, closures, in-process, and final materials; however, none of these employees received any training in quality control unit responsibilities."[17]
- "Firm's training of regulatory affairs personnel. consumer affairs personnel, territory business managers (sales reps) and customer service personnel fails to assure that they have the knowledge necessary to attempt to obtain all pertinent information from complainants in order to complete adequate investigation of complaints..."[18]

Training Plans

Next, we need to determine when it's appropriate and how to provide training, which we capture in training plans. Training plans should address at least three areas: onboarding, job skill training and ongoing/continued training.

For onboarding of personnel, the company, each site, and each department should have an appropriate onboarding program defined that encompasses the items defined in the curricula.

Corporate and site onboarding may be combined into one program managed at each worksite, or it may be managed separately if appropriate and sustainable. There should be an expectation set that onboarding training will be completed within an appropriate time window from the person's arrival in the company/on the site (two weeks, for example). Typical onboarding programs are managed by HR or Training departments, in conjunction with the other participating parties (i.e., EHS, IT, Security, etc.), and typically encompass a combination of instructor-led/classroom courses, self-study training (reading of policies/procedures), and computer-based training provided and owned by the responsible areas of the company/site.

For those personnel who will be working in GMP areas, companies may either include a GMP orientation program as part of onboarding, or manage it separately, typically through a quality-focused

Training department. Some companies require only those personnel who will be performing GMP functions to complete GMP orientation, while others require it of all personnel, to provide a basic understanding of the requirements the company must work within. However, it is a basic expectation of the regulators that all personnel performing GMP tasks complete any defined GMP training requirements prior to performing tasks independently.

And then, each department should have an orientation program for bringing newly hired personnel into the workgroup. Department orientation should be documented as part of the training process, and should include:

- A discussion with the manager, covering:
  - The work schedule and departmental work practices
  - A chance to ask any questions about the onboarding program content
  - An expectations message about the importance of, and working within, both the GMP and EHS requirements (including any of the specific "personnel responsibilities" defined in the regulations that are applicable to the individual's position)
  - A review of the new hire's job description, the departmental training plan and training process, and initial training assignments
- A tour of the work area and other important locations
- An introduction to other group and department personnel, as well as others the new hire is expected to interact with
- A confirmation of what equipment/supplies the new hire will need, and whether they are available or have been requested

Once onboarding is completed, the next step is job skill training (also termed "on-the-job training," or OJT). OJT requirements should be defined in a departmental training plan that documents the progression of tasks in the development of an employee through the variety of roles/tasks in that department (see Appendix 4.1, "Training Progression Samples"). It should be structured such that OJT builds on previous skills acquired earlier in the process and proceeds through tasks in a logical order (easier to more complex tasks/skills, daily tasks to less frequently performed tasks, etc.).

Then, in alignment with the defined curricula and training plans, but based on the individual and their specific experience and needs, we define and assign an individual training plan tailored to meet the individual's needs. In many cases, this happens through performance management and personal development planning discussions. The combination of a departmental and individual training plan allows for flexibility while individuals learn the skills to perform required tasks. What each individual needs to be able to meet the requirements may vary, but the task requirements and expectations should be the consistent for all those who perform the task.

Finally, the site needs a plan for ongoing/continued training. This should be defined on an annual basis, in a formal site training plan (see Appendix 4.2, "Sample Annual Site Training Plan") that is approved by site leadership and reviewed on an ongoing basis at management review meetings to ensure compliance. Encompassed in this process should be maintenance training (such as annual GMP, EHS, and aseptic refresher training, for example) as well as other larger-scale improvement initiatives (such as rolling out a new change management system, or upgrading an electronic system, for example). The annual site training plan should include:

- The training topic/type (i.e., annual GMP refresher, aseptic refresher, documentation management system rollout, onboarding, etc.)
- Planned timing for the training (i.e., July, 1st quarter, etc.)
- Target audience for the training (i.e., all GMP personnel, all laboratory personnel and support staff, all site management, etc.)

- Required completion date—as a time window from launch point (i.e., 45 days from assignment) or specific due date (i.e., end of 1st quarter, October 1) as appropriate.
- Approvals from the site's functional area leadership (i.e., Heads of Quality, Production, Facilities, Training, etc.)

The site training plan allows the various parts of the organization to plan for what training has been defined as required for specific audiences and provides a mechanism for management to hold personnel and areas accountable to expectations.

Regulators expect that the training assigned to any individual is appropriate to their position, as defined by appropriate organizational management. They also expect all personnel to complete their assigned training on time, and to stay current with changes or updates to their assigned training. The underlying expectation is that personnel are qualified to perform their tasks and do not undertake tasks without having completed both the GMP and task training defined as required for the task/role.

Citings Issued by the FDA in This Area Include

- "The Employee Training SOP states that 'employees shall receive cGMP training at least once a year.' There has been no cGMP training conducted since 8/1/11. Additionally, the QA Manager has not received cGMP training since 2009."[19]
- "The firm's president and quality director directly involved in the manufacturing of drugs are not trained on a continuing basis and with sufficient frequency to ensure that they remain familiar with cGMP requirements. Their last documented training was in 2006."[20]
- "Four QA Auditors performing...visual inspection failed to have the annual basic eye examination report required by SOP (redacted), Inspector Qualification Program, which reads in part, 'QA Auditors are requalified on an annual basis by passing a basic eye examination.'"[21]
- "There is no periodic GMP training provided to full time or temporary employees...."[22]
- "One validation manager is overdue for...training by more than 168 days."[23]
- "Temporary employees are given cGMP training by the temporary agency that employs them, they do not receive any additional training at this company such as job specific training."[11]
- "Employees are not given training in the particular operations they perform as part of their function. Specifically, requalification of the production operators within aseptic operations have not participated in media fills, as per SOP# 90-161-02, 'Validation of Aseptic Fill Challenges,' to ensure the operators remain current with relevant established procedures and cGMPs."[24]

Training Activities

Since we have now defined who to train on what, and what personnel need to be able to do when trained, we can now provide *appropriate* training activities. These may be provided in a variety of forms, which are defined in the instructional design process (see *Instructional Design*).

Regulators expect training activities to reflect the tasks and effectively prepare personnel to perform those tasks. They also expect that training is provided as needed or as defined in the site training plan. Additionally, they expect that training is successfully completed and utilized in performing the task—usually stated as training was "effective."

For training activities to be appropriate, the training being delivered must be accurate, designed to attain the desired goal, and provided by a Qualified Trainer. Most training effectiveness discussions typically consider the training activities because they're the most visible piece of the process, and we usually base effectiveness decisions on the *delivery* of the training and whether or not it met expectations. But basing judgment on this element alone overlooks many other things critical to our ability to provide effective training. The quality of the training activity directly affects training effectiveness, but it actually results from the combined outputs of three different process elements: Instructional Design, Accurate Content, and Qualified Trainers. (Further detail on these elements will be defined in those specific sections.)

The responsibility for ensuring that appropriate training activities occur, and subsequent verification of training effectiveness falls to the area management[6] but is usually accomplished with assistance from the Training department.

Citings Issued by the FDA in This Area Include

- "Multiple deficiencies were noted during review of the Design History File...We acknowledge your belief that the personnel...were appropriately trained in research and innovation capabilities; however, QA activities are not the same. If these employees had adequate experience as you have stated, we may not have discovered deficiencies which resulted in your firm voluntarily recalling product from the market."[25]
- "'Solution defects' for manual penicillin visual inspection include particulates per SOP (redacted); however, inspectors are not required to demonstrate the ability to identify this defect during qualification. An inspector observed an employee performing visual inspection who was qualified...and was unable to identify this defect in the test set."[26]
- "Cell bank technicians are not trained and challenged to identify microbiological contaminations while performing in-process testing of shake flask culture during the creation of cell banks."[27]

Instructional Design

The instructional design process enables us to define and build appropriate training and effectiveness measures. An instructional designer uses a specialized skillset to break a task down into its multiple components and determine how to effectively teach and assess each one. It begins with a needs analysis, which identifies what the training needs to include and accomplish—and whether training is actually needed at all. Then, the instructional designer, usually in conjunction with a subject matter expert (SME), designs and builds the content and practice activities, determines the most appropriate type of delivery for the training and the best type of assessment activities based on the intended use of the content, and then builds the assessments.

Training can be designed to be provided in a number of forms—instructor-led hands-on (usually OJT) or classroom training, self-study training such as e-learning (online/computer-based training packages or simulations) or reading policy or procedural documents. Each type has a place, and in many circumstances, a blended approach using multiple components of varying types (i.e., training on a new documentation management system that encompasses reading the procedures and attending instructor-led hands-on system training) provides the most appropriate training for a task. The form and delivery approach for the training should be defined during the instructional design process.

In addition, training activities may have different goals in mind—these also need to be considered in the approach. Training for awareness may simply require reading a procedure, while training for performance may require reading a procedure, along with hands-on OJT and a performance assessment. And the same training content may be used in different ways by different groups. For example, both Quality and Manufacturing personnel will require training on batch production activities, but Manufacturing will focus more on training that enables performance of the production activities, while Quality will focus their training more on understanding and reviewing the performance of those activities.

Regulators expect companies to provide well-designed training that matches the performance and procedural expectations for the task and enables personnel to perform to those expectations at the completion of training. The responsibility for ensuring that appropriately designed training exists falls to the process owners, typically area management,[2] but the instructional design process is usually completed through a combination of Training department personnel and an SME from the process owner's staff.

Citings Issued by the FDA in This Area Include

- "Recent training activities on numerous SOP revisions (some including major technical changes in process/equipment/test procedures) are grouped together in lengthy (100+) slide presentations provided online for 'read & understand' training by employees, without adequately assessing the training effectiveness and implementation of the changes."[28]

- "Your training SOP (redacted), Validation for Inspection, is deficient. This SOP is used to qualify employees performing visual inspections of your products. It does not require the visual inspection to occur in the same manner as done during production...."[29]
- "The inspection documented that the visual inspection certification program (VIC) for inspections of finished product does not adequately challenge the technician(s) performing the inspection. The...VIC program only requires that one of the five critical defects be included in the challenge set. Although the following are identified as critical defects: a vial with a crack neck, missing cap, missing stopper, high/low weight, and a foreign body, only a missing cap defect is included in the visual inspection program. This test will only show that the technician(s) is capable of detecting a missing cap, but it does not show that the technician is capable of detecting other critical defects. Additionally, the SOP does not require that the critical defect challenge vial selected be rotated to ensure that each inspector is challenged to detect each critical defect."[30]

Accurate Content

Effective training *must* provide accurate content. Training content should include and provide linkages to the procedures relevant to the task, appropriate background information relevant to the task (such as explanation of theory or the purpose of the task, where the task fits into the company's process, common errors to watch for, etc.), and references to regulatory expectations and guidance as appropriate. During the process of developing the training, at minimum an SME and the process owner, along with the QCU when appropriate, should review the training materials for accuracy and compliance with procedures, relevant GMP requirements, and other regulatory expectations. The training materials should be approved prior to implementation.

This review and approval should occur through a training content approval process that should also include a system to control the approved content and any changes to it. This process also needs to include defining the appropriate audience for the training, along with assessing the need for retraining personnel as part of the change process. Where approved content is used on a continual basis, it should undergo periodic review, and should also be reviewed when system or process changes are made, to ensure continued accuracy and appropriateness.

Regulators and process owners alike expect training to provide accurate, relevant information and skills the trainees require to perform the task correctly.

Citings Issued by the FDA in This Area Include

- "There are no criteria for establishing and maintaining the vial inspection qualification library, such as the number and type of defects required."[31]
- "Foreign matter is detected using a magnet and the naked eye. Analysts are trained using a training lot consisting of a sample material seeded with foreign matter. There is no procedure describing how to create the training lot (i.e., materials chosen based on type and color, foreign matter materials and size). Employee...was trained on this method using a training lot...The training lot used did not include foreign matter small enough...to fully validate the test method. This same employee performed this method...and recorded a passing result for significant foreign matter particles."[32]

Qualified Trainers

Next, Qualified Trainers must deliver our training. Qualified Trainers should be SMEs with the technical skills and knowledge that allow them to properly perform the task, provide appropriate task background and answer questions, and assess trainee performance of the task. Qualified Trainers also need training delivery skills and interpersonal skills similar to those who supervise personnel, because during the training process, the Qualified Trainer acts as a supervisor, providing guidance and direction, assessing performance, and providing feedback. Where, and what type of training the Qualified Trainer delivers will define their required skillsets, as providing one-on-one task training in an operational environment is very different than providing group training in a classroom.

The US GMPs explicitly state that training must be provided by Qualified Trainers. The regulators tend to define these as experienced personnel who have task-specific knowledge and a history of performing the task correctly—but also have the skills to assure the quality of the operation they're supervising as a trainer (which implies the training and supervisory skills are also required). Much of the previously stated expectation for the training system to "recognize and mitigate performance lapses" will fall to the Qualified Trainer providing the training, along with the area management monitoring both trainee and trainer performance.

A variety of individuals within an organization may be designated as Qualified Trainers—and the expectations for those providing knowledge-based and performance-based training may differ, along with the process for developing/qualifying the trainer. However, the site will be expected to provide a trainer qualification process that enables those chosen as trainers to provide evidence of qualification on both their content knowledge and their training skills, as well as providing evidence that they have been authorized to provide training on that topic by the area management or process owner. The responsibility for providing and conducting the trainer skill qualification process typically falls to the Training department, with input from functional area management. On occasion, it may also be desirable to include a QCU approval for competence on GMP or quality-related knowledge.

Citings Issued by the FDA in This Area Include

- "A manager is listed as the designated trainer for production. SOP (redacted), Trainer Qualification, states that supporting documentation of technical skills based on on-the-job experience will include his/her training record for the training task. The manager does not have documented training...as defined in SOP (redacted). Department management approved the manager to be a trainer based on their scientific understanding, GMP training, and the review of the necessary documentation. Department Management stated that a trainer does not have to be able to perform the actual manufacturing steps to be qualified to train others. The manager is documented as a trainer for 2 operators."[33]
- "The individual responsible for providing training to the Microbiological Laboratory personnel is a Chemist with limited background in Microbiology."[11]
- "The QC laboratory failed to review and approve QC laboratory trainers to assure the trainers are qualified...The Microbiology QC Manager and the QC Director confirmed there is no review and approval process for QC laboratory trainers."[8]
- "We observed a lab technician with beard hair exposed...because the beard cover worn was not appropriate to cover all his facial hair...He is also responsible for training new EM personnel on Aseptic Gown Qualification and EM Sampling Qualifications."[34]
- "During a laboratory investigation initiated...to investigate an OOS result...you concluded that the OOS result was caused by a pipetting error by the analyst. There is no record to indicate that the analyst received training in this technique. A year later...this same analyst was reported as providing training to other analysts and supervisors about correct glassware handling and pipetting as a corrective action after additional OOS results were attributed to pipetting errors."[35]

Assessments and Evaluations

Once training has been provided, we need to ensure that it accomplished our desired outcomes. To do this, we assess and evaluate both the trainee and the training program itself. This is the portion of the process where we evaluate training effectiveness, versus at the completion of delivery of the training event as discussed earlier.

When we assess and evaluate trainees at the completion of training, we should expect them to demonstrate that:

- They have the desired level of content knowledge to perform the task appropriately.
- They have developed and can use the skills required to perform the task.
- Where necessary, they can react appropriately to different situations they may encounter.

In order for Qualified Trainers to make these assessments—as well as to enable them to recognize and identify trainee performance lapses—a predefined standard or set of criteria must be defined, which the Qualified Trainer then uses to assess the trainee's level of performance.

It's important to use the right assessment type to get an accurate picture of the trainee's capability—assessments are not one-size-fits-all.

- For hands-on, task-oriented training, a performance assessment checklist (PAC) is a robust training assessment technique. PACs define the knowledge and performance standards required for competent performance of a task and documents the trainer's assessment of the trainee's level of competence against these criteria (See Appendix 4.3, "Sample Performance Assessment Checklist"). Another option, particularly where the training is intended to enable the use of a specific system, process, or tool (i.e., Failure modes and effects analysis (FMEA)), is a simulation where the trainee demonstrates their ability to use the system/process/tool to accomplish the task.
- For knowledge-based training, the most common assessment approach is a knowledge assessment (i.e., quiz) that demonstrates the trainee's level of understanding of the topic/content. These can be delivered on paper or electronically, during or at the completion of training. They can also be administered pre- and post-training, to assess the change in knowledge the training provided.

Whatever assessment(s) will be used for the training should be defined and created as part of the instructional design process, be approved as part of the training material approval process, and be subject to the same change control and periodic review process as the rest of the training materials.

Additionally, part of the instructional design process involves evaluation of the training program itself, which also provides value from the GMP standpoint. Training program evaluations typically follow the Kirkpatrick Model[36] or similar models to help identify whether the training program obtained the desired results, and if not, what areas to investigate to determine how to address it. As an example, the Kirkpatrick Model evaluates the following four levels:

- *Reaction*: Level 1, the first level in the Kirkpatrick Model, assesses trainee reactions to the training program, including whether the trainees saw the content as being relevant to their role/function. If this level scores low, the trainees likely did not get much benefit from the training program. The appropriateness of the content, delivery format, and the target audience should be reconsidered and the program redone.
- *Learning*: Level 2 assesses whether the trainees learned the knowledge or skill the training was intended to teach. This can be measured through a knowledge assessment (including pre- and post-training assessments), skill demonstrations, performance of a simulation, or other demonstration that learning has occurred. If the trainees don't show the ability to perform the skill or use the knowledge at the completion of the training, the design and the content of the training program should be assessed for appropriateness, along with the qualification of the trainer who provided the training.
- *Behavior*: Level 3 assesses whether the trainee uses the skills and knowledge from the training on the job, in their work environment. The manager makes this assessment in the operational area, by determining through oversight whether the trainee is performing the task correctly and utilizing the training content. PACs are one way of assessing and documenting evidence that the behavior learned in training is being used on the job. This means that the training must match the operation, which requires operational area involvement in the needs analysis, content identification, and design process. There must also be post-training follow-up to ensure the trainee is able to transfer the knowledge and skill into the operation, and support, which may include procedure updates, performance oversight, and communication of new

or changed expectations. If transfer isn't seen, consider whether the design and content of the training accurately reflected the task; also, consider whether the elements that drive personnel performance (support, oversight, procedures, and expectations) are in place.

- *Results*: Level 4 assesses the value the training provided through determining whether the new behavior enabled the desired change in the output of the operation—such as less deviations, less errors or improvements in operational quality post-training. Making this determination requires having metrics/data that can be directly correlated to the behavior and the training and has been tracked both before and after the training. If improvements are not seen here as a result of training, it may indicate that the metrics are measuring items that do not directly relate to the training, or that the expected change did not occur because something in addition to the behavior is in play in the situation.

Assessment and evaluation responsibilities often fall to a variety of personnel, depending on the type of training. The process owner will need to provide support personnel, along with the Training department. Training personnel and the instructional designer will have responsibilities throughout the process as well, along with management and the QCU.

Regulators expect personnel to have been "qualified" to perform the operations correctly—which includes a demonstration of capability to perform to the defined standards for the task, often the SOP-defined steps along with a verification that the person has the appropriate level of content and GMP knowledge to perform the task correctly—and that this is proven prior to the person being released to perform the task independently. Evidence should exist, in the form of records, that demonstrate the operator's correct performance of the task and possession of the appropriate knowledge, as appropriate. The level of assessment should be based on risk and reflect the difficulty and criticality of the task.

Citings Issued by the FDA in This Area Include

- "Your investigation confirmed that an analyst assigned to run the active air sampler did not set up and run it correctly, but labeled and incubated the plates anyway. Visual inspection of the incubated plates…did not show evidence of exposure in the air sampler."[37]
- "There is no assurance that operators execute the visual inspection of filled…syringes in a consistent manner and in accordance with the firm's written procedure....The execution of the visual inspection process was observed to be inconsistent in that…during the visual inspection… two operators performing the visual inspection were inconsistent in the amount of time they spent examining units."[15]
- "No evidence was provided that Quality Specialists can adequately identify all specific container/closure and product defects. Inspection technique competency is demonstrated by inspecting batches on-the-job, only identifying defects observed in those batches without qualification against all defect types."[26]
- "Your firm lacks adequate production/process controls to ensure consistent production of a… drug. Specifically, the most recent growth media simulations conducted to qualify two operators were not adequate for the following reasons:
  - The operator was not observed by a qualified person during hand washing, intermediate gowning, and preparation of components to evaluate adherence to procedures.
  - The operator was not observed by a qualified person during final gowning to evaluate proper gowning technique.
  - The operator was not observed by a qualified person when performing the final product vial assembly to evaluate adherence to procedures and aseptic technique."[28]

Records

The training system must generate the appropriate records to demonstrate the effectiveness of the system, along with the history of the training completed by individuals. As with anything else under GMP, if it wasn't documented, it wasn't done…and therefore can't be proven.

In addition to providing evidence of training completion, we should capture records of content approvals and change control, assessment results, curricula, training plans, and more. These records help demonstrate that the system is effective and training is happening appropriately, as well as providing proof of qualification to auditors. Training curricula or matrices should also be periodically reviewed to ensure all appropriate procedures/training are included, and that assignment to personnel is appropriate—this review should also be documented and included in personnel training files and curriculum management files.

Generation of records falls to the personnel responsible for the specific training activity—this may be the department providing the training, the process owner, or Training department personnel as appropriate—and it is the responsibility of area management to ensure that training that occurs in their area is appropriately documented.

Regulators expect to see records that have been defined throughout the training system process, including:

- Job descriptions and assigned duties
- Personnel curriculum vitaes (CVs) or resumes, demonstrating education, background, and prior work experience
- Training curricula (may be in the form of a training matrix, but should reflect role-based curricula) and site training plans
- Records of training activities (including topics covered, date of training, identification of the trainer, attendee signature sheets for instructor-led training, and records of assessments administered to trainees)
- Records of trainer qualification and traceability to topics/sessions taught
- Training system SOPs and associated records required by the site's defined process.

Citings Issued by the FDA in This Area Include
- "There are no training records for the Quality Control/Inventory Management worker and Quality Control Manager."[38]
- "Personnel training is not documented. Specifically, your firm lacks documented evidence of training...for personnel who perform operations related to the manufacturing activities... and/or quality system activities."[39]
- "Your Training SOP requires all employees to be trained 'to perform assigned responsibilities' and also requires maintenance of training records. No records were provided to demonstrate that employees who performed design control activities had been trained on the Design Control procedure. In fact, there were no training records at all for these three employees."[25]

WHAT PROCESSES SUPPORT THE TRAINING SYSTEM?

Having the elements of the system in place is a good start, but the system won't work without additional support processes in place and functioning appropriately.

Standardized, Documented Process

The most basic support to any GMP system is a standardized process documented in our operating procedures, because an effective system requires consistency of application and standards for operating the system.

A centralized GMP training system procedure should be put in place and followed by all groups on the site. Allowing groups to each write their own training procedures leads to inconsistencies in the training system, with can create gaps.

For a GMP training system, our procedure(s) should include standard descriptions of:

- Our training policy, including a general set of training expectations that align with regulatory expectations
- Our training system, and the processes included in the training system—including the definition and assignment of training plans/curricula, trainer qualification, training material

implementation/periodic review/change control, documentation of training, management of transfers, training waivers, management of training failures, and disqualification of previously trained personnel
- On-the-job training
- Standardized time frames for training completion and standard requirements to be completed
- Interfaces with the Learning Management System (as appropriate—see *Systems & Repositories*)

This often falls to a centralized Training department or the QCU to draft and manage these procedures/processes for the site. Often, there will be a "training liaison" in each functional area who works with the Training department to manage the training process in their respective area.

Regulators expect our defined process to be documented and followed and encompass the items listed above.

Citings Issued by the FDA in This Area Include

- "Your training for the qualification of employees for identifying colonies during EM is inadequate. There is no documentation describing the qualification process."[29]
- "Your firm has not established procedures that define employee training requirements, how training will be provided, when training will be required, and how training will be documented."[40]
- "SOP deficient, as follows: It does not identify a pass mark for the firm's consultant GMP training course, nor details for retraining and follow-up when an employee fails or does not take the exam; there is no description of cGMP training to be completed by new employees; ongoing GMP training, including on-the-job GMP training, does not exist."[41]

Appropriate Operational Procedures

Appropriate operational procedures are critical to an effective training process, because we derive much of our training content from them. Procedures should clearly define processes, responsibilities, and tasks to an appropriate level of detail and provide standard performance requirements for each process. Ambiguity of performance requirements or responsibilities, or the lack of documented processes, causes training effectiveness to suffer, as it's difficult to teach, learn, or assess a process that everyone does differently due to the lack of a defined standard. However, if procedures provide on-the-job reinforcement of items learned in training—even wording as simple as "at this point in the investigation, perform a root cause analysis to identify the root cause of the problem"—they automatically improve training effectiveness because they tie directly to what was learned and define when to use it. Trainees should be taught to use and always follow procedures when performing the task.

Area management and process owners, and the SMEs they appoint as procedure authors, have the responsibility to define the necessary operational procedures to the correct level of detail in order to enable consistent performance of tasks. Those SMEs should then be part of the training development and implementation process to ensure appropriateness and accuracy of the training process, content, and assessments.

Regulators expect procedures to provide enough specific detail to enable correct performance of tasks by personnel trained to perform the process/procedure, who follow the procedures, executing them as written when performing the task.

Citings Issued by the FDA in This Area Include

- "Written procedures…do not have descriptions in sufficient detail to ensure controlled, effective and consistent/reproducible cleaning results for a validated process. In one case, instructions read, 'Visually inspect the load for cleanliness at the completion of the cycle. If the equipment is not clean, then repeat the cleaning process.' In a validated cleaning process, established and proven process parameters render equipment clean. But in this case, the subjective decision-making of the operator is used. Another example is, 'Rinse all valve parts with water,' but no parameters (volume of water, time, water pressure or equipment used) are given."[42]

- "Written procedures do not sufficiently describe visual inspection of containers, closures and labeling as part of your receiving process. Instructions for collecting samples of raw materials, containers, and closures are not adequately described."[43]
- "Batch records do not contain specific instructions to prevent variability from operator to operator during manufacturing. Blending/milling instructions do not include specific instructions for the operators. There is no mention of what a 'suitable' container is, and there is no mention as to how uniformity of the blended material can be determined."[44]

(Electronic) Systems and Repositories

Systems and repositories (preferably electronic) ensure that we can manage the process, associated materials and records, and access the information we need. Having a location where people can access controlled, approved training materials and information provides the same benefit as a controlled documentation system—access to current, consistent information.

Best practice, due to the ease of management and access to information, is a centralized repository for the variety of types of training data that we need to maintain, as examples:

- Job descriptions should be centralized with HR and periodically reviewed for accuracy.
- Training materials (including sample test sets) should also be in a controlled repository, so that approved training materials are available to all Qualified Trainers approved to provide that training. If test samples are required, there should be a defined creation process to ensure they are made correctly and consistently each time. Training material approval and periodic review records and the like should also be maintained with the training materials.

  These should exist in the department that owns/is responsible for providing the training, accessible to Qualified Trainers who need to provide the training using these materials—but the Training department should be aware of where this is in the event of requests from auditors. Alternatively, the Training department may set up a centralized training material repository, to which Qualified Trainers are granted access.
- Curricula development, changes, approval, periodic review, and assignment records should exist in a centralized repository with the Training department, as this department typically manages the process of developing and assigning personnel curricula, particularly where learning management systems are in use. If this is done on paper, it's best to maintain this with the Training department as the single point of contact for curricula management.
- A file of training records (including assessments, CVs, and other personnel-specific information supporting their qualification and completion of assigned training requirements) should be in a centralized location, usually with the Training department or the QCU.

While training/process requirements and records can be successfully managed using a well-controlled paper system, electronic learning management systems (ELMS) and learning content management systems (LCMS) make these processes much easier to manage. For example, the ability to easily access records enables us to quickly verify an operator's qualification regarding a specific task prior to assigning the task, or to answer a regulator's request for evidence of training.

An ELMS/LCMS should be high on the list for any company to implement for the benefits to the levels of control, visibility, and efficiency the system provides to the GMP training process. ELMS/LCMS systems enable:

- Creation and assignment of role-based curricula
- Tracking and notification of training assignments and completions, with approvals if desired
- Notifications and escalation of any incomplete training requirements
- Hosting of electronic training content and assessments
- Identification of Qualified Trainers for specific topics

- Electronic/paperless documentation of training activities, with the ability to upload paper records as support/evidence of qualification
- Reporting and metrics generation capabilities
- Manager access to dashboards that show all assigned personnel and allow for individual management activities for each individual

The ELMS/LCMS chosen should meet the user requirements the company deems important, and fit with their defined training system. These systems may be locally owned, or vendor hosted/provided over a cloud-based or software-as-a-service (SaaS) system and can be scalable based on the company's size and needs.

ELMS/LCMS ownership and management typically should fall to the Training department. Procedures should describe the process and use of the system, which should be validated and subject to the appropriate computer system validation/Part 11/good automated manufacturing practice (GAMP) requirements and company change control processes—even if it's a vendor hosted system. There may be a need to have multiple administrators across the company/site, but this should be managed carefully. System administrators should understand the architecture and logic of the system, which comes from regular use of the system. Functional area personnel and management should be users of the system—allowing additional personnel "administrator" level access should be done only as needed, due to the potential for errors that can occur (usually restricted to the area "training liaison" mentioned earlier, if at all).

Regulators expect a standard library of training materials to be maintained for a variety of tasks, accessible to those who require them to perform training or qualify others on tasks. Reference materials (i.e., procedures, examples) should be available as needed. It is also an expectation that the training process is managed and reported on, and that an archive of records exists. (It is not required to use a computer system for these repositories, but if one is used, expectations for compliance with Part 11, along with the requirements for computerized systems captured in 21 CFR 211.68, including access controls, backups, and protection from loss/deletion of data will be applied to the system.)

Citings Issued by the FDA in This Area Include

- "The QC Laboratory uses 'A Training Guide for New Analysts,' which is not mentioned in either training procedure. This 'training guide' is not maintained in accordance with the training document retention requirement."[45]
- "A defect library containing a representative sampling of potential types of particulates that can and/or have been found in your products has not been developed to train your operators and inspectors who perform visual inspection activities."[46]
- "There are no criteria for establishing and maintaining the vial inspection qualification library, such as the number and type of defects required. The test library includes only (redacted) of which are rejects."[31]
- "Written procedures are maintained in a cabinet in management's office and are not easily accessible to production employees."[47]
- "Your firm utilizes experienced employees (QFEs) to accomplish OJT training, including training in the recognition of product defects. Your firm has established SOP..., 'Defect Recognition Manual,' which provides the training curriculum for the recognition of defects during production. The procedure requires the employee in training be provided samples of acceptable bags. The training is further delineated into area specific defects related to the particular defects expected to be encountered by the employee, with a requirement to provide the employee in training 'samples/photos of the defects for the appropriate area and explain the defects.' According to your Compliance Training Supervisor, QFEs are responsible for maintaining and providing any samples or photos to employees in training that are necessary for training. According to your QFE, while completing her duties, she provides OJT to employees in training in the packaging area. She displays and discusses reject samples as she observes them in the normal course of operations. The QFE stated that no standardized defect samples or photos are

maintained, no list or log of defects which have been discussed with the employee in training, and no assessment or evaluation by the QFE exists other than marking 'yes/no' to the question 'Were all reject bags placed in the appropriate bin?'[48]

- "Only (redacted) total employees have taken the recently implemented, web-based ISOtrain 'GMP Orientation All in One Lesson 4'... (redacted) of the 10 employees lack certification of the training."[46]

Management Support

Despite all of the previous system elements, management support has the largest impact on training effectiveness. But what does "support" mean? In a word: "expectations." The expectation for the training system—and everything encompassed by it—is to qualify personnel to perform their tasks correctly, and in compliant fashion. Which means that our management teams should expect that GMP-related training:

- Addresses those items supporting GMP-compliant performance
- Is provided on an ongoing basis, only by personnel qualified to provide training
- Is meaningful and provided in a way that provides the knowledge and skills required for task performance
- Is completed on time by all personnel performing work affecting Quality Systems—which is monitored and enforced by functional area management
- Provides results that are measured, reported, and acted on appropriately—including mechanisms to identify personnel who are not qualified to perform specific tasks
- Provides skills and knowledge that are used in functional area operations, which is ensured by the functional area managers
- Has the appropriate systems and support processes in place and functioning appropriately, with all personnel accountable for their parts of the process
- Is viewed as part of the job and ongoing employee performance management processes, and training performance is reviewed and discussed with personnel

Regulators expect that management personnel are qualified to oversee employees and operations in such a way that the quality of the product is assured—and, as a result, that management has a vested interest in the content, the quality, and the process of training and is performing the appropriate oversight of the personnel and the training process itself. The QS Guidance[2] clearly assigns responsibility for all aspects of training to management and requires senior leadership and management to define the desired work culture, provide policies and procedures—and then defines these topics for inclusion in our training courses and content. Regulators also expect management to provide sufficient qualified personnel to perform tasks, which may mean determining where additional resources are required, or extending training requirements to additional personnel to ensure enough task coverage exists for GMP processes. These responsibilities fall to senior leadership and all others throughout the company who are charged with process ownership or oversight of personnel performing GMP-related tasks.

Citings Issued by the FDA in This Area Include

- "The number of qualified personnel is inadequate to perform and supervise the manufacture, processing, packing, and holding of each drug product. According to the Laboratory Manager, they do not have the staff to adequately investigate OOS test results. In addition, the Quality Control Manager stated they need (redacted) people to conduct all of the testing—at the start of this inspection there were (redacted) laboratory staff members."[11]
- "Operator (redacted) was not qualified for visual inspection at the time of inspecting lots of (redacted), a sterile biologic product."[31]
- "Our investigators observed poor aseptic practices...For example, operators with exposed skin were observed making interventions over open product using a non-sterile (redacted).

Your response indicates that you will make changes to minimize the need for interventions. However, your response does not address the training of operators that is essential to ensure that all employees working on the filling line have been properly instructed on aseptic technique and cleanroom behaviors...Furthermore, your firm should ensure proper daily supervision and evaluate training effectiveness."[49]

- "Operators involved in cleaning operations/aseptic connections during filling were observed demonstrating incorrect aseptic techniques. We expect operators conducting operations within aseptic processing areas be properly trained and monitored to ensure that proper aseptic techniques are utilized during all operations."[50]
- "There is no oversight ensuring validation group employees complete required training."[23]
- "Training of employees is insufficient in that personnel are performing routine job functions without being trained on the current approved procedures. For example, a quality fill finish inspector performed AQL visual inspections on three lots of drug product without being trained on current version of the procedure."[51]
- "Failure to provide and document appropriate training on the operations employees perform.... Please provide a plan to investigate the extent of this deficiency and address the reasons why your manufacturing & quality management failed to detect these training deficiencies. This plan should also include procedures/provisions for proper quality oversight that ensures employees are adequately trained to perform their responsibilities with respect to cGMP."[52]
- "Testing Facility Management failed to ensure that personnel clearly understand the functions they are to perform."[53]
- "The current inspection noted the previous 2012 Observation #14 [documenting incidences where operators were not appropriately trained on procedures, not adequately following procedures and/or procedures were too difficult to follow] has not been adequately corrected. There have been approximately 1,070 incidences, including 280 deviations, of operators performing activities for which they have not been adequately trained impacting 256 vaccine batches to have been caused by 'Process procedure not followed' and/or 'Insufficient/unclear instructions in SOPs and Checklists,' and 'Operator error.'"[55]

CONTRACTORS AND CONSULTANTS

When specialized knowledge or service is required, many companies source consultants or contractors. Portions of the previous discussion address identifying training requirements for these individuals—which implies that they should be treated similarly to other employees in our training system. The key to understanding how to manage these personnel lies in recognizing who they are, what we're asking of them, and how these two roles differ from each other and from traditional employees.

Let's start by defining the two roles. Consultants are non-company employees hired on the basis of their knowledge or expertise in a particular subject matter—usually hired to advise or provide guidance on process development or improvement, or to audit to identify process gaps or weaknesses. Contractors are also non-company employees, but contractors are usually hired on the basis of having the technical skills needed to execute a specific task or project for the company—like performing an annual maintenance task on equipment, cleaning, or providing technical writing services. Temporary employees (including interns and personnel sourced through staffing agencies, as examples) may also be categorized as contractors.

These definitions provide some guidance on what training requirements are needed for both:

- Because a consultant is providing guidance based on their own knowledge/experience, minimal operational and GMP training should be required. By virtue of the fact that the person is a "consultant," they should already possess the expertise in their subject area and GMP requirements associated with it. The key is that they are providing guidance versus performing a task for the company.

Required training for a consultant should be in the form of an abbreviated new hire onboarding process that encompasses those items that are legally required for the person to be onsite—including training on basic safety requirements, critical company policies, the company's code of conduct, and other appropriate topics as necessary. The abbreviated process should not include training on employee-specific topics such as HR processes, benefits, corporate systems, and the like, as the consultant should not be expected to use these systems. In terms of operational training, for an advising consultant, minimal procedural training should be needed, but they should be expected to review the information that exists on the process on which they'll be advising.

- A contractor, however, is hired to perform a required task on behalf of the company, which means they require the same training on the task that would be expected of a company employee who would be performing that task.

  Contractor training may also utilize an abbreviated onboarding process similar to what a consultant may receive, due to the contractor's non-employee status. However, where this person will actually perform tasks, operational training on procedures, company systems, and the like will be required to enable the individual to perform their tasks in alignment with the company processes, but the scope of the training may vary based on the task and the person brought in to complete it (for example, contract personnel should not perform approvals on behalf of the company, so this may be eliminated from the training provided; alternatively, equipment training may not be required for a contractor who works for the equipment manufacturer). This may also include attending either a specialized contractor GMP training or participating in the GMP training defined for company employees, depending on the tasks required of the person.

For both consultants and contractors, however, companies are expected to obtain evidence to support the qualification of the person on the jobs they've been hired to perform. This should include a minimum of a CV/resume listing the person's name, address, and background (including work history and educational experience enabling them to perform the job), and a description from the company of the work they're being hired to provide (this may be a job description, consulting/service contract, statement of work or similar). Based on the individual's CV/resume, the company may decide to waive certain training (i.e., basic/annual GMP) based on the individual's experience/background; however, any decision to waive required training must be documented (with justification and supporting evidence) and approved by the QCU to ensure that it doesn't risk product or process quality.

The line blurs when we hire a consultant then subsequently ask them to function as a contractor. A good consultant will recognize and inform the company that their role has changed and state that training is needed for them to be able to perform the job, but this responsibility truly falls to the company—the process owner(s) charged with oversight of the operation(s) the consultant is performing must ensure the consultant is appropriately qualified.[2] Appendix 4.4 provides a sample of a decision tree that can be used to help define what training is required for the various types of personnel a company may use—full time, temporary, contract, and consultant—based on what the individual will be doing for the company.

Responsibilities for establishing these processes fall to a variety of personnel throughout the company—HR, EHS, Legal, QCU, and Training department personnel along with hiring managers—and in some cases the process owners if there are special requirements to be defined for the contracted personnel.

Regulators expect that companies ensure all contracted and consulting personnel they utilize are qualified to perform their assigned tasks, and that qualification is documented as directed in the GMPs. Further, the company is expected to provide the appropriate level of oversight of the contracted operation and personnel performing that operation on their behalf[2]—whether that occurs on- or off-site. Roles, responsibilities, expectations, and requirements should be spelled out in a quality agreement between the company and the contracted party (Refer to FDA Guidance to Industry *"Contract Manufacturing Arrangements for Drugs: Quality Agreements"*[57]).

Chapter 2 of the European GMPs, *"Personnel"* reflects similar requirements, but extend it a step further, to encompass visitors as a category of personnel as well. Visitors must be appropriately trained and escorted during the times that they can impact GMP areas.

In addition to earlier examples, further citings issued by the FDA in this area include:

- "The quality unit failed to establish approved procedures for the management of contract service providers with access to GMP areas. There is no documented quality unit oversight for personnel contracted to supply cleanroom garments (sterile gowns) to ensure there is no impact to GMP areas. Sterile gowns are used in all aseptic processing areas. (redacted) provides on-site coordinators to deliver garments to gowning rooms. No documentation could be provided to show when contracted employees were on site, or their designated reporting relationship to someone at (redacted)"[8]
- "A consultant was hired in 2012 which performed an internal audit on your behalf, but there is no documentation indicating the consultant was qualified based on their ability to meet specified requirements."[56]
- "Records are not maintained stating the consultant's qualifications and type of service provided Specifically, you do not have documentation of the qualifications and services provides for the consultant used.... Additionally, you do not have records documenting the consultant's qualifications, training and experience."[54]

SUMMARY

For such a short section of the regulations, the training and personnel behavior expectations carry a lot of weight into the rest of the GMP process. The general expectation is that each company has a plan for all personnel (both employee and non-employee populations) that ensures anyone having the opportunity to impact GMP operations is appropriately qualified, evidence of that qualification can be provided, and supervisory oversight ensures that personnel are correctly performing work that can impact product or process quality. A fully implemented GMP training system as described here will ensure that these expectations are met.

REFERENCES

1. CGMPs Preamble Federal Register, VOL. 43, NO. 190—Friday, September 29, 1978, Title 21-Food and Drugs CHAPTER I-Food and Drug Administration Department of Health, Education, And Welfare Subchapter C-DRUGS: General [Docket No. 75N-0339] Human and Veterinary Drugs Current Good Manufacturing Practice in Manufacture, Processing, Packing, or Holding.
2. FDA Guidance for Industry: Quality Systems Approach to Pharmaceutical Current Good Manufacturing Practice Regulations. U.S. Department of Health and Human Services Food and Drug Administration Center for Drug Evaluation and Research (CDER) Center for Biologics Evaluation and Research (CBER) Center for Veterinary Medicine (CVM) Office of Regulatory Affairs (ORA) September 2006.
3. FDA Guidance for Industry: Contract Manufacturing Arrangements for Drugs: Quality Agreements, November 2016.
4. Chesney David L., Vice President, Strategic Compliance Services PAREXEL Consulting, Waltham, MA USA, "Corporate Culture of Quality": IVT Quality Metrics and Management Week, Coronado, CA, February 22, 2016.
5. FDA Warning Letter 320-13-06, 12/17/12. FDA website. Accessed 25 Jan 2017. http://www.fda.gov/ICECI/EnforcementActions/WarningLetters/2012/ucm335195.htm
6. Whitepaper, "Achieve the Holy Grail of Training Effectiveness," Joanna Gallant. 2015, JGTA, LLC. JGTA website. Accessed 29 Jan 2017. http://www.jgta.net/?product=article-achieve-the-holy-grail-of-training-effectiveness
7. FDA Warning Letter, 7/2/10. FDA website. Accessed 25 Jan 2017. http://www.fda.gov/ICECI/EnforcementActions/WarningLetters/2010/ucm219001.htm

8. FDA 483, April 2014. FDA website. Accessed 25 Jan 2017. http://www.fda.gov/downloads/AboutFDA/CentersOffices/OfficeofGlobalRegulatoryOperationsandPolicy/ORA/ORAElectronicReadingRoom/UCM424825.htm
9. FDA 483, September 2015. FDANews (purchase required). http://www.fdanews.com/form483/49027-gopers-int-llc---september-30-2014
10. FDA 483, September 2014. FDANews (purchase required). http://www.fdanews.com/form483/49027-gopers-int-llc---september-30-2014
11. FDA 483, January 2011. FDA website. Accessed 26 Jan 2017. http://www.fda.gov/downloads/AboutFDA/CentersOffices/ORA/ORAElectronicReadingRoom/UCM244257.pdf
12. FDA Warning Letter 320-14-08, 5/7/14. FDA website. Accessed 28 Jan 2017. http://www.fda.gov/ICECI/EnforcementActions/WarningLetters/2014/ucm397054.htm
13. FDA 483, June 2011. FDANews (purchase required). http://www.fdanews.com/form483/40071
14. FDA 483, September 2014. FDANews (purchase required). http://www.fdanews.com/form483/48976-high-chemical-company---september-5-2014
15. FDA 483, August 2014. FDANews (purchase required). http://www.fdanews.com/form483/49008-amphastar-pharmaceuticals-inc---august-8-2014
16. FDA 483, August 2014. FDANews (purchase required) http://www.fdanews.com/form483/49094-xiamen-taft-medical-co-ltd---aug-1-2014
17. FDA 483, August 2013. FDANews (purchase required) http://www.fdanews.com/form483/44933-keystone-laboratories-inc---aug-8-2013
18. FDA 483, August 2010. FDA website. Accessed 28 Jan 2017. http://www.fda.gov/downloads/AboutFDA/CentersOffices/OfficeofGlobalRegulatoryOperationsandPolicy/ORA/ORAElectronicReadingRoom/UCM278326
19. FDA 483, April 2013. FDANews (purchase required) http://www.fdanews.com/products/44228
20. FDA 483, September 2014. FDANews (purchase required) http://www.fdanews.com/products/48982-aurora-medbiochem-company---september-4-2014
21. FDA 483, May 2013. FDANews (purchase required) http://www.fdanews.com/products/44713-jubilant-hollister-stier-llc---may-10-2013
22. FDA 483, January 2013. FDANews (purchase required) http://www.fdanews.com/form483/43520
23. FDA 483, December 2011. FDA website. Accessed 26 Jan 2017. http://www.fda.gov/ucm/groups/fdagov-public/@fdagov-afda-orgs/documents/document/ucm282550.pdf
24. FDA 483, May 2006. FDA website. Accessed 26 Jan 2017. http://www.fda.gov/AboutFDA/CentersOffices/OfficeofGlobalRegulatoryOperationsandPolicy/ORA/ORAElectronicReadingRoom/ucm059200.htm
25. FDA Warning Letter DEN-14-01-WL, March 17, 2014. FDA website. Accessed 26 Jan 2017. http://www.fda.gov/ICECI/EnforcementActions/WarningLetters/2014/ucm389625.htm
26. FDA 483, August 2014. FDANews (purchase required) http://www.fdanews.com/form483/48648-king-pharmaceuticals-llc---august-26-2014
27. FDA 483, August 2014. FDANews (purchase required) http://www.fdanews.com/form483/49385-cubist-pharmaceuticals-inc---july-10-2014
28. FDA 483, December 2012. FDANews (purchase required) http://www.fdanews.com/form483/42498
29. FDA 483, December 2013. FDANews (purchase required) http://www.fdanews.com/form483/45985-university-of-iowa-pharmaceuticals---dec-13-2013
30. FDA Warning Letter 320-12-01, October 2011. FDA website. Accessed 28 Jan 2017. http://www.fda.gov/ICECI/EnforcementActions/WarningLetters/ucm275960.htm
31. FDA 483, January 2015. FDA website. Accessed 26 Jan 2017. http://www.fda.gov/downloads/AboutFDA/CentersOffices/OfficeofGlobalRegulatoryOperationsandPolicy/ORA/ORAElectronicReadingRoom/UCM438176
32. FDA 483, September 2014. FDANews (purchase required) http://www.fdanews.com/form483/48894-l-perrigo-co---september-16-2014
33. FDA 483, September 2013. FDANews (purchase required) http://www.fdanews.com/form483/45668-sanofi-pasteur-limited---sept-20-2013
34. FDA 483, August 2013. FDANews (purchase required) http://www.fdanews.com/form483/45430-allergan-sales-llc---aug-2-2013
35. FDA 483, June 2001. FDA website. Accessed 26 Jan 2017. http://www.fda.gov/downloads/AboutFDA/CentersOffices/OfficeofGlobalRegulatoryOperationsandPolicy/ORA/ORAElectronicReadingRoom/UCM064086
36. Kirkpatrick Donald L. The Kirkpatrick Philosophy. Kirkpatrick Partners website. http://www.kirkpatrickpartners.com/OurPhilosophy/tabid/66/Default.aspx

37. FDA Warning Letter CBER-14-02, April 16, 2014. FDA website. Accessed 26 Jan 2017. http://www.fda.gov/ICECI/EnforcementActions/WarningLetters/2014/ucm394488.htm
38. FDA 483, June 2014. FDANews (purchase required) http://www.fdanews.com/form483/49006-surgical-design-inc---june-17-2014
39. FDA 483, June 2014. FDANews (purchase required) http://www.fdanews.com/form483/48625-xten-industries-llc---june-04-2014
40. FDA 483, March 2013. FDANews (purchase required) http://www.fdanews.com/form483/43813
41. FDA 483, March 2011. Private source. https://fdazilla.com/inspections/database/3002806423-20110304
42. FDA 483, August 2013. FDANews (purchase required) http://www.fdanews.com/form483/44931-oso-biopharmaceuticals-manufacturing-llc---aug-23-2013
43. FDA 483, October 2012. FDANews (purchase required) http://www.fdanews.com/form483/42082
44. FDA 483, July 2013. FDANews (purchase required) http://www.fdanews.com/form483/44920-formulation-technology-inc---july-18-2013
45. FDA 483, May 2013. FDANews (purchase required) http://www.fdanews.com/form483/44668-bayer-healthcare-pharmaceuticals-inc---may-24-2013
46. FDA 483, August 2012. FDA website. Accessed 26 Jan 2017. http://www.fda.gov/downloads/AboutFDA/CentersOffices/OfficeofGlobalRegulatoryOperationsandPolicy/ORA/ORAElectronicReadingRoom/UCM350766.htm
47. FDA 483, July 2012. FDANews (purchase required) http://www.fdanews.com/form483/42217
48. FDA 483, April 2011. FDA website. Accessed 28 Jan 2017. http://www.fda.gov/downloads/AboutFDA/CentersOffices/OfficeofGlobalRegulatoryOperationsandPolicy/ORA/ORAElectronicReadingRoom/UCM277366.htm
49. FDA Warning Letter 320-14-07, April 2014. FDA website. Accessed 28 Jan 2017. http://www.fda.gov/ICECI/EnforcementActions/WarningLetters/2014/ucm397240.htm
50. FDA Warning Letter 320-11-09, February 9, 2011. FDA website. Accessed 26 Jan 2017. http://www.fda.gov/ICECI/EnforcementActions/WarningLetters/ucm243561.htm
51. FDA 483, November 2009. FDA website. Accessed 28 Jan 2017. http://www.fda.gov/downloads/AboutFDA/CentersOffices/OfficeofGlobalRegulatoryOperationsandPolicy/ORA/ORAElectronicReadingRoom/UCM191991.htm
52. FDA Warning Letter 320-14-10, 7/7/14. FDA website. Accessed 26 Jan 2017. http://www.fda.gov/ICECI/EnforcementActions/WarningLetters/2014/ucm404316.htm
53. FDA Warning Letter 10-HFD-45-08-01, August 2010. FDA website. Accessed 28 Jan 2017. http://www.fda.gov/ICECI/EnforcementActions/WarningLetters/ucm222775.htm
54. FDA 483, September 2014. FDANews (purchase required) http://www.fdanews.com/form483/49027-gopers-int-llc---september-30-2014
55. FDA 483, October 2014. FDANews (purchase required) http://www.fdanews.com/form483/49056-glaxosmithkline-biologicals---oct-2-2014
56. FDA 483, October 2015. FDANews (purchase required) http://www.fdanews.com/form483/51721-cramer-products-inc---oct-26-2015
57. FDA Guidance for Industry: Contract Manufacturing Arrangement for Drugs: Quality Agreements. U.S. Department of Health and Human Services, Food and Drug Administration, November 2016. FDA website. Accessed 29 Jan 2017. http://www.fda.gov/downloads/drugs/guidances/ucm353925.pdf

SUGGESTED READINGS

- FDA Guidance for Industry:
  - Quality Systems Approach to Pharmaceutical Current Good Manufacturing Practice Regulations. U.S. Department of Health and Human Services, Food and Drug Administration, September 2006. FDA website. Accessed 25 Jan 2017. http://www.fda.gov/downloads/Drugs/.../Guidances/UCM070337.pdf
  - Sterile Drug Products Produced by Aseptic Processing—Current Good Manufacturing Practice. U.S. Department of Health and Human Services, Food and Drug Administration, September 2004. FDA website. Accessed 27 Jan 2017. http://www.fda.gov/downloads/Drugs/.../Guidances/ucm070342.pdf
  - Process Validation: General Principles and Practices. U.S. Department of Health and Human Services, Food and Drug Administration, January 2011, Revision 1. FDA

website. Accessed 7 Feb 2017. http://www.fda.gov/downloads/Drugs/Guidances/UCM070336.pdf

- Contract Manufacturing Arrangement for Drugs: Quality Agreements. U.S. Department of Health and Human Services, Food and Drug Administration, November 2016. FDA website. Accessed 29 Jan 2017. http://www.fda.gov/downloads/drugs/guidances/ucm353925.pdf
- USP, "USP <1116> Microbiological Control and Monitoring of Aseptic Processing Environments." USP 35 Volume 1, 2012, p. 697–707.
- Eudralex, Rules Governing Medicinal Products in the European Union; Volume 4: EU Guidelines for Good Manufacturing Practice for Products for Human and Veterinary Use.
  - Part 1, Chapter 2, "Personnel." European Commission, Health and Consumers Directorate-General, Public Health and Risk Assessment. 16 August 2013. EC website. Accessed 7 Feb 2017. https://ec.europa.eu/health/sites/health/files/files/eudralex/vol-4/2014-03_chapter_2.pdf
  - Annex 8, "Sampling of Starting and Packaging Materials." European Commission, Health and Consumers Directorate-General, Public Health and Risk Assessment. EC website. Accessed 7 Feb 2017. https://ec.europa.eu/health/sites/health/files/files/eudralex/vol-4/pdfs-en/anx08_en.pdf
  - Annex 16, "Certification by a Qualified Person and Batch Release." European Commission, Health and Consumers Directorate-General, Public Health and Risk Assessment. 12 October 2015. EC website. Accessed 7 Feb 2017. https://ec.europa.eu/health/sites/health/files/files/eudralex/vol-4/v4_an16_201510_en.pdf

APPENDIX 4.1: TRAINING PROGRESSION SAMPLES

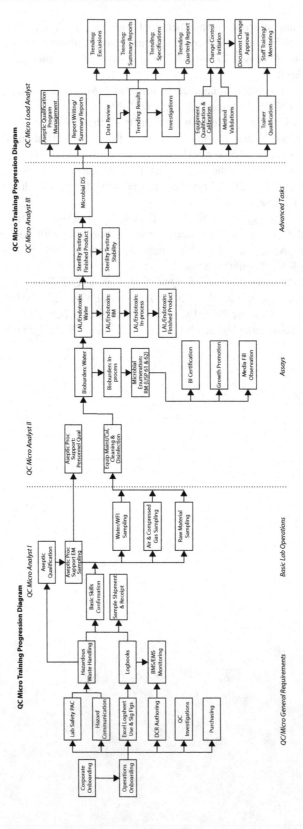

Formulation & Filling Training Progression Diagram

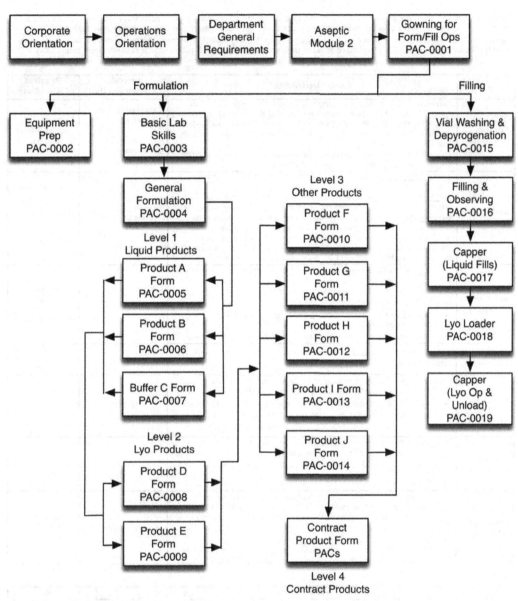

Source: JGTA, LLC, Hollis, NH.

APPENDIX 4.2: SAMPLE ANNUAL SITE TRAINING PLAN

The Annual Site Training Plan describes the minimum training that must be completed for all personnel specified. This training may include courses that encompass ongoing regulatory requirements or regulatory commitments, enable continuous quality improvements, improvement of employee skills, or any other topic that will protect or improve the quality of manufactured products or quality management processes. The planned series of training for the site in 2012 will include the courses listed below. Any additions or changes to the Site Training Plan will be approved.

Topic	Course Description	Schedule/ Completion Due	Required Attendees
New Hire Orientation	**Employees:** Provides basic onboarding training, including required corporate, HR, Safety and GMP training for new hires, preparing them to arrive into their assigned workgroups with basic training requirements completed. NHO includes time for review of basic SOPs and completion of computer-based GMP subpart training. **Contractors/Consultants:** E-learning session addressing basic company safety and compliance requirements, and corporate procedures.	Employees: Every other week Contractors & consultants: Upon arrival	All newly hired personnel
GMP Refreshers	**Area Specific GMP:** One hour, instructor-led training covering 1-2 relevant GMP topics specific to the area. **Standards:** E-learning sessions on newly developed corporate standards affecting a specific business group (i.e. QC, Validation, etc) will be assigned. **General GMP:** One hour, instructor-led training to cover any changes to the US/international regs since September of 2010 and current happenings in the industry. How the reg changes affect our jobs will be highlighted. Course will also focus on the general regulatory environment and news/industry trends from the past year, highlighting major CDs, WLs, and other enforcement actions.	Area Specific GMP: Q2 Standards: Per document issue date General GMP: Q3/Q4	All personnel
Root Cause Analysis	This workshop teaches a step-by-step approach for critical thinking and problem solving, with techniques to: • Identify specific factual issues and determine priority. • Gather relevant information on problems/decisions. • Develop well-rounded decisions, balancing creativity with a thorough evaluation of benefits and risks. • Create specific implementation plans that anticipate & address problems.	Monthly	Personnel who lead and are involved investigations
Aseptic Awareness	Address general principles and practices necessary to assure product sterility and safety related to aseptic processing.	July 2012	Manufacturing & targeted Quality personnel
Risk Management and Risk Assessment	Designed for personnel performing risk analysis, this course will cover: • Introduction to Quality Risk Management and the FMEA Tool. • Tools for use with change control: Comparison & Risk Estimation Matrices • Introduction to Preliminary Hazard Analysis (PHA) • Introduction to Hazard Analysis & Critical Control Points (HACCP)	Q1 2012	Personnel who lead and are involved investigations, Targeted Quality personnel
Trainer Qualification	Instructor-led course designed to provide the skills to deliver on the job training: • Recognize knowledge & performance components of good training • Deliver effective OJT/SOP training, through understanding learning styles & training effectiveness • Understand FDA's expectations of OJT, and the role of a trainer.	Monthly	Personnel who provide task training
PAC Authoring	Instructor-led course recommended for all employees writing, editing and/or reviewing Performance Assessment Checklists (PACs). Attendees will be able to: • Explain the role of the Subject Matter Expert in PAC authoring • Construct an effective PAC • Write specific/measurable learning objectives • Write specific/measurable performance evaluation criteria which provide evidence that the trainee can successfully perform prescribed tasks	Quarterly	Department SMEs who develop PACs

Approvals

Area	Name	Signature	Date
Development and Training			
Site Quality Head			
Site Head of Manufacturing			
Site Head/Plant Manager			

Source: JGTA, LLC, Hollis, NH.

APPENDIX 4.3: SAMPLE PERFORMANCE ASSESSMENT CHECKLIST (PAC)

PERFORMANCE ASSESSMENT CHECKLIST					
Document #:	PAC-xxxx	**Revision #:**	XX	**Effective Date:**	
Title:	Gowning for Formulation Operations				

Trainee's Name (Print): _____

Prerequisites

The following prerequisites must be completed prior to beginning this PAC. The supervisor, Qualified Trainer, or Training Coordinator/LMS Application Administrator (AA) must verify documented completion of these activities prior to the trainee beginning the assessment portion of this PAC.

Prerequisite Information			Verifier Information		
Type*	**LMS ID**	**Title**	**Initials**	**ID**	**Date**
SOP	SOP-xxx	Personal Health & Hygiene			
Course	TR-000081	Working In Controlled Environments: What You Must Know			

* Specify Module, Course, SOP, Curricula, etc.

Trainer Status Verification

Multiple Qualified Trainers may be involved in the training process. Anyone signing or initialing this PAC as a Qualified Trainer must be authorized as a Qualified Trainer on this PAC prior to conducting training.

The supervisor, Qualified Trainer or Training Coordinator/AA must verify each individual listed has Qualified Trainer status prior to conducting training, by ensuring each has entries in the LMS confirming that they have:

o   Completed the LMS module that qualifies them as an Area/OJT Trainer

o   Successfully completed this PAC themselves.

o   Been designated a Qualified Trainer for this PAC

(Supervisors using this PAC to document supervisory discussions with experienced operators do not need to list themselves as a trainer, and may N/A, initial and date this section.)

Trainer Information			Verifier Information		
Name (print)	**Initials**	**ID**	**Date Verified**	**Initials**	**ID**

Related Items

Upon completion of this PAC, the trainee will receive credit for this PAC and all items listed in this section.

Type*	LMS ID	Item Title
SOP	SOP-xxx	Gowning Requirements and Techniques
SOP	SOP-xxx	Clean Room Gowning Qualification
Drawing	SOP-xxx	Process Flow Diagram for Building X

* Specify Course, SOP, etc.

PERFORMANCE ASSESSMENT CHECKLIST			
Document #:	PAC-xxxx	Revision #: XX	Effective Date:
Title:	Gowning for Formulation Operations		

- o Gowning to enter the controlled non-classified area and Production hallways
- o Performing appropriate gowning changes in the Grade C area ante room
- o Gowning to enter the Grade C Production area
- Demonstrate appropriate degowning behavior within clean/controlled areas

Background/Rationale

Why gown?

We gown because we are required by regulations around the world to protect our products from contamination. As an example, the US GMPs require, in section 211.28, Personnel responsibilities:

(a) Personnel...shall wear clean clothing appropriate for the duties they perform. Protective apparel, such as head, face, hand, and arm coverings, shall be worn as necessary to protect drug products from contamination.

(b) Personnel shall practice good sanitation and health habits.

(d) Any person shown at any time (either by medical examination or supervisory observation) to have an apparent illness or open lesions that may adversely affect the safety or quality of drug products shall be excluded from direct contact with components, drug product containers, closures, in-process materials, and drug products until the condition is corrected or determined by competent medical personnel not to jeopardize the safety or quality of drug products. All personnel shall be instructed to report to supervisory personnel any health conditions that may have an adverse effect on drug products.

What is gowning supposed to accomplish?

The human body both supports a vast array of bacteria, fungi, and archaea on the surface of the skin, in saliva and oral mucosa, and in the gastrointestinal tract, and provides an unending source of skin flakes, oil, hair, clothing fibers and other bioparticles. Because of this, humans are the largest source of contamination in a cleanroom. A single instance of contamination during cell growth, purification, or fill/finish can result in our inability to provide our patients with life-saving medication and millions of dollars of loss to the company. Thus it is necessary to provide a barrier to protect cell growth, purification, and finished products and this is accomplished through proper gowning.

Why hygiene is important (from a microbiological perspective):

To protect our products, personnel must maintain their gowning quality and strictly adhere to gowning procedures and techniques, including always wearing clean clothing suitable for the manufacturing activity which they are involved in. Gowning is intended to minimize the spread of microbes in clean facilities, particularly around open processes, by providing a barrier between the individual and the controlled manufacturing area. We wear protective apparel such as head, face, hand, arm and leg coverings to protect product intermediates, active pharmaceutical ingredients (API's), clean areas and equipment from contamination.

People are the main source of contamination within our controlled manufacturing environments. We naturally shed skin particles into the air, and the amount of skin particles shed varies by person and time of day. These contaminants can get into our products and cause microbiological contamination. Gowning procedures begin at home with daily bathing or showering, shaving, brushing of teeth and hair, and the usage of skin moisturizers to reduce skin flakes. Personnel arriving for work must report problems that might increase contamination in the controlled areas such as flaking skin, dermatitis, sunburn or bad dandruff, cold, flu or chronic coughing; allergic conditions that cause sneezing, itching or scratching. These types of problems cause an increase in skin particles shed in the work area, and increase the risk of contamination to our products.

What do we use in gowning?

What you're going to wear:

- Goggles/safety glasses: Protective eye wear

PERFORMANCE ASSESSMENT CHECKLIST			
Document #:	PAC-xxxx	Revision #: XX	Effective Date:
Title:	Gowning for Formulation Operations		

How to Complete This Performance Assessment Checklist (PAC)

This PAC is designed to provide guidance, organization, and accountability to to the training process, and is designed to work in conjunction with modules/curricula set up in the LMS. This PAC ensures necessary background on this operation is provided, and that assessment of required knowledge and skills is conducted consistently across all trainees. All personnel will complete training before they are allowed to perform operations independently.
Instructions for conducting and documenting training are as follows:

— Qualified Trainer: The Qualified Trainer will:
- o Read this PAC in its entirety and review the applicable procedures/SOPs before beginning training.
- o Instruct and observe the Trainee as they perform these operations/procedures
- o Refer to SOP xxx (Good Documentation Practices SOP) for documentation requirements, as a procedure is performed during the training process where documentation is required (i.e. batch records, logs, etc.).
- o Document each checklist step when the Qualified Trainer has verified the Trainee is able to perform it independently.

— Trainee: Using this PAC and in accordance with the applicable SOPs, the Trainee will:
- o Read this PAC and the related SOPs in their entirety prior to observing the operation(s)
- o Observe the operation(s) being performed
- o Perform the operation(s) under a Qualified Trainer's direct supervision with the appropriate SOPs in hand or available. As the Trainee performs these procedures, the Qualified Trainer will observe and provide instruction and feedback as needed.
- o Complete documentation (i.e. batch record, log, etc.) as required in procedures being performed, in accordance with requirements defined in SOP xxx (Good Documentation Practices SOP).
- o Document each checklist step when the Trainee can attest to being able to perform it independently.

— Documenting Training and Authorization to Perform:
- o Record completion of each component in the checklist when the Trainee and the Trainer can attest to the Trainee's ability to perform the step independently.
- o When the Trainee is considered fully trained on all portions of this PAC, the Trainee's direct supervisor (or appropriate area management designee) provides the final signature, attesting to completion of this PAC and authorizing the Trainee to function as an "Operator".
- o At the discretion of their supervisor, an Operator can be designated as a Qualified Trainer on this PAC. Please refer to the requirements and the process for designating an individual as a Qualified Trainer described in SOP xxx (OJT Program SOP).

Learning Objectives

At the completion of this training, the Trainee will be able to successfully gown to access the Formulation & Fill area in accordance with SOP requirements.

The trainee will demonstrate the ability to:

- Identify and describe flow of personnel and where gowning/de-gowning occurs
- Identify where to locate gowning supplies, including additional supplies when needed, and what to do with damaged supplies
- Don primary and secondary gowning for entry into the Formulation & Filling area, in accordance with appropriate SOPs, including:

PERFORMANCE ASSESSMENT CHECKLIST

Document #:	PAC-xxxx	Revision #:	XX	Effective Date:
Title:	Gowning for Formulation Operations			

Why are there primary/secondary requirements?

Primary and secondary gowning both play roles in preventing contamination of the areas. Primary gowning is the gowning required to enter the area, while secondary gowning requirements are based on the classifications of the area, and are intended to reduce the likelihood of cross contamination, protect open operations, and/or ensure operator safety.

Why are there differences between rooms?

Clean areas for sterile product manufacturing are classified according to the required characteristics of the environment. Each manufacturing operation requires an appropriate environmental cleanliness level in order to minimize the risks of particulate or microbial contamination to the product or materials being handled. Determining the concentration of microscopic particles in air provides a measure of cleanliness: the lower the particulate concentration, the cleaner the air. The cleanest areas are termed as having the lower classification. (For example, a sterile environment is classified as ISO-5, while a non-sterile controlled area might be an ISO-7 or ISO-8.) Anything less filtered than ISO-8 is considered not classified.

The most common industry guidance documents include:

1. Federal Standard 209E designates cleanliness based on the number of particles ≥ 0.5 micron per cubic foot. Typically Class 100 areas are for sterile areas, Class 10,000 are for support areas, and Class 100,000 are for entrances to Class 10,000 areas. This standard is no longer in effect, but the names (classes) the standard uses are commonly used throughout the industry.

2. International Organization of Standards (ISO) 14611 designates cleanliness based on the log of the number of particles ≥ 0.5 micron per cubic meter. ISO-5 areas are where sterile processes occur, ISO-7 are support areas, and ISO-8 are for support to ISO-7 areas. We use this nomenclature to classify our controlled areas and biological safety cabinets (BSC).

3. EU Volume 4 Annex 1 designates cleanliness into four grades based on the type of operations performed in the area, using the ISO room grading system. Grade A areas are for high risk operations where absolute assurance of sterility is required (e.g. sterile filling, open vials, making aseptic connections), thus ISO-5 areas. Grade B areas are for aseptic preparation and filling, this is the background environment for the grade A zone and would use ISO-7 cleanliness standard. Grades C and D are clean areas for carrying out less critical stage in the manufacturing process. European inspectors prefer this method of classification.

Area Classifications

EU/Canadian/PICs GMP Grade	A		B		C		D	
	At Rest	In Operation	At Rest	In Operation	At Rest	In Operation	At Rest	In Operation
US Class*	100	100	100	10,000	10,000	100,000	100,000	Defined based on operation / process
ISO Classification	5	5	5	7	7	8	8	8
Bulk Biotech APIs/Drug Substances	Open manipulations performed in laminar flow hoods & biosafety cabinets, such as: • seed inoculation • additions to scale-up spinner flasks to maintain purity • open sampling/filling of containers following formulation to preserve low bioburden		Grade B—Not applicable to bulk biotech processing until the after the final bulk sterilization step.		• Purification chromatography • Formulation and preparation of solutions prior to filtration • Background environment for scale-up cell culture manipulations and formulation transfer/sampling		• Equipment & glassware cleaning and handling after cleaning • Media Prep • Closed processes (e.g., bioreactor rooms) • Background environment for cell culture dead-end sampling	

*Note: US Class comes from US Std. 209 which has been replaced by ISO Std. 14644-1.

PERFORMANCE ASSESSMENT CHECKLIST

Document #:	PAC-xxxx	Revision #:	XX	Effective Date:
Title:	Gowning for Formulation Operations			

- **Bouffant/head cover:** A covering worn on your head to limit shedding and microbial contamination
- **Beard cover:** Worn over beards, mustaches, or stubble
- **Gloves:** Worn over your hands to limit microbial contamination – no latex, only nitrile allowed
- **Coveralls:** Clean, non-shedding, single use garments worn over clothing/scrubs to limit microbial contamination
- **Scrubs:** Clean, single use garments worn instead of your personal street clothes to minimize contamination from outside sources
- **Shoe covers:** May be low or high topped (knee length), disposable or reusable, non-shedding used to cover shoes in order to prevent the spread of contamination carried on the shoes
- **Plant dedicated shoes:** Personal shoes, supplied by the company and worn in lieu of street shoes, which do not leave the gowning area to minimize contamination from outside the manufacturing area. Plant dedicated shoes must have a reinforced toe for safety purposes.
- **Lab coat:** May be disposable or reusable, commonly used as secondary gowning
- **Facemasks:** Worn over the nose and mouth to prevent contamination from nose or saliva. Commonly worn during critical processes.

What you're going to use to clean with:

- **Sanitizers:** Gloves, safety glasses, pens, and company issued cell phones must be sanitized with 70% isopropyl alcohol. Sanitizers designed for use on hands will leave moisturizers that will leave a coating on the gloves, and could cause contamination if used on gloves.
- **Lint free wipes:** Like a paper towel, but do not leave traces of lint or paper to contaminate the environment, used in cleaning safety glasses and other operations.
- **Tacky mats:** Essentially large sheets of adhesive tape, placed on the floor, sticky side up. Tacky mats are used to entrap particles from the bottom of shoes and wheels of carts.

Other helpful definitions

- **Contaminate:** To risk the cleanliness of the area by introducing viable or non-viable microorganisms and/or particulates from any source.
- **Particulate:** Any microscopic matter (microbes, viruses, skin flakes, dust, etc.) that can cause contamination.
- **Good hygienic practices:** These are behaviors that help lower the risk of contamination by minimizing outside contributing factors.
- **Don:** A synonym for the act of "putting on attire"
- **Environment:** Term used to describe the air, floors, walls, ceilings, and countertops of the manufacturing areas that are controlled
- **Airlock:** A transitional area or barrier between areas of different classification. Airlocks work to help provide air pressurization that is highest in the cleanest rooms and lowest in the "dirtiest" rooms, ensuring that particles are blown away from the cleanest areas.
- **Demarcation lines:** Lines, typically on the floor, that designate changes in area classifications, or differentiate between clean and "dirty" sides of gowning airlocks
- **Return grates:** Air return vents, found on the lower walls or at the base of hoods, used to recirculate air throughout a room and drive the appropriate airflow patterns in clean areas

What is the proper order for donning gowning? Why is there an order?

Hands must be washed, sanitized and gloved before handling gowning materials, and from there, gowning is typically put on from the top down (i.e. hair covers first). The reason that an order is established is to prevent contamination from one source from spreading to other gowning during the process.

PERFORMANCE ASSESSMENT CHECKLIST

Document #:	PAC-xxxx	Revision #:	XX	Effective Date:
Title:	Gowning for Formulation Operations			

- Gowning with unacceptable skin/health conditions (such as sunburned skin that is flaking, cold or flu like symptoms) – increases the likelihood of bacterial or viral contamination being introduced into controlled areas.

When should gowning be removed? Why do we care about degowning behavior?

Gowning should be removed after exiting the clean space, or leaving an area of higher classification to go to a lower classification area. Gowning should be changed when compromised (is ripped or torn, has touched an unclean surface or any production materials).

When degowning in classified areas, improper degowning behavior can cause contamination to be introduced. When removing secondary gowning, it should be removed in the reverse order than it was put on.

Best practice – confirm these things before leaving the gowning room for the clean area:

- No clothing is protruding out of your gowning
- All of your hair is covered by gowning, including any facial hair if present
- The bottom of your gown's legs are clipped or tucked in to prevent drag
- The button at the top of your gown's zipper is clipped
- Your safety glasses are sitting properly on your face
- Your ears are covered by the bouffant (hair cover)
- Your gloves are new or just cleaned with sanitizing agent

SAFETY WARNINGS:

- 70% IPA: 70% IPA is inflammable and may cause skin irritations. Spraying cleanroom gowning with 70% IPA is not allowed, as it may breach the garments and risk personnel safety.
- Foam Sanitizer: Foam sanitizer is flammable, and must be kept from fire or flame. It is also for external use only, so take care to avoid contact with eyes during use.

Performance Verification & Assessment

The following is an assessment of Trainee knowledge and skills:

Pre-Operation Action Assessment Trainee can successfully:	Trainee		Trainer	
	Initial	Date	Initial	Date
Explain proper behavior				
• Describe the procedures for the use of plant dedicated shoes, and describe what to do if you do not have plant shoes	Trainee Initial	Trainee Date	Trainer Initial	Trainer Date
• Explain what to do in the event you must leave the controlled area under emergency circumstances (i.e. a fire alarm)				
Describe area classifications used in (company name) operational areas, and their meaning	Trainee Initial	Trainee Date	Trainer Initial	Trainer Date
• Describe how to identify that the area classification is changing between areas				
Explain the flow of personnel and where gowning/degowning occurs	Trainee Initial	Trainee Date	Trainer Initial	Trainer Date
• Using a map of the controlled areas, correctly identify where the change areas are				
• Explain what to do in the event additional gowning supplies are needed				

PERFORMANCE ASSESSMENT CHECKLIST

Document #:	PAC-xxxx	Revision #:	XX	Effective Date:
Title:	Gowning for Formulation Operations			

What are good gowning practices/appropriate behaviors and why?

Appropriate behaviors and good practices are things that you can do to help control contaminants being introduced into controlled areas, and include:

- Showering before your work day, wearing clean clothing appropriate for your duties, and maintaining clean hair and skin throughout the work day – this reduces the potential contamination you may bring into an area on your body and clothing.
- Frequently using an alcohol based sanitizer such as 70% IPA on your gloved hands while working – this ensures that your gloved hands are always clean and are not contributing to cross contamination.
- Checking gowning for rips or stains prior to putting it on – this ensures that the gowning will be effective at controlling contaminants, and isn't contributing to the contamination in an area.
- Moving slowly and deliberately while working in controlled areas and while gowning – quick movements will disrupt airflow patterns and may circulate contaminants.
- Ensuring that gowning (gowns, gloved hands, etc.) does not contact the floor or any other surfaces – so you remain as clean as possible and do not introduce contaminants from dirty surfaces.
- Being aware of what demarcation lines indicate in gowning areas and ensuring you're operating appropriately in each area.
- Recognizing when you break technique and knowing how to react appropriately. o Changing tacky mats need to be changed when you see they are dirty – when they get dirty, they lose their effectiveness and may allow particles to be tracked into the controlled areas. o Being aware of surroundings and communicating with people around you.

Emergency evacuation & gowning

Evacuation is the most important concern. When notified to evacuate, do not take the time to degown. Proceed to the fire exit and to your muster point while gowned. All gowning worn outside the plant is to be removed upon reentry to the building and placed in designated bins as described in area procedures. Dedicated plant shoes must be sanitized according to area procedures prior to reentry.

What are poor practices/inappropriate behaviors and why?

Poor/inappropriate practices are any behaviors, clothing or personal practices that can generate or transfer contaminants. Some examples include:

- Sitting on the floor to don your gowning, kneeling on the floor while gowned, leaning against walls or surfaces while gowned – all of these cause your gowning to become contaminated, which can then transfer particulates to other areas.
- Coughing or sneezing (whether into your glove, gowned arm, or the air), letting hair fall out of your bouffant, using a ripped glove that exposes skin, opening your gown while in a clean area, or not buttoning your coverall/lab coat completely – these can all allow contamination to enter an area.
- Touching exposed product and/or product contact surfaces – do not break the sterile plane or contact materials/surfaces if at all possible, as it can allow particles/contaminants to be transferred
- Touching your face or any other exposed skin while gowned – transfers bacteria and particles to your gloves/gown, which may then be transferred to product, equipment or materials
- Holding or propping doors open – it compromises the differential pressures and changes the airflow between rooms.
- Blocking air return grates – this affects the process of recirculating the clean air and may compromise the ability to meet the required area classifications.
- Poor personal hygiene/preparation (i.e. beginning gowning process without washing hands, not practicing good hand sanitization on a regular basis, torn/ripped/dirty clothing, etc.) – increases the risk of contamination being introduced into clean areas.
- Unnecessary movement/proximity to others while gowning – causes shedding during gowning process

PERFORMANCE ASSESSMENT CHECKLIST

Document #:	PAC-xxxx	Revision #:	XX	Effective Date:
Title:	Gowning for Formulation Operations			

Review/Comments:

_____

_____

_____

_____

Trainee Statement of Readiness to Perform:

"I have completed training on the items listed in this PAC, participated in the indicated training, and have successfully completed the required objectives and actions set forth in this PAC. I am now able to independently perform the tasks outlined in this PAC."

Trainee Signature	Initials	ID	Date

Supervisor Release of Trainee to Perform as an "Operator":

Signing below designates that the Supervisor (or appropriate area management designee) has verified that the Trainee has been trained to perform this job in accordance with this PAC and is releasing him/her to perform it independently as an Operator.

Supervisor (or Designee) Signature	Initials	ID	Date

Supervisor Designation of Trainee as a "Qualified Trainer" for this PAC:

Signing below signifies the Trainee shall be designated as a Qualified Trainer on this PAC and receive that designation in the LMS. If the Trainee is not being designated as a Qualified Trainer at this time, N/A, initial and date this section.

Supervisor (or Designee) Signature	Initials	ID	Date

Forward completed PAC to Training Coordinator or Site Training Group for entry and filing.

Entry Type	Entered By		
	Initials	ID	Date
Operator			
Qualified Trainer			

PERFORMANCE ASSESSMENT CHECKLIST

Document #:	PAC-xxxx	Revision #:	XX	Effective Date:
Title:	Gowning for Formulation Operations			

- Explain what to do in the event gowning supplies become damaged
- Identify on the map what areas can or cannot be accessed, and explain why

Operational Action Assessment
Trainee can successfully:

	Trainee		Trainer	
	Initial	Date	Initial	Date
Don primary and secondary gowning for entry into the Formulation area				
Demonstrate proper hand sanitization technique prior to beginning gowning operation				
Inspect gowning for damage prior to donning, and explain common types of defects to look for				
In accordance with SOP xxx, demonstrate the ability to properly handle and don gowning for the controlled non-classified area and production hallways				
In accordance with SOP xxx, demonstrate the ability to perform proper gowning changes in the Grade C area anteroom, using proper technique				
In accordance with SOP xxx, demonstrate the ability to properly handle and don gowning for the Grade C Production Area				
Identify for each area the correct entry/exit flows for personnel, material and/or equipment				

Post-Operation Action Assessment
Trainee can successfully:

	Trainee		Trainer	
	Initial	Date	Initial	Date
Demonstrate appropriate degowning behavior within clean/controlled areas				
Demonstrate proper degowning technique within the controlled areas				
Demonstrate the proper techniques and handling of shoes while changing from plant shoes to street shoes				
In accordance with SOP xxx, demonstrate how to properly store plant shoes until used again				
Locate the collection bins for the different supplies and properly dispose of used gowning attire				
Explain the procedure for dealing with damaged or soiled gowning, and who should be notified of the damaged supplies				

Source: JGTA, LLC, Hollis, NH.

APPENDIX 4.4: SAMPLE TRAINING REQUIREMENT DECISION TREE

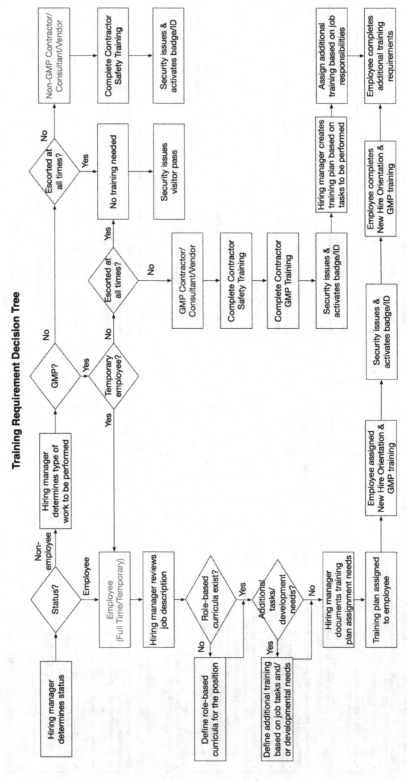

Source: JGTA, LLC, Hollis, NH.

5 Finished Pharmaceuticals
General Provisions

Graham P. Bunn

CONTENTS

§211.1 SCOPE

a. *The regulations in this part contain the minimum current good manufacturing practice for preparation of drug products (excluding positron emission tomography drugs) for administration to humans or animals.*

b. *The current good manufacturing practice regulations in this chapter as they pertain to drug products; in parts 600 through 680 of this chapter, as they pertain to drugs that are also biological products for human use; and in part 1271 of this chapter, as they are applicable to drugs that are also human cells, tissues, and cellular and tissue-based products (HCT/Ps) and that are drugs (subject to review under an application submitted under section 505 of the act or under a biological product license application under section 351 of the Public Health Service Act); supplement and do not supersede the regulations in this part unless the regulations explicitly provide otherwise. In the event of a conflict between applicable regulations in this part and in other parts of this chapter, or in parts 600 through 680 of this chapter, or in part 1271 of this chapter, the regulation specifically applicable to the drug product in question shall supersede the more general.*

c. *Pending consideration of a proposed exemption, published in the Federal Register of September 29, 1978, the requirements in this part shall not be enforced for OTC drug products if the products and all their ingredients are ordinarily marketed and consumed as human foods, and which products may also fall within the legal definition of drugs by virtue of their intended use. Therefore, until further notice, regulations under parts 110 and 117 of this chapter, and where applicable, parts 113 through 129 of this chapter, shall be applied in determining whether these OTC drug products that are also foods are manufactured, processed, packed, or held under current good manufacturing practice.*

[43 FR 45077, Sept. 29, 1978, as amended at 62 FR 66522, Dec. 19, 1997; 69 FR 29828, May 25, 2004; 74 FR 65431, Dec. 10, 2009; 80 FR 56168, Sept. 17, 2015]

Section 201(g) of the FD&C Act (21 USC 321[g]) provides that the term "drug" means:
(A) articles recognized in the official *United States Pharmacopoeia*, official *Homoeopathic Pharmacopoeia of the United States*, or official *National Formulary*, or any supplement to any of them; (B) articles intended for use in the diagnosis, cure, mitigation, treatment, or prevention of disease in man or other animals; (C) articles (other than food) intended to affect the structure or any function of the body of man or other animals; and (D) articles intended for use as a component of any articles specified in clause (A), (B), or (C).

Prescription and OTC drug products and manufacturing have clearly been included in the GMP scope as well as repackaging and relabeling operations. For a time, OTC products were under some contention, but Sec. 450.100 CGMP Enforcement Policy—OTC vs. Rx Drugs (CPG 7132.10)—makes it very clear. (CPG Sec. 450.100 CGMP Enforcement Policy—OTC vs. Rx Drugs)

BACKGROUND

Because of increased visibility and promotion of certain OTC preparations, there are periodic inquiries from division offices within the Office of Pharmaceutical Quality Operations (OPQO) regarding whether or not the enforcement policy for CGMP regulations is the same for OTC drug products as it is for prescription (Rx) drug products.

Section 501(a)(2)(B) of the FD&C Act requires drugs to be manufactured in conformance with CGMP. This section does not differentiate between OTC and Rx products, and it was not intended by Congress to do so. A prescription drug may be toxic or have other potential for harm, which requires that it be administered only under the supervision of a licensed practitioner (Section 503(b)(1) of the Act). For this reason, problems associated with its manufacture are generally more likely to cause serious problems.

POLICY

The CGMP regulations apply to all drug products, whether OTC or Rx.

REGULATORY GUIDANCE

The selection of an enforcement action to be applied will be based on the seriousness of the deviation, including such factors as potential hazard to the consumer. (Issued: 4/1/82)

DIETARY SUPPLEMENTS

Although outside the immediate scope of this book, it is worth briefly mentioning some information concerning dietary supplements.

BACKGROUND

Under the Dietary Supplement Health and Education Act of 1994 (DSHEA), dietary supplement manufacturers have the essential responsibility to substantiate the safety of the dietary ingredients used in manufacturing a product. Manufacturers are also responsible for determining that any representations or claims made about their products are substantiated by adequate evidence to show that they are not false or misleading. FDA is responsible for taking action against any unsafe dietary supplement product after it reaches the market. FDA accomplishes its responsibilities through monitoring safety literature; dietary supplement adverse event reports; and product information, such as labeling, claims, package inserts, and accompanying literature.

As part of DSHEA, Congress gave the Secretary of Health and Human Services and the FDA by delegation the express authority to issue regulations establishing CGMPs for dietary supplements. The FDA has issued a final rule establishing requirements for the production of dietary supplements.

SPECIFICALLY THIS RULE

- Requires certain activities in manufacturing, packaging, labeling and holding of dietary supplements to ensure that a dietary supplement contains what it is labeled to contain and is not contaminated with harmful or undesirable substances such as pesticides, heavy metals, or other impurities.
- Requires certain activities that will ensure the identity, purity, quality, strength, and composition of dietary supplements, which is a significant step in assuring consumers they are purchasing the type and amount of ingredients declared.

On June 25, 2007, FDA published in the *Federal Register* a final rule that established a regulation (21 CFR Part 111) entitled Current Good Manufacturing Practice (CGMP) in Manufacturing, Packaging, Labeling, or Holding Operations for Dietary Supplements (72 FR 34752). The Dietary Supplement (DS) CGMP rule in 21 CFR Part 111 ("the DS CGMP rule") requires persons who manufacture, package, label, or hold a dietary supplement to establish and follow CGMP to ensure the quality of the dietary supplement and to ensure that the dietary supplement is packaged and labeled as specified in the master manufacturing record.

In the same issue of the *Federal Register* (72 FR 34959), FDA also issued an interim final rule (the identity testing interim final rule) setting forth a procedure for requesting an exemption from a requirement of the DS CGMP rule for the manufacturer to conduct at least one appropriate test or examination to verify the identity of any dietary ingredient that is a component of a dietary supplement. The provisions of the identity testing interim final rule have the full force of law, but FDA provided a 90-day comment period on those provisions through September 24, 2007. On September 17, 2007, FDA published a notice in the *Federal Register* to extend the comment period to October 24, 2007.

The DS CGMP rule and the identity testing interim final rule were effective as of August 24, 2007.

FDA has prepared this Small Entity Compliance Guide in accordance with Section 212 of the Small Business Regulatory Enforcement Fairness Act (Public Law 104-121). This guidance document restates in plain language the legal requirements set forth in the DS CGMP rule (21 CFR Part 111). The DS CGMP rule is binding and has the full force and effect of law.

FDA's guidance documents, including this guidance, do not establish legally enforceable responsibilities. Instead, guidances describe the Agency's current thinking on a topic and should be viewed only as recommendations, unless specific regulatory or statutory requirements are cited. The use of the word *should* in Agency guidances means that something is suggested or recommended, but not required.

Compliance to the 21 CFR 111 rule were phased in over three years on June 26, 2008, 2009, and 2010 depending on the number of full-time employees in the company. Table 5.1 below covers the subpart subjects and which reflect the 21 CFR 211 requirements for finished pharmaceuticals written as a series of questions with the corresponding rule responses.

Following the effectiveness of the GMP rule requirements there have been several FDA483 and warning letters issued to companies who were either unaware of the requirements or did not implement them before the effective date of the rule.

TABLE 5.1

Subparts of the Dietary Supplements CGMP Rule

Subpart	Subject of Subpart
A	General Provisions (including coverage and definitions)
B	Personnel
C	Physical Plant and Grounds
D	Equipment and Utensils
E	Requirements to Establish a Production and Process Control System
F	Production and Process Control System: Requirements for Quality Control
G	Production and Process Control System: Requirements for Components, Packaging, Labels and for Product that You Receive for Packaging or Labeling as a Dietary Supplement
H	Production and Process Control System: Requirements for the Master Manufacturing Record
I	Production and Process Control System: Requirements for the Batch Production Record
J	Production and Process Control System: Requirements for Laboratory Operations
K	Production and Process Control System: Requirements for Manufacturing Operations
L	Production and Process Control System: Requirements for Packaging and Labeling Operations
M	Holding and Distributing
N	Returned Dietary Supplements
O	Product Complaints
P	Records and Recordkeeping

HOMEOPATHIC DRUGS

If "finished homeopathic drugs" are offered for the cure, mitigation, prevention, or treatment of disease conditions, they are regarded as drugs within the meaning of Section 210(g)(1) of the Act. This would apply whether or not they are official homeopathic remedies listed in the Homœopathic Pharmacopœia of the United States (HPUS). As drugs, they are patently subject to the CGMPs with some reservations. Homeopathic drugs generally must meet the standards for strength, quality, and purity set forth in the Homeopathic Pharmacopeia. Section 501(b) of the Act (21 USC 351) provides in relevant part:

Whenever a drug is recognized in both the United States Pharmacopeia and the Homeopathic Pharmacopeia of the United States it shall be subject to the requirements of the United States Pharmacopeia unless it is labeled and offered for sale as a homeopathic drug, in which case it shall be subject to the provisions of the Homeopathic Pharmacopeia of the United States and not to those of the United States Pharmacopeia.

Under U.S. law, homeopathic drugs are required to meet the same approval rules as other drugs. But under a policy Sec. 400.400 adopted in 1988, the agency has used "enforcement discretion" to allow the items to be manufactured and distributed without FDA approval. The FDA compliance policy guide Sec. 400.400 Conditions Under Which Homeopathic Drugs May be Marketed (CPG 7132.15) provides supplemental information regarding homeopathic drugs relating to import, export, and interstate commerce in such products.

FDA issues a draft guidance for industry "Drug Products Labeled as Homeopathic" in December 2017 and has since proposed a risk-based enforcement approach with specific focus on:

- Products with reported safety concerns
- Products that contain or purport to contain ingredients associated with potentially significant safety concerns
- Products for routes of administration other than oral and topical

- Products for vulnerable populations such as those with compromised immune systems, infants and children, the elderly, and pregnant women
- Products intended to be used for the prevention or treatment of serious and/or life-threatening diseases and conditions
- Products deemed adulterated under Section 501 of the FD&C Act.

§211.3 DEFINITIONS

The definitions set forth in §210.3 apply in this part.

EXAMPLES OF OBSERVATIONS FROM FDA CITATIONS

- Your batch production records (BPRs) failed to include complete information relating to the production and control of each batch, as required by 21 CFR 111.255(b) and 21 CFR 111.260. Specifically, your firm's Fill Worksheet and Packaging Check List that are used to document the packaging of finished dietary supplements into retail packaging for confidential information redacted fail to include the following:
    - The identity of equipment and processing lines used in producing the batch (21 CFR 111.260[b])
        - The date and time of maintenance, cleaning, and sanitizing of the equipment and processing lines used in producing the batch or a cross reference to records, such as individual equipment logs, where this information is retained (21 CFR 111.260[c])
        - Documentation that the finished dietary supplement meets specifications established in accordance with 21 CFR 111.70(g) (21 CFR 111.260[i])
    - Documentation, at the time of performance, of packaging and labeling operations, including:
        - The quantity of the packaging and labels used (21 CFR 111.260[k][1]);
        - The results of any tests or examination conducted on packaged and labeled dietary supplements or a cross-reference to the physical location of such results (21 CFR 111.260[k][3]).
    - Documentation, at the time of performance that quality control personnel:
    - Reviewed the batch production record (21 CFR 111.260[l][1])
        - Approved or rejected any reprocessing or repackaging (21 CFR 111.260[l][2])
        - Approved and released, or rejected, the batch for distribution (21 CFR 111.260[l][3])
        - Approved and released, or rejected, the packaged and labeled dietary supplement, including any repackaged or relabeled dietary supplement (21 CFR 111.260[l][4])
- We found serious violations of the CGMP in Manufacturing, Packaging, Labeling, or Holding Operations for Dietary Supplements regulation, Title 21, Code of Federal Regulations (CFR), Part 111 (21 CFR Part 111). These violations cause your dietary supplement products redacted to be adulterated within the meaning of Section 402(g)(1) of the Federal Food, Drug, and Cosmetic Act (the Act) (21 USC § 342[g][1]) in that the dietary supplements have been prepared, packed, or held under conditions that do not meet CGMP requirements for dietary supplements.
- You failed to make and keep records that laboratory methodology established in accordance with subpart J is followed, and the person who conducts the testing and examination is documenting at the time of performance that laboratory methodology established in accordance with subpart J is followed, as required by 21 CFR 111.325(b)(2)(i). Specifically, your quality control unit's chemist did not accurately document use of the High-Performance Liquid Chromatography (HPLC) equipment from February 24, 2016 through April 18, 2016. The results obtained from use of this equipment were used to release and distribute products.

ment indicated that you had only one survey available out of the ten supplier surveys
the investigator requested during the inspection. In addition, you accepted some components, such as homeopathic attenuations, without a certificate of analysis (COA) and did
not conduct identity testing. As a result, you lack assurance that your components meet all
appropriate specifications.

SUGGESTED READINGS

- FDA Guidance for Industry: Drug Products Labeled as Homeopathic, FDA December
2017.
- Current Good Manufacturing Practice (CGMP) In Manufacturing, Packaging, Labeling,
or Holding Operations for Dietary Supplements (72 FR 34752).
- SEC. 400.400 Conditions Under Which Homeopathic Drugs May Be Marketed (CPG 7132.15).

6 Production and Process Controls

Jocelyn A. Zephrani

CONTENTS

§211.100 WRITTEN PROCEDURES; DEVIATIONS

a. *There shall be written procedures for production and process control designed to assure that the drug products have the identity, strength, quality, and purity they purport or are represented to possess. Such procedures shall include all requirements in this subpart. These written procedures, including any changes, shall be drafted, reviewed, and approved by the appropriate organizational units and reviewed and approved by the quality control unit.*
b. *Written production and process control procedures shall be followed in the execution of the various production and process control functions and shall be documented at the time of performance. Any deviation from the written procedures shall be recorded and justified.*

With the clear objectives of the current good manufacturing practices (CGMPs), it is perhaps surprising that they needed to include such details that there must be written procedures since no one can be expected to remember everything. Then there is a requirement to follow these written procedures, which seems to state the obvious. However, the FDA has used these requirements to issue repeated inspection observations as FDA483s and warning letters, because some organizations do not have procedures that they need, and even if others do have procedures, they are not followed.

Written standard operating procedures (SOPs) must provide the reader/operator and executor of the responsible steps with clear instructions for performing operational activities and also direct the content of documented evidence that the procedures have been performed. They also provide a basis for the training of personnel; see Chapter 4, "Organization and Personnel and Training". Procedures are an essential part of quality systems covering all aspects of GMP operations.

The SOP providing detail on the requirements of SOPs, describes the overall procedural requirements, process, and content for the preparation, approval, and revision. It also includes their distribution and control, as well as the archiving of all GMP documentation and records within a department, all critical for a robust quality system. This SOP defines how to initiate/revise an SOP, provide direction regarding formatting of documents, defines who should review and approve documents, provides the frequency of routine review (often every two to three years), and describes the methodology for issuing and replacement of outdated versions, training, archiving, and destruction. Documents must be uniquely identified, including a version number, as appropriate. When a document has been revised, a system must be in place to prevent the inadvertent use of superseded documents (e.g., only current documentation should be available). The life cycle of a document (creation, distribution, use, archiving, and destruction) must be considered when establishing the control system. Many companies now use automated, validated documentation systems that provide a high level of document control during the review, approval, and distribution processes. Electronic documentation systems provide current versions of SOPs electronically for review by trained, qualified personnel. Hard-copy printouts are date-stamped and accompanied by a statement such as "copy only valid for xx/xx/xx" (that day only). Note that the computerized documentation control systems must be validated and their qualification carefully and fully documented. Manual or paper systems are also common, and if planned/executed carefully, the document control system can be effective. Version and distribution control issues (especially forms and attachments), provide additional challenges when developing a manual document control system. Various methodologies are used to compensate for tracking documents via manual systems. The Document Control department is responsible for issuing records and numbered official copies to identifiable recipients. In a manual documentation control system, the use of logbooks to keep track of the transaction is prevalent. The uncontrolled copying of distributed SOPs is not permitted, so the copying may be monitored by printing the document on different colored paper, so that a photocopy is obvious. Borders or unique stamps on the documents is another way of ensuring that only originals have been distributed and to avoid uncontrolled photocopying. Issuance of a unique number to forms provides traceability and accountability, which forms part of document control and is linked to data integrity (restricting the unauthorized duplication of documents); see Chapter 24, "Data Integrity and Fundamental Responsibilities". Other areas that must be addressed include the storage of critical records, which must be secure and assembled in a defined manner, with their access limited to authorized individuals. Documents must be stored in such a way that they can be easily and efficiently retrieved, especially during an FDA inspection. The storage location must ensure adequate protection from loss, destruction, or damage. Electronic documents and paper records must be adequately protected against misfiling and loss.

A typical SOP format includes sections for the following:

- Introduction
- Purpose
- Scope
- Definitions
- Responsibilities

- Description of the Procedure steps
- References: Other Procedures
- Attachments (forms related to the described work process)
- Brief Change History

Operational-specific SOPs should be written by the department and function (e.g., Manufacturing, Packaging, QA) to accurately describe activities and requirements of the task and personnel. Quality systems that are relevant to multiple departments, for example, investigations, corrective and preventive action (CAPA), Change Control, or Annual Product Review require cross-functional SOPs and are usually written by the Quality Unit.

Elements to keep in mind when designing and implementing effective SOPs include preparing an outline of the task to be performed before beginning to write the procedure. A list of important steps that relate to the task will provide a concise and clear summary for the reader. It is important to remember when creating the document that it should be at a level that is easy to understand and that not everyone may have a clear idea of the process that is being described. The use of visual tools, such as process flow charts, symbols, and pictures may also help to communicate clear requirements.

Master production and control records, which define sequential steps for manufacturing and packaging/labeling and their process parameters, are basically SOPs with places to record parameters, results, settings, weights, etc. As with any SOP, the detail provided needs to be sufficient to ensure that the process will be followed consistently, but not overly complex as to be incomprehensible. See Chapter 7, "Records and Reports".

Every employee engaged in GMP activities must be appropriately trained on all relevant written procedures according to training curriculums. See Chapter 4, "Organization and Personnel".

Internal quality audits, headed by the Quality Unit, support the identification and evaluation of compliance to written procedures. The report following the summation of the audit provides information pertaining to the scope and purpose of the audit, a summary of the observations found, as well as providing an overall audit outcome (good, satisfactory, action required, or at risk/action required). An executive summary is included in the audit report as well, as it is essential that senior management is aware of the state of compliance of the quality systems/operations.

External audits, involving personnel from another firm or facility, add an additional layer to compliance assessments. Included in this category are regulatory audits, such as those performed by the Food and Drug Administration (FDA). The FDA in its Compliance Policy Guide "FDA Access to Results of Quality Assurance Program Audits and Inspections (CPG 7151.02)" announced the "FDA will not review or copy reports and records that result from audits and inspections of the written quality assurance program, including audits conducted under 21 CFR 820.22 and written status reports required by 21 CFR 58.35(b)(4). The intent of the policy is to encourage firms to conduct quality assurance program audits and inspections that are candid and meaningful." In other words, the FDA encourages the use of internal audits, but it must be kept in mind that in the event of litigation, requests may be made to see such records.

Audits, whether internal or external in nature, are used to assess compliance in regards to the regulatory requirements of CGMPs. CAPAs are used to manage audit observations to ensure adequate implementation of changes by a responsible person by a defined date. Repeated findings of similar noncompliance issues require immediate action to correct and prevent their reoccurrence. The root cause of a non-conformance can be due to a broad range of issues, such as deficient procedures, inadequate training, or insufficient emphasis by management to address a problem. The root cause needs to be identified so that appropriate CAPAs can be assigned. Quality assurance should work with the stakeholders to ensure the corrective action will result in obtaining or restoring systems in a state of control and compliance with regulatory requirements/expectations.

The requirement that execution of the various production and process control functions shall be documented at the time of performance has received increasing regulatory authorities' attention and observations relating to data integrity in recent years. The significance of this, although not new to FDA-regulated industries, is described in depth in Chapter 24, "Data Integrity and Fundamental Responsibilities".

From time to time, changes to written procedures are needed and are managed with a document change control process. In order to ensure that the planned change is suitably reviewed, approved, implemented, and documented by appropriate personnel, the management of changes must be adequately controlled. Written procedures detailing the identification, documentation, appropriate review, and approval of changes to fulfill regulatory requirements for change reporting must be in place. A change coordinator routinely monitors the change to facilitate its movement through the process in a timely manner.

DEVIATIONS

Unplanned events or a departure from an approved process or procedure is handled as a deviation or a non-conformance, depending on the event's criticality. A critical deviation represents a significant failure of a quality system and has a high potential to adversely affect the safety, identity, strength, quality, or purity of materials or products. Immediate action must be taken to isolate a potentially affected process or product involved in a deviation. An investigation must be undertaken whenever there is a failure to comply with relevant documentation or regulatory requirements. The deviation is evaluated using a risk management approach, as the outcome of the assessment determines the required response as CAPA actions. The root cause must be identified and an assessment made as to whether the deviation is part of a trend. The Quality Unit will review deviations on an on-going basis, to detect early-stage trends. Unfavorable trends need to be escalated, so that corrective and preventative actions can be put in place to prevent a reoccurrence of the deviation. Adequate time and resources for root cause investigations of deviations, including complaints, must be allocated by management with timely completion and appropriate CAPAs. Incomplete investigations with inadequate root cause(s) create CAPAs that do not address the problems. Ultimately these problems resurface with significant impact to the quality systems and company with ever-increasing attention from regulatory authorities.

§211.101 CHARGE-IN OF COMPONENTS

Written production and control procedures shall include the following, which are designed to assure that the drug products produced have the identity, strength, quality, and purity they purport or are represented to possess.

a. *The batch shall be formulated with the intent to provide not less than 100% of the labeled or established amount of active ingredient.*
b. *Components for drug product manufacturing shall be weighed, measured, or subdivided as appropriate. If a component is removed from the original container to another, the new container shall be identified with the following information:*
   1. *Component name or item code*
   2. *Receiving or control number*
   3. *Weight or measure in new container*
   4. *Batch for which component was dispensed, including its product name, strength, and lot number*
c. *Weighing, measuring, or subdividing operations for components shall be adequately supervised. Each container of component dispensed to manufacturing shall be examined by a second person to assure that:*

1. *The component was released by the quality control unit.*
2. *The weight or measure is correct as stated in the batch production records.*
3. *The containers are properly identified.*
  d. *Each component shall be added to the batch by one person and verified by a second person.*

It is important to clarify that the intent of the statement: "The batch shall be formulated with the intent to provide not less than 100% of the labeled or established amount of active ingredient" does not mean that it is required to calculate by assay the exact amount of active ingredient, per batch. Generally, a batch is accepted if analytical results are within specifications, as usually, the results of the assay do not calculate to exactly 100% due to inherent errors (measurements in weighing, analytical methodology). Some manufacturers may have thought that formulating a product at 98% would save them 2% of the active pharmaceutical ingredient but still produce a product that passed the specification of 97% to 101% of stated amount. A financial incentive not a quality focus. Dispensing is a critical step in the manufacturing process whereby materials, released by the Quality Unit, are measured and transferred for processing for a specific batch as defined in written procedures. Adequate identification of components is an essential GMP requirement and the labeling of component containers needs to provide sufficient information to ensure traceability. While 211.101(b) specifically requires labeling of new containers, with the component name, control number, weight, and batch to which the component is being dispensed, it is the usual practice that all dispensed materials are labeled accordingly. In addition, while not specified in the regulations, additional information may be added to the label including lot number, dispensing date, and container number. As part of the dispensing process, all secondary containers are to be examined before use to assess the absence of foreign particulates and to ensure the integrity of the container. The requirement that "each container of component dispensed to manufacturing shall be examined by a second person" (§211.101 [c]) can be interpreted to mean that a second person adequately supervises by examining and ensuring that the component has been released by the Quality Unit, that the weight/measure of the component matches the batch record requirements and that the component has been properly identified. This verification by a second person is needed when the dispensing process is a manual one. In the case where the use of a validated, automated dispensing system is in place, a second operator check is not required. Refer to 21 CFR 211.68. Throughout the operation, the materials must be clearly identified, and their status and location must be recorded. This can be done manually by maintaining paper documents or entering the information into a material management program. Increasingly, data gathering is being accomplished using bar codes and scanners and radio frequency (RF) interfaces. The data gathered from these systems can be entered automatically into the inventory control system while increasing accuracy. The same logic applies to the need for a second check when verifying components in production. Once again, if the addition of components is manual, a second human check is required, while the use of a validated automated system will permit a single operator to perform the dispensing operation.

§211.103 CALCULATION OF YIELD

Actual yields and percentages of theoretical yield shall be determined at the conclusion of each appropriate phase of manufacturing, processing, packaging, or holding of the drug product. Such calculations shall be performed by one person and independently verified by a second person.

Theoretical yield defined in Section 210.3(b)(17) is defined as the maximum quantity that could be produced, based on the quantities of components assigned to a batch, in the absence of any loss or error in production.

All materials assigned to a batch need to be compared to the actual yields at appropriate process steps. On the basis of historical, validated data, an acceptable range for the actual yield at each appropriate stage can be calculated. By assigning an acceptable range at various stages of the process, process control trends can be generated. In addition to assessing the theoretical yield, calculating the acceptable product yield provides a better tool for evaluating process changes. Although different lots of a batch could have identical theoretical yields, their acceptable product yield could vary widely, as for example in the case of waste. Without further examination of the acceptable product yield percentages, investigation into potential problems within a process could theoretically be overlooked.

As required by the GMP regulations, yield calculations involve reporting the following data/calculations at each appropriate phase:

- Actual yield (kg)
- % of theoretical yield = (actual yield/theoretical starting quantity) × 100
- While the percent acceptable product yield is not a GMP requirement, it provides additional information to alert personnel of potential process control issues
- % acceptable product yield = ([acceptable product]/theoretical yield) × 100.

§211.105 EQUIPMENT IDENTIFICATION

a. *All compounding and storage containers, processing lines, and major equipment used during the production of a batch of a drug product shall be properly identified at all times to indicate their contents and, when necessary, the phase of processing of the batch.*

This requirement is clear in requiring identification and traceability during production process. Status labels or tags must always be attached to equipment, process lines, and containers and provide information regarding its contents (product/material, batch number), the status of cleanliness (to be cleaned/clean), and process stage (granulation). Multiple pieces of equipment that are cleaned and used in a train within a suite may have a status tag generated for the room, rather than for each individual piece of equipment. The use of equipment logbooks, in addition to status tags, can provide a permanent record and additional support information (type of cleaning performed, time/date of cleaning, personnel responsible). This information is needed in cases whereby a batch or process is under investigation.

In-process materials are required to be labeled with the product, batch number, and stage of processing, and if multiple containers are used, sequentially numbered.

b. *Major equipment shall be identified by a distinctive identification number or code that shall be recorded in the batch production record to show the specific equipment used in the manufacture of each batch of a drug product. In cases where only one of a particular type of equipment exists in a manufacturing facility, the name of the equipment may be used in lieu of a distinctive identification number or code.*

The intent of this subsection is to allow identification and traceability of equipment involved in the production process. This is particularly important where several different pieces of the same equipment are used for the process, as the same type of equipment does not ensure that they will all process identically. In the case where there is only one piece of equipment, it is sufficient to record the name of the equipment in the batch record.

§211.110 SAMPLING AND TESTING OF IN-PROCESS MATERIALS AND DRUG PRODUCTS

a. *To assure batch uniformity and integrity of drug products, written procedures shall be established and followed, which describe the in-process controls, and tests or examinations to be conducted on appropriate samples of in-process materials of each batch. Such control procedures shall be established to monitor the output and to validate the performance of those manufacturing processes that may be responsible for causing variability in the characteristics of in-process material and the drug product. Such control procedures shall include, but are not limited to, the following, where appropriate:*

1. *Tablet or capsule weight variation*
2. *Disintegration time*
3. *Adequacy of mixing to assure uniformity and homogeneity*
4. *Dissolution time and rate*
5. *Clarity, completeness, or pH of solutions*

b. *Valid in-process specifications for such characteristics shall be consistent with drug product final specifications and shall be derived from previous acceptable process average and process variability estimates where possible and determined by the application of suitable statistical procedures where appropriate. Examination and testing samples shall assure that the drug product and in-process material conform to specifications.*

c. *In-process materials shall be tested for identity, strength, quality, and purity as appropriate and approved or rejected by the quality control unit, during the production process, for example, at commencement or completion of significant phases or after storage for long periods.*

Statistically sound sampling criteria must be used to determine the variability of key product parameters. These tools should be used in all stages of the production system. A documented sampling plan, approved by the Quality Unit needs to be in place and an acceptable quality level (AQL) is assigned to each defect type to ensure the safety and quality as established by product performance and quality requirements. Samples are representative of the whole, and sample locations or time points in the process are described or determined by the most stressed part of the process (e.g., beginning or end of process).

Process validation is performed to "establish(ed) and monitor the output and to validate the performance of those manufacturing processes that may be responsible for causing variability in the characteristics of in-process material and the drug product." The requirements for this validation are set out in 21 CFR Part 211.100 (a) which the FDA calls the regulatory "foundation for process validation." Manufacturers are required to have production and process-controls procedures in place that are "designed to assure" drug products have a certain level of quality and that their products are manufactured safely, effectively, and purely.

PROCESS VALIDATION

In January 2011, FDA revised its guidance for industry on Process Validation: General Principles and Practices. The guidance aligned process-validation activities with the product life-cycle concept and with existing harmonized guidelines. The guidance now defines process validation as "… the collection and evaluation of data, from process design through commercial production, which establishes scientific evidence that a process is capable of consistently delivering quality products." The activities involved in process validation occur over the entire life cycle of a product and can be divided into three (3) distinct stages.

STAGE I—PROCESS DESIGN

The commercial manufacturing processes are defined during Stage I, based on knowledge gained through development of the process, site transfer, and scale-up activities. Process knowledge and understanding lead to the development of appropriate process controls, which can be used to address variability in the process. It is essential to understand the sources and impact of the variation to be able to detect the degree of variation in the process. Control of the variation should be in proportion to the risk that it potentially presents to the process or product. The information gathered during Stage I will be incorporated into the designed manufacturing process and will then be confirmed during Stage II.

Process design and development represents the first stage of the process validation life cycle. In the case of product transfer and scale-up, this stage begins during the planning of a site transfer and continues through the verification of the manufacturing process at the transfer location. Site transfer and scale-up activities must be well defined and documented. They should be based on knowledge gained from other similar processes and products as well as from development reports generated by the originating site. Thorough documentation is needed in order to fully understand the process and all potential factors, which may impact it.

Process steps and operating parameters are defined during the process design stage. The impact of process parameters and material interactions on process performance and product quality must be evaluated. Initial identification of Critical Process Parameters (CPPs) and material attributes are defined based on data obtained during development.

The functionality and limitations of commercial manufacturing equipment must also be considered in the process design stage. Other factors to consider include the possible contribution to variability that may be caused by different production lots, production operators, environmental conditions, and measurement systems in the production setting. Usually all the input variability that is typical of commercial production is not known at this stage. An assessment of the identified CPPs and material attributes must be performed at each scale-up step through commercial manufacturing in order to estimate process variability.

GMP documents need to be defined before the process performance qualification (Stage II) can start. A defined target profile for the product will have been identified, with target settings, and will be adhered to in order to show process consistency. A detailed assessment of product quality attributes and process parameters to establish specifications will have been determined. Control limits and ranges will have been established and verified during scale-up activities. Documentation including process flow diagrams with information regarding critical set points, inputs, and the expected outputs will be established. A risk assessment to select critical process steps and parameters and to assess process robustness and process risk will have been performed, following local procedures or guidances. Master manufacturing documentation will have been drafted by the process owner for use during commercial-scale process performance qualification batches.

STAGE II—PROCESS PERFORMANCE QUALIFICATION

During this stage, the process design is evaluated to determine if it is capable of reproducible results during commercial manufacturing. There are numerous prerequisite activities that must occur prior to the actual process qualification. Process performance qualification, which is equivalent to process validation, must be done according to a preapproved protocol, and sampling is to be performed to a higher level than the normal quality sampling of a batch. The approach to this stage should be based on an understanding of the process and of sound scientific basis. The completion of Stage II is the equivalent of reaching a "validated state" for the process.

Number of Validation Batches

The number of batches required for validation must be scientifically justified, using statistical measures to achieve adequate assurance. Factors that affect the number of batches required include the complexity of the process and the level of process variability.

New products for launch or transferred from another site may be validated with a minimum of three batches or via a matrix approach. Other validated products may be produced on the equipment in between the validation batches for the new product. Until the three consecutive validation batches (or then number of batches defined in the protocol have been completed), no additional batches of the new product shall be manufactured.

If a validation study is required involving a product with multiple dosage strengths, product sizes, and/or batch sizes, a bracketing or matrixing approach may be utilized to address the entire product family. If this approach is selected, it must be justified, documented, and approved.

Results from Stage II verifications should include a successful process validation (PV) with an approved PV report and confirmation of all proposed critical material attributes, critical quality attributes, critical process parameters, and in-process controls. Risk assessments and process validation plans shall be updated as applicable. Process validation-related documentation, such as SOPs or master batch records (MBRs), which were in draft form prior to the execution of the PV will be revised, approved, and trained prior to release of the process.

STAGE III—CONTINUED PROCESS VERIFICATION

Continued Process Verification provides assurance that the manufacturing processes are in a continued state of control during routine commercial production. A program is established to collect and analyze product and critical process data on a regular basis. Inter- and intra-batch variability must be evaluated in order to be able to monitor process controls. Monitoring and sampling needs to be performed at the same level as during Stage II until there is sufficient data to provide a level of confidence that the process is in control and statistically-significant variability estimates can be generated. At that time, monitoring can be adjusted based on data collected.

Annual review of validation status is also an important part of this process. Review of deviations, investigation results, product failures, complaints, and other product performance and quality indicators shall be included as a component of the Continued Process Verification program.

Annual Monitoring/Validation Batch

The validation status of a drug product is regularly updated by performing at least one annual monitoring/validation batch, in alignment with the annual product review (APR) cycle, as part of continuous process validation. If the process has been revalidated during that year or the product was not produced within that time period, the annual monitoring/validation batch is not required. The annual monitoring/validation batch must be included in the stability program.

If significant deficiencies are identified during review of the current validation package, the need for complete revalidation must be assessed.

Change Control and Revalidation

All changes to equipment, systems, utilities, processes, materials, specifications, methods, and procedures must be assessed for their impact on the validated state and are subject to the change control process.

A process may require revalidation based on review of Continued Process Verification data (e.g., due to an increase in variability) or due to a change in the process. When a process change is proposed, the extent of revalidation required, if any, must be based on an assessment of the impact of the change to the critical quality elements of the process. At a minimum, the following must be considered:

- Change of manufacturing or supporting processes
- Changes in the master manufacturing formula, procedure, or batch size
- Changes in validated ranges of process parameters
- Raw materials, specifications, grade, reference standards, or test methods
- Changes to container closure system
- Changes to equipment, instrumentation, or computerized systems or their maintenance
- Changes to facilities or utilities
- Changes to the quality system, including deviations, investigation results, product failures, complaints, or other quality indicators
- Trends, for example, from Continued Process Verification and Annual Product Reviews

Revalidation covers either the entire scope of the original validation or is limited to specific process parameters or steps, depending on the justification described in a validation protocol. The impact of limiting the scope of revalidation with respect to its impact on other steps should be carefully assessed. Process assessment will include a review of the current process and its data, all historic validation and revalidation activities, and current issues, as applicable. The process assessment report will summarize recommendations for process improvements, if required, and further steps to be taken.

Process Validation Approach

There are three possible approaches to process validation: prospective, concurrent, and retrospective.

Prospective validation must be applied to new processes, including existing, approved processes transferred from other sites, and process, material, or equipment changes, under change control, as documented through the change control process. Validation batches must be at the intended commercial scale, utilizing final process parameters on equipment to be used for commercial production. Prospective validation activities, including approval of final reports, must be complete prior to commercial distribution of the final product.

Concurrent validation involves release of product for commercial distribution prior to the completion of all validation activities. This approach is acceptable only in exceptional cases such as infrequent production (i.e., one or two batches per year) or established processes that have not been validated to current standards. The rationale/justification for the approach must be documented and approved by Quality in advance. Batches may be released after approval of an interim report. Concurrent validation may also be used for revalidation of legacy products where there has been no change from the current process.

Retrospective validation involves the review of historical data and includes all batches made during a review period. This approach is not acceptable for the validation of new products. New processes and changes to existing processes may not be retrospectively validated. Retrospective validations for existing (legacy) processes must be replaced with prospective validation studies in order to meet current standards and expectations.

§211.111 TIME LIMITATIONS ON PRODUCTION

When appropriate, time limits for the completion of each phase of production shall be established to assure the quality of the drug product. Deviation from established time limits may be acceptable if such deviation does not compromise the quality of the drug product. Such deviation shall be justified and documented.

The main purpose of this regulation is to indicate that products need to remain stable before processing to the next stage. Maximum allowable hold times are established as part of a pilot plant study or validation exercise for starting materials, intermediates, and bulk and finished products to ensure materials are not adversely affected by in-process or storage conditions. Hold-time studies establish the time limits for maintaining materials during different stages of production to ensure the quality of the product does not deteriorate over time. The containers used to hold the hold-time samples need to simulate the containers that are used in production, and in the case of bulk product, the headspace needs to be in proportion to the bulk product stored during manufacturing. The environmental conditions of the hold-time studies should reflect the actual manufacturing conditions being tested. Products that are undergoing hold-time studies should also be put up to long-term stability testing.

The determination of maximum hold-time limits is critical where product is sensitive to environmental conditions, as an example: moisture, oxidation, or microbial attack. In these cases, it is critical that the maximum allowable hold times be determined and clearly specified in the manufacturing batch records. The batch record will then provide evidence through the recording of date and time by the operator that the product has not exceeded its time limitations as determined in the validation study. It is acceptable for validated time limits to be revisited and extended, as long as the subsequent validation studies show that the product has remained stable, with no adverse impact to the quality, safety, or efficacy of the drug product.

§211.113 CONTROL OF MICROBIOLOGICAL CONTAMINATION

a. *Appropriate written procedures, designed to prevent objectionable microorganisms in drug products not required to be sterile, shall be established and followed.*

For most products other than injections and eye preparations, there is no need for sterility. For these products, the presence of microorganisms could still constitute a problem since certain microorganisms are associated with human illness and must be absent. For example, oral suspensions and solutions should be tested for freedom from *Escherichia coli;* products for topical application should be tested for freedom from *Pseudomonas aeruginosa* and *Staphylococcus aureus.*

Some products may also be prone to microbial degradation resulting in loss of active ingredient or breakdown in physical characteristics, such as emulsions. In such cases, it may be necessary to have a specification for total viable microorganisms.

The USP 29 General Information Chapter *<1111> Microbiological Examination of Nonsterile Products: Acceptance Criteria for Pharmaceutical Preparations and Substances for Pharmaceutical Use* addresses total plate count criteria for bacteria and yeasts/molds. In addition, it discusses evaluation of other microorganisms recovered in terms of the following:

- The use of the product (e.g., route of administration)
- The nature of the product as it relates to supporting growth
- The method of application
- The intended recipient (e.g., neonates, infants, the debilitated)
- The use of immunosuppressive agents
- The presence of disease, wounds, organ damage

The presence of certain microorganisms in nonsterile preparations may have the potential to reduce or even inactivate the therapeutic activity of the product and has a potential to adversely affect the health of the patient.

Chapter <1111> gives examples of total plate count limits as well as the absence of certain microorganisms based on route of administration. For example, as taken from Table 6.1 in Acceptance Criteria for Microbiological Quality of Nonsterile Dosage Forms, the total plate count criteria for nonaqueous preparations for oral use are less stringent than those for oromucosal use products.

The procedures and conditions required to assure adequate microbial control will vary according to the specific products but are likely to include some, or all, of the following:

1. Microbial monitoring of potentially susceptible raw materials. This may require special negotiation with the supplier if a microbiological specification is not a normal requirement for his other customers. Current practices involve the setting of microbial specifications for materials of natural (animal, vegetable, or mineral) origin, those likely to support microbial growth, and materials to be used in product formulations with rigorous microbial specifications, such as injections.
2. Equipment sanitation procedures that have been proven effective, especially for any specific known deleterious or objectionable microorganisms.
3. Processing conditions that minimize the potential for microbial growth.
4. Environmental control including covers over equipment; laminar flow at susceptible points, wearing of protective clothing such as gloves and masks, and clearing filling lines at breaks.
5. Formulations to include preservatives.

TABLE 6.1
Acceptance Criteria for Microbiological Quality of Nonsterile Dosage Forms: May 1, 2009

Route of Administration	Total Aerobic Microbial Count (cfu/g or cfu/mL)	Total Combined Yeasts/Molds Count (cfu/g or cfu/mL)	Specified Microorganism(s)
Nonaqueous preparations for oral use	10^3	102	Absence of *Escherichia coli* (1 g or 1 mL)
Aqueous preparations for oral use	10^2	101	Absence of *Escherichia coli* (1 g or 1 mL)
Rectal use	10^3	102	—
Oromucosal use Gingival use Cutaneous use Nasal use Auricular use	10^2	101	Absence of *Staphylococcus aureus* (1 g or 1 mL) Absence of *Pseudomonas aeruginosa* (1 g or 1 mL)
Vaginal use	10^2	101	Absence of *Pseudomonas aeruginosa* (1 g or 1 mL) Absence of *Staphylococcus aureus* (1 g or 1 mL) Absence of *Candida albicans* (1 g or 1 mL)
Transdermal patches (limits for one patch including adhesive)	10^2	101	Absence of *Staphylococcus aureus* (1 patch)

Although there may be a need for limits for liquid products, especially aqueous products, there would seem to be less value for solid oral dosage products. Microbial contamination has not been a problem except for products involving materials of natural origin. The USP General Information Chapter <1112> *Application of Water Activity Determination to Nonsterile Pharmaceutical Products* addresses water activity in relationship to Microbial Limit Testing strategies. This chapter notes that determination of water activity of nonsterile pharmaceutical dosage forms aids the decision-making process regarding optimized product formulations, susceptibility to microbial contamination, frequency of microbial limit testing, etc. It points out that nonaqueous liquids and dry solid dosage forms will not support microbial growth due to low water activity.

b. *Appropriate written procedures, designed to prevent microbiological contamination of drug products purporting to be sterile, shall be established and followed. Such procedures shall include validation of any sterilization process.*

Sterile products are manufactured using either terminal sterilization or aseptic processing. The level of sterility assurance is significantly higher with terminal sterilization; autoclaving at 121°C can result in a 10^{-6} microbial survivor probability, whereas aseptic processing tends to result in the order of 10^{-3}. Because of these significant differences in assurance levels, terminal sterilization should be the method of choice. Some products cannot withstand the temperature conditions of autoclaving, the ingredients may be heat labile or the package may be physically affected by the pressure changes (e.g., prefilled syringes), and aseptic processing may then be necessary. A useful compromise situation is a combination of aseptic processing with some level of heat treatment that could effectively kill off vegetative organisms without adversely affecting chemical stability or physical integrity.

The subject of aseptic processing versus heat sterilization or the compromise of aseptic plus some heat treatment can be very complex, especially for those products that have some degree of heat lability. The possible permutations of temperature and time are almost limitless. Also, the relative benefits/disadvantages of aseptic processing with low levels of degradants and some heat treatment with higher levels of sterility assurance but also higher levels of degradants need to be evaluated.

Whichever process is used, the probability of having a nonsterile unit will be extremely low. Consequently, assurance of sterility cannot be demonstrated by testing a limited number of samples. For example, when sterility testing 10 units, lots with 0.1% contaminated units could be passed as sterile 99 out of 100 times. Increasing the sample size to 100 still leaves a 91% chance of passing a contaminated batch. Also, if the sample size is increased, the potential for false positives also increases. This then places a greater emphasis on the need to validate the sterilization process and to ensure that the defined process is followed for every batch of product. The key parameters to be evaluated for the different types of sterilization are outlined below; whichever process is used, the same basic steps outlined previously for process validation are also to be included: product/process design, equipment qualification, services qualification, process performance, and revalidation. Validation of heat sterilization (dry heat or autoclave) includes:

1. Heat distribution within the empty sterilization chamber
2. Heat penetration within the units of product for the various loading cycles to be used
3. Lethality calculations based on the known numbers of resistant bacteria or spores killed, usually *Geobacillus stearothermophilus* spores placed in units that receive the least heat treatment
4. Bioburden data showing the numbers and types of organisms, with particular reference to resistivity, likely to result from the components and the process prior to sterilization
5. Perform studies outside the ranges of conditions that will routinely be used for sterilization cycles

VALIDATION OF ASEPTIC PROCESSING

1. Treatments of product components and processing equipment to remove particulate matter, sterilize, and depyrogenate are critical to effective aseptic processing. This include ampoules, vials, stoppers, filters, intermediate storage vessels, tubing, filling equipment, gowns, masks, and gloves. The processes for each of these must be validated.
2. Environmental qualifications must include:
   a. *Air quality.* At the point of use (e.g., filling), air should be supplied by high-efficiency particulate air (HEPA)-filtered laminar flow air at about 90 feet per minute and with a pressure differential to adjacent areas of different classification of at least 10–15 Pa with doors closed. Nonviable particle counts should be less than 100 per cubic foot equal to or larger than 0.5 µm (Class 100/grade A or ISO 5); viable particles should be not more than one colony forming unit per 10 cubic feet. Where an aseptic processing room is adjacent to an unclassified room, an overpressure of at least 12.5 Pa from the aseptic processing room should be maintained according to the 2004 *FDA Guidance for Industry—Sterile Drug Products Produced by Aseptic Processing—Current Good Manufacturing Practice.*

      Away from the critical filling area, where product is not exposed to the environment, less stringent requirements are necessary but must still be controlled in order to minimize the bioburden load. The Class 100,000 (ISO 8) (not more than 100,000 particles per 0.5 µm or larger and not more than 25 colony-forming units per 10 cubic feet) should be adequate. Air filter integrity and efficiency testing should be included.
   b. *People.* The presence of people in an area or room will have an impact on air quality. The validation study should include the maximum number of people expected to be present at any time during the process. Other people-related activities to be examined would be training programs, especially with respect to microbiological understanding,

aseptic techniques, and gowning techniques. The effectiveness of these techniques can be evaluated by the use of swabs, contact plates, and touch plates.

c. *Time limitations.* Liquid preparations and wet components are prone to microbial multiplication, including the possibility of microorganisms passing through filters. Maximum time frames for key steps need to be confirmed.

d. *Product filtration.* The filtration system used to "sterilize" the drug product, usually 0.22 μm, should be challenged using a suitable small organism, usually *Brevundimonas diminuta.* The number of organisms used in the challenge will be in excess of the maximum bioburden levels measured in unfiltered solutions.

e. *Media fills.* The overall effectiveness of the aseptic process is then validated using liquid media fills.

    1. Initially, three media fills are considered desirable.
    2. According to the 2004 *FDA Guidance for Industry, Sterile Drug Products Produced by Aseptic Processing—Current Good Manufacturing Practice,* the starting point for a media fill run size is 5000 to 10,000 units. For production sizes under 5000, the number of units should be at least equal to the batch size.
    3. Each shift and each employee used for aseptic processing should be included in the media fills.
    4. According to the guidance, the recommended criteria for assessing the state of aseptic line control are as follows:
        • When filling fewer than 5000 units, no contaminated units should be detected.
            • One (1) contaminated unit is considered the cause for revalidation, following an investigation.
        • When filling from 5000 to 10,000 units:
            • One (1) contaminated unit should result in an investigation, including consideration of a repeat media fill.
            • Two (2) contaminated units are considered the cause for revalidation, following investigation.
        • When filling more than 10,000 units:
            • One (1) contaminated unit should result in an investigation.
            • Two (2) contaminated units are considered the cause for revalidation, following investigation.

f. *Revalidation.* As with any process, revalidation should be considered whenever there is a change in the product, components, process, facility, equipment, or people. Additionally, since the aseptic process is so people dependent, regular revalidation is essential. This routine revalidation should normally be performed every six months on each different type of process and for each shift; every operator should be included in a revalidation at least every 12 months.

The routinely collected data on bioburden levels and environmental conditions will also serve to confirm that the process is being maintained under control.

The greatest potential source of microbial contamination in an aseptic environment is people. The interaction of people and process is also not consistent. One way to significantly minimize this potential microbial exposure and variability is to separate the people from the process. Newer aseptic installations and upgrades are introducing barrier technology. This technology maintains the environmental conditions around the product at Class 100 or better while allowing personnel access only by way of glove ports. Consequently, there is no direct interaction of people and process. This approach greatly enhances the potential for sterility assurance—from about 10^{-3} to 10^{-5} or 10^{-6}.

The 2004 *FDA Guidance for Industry, Sterile Drug Products Produced by Aseptic Processing—Current Good Manufacturing Practice* discusses various aspects of maintenance, design, and monitoring of Aseptic Processing Isolators in Appendix A and Blow-Fill-Seal Technology in Appendix B.

Another benefit of the use of barrier technology is that the high-quality air needs to be supplied only to the product operational area and not to the entire room.

VALIDATION OF ETHYLENE OXIDE STERILIZATION

This process is used for the sterilization of components but *not* for products. Because of the inherent health hazards associated with the use of ethylene oxide, its use is diminishing. Key parameters to be included in the validation study include:

1. Distribution of temperature, ethylene oxide, and humidity in the sterilization chamber
2. Penetration of gas and moisture of the material to be sterilized
3. Lethality calculations based on the known numbers of resistant bacteria or spores killed
4. Removal of ethylene oxide and ethylene glycol residues

VALIDATION OF RADIATION STERILIZATION

Gamma radiation using Cobalt-60 is used for the sanitization and sterilization of many pharmaceutical raw materials and products. Usually, these are solids or nonaqueous preparations because water when irradiated generates free radicals, which tend to cause degradation. Gamma radiation is easy to use since time is the only variable once dosage has been established. There is also some evidence that gamma irradiation can reduce endotoxin levels.

The validation of a gamma irradiation sterilization process involves three stages.

1. Product qualification evaluates the impact of radiation on the product. Three levels of radiation may be determined: (i) maximum tolerated level—the highest dose that fails to induce an unacceptable change in the product; (ii) maximum process dose—based on the defined sterilizing dose—to be applied and the highest level of exposure in any unit of product; (iii) minimum process dose—the opposite of (ii). The optimum situation is for maximum and minimum process values to be close but significantly lower than the maximum tolerated level.

   Assessment of impact must use real-time stability studies, since accelerated conditions may result in more rapid degeneration of free radicals and give an impression of greater stability.
2. Equipment qualification is normally performed by the operator of the facility and should address design, installation, operation, and maintenance.
3. Process qualification should include:
   a. Sterilization approach, of which there are three: (i) overkill, which usually involves radiation doses in excess of 25 kGy and can only be used for products that are radiation stable; (ii) bioburden, which relies on a lower level of radiation based on the known and constant bioburden of the product; and (iii) species-specific, which uses an even lower radiation dosage and is particularly useful for products with a low, nonresistant bioburden such as pharmaceuticals.
   b. Dose distribution in the loads using well-defined loading patterns.
   c. Biological challenge using *Bacillus pumilis*.
   d. Cycle interruption studies.

§211.115 REPROCESSING

a. *Written procedures shall be established and followed prescribing a system for reprocessing batches that do not conform to standards or specifications, and the steps to be taken to ensure that the reprocessed batches will conform to all established standards, specifications, and characteristics.*

b. *Reprocessing shall not be performed without the review and approval of the quality control unit.*

Reprocessing is defined as the introduction of a product or material back into a manufacturing process. This is an exception in a process and must not be conducted without first formally investigating the issue. The quality system, which defines reprocessing steps, must be defined in approved written procedures. If a proposal has been made to reprocess a material, the decision must be documented by the Quality Unit in a deviation report and an investigation performed. The reprocessing material cannot be released until the investigation has been completed as defined in the SOP and approved. Reprocessed material must be supported by process validation and stability, as well as being permitted by the product license. If there is no existing supporting stability data, the batch must be put on stability testing prior to release. Release testing must be performed for reprocessed products and the need for additional testing must be considered as the normal release standards will not necessarily be sufficiently robust to evaluate the reprocessed batch.

If the reprocessing becomes a common recurrence, then the adequacy of the manufacturing process needs to be assessed and appropriate improvements be taken.

EXAMPLES OF OBSERVATIONS FROM FDA CITATIONS

- The processes used to manufacture your (b)(4) drug products have not been shown to be consistent and reliable, and consequently batches of your drug products are likely to significantly vary in strength, quality, and purity.
- FDA collected samples of your (b)(4) batch #(b)(4) at the port of entry. FDA laboratory analysis found that your (b)(4) did not contain any of the labeled active ingredient, (b)(4). FDA denied entry of the shipment accordingly and notified your customer, (b)(4), which filed a complaint with you.
- Your subsequent investigation into the customer complaint for batch #(b)(4) revealed that, during (b)(4) of components, you added the wrong ingredient, (b)(4), instead of the active ingredient.
- No restricted access to the microbial identification instrument. Further, you lacked restricted access to the external hard drive used for backup of this instrument. All users could delete or modify files. In your response, you commit to limit access to the system and external hard drive. However, your response is inadequate because you did not provide a retrospective risk assessment of the impact and scope of inadequate system controls at your firm.
- Your master batch records lacked a statement of theoretical yield, percentage of theoretical yield, and statements of limits beyond which an investigation is required. Without calculating theoretical yield, you may be missing important indications of possible error throughout your manufacturing process.
- In January 2013, multiple in-process and finished product batches of xxxxxx USP failed to meet release specification for (b)(4). Failure to meet (b)(4) specifications may reduce the effectiveness of products administered as nasal sprays. You rejected these batches and corresponding finished products and undertook an investigation into the (b)(4) failures. Your investigations (b)(4) and (b)(4) stated that "the root cause can be attributed to the raw material... (b)(4)..." but offered no further explanation for the failures and did not specify the basis for your conclusion.

- Following these investigations, you began manufacturing (b)(4). However, you have never revalidated your manufacturing process to account for the variability in your finished product that you initially attributed to (b)(4).
- Bulk (b)(4) used in solid (b)(4) dosage form manufacturing were held for excessive periods during commercial batch manufacturing without adequate hold-time studies or scientific justification. For example, in many instances, bulk (b)(4) for multiple drug products were held for longer than (b)(4), including some held significantly beyond (b)(4). Despite these excessive (b)(4) hold times, you released the (b)(4) for (b)(4), and rarely placed the finished product batches in your stability program.
- Your smoke studies do not support your assertion that you maintain unidirectional airflow for all aseptic operations. At times, the smoke volume was too low to accurately demonstrate airflow. You did not inject the smoke in areas that showed the effects of operator interventions on the unidirectional air stream. These smoke studies do not demonstrate that your line is designed to prevent microbiological contamination, or to provide high assurance of product sterility.
- There were no SOPs for the QA investigations of product failures, laboratory failure investigations, and stability investigations.

SUGGESTED READINGS

- FDA Guidance for Industry: Q8(2) Pharmaceutical Development. Rockville, MD, U.S. Dept. of Health and Human Services, May 2009.
- FDA Guidance for Industry: Q8, Q9, and Q10 Questions and Answers (R4), November 2011.
- FDA Guideline on General Principles of Process Validation, January 2011.
- FDA Draft Guidance for Industry: Powder Blends and Finished Dosage Units—Stratified In-Process Dosage Unit Sampling and Assessment, November 2003.
- FDA Guideline on Sterile Drug Products Produced by Aseptic Processing, September 2004.
- Agalloco JP, Carlton FJ. *Validation of Pharmaceutical Processes Sterile Products.* 2nd ed. 1998.
- Wachter AH, Nash RA. *Pharmaceutical Process Validation.* 3rd ed. New York, Marcel Dekker, 2003.
- Subchapter 490 Validation Sec. 490.100 Process Validation Requirements for Drug Products Subject to Pre-Market Approval (CPG7132C.08) Issued: 8/30/93, Revised: 03/12/2004.
- Subchapter 420 Compendial/Test Requirements Sec. 420.100 Adulteration of Drugs Under Section 501(B) And 501(C) of The Act [Direct Reference Seizure Authority for Adulterated Drugs Under Section 501(B)] (CPG 7132A.O3) Issued: 6/20/85, Reissued: 9/4/87, 3/95.
- PIC/S Recommendation on the Validation of Aseptic Processes, January 2011.
- ISO 13408-1:2008 Aseptic processing of health-care products—Part 1: General requirements (parts 2–8 also deal with aseptic processing).
- PDA Technical Report No. 28 Process Simulation Testing for Sterile Bulk Pharmaceutical Chemicals, January 2006.

7 Records and Reports

Graham P. Bunn

CONTENTS

This introduction to the FDA requirements for Electronic Records: Electronic Signatures is provided for the history and as a general description. It is not intended as an interpretation because detailed explanations are provided in other resources.

When the current good manufacturing practice (CGMP) regulations were originally effective in the late 1970s, paper records and pen signatures on paper were the only records. With advances in computer technology and the storage of data and information electronically, the amount of paper records decreased but the securing and authenticity of electronic data/information significantly increased. There was also the additional requirement to log into the computers using user name and password.

In 1994 the FDA issued a Proposed Rule covering electronic records and signatures and the final rule in 1997, 21 CFR Part 11 "considers electronic records, electronic signatures and handwritten signatures executed to electronic records, to be trustworthy, reliable, and generally equivalent to paper records and handwritten signatures executed on paper." Part 11 works together with a predicate rule, which refers to any FDA regulation that requires organizations to maintain records. There was an obligation to ensure that the computer systems and software used in these operations were validated and revisions histories of software maintained by the users. As a result of comments from the industry, the FDA reexamined the requirements and in the *Federal Register* of February 4, 2003 (68 FR 5645), they announced the withdrawal of the draft guidance entitled "Guidance for Industry, 21 CFR Part 11; Electronic Records; Electronic Signatures, Electronic Copies of Electronic Records." The FDA noted that it wanted to minimize industry time spent reviewing and commenting on the guidance, which might not ultimately have been representative of FDA's approach under the CGMP initiative. Then in the *Federal Register* of February 25, 2003 (68 FR 8775), FDA announced the withdrawal of the part 11 draft guidance documents on validation, glossary of terms, time stamps, maintenance of electronic records, and CPG 7153.17 Enforcement Policy: 21 CFR Part 11; Electronic Records, Electronic Signatures. The final rule covering the revised requirements was issued in the *Federal Register* 62 FR 13464, Mar. 20, 1997 covering the following major subparts:

Subpart A—General Provisions
11.1 Scope
11.2 Implementation
11.3 Definitions
Subpart B—Electronic Records
11.10 Controls for closed systems
11.30 Controls for open systems
11.50 Signature manifestations
11.70 Signature/record linking
Subpart C—Electronic Signatures
11.100 General requirements
11.200 Electronic signature components and controls
11.300 Controls for identification codes/passwords

§211.180 GENERAL REQUIREMENTS

a. *Any production, control, or distribution record that is required to be maintained in compliance with this part and is specifically associated with a batch of a drug product shall be retained for at least 1 year after the expiration date of the batch or, in the case of certain OTC drug products lacking expiration dating because they meet the criteria for exemption under 211.137, 3 years after distribution of the batch.*
b. *Records shall be maintained for all components, drug product containers, closures, and labeling for at least 1 year after the expiration date or, in the case of certain OTC drug products lacking expiration dating because they meet the criteria for exemption under 211.137, 3 years after distribution of the last lot of drug product incorporating the component or using the container, closure, or labeling.*
c. *All records required under this part, or copies of such records, shall be readily available for authorized inspection during the retention period at the establishment where the activities described in such records occurred. These records or copies thereof shall be subject to photocopying or other means of reproduction as part of such inspection. Records that can be immediately retrieved from another location by computer or other electronic means shall be considered as meeting the requirements of this paragraph.*
d. *Records required under this part may be retained either as original records or as true copies, such as photocopies, microfilm, microfiche, or other accurate reproductions of the original records. Where reduction techniques, such as microfilming, are used, suitable reader and photocopying equipment shall be readily available.*
e. *Written records required by this part shall be maintained so that data therein can be used for evaluating, at least annually, the quality standards of each drug product to determine the need for changes in drug product specifications or manufacturing or control procedures. Written procedures shall be established and followed for such evaluations and shall include provisions for:*
   1. *A review of a representative number of batches, whether approved or rejected, and, where applicable, records associated with the batch*
   2. *A review of complaints, recalls, returned or salvaged drug products, and investigations conducted under 211.192 for each drug product*

f. *Procedures shall be established to assure that the responsible officials of the firm, if they are not personally involved in or immediately aware of such actions, are notified in writing of any investigations conducted under 211.198, 211.204, or 211.208 of these regulations, any recalls, reports of inspectional observations issued by the Food and Drug Administration, or any regulatory actions relating to good manufacturing practices brought by the Food and Drug Administration.*

Records as required by subsections (a) and (b) would be available for review for a "reasonable" time as defined by the number of years specific to the product after its expiration date. Conscientious companies maintain records until the statute of limitations runs out to ensure coverage of any liability to the consumer. The FDA reviews records under its inspection authority defined in Section 704 of the Federal Food, Drug, and Cosmetic Act. This was further extended in the 1953 amendments contained in Public Law 82–217, which established Section 704(a), and in the Drug Amendments of 1962 contained in Public Law 87–781 (1961). The FDA does not have the authority to inspect records regarding the manufacture of non-prescription drugs that are not "new drugs" as defined in Section 201(p) of the Federal Food, Drug, and Cosmetic Act. However, the manufacture of any drug product that is not in compliance with CGMP requirements makes the product adulterated under Section 301(b) of the Act and a federal crime under Section 303 of the Act. If FDA has reliable information that a non-prescription or old drug product was being manufactured in violation of CGMPs, they could obtain a search warrant authorizing inspection of the records to identify any evidence.

Subsections (c) and (d) relate to the electronic storage and retrieval of records (paper and electronic). Although the regulations do not directly require retention of original records, they can be retained as true copies, such as on microfilm/microfiche (at the time of writing this edition, these are almost unheard of and there are probably fewer records currently supporting products currently on the market) or portable document format (PDF) files are permitted.

Older/outdated equipment used to archive documents must still be available and functional to read the documents and provide paper copies. It is the document owner's responsibility to ensure that documents are "readily" available when requested by the FDA. The records relating to the product and components, drug product containers, closures, and labeling must be available at the location at which they were generated. The FDA acknowledges the practicality of storing archived documents at another location (company site or specialist company) or electronically. Specialized companies will manage archived records off-site, but these records must be readily available within a "reasonable" time either as the hard copy or electronically. The retrieval time for archived documents needs to be periodically challenged and be included in the internal audit of the Document Management System. During regulatory inspections it may be appropriate to inform the requestor that the document is being retrieved from the archive and when to expect it. The apparent delay of providing the document because it is off-site without adequate explanation does not do well to support inspections. Retrieval from storage must be within a "reasonable" time, and be sure to inform the requestor that the document could take a few hours to obtain due to storage off-site. Ensure that storage is at an approved facility and the document retrieval is periodically tested for effectiveness and suitable time to retrieve.

The amount of documentation supporting the production of prescription and OTC products has increased significantly over the years and so has the ability to store the information/data electronically. Data is also captured in electronic files and with the availability of faster scanners enables documents to be maintained and stored more easily. A robust and secure document archiving system is essential to manage, track, catalog, and secure documents but still provide reasonable access to these documents.

In 2014 FDA issued a guidance for industry (Circumstances that Constitute Delaying, Denying, Limiting, or Refusing a Drug Inspection) with a specific section relating to "Delay Producing Records." There needs to be a standard operating procedure (SOP) defining the process for responding to the FDA requests, which also include endorsement of the document copies by QA and by implication to remove the copies from the premises. Unless copies contain information relating to "trade secret" (21 CFR 20.61), they can be released under the Freedom of Information Act.

Subsection (e) contains an important requirement that at least once a year a review of the quality standards for each drug product are performed to determine if there is a need for changes in drug product specifications or manufacturing or control procedures. The requirements for annual reporting are defined in 21 CFR 314.70(d) and 314.81(b)(2) and need to be defined in a SOP with specific responsibilities. While Regulatory Affairs may coordinate the review, there are key responsibilities for data and information review by other department subject matter experts of a representative number of product batches. These include approved and rejected batches and, where applicable, records associated with each batch. This review provides the opportunity to evaluate all of the data from the product and identify opportunities for product and quality improvements. Although ongoing reviews are performed through the Quality Management Systems requirements, additional overall review may identify other requirements. The data also includes review of complaints, recalls, returned or salvaged drug products, and investigations conducted under §211.192 for each drug product. The review process should be distributed throughout the year to ensure that all products are covered within the required time period according to a schedule.

Subsection (f) requirements relate to the officials (directed to senior management) of the firm to be informed in writing (unless they were involved or immediately aware) of investigations relating to complaints, returned drug product, salvaged drug product, recalls and any inspection observations (FDA483, warning letters) and regulatory actions relating to CGMPs (delayed drug approvals, import alerts, etc). There are two historical court cases involving senior management relating to shipment of adulterated and misbranded drugs in interstate commerce in *United States v. Dotterweich* (320 U.S. 277, 1943 and unsanitary conditions in *United States v. Park* (421 U.S. 658, 1975). Management must be kept informed of the CGMP regulatory compliance status of each facilities' operations at all times, as they hold the positions that can affect change immediately through the deployment of people and financial resources. Not only does this enable mitigation of compliance risk but also patient safety. Quality orientated and forward-thinking companies will have procedures ensuring senior management is regularly informed of quality issues. Additionally, procedures require notification early quality indicators enabling proactive steps to be taken to avoid major events. Sometimes immediate notification to senior management is necessary and must be effective and efficiently implemented for potential non-compliance or confirmed/potential impact to patient safety. Companies establish Quality Councils comprising of site senior management who regularly review data/information (metrics) from the Quality Management Systems with recommendations and discuss appropriate actions. This includes regulatory compliance and product quality issues, which are also provided to corporate management so that site trends and changes can be monitored across the company. The FDA expects corporate management to proactively monitor compliance and quality issues and also take actions, especially when a site has received a FDA483 or warning letter to determine if similar gaps exist at other sites. Receiving another regulatory observation for the same or similar compliance issue at another site does not project conscientious management to any regulatory authority. See also Chapter 3, "Management Responsibility and Control".

§211.182 EQUIPMENT CLEANING AND USE LOG

A written record of major equipment cleaning, maintenance (except routine maintenance such as lubrication and adjustments), and use shall be included in individual equipment logs that show the date, time, product, and lot number of each batch processed. If equipment is dedicated to manufacture of one product, then individual equipment logs are not required, provided that lots or batches of such product follow in numerical order and are manufactured in numerical sequence.

In cases where dedicated equipment is employed, the records of cleaning, maintenance, and use shall be part of the batch record. The persons performing and double-checking the cleaning and maintenance shall date and sign or initial the log indicating that the work was performed. Entries in the log shall be in chronological order.

This is an important section to understand the requirements as citations in regulatory actions have been made. First, note that this section specifically refers to "major" equipment, and therefore each company needs to clearly define what is within this scope, as there is no requirement to include smaller equipment items like stirrers and scoops. Cleaning of reused non-major items is still required to be documented as evidence that the steps were performed. It is expected that bound numbered pages are used as logbooks issued by Document Management as controlled documents after QA approval. There are also specific requirements relating to chronological order (time/date) and signature or initials (often the requirement in the CFR is to "document").

Although the section excludes routine maintenance and adjustments, it is recommended for completeness and can also meet the requirements of §211.67 Equipment Cleaning and Maintenance. Dedicated equipment cleaning is incorporated into the batch record and hence readily available during the review process prior to batch release. Maintaining the complete history of equipment in a single logbook minimizes loss of information and makes verification and traceability easier, especially during annual review of equipment function, reliability, and calibration.

§211.184 COMPONENT, DRUG PRODUCT CONTAINER, CLOSURE, AND LABELING RECORDS

These records shall include the following:

a. *The identity and quantity of each shipment of each lot of components, drug product containers, closures, and labeling; the name of the supplier; the supplier's lot number(s) if known; the receiving code as specified in §211.80; and the date of receipt. The name and location of the prime manufacturer, if different from the supplier, shall be listed if known.*
b. *The results of any test or examination performed (including those performed as required by § 211.82(a), § 211.84(d), or § 211.122(a)) and the conclusions derived therefrom.*
c. *An individual inventory record of each component, drug product container, and closure and, for each component, a reconciliation of the use of each lot of such component. The inventory record shall contain sufficient information to allow determination of any batch or lot of drug product associated with the use of each component, drug product container, and closure.*
d. *Documentation of the examination and review of labels and labeling for conformity with established specifications in accord with §211.122(c) and §211.130(c).*
e. *The disposition of rejected components, drug product containers, closure, and labeling.*

Section (a) provides the minimum information to trace components, product containers, closures, and labeling back to the producer/manufacturer. If the producer is unknown, the supplier must be identified. Sometimes distributors are not prepared to identify their manufacturing source, which can be a problem if deviations need data for investigations. Although this can have a greater impact on raw materials, due to variations in manufacturing processes that could still meet required specifications but in practice not be able to produce a product meeting specifications. A risk assessment of the supplier/component needs to be performed when the manufacturer is unknown and also maintain compliance with the supplier qualification process. Primary components can require on-site audits, but this may not be possible in all cases. However, alternative suppliers with known manufacturers should always be considered.

Subsection (b) requires the testing data and conclusions to be retained. Without evidence of assessment of suitability for use against requirements (specifications), there is no evidence for acceptance of the components/materials/containers/labeling/packaging.

Subsection (c) requires inventory records of each component, drug product container, and closure and additionally reconciliation of usage for each lot of components. This is to ensure there is sufficient information in the event of a customer complaint or a deviation requiring investigation. Labels and labeling are covered by the requirements in subsection (d) and disposition of rejected components, drug product containers, closures, and labeling in subsection (d). This ensures that there is accountability for usage and rejection (documented disposal/returns) for all components, drug product containers, closures, and labeling.

§211.186 MASTER PRODUCTION AND CONTROL RECORDS

a. *To assure uniformity from batch to batch, master production and control records for each drug product, including each batch size thereof, shall be prepared, dated, and signed (full signature, handwritten) by one person and independently checked, dated, and signed by a second person. The preparation of master production and control records shall be described in a written procedure, and such written procedure shall be followed.*

Master production and control records for each drug product batch size are required so that the potential for calculation errors is minimize for different batch sizes. The detail associated with this subsection requiring the preparation by one person and an independent check by a second person highlights its importance. Although the writing and review are fundamental requirements, the inference is that the accuracy and completeness of this document is significant. As the Quality Control Unit has the responsibility for the approval of all procedures, the second signature is expected, although not defined, to be Quality Assurance. However, Production, Technical Services, and Regulatory Affair also have responsibilities for the content of the record, and these approvals can be captured in the document change approval process.

This document has the specific requirement to use full signatures and not initials on the document. Note this is the only place in the 21 CFR 211 CGMP regulations that this is defined. Most companies require registration of signatures and initials so that identification of individuals can be more easily performed. Names can also be printed by the individuals as the document is signed to add further clarification. Quality-orientated companies require individuals participating in the execution of the master production and control records (Production and Packaging) to register their signature and initials with the date in a table incorporated into the record to ensure traceability/identification throughout the document.

The checking of the document by an independent second person and "signed" is interpreted to require a full signature and at the time the CGMPs were first issued stressed the importance placed on the these specific responsibilities.

With advancements in computer technology, the requirements relating to signing were codified in 21 CFR 11 covering electronic records and electronic signatures. The electronic signatures are equivalent to handwritten signatures (often referred to as "wet" signatures), initials, and other general signings required by predicate rules. Part 11 signatures are used to document actions occurred in accordance with the predicate rule (e.g., approved, reviewed, and verified).

The reference to performing actions and the associated responsibilities with documented evidence is required to be in writing and traceable. These every day actions are confirmed by signatures/initials as directed by "Good Documentation Practices," which is a core SOP in the FDA-regulated industries of GMPs, good laboratory practices (GLPs), and good clinical practices (GCPs) (GxP). The procedure covers prohibited items (pencil, white out, pre/back dating, signing for another person [forgery], fraud, cross outs, etc.). It also covers date and time format, corrections with single line and no obliteration of information, indelible ink, explanations for corrections, and several other requirements. It is worth noting that the SOP is essential to virtual companies of five employees to multinational pharmaceutical, device, and biopharmaceutical companies alike. The requirements are basically the same for all aspects of GxP and independent of company size, type of operations, and also includes contractors providing manufacturing, packaging, and testing services to other companies. Documents provided by contractors need to meet the same requirements of the "Good Documentation Practices" SOP. Linked to this SOP is data integrity, which is discussed in more depth in Chapter 24, "Data Integrity and Fundamental Responsibilities".

The requirements of the master document generated to document manufacturing of the batch are defined by the following:

b. *Master production and control records shall include:*
1. *The name and strength of the product and a description of the dosage form.*
   This is normally the proprietary name and the description of the dosage form refers to tablet, capsule, or injection. The strength must be used consistently throughout the record and all the supporting documents including any certificates of analysis to avoid any confusion or errors.
2. *The name and weight or measure of each active ingredient per dosage unit or per unit of weight or measure of the drug product and a statement of the total weight or measure of any dosage unit.*
   The details of the active ingredient(s) per dosage unit refers to solid dosage forms (tablets and capsules), but for injections this could be % w/v or v/v or weight/units per mL. Ensure that documents comply with the FDA requirements defined in "Strength Conversion in Drug Listing" defined on the website for the current version (www.fda.gov).
3. *A complete list of components designated by names or codes sufficiently specific to indicate any special quality characteristic.*
   Components are specified by name or code, providing some flexibility for identification, but the specific quality characteristics are in reference to pharmacopeias or other designated grades. The requirement is for a "complete list" of all components, even those that do not appear in the final dosage form, for example, water used in the coating solution for tablets or to dissolve other components in injections before freeze drying, nitrogen overlay or used for purging the oxygen from injections.
   Acids and bases are also designated as components when used to adjust the pH of solutions with the quantities used being documented in the record. A regulatory expectation based on the validated process is that the range of acid or base expected to be used for the specific batch size is defined in the production control record. Beyond the defined range, an investigation is required, since something has changed in the production process resulting in the batch being atypical, that is, not what is "normally" seen.
4. *An accurate statement of the weight or measure of each component, using the same weight system (metric, avoirdupois, or apothecary) for each component.*
   The types of weight system in brackets is based on historical values, which are seldom used now but more importantly is the use of decimal places, for example, 0.05 Kg would be less likely to be misread if it was written as "50g." Although trained and experienced operators would be performing the measurement of each component with an independent second check performed, it has been record that errors in the weighing due to misreading the numerals has occurred and also been checked incorrectly.
5. *A statement concerning any calculated excess of component.*
   Theoretical variations in the quantity of components are permitted, provided they are justified in the records. Some active pharmaceutical ingredients may vary in their potency based on water variations and calculations need to be provided for the operators to determine the weight required using the values from the certificate of analysis for the specific batch.

6. *A statement of theoretical weight or measure at appropriate phases of processing.*

   These values are based on the process validation, and the justification for the "appropriate phases" should be in approved supporting documents.

7. *A statement of theoretical yield, including the maximum and minimum percentages of theoretical yield beyond which investigation according to §211.192 is required.*

   The requirement to investigate yield outside the theoretical at the critical process phases, which are developed from historical data and set at scientifically justified limits, provide a reasonable and measurable monitoring process. Prudent manufacturers will monitor results and respond accordingly to trends and perform prompt investigations for out of limits results. An erratic or trending yield indicates that the process is not completely in control and requires further technical investigation. Loss of material resulting in low yield may be explainable when unexpected events occur, but equally, yields above expectation must be investigated, as material has been added, for example, liquid remaining in the process/transfer equipment from cleaning.

8. *A description of the drug product containers, closures, and packaging materials, including a specimen or copy of each label and all other labeling signed and dated by the person or persons responsible for approval of such labeling.*

   The definition of "label" and "labeling" is found in 21 CFR 321:

   (k) The term "label" means a display of written, printed, or graphic matter upon the immediate container of any article; and a requirement made by or under authority of this chapter that any word, statement, or other information appear on the label shall not be considered to be complied with unless such word, statement, or other information also appears on the outside container or wrapper, if any there be, of the retail package of such article, or is easily legible through the outside container or wrapper.
   (l) The term "immediate container" does not include package liners.
   (m) The term "labeling" means all labels and other written, printed, or graphic matter (1) upon any article or any of its containers or wrappers, or (2) accompanying such article.

   Note the requirement for the labeling to be signed/dated for approval: it is not just attached, as the action of including "signed" signifies authenticity. Actual labels from each batch run are required and include the first from the rolls during the packaging process. These labels are essential when performing investigations relating to labels. Samples of patient information leaflets are also included. Control and management of labeling is critical to ensure that the correct label is used and there are no mix-ups. Controls include restricting access to labeling so that only authorized personnel are responsible for the handling, labeling requests in writing with labeling delivered to the packaging floor in locked cages with verification and signature for receipt and overall accountability. Any changes to labeling require a change control, which must include production and Regulatory Affairs to ensure that the product filing information is accurately maintained.

   In *Kordell v. U.S.* (164 F. 2d 913 and 335 U.S. 345), it was determined that labeling may have a variety of meanings. Any printed or verbal claims relating to a drug product's efficacy or use and that are available to potential customers may be defined as labeling. Labeling does not have to directly accompany the drug product in interstate commerce or be shipped simultaneously with the container. An integrated or related transaction with the function of promotion is sufficient to constitute labeling. All labeling must be controlled and care exercised in relation to all types of communication and advertising relating to the products so that compliance with the Act is maintained.

9. *Complete manufacturing and control instructions, sampling and testing procedures, specifications, special notations, and precautions are to be followed.*

The master production and control records must be written with direct instructions in sufficient detail so that adequately trained personnel can consistently perform the required actions/tasks. Too much detail loses the objectivity, and insufficient detail probably results in personnel only knowing what to actually do because they were shown or told by another "more experienced" operator/supervisor: they remembered how to do it. This results in variations in implementation of the instructions and can potentially impact the product but may not be readily detected. Clear, concise, and unambiguous instructions that can be consistently executed with adequate space to record data/information/results need to be incorporated into every batch production and control record with care and precision. Errors can and do occur but may not be readily detected by testing or record review but could impact the product the patient receives.

Sampling performed by manufacturing personnel during batch production needs to be clearly defined in the record with the methodology, sampling apparatus, location(s), and the type of container with label requirements.

Some testing is performed during manufacturing and includes, for example, tablet weights/hardness and container fill volumes, which are clearly defined with specification and actions to be taken if the limits are exceeded. Precautions relating to handling of materials or safety requirements when processing are also included and must comply with applicable laws and regulatory requirements. Other minimum requirements are defined in 21 CFR 188.

Although the title of this subpart relates to the production process, the packaging process must also be defined in the same level of detail with adequate instructions for execution and space to document and verify/check each significant step.

The format/layout of the record contributes to the successful execution of the steps as intended and must provide basic elements of adequate space to document results/settings, provide consistent arrangement of columns in tables so that the blank spaces can be completed, minimize repetition on entries to minimize potential documentation errors, use of pictures and icons to reduce voluminous text and reduce misunderstanding, and clear identification of who does what, when, and the documented evidence supporting it with actual time performed as necessary.

§211.188 BATCH PRODUCTION AND CONTROL RECORDS

Batch production and control records shall be prepared for each batch of drug product produced and shall include complete information relating to the production and control of each batch.

These records shall include:

a. *An accurate reproduction of the appropriate master production or control record, checked for accuracy, dated, and signed.*

Note that the "Master..." document is approved and the Batch Production and Control Records (BPCR) are an accurate reproduction of the "Master..." After photocopying, the BPCR are checked to ensure that they are accurate and confirmed with a signature/date (one of the few requirements in 21 CFR 211 for a "signature" not initials). Should the BPCR be generated from a validated electronic system with approved master copies, it still must be checked for accuracy before being issued. This includes checking that the information is readable and no extraneous "marks" are present, especially in relations to numerical figures: a "6" can look like an "8" if the printer inadvertently adds an erroneous mark. These records are used by the production and packaging operators during the manufacturing/packaging of the batch and must be accurate and complete. Reliance on the operators to detect an error (extraneous mark or other) is unacceptable, as checks and balances must be in place to minimize the risk of errors. A unique batch number is entered on each page of the BPCR prior to issuance by Document Control. Since the records contain all the required steps, they may be executed simultaneously in difference physical locations in the facility, for example, preparation of the tablet binding solution and weighing of the tablet ingredients. Records must be available for the operators to enter data/information and initials/dates concurrently (at the time of performance) and therefore record sections are separated. Since the record contains executed information/data specific to the batch, it must be controlled at all times so that pages and supporting records are not lost or misfiled with other records. Management and control of each unique batch record is critical during the execution process. In addition to data/information being entered by operators and covered by the SOP on "Good Documentation Practices," printouts from equipment, for example, balances and temperature monitors, will also be generated and must be attached to the BPCR in the appropriate place and annotated with the operator's initials/date across the printout and record (so that if it is removed/lost it is obvious that the printout was once attached).

The BPCR must be protected from damage and potential contamination from the active ingredients/product during execution. Requests for additional or damaged pages must be documented/accounted for and approved in writing.

b. *Documentation that each significant step in the manufacture, processing, packing, or holding of the batch was accomplished, including:*
  1. *Dates*; using the required format: note that outside the United States the dates are sometimes written dd/mmm/yyy or even yyy/mmm/ddd.
  2. *Identity of individual major equipment and lines used*; equipment identity is usually the company uniquely allocated number and filling lines are assigned numeric or alpha identifications.
  3. *Specific identification of each batch of component or in-process material used*; these identifications are assigned at receipt or during processing for traceability.
  4. *Weights and measures of components used in the course of processing*; this was discussed above and includes the standardization of the units.
  5. *In-process and laboratory control results*; the in-process results being generated by production and the laboratory ones from specific testing; these results must be provided in writing with signatures by the laboratory: verbal and email communications are unacceptable since production are normally making a decision based on these results.
  6. *Inspection of the packaging and labeling area before and after use*; this is a critical step since the lines are often used for multiple products and strengths and a tablet can become trapped in the filling equipment but then dislodged during the filling of another product, even though cleaning of the equipment would have taken place. Clearance includes all the components used for the batch; there are some logistical variations to this when the components are allocated to more than one batch of the same product and strength. Procedural control is important in maintaining the correct allocation of components for each batch and so that they are traceable. The reader is encouraged to review the recalls on the FDA website for examples of line clearance failure results. The importance of this critical step should not be underestimated, and it takes time to perform correctly with an independent verification by a second person. Often the production floor quality group perform the verification when production have completed and documented their step. Detailed procedures define where and how the inspection is performed for consistency with supporting diagrams as needed. Use of flashlights aids the physical inspection and must also include counters and electronic equipment, which could contain the previous batch information. The author has experienced line clearance failures due to documents, components, and product being found in the most unexpected locations.
  7. *A statement of the actual yield and statement of the percentage of theoretical yield at appropriate phases of processing*; this is essential since commercial products are produced by validated process and therefore the yield limits are based on process

capability and historical data. Should an out of limit or atypical yield be obtained, an investigation must be performed. This is especially important when the yield is higher since something unexpected has changed and more material/product, at least in theory, has been produced. Subsequent analysis of the material/product may identify that the potency is out of limits and/or there is also contamination present.

8. *Complete labeling control records, including specimens or copies of all labeling used*; this has been previously discussed in this chapter.

9. *Description of drug product containers and closures*; this must be aligned with the regulatory filing and be adequate so that warehousing can retrieve the required container/closures, and operations personnel can confirm that they are correct against the records.

10. *Any sampling performed*; this was previously discussed. Production must be adequately trained to perform the sampling according to the defined procedure so that the sample is representative of the batch. Incorrect sampling, handling, storage, and transportation to the QC laboratory or the in-process testing location in production could render the samples "non-representative" of the batch. The potential for out of specification or atypical results then exists or a bias introduced so that the sample is no longer representative of the batch.

11. *Identification of the persons performing and directly supervising or checking each significant step in the operation*; a sign-in page with printed name, initials, and signature is essential in the manufacturing and packaging records so that the identification of every person entering information in the records can be easily identified. Steps/tasks are allocated in "blocks" (defined as "significant" in the regulations) with corresponding initials/date for performance. Practicality and logistics are balanced with maintaining contemporaneous confirmation of the steps being performed. The operator performing the step then either requires a checked (confirmation) or verified (normally taken as "seen" or "witnessed": to visually see) by a second person. The second person must be independent of the performance; otherwise, it can be interpreted as a having a vested interest in completing the step.

    An example of this is provided in Charge-in of Components: 21 CFR 211.101(d) "Each component shall either be added to the batch by one person and verified by a second person or, if the components are added by automated equipment under 211.68, only verified by one person." Note that the addition is "verified," which is normally interpreted as being witnessed. Hence, the "confirmation" or "implication" that the complete material/component had been added to the batch because the container it was in is empty is unacceptable. The SOP "Good Documentation Practices" needs to define the critical terms "performed," "verified," "checked," and "reviewed" and all personnel trained so that there is no misunderstanding. Note also that there is an expectation that supervisors are actively performing oversight and verifications/checks during productions/packaging activities and are required to confirm this by being identified by initials/signature in the records.

12. *Any investigation made according to §211.192*. This is covered in more details in the subpart below.

13. *Results of examinations made in accordance with §211.134*. This is covered in more details in the corresponding subpart.

§211.192 PRODUCTION RECORD REVIEW

All drug product production and control records, including those for packaging and labeling, shall be reviewed and approved by the QCU to determine compliance with all established, approved written procedures before a batch is released or distributed. Any unexplained discrepancy (including a percentage of theoretical yield exceeding the maximum or minimum percentages established

in master production and control records) or the failure of a batch or any of its components to meet
any of its specifications shall be thoroughly investigated, whether or not the batch has already been
distributed. The investigation shall extend to other batches of the same drug product and other
drug products that may have been associated with the specific failure or discrepancy. A written
record of the investigation shall be made and shall include the conclusions and follow-up.

Although this is one of the shorter subparts of 21 CFR 211, it contains two major requirements:

a. Review of all the production and packaging records to determine compliance with all established approved written procedures—this is more than looking for blank spaces, checking
   calculations, and ensuring compliance with the SOP "Good Documentation Practices."
b. Thorough investigation of any discrepancies or failure of the batch/components to meet
   specifications—this is more than two lines of text concluding that it was an isolated incident or the cause could not be identified.

The significant words have been underlined above and the two major requirements are now discussed in more depth.

BATCH RECORD REVIEW

This section requires that a product be released only after review by the QCU of the entire batch
record for compliance with approved written procedures, which are found acceptable. Otherwise, the
QCU has the authority to reject the batch. There must be written evidence that every requirement of
this section has been performed, and this is usually documented by the use of some form of checklist
to ensure consistency. However, the Reviewer must use Quality experience, expertise, and a broad
understanding of the regulatory requirements and quality context to go beyond the checklist. The
same approach is undertaken in performing audits using a checklist, which most seasoned industry
professionals can do. The checklist defines the specific documents supporting or contained within
the batch record and describe the checks that need to be performed on each document or Quality
Management Systems (change control, investigations). If the release criteria are not stated on the
batch record, they should be included on the checklist, which would include but not be limited to:

1. Batch production and control record is current and approved as an accurate copy.
2. Correct, released, components were used in manufacturing.
3. Correct quantities of components were used in manufacturing.
4. All components were within the retest dating period.
5. Batch production and control record (Manufacturing) is properly completed.
6. Sampling was performed as required.
7. Any in-process testing was performed as directed and results are within defined limits.
8. Correct product was packaged.
9. Correct packaging components were used.
10. Labeling contains the correct control/batch number, expiry date, and is the current version.
11. Yields and accountability are within action levels.
12. Batch production and control record (Packaging) was properly completed.
13. Test data, in-process, and control laboratory are within specifications.
14. Retained samples have been taken.
15. Written investigation of any deviation from procedure or requirement are included with
    any approvals and data to support remedial action.

A comprehensive review of the manufacturing, packaging, and control documentation is time consum-
ing and occasionally identifies more than the absence of signatures or the misplacement of a document.

The responsibilities for the execution and verification of the data/information in the batch record and supporting documentation generated during manufacturing or packaging of the product clearly belong to personnel executing, performing a second check/verification, and supervisor/management review. Since production/packaging owns their record, they are responsible for the initial review of these documents and written evidence that it has been performed. Subsequent reviews by administrative personnel to collate documents and ultimately the QCU (often defined as Quality Assurance) do not transfer or negate production's responsibility. Reliance on other department personnel checking the documents is unacceptable. Since other departments will provide supporting documents, they are responsible for content accuracy and completeness of their own documents. All personnel must understand the importance of record execution, procedures, and the need to follow them or document atypical or non-complying situations. Supervisors and managers must provide sufficient time for record review for themselves and other personnel before they can be transferred to the QCU for their independent review. Quality-oriented production management monitor the first-time right success rate of record execution, provide feedback to their personnel, and take responsibility for implementing their own actions to permanently correct the problems before being informed by the QCU. The responsibilities of the Quality Control Unit are also discussed in Chapter 4, "Organization and Personnel".

When production deviations occur they must be documented, investigated, and management involved in the review of the decision-making, supporting evidence, and conclusions.

Thorough investigation of any discrepancies or failure of the batch/components to meet specification must be performed and adequately documented with suitable approvals.

EVENTS, DEVIATIONS, AND INVESTIGATIONS

The following is intended as a guide to investigations and not as an all-inclusive methodology. There are numerous training workshops and books written that cover all aspects of performing investigations and written/facilitated by people who have spent their entire careers understanding and performing root cause analysis, documenting the results, and identifying appropriate actions.

Although these events are called many things by many people, they will always occur and there is no simple solution. There are no boundaries limiting them to the size of the operations, number of employees, types of products, counties, or event particular industry: pharmaceutical, biological, device or dietary supplement. Deviations, events, incidents, problems, or whatever you wish to call them are fundamentally departures from the planned/expected requirements. Those events that look simple are not, and those that are easily managed may not reoccur. Be wary of those appearing as if they can be simply addressed, as they often come back again and cause irreparable damage and costs (time and money) to the operations and ultimately company/share holders. The investigation process is not limited to FDA-regulated industries because safety, transport, criminal, and other professions all use the same approach; the content may be different, but the process is still the same.

The focus on investigations has increased significantly over the last 15 years and is reflected by the citations in FDA483s and warning letters. Changes in the global sourcing of FDA-regulated products have added to the number of citations. Astute companies have learned from other company's mistakes and have developed their personnel skills to perform comprehensive in-depth investigations that more clearly identify the root causes enabling effective actions to be implemented to minimize the probability for a repeat occurrence. Costs associated with each investigation (people, holding of batches, etc.) are reduced and overall a well-executed and efficient process has proven cost effective.

Companies that fail to understand the importance of the investigation process and/or do not want to dedicate the adequate resources (dedicated personnel, electronic system, supporting subject matter experts providing input, adequate time for personnel to plan and execute remediation actions, and holding people accountable when actions are overdue) often have repeat events and subsequently become the focus of FDA regulatory actions.

There needs to be a robust investigation process integrated with the system, which manages and provides the opportunity for the desired outcome. Understanding how an inadequate investigation system fails to support the Quality Management System provides opportunities for improvement by senior management. Not only is it in the overall interest of the company through cost and time savings, which site management can report to corporate through metrics and oversight audits, but it is a regulatory requirement that is often placed as a low priority by companies.

Key investigation steps include:

1. Identification: All personnel need to understand the definition of an event (trigger of the deviation). The most advanced investigation system cannot replace the understanding, inquisitiveness, alertness, and diligence of "hands on" personnel who are astutely aware that something was "not right" or "unusual" and immediately notified their manager.
2. Report: The requirement to take immediate action.
3. Document and retain evidence: Promptly and accurately record who, what, when.
4. Collect further information/data: From testing as needed.
5. Investigate: Using tools.
6. Conclusions: Based on the evidence/data with rationale.
7. Identify root cause(s): Supported by conclusions.
8. Assign actions: Responsible personnel and timelines.
9. Confirm actions: Completeness with documented evidence.
10. Verify effectiveness of actions: At suitable timeline with evidence.

There are generally three main sources of events: laboratory, customer complaints, and manufacturing (including other departments/functions outside the QC laboratory). Laboratory investigations are discussed in Chapter 18, "Laboratory Controls".

Areas of an investigation system failures and remediation are shown in the table below for further consideration (Table 7.1).

TABLE 7.1
Areas of Investigation System Failure and Potential Remediation

Failures	Potential Remediation
(a) There is no investigation system or corrective/ preventive action system	Management/QA is unaware of the need/requirement: implement system Management/QA is aware, but it is of low priority: consider changing management/QA since this is a fundamental regulatory requirement.
(b) System is inadequate	No time/resources to enhance: Management needs to assign sufficient resources
(c) System exists but few events documented relative to the operations	The majority of personnel are not trained/aware of their responsibilities for reporting potential events that could lead to deviations: implement training "awareness" for all personnel and provide periodic focused training sessions. The requirement for the training may not be clearly understood and/or implemented. Additionally, the "trigger" in the investigation SOP may be unclear/omitted and needs to be revised.
(d) Repeat events frequently occur	Inadequate root cause analysis and/or incorrect CAPAs: train personnel or hire/reassign personnel with the required skills.
(e) Investigations are overdue without justification	Inadequate resources: Management needs to dedicate adequately skilled resources
(f) CAPAs are overdue	Inadequate resources, inadequate Management priority: Management needs to assign sufficient time to complete the required actions within the approved timeline (personnel to implement CAPAs and/or allocate budget spending/enhancement of Quality Systems). Action completed by a specific date is linked to the content and urgency of the root cause. Exceeding the date results in an increase in the probability that the event leading to the deviation/investigation will reoccur. Disregarding the need to complete the action/timeline indicates Management does not take commitments seriously.

Complaints are managed according to §211.198 in terms of the content reviewed, but the manufacturing investigation process still follows the same system steps discussed below.

A manufacturing investigation is initiated from the laboratory after any known laboratory error has been eliminated by an investigation. Investigations are also initiated for events/deviations occurring during processing, holding, and distribution of product.

IDENTIFICATION AND NOTIFICATION

Events are often defined as potentially impacting the drug product safety, identity, strength, quality, and purity that it purports or is represented to possess. The event can also be departure from a defined requirement or expectation as defined in a procedure and hence is impacting compliance with the requirement(s) and/or with CGMPs.

An event occurs and the person observing (either in real time—time actually occurred—or sometime after the event occurred, by observing it) has the responsibility to immediately report the details to management. During the training for this requirement, which impacts employees involved with CGMP operations sitewide, the focus is on the potential impact to product or procedural compliance, as the observer does not need to have data to support or confirmation that the event is reportable. Any company can have the most advanced investigation management Quality System, but without the conscientious due diligence and astute observations from employees, events will not be reported. It is unimaginable what potential events have been ignored, cannot be identified through lack of awareness, or dismissed as unimportant. Consequences of unreported critical events could potentially have immeasurable for the company and patients. Equally important is the ability to respond to the event promptly with the correct resources; forward-thinking management acknowledges that QA and subject matter experts must be deployed to promptly assess the event for the following reasons:

1. Data and information will be lost with delay.
2. Evidence and the "scene" of the event are changing with time, especially when this involves production-related events.
3. Employees involved will be challenged to recall details, which can be critical to the investigation when interviews are performed days later.
4. Some evidence can be lost if there is a need for containment or response to remove unsafe conditions, for example, water system leakage flooded area. Containment could be quarantine of batch(es), additional labeling, or isolating the impacted area/room/system.

Some company management has identified the need to deploy a SWAT team (Area Manager, QA Investigator, Maintenance, Safety, Technical Services, and Mechanic) to events immediately after they are observed to assess and document them. Quality Assurance can then perform the initial potential impact analysis with input from other subject matter experts. Dedicated investigators assigned to specific departments/Quality Systems are of significant benefit to the functionality of the operations.

The event details need to be submitted to Quality Assurance promptly, normally within one business day of the observation. The reason for the urgency is that QA continues to disposition product, and at this time, the impact of the event on the pending shipment batches is unknown. Additionally, if the event has critical impact to the product (e.g., wrong label on final container), it could also be impacting products already released to market.

DETAILS AND MORE DETAILS

It is imperative that the event details are captured promptly (often within minutes of the observation) so as to maintain accuracy and completeness through interviewing personnel involved. Recalling adequate information details days later is unrealistic to obtain an accurate account as memory of the event fades with time.

DESCRIPTION OF THE EVENT

At 6:30 a.m. in manufacturing room A7, operator JS was preparing to sample the final blend of Garfeneri 100mg tablets batch # 17–897 according to step 34c of the batch record. Upon opening the lid to the blender there was a piece of blue material on the surface of the powder about 1" diameter as shown in the picture (attachment 1)." Note that the details must include when, where, who, and what related to the observation and also the corresponding details relating to event occurrence if this is known. Although occurrence and observation can be the same time point (e.g., water started leaking from the pipe), there can be a distinct difference: a rouge tablet was identified in the in-process sample bottle on February 3, 2017 at 3:45 p.m. However, when the rouge tablet entered the bottle is unknown at this time and could have occurred during the manufacturing compression stage or the bottle-filling step.

The next step of "Immediate Actions" needs to be detailed so that the necessary urgency and control of the situation can be documented: "The Manufacturing Supervisor and floor QA were immediately notified. The blue material was removed with the sampling thief, placed in a sealed plastic bag, and labeled with the product description, container number, batch number, and initials/date. The operator, Manufacturing Supervisor, and floor QA annotated the batch record at step 34c with the details of the observation. Sampling of the other containers continued per the requirements of step 34c, the blend was transferred to the holding area per the batch record, and QA added a note to the batch comments in the Materials Management System (see attached).

Note there are three dates/times:

1. Time of occurrence (if known). In the above example, the exact date/time is not known. It may, however, be limited to a time period (floor was dry at 4:00 a.m. but wet at 6:00 a.m.).
2. Date/time of observation. When it was detected/seen by an employee.
3. Date/time event opened in the Quality System. Available software can capture all this information, the last being when the details were entered into the software by the Initiator. Industry standard and current Regulatory Authority expectation is that the investigation will be closed within 30 business days after opening unless justified and approved by QA.

EVALUATION/TRIAGE

QA makes an initial impact assessment from the details provided to determine initial impact, normally within 24 hours of notification. This is made on a risk management approach and includes severity, frequency, and detectability. See also Chapter 2, "Quality Systems and Risk Management". At this time, a unique tracking number is assigned. QA will also:

a. Identify if other batches of the same product could be impacted.
b. Identify if other products could be impacted.

Evaluation results could result in additional batches being placed on hold status and linked to the investigation.

Using the details provided, QA then triages the event to either:

1. Minor event—no product or compliance impact. May require limited immediate action but does not require an investigation. Minor reportable events are tracked for repeat occurrences or trends. Multiple recurrences would generate a trend investigation.
2. Major investigation—potential product/GMP compliance impact, requires an investigation, root cause analysis, and corrective and preventive action (CAPA).
3. Critical investigation—potential adverse product impact or failure, requires an investigation, root cause analysis, CAPA, and senior management notification.

Some companies have different definitions of the above and also include a Minor Deviation/ Investigation.

INVESTIGATION

Performing a robust and meaningful investigation is a skill no different than having or attaining a skill in other professions. Some people have a natural ability, and some can be taught the theory and with practice will become proficient. Remaining personnel are more usefully deployed by management in using their skills for other tasks. A skill can be defined as the "ability to do something well usually gained through training and experience." It usually takes time and adequate resources to attain a sufficient skill level that can be consistently applied in attaining the desired outcome.

Swimming can be taught by a coach, but not everyone is a good swimmer or even wants to swim. Many can just keep their heads above the water and when panic sets in they grab anything that will help them survive—if you are unable to identify the root cause, you will write down many "ideas" with the hope that at least one may just be the right one. The ability to identify potential root causes and then create appropriate CAPAs are no different. A few dedicated investigators are worth more than a room of people frantically trying to identify something that possibly relates to the event as a cause and usually result in identification of multiple symptoms. Most people can probably identify some symptoms, but only a few know what a true root cause is. There is then a rush to revise the SOP or retrain the operators as the resulting CAPAs. Neither of which will prevent event reoccurrence because they were not actually related to the root cause of the event.

Some companies assign some QA resources to perform the investigations and their other responsibilities. However, forward-thinking company management understand that to perform adequate investigations requires focused, dedicated, and adequately trained investigators. Many companies do not allocate sufficient time for robust and thorough investigations but will find time to perform another investigation when a repeat occurs for the same type of event. This may be assigned to inadequate root cause analysis and/or CAPAs.

Investigations need to be prioritized so that the critical ones with the greatest potential impact to product quality/patient or compliance risk are performed first, but that does not mean that the others are never done. Performing an investigation soon after the incident occurs is more productive that retrospectively months later.

INVESTIGATION TOOLS

Data, interviews, and information is collected for the investigation, and the following tools can be used to support the investigation:

- "6M" or Fishbone analysis: Products/Materials, Process/Method, Personnel/Man, Equipment/Instrument/Machine, Environment/Mother Nature, Measurement
- 5 Whys: asking why the event occurred and repeating this normally up to four additional times
- Failure Mode Effects Analysis
- Fault Tree Analysis
- Interviews
- Flow charts
- Pareto charts

An example of a comprehensive, stand-alone investigation report is presented in the following table (Table 7.2).

Identification of the most probable or root-cause analysis part of the investigation is critical so that meaningful CAPAs can be developed with appropriate timelines. The process is often stopped before the true root cause is identified because of time limitations, cost of permanent actions/fixes, and sometimes management focus on getting investigations closed. The focus can originate from the necessity to close the investigation to disposition the batch, to reduce the number of open investigations for the

TABLE 7.2

Investigation Report Content

Section	Content
Description	Complete concise description of the event including what was deviated from or not in compliance with.
Immediate action	Details, as necessary, to capture date, location, who observed, when, and how of event notification including any decisions made and actions taken.
Background	Information needed to put the event into context. Section should be designed to give an independent reader enough information to fully understand the event and related facts.
Chronology	Outlines the sequence of events (days/hrs/mins) before, during, and after the event.
History/trends	Based on database queries a history of prior or related events is presented along with a conclusion of how it relates to the current investigation.
Scope	Determine if there a potential impact on other products and/or other batches of the same product. Justify and exclusions.
Investigation text: analysis of events	See above tools and use of data and information
Conclusions	Use scientific rationale supported by evidence.
Impact	GMP/compliance, material or batch impact is evaluated based on the investigation scope and facts. Impact to product and patient safety, especially if other products/batches that are on the market.
Root cause	Use investigation tools.
CAPA	Actions that in total provide a correction, a corrective action (includes elimination of recurrence), and if applicable a preventive action (e.g., trends indicate a potential failure).

weekly metrics, but again, quality-focused management will deploy resources to timely closure with appropriate CAPAs. It's easy to close an investigation by using human error as the root cause, although it is seldom actually true.[1] The subsequent CAPA includes "retraining the person" often as rereading the SOP. However, this has little to no impact on the ability of the person to execute the step without error again or anyone else. It is a paper exercise to close the investigation. If the investigator is challenged during a regulatory inspection to identify when the person became "untrained" or "inadequately" trained, a difficult conversation will follow, as there is no answer to the question.

It is interesting that there is no mention of corrective and preventive actions in 21 CFR 211, but the reference in the last sentence of this subsection (21 CFR 211.192) to "...follow up" is interpreted to include the subsequent actions to the investigation.

ISO 9000:2005(E) definitions:

- Correction—eliminate a *detected* non-conformity
- Corrective action—action to eliminate the cause of a *detected* non-conformity or other undesirable situation
- Preventive action—action to eliminate the cause of a *potential* non-conformity or other undesirable situation

In 21 CFR 820 Quality System Regulation covering medical devices, subsection "820.100 Corrective and Preventive Action" defines nine requirements to be defined in procedures including the analysis, investigation, dissemination of information, and reporting to management. When referring to CAPA in relation to medical devices, it is the entire system (identification, investigation, root cause, actions) but with pharmaceuticals, CAPA is normally only focused on the actions within the investigation system.

EFFECTIVENESS CHECKS

When the investigation process/report are complete, and the appropriate CAPAs/timelines have been identified, the effectiveness of the CAPAs needs to be defined. This includes what is to be measured/

monitored, when (time or quantity) and the acceptance criteria. The effectiveness check needs to be scientifically sound, that is, after the next three batches or three months. There is no value to using three months when the product is only made every six months. Once the effectiveness has been defined, the final report and information can be reviewed and approved for technical content. Often there are Reviewers assigned and then at least one Approver. The documents are then submitted to QA for review to determine if it complies with the investigation SOP, is it understandable/readable, accurate, complete, and are the CAPAs aligned with the root cause(s) with appropriate timelines and the effectiveness checks appropriate for the CAPAs. This is not an easy task for any complicated failure investigation, and the skills required to perform this come from training and experience. The responsible QA personnel must complete their review and approval independent of the batch release function.

Management can easily identify employees to perform investigations by using anyone who is available but these often do not have the required skills set. Outstanding investigators, as with many other skills, are not easy to find and probably even harder to retain. Mainly because they have the "gift" of curiosity and are relentless in their pursuit of the root cause. Sherlock Holmes, the famous detective, had several quotes. Here are two that are considered pertinent: "How often have I said that when you have excluded the impossible, whatever remains, however improbable, must be the truth" and "It is a capital mistake to theorize in advance of the facts. Insensibly one begins to twist facts to suit theories, instead of theories to suit facts."

Management that supports having dedicated well-trained investigators focusing on investigations and assigning CAPAs are providing their commitment and support to a more effective and compliant process support the overall quality management system. Adding this responsibility to another role/position does not work well, as there are always other competing priorities. Attention is then only refocused when there is a regulatory observation for the lack of thoroughness/in-depth investigation, but it's too late. It will cost many times more to correct this situation than to do it right the first time.

§211.194 LABORATORY RECORDS

a. *Laboratory records shall include complete data derived from all tests necessary to assure compliance with established specifications and standards, including examinations and assays as follows:*
   1. *A description of the sample received for testing with identification of source (that is, location from where sample was obtained), quantity, lot number or other distinctive code, date sample was taken, and date sample was received for testing.*

      Sample management is critical in maintaining integrity of the sample so that it is not compromised during transport, storage, handling, or preparation prior to the analysis being performed. Sample chain of custody including laboratory receipt is essential so that it can be traced from acceptance, log in, storage (under the required conditions), and subsequently prepared following the required method. Sample description is to identify through a "title" (5g xxxxx tablet blend lot # 637 sampled by GB 1/12/18) and not related to the methodology for the visual appearance of the sample. A sampling plan/protocol is required so that the person (QC or production) has clear directions for the sampling method including tools, amount, location, number of containers, sample container description, labeling requirements including storage, and any specific precautions. The remaining requirements are clearly defined in the regulation above.

   2. *A statement of each method used in the testing of the sample. The statement shall indicate the location of data that establish that the methods used in the testing of the sample meet proper standards of accuracy and reliability as applied to the product tested. (If the method employed is in the current revision of the United States Pharmacopeia, National Formulary, AOAC International, Book of Methods, or in other recognized standard*

references, or is detailed in an approved new drug application and the referenced method is not modified, a statement indicating the method and reference will suffice). The suitability of all testing methods used shall be verified under actual conditions of use.

Since the content of the method can be revised, it is important to be able to confirm exactly which revision or date version was used at the time of the analysis. Method suitability and being verified are referring to method validation or qualification in relation to monograph testing. Analytical methodology must be validated, and the validation data must be retained. As written, the regulations would require that for each method used the records for each sample tested should reference the location of the validation data. This would seem to be onerous and unnecessary provided the monograph, or some other procedure, indicates the location. It is assumed that "official" methods have been validated, and reference to the official source is considered to be adequate. However, for both official methods and for methods validated in another laboratory, it is necessary to verify suitability in the individual laboratory (§211.165[e]). The degree of work to verify suitability may vary with the complexity of the method. It may be sufficient to perform the method with samples of known composition or that have previously been analyzed.

3. *A statement of the weight or measure of sample used for each test where appropriate.*
4. *A complete record of all data secured in the course of each test, including all graphs, charts, and spectra from laboratory instrumentation properly identified to show the specific component, drug product container, closure, in-process material, or drug product, and lot tested.*

Simply noting that the method was followed is inadequate since in the event of an out of specification (OOS) result and an investigation there would be no evidence of the actual measure/weight of sample to be confirmed. It is interesting to note that "a complete record of all data secured in the course of each test..." has been a requirement since the late 1970s, but FDA warning letters report deletion of analytical data or selective reporting. See www. FDA.Gov. Also Chapter 24, "Data Integrity and Fundamental Responsibilities" and Chapter 18, "Laboratory Controls".

5. *A record of all calculations performed in connection with the test, including units of measure, conversion factors, and equivalency factors.*

This provides confirmation of the management and use of the data by the analyst for the independent reviews.

6. *A statement of the results of tests and how the results compare with established standards of identity, strength, quality, and purity for the component, drug product container, closure, in-process material, or drug product tested.*

Use of automatic calculation methodology is acceptable, and it minimizes the potential for potential calculation errors. Comparing the results with standards for the established test criteria provides a decision step to determine if the result(s) is/are within the limits or not. Although primarily performed by Quality Control (QC), it can be performed by production for in-process testing provided they are trained and qualified to perform the testing. The test results determine if the sample passes the test or not and may also indicate a trend when compared to historical data. Atypical results may also be within limits but require further investigation since something has changed.

7. *The initials or signature of the person who performs each test and the date(s) the tests were performed.*

8. *The initials or signature of a second person showing that the original records have been reviewed for accuracy, completeness, and compliance with established standards.*

The requirements in 7 and 8 are fundamental GMP requirements and covered by the Good Documentation Practices SOP and signature registration for identification/traceability. It is important to be able to clearly identify all personnel participating in the analysis, review, and approval.

b. *Complete records shall be maintained of any modification of an established method employed in testing. Such records shall include the reason for the modification and data to verify that the modification produced results that are at least as accurate and reliable for the material being tested as the established method.*

The need for these requirements originates from endless method changes without justification/reasons, and therefore a Reviewer/Regulatory Agency is left to work out why changes were made. Analytical methods require change management with history and also including justification.

c. *Complete records shall be maintained of any testing and standardization of laboratory reference standards, reagents, and standard solutions.*

Traceability in case of investigation or atypical results and the methodology must be established and consistently followed.

d. *Complete records shall be maintained of the periodic calibration of laboratory instruments, apparatus, gauges, and recording devices required by §211.160(b)(4).*
e. *Complete records shall be maintained of all stability testing performed in accordance with §211.166.*

Calibration and stability are addressed in §211.160(b)(4) and §211.166, respectively. See also Chapter 11, "Equipment".

§211.196 DISTRIBUTION RECORDS

Distribution records shall contain the name and strength of the product and description of the dosage form, name and address of the consignee, date and quantity shipped, and lot or control number of the drug product. For compressed medical gas products, distribution records are not required to contain lot or control numbers.

In the event of a product recall, the above information is essential to implement an effective recall of the impacted product. Use of electronic distribution records enables this data to be quickly and accurately retrieved provided the SOPs are accurate/complete and being followed. The retrieval of distribution records is often only "visible" during a recall and under those conditions often highlights inaccuracies, lack of effectiveness, and is incomplete. Management needs accurate and complete records promptly when dealing with recalls and does not want to be in discussion with FDA without them. Retrieval of records must be part of the internal annual audit program and periodic mock recalls need to be performed to confirm the process works as intended.

§211.198 COMPLAINT FILES

a. *Written procedures describing the handling of all written and oral complaints regarding a drug product shall be established and followed. Such procedures shall include provisions for review by the QCU of any complaint involving the possible failure of a drug product to meet any of its specifications and, for such drug products, a determination as to the need for an investigation in accordance with §211.192. Such procedures shall include provisions for review to determine whether the complaint represents a serious and unexpected adverse drug experience, which is required to be reported to the FDA in accordance with §310.305 and §514.50 of this chapter.*

b. *A written record of each complaint shall be maintained in a file designated for drug product complaints. The file regarding such drug product complaints shall be maintained at the establishment where the drug product involved was manufactured, processed, or packed, or such file may be maintained at another facility if the written records in such files are readily available for inspection at that other facility. Written records involving a drug product shall be maintained until at least one year after the expiration date of the drug product, or one year after the date that the complaint was received, whichever is longer. In the case of certain OTC drug products, lacking expiration dating because they meet the criteria for exemption under §211.137, such written records shall be maintained for three years after distribution of the drug product.*

1. The written record shall include the following information where known: the name and strength of the drug product, lot number, name of complainant, and reply to complainant.
2. Where an investigation under 211.192 is conducted, the written record shall include the findings of the investigation and follow-up. The record or copy of the record of the investigation shall be maintained at the establishment where the investigation occurred in accordance with 211.180(c)
3. Where an investigation under §211.192 is not conducted, the written record shall include the reason that an investigation was found not to be necessary and the name of the responsible person making such a determination.

This is a critical quality system that must be managed with adequate resources, precision, and timeliness. Patients, prescribers (physicians), health-care professionals, distributors, and patient support personnel may be reporting a potential significant finding related to the drug product and as such it must be managed with the appropriate urgency. The initial review and triage must be performed to determine the potential impact, especially in relation to patient safety. Companies assign complaints into critical, major, and minor depending on the potential to impact patient safety determine by a risk assessment. Drug products that fail to meet any of the required specification, user quality attributes e.g., "appears different, does not have the same effect, package cannot be opened, product blocked needle," including lack of effect reported by the patient, must be evaluated. Although reading this statement makes sense from quality and business perspectives, there are frequent citations in FDA483s and warning letters of companies having numerous complaints that have not been evaluated for several months. Patient risk cannot clearly be assessed without knowing what has been reported by customers (patients, health-care providers).

All notifications are treated with "respect" no matter how "trivial" the complaint may appear, as the person reporting it is expressing concern about the product for what they believe is worth them making the effort. Consider if no one complained or people were deterred from complaining there would be nothing to investigate or correct/prevent, and manufacturers would never know there was a problem. Prescribers and patients would stop using the product, and sales would decline without the reason being known.

Regardless of the method (verbal or written) that the complaint was received, it is managed by the same process, logged into a system, and assigned a unique tracking number. This unique number is "attached" to an outer container, that is, plastic sealable bag containing the returned medication/packaging and stored under the required conditions.

The complaint must be triaged promptly since a potential serious or unexpected event could also impact other patients taking or being administered the product. The recipient of a verbal complaint must obtain as much information about the complainant and the description of the complaint as possible including lot numbers and related concerns. It is sometimes not easy obtaining precise information to support the initial assessment; however, all complaints require repeated and diligent efforts for return of the product to ensure that every effort and method is used to return the container and/or product to facilitate the investigation. It is essential that all the efforts and details are documented to prove due diligence, which is usually a total of three attempts to obtain further information and/or return of the complaint container/medication. The assessment\investigation continues while the product is in the process of being returned, and the investigation process followed according to the SOP as far as possible with the information received, even if the product is never returned. Failure to return a complaint product or obtain further information is not a justification for not following the complaint SOP. Equally, once a compliant is received in must be logged and assigned a tracking number and cannot be canceled or deleted if the product is not returned or incomplete information is obtained. See subsection (b) below for justification for not performing an investigation.

Based on the complexity of the manufacturing and distribution network for the product, the investigation may involve multiple, separate, but interconnected investigations by different facilities (e.g., a contract manufacturer, a separate packaging facility, and a distribution center).

Subsection (a) above notes the requirement to determine if the complaint represents a serious and unexpected adverse drug experience, which is required to be reported to the FDA. The reaction may have resulted from adulteration of the product, specific reaction of the patient to the product, reaction of the patient because of their current medical condition, and/or the other medications taken with the product. A qualified physician evaluates the medical aspects of the potential serious or unexpected adverse drug reaction.

Subsection (b) contains the minimum requirements of the complaint documentation and includes the need for an investigation under §211.192 relating to the manufacturing, packaging, testing, and holding of the product. However, there is a provision included that an investigation does not always need to be performed provided it is adequately and completely justified. The justification needs to be rational and plausible to a reader with scientific background. The requirements for documenting the decision are reasonable to quality-orientated professionals who want to explain the reasoning supporting the decision. Even if the batch number is not reported, a historical review of the product complaints can be performed and the results documented. As with all deviation/complaint investigations, all the information and data is evaluated, no matter how limited or "trivial" it may initially appear; it may just be the "piece of the puzzle" that completes the picture to identify the root cause.

Fundamental information relating to complainant, patient, dates, other medication, dates, times, contact details, and other information is recorded and protected according to the data protection of personal information. Pseudonyms or codes are used when reporting information to regulatory authorities.

Following the initial triage of the complaint as shown above there may be a parallel path of medical evaluation and manufacturing related investigation performed. A review of trends for the product, strength, and other batches is also performed. Complaints will be received at some time for Lack of Effect/Efficacy (either the prescriber makes the determination or the patient reports it) and will be managed no differently that other types of complaints. Patients may receive a generic brand and feel that it does not "work" as well as the originator. Hence, they report a lack of the effectiveness compared to previous medications.

Complaints may be closed at any stage of the processing, provided an explanation is documented with management approval. Additionally, the complaint SOP will include reference to complaint information/situations (potential and confirmed), which require immediate escalation to Executive Management, for example, potential sterility failure of a sterile product, tampering, or counterfeiting. The detailed process steps and notification item lines are included in a SOP, which also covers other situations when Executive Management is informed and also linked to the recall SOP as complaints may initiate a product recall from the market.

Since the manufacturing-related investigation system already exists, the process is still the same, although it may be performed by different personnel but still includes all the available data and information for the specific product and related investigations. The complaint history of the product for all the dosage strengths are reviewed to determine if there is a trend related to the product or if there are any related complaints that can provide supporting data/information.

Production and packaging records for the particular batch are reviewed each time to determine if there were any abnormal occurrences or potentially related deviations during processing.

Testing of any description needs to follow an approved plan with documented results, as it is part of the Quality Management System. Retained samples and the sample label provide evidence of labels and containers from which to compare the returned complaint. Physical examination of the product against the description determines if the sample still meets the requirements or if it could be counterfeit. If the actual medication cannot be obtained, photographs of it and where possible all packaging as well may be able to establish initially if the medication is genuine and actually manufactured/marketed by the complaint receiver. An important part of the manufacturing investigation will determine if the complaint is plausible. For example, a comingled product with a product not packaged in the facility is highly unlikely since SOPs do not allow employees to take medication to GMP areas, the tablet slots on the filling machine may not physically allow the tablet to enter the bottle (proven by physical measurements), and the weight checker may have also identified it as an unacceptable container weight. Although this does not exclude someone intentionally placing the tablet in the bottle, there is substantial evidence that the tablet was introduced after the bottle left the custody of the packaging facility. Additional factors to consider are other medication, including over the counter, which the patient is taking and when this can be confirmed.

If the complaint drug is returned, then the QC laboratory can perform testing according to the finished product test methods and review against specification, including visual appearance. Examination of foreign materials associated with the product may require use of specialist laboratory testing at a contract laboratory. The report of this examination/testing is reviewed and attached to the investigation and used to support the conclusions. Timelines for complaints closure usually follow the deviation/investigations of 30 business days, but extensions can be approved by Quality with adequate justification.

Recurring complaints need to be investigated in depth, as any resulting CAPAs do not appear to be effective or root cause was incorrect. See investigation discussion previously in this chapter. The FDA may issue an observation for ineffective CAPAs or timeline taken to resolve deviations resulting in complaints, especially if there is any risk to patient safety, for example, sterile products or foreign tablets (line clearance failures).

Some complaints have ultimate longer-term benefits for patients, as improvements for the patient in use of the product result in better compliance with the dosing requirements.

After closure of the overall complaint investigation with appropriate CAPAs, the complaint file can be closed with response to the complainant after review by Quality and sometimes legal counsel.

There are also specific reporting requirements in §314.81 for new drug application (NDA) and abbreviated new drug application (ANDA) post marketing reports:

- (a) Applicability. Each applicant shall make the reports for each of its approved applications and abbreviated applications required under this section and section 505(k) of the act.
- (b) Reporting requirements. The applicant shall submit to the Food and Drug Administration at the specified times two copies of the following reports:
  - (1) NDA—Field alert report. The applicant shall submit information of the following kinds about distributed drug products and articles to the FDA district office that is responsible for the facility involved within three working days of receipt by the applicant. The information may be provided by telephone or other rapid communication means, with prompt written follow-up. The report and its mailing cover should be plainly marked: "NDA—Field Alert Report."
    - (i) Information concerning any incident that causes the drug product or its labeling to be mistaken for, or applied to, another article.
    - (ii) Information concerning any bacteriological contamination, or any significant chemical, physical, or other change or deterioration in the distributed drug product, or any failure of one or more distributed batches of the drug product to meet the specification established for it in the application.
  - (2) Annual report.
    See previous discussion in this chapter.

Note the timeline to file the field alert report is three working days, and at that stage there is often limited information and no sample to examine. The requirements in §314.81 for NDA and ANDA post-marketing reports are specific and while unnecessary filings overburden companies with documentation, the failure to file or omit to file within the timeline is a deviation from regulatory requirements and will result in an observation as a FDA483 or warning letter.

There is no specific reference to adverse drug reactions in this subsection, but the initiation of a manufacturing investigation could also be from an adverse drug reaction complaint.

The recording of complaint data should allow examination by product, lot number, complaint type (often from a defined list), and packing type/size. Software used for tracking complaints enables them to be logged and circulated to the required personnel promptly with electronic signatures and data/information entered as the investigation proceeds. Assignment of root cause(s) with appropriate corrective/preventive actions can be part of the same work flow. Historical trending of previous complaints and other potentially related manufacturing investigations is also possible and enables a robust investigation to be performed. Complaint trending metrics are presented to senior management regularly at the Quality Council meetings and can be extracted from the complaint database so that any appropriate actions can be taken/endorsed.

Minutes of any discussions and decisions made regarding the management of complaints should also be maintained.

EXAMPLES OF OBSERVATIONS FROM FDA CITATIONS

- Your firm failed to prepare batch production and control records with complete information relating to the production and control of each batch of drug product produced (21 CFR 211.188).
- Failure to ensure that all quality-related activities are recorded at the time they are performed. In the production area, our investigators witnessed an employee backdating production batch records for seven batches of (b)(4) (batches [b][4] to [b][4]) and transcribing data from a master template record. Furthermore, analysis of the transcribed data for these seven (b)(4) batches and for approximately 40 batches of (b)(4) active pharmaceutical ingredient (API), indicated that you did not record data contemporaneously and that missing data was later falsified so the official records would appear complete.
- You failed to analyze product and process data for commercial batches of xxx to identify adverse trends. Our review of the stability summary data for the 15 lots of xxx produced in 2014 identified quality attributes that are inconsistent with the specifications in your approved new drug application for xxx.
- Your firm failed to maintain adequate written records of major equipment maintenance (21 CFR 211.182). The FDA investigators identified two maintenance logbooks that included multiple entries describing significant equipment malfunctions, but for which no investigation into the potential effect on product quality was performed. In addition, your records do not always include information on repairs following these malfunctions. For instance, no maintenance actions or product impact investigations were recorded for out-of-limit findings during equipment calibration. In other cases, your firm determined that there was no product impact without justification. In addition, we note that ten serialized entries had been torn out of the logbooks. Your staff could not locate these records during the inspection and reported to our investigator that the entries had likely been destroyed.
- You do not have master production and control records for any of your drug products. Furthermore, you do not prepare batch production and control records for any of your drug products. Instead, you provide verbal manufacturing instructions to your staff.
- Your firm failed to follow adequate written procedures for the preparation of master production and control records designed to assure uniformity from batch to batch. (21 CFR 211.186[a]). Our investigators found quality-related documents in a waste bin. Among these documents were an incomplete sterility test data sheet, a form used to track the movement of (b)(4) samples, a media fill incubation card, and others. The incomplete sterility test data sheet had been filled out to track information about a "(b)(4)" sterility check. After an error was observed on the original data sheet, the record was torn and discarded with no written explanation.

- Your firm lacked batch records for all drug products you manufactured from May 2015 to February 2017. You did not document significant production details, including but not limited to the personnel, dates, equipment, raw material identity, and labeling, for each batch. We acknowledge that you created a batch record template during the inspection for your xxx drug product. However, this batch record template lacked provisions for data on processing, filling, and packaging operations. Such data is necessary to establish that the manufacturing process was followed and is reproducible.
- Failing filter integrity test results are not reported by procedure xxx. After failures, the tests are repeated without documenting the failing results, the actions taken, or the reasons for invalidating the original results.
- You failed to investigate customer complaints thoroughly. In 2016, you received 32 customer complaints concerning drugs intended for the U.S. market. These complaints included (redacted) irritation, burning, pain, and discharge after using (redacted) ointment and (redacted) ointment. Our investigator reviewed three investigation reports for (redacted) ointment. Each of your investigations consisted of testing "storage samples" and applying drug product from at least three implicated complaint lots on your employees as "test subjects." Your investigations lacked critical elements that help determine root causes. For example, the three investigations lacked an evaluation of the manufacturing process and associated records. You also did not routinely test complaint lots for all relevant quality attributes (e.g., sterility). Despite missing critical elements, your investigation concluded that "there are no problems" with the implicated lots. Without thorough investigations, your quality unit lacks sufficient information to make reliable decisions on root causes and take effective action.

From January 2012 to August 2016, your firm received numerous (approximately 1,500) consumer complaints related to leaking, empty, and under-filled sterile (redacted) solution (redacted) % bottles. Your firm's investigation indicates this persistent critical quality defect is due to a filling machine issue in which the (redacted) is improperly placed into the bottle (redacted). Because of this recurring malfunction, operators frequently perform aseptic interventions at the insertion station when they detect stuck (redacted) defects. These defects are not easily detected, and the line has produced finished, capped units with non-integral container-closures. In addition, in some cases, (redacted) cracks do not immediately occur in finished units, but instead develop days later. Specifically, your investigation states, "…it is evident that a wrong placement of the (redacted) on the bottle on the filling machines must be resulting in a damaged or cracked (redacted) which does not occur immediately and occurs on standing for a few days." Because of the location and delayed timing of these defects, they are not readily detectable by final manual or automated inspections.

REFERENCE

1. Human Error Is The Leading Cause Of GMP Deviations – Or Is It? Pharmaceutical on Line, May 1, 2014: J. Gallant.

SUGGESTED READINGS

- Guidance for Industry Part 11, Electronic Records; Electronic Signatures—Scope and Application; U.S. Department of Health and Human Services Food and Drug Administration Office of Regulatory Affairs (ORA), August 2003.
- Andersen B, Natland T. *The ASQ Pocket Guide to Root Cause Analysis*. Milwaukee, WI, ASQ Quality Press, 2013.
- FDA Guidance for Industry: Circumstances that Constitute Delaying, Denying, Limiting, or Refusing a Drug Inspection, U.S. Department of Health and Human Services Food and Drug Administration, October 2014.
- Data Integrity and Compliance with CGMP, Draft Guidance for Industry, U.S. Department of Health and Human Services, FDA April 2016.

8 Clinical Trial Supplies

David Stephon

CONTENTS

INTRODUCTION

Good manufacturing practices (GMPs) represent good documentation, good housekeeping, and good scientific practices, regardless of the ultimate user of drug products. The unique requirements of the investigational supply process create an opportunity for innovative approaches to regulatory compliance. Moreover, because of potential problems with similar look-alike containers and packaging with look-alike labels, creative adoption of current good manufacturing practice (CGMP) principles and concepts in the clinical trial material (CTM) supply process is just good business practice.

Many factors have contributed to heightened awareness of the applicability of current GMP regulations to the preparation of CTMs. These include:

- The proliferation of numerous, small biotech and pharmaceutical companies that have used third-party contract manufacturing organizations (CMOs) or have hired expert consultants to manage and coordinate clinical supply operations
- The increased number of FD483 inspectional observations dealing with CGMP deficiencies found during inspections of clinical supply operation entities or during the review of late-phase CTM documentation during the pre-approval inspection (PAI) process
- The routine and for cause Food and Drug Administration (FDA) inspections of firms that manufacture CTM
- The development of educational forums and training classes that focus on CTM and the clinical supply process

THE UNITED STATES CGMP REGULATION AND
APPLICABILITY TO CLINICAL TRIAL MATERIAL

It is well recognized that the 1978 CGMP regulations were purposefully written with a lack of specificity. On one hand, this was done to promote innovation as well as compliance by industry, through a wide variety of approaches of *what* to do rather than *how* to do it. In other words, the CGMP regulations were written to be flexible enough to allow sound judgment and permit innovation, yet explicit enough to provide clear understanding of what is required. On the other hand, intentional lack of specificity in the CGMP regulations also allowed considerable discretion in achieving the necessary level of controls appropriate for diverse pharmaceutical manufacturing operations, warehouse operations, or quality control laboratories, including the production of CTMs.

The CGMP regulations were, in many ways, originally promulgated for commercial drug products. These, by definition, involve routine, repetitive procedures whereby the significant amounts of scientific supportive data that have been generated for regulatory approval are used to define optimal manufacturing and testing or drug products and the corresponding active pharmaceutical ingredient (API). In this case, a well-defined product fully identified with a distinctive size, shape, color, or logo is processed and packaged on specific, often dedicated, equipment. Manufacturing procedures, specifications, standard operating procedures (SOPs), facilities, and equipment have already been evaluated, determined, and validated. Changes to these established procedures and fine tuning are not often required, and if they are, 21 CFR 211.100(b) allows deviations, provided the nature, rationale, and approval of such deviations are investigated, documented, and most importantly, justified.

Even though we stated the CGMPs were intended in many respects for commercial product manufacture, it is important to understand that the CGMP regulations clearly state the applicability to CTM. GMPs are enforced in the United States by the US FDA, under Section 501(B) of the 1938 Food, Drug, and Cosmetic (FD&C) Act (21 USC 351).[1] The regulations use the phrase "current good manufacturing practices" to describe these requirements. Courts may theoretically hold that a drug product is adulterated even if there is no specific regulatory requirement that was violated as long as the process was not performed according to industry standards. Under FDA regulations, clinical trial investigational materials are required to be manufactured under CGMPs. This statement is based on the following premise and interpretation:

- The CGMP regulations, Title 21 of the Code of Federal Regulations (21 CFR), Parts 210 and 211, are binding regulations. This means they have the force and effect of law. The regulations interpret the statutory requirement for production of drugs in compliance with CGMPs, found in Section 501(a)[2] (B) of the FD&C Act. The Act itself makes no distinction between finished pharmaceuticals, APIs, clinical supplies, and commercial products. GMP compliance is required for all products meeting the definition of a drug in Section 201(g) of the Act.[2]
- The definitions in 21 CFR, Part 210 are legally binding for all drugs. This includes APIs, investigational APIs, finished clinical supplies, and, of course, commercial products.
- The CGMP regulations for finished pharmaceuticals, meaning dosage for drugs (whether or not in packaged form), found at 21 CFR, Part 211, are legally binding for all finished drug products, whether for commercial sale or for use in clinical trials.

FDA's position on the applicability of the GMP regulations to clinical supplies is clear, and it has been for many years. In the Federal Register of 29 Sep 1978, FDA published a major revision to the CGMP regulations for finished pharmaceuticals, 21 CFR 210 and 211. In the preamble section of that announcement, FDA addresses the applicability of 21 CFR 210/211 to the manufacture of clinical investigational drugs under Comment 49. This states: "The Commissioner finds that, as stated in section 211.1, these GMP regulations apply to the preparation of any drug for administration to humans, including those still in the investigational stages. Further, it is also implicit in the definition in 21 CFR 210.3(b)[4] that the regulations apply to clinical supplies because the definition found there specifically states (in part).... The term also includes a finished dosage form that does not contain active ingredient but is intended to be used as a placebo." Therefore, the specific inclusion of placebos reflects the applicability of the GMP regulations to clinical supplies, because placebos are primarily used in clinical trials.[3]

UNIQUENESS OF INVESTIGATIONAL CLINICAL TRIAL MATERIAL

The preparation of CTM is governed by diametrically different principles of requirements and essentially is a mini-production operation in an R&D environment. Formulations and manufacturing processes are evolutionary, and dosage strengths often change as new toxicology and clinical information become available. During the initial stages of clinical development, these prototype products are incompletely characterized, and there is an anticipated learning curve as processes, quality control tests, and controls are developed. CTM, especially supplies manufactured for Phase I and II studies, are rarely manufactured or packaged in a set routine. As development proceeds and as clinical studies are expanded, scale-up to larger batch sizes frequently mandates changes in the formulation and/or manufacturing and control process. As commercialization approaches, starting in late Phase III studies, seemingly minor modifications to address trade dress and market image requirements represent an additional change that must be proven not to influence the extensive clinical database generated from the use of pivotal clinical study (i.e., Phase III) CTM.

The packaging and labeling of CTMs are customized to meet specific clinical studies. Unique label requirements, especially identically appearing copy on several different product containers, require scrutinizing quality control to address this increased complexity. Unlike marketed products, mix-ups in look-alike CTM cannot readily be detected in the field. Therefore, good scientific practices, good housekeeping practices, good documentation practices, and good manufacturing practices must be conducted following a zero-defect tolerance in an environment of continual change. SOPs must be general and typically supplemented by written work instructions in many cases that specify what will be done each time an operation is performed. A proactive, comprehensive manufacturing, packaging, and labeling protocol that clearly defines what, who, when, and how is especially helpful.

APPLICATION OF A CGMP CONCEPTUAL MODEL TO CTM PRODUCTION

FDA and industry trade associations purport an incremental approach to CGMP compliance for CTM.[4] This approach recognizes which controls are needed and the extent of difference between CTM and commercial manufacturing. It also recognizes the controls necessary and the extent those controls differ between the various phases of clinical studies. This model calls for well-defined procedures, adequately controlled equipment, and accurate recording of all data. Often use of disposable equipment and process aids, prepackaged process, for example, water for injection (WFI), and sterilized containers are incorporated into the manufacture of CTM to not only ensure consistent control, assure CGMP compliance, but also lessen CGMP burden. Often firms use contract manufacturing organizations and testing facilities to better ensure consistent quality requirements, especially when CTM supplies are made on a less frequent basis as well as smaller scale, than routine commercial production. Other requirements in CTM manufacturing include well-designed cross-contamination controls and appropriate microbiological control for production of sterile processed products. Personnel training is a CGMP requirement on a continuous basis, and review of key written procedures is also an attribute that CTM manufacture shares with commercial production. Let's take a closer look at some of the other CGMP controls required for CTM manufacture.

Tables 8.1 through 8.4 depict an example of an incremental approach to CGMP requirements for several parameters as a function of Clinical Development Phase, including preclinical. This truly shows the thought process a company manufacturing CTM would consider to apply the correct degree of CGMP oversight commensurate with control requirements.

CGMP Development Levels (Incremental Approach)

TABLE 8.1
Definition of Development Phase Levels

A	B	C	D
API Intermediates and Final API	API Intermediates and Final API, Bulk Drug and Finished Product	API Intermediates and Final API, Bulk Drug and Finished Product	API Intermediates and Final API, Bulk Drug and Finished Product
Laboratory scale	Initial pilot (kilo)	Continuing pilot (kilo) and initial scale-up batches	Commercial manufacturing process defined
Preclinical explorative study (non-GLP) support or reference standards	Advanced preclinical (GLP) studies		Process equivalent to proposed commercial process
Toxicology studies; preliminary (non-GLP) explorative	Preliminary stability batches (to support GLP nonclinical studies and Phase I Clinical Studies)		
	Phase I clinical trials	Phase II–III clinical trials	Phase II–III (pivotal) clinical trials

TABLE 8.2
Minimal Quality Standards for Source Document Review Requirements for API Intermediates and Final API

A	B	C	D
Review of Process Description in Laboratory Notebooks or Batch Manufacturing Instructions by Production and Quality Unit	Review of Master Batch Record; and Review and Approval of Executed Batch Record by Production and Quality Unit	Review of Master Batch Record; and Review and Approval of Executed Batch Record by Production and Quality Unit	Review and Approval of Master and Executed Batch Record by Production and Quality Unit
Review of documents related to materials, equipment, processing, collection of data	Review and approval of documents related to materials, equipment, processing, collection of data, and QC test results; Formal stability protocol and reports required	Review and approval of documents related to materials, equipment, processing, collection of data, and QC test results; Formal stability protocol and reports required	Review and approval of documents related to materials, equipment, processing, collection of data, and QC test results; Formal stability protocol and reports required
Deviations (including OOS) are reviewed and process improvements included in production instructions and scientific observations are reviewed	Deviations (including OOS) are documented	Deviations (including OOS) are required to be formally investigated, reviewed, and approved	Deviations (including OOS) are required to be formally investigated, reviewed, and approved
Changes are required to be documented	Changes are required to be documented	Formal Change Control Management system required	Formal Change Control Management system required
Formal release (e.g., Certificate of Compliance) is not required for product release	Formal release (e.g., Certificate of Compliance) is required for product release	Formal release (e.g., Certificate of Compliance) is required for product release	Formal release (e.g., Certificate of Compliance) is required for product release

TABLE 8.3

Minimal Standards for Source Document Review Requirements for Bulk Product and Finished Product

A	B	C	D
N/A	Review of Master Batch Record: and Review of Approval and Executed Batch Record by Production and Quality Unit	Review of Master Batch Record; and Review and Approval of Executed Batch Record by Production and Quality Unit	Review and Approval of Master and Executed Batch Record by Production and Quality Unit
N/A	Review and approval of documents related to materials, equipment, processing, collection of data, and QC test results; Formal stability protocol and reports required	Review and approval of documents related to materials, equipment, processing, collection of data, and QC test results; Formal stability protocol and reports required	Review and approval of documents related to materials, equipment, processing, collection of data, and QC test results; Formal stability protocol and reports required
N/A	Deviations (including OOS) are reviewed/approved and process improvements included in production instructions	Deviations (including OOS) are required to be formally investigated, reviewed, and approved	Deviations (including OOS) are required to be formally investigated, reviewed, and approved
N/A	Changes are required to be documented	Formal Change Control Management system required	Formal Change Control Management system required
N/A	Formal release (e.g., Certificate of Compliance) is required for product release	Formal release (e.g., Certificate of Compliance) is required for product release	Formal release (e.g., Certificate of Compliance) is required for product release

N/A: not applicable

TABLE 8.4

Minimal Standards for Method Qualification and Validation Requirements for Intermediates, Final API, Bulk, and Finished Product

A	B	C	D
Method Development	Method Qualification Required	Method Validation Required	Method Validation Required
N/A	Accuracy Precision (Repeatability) Specificity Linearity Solution Stability Forced Degradation LOQ LOD	Accuracy Precision (Repeatability) Specificity Linearity Solution Stability Forced Degradation LOQ LOD	Accuracy Precision (Repeatability, Intermediate, Precision) Specificity Linearity Solution Stability Forced Degradation LOQ LOD Range Robustness
Documentation requirements satisfied by laboratory notebook	Documentation requirements satisfied by laboratory notebook	Documentation requirements satisfied by formal protocol and reports	Documentation requirements satisfied by formal protocol and reports

QUALITY UNIT

A quality unit function is required during the manufacture of CTM. All CTM production areas and quality control laboratories should have basic quality assurance programs under the direction of an empowered quality unit function. The quality unit's responsibilities for a CTM supply process should include:

- Approve/reject raw materials, intermediates, and the final API
- Approve/reject all procedures or specifications impacting the identity, strength, quality, and purity of the finished CTM
- Review for approval/rejection all production records to determine compliance with all established, approved written procedures before a batch is released or distributed
- Review production records to ensure no errors have occurred; if an error has occurred, conduct an appropriate investigation to determine the reason for the error any probable effect(s) on the CTM
- Approve/reject materials produced by a third-party contractor
- Ensure adequacy of laboratory facilities
- Review, approve, and ensure that all written procedures for production and process controls are appropriate
- Review and approve specifications, standards, sampling plans, test procedures, laboratory control methods, and procedures, including any changes
- Ensure good documentation practices
- Conduct appropriate training of personnel, along with proper documentation and record keeping

STANDARD OPERATING PROCEDURES

Written production and control procedures should be developed during the investigational new drug (IND) stage of drug development. In early clinical phase (e.g., Phase I or Phase IIa), these procedures may be general, but as knowledge and experience with the new API and dosage form are gained, the procedures and controls usually are required to undergo considerable refinement. All written procedures are required to be approved by the appropriate units (laboratory, warehouse, production) with final review and approval by the quality unit, prior to implementation.

Procedures must be followed during CTM production and documented evidence of compliance to these procedures by the execution of records of reports. Actual specific process control procedures and conditions, such as timing, temperature, pressure, and adjustments (e.g., mixing, filtration, or drying) is required to be documented. Proper documentation will allow review and approval by the quality unit.

CHANGE CONTROL AND CLINICAL DEVELOPMENT

A change control system is also required during clinical development, even though the final process has not been established to be on state of control through validation. This system becomes critical as clinical development progresses to the manufacture of the CTM that will be used in multi-center trials in support of the drug application. The change control system in this stage facilitates the writing of key documents that will be reviewed later during the PAI, such as the Product Development report.[5] Change control during clinical development is utilized to capture key changes that occur in formulation, equipment, quality control methods, and specifications. Classification of change during clinical development is geared toward regulatory filing categories that communicate these changes by way of an annual report for less critical changes to amendment for more critical changes, to the IND application. This is in contrast to the change control system that would be in place for routine commercial production, where escalating change criticality classification requires FDA notification to the approved New Drug Application (NDA) by way of the annual report, the various changes-being-effected categories, or prior approval supplement.

BUILDINGS AND FACILITIES

Although commercial production facilities can be used for the production of CTM, they usually are not. One reason is that production equipment is often too large for the CTM production scale required. Another reason is that the CTM may contain components that are not yet fully characterized with regard to cleanability or toxicology, and therefore are not desirable to contaminate commercial production equipment. That said, the product life cycle for a CTM can start "on the bench" to pilot plant production and then to a commercial manufacturing facility, prior to commercial launch upon successful application approval and PAI.

CTM usually are manufactured in facilities that are designed for that purpose. Nonetheless, the facilities are required to meet the general guidelines for design and construction, including adequate lighting, plumbing and HVAC, allow for maintenance, cleaning and sanitization, and be designed for the flow of materials that avoids contamination or mix-ups. In this way, the physical infrastructure that is required to manufacture CTM is no different than would be required for commercial production. Typical of CTM manufacturing is that the variety of the operations required to support drug development programs demands that the facility be as flexible as possible, so the equipment is often small scale and portable.

EQUIPMENT

In early clinical development, many different new chemical entities (NCE) and their formulated analogs will be processed intermittently on a wide spectrum of equipment trains and configurations depending on the CTM supply chain requirements. Equipment for the manufacture of CTM should be appropriate for its intended function, properly maintained, calibrated, cleaned, and sanitized following written procedures at appropriate intervals. Equipment product contact surfaces should not contaminate or be reactive, additive, or absorptive with CTM product. Of course, as with commercial production, equipment should be identified and documented in production records.

In addition, the clinical development manufacturing environment is characterized by frequent equipment turn over, where a well-defined cleaning program is required. Challenges to the equipment cleaning program during CTM manufacture include defining acceptance criteria when toxicology of the NCE is still evolving. During CTM manufacture, the cleaning process is typically in the cleaning verification stage, where "clean until clean" is reasonable and practical. The cleaning verification process development and test results later form the basis for the development of the cleaning validation program, completed at least prior to commercial launch.

To validate the cleaning of any equipment, acceptable levels of cleanliness must be established. This is usually based on a fraction of the therapeutic dose of an active compound. Cleaning validation for multiple compounds may be performed using a matrix approach. This matrix generally will be applicable for classes of compounds and must consider their solubility in the cleaning solvents utilized.

Other considerations for equipment controls during CTM manufacture include establishing an equipment qualification program. For CTM manufacture, installation qualification and operational qualification, often combined under the "Installation and Operational Qualification (IOQ)" approach, establishes the equipment as meeting the manufacturer's criteria for installation and operation. Manufacturing equipment should be qualified before any pilot or larger-scale production of the CTM is performed.

PROCESS CONTROLS

During early clinical development, where typically a single lot of API provides an inventory to manufacture one or more small batches of CTM drug product, significant process and formulation changes often allows for inherent variability in batch replication. Heightened in process sampling provides an explorative process understanding to further allow adjustments to formulation and processing parameters. By the time late-stage clinical development (e.g., Phase III) is initiated, it is expected that the process for API synthesis as well as CTM drug production are in the final defined form, and the process that has been successively replicated represents the proposed commercial process that will subsequently undergo process validation prior to commercial launch.

When systems, such as HEPA filtration, sterilization, and the production of process water are utilized to protect the CTM from contamination, it is expected that these critical utilities be validated and therefore established in a state of control.

PACKAGING AND LABEL CONTROL

Components used for packaging and labeling of CTM require the same degree of control as those package and label commercial products. There are some differences, however, in the areas of labeling and expiration dating.

Labels for CTM are often one-of-a-kind because they contain unique subject numbers. Clinical labels are usually cut labels that are hand applied. The labeling and collation of CTM patient kits often involve the use of more than one drug product. These differences demand that the preparation of the CTM trial labels and the labeling of CTM be given extra care and attention.

The use of cut labeling, which is usually hand applied, requires that each drug unit be inspected independently by two (2) qualified personnel to verify correct labeling. This in addition to the usual 200% inspection that the labels have been given during the printing process before they are issued to the production room.

Clinical labels differ in another way as well. The expiration date that is required on all drug product labels in accordance with 21 CFR 211.127(b) is waived by the supplement regulation under 21 CFR 211.137(g). This waiver of the expiration date for CTM is not without additional obligation, however. If the expiration date is not shown on the CTM label, then an ongoing stability study must demonstrate that the CTM in use in the clinic continues to meet standards for identity, strength, potency, and quality that are listed in the IND, throughout its use period. The label for a CTM produced for use in the US must also include the statement "Caution: New Drug-Limited by Federal (or United States) Law to Investigational Use."

LABORATORY CONTROLS

Laboratory controls supporting CTM manufacture are required to have adequate facilities, equipment, procedures, methods, controls, and qualified personnel to analyze and evaluate development products for conformance with proposed and evolving specifications, tests, and methods.

A laboratory metrology program should consist of calibration and maintenance of analytical instruments, apparatus, gauges, and recording devices performed at defined intervals in accordance with the manufacturer's requirements, where available, and in accordance with written procedures. Complex analytical instrumentation, such as HPLCs, GCs, and FT-IRs, should have an installation and operational qualification program. The program should have provisions for remedial action when the established acceptance criteria are not met.

Review and approval must occur for all specifications, standards, methods, and other laboratory control mechanisms, including any changes to such criteria. Final approval for all of these described controls remains the responsibility of the quality unit, as it does for commercial production. Written procedures should also exist for sampling and testing. Acceptance criteria must be based on development data and demonstrate a correlation between the methods and the controls used in Product Development for CTM.

The evolution of analytical methods and controls during CTM manufacture are required to show correlation between Product Development stages and those eventually transferred to commercial production. Changes to methods and controls are required to be supported by data and be approved before implementation.

A written program to evaluate the stability characteristics of the CTM API and finished drug product must also be established. The stability test results will support the container closure as well expiry dating of the CTM. Data must be available to support the stability of the CTM finished drug product in the proposed container/closure system and storage condition throughout the time that it will be used in the clinic.

A reserve or retention sample for each lot of CTM API and batch of CTM finished drug product is required to be retained. 21 CFR 211.170 requires that the quantity of retained sample taken is twice the amount of product to conduct all tests necessary to determine whether the drug meets its specifications. Retention samples are required to be stored under conditions consistent with current product labeling and in the container/closure system representative of that used when shipped and stored at the clinical site. Finally, a visual inspection is required to be conducted on reserve samples at least annually to determine signs of potential deterioration.

YIELDS

A variety of factors, including the preparation of relatively small batch sizes during CTM manufacture and often the subdividing of in process material for further research and development work, often results in significant yield discrepancies. Nonetheless, these discrepancies should be investigated during CTM manufacture since other factors may have contributed to the discrepancies and could potentially signal a processing error. Specifications for theoretical yield that would trigger an investigation in the quality system are typically wider initially than in later stages of Product Development. Initial theoretical yield specifications should be initially set during CTM manufacture using known process controls to ensure the final CTM product meets the specifications for identity, strength, quality, and purity. As CTM drug production progresses through Phase I to Phase III, yield specifications will be narrowed in order to define adequate process control as the product approaches commercial production scale.

OTHER CONSIDERATIONS

Other quality system components that are required to support CTM manufacture and control include systems for complaint handling and investigations of deviations. An adequate complaint management system is essential during the CTM manufacture stage of Product Development. During a clinical study, the customer base is composed principally of the clinical subject, study coordinator, principal investigator , or the clinical pharmacy personnel. The sponsor of the clinical study must have adequate systems in place to readily investigate and mitigate risk to the patient. Examples of type of complaints received during CTM manufacture and the conduct of a clinical study include but are not limited to (a) miscounts of tablets or capsules, (b) missing desiccant, (c) mislabeling, (d) discoloration or chipping of tablets or "hazing" of capsules, (e) turbid solution, or (f) particulate matter observed in parenteral CTM finished drug product. The complaint system should require procurement of field samples wherever possible and an investigative component that strives for root cause and remediation.

Quality investigations for laboratory or process anomalies are required to be conducted for the manufacture of CTM in compliance with 21 CFR 211.192. The degree of investigational analysis and required documentation should be designed using an incremental-based approach as depicted in Tables 8.3–8.4. Certainly, as the CTM development program progresses from Phase IIa to Phase III, the formality of investigations of deviation and aberrant laboratory test results would be equivalent to what would be required during commercial production. When third-party CMOs are employed for some or all of the CTM production and packaging and labeling, quality agreements are required to outline the roles and responsibilities between the sponsor and CMO, including requirements for quality investigations.

DISTRIBUTION AND STOCK RECOVERY

Good distribution practices for CTM should describe the transport of the CTM product from the point of production to product to the patient/subject for consumption. Distribution records should allow for traceability and accountability. The holding and distribution of CTM requires the same care and documentation as commercial materials. However, because CTM are distributed to sites by subject number, the recordkeeping is somewhat more complicated. Nevertheless, the CGMP requirements for quarantine, until released by the quality unit for storage at appropriate conditions of temperature, humidity, and light and the need for written distribution procedures, apply to CTMs as they do to commercial products.

Procedures are required during CTM production for conducting recall of product, just as in the case for commercial product. However, the phrase "stock recovery" is more aptly employed during the CTM production and distribution phase, as opposed to the phrase product recall. Just as with a commercial product call system, a CTM stock recovery process would include classifications of defects, as described under 21 CFR 211.7. In an analogous manner to commercial product, CTM that needs to be recovered due to a determined product defect would require distribution channels and levels, as well as effectiveness checks to be performed.

CONCLUSION

The goal of CGMP during CTM is to assure safe CTMs as well as assure the quality of CTM. The sponsor of the clinical trial should have the ability to reproduce CTM within a trial, between trials, and throughout development to commercial manufacture. The importance and cost of conducting clinical research necessitates the preparation of CTM in a controlled and CGMP compliant manner. It is important to recognize that while the CGMP regulations apply to CTM, just as for commercial products, there are distinct differences in interpretation and implementation of CGMP in the CTM production environment.

REFERENCES

1. *Federal Food, Drug, and Cosmetic Act,* as amended, 21 USC 301 *et seq.*, Sections 201(g) (21 USC 312[g]) and 501(a)(2)(B) (21 USC 351[a][2][B]).
2. "Current Good Manufacturing Practices for Finished Pharmaceuticals," 21 CFR 210 and 211.
3. *Federal Register*, 29 September 1978, Vol. 43, No. 190, pp. 45013–45336.
4. FDA Guidance for Industry: CGMP for Phase 1 Investigational Drugs, July 2008.
5. FDA Compliance Program 7346.832, PreApproval Inspections/Investigations.

9 Contracting and Outsourcing

Joseph C. Near

CONTENTS

One thing that is common to the small virtual company (those with only "office-based" personnel) and the multinational company marketing commercial product is that they both use contractors and outsource one or more operations. The virtual company with its first product in development is solely dependent on contractors and, because of this, needs to minimize any potential regulatory-related risks that may jeopardize product development or regulatory submission review. The multinational company can have product manufactured and/or packaged and analyzed by a contractor; here too there is a regulatory risk associated with the operations if they are not in compliance with the regulatory filing or current good manufacturing practice (CGMP) requirements and regulatory expectations. While the contractor would be required to respond to any observations observed during a regulatory inspection, there is also an impact for the client (also commonly referred to as the "owner" or "sponsor"), virtual or commercial, having their product manufactured at the facility.

The Food and Drug Administration (FDA) in its Guidance for Industry entitled *Contract Manufacturing Arrangements for Drugs: Quality Agreements*[1] clearly states that each party engaged in the manufacture of a drug is responsible for ensuring compliance with CGMP for the manufacturing activities it performs, but the FDA also states that outsourcing a process to a contractor does not devoid the client of responsibilities for compliance. This includes the client's quality unit's legal responsibility for approving or rejecting drug product manufactured by the contract facility. The FDA

Guidance for Industry: *Q10 Pharmaceutical Quality System*[2] states that, as part of a pharmaceutical quality system, the pharmaceutical company/client is ultimately responsible for ensuring that "processes are in place to assure the control of outsourced activities and quality of purchased products."

During the last 15 years, there has been a significant change in the way pharmaceuticals are developed and brought to market for the consumer/patient. One of the biggest changes is the expanded use of contractors for one or more of the developmental steps (premarket) and, increasingly, for the entire process. The outsourcing industry used to support virtual companies with no/limited capabilities of their own, and some products from large companies were contracted out because of logistics and limited in-house capabilities. Today, there is increasing demand for commercial products to be produced by contractors and also by business alliances.

The last several years have also seen a number of major acquisitions and mergers involving larger pharmaceutical companies, which has resulted in demands for cost constraints. An outfall of this is amalgamation of capabilities (production, analysis, packaging/labeling, and distribution) and selling selected facilities. Additionally, executive management uses the opportunity to streamline the drug development processes, resulting in increased demand for contractor capabilities.

Contractors have gained knowledge and experience over the last 15 years enabling them to manage the requirements/requests from multiple clients simultaneously. New operations attract experienced management personnel to successfully exceed client expectations. Outsourcing operations offer distinct advantages that have to be utilized to their maximum benefit.

While there has always been a need for clinical trial supplies contractors, the increase in business, regulatory, and public expectations for rapid time to market has had a significant impact on this section of the industry. Additionally, regulatory authorities are requiring increased data and information from clinical trials to support product indications. Clinical studies have increased in complexity and resulted in additional control requirements during packaging. Increased safety focus added additional requirements for further and more complex studies.

Key support companies identified the need for specialized services, for example, clinical supplies labels with all the complexity and controls for blinded labels. This service not only covers initial issuance of thousands of labels but may also include different languages and different arms of a study, that is, development drug, comparator drug, and sometimes two placebos. Additionally, analytical testing and manufacturing capabilities have expanded from "conventional" pharmaceuticals to more complex biological systems used for the generation of therapeutic treatments. Biopharmaceutical contractors have gained valuable experience and expertise and are now able to offer a wide range of services covering today's product requirements.

OUTSOURCING

The following chapter discusses different topics related to outsourcing manufacturing operations and can be adapted for individual processes that are outsourced to a contractor.

There are also relevant and valuable CGMP recommendations with respect to contract manufacturing in the following guidance documents:

- *Q7 Good Manufacturing Guidance for Active Pharmaceutical Ingredients*
- *Q9 Quality Risk Management*
- *Q10 Pharmaceutical Quality System*

Key reasons to consider outsourcing include the following:

1. Capabilities outside company facilities/operations or portfolio: for example, a pharmaceutical company with a biotechnology product needs to develop an injectable formulation.
2. Specialized facilities/operations needed: for example, filling/lyophilizing, containment requirements.

3. Accelerate drug development.
4. Reduce time to market.
5. Production capacity exceeded or fluctuates with seasonal demand.
6. Capital investment limited or not prepared to be committed at this stage of development. Purchasing or building facilities specifically for a product that later fails to meet acceptance criteria can ultimately result in an empty building and loss of capital investment, which could have been utilized in developing other products.
7. Greater return on investment.
8. Maximize patent life by decreasing time to initiate clinical studies and accelerate decision points.
9. Flexibility and ability to respond to changing developmental requirements based on marketing and clinical responses.
10. Finances redeployed to other strategic areas, including product development.
11. Complement or provide redundancy in the supply chain.
12. Support uncertain product approvals without tying up internal resources.
13. Smaller volume products.

Companies are using contractors' capabilities to free internal resources for other drug product development projects. Another advantage that contractors offer is the ability to provide specialized services (e.g., containment, biological handling, and lyophilization), which would take capital investments, other resources, and mainly time. A contractor has the ability to initiate services in a fraction of the time taken at a company facility and can do so with highly experienced staff. This has a distinct time-saving advantage for the company. Additionally, if development of the product is stopped (either for clinical or business development reasons), the company can, with the appropriately worded contract, stop development and associated expenditure promptly.

TYPES OF OUTSOURCING

Contract facilities can perform a variety of manufacturing operations and activities, including but not limited to:

- Formulation
- Fill and finish
- Chemical synthesis
- Cell culture and fermentation, including for biological products
- Analytical testing and other laboratory services
- Packaging and labeling
- Sterilization or terminal sterilization, and lyophilization

Virtual companies having no facilities of their own for developing, manufacturing, packaging/labeling, and testing and distribution of products rely solely on contractors. One or more of these operations are contracted to one or more contractors. It is not uncommon for commercial operations involving multiple steps (e.g., granulation, pelletization, tableting, liquid formulation, and vial filling) to involve more than one company at locations that can be in different countries. The complexity of coordinating with one contractor is multiplied several times when another is required for a specific processing step.

A larger pharmaceutical company may choose to manufacture an oral solid product at a contractor and ship to one of its own facilities for final manufacturing steps or packaging/labeling.

The decision to develop an injectable formulation for an existing drug can represent unique challenges. If formulation development is successful, there is still the logistics of finding a suitable sterile clinical trials contractor. To build a sterile manufacturing facility requires capital and enormous running cost and commitment. The last thing a company needs when a drug development program is cancelled is an empty facility drawing cash from the budget. A specialized sterile clinical trial manufacturing/packaging contractor can offer the ability to deliver sterile dosage forms. However, there are a limited number of these facilities available because of the overhead costs, specifically trained personnel, and other factors. Selecting a contractor, especially for long-term projects, must be performed with a systematic evaluation.

OUTSOURCED PROCESSES

Key processes that are commonly outsourced include the following:

ENTIRE PROCESS

This is where the client of the regulatory filing (Investigational New Drug or New Drug Application) performs no operations within their facilities. The client could be a virtual company or one that does not have the specific capabilities. The process may be performed at one or more contractors.

MANUFACTURE OF THE ACTIVE SUBSTANCE AND UNIQUE EXCIPIENTS

Both of these types of components are often sourced from contractors. There has been a significant change in the outsourcing of active substances (also commonly referred to as active pharmaceutical ingredients [APIs]) to contractors, especially the Far East and India. Many large and smaller pharmaceutical companies no longer choose to maintain facilities and operations for the production of active substances. Additional challenges are generated when sourcing from any company outside the United States. It is the client's responsibility to ensure that they have sufficient confidence through physical verification and discussions with the contractor that their specific requirements are completely understood.

MANUFACTURE OF INTERMEDIATES AND FINAL DOSAGE FORMS

Intermediates may be manufactured at a contractor and either sent to another contractor for process completion or sent to the client's facility.

Manufacture of the dosage form can be initiated at any stage following discovery, production of the initial dosage form for clinical phase I studies, and through all subsequent phases of development to commercialization. Ideally, all this type of work should be performed at a single contractor, but it is not uncommon for more than one contractor to be involved. Formulation work, including analytical testing, may be performed by one contractor and transferred to another because of logistics of scale or other factors. Some specialized testing may be performed at another contractor. Stability storage and testing can be performed at yet a different contractor. Clinical trial supplies are often packaged by more than one contractor because of timelines, logistics, specialized equipment, and capabilities. Add to this the complexity that any one of these functions could be performed in a different country. The management of the contractors just increased significantly.

The entire process from compilation of pre-human testing, formulation/development, stability studies, and clinical study results through to the inclusion of all the required information/data as defined by regulatory requirements and reviewers are shown in Figure 9.1.

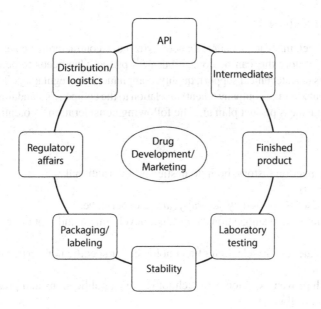

FIGURE 9.1   Contractor capabilities.

OUTSOURCING PROCESS

The process for outsourcing generally involves the following steps:

- Needs Assessment
- Contractor Identification
- Request for Proposal
- Contractor Evaluation (including Audit) and Selection
- Agreements (Service Agreement and Quality Agreement)
- Ongoing Performance Evaluation, Management and Process Improvement

A standard operating procedure (SOP) must define the process, requirements, and responsibilities for the selection, evaluation and approval, and ongoing management/oversight of contractors.

NEEDS ASSESSMENT

The decision to outsource one or more processing capabilities originates from strategic business development or commercial logistics. A company either cannot or does not want to provide the resources (facilities, equipment, personnel, etc.) necessary to progress development of the product to the next phase or support the supply of a commercial product. A commercial product may not be financially viable although there is a patient need. These types of products are designated "orphan drugs" by the FDA. A company will supply the product because of multiple reasons, including compassionate use and good public relations. In this case, the company may elect to use a contractor for the manufacturing and packaging of the product. This releases company scheduling, space, capital investment, and other resources.

There are risks (legal, financial, regulatory, etc.) associated with any outsourcing, and this needs to be evaluated and managed so as to minimize this for the client. The later the product is in development, that is, phase III or it is a commercial product, the greater the risk to the client, as delays and problems have greater and more visible impact to regulatory authorities, public, and shareholders.

CONTRACTOR IDENTIFICATION

Once a decision has been made to outsource an activity(ies) to a contractor(s) the next step is to identify potential contractors. Before this can be done, a business project plan needs to be defined with input from multiple sources (e.g., technical support, quality, compliance, and regulatory). The plan defines the requirements of the outsourcing company (client) in relation to the company's standards and expectations.

Based upon the business project plan and the following considerations, potential contractors can be identified:

- Reputation.
- Regulatory inspection history, both domestic and international.
- Financial stability.
- Broad client base, supported by several years of experience.
- Can provide innovative suggestions to product development and input to resolve technical problems.
- Ability to provide a wide selection of technologies for specific nonsterile and sterile product requirements.
- Personnel with proven experience in technology (e.g., publications and presentations) and management/coordination.
- Potential to provide international shipments through partnerships or other facilities of the company.
- Reliability.
- Ability to meet and manage timelines.
- Strong communicator.
- Accountable for commitments.
- Complete understanding and commitment to quality. This is a critical component because of regulatory implications.
- Sufficient staffing and equipment to perform the specific work.
- Openness.
- Preparedness to build and maintain a strong and lasting business relationship.

REQUEST FOR PROPOSAL

After a list of companies potentially fitting the business plan requirements has been compiled, preliminary discussions take place between the client and the contractors, including a request from potential contractors to submit business proposals based on the client's requirements. This step of the process may necessitate the joint signing of confidentiality disclosure agreements (CDAs) between the companies. Some discussions may take place without a CDA in order to decrease the resource requirements utilized to identify the top two or three potential contractors. The technical capabilities of the companies determine potential candidates. This stage of the process is often referred to as Due Diligence and generally involves determining the following:

- Business history, including financial
- Regulatory history
- Capabilities for current project requirements and potential to accommodate expansion of capacity/volume
- Ability of contractor to listen to client's needs
- Ability of contractor to develop a long-term business relationship/partnership
- Any liabilities or pending litigation

It is also common that a technical assessment, potentially involving a site visit, be undertaken by manufacturing, product development, and laboratory personnel from the client.

CONTRACTOR EVALUATION (INCLUDING AUDIT)

There is both a business and compliance risk if regulatory action is taken against the contractor. This in turn could be linked to the client. It is therefore essential that a GMP quality assessment be performed to establish the regulatory compliance status of the selected company/companies.

Once the two or three potential contractors have been identified based upon evaluation of business proposals, discussions between the client and the contractors, and the outcome of any technical assessments, the compliance function of the client typically arranges and performs a compliance quality assessment against CGMP requirements and company standards. This may not be required based on previous use and qualification of the contractor; however, the requirements for qualification of a contractor and any required audits should be detailed in an SOP. It is essential that the results of the assessment be analyzed for potential regulatory risks, and recommendation for use or not is issued. There may be limited choices of companies when specialized capabilities are required, but compliance gaps/observations are identified. As with all business partners, it is essential that the contractors work with them to ensure that there is complete understanding of expectations/requirements. This can take on several forms, from independent function of the contractor to a significant Quality Assurance (QA) oversight by the sponsor. The "quality" function makes the final recommendation for use of the contractor.

There will be times when the client will have no opportunity to select the contractor because there is only one having the required capabilities. Contractors who provide specialized services clearly appreciate they have a niche in the market with "captured" clients but do not necessarily use this to their unfair advantage.

AGREEMENTS

To successfully outsource a process it requires careful planning, selection, communication, maintenance, and above all management of the contractor.

In addition to business and legal agreements (e.g., Master Services Agreement), there must be a clear understanding of responsibilities relating to CGMP defined in a quality agreement. Agreements define essential requirements of the project and the process for managing when things do not go according to plan. The content of the quality agreement must be clearly understood and signed/approved by appropriate personnel (senior management, production, and QA) of both parties. The FDA's expectations regarding quality agreements can be found in the FDA Guidance for Industry: *Contract Manufacturing Arrangements for Drugs: Quality Agreements.*[1] The content of a quality agreement is dependent to a certain extent on the type of outsourcing; however, key sections of a quality agreement typically include but are not limited to the responsibilities, timelines, and documentation for the following:

- Regulatory
    - Authority interaction and notification to client: need to define process for notification of the client if a regulatory agency indicates that they are inquiring or on-site for the client's product.
    - Statement of the regulatory requirements to which the process defined in the agreement is to be performed.
- Clear definition of the processes, tasks, and especially any limitations/exclusions and scope.
- Facility addresses.
- Contact personnel of both parties with titles, e-mail, and telephone numbers (with designees).
- Identification of the party responsible for performing each process/task or other key steps.
- Change control requirement notifications to the client: Provide examples of changes that need to be promptly notified to the client in writing. Emergency changes will be

notified retrospectively. A client may request that their next batch be delayed until they have reviewed and agreed with the changes. The changes need to be assessed in the client's change control system with the appropriate internal approvals.

- Recall responsibilities and the process steps with timelines.
- Notification of client for significant events (e.g., failures of sterility, environmental, out-of-specification results, and manufacturing deviations) with timelines. Provide examples and ensure the contractor is clear of expectations. The process/timelines for client review and comment need to be defined, and also how the deviation/investigation is closed.
- Annual product review: define in sufficient detail the data/information that the contractor is required to supply and the due date.
- Complaint management: normally, the client handles the initial contact and contacts the contractor if the problem could be related to the operations performed by the contractor. Equally, if the contractor receives a complaint, they are required to notify the client immediately with follow-up documentation.
- New Drug Application field alert responsibilities.
- Material/product release responsibilities.
- Storage and shipment requirements.
- Timelines for key milestones in the process or for achieving each sub-step in the process. This would also include delivery of intermediates, product, and other materials. Include key performance indicators by which the contractor will be measured. These may include defined timelines and number of batch documentation errors requiring correction.
- Definition of the documentation and materials/components to be supplied by the client and those to be supplied by the contractor. This ensures that there are no gaps in the exchange of information/data between the two parties.
- Agreement for the client to perform quality assessments. These are normally performed at least every two years and "for cause" as necessary.
- Integrity of electronic information/data exchange between the two parties.
- Use of subcontractors by the contractor: this is normally prohibited without prior approval from the client.
- Confidentiality and intellectual property ownership are often included in the business agreement, which also contains details of payments, penalties, and other business-related items.

Agreements are controlled documents, and as such must be version-controlled, signed by appropriate management of both parties, and contain an effective date. These must be revised as needed to reflect changes in the agreement and at least every three years. Ensure that the contractor has trained appropriate personnel on the requirements of the agreements, and the client has an equal responsibility to ensure their personnel are trained. It is not only embarrassing to either party if the other identifies that an agreement requirement has not been met due to lack of awareness, but also detrimental to the business relationship.

Dispute resolution should be managed at early stages to prevent escalation and "finger pointing" to assign blame. If the quality agreement does not address the issue and it cannot be resolved through discussion with regular contracts, then it needs to be managed through dispute resolution as defined in the legal agreement.

ONGOING MANAGEMENT, OVERSIGHT AND PROCESS IMPROVEMENT

Never underestimate the resources needed to adequately monitor and manage contractors. Failure to provide the required resources will be detrimental to the client. The management varies according to the type of outsourcing and the individual contractors. Frequent and in-depth management of operations at the contractor at the initiation of the project should be able to be decreased in frequency, as confidence and business relationships are strengthened. Regular meetings and monitoring visits ensure operations run according to plan. There should be infrequent surprises for either party with open communication. Contractors welcome open and honest clients to build long-lasting business relationships. Management of the contractor is critical in maintaining compliance with regulatory commitments and the regulatory filing of the product. It is critical that the client does not squeeze the budget putting the contractor in a position of cutting cost that impacts on the quality of work and staff morale.

Due to the degree of outsourcing, complexity of the process, and degree of risk, some companies are dedicating resources specifically to manage contractors. While this is a distinct advantage, many companies cannot afford the expense, especially small virtual companies. For these companies, there are major obstacles to managing contractors with personnel in different departments with sometimes an ineffective process. One of their largest challenges is communication and contractor management.

Some contractors also dedicate a contact person (customer project manager) within their organization who is responsible for interfacing with clients. Although this does not prevent direct contact with key personnel, for example, QC laboratory manager, it may appear that the contractor is preventing access to specific personnel. Without the customer project manager, there is the potential for breakdowns in communications and multiple requests/questions being delivered to the wrong personnel. The customer project manager has a critical role in ensuring that customer needs are met, questions resolved, and meetings held with appropriate key personnel. An organized and client-focused contractor employs dedicated customer project managers.

Technical transfer is the process of transferring knowledge from the client to the contractor efficiently, completely, and with clarity, without ambiguity is essential for everyone's success. Contractors are conscious of the client's success and want to share in it. A contractor's goals include those clients with products that were brought from development to commercial approval in their facilities. The contractor's reputation in the industry is enhanced each time one of their clients obtains product regulatory approval. Regular on-site meetings with the appropriate key client personnel are necessary to establish business relationships, respect, and to clarify details of logically working together. Regulatory compliance with the filing and CGMPs is part of the overall package between the two companies. Without understanding each other's requirements, the product life cycle will surely fail to meet criteria and expectations. While the client needs the assurance that development/production is meeting timelines without major compliance problems, the contractor needs to be informed of proposed changes and above all if they are not meeting client requirements. These points can only be met by open and honest communication and by putting everything in writing.

At the center of a long-term business relationship between the client and the contractor is a degree of trust. This does not mean that the need to confirm requirements is not in writing, because communication and agreement are as essential as trust. The client must build an open and strong rapport with the contractor, and they will respond accordingly, as it is in their business and financial interest to keep clients and build long-term partnerships. The client is ultimately responsible for compliance relating to their products. Data-related questions concerning compliance to CGMP requirements could seriously impact a drug application under review by the FDA. Equally, if the FDA issues FDA483s or even more importantly a warning letter to the contractor where a commercial product is being processed or analyzed, there is a risk to the client. This risk must be assessed promptly to determine if there is any potential impact to the client's product. Observations in FDA483s and warning letters can be related to quality system failures, and although not always directly mentioned against the client's product, they can still have a significant impact because system problems normally have no restrictions. Additionally, further regulatory actions could jeopardize the capabilities of the contractor.

Monitoring client operations when in progress is part of the ongoing relationship with the contractor. All contractors welcome clients to their facilities because without this welcome there is no business relationship. While the client does not want to disrupt operations, there is the understanding that the client has a need and to an extent an invitation to monitor their product being processed.

The visit is normally preplanned and may be for specific steps in the process. Some clients have arrangements to have personnel on-site continually monitoring the process. Key to monitoring is confidentiality and communication. Confidentiality is needed because it is almost impossible to be in a facility and not detect/identify some form of information from another client. It is not difficult because that is the business the contractor is in: managing multiple clients simultaneously. Respect confidentiality and ensure that the contractor is promptly aware of any concerns that may arise during on-site monitoring.

The client must not be under any illusion of the magnitude of resources needed to maintain a business relationship with a contactor. Initial audit and any remediation, agreements, defining and organizing materials/components, confirming timelines, approving final labels, and regular meetings with defined agendas/actions are initial examples. At some point in the growth of contracting, the sponsor organization may want to consider dedicated staff for contract administration. This threshold can be reached unexpectedly with the surprise of a failed project/batch or major delay.

While cost is also a determinant for selecting a service provider, it typically ranks at or near the bottom of survey responses for outsourcing selection criteria.

OTHER TYPES OF CONTRACTORS

Other areas where contractors are used are as consultants (outside the scope of this chapter) in performing functions relating to engineering or technical support. The latter areas cover instrument calibration, weight certification, high-efficiency particulate air (HEPA) filters, equipment maintenance, and calibration. The process for the selection of services from a contractor in this category has the same approach as those for the manufacturing.

- Define project requirements and scope.
- Perform due diligence to identify potential contractors who can provide the required services.
- Perform selected audits of contractors with a team comprising of quality CGMP, technical, and engineering experts. This may be performed initially by a questionnaire, depending on the SOP for contractor approval, and based on a risk assessment. Additional documentation from the contractor can also be requested in support of the selection.
- Write the audit report and make recommendations.
- Select contractor and obtain written agreement for scope of service and requirements.
- Manage the contractor according to SOP requirements.
  - *On-site visit by contractor.* It is essential that the contractor is adequately supervised while on-site. This includes following site procedures for security, safety, and access to specific areas. Contractors should have some degree of training (documented) on the requirements of performing work on-site. Escorting and closely supervising contractors are essential in maintaining controlled environment/conditions. Often, contractors will send the same person for the periodic work, which enables the host to have consistency, as the contractor is aware of the client's requirements.
  - *Separate operating facilities.* These include those providing services (e.g., calibration and weight verification), where the product is shipped back to the client for completion of operations (packaging/labeling) or further processing. Equipment can be shipped back to a vendor/manufacturer for maintenance and calibration.

DOCUMENTATION/DATA REVIEW AND ACCEPTANCE

It is the ultimate responsibility of the client to ensure that all the documentation and data received from the contractor is acceptable. The quality agreement must define the documents, contents, approvals, and timelines for delivery. Copies of manufacturing/packaging records may be reviewed on-site, perhaps initial batches, and then periodically as agreed in writing with the contractor. The objective is to build confidence with the documentation produced to support the client's product. Minimum documentation requirements to release the batch must be clearly defined.

Specific testing results are added to the core template contents as shown below and Certificates of Compliance usually contain the following:

- Product description/strength and batch number.
- The regulatory requirements under which the product was made.
- List the number of each deviation, investigation, and out-of-specification investigation related to this product and the status (open or closed). The client needs to confirm all of these by obtaining copies for review.
- Name, job title, and signature of the author/date.
- Name, job title, and signature of QA representative/date.

The documentation and data must meet at least the requirements of the client's SOP for documentation principles. The contract will define the requirement to provide the raw data, including copies of charts, printouts, and laboratory records. The contractor's QA unit must review and approve all documentation, including release of the batch to the client according to the contractor's SOP.

If it can be shown that the contractor's "quality" unit released product for distribution, even though it is aware of CGMP deviations, (e.g., it is aware that the test methods used by the contractor have not been validated), it then would be appropriate to cite the manufacturer for the CGMP deviation of releasing the inadequately tested drug.

In both cases, the contracting firm also could be held responsible for shipping adulterated drugs in interstate commerce.

CHANGE CONTROL

Compliance with regulatory requirements includes managing changes. This applies equally to the contractor with respect to operations/products and to the client for informing the contractor. The contractor will have a change control SOP, which must be reviewed, and any concerns responded to before operations commence. It must be remembered that the contractor needs to be able to work daily with the SOP. The contractor's SOP will then interface with the specific change requirements, especially the scope of notification to individual clients. These requirements are defined in the quality agreement, and the client needs to confirm with the contractor how their staff will consistently implement the requirements. Clients must ensure specific requests are managed by the contractor and fully incorporated into their systems. Ask, clarify, and confirm before work begins. Monitor progress and resolve any concerns with the contractor.

CONTRACTOR CERTIFICATION

Although there is no specific GMP regulatory requirement for a contractor certification program, there is an expectation that clients will evaluate contractors to ensure that they can meet requirements. Evidence that the contractor has been evaluated may be requested during a regulatory authority inspection. It is essential that the program is defined in an SOP and its scope clearly defined and implemented with supporting documentation. A program for certification should include the process for the initial evaluation of the contractor and recommendations. The recommendation may be: Approved, Improvement Needed, and Not Approved. Where improvements are required, these should be discussed with the contractor to ensure that expectations are clear. Some improvements may need to be compromised in content and timelines, but this does not relate to unacceptable risk. It is critical to assess the potential risk factor, as this can result in holding operations until the required changes have been made and confirmed.

Ongoing monitoring of contractors for compliance with CGMPs and agreement requirements is performed and documented by the client. Deviations and concerns need to be promptly discussed and resolved. Failure to resolve these problems can result in changes to a contractor's status. Appropriate action, including informing senior management, must be defined in a SOP. The client and contractor should work together to resolve differences. Sometimes, the client may make the decision to transfer operations to a new contractor.

CONCLUSIONS

Clients need contractors to meet their company goals for increased productivity and, above all, for making a profit. Consumers/patients in turn rely on these clients to make products available at competitive prices at the right time. Both parties rely on service and quality products.

Clients are responsible for ensuring that the contractor has a clear understanding of the scope and content of the project. Contractors are responsible for working with their clients to understand their specific requirements. It should be remembered that contractors have multiple clients "pulling" them in many different directions at the same time. Communication is at the center of all the projects and the responsibility of both parties. If there is any doubt, ask the other party to confirm in writing. A lost batch because one person failed to inform another about a required change is a lost opportunity to continue building a strong business relationship. Be open with the contractor, and they will in turn want to keep an open rapport with clients. It is in everyone's interest to build and not erode relationships.

RESPONSIBILITIES AS A CONTRACTOR

Drugs must be manufactured in conformance with CGMP. The FDA is aware that many drug manufacturers use independent contractors, such as production facilities, testing laboratories, packagers, and labelers. The FDA regards contractors as extensions of the manufacturer.

You and your customer, have a quality agreement regarding the manufacture of drug products. You are responsible for the quality of drugs you produce as a contract facility, regardless of agreements in place with application sponsors. You are required to ensure that drugs are made in accordance with section 501(a)(2)(B) of the FD&C Act for safety, identity, strength, quality, and purity. See the FDA's guidance document, *Contract Manufacturing Arrangements for Drugs: Quality Agreements*, at https://www.fda.gov/downloads/drugs/guidances/ucm353925.pdf.

COMMUNICATIONS WITH SPONSOR

You are responsible for ensuring that your firm complies with all applicable requirements, including the CGMP regulations. You should immediately notify the drug application sponsor of changes to the manufacturing or testing of the drug product, and any relevant drug master file updates, so they can file an appropriate submission to the application (supplement or report in annual report). A major change should not be implemented until a prior approval supplement is approved by the FDA.

DISTRIBUTOR'S RESPONSIBILITIES

The following was from a warning letter issued in 2013 to a dietary supplement manufacturer and made reference to incidents from 1943 and 1975, which are well-known cases.

As a distributor that contracts with other manufacturers to manufacture, package, or label dietary supplements that your firm releases for distribution under your firm's name, your firm has an obligation to know what and how manufacturing activities are performed so that you can make decisions related to whether your dietary supplement products conform to established specifications and whether to approve and release the products for distribution. [72 Fed. Reg. 34752, 34790 (June 25, 2007)]. Your firm introduces or delivers, or causes the introduction or delivery, of the dietary supplement into interstate commerce in its final form for distribution to consumers. As such, your firm has an overarching and ultimate responsibility to ensure that all phases of the production of that product are in compliance with dietary supplement CGMP requirements.

Although your firm may contract out certain dietary supplement manufacturing operations, it cannot, by the same token, contract out its ultimate responsibility to ensure that the dietary supplement it places into commerce (or causes to be placed into commerce) is not adulterated for failure to comply with dietary supplement CGMP requirements, see United States v. Dotterweich, 320 U.S. 277, 284 (1943)[3] (explaining that an offense can be committed under the Federal Food, Drug, and Cosmetic Act (FD&C Act) by anyone who has "a responsible share in the furtherance of the transaction which the statute outlaws"); United States v. Park, 421 U.S. 658, 672 (1975)[4] (holding that criminal liability under the FD&C Act does not turn on awareness of wrongdoing, and that "agents vested with the responsibility, and power commensurate with that responsibility, to devise whatever measures are necessary to ensure compliance with the Act" can be held accountable for violations of the FD&C Act). In particular, the FD&C Act prohibits a person from introducing or delivering for introduction, or causing the delivery or introduction, into interstate commerce a dietary supplement that is adulterated under section 402(g) for failure to comply with dietary supplement CGMP requirements (see 21 USC §§ 342[g] and 331[a]). Thus, a firm that contracts with other firms to conduct certain dietary supplement manufacturing, packaging, and labeling operations for it is responsible for ensuring that the product is not adulterated for failure to comply with dietary supplement CGMP requirements, regardless of who actually performs the dietary supplement CGMP operations.

EXAMPLES OF OBSERVATIONS FROM FDA CITATIONS

- Your response was inadequate because you did not adequately investigate and address the impact on the drug product already distributed to the U.S. market. Your response also does not indicate whether your contract packaging facility plans to use the blister line that still lacks adequate humidity controls to repack products for the U.S. market.
- As a contract laboratory, you must comply with the CGMP regulations that apply to operations you perform, including but not limited to those that address the operations of your quality control unit, laboratory, investigation systems, documentation systems, and other facets of your operation. As set forth in FDA's guidance for industry, *Investigating Out-of-Specification (OOS) Test Results for Pharmaceutical Production*, following an OOS result, the laboratory should conduct an initial assessment to determine whether there was a meaningful error in the analytical method. Following such assessment, "[f]or contract laboratories, the laboratory should convey its data, findings, and supporting documentation to the manufacturing firm's quality control unit..." FDA considers contractors as extensions of the manufacturer's own facility. Your failure to comply with CGMP may affect the quality, safety, and efficacy of the products you test for your clients. It is essential that you understand your responsibility to operate in full compliance with CGMP, and to inform all of your customers of significant problems encountered during the testing of these drugs. Your clients (e.g., drug manufacturers, application sponsors), in turn, must provide you with all of the scientific data and information needed to support reliable method implementation.
- You and your customer, **(b)(4)**, have a quality agreement specifying the testing method that must be used for your drug product. Your firm failed to follow the procedure set forth in your quality agreement regarding the use of the United States Pharmacopeia for drug component testing. You also failed to obtain prior approval from your customer before changing the test method, as required in your quality agreement.

REFERENCES

1. FDA Guidance for Industry: Contract Manufacturing Arrangements for Drugs: Quality Agreements, November 2016.
2. FDA Guidance for Industry: Q10 Pharmaceutical Quality System, April 2009.
3. United States v. Dotterweich, 320 U.S. 277, 284 (1943).
4. United States v. Park, 421 U.S. 658, 672 (1975).

10 Buildings and Facilities

Robert Del Ciello

CONTENTS

§211.42 DESIGN AND CONSTRUCTION FEATURES

a. *Any building(s) used in the manufacture, processing, packing, or holding of a drug product shall be of suitable size, construction, and location to facilitate cleaning, maintenance, and proper operations.*

Regarding buildings and facilities, there are two major areas of concern: the external environment and the internal environment. The external environment must be amenable to the location of well-designed and constructed buildings. It is insufficient that the buildings in which the production operations are to occur are clean and orderly and are of suitable size and construction. If the land, air, or water resources that surround the plant offer the potential for water damage, infestation, or contamination of any type, the facilities are in jeopardy of being judged unsuitable.

Several professional resources and functions will be involved in site selection. These are likely to include legal, real estate, state and local government agencies, utility companies, engineers, and architects. These functions not only provide professional expertise but also are able to identify possible sources of financial incentives for building in specific geographical locations.

Pertinent consideration prior to purchase, construction, or alteration of existing facilities includes the following:

1. Adequate space for future expansion
2. Zoning laws to allow anticipated development while restricting undesirable developments in the vicinity
3. Availability of water (quality and quantity), power, fuel, sewage, and waste-stream removal
4. Accessibility for employees (availability of public transportation), materials, and visitors (customers and suppliers)
5. Environmental issues such as site history; soil, water, and air quality; and geological and topological issues (potential for flooding, earthquakes, and foundation instability)

6. Proximity of undesirable activities—such as other industries, disposal sites, or open mining—that are likely to pollute or act as a source of vermin, insects, odor, or microorganisms
7. Availability of a suitable labor force (people, skills, wage expectations, labor relations and attitudes, and access to further education sources)
8. Ability to provide adequate security arrangements
9. Proximity or accessibility to interrelated operations of the company—research and development (R&D), marketing, and internally produced intermediates or components
10. Political situation—government stability, trade policies and taxation (for foreign-based operations), and financial incentives

Having identified a suitable location for the facility, the site-development plan is prepared and will include:

1. Compliance with appropriate laws and regulations and any additional company standards
2. Site resources and infrastructure, such as amenities, green spaces, parking for employees and visitors' vehicles and delivery and distribution vehicles, road and rail access, recreation areas, site utilities, tank farms and other external storage, and protection of wetlands and other restricted environments
3. Storm water and waste management
4. Site security and access—fences, guard posts, and cameras
5. Buildings—siting, layout, usage, function interrelationships for efficiency, possible expansion, and surface finishes
6. Utilities—design, layout, and backup (especially for critical utilities as electricity and nitrogen for some chemical operations)
7. Equipment—design, layout, spares, and capacity
8. Traffic flow—pedestrian arid vehicular (internal and external)
9. Safety—for personnel and equipment, containment for hazardous materials, sprinkler system, emergency egress, and emergency services access
10. External architecture to take into account local environmental conditions (wind, snow, and humidity) and aesthetic appearance blending with the local atmosphere, comparative image, and functionality
11. Ease of maintenance—accessibility to services (service ducts), ease of cleaning, and access for equipment
12. Selection and use of experienced contractors
13. Identification of project management responsibility
14. Validation plans and an effective change control procedure. Provision of design and "as-built" drawings
15. Construction materials
   The choices of materials of construction for manufacturing facilities are numerous. Some examples are presented subsequently. It is important, when choosing a material, to keep in mind the characteristics of the manufacturing process. Parenteral manufacturing operations have different requirements than oral-dosage manufacturing operations. Similarly, biotech and vaccine manufacturing operation requirements can differ. It is imperative that these requirements be considered when specifying wall, floor and ceiling construction, and finishes. The ISPE Guides provide guidance on these choices (refer to Suggested Readings).
   a. *Walls.* The position of the walls should provide an orderly movement of production and waste materials, personnel, and should take into account noise levels to provide acceptable working conditions. The interrelationship of different operations should minimize the potential for cross-contamination and component mix-up during storage and interdepartmental shipping.

Walls in manufacturing areas, corridors, and packaging areas should be of plaster finish on high-quality concrete blocks or gypsum board. The finish should be smooth, usually with enamel or epoxy paint.

Prefabricated partitions may be used in packaging areas where flexibility of layout is important. Prefabricated units have also been used in other areas, including sterile suites where panel joints must be given particular attention. Where possible, walls should be flush and projections should be avoided if possible. Wall penetrations and protrusions are to be properly sealed and minimized.

b. *Floors.* Floor covering should be selected for durability as well as for cleanability and resistance to the chemicals with which it is likely to come into contact.

    i. Terrazzo provides a hard-wearing finish; both tiles and poured-in-place finishes are available. The latter is preferable for manufacturing areas; if tiles are used, care must be taken to ensure effective sealing between the tiles, which, otherwise, could become a harboring area of dirt and microorganisms.

    ii. Usually, ceramic and vinyl tiles are not recommended for production areas. However, if used, the between-tile sealing should be flush and complete.

    iii. Welded vinyl sheeting provides an even, easy-to-clean surface. This is not practical for heavy traffic areas but can be of value in production areas, especially for parenteral and biotech products. Here, the lack of joints improves the ease of cleaning and sanitation.

    iv. Epoxy flooring provides a durable and readily cleanable surface. However, the subsurface finish is extremely important.

c. *Ceilings.* Suspended ceilings may be provided in office areas, laboratories, toilets, and cafeterias. They usually consist of lay-in acoustical panels of nonbrittle, nonfriable, nonasbestos, and noncombustible material.

    Manufacturing areas require a smooth finish, often of seamless plaster or gypsum board. All ceiling fixtures, such as light fittings, air outlets and returns, communication system, and sprinkler heads should be designed to assure ease of cleaning and to minimize the potential for accumulation of dust.

d. *Services.* In the building design, provisions must be made for drains, water, steam, electricity, and other services to allow for ease of maintenance. Access should, ideally, be possible without disruption of activity within the actual rooms provided with the services. A common practice is to have a utility are adjacent to the manufacturing space. In this manner, maintenance type operations can be conducted without affecting the environment within the controlled manufacturing space.

b. *Any such building shall have adequate space for the orderly placement of equipment and materials to prevent mix-ups between different components, drug product containers, closures, labeling, in-process materials, or drug products and to prevent contamination. The flow of components, drug product containers, closures, labeling, in-process materials, and drug products through the building(s) shall be designed to prevent contamination.*

The requirements of this section involve the design and layout of the facility, which must minimize the possibility of mix-ups or contamination. Sufficient space must be provided to allow adequate separation of adjacent equipment and operations. An example of this includes the spatial separation of packaging lines so that packaging components, bulk product, and finished product cannot intermix between lines and that dust or spillage from one line cannot result in the contamination of adjacent equipment. For example, a common practice is to introduce a physical barrier between the packaging lines. This need not be a permanent wall; a moveable partition serves the purpose.

The layout of the manufacturing and support operations must account for efficient material, personnel, and equipment flow patterns. Adequate access control is required to restrict entrance to manufacturing areas. The most efficient and compliant flow pattern is the one that provides for unidirectional flow. This methodology minimizes backtracking and thus the potential for cross-contamination and mix-ups during all manufacturing and support (cleaning) operations. The separation of visitor and employee entrances to the manufacturing building should be considered. Visitor entrances to the manufacturing and support areas should be minimized and restricted to a single point.

c. *Operations shall be performed within specifically defined areas of adequate size. There shall be separate or defined areas or other such control systems for the firm's operations as are necessary to prevent contamination or mix-ups during the course of the following procedures:*
   1. *receipt, identification, storage, and withholding from the use of components, drug product containers, closures, and labeling, pending the appropriate sampling, testing, or examination by the quality control unit before release for manufacturing or packaging*
   2. *holding rejected components, drug product containers, closures, and labeling before disposition*
   3. *storage of released components, drug product containers, closures, and labeling*
   4. *storage of in-process materials*
   5. *manufacturing and processing operations*
   6. *packaging and labeling operations*
   7. *quarantine storage before release of drug products*
   8. *storage of drug products after release*
   9. *control and laboratory operations*

This subsection has, on occasion, been interpreted to mean that separate discrete areas must be provided for each of the listed operations. Although there is no dispute with respect to (5), (6), and (9), the other areas are more controversial. However, in the preamble to the regulations, it is specifically stated that "separate or defined is not intended necessarily to mean a separate room or partitioned area, if other controls are adequate to prevent mix-ups and contamination." The Federal Register of February 12, 1991 (56 FR 5671) proposed the inclusion of "as necessary" to qualify the requirement for separate or defined areas. This was to clearly indicate that separate rooms or partitioned areas are not necessary if other controls exist to prevent mix-ups or contamination. This clarification is also present in the preamble to the 1978 final rule. The intent has now been confirmed in the revision (effective February 21, 1995) that added the words "or other control systems." Facilities and equipment should be designed and operated to minimize the potential for mix-ups or contamination. Where there is reliance on systems, paper, or computer, it must be demonstrated that such systems are effective and followed. As with all key systems, employees must be fully trained in their use, and routine audits should be performed. Systems control of storage, flow of materials, and product, may be more effective than physical separation and is certainly more efficient with respect to space utilization and materials handling. Physical movement of materials into and out of quarantine, for example, not only adds cost but, by adding another action, actually increases the potential for error. The further sophistication of barcoding materials throughout the various plant operations and linking this into a computer materials handling procedure greatly minimize the chance of unreleased or substandard materials being used inadvertently.

Some companies have found segregation using flexible physical areas to be a satisfactory alternative. For example, in a warehouse, a quarantine area can be designated around the goods simply by roping off the quarantine goods or by placing floor markings. This arrangement allows easy expansion or contraction of the area to meet changing volumes.

It should be noted, however, that even physical separation will be ineffective in preventing mix-ups and contamination, unless accompanied by adequate support procedures and training of personnel.

Although segregation of materials by systems is acceptable, appropriate specific storage conditions, such as low temperature or controlled humidity, must be provided. Receiving areas, where materials are unloaded from delivery transportation, are an access point for airborne contamination, such as dirt, dust, insects, vermin, birds, and even engine fumes, from the delivery vehicles themselves. Where possible, these access points should be protected by flexible curtains to minimize the gap between the truck and the physical facility to the outside when vehicles are unloading; air curtains between the receiving bays and the warehouse proper may also be used to provide additional protection to the warehouse environment. Insect and rodent traps are commonly required.

Sampling, particularly of chemical components, requires separate comment. When containers of components are opened for sampling purposes, the contents are exposed, albeit for short periods, to ambient conditions. It should be demonstrated that normal warehouse conditions do not expose the materials to unacceptable contamination from other components, particulate matter, or microorganisms. Otherwise, separate facilities will need to be provided for sampling. This is addressed in Section 211.80(b).

Traditionally, most warehouses for components and finished products have been operated under ambient conditions. Generally, this has been adequate since most pharmaceutical products are sufficiently stable under such conditions, and stability data are available to support defined shelf lives. The prevailing conditions in a warehouse must be monitored, and any particularly sensitive products or components should be provided appropriate environments. For relatively stable products, it has been a common practice to omit any specific storage conditions on the labeling; it was then assumed that the United States Pharmacopeia (USP) conditions of "room temperature" applied. Recently, some sections of the Food and Drug Administration (FDA) have been insisting that in order to obtain approval for new products, defined storage conditions must be stated on the labeling of all products. This has been further complicated by the revision to the USP definition of Controlled Room Temperature, from 15°C to 30°C to "A temperature maintained thermostatically that encompasses the usual and customary working environment of 20°C–25°C (68°F to 77°F); that results in a mean kinetic temperature calculated to be not more than 25°C and that allows for excursions between 15°C and 30°C (59°F and 86°F) that are experienced in pharmacies, hospitals and warehouses. Articles maybe labeled for storage at 'controlled room temperature' or at 'up to 25°C' or other wording based on the same mean kinetic temperature." Although it may seem relatively easy to calculate the mean kinetic temperature, in practice, this is not so simple. Products remain in facilities for differing lengths of time and it is possible, for example, that a batch of product stored in a warehouse for three summer months may be exposed to a higher mean kinetic temperature than if it were stored for three summer and three fall months. The impracticality of evaluating mean kinetic temperatures for the storage of individual batches is obvious, and it is hoped that a general calculation possibly based on average storage periods will be acceptable. This revised definition, which does not allow excursions above 30°C, is also resulting in many warehouses having to install air conditioning, at considerable expense, to control relatively brief exposure to higher temperatures in summer months.

The issue of labeling is still unresolved. It is considered that the use of the term "controlled room temperature" would be meaningless for certain areas of trade that are not aware of the USP. The more extensive wording of USP, Controlled Room Temperature, is too verbose for most labels and incomprehensible to many areas of the trade. Many companies have retained the old USP definition (15°C–30°C) on their labeling until this is resolved by the FDA.

The subject of stability studies is addressed in more detail in Section 211.66, and since the International Council for Harmonisation of Technical Requirements for Pharmaceuticals for Human Use (ICH) agreement, future stability studies will be performed at $25 \pm 2°C$.

The storage period for rejected materials awaiting destruction should be kept as short as possible. These materials take up valuable space, and there is always a risk that they may be inadvertently used. Even with the use of a validated storage procedure, it may be advisable to maintain physical segregation. FDA investigators have found reference to stored reject materials a useful way to identify production deviations.

Many FDA investigators consider that the presence of reject materials and products demonstrates failure with procedures and, consequently, is evidence of good manufacturing practice (GMP) violations. Rejections of materials could be due to inadequate definition/agreement of specifications, different test methodologies used by the supplier and the customer, nonvalidated analytical methods, nonvalidated production procedures at the supplier resulting in variable quality, use of untrained analysts, or expected data variability around a specification limit. For products, many of the same potential causes apply plus noncompliance with procedures. Frequently an investigator will consider product rejection evidence of an inadequately validated process. Obviously, the cause of any rejection does need to be thoroughly investigated and appropriate corrective action taken and documented.

The degree of separation of individual manufacturing and processing operations will be dependent on the nature of these operations. Raw materials are usually dispensed in an area specifically designed to minimize the potential for mix-ups and cross-contamination. Scales are separated by partitions and supplied with dust extraction and sometimes unidirectional airflow. Where a manufacturing process requires several different pieces of equipment (e.g., blender, granulator, and dryer), these may all be contained in one room or suite of rooms. Processes for different products should use completely segregated facilities. Where this is not possible, adequate physical separation should be maintained along with documented evidence to demonstrate the adequacy of the arrangement. This evidence could include data from the analysis of air samples, which confirms that the potential for cross-contamination is negligible. However, where such arrangements are necessary, it would be advisable to provide separate facilities for any particularly potent or sensitive products or manufacture in campaigns.

Packaging and labeling operations are usually kept separate from manufacturing. Even when a highly automated process is used, and packaging immediately follows manufacturing, the packaging is usually performed in an adjacent area.

The need to provide physical barriers between packaging lines has already been mentioned. Particular attention needs to be paid to the online storage of bulk product, labeling, and filled but unlabeled containers. During packaging operations, it is not uncommon for individual pieces of line equipment to break down. Under these circumstances, it may be economically viable to continue the operation and to accumulate part-packaged product until the effective unit is repaired. When the labeling unit breaks down, special care must be taken to ensure that unlabeled containers do not get onto another line, or even intermixed with a different batch of the same product. Where possible, accumulation tables should be an integral part of a packaging line, thereby enabling short downtimes on equipment to be handled without the need to remove part-packaged product from the line. Protracted breakdown of labeling equipment may, on occasion, result in amounts of unlabeled product in excess of the capacity of accumulation tables. Also, some processes are designed to produce filled unlabeled product. This includes sterile products such as syringes, and vials, which are labeled outside of the sterile suite. Obviously, in such situations, great care must be taken to prevent mix-ups. When labeling is to be performed later, security can be enhanced by holding the unlabeled product in sealed or locked containers (see also Chapter 17).

The requirement of separate areas for control and laboratory operations does not preclude the use of in-process testing within the manufacturing and packaging areas. However, the environmental conditions in these areas must be suitable for the proper operation of the testing equipment and performance of the test. In some instances, it may be necessary to site in-process test equipment in designated areas or rooms within the manufacturing or packaging facilities.

10. *Aseptic processing, which includes as appropriate:*
   i. *floors, walls, and ceilings of smooth, hard surfaces that are easily cleanable*
   ii. *temperature and humidity controls*
   iii. *an air supply filtered through high-efficiency particulate air (HEPA) filters under positive pressure, regardless of whether flow is laminar or nonlaminar*
   iv. *a system for monitoring environmental conditions*
   v. *a system for cleaning and disinfecting the room and equipment to produce aseptic conditions*
   vi. *a system for maintaining any equipment used to control the aseptic conditions*

This subsection emphasizes the special requirements associated with aseptic processing. Some companies also apply aseptic processing techniques during the production of terminally sterilized products. In these cases, compliance with the regulations is not mandatory, although it does make good business sense. The absence of a terminal sterilization process and the relative ineffectiveness of end product sterility testing place a critical reliance on the environmental conditions associated with aseptic processing. Recognizing the importance of aseptic processing in the production of injections, the FDA issued a "Guideline on Sterile Drug Products Produced by Aseptic Processing—Current Good Manufacturing Practice" in 1987, revised in 2004, With respect to facilities, the guide provides guidance on air quality, airflow, pressure differentials, and layout. There is no information on surface finishes.

Floors, walls, and ceilings in sterile suites are subject to intensive and frequent cleaning and sanitization; they must be composed of smooth, hard surfaces with a minimum of joints. Additionally, they should be resistant to abrasion, not shed particles, free from holes, crevices, and cracks, sufficiently flexible to accommodate building normal structural movement, and impervious to water and cleaning and sanitization solutions. Regular examinations should be performed to identify and repair any cracks in the surfaces or around service fittings and windows. Critical rooms, such as those for filling of final containers, should preferably have windows to allow supervision without the necessity for access. All service fittings should be flush with surrounding surfaces for ease of cleaning and sanitization.

Temperature and humidity need to be controlled primarily for the comfort of operators. The gowning requirements to minimize the potential for microbial contamination from operators are rather stringent and can easily cause personal discomfort, which could, in turn, adversely impact the aseptic processing. Conditions in the order of 68°F and 45% relative humidity have been found to be suitable.

The most critical factor in aseptic processing is the microbial and nonviable particulate condition of the air. This air is provided by way of high-HEPA filters, and the quality of the air is adjusted to meet the varying needs of the different processing areas. The requirements of the environment in these areas vary slightly between the FDA and European Union (EU) regulations. It is important to understand these requirements and the differences between these regulations. It is recommended that one refers to the ISPE Guide on Sterile Manufacturing Facilities.

Such heavy emphasis on air quality necessitates appropriate systems and procedures for monitoring. This will include evaluation of pressure differentials between rooms, particulate levels (viable and nonviable), and also temperature and humidity.

Air-pressure differentials should be monitored automatically, documented, and audible or visual warning alarms are an added advantage. The number of rooms interlinked in a sterile suite makes the balancing of air-pressure differentials very difficult. Movement of people and materials, involving opening and closing of doors, adds to the complexity. Computer control can provide a more rapid response to these changing conditions. HEPA filters must be tested at regular intervals for the presence of leaks; such leaks would also be likely to affect pressure differentials. Particulate levels are usually monitored during each work shift or part shift when operators leave and return; air-sampling devices are most commonly used since they do provide a quantitative measure of the volume of air sampled. However, for microbial evaluation, settle plates can also be of value since they provide a measure of the microbial impact over a more protracted period.

Cleaning and disinfection of aseptic facilities and equipment are of obvious importance, especially in the critical areas. Procedures must be validated with respect to both removal of previous product and to demonstrate effective disinfection. Residual amounts of any cleaning or disinfectant agents should be at an acceptably low level. In order to minimize the possibility of microbial resistance, the disinfectant should be changed periodically. After cleaning and disinfecting, rooms and equipment must be maintained in such a manner that these conditions are not impaired.

For certain pieces of equipment, a "clean-in-place" procedure is most effective. This is particularly valuable with tanks and pipelines where access or dismantling may be difficult. The procedure basically consists of applying sequential wash, sanitization, and flush cycles to the assembled equipment. Sanitization is often accomplished with high-pressure steam.

Having established suitable conditions for aseptic processing, it is necessary to have a defined maintenance program for equipment and facilities. In addition to the servicing of HVAC equipment and checking of ducts, filters, and service ports for leaks, the physical condition of walls, floors, and ceilings should be monitored. Slight shifts in building position, which are not uncommon, can result in cracks, which then need to be repaired.

The environmental conditions are essentially established by flushing the area with high-quality air. Any disruption in this flushing process will affect pressure differentials and possibly adversely affect the conditions. Consequently, the provision of auxiliary generating capacity to maintain essential air-handling equipment can be a valuable asset. This equipment should switch on automatically in the event of a power failure and will allow completion of ongoing sensitive operations and maintain the environment until normal power is restored. Where such auxiliary power is not available, aseptic operations should cease immediately if there is a power failure, and restarting will not be possible until the reestablishment of the defined condition has been confirmed.

The industry is utilizing barrier technology systems as a means of enhancing levels of sterility assurance and, for new facilities, reducing costs. Two main variations exist: barrier isolation systems, which protect the product from the operators and the external environment, and barrier containment, which additionally protects the operator from the product. Barrier containment is frequently used when handling high hazard or cytotoxic agents. Both systems contain the aseptic operating environment within a closed system with no direct access to operators. Access is via glove ports with sterilized components being fed directly from a sterilizing/depyrogenizing tunnel or after batch processing via a rapid transfer port. Clean and sterilize in place procedures are required.

The space required to be maintained at a Class 100 (Class A) level is significantly less than that for traditional aseptic rooms, and this can have important cost implications. The overall facility can be smaller, the Class 100 (Class A) space costs less than one-quarter the cost of clean space, and gowning areas can be eliminated. Additional benefits include more consistent assurance of sterility since the microbial and nonviable particulate content of the processing environment is constant—no operator involvement and more comfortable working conditions for employees. The actual level of sterility assurance should be greatly enhanced, possibly from 1×10^{-3} to 10^{-5} or 10^{-6}.

    d. *Operations relating to the manufacture, processing, and packing of penicillin shall be performed in facilities separate from those used for other drug products for human use.*

This is the first of several portions of the regulations that pertain specifically to the production of products containing penicillin (see also Sections 211.46[d] and 211.176).

    The industry has taken the steps to have completely separate manufacturing facilities, and usually manufacturing sites, for these types of products rather than attempt to separate these operations in the same building. This is due to the fact that it has been almost impossible to prevent the migration of penicillin products throughout the building.

§211.44 LIGHTING

Adequate lighting shall be provided in all areas.

    In order to meet lighting requirements, it is necessary for the manufacturer to define the term "adequate." It is defined as the amount of light (lux or foot-candles) reaching the working surface for each area involved in the production of pharmaceuticals. Public standards exist for some types of work. Normally, a range of 30–50 foot-candles ensure worker comfort and ability to perform efficiently and effectively; however, 100 foot-candles may be needed in some areas, as well as special lighting for some operations, such as inspection of filled vials. Once the light levels have been defined, it is necessary that they be measured periodically and the results recorded. The specifications should call either for replacement of light sources when some level above the established minimum has been reached or, alternatively, routine replacements of light sources on some schedule that has been shown adequate to ensure that light levels do not drop below the established minimum.

§211.46 VENTILATION, AIR FILTRATION, AIR HEATING, AND COOLING

    a. *Adequate ventilation shall be provided.*
    b. *Equipment for adequate control over air pressure, microorganisms, dust, humidity, and temperature shall be provided when appropriate for the manufacture, processing, packing, or holding of a drug product.*
    c. *Air filtration systems, including prefilters and particulate matter air filters, shall be used, when appropriate, on air supplies to production areas. If air is recirculated to production areas, measures shall be taken to control recirculation of dust from production. In areas where air contamination occurs during production, there shall be adequate exhaust systems or other systems adequate to control contaminants.*
    d. *Air-handling systems for the manufacture, processing, and packing of penicillin shall be completely separate from those for other drug products for human use.*

The regulations provide minimal guidance by stating that ventilation should be adequate. It is then up to the producer to demonstrate adequacy with respect to the operations being performed. The conditions necessary for aseptic processing have already been described (Section 211.42[c][10]).

    Air-handling systems should consider the following factors.

    1. Placement of air inlet and outlet ports. These should be sited to minimize the entry of airborne particulates or odors from the surrounding areas. Outlets should not be sited near inlets.

2. Where recirculation of air is acceptable, adequate precautions must be taken to ensure that particulates from a processing area are removed. This will usually require an alarm system or an automatic cutoff in the event that a filter develops a hole. Dust extraction systems should be provided, where appropriate, to further minimize this potential problem.
3. The degree of filtration and the air volumes should be based on the operations involved. Specific product manufacturing process requirements are to be addressed in the design.
4. Temperature and humidity conditions should provide personnel comfort, which will enhance employee performance.
5. Where differential pressures are required between adjacent areas, suitable monitoring equipment must be provided. For example, solids manufacturing areas are usually maintained at a negative pressure in relation to adjacent rooms and corridors in order to minimize the possibility of dust migration to these other areas. As indicated, specific product manufacturing process requirements are to be incorporated into the design.
6. The siting of final air filters close to each room being serviced eliminates concerns regarding the possibility of small leaks in the air duct system. Air usually enters rooms near the ceiling and leaves from the opposite side near the floor.

As with all systems, operating requirements should be defined and monitored at appropriate frequency to ensure compliance. If conditions are shown to have fallen below the required standards, it may be necessary to more thoroughly evaluate any products that were produced during the period in question.

It is important to monitor filters to ensure proper operation. After initial mounting and testing with a smoke generator of defined particle size range, the use of a differential manometer to monitor pressure drop across the filter gives warning of both breaks in the filter and buildup of retained particulates necessitating filter replacements. A specification of maximum permissible pressure drop before replacement should be defined.

As indicated previously for sterile areas, computer control of HVAC systems is more likely to allow the delicate balancing of the various air pressures, airflows, temperatures, and humidity. When this is expanded to the entire plant systems, the computer control can additionally optimize energy utilization, thereby reducing costs.

The regulations also make specific reference to the handling of penicillin products (211.46[d]). Not only shall such operations be performed in separate facilities from those for other drug products for human use (211.42[d]), but they must also have separate air-handling systems.

§211.48 PLUMBING

a. *Potable water shall be supplied under continuous positive pressure in a plumbing system free of defects that could contribute contamination to any drug product. Potable water shall meet the standards prescribed in the Environmental Protection Agency's (EPA's) Primary Drinking Water Regulations set forth in 40 CFR Part 141. Water not meeting such standards shall not be permitted in the potable water system.*
b. *Drains shall be of adequate size and, where connected directly to a sewer, shall be provided with an air break or other mechanical device to prevent back-siphonage.*

The Public Health Service Drinking Water Standards are administered by the EPA. The standard is somewhat variable in that the frequency of examination of the water is dependent on the size of the population served. This leads to some uncertainty in water quality if potable water becomes part of a pharmaceutical product. This problem does not arise for products of the official compendia (USP and National Formulary), for which purified water is always required. The text of the drinking water standards is found in 40 CFR 141.

The FDA usually will not inquire into whether the potable water does meet the standard, if the manufacturer connects the potable waterline to a public supply that meets the standard. A quality control problem arises, however, in that the public supply ensures the quality only to the edge of the manufacturer's property, and even then tests, usually, only at the central reservoir. The water can lose quality in transmission through the public piping system and, of course, through the manufacturer's system. The prudent manufacturer will test potable water periodically. If potable water is obtained from wells under the control of the manufacturer, periodic testing is mandatory.

Drains, particularly those in production areas, can be a potential source of microbial hazard. The requirement to include an air break between drain and sewer is an attempt to minimize this by eliminating the chance of back-siphonage. Drains should also be regularly disinfected.

§211.50 SEWAGE AND REFUSE

Sewage, trash, and other refuse in and from the building and immediate premises shall be disposed of in a safe and sanitary manner.

A pharmaceutical plant may consider disposal in several different ways.

1. *Product Disposal.* Any product requiring disposal should initially be separated from its packaging if appropriate. For example, any product to be disposed of in an approved landfill site should not be left in impermeable glass, plastic, or other containers, which would significantly delay destruction. There are risks associated with the destruction of products—potential for the product to get diverted, legitimately or otherwise, during the disposal sequence and contamination of groundwater. Disposal procedures should involve agents with a proven record of dealing with such sensitive materials or the use of company personnel to accompany the material from plant to disposal. Ideally, incineration procedures have preference over landfill. Where incineration is used, product in plastic or other flammable packaging may not need to be returned to bulk.
2. *Printed Packaging Disposal.* The disposal of printed packaging components including labels, inserts, and cartons poses no health risk. However, ineffective disposal, such as into public landfill, can give rise to public concern that product may be associated with the packaging. Such materials should preferably be incinerated.
3. *General Trash and Sewage.* Normal local services will usually be adequate for trash and sewage. However, internal procedures should be sufficiently rigorous and monitored, to ensure that product and packaging waste do not get intermixed. Containers used within the plant to accumulate waste materials should be clearly marked to denote their designated use.

§211.52 WASHING AND TOILET FACILITIES

Adequate washing facilities shall be provided, including hot and cold water, soap or detergent, air driers or single-service towels, and clean toilet facilities easily accessible to working areas.

In addition to GMP regulations, Occupational Safety and Health Administration regulations impact on washing and toilet facilities (see 29 CFR 1019.141). These require toilet rooms to be separate for each sex except where individual locked toilet rooms are available and also define the minimum number of water closets based on the number of users. The legal requirements of GMPs specify minimum facilities for personnel. Management concern with employee morale and extra measures to ensure minimum probability of contamination suggest additional emphasis and activities.

1. Eating facilities:
   a. Eating and drinking are permitted only in separate eating facilities, well segregated from all production areas (see also 29 CFR 1910.141[s][g][2]). Smoking is now usually prohibited in the manufacturing building due to cultural changes concerning health issues.
   b. Prominent signs indicating these rules are posted at entrances to production areas.
   c. Enforcement procedures against violators are taken by management.
   d. Permanent facilities for breaks and people bringing lunches are required. Cafeterias serving hot meals are ideal to reduce the amount of food, a potential contamination source, being brought into the plant.
2. For production and materials processing areas:
   a. Drinking, eating, smoking, tobacco chewing, and expectoration are prohibited.
   b. Tissues and closed disposal containers are readily available.
3. Lavatories and lockers:
   a. Adequate in number for the number of personnel employed.
   b. Conveniently located at all areas.
   c. Hot shower facilities are provided (see also 29 CFR 1910.141-[s][d][d]).
   d. Disinfectant soaps are utilized.
   e. Adequate ash and waste receptacles are provided.
   f. Periodic cleaning of the area during each shift with logging of times and conditions is mandatory.
   g. Complete cleaning with cleansing and disinfectant agents daily. Follow-up inspection by supervisory personnel is logged.
   h. Specific rest areas for female employees are provided.
   i. Eating and drinking are not permitted. Foods and beverages for meals and breaks may be stored only in lockers and then removed to a separate eating area.
   j. Areas separated from all aseptic spaces by an air lock.

§211.56 SANITATION

a. *Any building used in the manufacture, processing, packing, or holding of a drug product shall be maintained in a clean and sanitary condition. Any such building shall be free of infestation by rodents, birds, insects, and other vermin (other than laboratory animals). Trash and organic waste matter shall be held and disposed of in a timely and sanitary manner.*

b. *There shall be written procedures assigning responsibility for sanitation and describing in sufficient detail the cleaning schedules, methods, equipment, and materials to be used in cleaning the buildings and facilities; such written procedures shall be followed.*

c. *There shall be written procedures for the use of suitable rodenticides, insecticides, fungicides, fumigating agents, and cleaning and sanitizing agents. Such written procedures shall be designed to prevent the contamination of equipment, components, drug product containers, closures, packaging, labeling materials, or drug products and shall be followed. Rodenticides, insecticides, and fungicides shall not be used unless registered and used in accordance with the Federal Insecticide, Fungicide, and Rodenticide Act (7 USC 135).*

d. *Sanitation procedures shall apply to work performed by contractors or temporary employees as well as to work performed by full-time employees during the ordinary course of operations.*

This requirement relates to the availability of effective cleaning and sanitation programs and confirmation that they have been followed. No details are given, nor should they be, on how to achieve the desired conditions. Cleaning and sanitation programs should be adjusted to meet the specific needs of each facility. In addition to the cleaning of floors, walls, and ceilings, there should be attention to dust extraction and air input systems. Ductwork, especially for dust extraction systems, can become a potential explosion hazard if dust is allowed to accumulate.

Cleaning procedures should be written in sufficient detail, with respect to materials, equipment, process, and frequency, such that they are unambiguous. Where appropriate, data should be accumulated to confirm the adequacy of the cleaning procedure.

The total elimination of rodents, birds, and insects is virtually impossible and the regulations do refer to freedom from "infestation." The use of rodenticides, fungicides, fumigating agents, and other techniques should be combined with good hygienic practices. Spilled materials, such as sugar, that might attract creatures should immediately be eliminated. Holes in buildings that could provide additional means of access should be blocked.

Where traps and other lethal techniques are used, there should be frequent examination and removal of "corpses," which could in time become a source of further contamination. If these traps consistently yield results, attempts should be made to identify and eliminate the source of the problem.

Frequently, rodenticides and other treatments are contracted out. As with any contracted service, the company must assure that the procedures used are viable, achieve the desired results, and that they are followed.

§211.58 MAINTENANCE

Any building used in the manufacture, processing, packing, or holding of a drug product shall be maintained in a good state of repair.

Deterioration of buildings not only presents a poor image of the facility but can also impact product quality. Cracks and holes in walls, floors, or ceilings can provide access for insects, rodents, birds, dirt, or microorganisms. They can also hinder cleaning and sanitation, thereby increasing the potential for cross-contamination or microbial multiplication. Floor cracks can also become a safety hazard for people or even dislodge materials from trucks.

The ingress of water from roof leaks can cause significant damage to materials and equipment, give rise to electrical failures and fires, and result in damage to the basic structure of the building. Additionally, holes in the roof or near the tops of buildings provide ready access to birds, which may then be encouraged to nest within the building.

BUILDINGS AND FACILITIES

Damage to insulation or pipes and ductwork will detract from the basic purpose of such insulation. It may also result in freezing and eventual leakage of pipes and in the shedding of insulation material into product and equipment.

Light fittings need regular cleaning to remove any accumulated dust, which can act both as a potential source of contamination and reduce light intensity.

Where the proper correction of building deficiencies requires shutdown of the area, it may be necessary to resort to temporary repair until adequate time can be made to enact a permanent repair. Building inspection and maintenance programs should be defined in writing and a record kept confirming compliance and referencing any repairs performed.

This regulation specifically refers to buildings, whereas Section 211.67 relates to equipment. This appears to ignore the maintenance of services, some of which are included in other sections of Subpart C, but without reference to maintenance. Clearly, services can impact directly on processing and product quality, and they must undergo routine maintenance. Essential services will include HVAC, water (all types), steam, vacuum, compressed air and other gases, electricity, dust extraction, product/material pipelines, drainage, and sprinkler system.

GENERAL OBSERVATIONS

Building new or renovating present pharmaceutical or related manufacturing facilities represents challenges that require special expertise. A number of architectural and engineering firms take on the majority of such projects. They should be selected with great care, and ongoing review of the project, by the internal team, should be the rule.

The firm should be selected based on the firm's experience with the type of project (manufacturing, laboratory, warehouse, etc.) as well as the experience of the individual team members being proposed by the firm. The firm's project manager will usually be supported by a project architect, project mechanical services engineer, project electrical engineer, project structural engineer, project civil engineer, and project landscape architect on a large project.

Every project starts out with the objective of being a successful endeavor. However, the owner should be prepared for negative experiences. Some of the typical issues include "unbalanced" air systems, undersized exhaust fans, problems with heat exchangers, insufficient light levels, pressure monitoring problems, seal dampers not meeting specifications, inadequate roof or room drains, condensate problems, undersized electrical systems, improper laminar flow hoods, flawed water supply, and inadequate geologic surveys.

Obviously, close supervision must be accomplished by knowledgeable employees and agents of the owner. Otherwise, the requisite expansion may become a large drain swollen by lost time and financial resources. In addition, of course, failures in planning, equipment, and personnel burdened by these events may result in the following FDA citations:

EXAMPLES OF OBSERVATIONS FROM FDA CITATIONS

- "The sterility test room was not designed and constructed to facilitate cleaning and disinfection."
- "The HVAC and dust collection systems are not validated."
- "The direction of airflow is not monitored in the manufacturing rooms."
- "There are no approved procedures for maintaining the HVAC and dust control systems throughout the plant."
- "The WFI system is not designed in a manner to minimize microbial contamination and endotoxin load. For example, in the past year, there have been 10 incidents of WFI samples that exceeded specifications for microbial contamination."
- "The written procedures covering pest control within the buildings are not signed or dated by the personnel who prepared and authorized them."
- "Inspection of the reverse osmosis water system revealed dead legs, which are potential sites for microorganisms to lodge, multiply, and enter the effluent."
- "There are no temperature or humidity specifications for the area."
- "Sensors for monitoring warehouse temperature have not been calibrated since their installation three years ago."
- "Air recirculated in the compressing area has never been tested for particulate matter. Validation of the air-handling system is inadequate—samples for cross-contamination were collected from only...cubicles in the compressing area."

SUGGESTED READINGS

- International Standard ISO 14644, Cleanrooms and Controlled Environments, latest revision.
- Mead WJ. Maintenance: Its interrelationship with drug quality. *Pharm Eng* 1987; 7:29–33.
- Fornalsaro T. Design and operation of a new sterile manufacturing facility. *Bull Parent Drug Assoc* 1970; 24:110.
- Goddard K. Designing a parenteral manufacturing facility. *Bull Parent Drug Assoc* 1969; 23:69.

- Loughhead H. Parenteral production under vertical laminar flow. *Bull Parent Drug Assoc* 1969; 23:17.
- FDA. Guideline on Sterile Drug Products Produced by Aseptic Processing. September 2004.
- Haas PJ. Engineering design considerations for barrier isolation technology. *Pharm Technol* 1995; 19(2):26.
- Wintner B, Divelbiss JD. Isolator evaluation using computer modeling. Part I. Airflow within the minienvironment. *Pharm Eng* 1994; 14(6):8.
- Divelbiss J, Wintner B. Isolator evaluation using computer modeling. Part II. Hydrogen peroxide sterilization with two diluent fluids. *Pharm Eng* 1995; 15(2):84.
- Melgaard HL. Barrier isolation design issues. *Pharm Eng* 1995; 14(6):24.
- Blanchard JA, Signore AA. Cost effective CGMP facilities. *Pharm Eng* 1995; 15(2):44.
- Brader WR, Hsu PT, Lorenz BJ. Impact of implementing barrier technology on existing aseptic fill facilities. *Pharm Eng* 1995; 15(2):30.
- Collentro WV. USP purified water and water for injection storage systems and accessories, Part I. *Pharm Technol* 1995; 19(3):78.
- Stark S, Vichl S. Laboratory facility renovations: 15 considerations that can't be ignored. *Pharm Eng* 1995; 15(1):28.
- Collentro WV. USP purified water systems: Discussion of ion exchange. Part II. *Pharm Technol* 1994; 18(10):56.
- Wood JP. *Containment in the Pharmaceutical Industry*. Marcel Dekker, New York, 2001.
- Avis KA, Liebermann HA, Lachman L. *Pharmaceutical Dosage Forms*, Vols 1–3. Marcel Dekker, New York, 1993.
- DeSpautz JF. *Automation and Validation of Information in Pharmaceutical Processing*. Marcel Dekker, New York, 1998.
- Signore AA, Jacobs T. *Good Design Practices for GMP Pharmaceutical Facilities*. Marcel Dekker, New York, 2005.
- ISPE Baseline Guide: Active Pharmaceutical Ingredients, Vol. 1, ISPE
- ISPE Baseline Guide: Oral Solid Dosage Forms. Vol. 2, ISPE.
- ISPE Baseline Guide: Sterile Manufacturing Facilities. Vol. 3, ISPE.
- ISPE Baseline Guide: Water and Steam Systems. Vol. 4, ISPE.
- ISPE Baseline Guide: Commissioning and Qualification. Vol. 5, ISPE.
- ISPE Baseline Guide: Biopharmaceutical Manufacturing Facilities. Vol. 6, ISPE.
- ISPE Baseline Guide: Risk-Based Manufacturing of Pharmaceutical Products (Risk-MaPP), Vol. 7, ISPE.
- Designing a Facility with Both Good Manufacturing Practice (GMP) and Biosafety in Mind: Synergies and Conflicts; Vibeke Halkjaer-Knudsen; Applied Biosafety 2007.
- Designing GMP Manufacturing Areas, Eric Bohn, PharmTech, March 25, 2015.
- Chi YT, Chu PC, Chao HY, Shieh WC, and Chen CC. Design of CGMP production of 18F- and 68Ga-radiopharmaceuticals. BioMed Research International 2014; Research Article (8 pages), Article ID 680195, Volume 2014.
- GMP Facility Design, Construction, Commissioning and Qualification to Meet International Regulatory Expectations. March 14, 2014, Validation Technologies, Inc.
- Why Good Facility Design is Crucial for GMP Compliance, Richard Soltero, September 29, 2014, Nutritional Outlook.
- Commissioning and Qualification: A New ASTM Standard—GMP Regulations, Robert Chew and David Petko, Pharmaceutical Engineering, November/December, 2007.

11 Equipment

Robert Del Ciello and Joseph T. Busfield

CONTENTS

INTRODUCTION

The specification, design, qualification, and use of equipment in the various manufacturing processes have taken on more technology-driven characteristics since 2000. With the advent of a systems approach to compliance, the attributes of equipment that need integration with other quality systems have been emphasized. This has occurred in the areas of specification through a stronger integration with process validation, instrumentation having a stronger integration with the calibration/maintenance quality system, and embedded controls that enable continuous improvement programs. These programs have sprung from different points. The Food and Drug Administration (FDA) has initiated the Process Analytical Technology (PAT) program. This program's objectives encompass a thorough knowledge of the manufacturing process coupled with the appropriate instrumentation and controls that address the critical processing parameters (CPPs) in such a manner so as to allow improvements in the manufacturing process without significant regulatory filings.

The advent of an integrated commissioning and qualification approach to the start-up and qualification of new equipment has streamlined this entire process. The focus of this program is to test the equipment system according to procurement specifications during commissioning and then verify whether the equipment systems operate according to manufacturing process requirements for qualification. In some circumstances, additional qualification testing may not be conducted if the commissioning testing adequately demonstrates that the equipment supports the product manufacturing process critical quality attributes (CQAs). A risk-based approach to qualification testing has become mainstream. This is an outgrowth of the overall industry risk-based approach developed over the last 10 years.

The development of Good Automation Manufacturing Practice (GAMP) guidelines and calibration program guidelines has substantially transformed the process used, not only for the procurement and qualification of computer systems but also the entire system for the acquisition of equipment and systems.

§211.63 EQUIPMENT DESIGN, SIZE, AND LOCATION

Equipment used in the manufacture, processing, packing, or holding of a drug product shall be of appropriate design, adequate size, and suitably located to facilitate operations for its intended use and also for its cleaning and maintenance.

In order to properly specify equipment and systems, the pharmaceutical manufacturer needs to identify the manufacturing process. This requires that during the development of the product, the CQA of the product, and the associated CPPs that directly affect the attributes, be identified and the effect of the parameters on the attributes be understood. These requirements are to be included in a user requirements specification (URS) of the equipment/system. This specification is to focus only on the manufacturing requirements, for example, range of CPPs, sensitivity of the control system to maintain these parameters, and so on. The purpose of this focus is to ensure that the qualification testing is limited only to the equipment capabilities that are required to manufacture an effective product.

In the past it was common to have qualification testing address all equipment/system capabilities. However, this type of testing is normally addressed during the start-up and commissioning of the equipment/system. Only capabilities that affect the manufacturing characteristics are tested during qualification. Therefore, commissioning tests the equipment/system against the requirements of the purchased specification, whereas the qualification testing addresses those requirements included in the URS. As indicated above, in certain circumstances, the commissioning testing is leveraged or replaces the qualification testing.

An important tool used during the selection of equipment is to perform an impact assessment. The impact assessment provides a scientific rationale to the effect the equipment system has on the quality attributes of the product being manufactured. The assessment segregates equipment systems into a minimum of two categories: direct impact and no impact. This categorization enables the appropriate attention to be directed towards the specification, installation, and qualification of equipment systems. Some industry professionals also utilize an "indirect impact" category. With the advent of the risk-based approach, this category is slowly being phased out of the initial assessments.

Once the use of equipment system has been properly identified, several parameters are to be considered when evaluating the equipment:

1. Availability of *spares and servicing.*
2. The frequency and ease of *maintenance* will significantly impact on productivity and even quality. Equipment breakdown during processing could adversely affect quality. Included in the maintenance evaluation should be the cleanability of the equipment. This will involve accessibility to the parts to be cleaned and the relative ease of disassembly and reassembly.
3. *Environmental issues* are important constructions. Is the design of the equipment conducive to the application? Such attributes as the ability to contain toxic products, the ability to contain dust, the ability to maintain aseptic conditions, etc. need to be reviewed.
4. *Construction materials and design* (see §211.65 below).
5. The type of *process controls* such as automatic weight adjustment on tablet presses and temperature recorders on ovens. The use of these controls has become a routine and is expected in today's manufacturing environment. The PAT initiative depends upon these controls to demonstrate that the manufacturing process is under control and to facilitate a continuous improvement program. Many such systems are integrated into a sitewide process control computer of distributed control system. Such integration adds to the complexity

and validation required, but the benefit of being able to see and control all the aspects of a process from an integrated system will outweigh the added complexity and validation requirements.

New equipment should not be used for commercial production until it has been qualified and the process in which it is to be used has been validated; this applies equally to laboratory and other test equipment. All equipment should be appropriately identified with a unique number to allow reference in maintenance programs and in batch records (see also §211.105[a]).

The location of the equipment in the facility must enable an efficient flow of the manufacturing process. Manufacturing trains should be unidirectional whenever feasible. Backflow or crossflow within the process are to be minimized, as these incidences inherently have a high capability to cause mistakes.

The equipment system is to be placed in such a manner so as to enable all parts requiring maintenance, instrumentation, and calibration to be easily accessible. The key is easily accessible. Locating equipment in areas that are inaccessible usually means the maintenance and cleaning operations are not performed adequately, and thus leads to errors during the manufacturing of products.

§211.65 EQUIPMENT CONSTRUCTION

a. *Equipment shall be constructed such that the surfaces that come into contact with components, in-process materials, or drug products shall not be reactive, additive, or absorptive so as to alter the safety, identity, strength, quality, or purity of the drug product beyond the official or other established requirements.*

The pharmaceutical manufacturer is required to fully understand the manufacturing process and all its constituents. This subpart requires that all product contact surfaces be inert with regards to the active ingredients, excipients, and critical utilities, that is, water (USP or WFI), compressed gases, and so on. Traditionally, product contact surfaces are constructed of stainless steel (usually a 316 grade to facilitate cleaning), Teflon®, viton (or other inert elastomer), or other inert material. The choice of the material depends upon the unit operation within which the equipment will be placed. For example, for bulk chemical active pharmaceutical ingredients (API) operations, reaction/crystallization vessels can be constructed of stainless steel, hastelloy C, or glass for the chemical reactions to manipulate molecules and develop the active ingredient. For bulk biotech API operations, the equipment is usually constructed of 316L stainless steel for cleaning of proteins due to the inert nature of the stainless steel with respect to the biological processes. Formulation and filling operations, whether for parenteral, biotech, or oral dosage forms, have been and still are constructed from 316L stainless steel. Again, stainless steel is used primarily because of its inert nature as well as its ability to be cleaned and sterilized.

b. *Any substances required for operation, such as lubricants or coolants, shall not come into contact with components, drug product containers, closures, in-process materials, or drug products so as to alter the safety, identity, strength, quality, or purity of the drug product beyond the official or other established requirements.*

This requirement affects the design, construction, and placement of the manufacturing equipment. Motors, drive belts, gears, and other potential sources of lubricant contamination should be located away from equipment, vessel, or package openings that could result in product contamination. For the equipment where this is not possible, such as some mixers, tablet, and encapsulating machines, lubrication needs to be controlled and monitored. Lubricants are to be of good grade to minimize the impact of a contamination.

Gaskets and other connecting surfaces should be monitored to ensure that they do not break down, thereby allowing environmental contamination or gasket particles into the product.

§211.67 EQUIPMENT CLEANING AND MAINTENANCE

a. *Equipment and utensils shall be cleaned, maintained, and sanitized at appropriate intervals to prevent malfunctions or contamination that would alter the safety, identity, strength, quality, or purity of the drug product beyond the official or other established requirements.*

This subsection requires the establishment of a cleaning/sanitization program and a maintenance program, two separate and significant elements of the overall quality system. It is of interest to note that the regulation provides two rationales for the establishment of these programs—proper functioning of the equipment and the potential for cross contamination. Therefore, these concepts need to be at the core of each program.

Sections (b) and (c) go on to provide additional details of the content of the two programs.

b. *Written procedures shall be established and followed for cleaning and maintenance of equipment, including utensils used in the manufacture, processing, packing, or holding of a drug product. These procedures shall include, but are not necessarily limited to, the following:*
   1. *Assignment of responsibility for cleaning and maintaining equipment*
   2. *Maintenance and cleaning schedules, including appropriate sanitizing schedules wherever required*
   3. *A description in sufficient detail of the methods, equipment, and materials used in cleaning and maintenance operations, and the methods of disassembling and reassembling equipment as it is necessary to assure proper cleaning and maintenance*
   4. *Removal or obliteration of previous batch identification*
   5. *Protection of clean equipment from contamination prior to use*
   6. *Inspection of equipment for cleanliness immediately before use*
c. *Records shall be kept for maintenance, cleaning, sanitizing, and inspection as specified in §211.180 and §211.182.*

There are various quality system element processes that can be utilized in each of these programs. The details of each depend upon the products being manufactured, business approach utilized, and the preferences of the operating unit. No matter what the process is, each program needs to have distinct attributes.

CLEANING PROGRAM

The cleaning program requirements also need to be documented in standard operating procedures (SOPs). In addition, the cleaning processes are required to be validated. The cleaning program identified in this subpart refers to equipment and utensils used in the manufacturing process. It is of note that this subpart identifies utensils. Any utensil, such as scoop, used in a weighing operation or other processing step must also be part of the cleaning program. Many firms utilize disposable utensils. This has proven to be the most cost-effective approach to ensuring the cleanliness of utensils in certain cases. It is recommended that a review of both approaches be conducted to determine the best approach. Facility cleaning and sanitization is covered in subpart 211.56.

The cleaning program consists of two parts—the validation of the processes and detergents/sanitization agents and the day-to-day use of the validated processes and qualified detergents and sanitizers. Many cleaning processes are automated. These fall into two classes: clean in place (CIP) and clean out of place (COP). The CIP systems have their equipment provided with hard-piped services with cleaning solutions. The cleaning process is automated and usually is documented through a printout of the automation system. The COP systems consist of bringing the equipment to a cleaning station or placing the equipment in an automated washer. Again, the cleaning process is automatic with the appropriate documentation of the cleaning batch. CIP and COP cleaning processes are validated.

While the best cleaning systems involve automated process and/or washers, many cleaning processes are manual. The manual systems are executed by operators on a daily basis. Because of the variability of having operators execute the cleaning processes, these cleaning process cannot be truly validated in the same manner as the CIP or COP systems. Manual processes are usually qualified along with the qualification of the operators.

The following attributes are to be addressed in setting up a cleaning program:

1. An equipment and utensil list containing the product contact surfaces, their materials of construction.
2. Justification of sampling site locations based on which criteria—worst case, most difficult to clean, solubility of active, and so on. An important item to be addressed in providing the rationale for sampling sites is why certain other sites are not included.
3. Identification of operating cleaning procedures.
4. Rationale or justification for the cleaning agents selected. A list of approved cleaning agents, including the active ingredient or residual component tested, test method used, cleaning agent concentration, or effectiveness testing performed (to verify temperature, pressure, and time of working concentration, etc.) is to be identified.
5. Critical parameters to be monitored and controlled (i.e., wash and rinse temperatures, pressures, and times) for automated processes.
6. Validated analytical and microbial test method identified.
7. Scientific rationale rinse and swab sampling acceptance limits, including calculations, pre-established acceptance limits, with references.
8. For finished pharmaceutical dosage forms, the cleaning limit is based on allowing not more than a fraction of a therapeutic dose to be present in subsequent products. A scientific rationale or justification is to be developed for residual values.
9. Interferences are to be determined for the cleaning agent and product(s) test methods.
10. A scientific rationale that describes the worst-case challenge selection process is to be developed.
11. Scientific rationale describing the product/ingredient matrix.
12. Definition of hardest-to-clean areas is to be provided.
13. Swab selection criteria and rationale. Criteria used for swab selection including:
    a. extractables, minimal interferences with analytical method sensitivity-low carbon extracting swabs
    b. surface-cleaning ability—soluble and insoluble challenges
    c. abrasion resistance—ease of the sorptive material to be removed by surfaces
    d. solvent resistance
    e. sorption and retention properties
14. Cleaning agent selection criteria and rationale including:
    a. cleaning effectiveness—ability to remove product residue
    b. cleaning capability—statistical limits based on historical data from acceptable study runs (prevalidation activities)
    c. safety assessment—relative to the equipment, determine if the cleaning agent causes pitting or microscopic deterioration
    d. solubility studies—ease of cleaning agent removal after final rinse
    e. process clearance capability—limits based on removal of residues by the process itself, determining if the cleaning agent is the hardest to remove residue
    f. validated analytical method—limit of detection and quantitation
    g. toxicity of material based on LD50 value

15. Parameters affecting cleaning effectiveness or attributes of the cleaning process.
    a. coverage of cleaning agent
    b. wash and rinse temperatures, pressures, and times
    c. storage conditions and testing of the cleaning agent working solution
16. Criteria for acceptance after cleaning, including supporting documentation.
    a. Rationale for maximum limit set for product and cleaning agent residues
    b. Approved method of sampling (based on swab and cleaning agent profiles and recovery study data)
    c. Validation of the analytical and microbial test methods, including limit of detection (LOD) and limit of quantitation (LOQ)
17. Recovery criteria for sampling methods.
18. The cleaning procedures used during protocol execution are to be listed, and an evaluation of the procedures' effectiveness provided.

OVERVIEW—CONTROL OF MAINTENANCE/CALIBRATION PROGRAMS

1. All equipment and instruments are to be provided with unique identification. This can be of any format but usually is an alphanumerical identifier, which can be easily utilized by a computer planning system. Although not mandatory, a computer management system is usually used for the schedule of preventive maintenance (PM) and calibration tasks and the record keeping for calibration data. There are numerous systems available varying widely in cost. If such a system is used, it will require validation.
2. All preventive, maintenance, and calibration tasks and regimes are required to be documented as SOPs. These SOPs are to be managed according to the site documentation quality system program.
3. Additions, modifications, and deletions to and from the maintenance and calibration program must be processed by a process designed to control the change and secure appropriate approvals for the changes. This process can be a "delegated" change control process or subset of the site Change Control program.
4. The maintenance and calibration programs are to address both PM activities as well as corrective maintenance activities.
5. The PM and calibration activities are to be documented in SOPs. The frequencies of conducting these activities are to be placed in a scheduling system (whether manual/computerized). A method of documenting the PM and calibration task that has been completed is required.
6. Systems are required to identify how corrective maintenance and calibration activities are conducted. These systems are to be documented in SOPs. Many firms use a work order (WO) system to document corrective activities. Appropriate approvals of the WOs are required.
7. There is to be a process of entering new equipment and instrumentation items into the maintenance or calibration system. These processes are to be documented in SOPs. The processes are to identify what information is required before an equipment item can be entered. Information such as, but not limited to:
    a. unique identifier
    b. equipment assessment or instrument classification
    c. URS
    d. procurement specification
    e. recommended spare parts
    f. recommended lubricants
    g. vendor manuals and drawings

8. A history of maintenance and calibration work is to be kept for each equipment and instrument item.
9. Process to report abnormal situations, that is, out of tolerance for instruments, unapproved parts for maintenance. The system procedures are to identify the conditions that are considered abnormal.
10. Supporting these systems is a replacement parts program. This program is to address the specification, acquisition, storage, and issuance of replacement parts—including lubricants. How replacement parts are approved and how "like-for-like" or functional equivalent replacements are evaluated need to be included in the system SOP.

In the editor's experience, the important aspects of a well-run and compliant maintenance and calibration program is poorly understood in this industry. The following additional sections go into some needed detail regarding compliant programs.

MAINTENANCE AND CALIBRATION PROGRAMS

Maintenance and its specialized subset, calibration, are integral parts of all manufacturing industries. The need to maintain equipment and calibrate process controls is not based on any law or regulation of man; rather, it is a natural result of the second law of thermodynamics. Without getting too technical, the second law simply states that all things wear out. Everything goes from a state of order to a state of greater disorder. In this context, it is readily seen why regulatory agencies, which have an interest in equipment operation correction, require maintenance and calibration programs to counter the effects of the second law and (in the pharmaceutical and related industries) to maintain the validated state of the equipment as required in 21 CFR 211.67 on cleaning and maintenance, and 21 CFR 211.68a on automatic, mechanical, and electronic equipment.

One of the more interesting quirks of the pharmaceutical and related industry is that while the CFR is often open to interpretation in many areas, allowing for the development of the "C" (current) in current good manufacturing practices (CGMPs), there are more specific directions in the maintenance and calibration areas. Yet, these areas are very often overlooked when developing compliance programs. Too often these areas are dismissed as "cost centers" and not considered as part of the compliance program. This ought not to be. A manufacturing site can run 24 hours a day, 365 days a year, and not allow time for maintenance or calibration. It will make lots of money but be completely out of compliance. On the other hand, a site can perform maintenance and calibration according to written programs and schedules but not have any production, and the site will be in compliance but out of business shortly. There needs to be a balance that incorporates maintenance and calibration efforts into the compliance program, as much as any other quality system element, but works within the needs for production. The program elements described in this section are designed to do just that. Certainly, there may be other ways to maintain compliance in maintenance and calibration programs, but this section will provide considerations for compliant maintenance and calibration programs that have worked at many sites.

COMMON CONSIDERATIONS

In general, compliance programs need at least three components: procedures, practices, and paperwork. It needs *procedures* to provide instructions on what to do and how. It must have *practices* that follow the approved procedures. And there must be *paperwork,* which demonstrates that the practices were completed as per the procedures. The need for these three components is just as true in the maintenance and calibration areas. There is the need for procedures (SOPs) to define the administration of the program as well as the actions required to maintain/calibrate specific equipment. Certainly, the procedures must be followed by the practices in the field and office to maintain the equipment and program. And finally, these activities or practices must be documented (paperwork) to maintain a history or evidence of performing the required tasks.

Beyond the requirements common to compliance programs in general, there are several areas of additional requirements or requirements specific to maintenance and calibration that they share.

First, there is the need for the program to be codified in procedures. These procedures are a written program that outlines such areas as:

- Responsibilities of equipment owners, technical personnel, and Quality Unit
- Procedures, forms, and approval for adding, deleting, and modifying equipment in the maintenance or calibration program
- A scheme to uniquely identify equipment (if this scheme is not included in the validation program)
- Directions for a risk-based system of classifying equipment and instruments
- How to add, change, or remove replacements parts from inventory, including functionally equivalent parts and lubricants evaluation
- Directions for establishing and modifying schedules for PM and calibration based on a risk assessment
- Baseline instructions on performing the work. For example, identification of calibration points, handling corrective WOs and emergency WOs, guidelines for closing notes for WOs, and so on
- Identification of reports and metrics that need to be regularly generated and reviewed
- Instructions how to handle abnormal events, for example, out-of-tolerance calibrations, equipment malfunctions that could impact product, and so on
- Establishing qualification requirements for technicians and documenting such
- Establishing training requirements for technicians
- Guidelines on technically qualifying contracted companies and their employees

Both maintenance and calibration programs need procedures that follow the life cycle of the equipment (of facility) from addition to the program of retirement and scrapping.

In addition to the program-defining procedures or administrative procedures, there is the requirement for specific procedures governing how to maintain or calibrate equipment. What is the PM procedure for a tablet press? A lyophilizer? How is a pressure indicator calibrated? Or a conductivity meter? The CFR is specific in requiring procedures for the actual maintenance activities performed on equipment (see 21 CFR 211.67), and it is not only compliant to have such procedures established and approved but also just good business.

Another area that the maintenance and calibration programs have in common is the need for the Quality Unit input into the approval process for specific maintenance and calibration procedures. There is often a cry that Quality does not have the background to evaluate maintenance or calibration procedures, and this area should be left to the engineering folks to evaluate apart from Quality. Of course, the same could be said for a procedure to operate a lyophilizer or purified water system. Quality personnel are not the subject matter experts (SMEs) on most of the procedures they are called upon to evaluate and approve. But the CFR requires procedures for maintenance and calibration. And the CFR requires the Quality Unit to approve all procedures that could impact product (21 CFR 211.22c), and certainly maintenance and calibration procedures can impact product. Rather than avoiding the requirement for the Quality Unit to approve maintenance and calibration procedures, the programs must include requirements for what each approver specifically evaluates.

Qualifications

Maintenance and calibration technicians must be qualified by education, training, or experience to perform their functions. This includes contracted technicians.

Each technician should have a file containing the qualifications of the person to perform the assigned functions. This file can include any education, training, and experience records that demonstrate the qualification of the technician. Likewise, outside technicians require a review of their qualifications to do the work. Even manufacturer's representatives need to be qualified to some extent. The author once interviewed an original equipment manufacturer (OEM) technician who, as it turned out, had only worked for the OEM manufacturer two weeks and came to the manufacturer from an unrelated industry. He was not qualified to do the work, regardless of the business card that had the OEM manufacturer's logo imprinted. A company does not fulfill its compliance requirements by signing a purchase order. A purchase order is not a regulatory document. Suppliers do not get 483s but are a "privilege" reserved for the drug or related product manufacturer. That is the entity responsible for the quality of the product, not the Ajax Maintenance, Calibration, and Chimney Sweep Company!

Although maintenance and calibration share many activities and have common requirements, there are also areas where they have specific requirements. Some of those specifics are identified in the following sections.

MAINTENANCE PROGRAMS

Maintenance programs in the pharmaceutical or related industry have some specific requirements for approvals and documentation that should be incorporated in the program to ensure compliance.

Preventive Maintenance

One of the first requirements is (as has been mentioned) the need for a procedure for PM of specific equipment. It is most common that the preventive (and corrective) maintenance procedures are incorporated in a Computerized Maintenance Management System (CMMS) at the site. Thus, the PM procedure is developed as a series of tasks and frequencies. For example, an air handler could have a PM such as (Table 11.1).

TABLE 11.1

Example of an Air Handler PM Schedule

Frequency	Task
3 months	Check belts for wear, tension, and alignment
3 months	Check pre-filters for blockage
6 months	Replace pre-filters
6 months	Lubricate bearings
12 months	Clean coils

There needs to be a defined method to add (or modify) equipment and the tasks to be performed into the system, supported by change management. This method must be a documented system, provide the history for any changes, and have appropriate approvals. Generally, the approvals are technical management, operations (or owner) management, and Quality Assurance. Once equipment has been identified and its "boilerplate" documented—model and serial number, manufacturer, location, and so on—the requirements for maintenance have to be defined. These maintenance requirements are based on the manufacturer's recommendations and supplemented by the site's experience, conditions, and operating load for the equipment. These maintenance requirements must be developed by someone familiar with PM and the type of equipment. In practice, many PMs can be reduced to common activities across many types of equipment. As examples:

- Hard-to-hard (metal-to-metal) moving contact surfaces require lubrication (e.g., bearings).
- Hard-to-soft (metal-to-rubber) moving contact requires inspection and replacement of the softer surfaces (e.g., belts).
- Filters require inspection/testing for leakage and/or blockage.
- Hydraulics require inspection for leakage, level, and/or fouling, and so on.

Using such basic building blocks, one can construct a simplified maintenance regimen that recognizes the commonality among seemingly different types of equipment. One can also develop basic instructions to use as a pick list to develop a PM procedure. Using such a pick list would ensure common terms and prevent variation based on individual language styles and ensure comprehensive statements of maintenance activities. For example, every time a PM calls for an inspection of belts, common language can be inserted, such as "Inspect belts for glazing, cracking, alignment, and tension. Replace belt(s) if any deterioration is found, replacing full sets only as required." Developing such building blocks will help ensure that belts (or whatever the common task is) will be maintained the same way across different equipment that have belt drives in common.

Once the PM regimen has been developed, it needs to be reviewed and approved by a technical representative for appropriate content and schedules. It should also be reviewed and approved by an operations person familiar with the operation to ensure any concerns around equipment availability and cleaning are considered. It should also be reviewed and approved by a Quality representative to ensure the requirements of the program and overall compliance requirements are being met.

Often the Quality approval is a "sticking point," especially if a site uses a CMMS. But think about this: Quality is required to approve all procedures that can impact product, and maintenance activities are required to be performed against written procedures. Suppose Company A did not have a CMMS but performed PM through the use of SOPs. Such procedures would be typed into a word processing program, printed, and approved as a SOP. Now, Company B has a validated state-of-the-art CMMS, and the procedures are typed into it instead of a word processor. Too often, companies think that using a CMMS somehow enables bypassing the approval process that a regular SOP would require. The approval requirements do not depend on the software on the screen when preparing a PM regimen. There is an appropriate Quality review required of PM activities, not as an SME, but as a compliance gatekeeper, and this role needs to be outlined in the administrative procedures of the maintenance program.

Note that the same rigor applied to adding equipment to the maintenance program must be applied to changes in PM regimens and removing equipment from the program.

Once a PM regimen has been established (the procedure), it must be executed (the practice). PMs must be performed by technicians qualified to do so, completed in a timely manner, done with regards to operations considerations, and documented (the paperwork). There are several caveats of which to be aware when performing PMs. First, that which is stated on the procedure is that which is done. No more, no less. If a PM instruction is wrong, it should be noted and the process to correct or modify the regimen followed before the next PM is due. Second, if additional work is necessary, a corrective WO should be generated to cover that work. The problem may be corrected at the time of the PM, but should be done via the corrective WO, else the history of that equipment is "muddied" and difficult to follow if one has to sort through PM notes to identify corrective work. Third, the technician must be indoctrinated to report any findings that could potentially have impacted product prior to maintenance, for example, a seal-leaking lubricant into the product. If a technician sees such a problem, a "monkey" jumps on his back! They have to find a more suitable home for the "monkey," and there should be documented evidence that the "monkey" was transferred to Operations and/or Quality management. Finally, the PM must be recorded in an equipment logbook. Not in detail—leave that to the PM sheet—but referenced by date and PM WO number.

PMs are often checklist-type operations with a space for comments. These completed PMs must be reviewed by a supervisor to ensure completion of all the activities and to initiate or verify any remediation required—either to the PM regimen or the equipment.

Preventive maintenance is performed for a reason with a defined due date and as such should rarely be overdue because it is a planned procedural commitment. Every effort should be made to complete them on time to maintain compliance. Not doing them as scheduled is a deviation from the commitment in a procedure. Some organizations have gone to taking equipment out of service if the PM is overdue, the same way instruments are generally taken out of service if the calibration is overdue. Certainly, this approach cannot be faulted as "inadequate," but it may be too much. PMs tend to self-correct to some extent. If a belt is not checked or replaced, it will break and the machine will stop—neither a desirable effect nor one indicating control, but obvious. Calibration failures, on the other hand, are not readily visible and are more insidious. Thus, the requirement to take equipment from service if a PM is not completed on time may be mitigated by this consideration. Reported? Absolutely. Remedied? Absolutely. Production stopped? You decide.

Much more can be said about PM, indeed about all the topics in this chapter, but the intent is to provide broad concepts and things to ponder.

Corrective Maintenance

Corrective maintenance differs because it has no preset steps to follow. It depends upon the skill of the technician to troubleshoot a problem and/or replace a part. There is the requirement to have the program defined, but it cannot prescribe the specific corrective work. As part of that program definition, there needs to be such items as priority setting, responding to emergencies, prohibiting unauthorized changes to equipment, and recording of the work done.

Setting priorities is straightforward but has been complicated by the ability to define them to the nth degree in modern CMMSs. Basically, there are two priorities: do it now or do it later. Since a modern CMMS will allow 6.02×10^{23} priorities (maybe a slight exaggeration), some feel it necessary to develop that many priorities. Limit the number of priority classifications to those that are really useful.

There should be a definition of how to respond to emergencies—not only shift considerations but availability of the CMMS, a Quality representative if required, parts, and so on. There also needs to be regular reinforcement of the prohibition against unauthorized changes to equipment by technicians. Beware of the well-meaning, second-shift mechanics who want to get the equipment running. They are on the second shift but do not have all the support framework available to the day-shift workers. As mechanics, they have the tools, but the tools can really mess things up. They have to know that no changes can be made to the equipment, regardless of how loudly the production folks yell, regardless of how easy it would be to fix, and regardless of how sure they are that the change will not impact anything.

Recording the work done takes on special significance with corrective maintenance. Since it cannot be defined as PM prior to doing the work, its recording is more critical. Technicians need to record four basic things:

- A technical description of the problem (more than the originator's "it does not start")
- A technical description of the solution and testing (if required)

- Who did it and when
- What parts were used

Technicians should be discouraged from incorporating any editorial comments in the closing notes of the WO, such as:

"This equipment never worked and never will!"
"The engineer who installed this got a degree from a cereal box!"
"If the operators knew what they were doing, we would not have such problems!"

Remember, the first person to review the closing notes should be the supervisor. The next person to do so could be a regulatory inspector.

Training: Training for maintenance technicians is peculiar. In the calibration arena, there are usually SOPs for calibrating devices. Although maintenance may have the equivalent in the PM regimens, they are usually much more varied and numerous. As a result, often maintenance technicians are trained on general GMPs, documentation, access, and so on, but not on their specific job functions. Training on 4000 PM regimens would leave no time for actually performing the work. A suggestion is to draw on the commonality of PM activities and train on the general skills required to perform maintenance. For example, regular training sessions could be conducted on such topics as:

- Basics of lubrication
- Shaft and belt alignment
- Electrical contact maintenance

Using this scheme would provide training on the functions required to perform their jobs, but avoid 4000 training sessions. It also has the advantage of being able to use vendors as training resources.

As usual, much more detail could be provided, but space limitations allow only some basic considerations for a compliant maintenance program.

CALIBRATION PROGRAMS

Calibration is the specialized subset of maintenance. It usually employs the most highly trained technicians and has more visibility than maintenance. This is because the program usually employs stickers that should be checked regularly by the operators to ensure that the instrument is in calibration, and the devices themselves are often meant to be read and readings recorded. Similar yet different requirements are placed on a calibration program. There still needs to be a methodology to add, modify, and delete instruments. There needs to be a rigorous approval of all such actions. There needs to be documented evidence of all such activities. Different data are required to add (modify or delete) a device to the program in the calibration area than in maintenance.

Classification

Instruments are generally classified according to their potential impact on product using a risk-based approach. The FDA Guidance for Industry, Q9 Quality Risk Management (June, 2006) states: *"It is neither always appropriate nor always necessary to use a formal risk management process (using recognized tools and/or internal procedures, e.g., standard operating procedures). The use of informal risk management processes (using empirical tools and/or internal procedures) can also be considered acceptable."* So hold back on performing a full-blown Failure Mode Effects Analysis for each instrument (or piece of equipment in the case of PM). An empirical method can be developed to determine the risk presented by an instrument out of calibration and thus its classification.

There are varying classification schemes out there. Some with two categories, some with three. Presented here is a logical three-tier scheme. After the initial categorization of an instrument (device or loop) as GMP—used in or to support the manufacture of a drug or related product—the instrument can be placed into one of three the classifications: GMP critical, GMP non-critical, or GMP utility.

A GMP critical instrument is one that monitors or controls a parameter that can have a direct impact on product quality, identity, purity, and so on. The terms "direct impact" and "indirect impact" are currently in vogue in the pharmaceutical and related industry but still leave room for interpretation. A more complete definition could be:

GMP Critical Instrument: An instrument, which measures, monitors, records, or controls a critical parameter or any parameter with the potential to impact product; any instrument used to test or determine product quality; and/or any instrument used to produce data used in a regulatory document. This includes all calibration standards and all critical instruments referenced by a validation protocol or study.

GMP Non-Critical Instrument: An instrument that may reasonably and frequently be used by maintenance, production, R&D, laboratory, or technical services personnel to troubleshoot or anticipate changes in critical parameters and is not used to determine product quality.

GMP Utility Instrument: An instrument is classified as GMP utility if it monitors or controls a local facility utility supply to a GMP process, an on/off condition, or provides an indication of a non-critical parameter on a piece of GMP equipment.

Other circumstances that may warrant GMP utility classification include:

- Visibility to maintenance personnel only for troubleshooting purposes
- Very coarse scaling factors relative to the parameter measured (gross readings only)
- Instruments with low accuracy ratings
- Devices in the output circuit of a control loop

As an aside, note that the last category is *not* called "for reference only." It is a personal quirk of the author who thinks that a device used for reference should have some accuracy basis and not a category that ignores ongoing calibration. After all, who wants an encyclopedia for reference that is not accurate? It is also worth noting that just because a device is classified as GMP utility (or even non-GMP) it is not exempt from the second law of thermodynamics. It still wears out! There is no use in installing an instrument in a system and then never checking its calibration or operation. If it is never checked, it should never be installed, because the laws of creation tell us that it will wear out. However, the devices in this classification are often very nominal, sometimes a pressure gauge that is color coded red and green with no or very coarse scaling factors. Perhaps it is only used to provide an indication of a gross blockage in a compressed air filter, or the on/off condition or a control solenoid, or the pressure of the water feed, and return of a water-sealed vacuum pump. These devices should not be ignored but do not require a rigorous calibration. Some may be well served by a simple operation check to make sure that they are not stuck in one position. Stroking a valve to see if it goes through its full range of motion in response to a spanning of the input signal may be the most appropriate check. The bottom line is devices used in the manufacturing, or to support the manufacturing of a drug or related product, are required to be in a maintenance/calibration program. Do not ignore the GMP utility devices because they are "unimportant." If a device is not in the program, perhaps it should not be in the facility!

A statement worth remembering is "Complexity that does not enhance compliance is a compliance risk." Thus, if the effort is expended to classify instruments, there should some rationale for such an activity. Once instruments and devices are classified, that classification can be used as a basis for limiting the number of out-of-tolerance (OOT) events by first applying the OOT requirements to only the GMP critical devices (those that have a direct impact on product) and second, by setting limits as triggers for the OOT events that are based on the process—not the instrument—and applying these limits to only the GMP critical devices.

Calibration Limits

There are several different limits to be considered in a calibration program. The most basic limit of accuracy (or uncertainty) is that provided by the manufacturer—the instrument accuracy limits. These are the advertised values that manufacturers are constantly making tighter so that the instrument is seen with a better quality. However, these may not be a good thing for the pharmaceutical industry. Extreme accuracy, like apple pie, is hard to argue against, but the necessity of such accuracy needs to be evaluated. Why would one install a device with an accuracy of $\pm0.1\%$ on a process that can vary $\pm5.0\%$ with no impact on output quality? The calibration program should be based on the needs and requirements of your process and not the best technology of an instrument manufacturer! That leads to another set of limits, the calibration limits.

The calibration limits are those values used to determine if an instrument requires adjustment during a calibration. As such, they are functions of the instrument, though these calibration limits may be set wider than the instrument accuracy limits of the manufacturer. In the hypothetical example given above (the $\pm0.1\%$ instrument accuracy limits on a process that can vary $\pm5.0\%$ with no impact on output quality), there is no value to calibrating the device to the manufacturer's limits. The manufacturer probably only makes instruments meeting these rigid specifications, and requests for more reasonable specifications to match the customer's needs will fall on deaf ears. Using the preceding values, calibration limits of $\pm0.5\%$ or even $\pm1.0\%$ would make sense and avoid unnecessary adjustment and out-of-calibration events. Thus, the guidance is to set calibration limits as a function of the instrument, but related to the customer's use of the instrument. Note that an inexpensive pressure gauge may have an instrument accuracy limit of 2.0%, and enlarging this limit may not be prudent. As a guide, electronic devices often have manufacturer's accuracy tighter than required, but mechanical devices have not seen the same advances in accuracy limits, and there may not be an opportunity to increase the instrument accuracy limits when setting calibration limits.

There is a third set of limits. Often these limits are referred to as process calibration tolerances (PCTs). They should not be called process tolerances, since process tolerances are related to the process design and not calibration per se, though there is an indirect relationship. PCTs are those values beyond which the product quality *may* be compromised. Since only GMP critical instruments can directly impact product quality, only they should have this secondary calibration tolerance applied. PCTs are recognition that the industry uses off-the-shelf instruments in particular applications, and the calibration program should identify limits related to the process, not the instrument manufacturer's technology. PCTs are triggers for OOT events, based on the process needs, and applied only to GMP critical devices. PCTs are significantly less than process tolerances to protect the process, but are yet broader than the calibration limits (They may be equal to the calibration limits if PCTs have not been established).

How are PCTs determined? In the best of all possible worlds, they would be derived from process development studies and the process tolerances. But often we are not in the best of all possible worlds. We still have hope. The operation folks should know (and are responsible for determining in any case) the limits of the process they operate before the quality of the product suffers. These limits may even be incorporated in an SOP and can be extracted from that SOP. Another source for determining PCTs is past investigations. If an investigation determines that a calibration error of 2% does not have a direct impact on product quality, there is no sense in issuing an OOT the next time when the calibration is out by 1%! Change or apply a PCT of 2%. Do not do the same thing and expect different results.

Frequency of Calibration

Another calibration parameter to be tied to the classification is the frequency of calibration or the inverse, the calibration period. It stands to reason that if a device is GMP critical and its inaccuracy can impact product quality, it should have its accuracy checked more frequently than devices that cannot directly impact product quality. For example, one scheme would be to set the default calibration frequencies to quarterly for GMP critical, semi-annually for GMP non-critical, and annually for GMP utility device checks. These frequencies can be modified as experience is gained with a particular device, though there should be upper limits, that is, no less frequently than semi-annually for GMP critical devices, no less frequently than annually for GMP non-critical devices, and no less frequently than bi-annually for GMP utility devices. A shorter time frame for GMP critical instruments means a shorter window for investigation impact to product when the instrument is found OOT. The financial savings from having a shorter window to test (or worse case, recall) product would easily pay for performing the calibration quarterly as opposed to every six months.

Out-of-Tolerance Events

In the pharmaceutical and related industry, there is a requirement to investigate any impact that a badly out-of-calibration instrument may have had on past production. "Badly out-of-calibration" is often termed as out-of-tolerance (OOT) to distinguish it from the normal adjustments to bring an instrument closer to the "true" value of the standard. Out-of-tolerances are a fact of life. They must be generated by the person finding the OOT immediately, but then they must notify the owner of the process (and quality) of the event. Until there is a formal, documented notification of an instrument found OOT, the burden of this knowledge is with the calibration technician. The "monkey" is on their back. They need to transfer custody of this "monkey" to the operations and quality personnel in an immediate and documented way, and then they have completed their responsibility. The calibration technician is not qualified by education, training, or experience to evaluate the impact of the calibration error for any parameter on product quality. That has to be the purview of the personnel who know the process and the chemistry or biology of the product, not the calibration technician. The calibration technician's role is that of the fabled "Greek messenger"—they are the bringer of bad news but not the one responsible for remediating the bad news.

There are some reactions to an OOT event that are within the purview of the calibration department. First, if an instrument is found out-of-tolerance, it is less than wise to wait a full calibration cycle to check the calibration again. One approach is to schedule a demand calibration halfway through the next normal calibration period. Thus, if a GMP critical device was found OOT during a normal quarterly calibration, an "extra" demand calibration would be scheduled six weeks (one and one-half months) after the OOT event. This OOT remediation calibration would help determine if the OOT event was singular or a sign of the device's continuing failure. If the device was found OOT again at the shortened period calibration, there is less product in jeopardy and the process to replace the device can be initiated (as the device is checked at an ever-increasing frequency to ensure production as required).

A second reaction to an OOT event that is within the scope of the calibration department is evaluation of the history of the device's calibration. For example, if a review of the device's history shows it has failed twice in the last four calibrations, the process to replace the device should be initiated. The calibration department should be proactive in identifying and taking steps to remove them. Few instruments have a monetary value equal to the cost of a product investigation or, worse case, product recall.

The calibration department should also conduct a review of the history of all devices that failed calibration—not OOTs per se, just found out-of-calibration, GMP critical, and GMP non-critical devices alike. In these cases, an out-of-calibration can trigger a review of the records, and heuristic rules can be established to address the failed calibrations. Perhaps, if a device is found out-of-calibration two of the last four times, the frequency of the calibration should be increased.

There are several more areas of interest in a calibration program: device calibration SOPs, test points, loop calibrations, test accuracy ratios.

Device Calibration SOPs

Devices that are calibrated need to have a procedure to do so. But a site may have thousands of instruments. Does that require thousands of SOPs? One hopes not. What a training nightmare! Rather, a site can develop core or type SOPs. For example, rather than having one SOP for calibrating a 0 to 100 psig Ajax brand pressure gauge, and another for a 0 to 150 psig Ajax brand pressure gauge, and yet another for a 0 to 100 psig Zenax brand pressure gauge, a single SOP for calibrating pressure gauges can be developed. It would include setting up the calibration apparatus, requirements for getting As-Found data. It would also include the checkpoints as percentages (e.g., 10%, 30%, 50%, 70%, 90%) or fixed values of the range. Checks for repeatability would be included, and general adjustment procedures would be specified, such as adjust the zero, adjust the span, when no more interaction, and adjust linearity if such an adjustment is available. The SOP would continue with the As-Left verification and recording of values and any paperwork or OOT requirements. What these core SOPs would not have is specific data, such as calibration limits, PCTs, or test points. These data would have to be provided to the technician via an alternative method, apart from the SOP. One method would be to develop and approve a specific calibration sheet when the device is added to the program and controlled copies would then be provided to the technician when the calibration is performed. Or, as part of the original approval process, the calibration parameters are entered into the CMMS (or the CCMS, Computerized Calibration Management System) if the system is robust enough to accept such data, can provide the data at the time of the calibration, and is properly validated. In any case, developing and maintaining 20 SOPs is easier and less prone to compliance variations than maintaining 4000. Beware that some devices will have calibration procedures too specific to fit into a core SOP, such as those that require pressing certain buttons to enter the programming of a device, but even accounting for these types (e.g., conductivity meters) the site is well below 4000 SOPs.

Test Points

The points at which a calibration is verified or adjusted, the test points, was alluded to in the preceding paragraph. There are a few things to consider regarding the test points. First, most calibrations are based on a linear model. One cannot verify linearity with a single point. It takes at least three points to determine a nominally straight line. Five points would be a better determination. A single point check is not a calibration and should not be declared as such. Many devices also require a repeatability challenge to ensure that the same input will result in the same output each time. The most popular example cited for the need for a repeatability check is hysteresis, or mechanical binding of moving parts, especially when a reading is approached from a value below the reading and a value above the reading. Hysteresis is not the only repeatability issue, but it is a major consideration and thus mechanical instruments in particular should incorporate a repeatability challenge in their calibration regimen. Electronic devices can also exhibit repeatability errors, though generally to a lesser degree. Depending on the repeatability specification of the device, repeatability may be a negligible consideration for these devices.

The program should also consider how to handle test points at the extreme of the range of the device. Should the zero adjust test point be 0% or 10%? The span adjust test point be 100% or 90%? The answer is based on whether the device has a "live" zero or full-scale reading. If one can input 0% and know that if the reading is less than zero, it will be apparent, then use the 0% value. For example, if one was calibrating an resistance temperature detector (RTD) transducer with an input of 0°C–100°C and an output of 4 to 20 ma (live zero and span points), it is given that if the device is not calibrated correctly an input of 0°C can generate an output of 3.8 ma, thereby verifying the out-of-calibration condition. Not all devices have a live zero (or full-scale) reading. Pressure gauges may have mechanical stops at the low and/or top ends that inhibit the output from reflecting the input accurately. Programmable logic controllers (PLCs) may have electronic "clamps" at the limits.

So, inputting 21 ma would still only result in a 100% reading just as a 20 ma would. In such cases, the best practice would be to use zero and span test points values removed from the extremes, thus using the common 10% and 90% test points at the limits of the range.

The preceding paragraph notwithstanding, every effort should be made to avoid limited range calibrations. Yes, the device may not be used over the full range, but the calibration adjustments may be designed to be used as the extremes (within 10%). Someone once challenged this by saying they had a 0 to 120 psig pressure gauge that was used only for reading 30 psig. Why not calibrate it 0 to 60 psig? The response is threefold. First, the gauge is not correct for the application. In general, instruments should be routinely read around the midpoint of their range, say 35%–65%. Regularly reading 30 psig on a 120 psig range gauge is not a good practice. Second, if one finds an error at 60 psig, what does one adjust? The zero or the span adjustment? Neither was designed to be used as a midrange adjustment. Third, if one uses an inexpensive pressure gauge with a ± 2.0% of full-scale accuracy, the accuracy of the gauge is ±6 psi. Since this accuracy is given as a full-scale value, the ± 6 psi is valid throughout the range, thus reading 30 psig provides a potential error of ± 6 psi or ± 20%—a reading of questionable value to the process with that kind of built-in error.

Loop Calibrations

Loop calibrations? Why not? Why not calibrate the instrument system the way it is used? After all, the basic thing the operator wants to know is: "Does the reading on the panel accurately reflect what the parameter value is in the tank?" The best way to verify that is to calibrate the system as a loop. Take the RTD out of the pipe and put it in a bath and see if the temperature of the recorder is correct. The magic in between is of no interest to the operator. If the loop reads correctly at all points and is repeatable, this is a valid calibration check. Many discrete devices are themselves made up of loops, internal to the enclosure of the instrument perhaps, but loops nonetheless. However, a calibration failure of a loop does necessitate disassembling the loop and calibrating each component, reassembling the loop, and rechecking the loop as a whole. At the end of the day, this methodology provides a calibration that is most related to the use of the system and can save on calibration resources.

Test Accuracy Ratios

The ratio of the accuracy of the unit or system under test to the accuracy of the standard used to test is called the test accuracy ratio (TAR) or test uncertainty ratio. A calibration industry heuristic rule is that a TAR of 4:1 should be maintained. Thus, if one has a standard with an accuracy of ±0.1% and is used to calibrate a device with a calibration limit of ± 1.0%, the TAR is 10:1, greater than required but a good ratio. However, if the standard accuracy is only ± 0.5%, the TAR is reduced to 2:1, less than generally accepted. If the calibration limit for a device being calibrated with the ± 0.5% standard is ± 0.4%, the TAR has dropped below 1:1 and the device is being "de-calibrated." An unacceptable situation. The standard used to calibrate a device must be more accurate than the device it is calibrating.

Beware of two situations regarding TARs. First, the TAR of the standard may have to include auxiliary devices used with the standard. For example, if one has a field calibrator with ± 0.2% stated accuracy, but an RTD is plugged into the calibrator that has an accuracy of ± 1.0%, both accuracies must be considered when establishing the TAR. The most common method for assigning an accuracy to a loop (which includes a standard and auxiliary components) is the root of the sum squared, but there are other methods. The main point is to be aware of the effect of auxiliary components on the accuracy of the standard train and include it in the TAR calculations.

The second situation occurs when an organization makes the statement in the SOPs that all calibrations with be done with a TAR of 4:1 but fails to verify that this is happening. There is no verification of the TAR on calibration sheets, or no tools or training provided to the technicians to ascertain the TAR. This is certainly a compliance risk. If the program sets a TAR requirement—as it should—but it is never verified, the program has a glaring gap. There must be a way for calibration technicians to verify the TAR they are being required to maintain.

MAINTENANCE AND CALIBRATION METRICS

After a program has been established, there should be metrics to monitor the effectiveness of the program. A modern CMMS and CCMS can provide a vast plethora of metrics. Just because they can tell you the color of the eyes of the last technician who worked on the equipment does not mean you should track that data. Just because it can be done does not mean that it should be done! It is useful to divide the data or metrics to be used into two categories: compliance and business. While all compliance-based metrics have a business justification, all business-based metrics do not necessarily have a compliance component. So generate metrics cautiously, lest you get buried in relatively meaningless paper required by wayward statements in SOPS.

The most basic compliance needs are two for each: maintenance and calibration. For maintenance activities, the two basic metrics are (1) overdue or late PMs and (2) open corrective WOs. For calibration, the two basic metrics are (1) overdue or late calibrations and (2) OOTs issued. The first item of each of these two sets provide paperwork to tell how well your practices are complying with your procedures. The second item in each set, maintenance and calibration, reports on perturbations in the system and provides insight on how well they are handled. More metrics may be useful to run the business, but it is suggested that they may not be part of the compliance SOPs to avoid compliance constipation.

SUMMARY

All that can be said about maintenance and calibration programs in the pharmaceutical and related industries has not been said in this chapter section. The goal was to provide points to consider when designing a program and a vision of a path forward, not a detailed program for each area. Lots of details can be implemented in various ways. A calibration review team may be established to review calibration parameters, or the parameters can be routed for approvals to different folks without establishing a team. Parts equivalency can be done via a risk-based technical review and approval (lower case *change control*) for functionally equivalent parts or via major Change Control if the replacement part changes the operation and/or validated state of the equipment. The major considerations are outlined here; the details can be developed as best suits your circumstances.

§211.68 AUTOMATIC, MECHANICAL, AND ELECTRONIC EQUIPMENT

a. *Automatic, mechanical, or electronic equipment or other types of equipment, including computers, or related systems that will perform a function satisfactorily, may be used in the manufacture, processing, packing, and holding of a drug product. If such equipment is so used, it shall be routinely calibrated, inspected, or checked according to a written program designed to assure proper performance. Written records of those calibration checks and inspections shall be maintained.*

b. *Appropriate controls shall be exercised over computer or related systems to assure that changes in master production and control records or other records are instituted only by authorized personnel. Input to and output from the computer or related system of formulas or other records or data shall be checked for accuracy. The degree and frequency of input/output verification shall be based on the complexity and reliability of the computer or related system. A backup file of data entered into the computer or related system shall be maintained except where certain data, such as calculations performed in connection with laboratory analysis, are eliminated by computerization or other automated processes. In such instances, a written record of the program shall be maintained along with appropriate validation data. Hard copy or alternative systems, such as duplicates, tapes, or microfilm, designed to assure that backup data are exact and complete and that it is secure from alteration, inadvertent erasures, or loss shall be maintained.*

As indicated in 211.68(a) above, the use of automated controls is not only allowed but also expected to be used in the equipment used in the manufacture of pharmaceutical products. While the use of such devices is not mandatory, it is difficult to acquire equipment today that does not have some type of computer/automated control. As stated in section (a), the control unit needs to be calibrated and verified to be working correctly. This last part is the essence of qualification. As with other systems, written records need to be maintained. In paragraph (b) above, the regulation goes on to specify what needs to be verified in the testing, that is, input and output (I/O), backup systems, and calculations.

With a careful reading of the above requirements, it can be seen that there are two phases to complete computer system (or control system) validation. These are the equipment qualification and the software validation. The hardware itself needs to be qualified, as does any other process equipment. In addition, 21 CFR 11 (Electronic Records; Electronic Signatures—Scope and Application, Guidance for Industry FDA 2003) and requirements overlap both the hardware and the software aspects of the systems.

Based on the two major aspects of automated controls and computer-controlled systems and processes there are again two areas to be considered. These are known as the structural validation and the functional validation stages of qualification/validation.

Structural qualification/validation is primarily set to deal with the development of the software source code, the capabilities and qualifications of the programmer, and the related software functions (e.g., version control). The functional qualification/validation aspect of the program, as the name implies, involves the qualification of the hardware to operate under the conditions it is designated for as well as the actual validation of the entire unit (hardware and software with associated devices/equipment).

Software validation of control systems (hardware and software) has developed to a mature level with the advent of such documents as GAMP (latest revision) and the FDA's "Guide for the Validation of Automated Systems." These documents (and others) provide a structured approach to the design, specification acquisition, installation, and validation of computer/control systems. The level of qualification required in the GAMP approach is dependent upon the type of control system and the categorization of the software used for the control system as follows (Table 11.2).

The GAMP approach can be tied directly into the life-cycle approach to software development and computer control qualification. It is not meant to be a stand-alone approach but one that ties all aspects of the qualification process together. Figure 11.1 shows the life-cycle approach to computer system validation. This includes both software and hardware qualification.

The maintenance of the control system is handled within the maintenance/calibration programs as discussed above. Additional skills are required as the complexity of the control system increases,

---

TABLE 11.2
Level of Qualification Required in the GAMP Approach

Category	Example Software/System Type	Basic Level of Validation
Operating systems	Windows, DOS, Unix providing operating platform for a system	None
Firmware	Micro controllers and discrete devices. Process instruments controlling or recording, for example, temperature, flow, pressure, conductivity, level, and pH	Minimal
Commercial off-the-shelf	Standard application software. Source code not supplied/ established customer base	Basic
Configurable software	Customized application software source code not supplied/ established customer base. Generic software configured to client needs for example, DCS	Intermediate
Custom (Bespoke) software	Source code developed to client needs for example, PLC	Complete

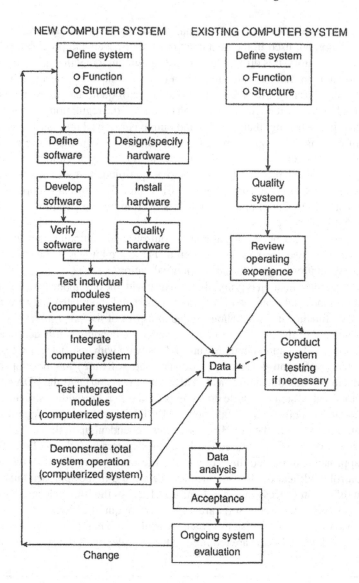

FIGURE 11.1   Validation life cycle.

from a simple embedded firmware controller to a distributed control system that operates the entire manufacturing process. Appropriate personnel are needed to support these systems.

§211.72 FILTERS

Filters for liquid nitration used in the manufacture, processing, or packing of injectable drug products intended for human use shall not release fibers into such products. Fiber-releasing filters may not be used in the manufacture, processing, or packing of these injectable drug products unless it is not possible to manufacture such drug products without the use of such filters. If use of a fiber-releasing filter is necessary, an additional non-fiber-releasing filter of 0.22 μm mean porosity (0.45 μm if the manufacturing conditions so dictate) shall subsequently be used to reduce the content of particles in the injectable drug product. Use of an asbestos-containing filter, with or without subsequent use of a specific non-fiber-releasing filter, is permissible only upon submission of proof to the appropriate bureau of the FDA that use of a non-fiber-releasing filter will, or is likely to, compromise the safety or effectiveness of the injectable drug product.

As indicated in the previous version, this subsection has restricted applicability to the manufacture of injectable products for humans. The later introduction of limits on particulate matter in injectables encouraged the move away from fiber-releasing filters. The ban on use of asbestos filters, without FDA approval, relates not only to a reduction in particulate matter in injections but also to a minimization or elimination of worker exposure to airborne asbestos fibers.

More important for sterilizing filters are extractables and validation of filtration effectiveness. Many companies, with the support of the filter manufacturers, have used a matrix approach to address these issues, provided there is a scientific justification.

EXAMPLES OF OBSERVATIONS FROM FDA CITATIONS

- Worst-case conditions are not undertaken during the validation study.
- Cleaning failures noted in the ongoing cleaning validation program are not investigated and corrected.
- The maintenance support group was using an obsolete SOP for maintenance and calibration of equipment.
- The firm's cleaning validation program has not addressed how long a product can remain in the processing equipment before the equipment must be cleaned.
- There are no maintenance records for the tableting machines to indicate when routine repair and replacement of parts is performed.
- Filters used to sterilize bulk drug solutions are not being subjected to a prefiltration integrity test.
- There are no written procedures for calibration and PM of laboratory instrumentation.
- The record generated during the calibration of the fluid bed dryer sensors and chart recorder appear inadequate in which there is no written protocol for this operation; the probes of the original Digistrip recorder used to calibrate the Digistrip thermocouples had not been calibrated since.
- There are no qualification studies performed on equipment to assure that they perform as intended.

SUGGESTED READINGS

- Mead WJ. Maintenance: Its interrelationship with drug quality. *Pharm Eng* 1987; 7:29.
- Branning RC. Computer system validation: How to get started. *Pharm Eng* 1987; 7:11.
- Fry EM. FDA regulation of computer systems in drug marketing. *Pharm Eng* 1988; 8:47.
- DeRisio R. Equipment design: Moist heat sterilizer. *Pharm Eng* 1987; 7:43.
- Harris JR et al. Validation concepts for computer systems used in the manufacture of drug products. *Pharm Technol* 1986; 10:24.
- Chapman KG, Harris JR, Errico JJ. Source code availability and vendor-user relationship. *Pharm Technol* 1987; 11:24.
- FDA. Guide to Inspections of Validation of Cleaning Processes. Washington, DC: U.S. Department of Health and Human Services, July 1993.
- Fourman GL, Mullen MV. Determining cleaning validation acceptance limits for pharmaceutical manufacturing operations. *Pharm Technol* 1993; 17(4):54.
- Smith JA. A modified swabbing technique for determination of detergent residues in clean-in-place systems. *Pharm Technol* 1992; 16(1):60.
- Jenkins KM, Vanderwielen AJ. Cleaning validation: An overall perspective. *Pharm Technol* 1994; 18(4):60.
- PhRMA. Computer system validation: Auditing computer systems for quality. *Pharm Technol* 1994; 18(9):48.

- Agalloco J, Mascherpa V. Validation of a computerized system for autoclave control. *Pharm Technol* 1995; 19(1):42.
- Tetzlaff R, Shepherd R, LeBlanc A. The validation story. *Pharm Technol* 1993; 17(3):100.
- Rohsner D, Serve W. The composition of cleaning agents for the pharmaceutical industry. *Pharm Eng* 1995; 15(2):20.
- Paul BO. Continuous bagging eliminates dust, powder handling. *Chem Process* 1995; 47.
- PMA. Validation concepts for computer systems used in manufacturing of drug products. *Pharm Technol* 1986; 10(5):24.
- Double ME. The role of quality assurance in the validation process. *Pharm Eng* 1991; 27(5):50.
- Chapman KG. A history of validation in the United States: Part 1. *Pharm Technol* 1991; 15(10):82.
- Chapman KG. A history of validation in the United States: Part 2. Validation of computer-related systems. *Pharm Technol* 1991; 15(11):54.
- PMA. Computer system validation—staying current: Software development testing strategies. *Pharm Technol* 1989; 13(9):142.
- PMA. Computer system validation—staying current: Change control. *Pharm Technol* 1990; 14(1):20.
- McKinstry PL, Atwong CT, Atwong MK. An application of a life cycle approach to computer system validation. *Pharm Eng* 1994; 14(3):46.
- PMA. Computer system validation—staying current: Installation qualification. *Pharm Technol* 1990; 14(9):88.
- PMA. Computer system validation—staying current: Security in computerized systems. *Pharm Technol* 1993; 17(5):48.
- Chapman KG, Harris JR, Bluhm AR, Errico JJ. Source code availability and vendor—user relationships. *Pharm Technol* 1987; 11(12):24.
- FDA. Computerized drug processing; source code for process control. Compliance Policy Guide (7132a.15), 1987.
- Levehuk JW. Good validation practices: FDA issues. *J Pharm Sci Technol* 1994; 48(5):222.
- PDA. Validation of computer related systems. Technical Report No. 18, 1995.
- George JM. Lessons from the field, real-life experiences in computer system validations. *Pharm Technol* 1994; 18(11):38.
- Wood JP. *Containment in the Pharmaceutical Industry.* New York, Marcel Dekker, 2001.
- Avis KA, Liebermann HA, Lachman L. *Pharmaceutical Dosage Forms*, Vols 1–3. New York, Marcel Dekker, 1993.
- DeSpautz JF. *Automation and Validation of Information in Pharmaceutical Processing.* New York, Marcel Dekker, 1998.
- Signore AA, Jacobs T. *Good Design Practices for GMP Pharmaceutical Facilities.* New York, Marcel Dekker, 2005.
- ISPE. ISPE Baseline Guides, Commissioning and Qualification. Vol. 5. ISPE, 2001.
- GAMP Good Practice Guide, Calibration Management. ISPE, 2001.
- Nassani M. Cleaning validation in the pharmaceutical industry. *J Valid Technol* 2005; 11(4).
- Busfield J. CGMP Maintenance Program Considerations. *J Valid Technol* January, 2013.
- Busfield J. CGMP Equipment, Instruments, and Calibration. *J Valid Technol* February, 2013.
- FDA Guidance for Industry: Q9 Quality Risk Management, Washington, DC, U.S. Department of Health and Human Services, Food and Drug Administration, Center for Drug Evaluation and Research (CDER), Center for Biologics Evaluation and Research (CBER, June, 2006.

- E2500-07, Standard Guide for the Specification, Design and Validation of Pharmaceutical and Biopharmaceutical Manufacturing Systems and Equipment, ASTM, 2009.
- ICH Q8, Pharmaceutical Development Q8(R2).
- ICH Q9, Quality Risk Management.
- ICH Q10, Pharmaceutical Quality System.
- FDA Pharmaceutical cGMPs for the 21st Century—A Risk-Based Approach.
- GAMP 5: Risk-Based Approach to Compliant GxP Computerized Systems.
- GAMP Good Practice Guide: A Risk-Based Approach to GxP Process Control Systems (GPCS).

12 Control of Components and Drug Product Containers and Closures

Graham P. Bunn

CONTENTS

§211.80 GENERAL REQUIREMENTS

a. *There shall be written procedures describing in sufficient detail the receipt, identification, storage, handling, sampling, testing, and approval or rejection of components and drug product containers and closures; such written procedures shall be followed.*
b. *Components and drug product containers and closures shall at all times be handled and stored in a manner to prevent contamination.*
c. *Bagged or boxed components of drug product containers or closures shall be stored off the floor and suitably spaced to permit cleaning and inspection.*
d. *Each container or grouping of containers for components or drug product containers or closures shall be identified with a distinctive code for each lot in each shipment received. This code shall be used in recording the disposition of each lot. Each lot shall be appropriately identified as to its status (i.e., quarantined, approved, or rejected).*

When these regulations were written over 40 years ago the general expectation perhaps was slightly different in that procedural requirements were not always written. Today there is no question that directions/instructions—standard operating procedures (SOPs)—protocols, methods, specification, and any other requirement must be written down.

The process from the time of receipt (delivery at the receiving dock) through the life of storage needs to be defined and also the materials (components, drug product containers, and closures) must be prevented from contamination during handling and storage. Outer containers range from metal drums to cardboard boxes and paper "sacks." The physical durability during shipment and warehouse handling needs to be appropriate and some degree of care exercised during movement, especially with forklift trucks.

Containers must be clean from "transport debris" and dirt before they enter the sampling area. Vacuum removal of debris and wiping are part of normal procedures. The second stage is the inspection of the individual containers and sampling by the incoming inspection team, which is often part of the Quality Control (QC) group. Since the working warehouse needs to accommodate potentially large shipments of cardboard/metal drums, packages, and shippers, it is busy and not surprisingly outside dust and dirt is brought in. Daily, weekly, and equally important monthly cleaning of the warehouse facility, including the receiving and shipping docks is essential in maintaining cleanliness of the building and operations. Outer container must be stored on pallets at all times to minimize potential for contamination and also damage since most are transported by forklifts. Many incoming warehouses are maintained impeccably. Sweeping floors, clearing up trash, and moving pallets out of the bays on a rolling time basis for cleaning is performed and documented.

Double warehouse doors, often with air curtains, minimize temperature/humidity fluctuations from the outside environment, which can vary immensely from summer to winter depending on geographical location. The roller doors also prevent rodents, flying/crawling insects, and birds from entering, and a well-run pest control program by a professional company is essential. Pest control companies are required to be registered with the state and have current licenses and insurance, and the technicians have individual licenses. Normally a pest control book is supplied with the chemical treatment for perimeter and traps on the inside perimeter of the building, especially at entrances/exits. Ensure that the technicians are trained with adequate evidence on the site Pest Control Program SOP, as it needs to contain the current map location of all the flying insect light traps, baits, and documentation requirements. Maps can be updated, but ensure that the SOP is also revised with required training. Normally on-site maintenance/facility personnel accompany the technicians, check the report provided, and sign/date for acceptance by the company. Reports are filed and any recommendations (often repairs to facilities to prevent ingress of pests, e.g., sealing gaps, and replacing door jams) must be followed up for action within suitable timelines. Any unusual pest activities need to be promptly addressed by management. Appropriate temperature control and humidity monitoring need to be performed constantly. See also Chapter 13, "Holding and Distribution". Some companies have implemented requirements that employees notify quality if a pest is sighted within the facility so that appropriate action can be taken and the incident and remediation are documented. Periodic review of the reports is performed by Quality Assurance and a summary with any recommendations is submitted as part of the quality council meetings.

Containers opened for sampling must have identification of who performed the sampling and the signature/date it was performed attached to each container. A statistical sample of the material/component (sampling plan) is taken in a controlled conditions in a suitable room with appropriate gowning (the requirements are the same as that in which the initial dispensing of the material/component will be taking place). This is to preserve the fitness for use of the remaining containers or closures as well as to ensure sample integrity, if they are to be examined for microbial contamination. At a minimum, any sampling should be performed in a manner to limit exposure to the environment during and after the time samples are removed (i.e., wiping outside surfaces, limiting time that the original package is open, and properly resealing the original package). It is essential that there is no potential cross contamination during sampling: use of disposal sampling utensils/gowns and cleaning the room between sampling with a room logbook is expected. When disposable sampling utensils are not use there needs to be adequate documented evidence that the cleaning procedure is sufficient. Samples must be placed in suitable containers to maintain the environment with correct storage conditions and appropriately labeled before being submitted for testing with approved methods and specifications.

After the initial acceptance the shipment is entered into the validated Enterprise Resource Planning (ERP) program, which captures details of the supplier, dates, quantities, and also captures the user of the system before assigning a unique number for each batch. Delivery of the same batch on another day will be allocated another unique number. This unique number allows the company to trace the material through the receipt, quarantine, sampling, testing, and release/rejection process. Each container of the same batch in the shipment is labeled with distinctive number. In the event of an investigation or need for a recall, all the batches of finished product that used a specific batch of containers can be efficiently/effectively identified.

Status (quarantine/released/rejected/hold) is still acceptable by attaching labels to each container. However, since the introduction of ERP systems this status identification has been performed electronically in a qualified system. The ERP knows the location in the facility of every outer container, and the status of each container is controlled by authorized access via unique bar codes on each container and reader. All outer containers are received authorized user access into the system in a "quarantine" status, and only Quality is authorized to change the status. The ERP knows when and who change the status and if the bar code is read for the location and the container it will not permit it to be relocated (for use in production) unless it is in a released status. Hence, there is no need to have the status label on the containers because the ERP controls it.

§211.82 RECEIPT AND STORAGE OF UNTESTED COMPONENTS, DRUG PRODUCT CONTAINERS, AND CLOSURES

a. *Upon receipt and before acceptance, each container or grouping of containers of components, drug product containers, and closures shall be examined visually for appropriate labeling as to contents, container damage or broken seals, and contamination.*
b. *Components, drug product containers, and closures shall be stored under quarantine until they have been tested or examined, as appropriate, and released. Storage within the area shall conform to the requirements of Section 211.80.*

Note that the examination requirement is before acceptance by the warehouse. Warehouse personnel review delivery notes against their purchase information and perform count of the items/containers and an external check of the shipment for physical damage and also potential contamination. They may refuse delivery if the physical appearance is unacceptable, including broken seals (often with tracking numbers listed on the delivery note) container contamination, and leakage of the contents. The results are documented and Quality Assurance (QA) notified. Depending on the contract with the supplier, the shipment may be rejected at the premises door and sent back with the shipper and the shipment is documented as never being accepted at the premises. Who pays for the shipment and returns is usually predefined.

Confirmation of the supplier name is critical for traceability as often "agents" are brokers for several suppliers, and the name on the label may be a distributor (taking bulk packages and breaking them down into sublots) this is elaborated upon in §211.84. The certificate of analysis (CoA) for the components, containers, and closures needs to be reviewed for accuracy and completeness against the incoming inspection specifications and also against the results of testing (dimensional, limit tests, etc.) to ensure the requirements are met. The supplier identification is also a requirement against the approved supplier list, and any discrepancies need to be notified to QA before any components, containers or closures can be accepted.

As mentioned in §211.42(c) above, container labeling with the status and changes as necessary are required or a qualified/validated ERP system. Spatial separation of quarantined and released items including excipients and active pharmaceutical ingredients is acceptable with the ERP. Rejected items are clearly labeled on each container and stored in a physically restricted access area.

§211.84 TESTING AND APPROVAL OR REJECTION OF COMPONENTS, DRUG PRODUCT CONTAINERS, AND CLOSURES

a. *Each lot of components, drug product containers, and closures shall be withheld from use until the lot has been sampled, tested, or examined, as appropriate, and released for use by the quality control unit.*

The need to withhold use of any item (components, containers, closures, and excipients/active pharmaceuticals) is not only based on logical quality decision making but also equates to strategic business sense: making a batch with unreleased items runs a risk of rejection. However, there are occasions when, for various reasons, an exceptional situation arises where product is in short supply for patients and delay in initiating the production could result in significant delay to shipping may justify using unreleased items. When the 21 CFR 211 regulations were proposed and they were published for comment, there were responses that challenged this requirement. The commissioner responded in the preamble:[1] "As a general principle, such procedures would violate the precepts of good quality control because untested and possibly noncomplying materials would be used in drug product processing. Although initially it would appear that the manufacturer merely assumes the risk of having to recondition or destroy a processed lot that was found to contain unsatisfactory components, containers, or closures, the Commissioner is concerned that processing while testing substantially increases the risk to the consumer that an unsatisfactory lot might erroneously be released. The Commissioner cannot accept such risks or these suggestions."

Although the FDA has commented to this effect, there are instances when this situation may occur. These rare instances must be managed as a deviation with a risk assessment and appropriate root cause analysis with corresponding corrective and preventive actions (CAPAs). Approval by executive management from production and quality is required. The batch cannot be released until all testing is complete and the results meet specifications and all documentation is completed according to SOPs.

b. *Representative samples of each shipment of each lot shall be collected for testing or examination. The number of containers to be sampled, and the amount of material to be taken from each container, shall be based upon appropriate criteria, such as statistical criteria for component variability, confidence levels and degree of precision desired, the past quality history of the supplier, and the quantity needed for analysis and reserve where required by §211.70.*

Testing or examination of the samples is intended to cover physical (dimensions) and visual, chemical, and microbiological of each shipment. Even if the same batch is received again, the sampling and testing must be performed. Additionally, the second batch would have a different receiving number for traceability. Other tests may be performed depending on the origin, intended use, and official reference standard. The number of containers sampled must be statistically based. Testing requirements, including any reduced testing plan, need to be justified and documented. Samples are usually a quantity of the item at least twice the size needed for complete testing, and any exceptions need to be justified. This sample size allows for retesting if an out of specification result is obtained or loss of sample during testing. During the qualification process for new suppliers, the qualification procedure may require more testing/sampling, and ultimately a report is issued, justifying any changes to reduce the number/frequency of the tests performed.

c. *Samples shall be collected in accordance with the following procedures:*
   1. *The containers of components selected shall be cleaned, where necessary, by appropriate means.*
   2. *The containers shall be opened, sampled, and resealed in a manner designed to prevent contamination of their contents and contamination of other components, drug product containers, or closures.*
   3. *Sterile equipment and aseptic sampling techniques shall be used when necessary.*

4. *If it is necessary to sample a component from the top, middle, and bottom of its container, such sample subdivisions shall not be made into composites for testing.*
5. *Sample containers shall be identified so that the following information can be determined: name of the material sampled, the lot number, the container from which the sample was taken, the date on which the sample was taken, and the name of the person who collected the sample.*
6. *Containers from which samples have been taken shall be marked to show that samples have been removed from them.*

Requirements (c)(1) and (2) have been previously discussed in this chapter.

Items requiring the use of sterile equipment and aseptic sampling may occur, but manufacturers avoid these types of situations wherever possible by managing the items quantities. If there are no other options, the sampling is performed under rigorous conditions so as to not produce a false positive result or potentially contaminate the items intended for production use.

The regulations do not preclude the composing of samples for testing, except as detailed in (c)(4). If the objective is to determine homogeneity of an item/component, then pooling the samples defeats this objective.

As defined in (c)(5), a sample container must contain the requirements listed above and also as needed include any specific storage (temperature/light/nitrogen overlay) or hazard warnings. The container must also be suitable for preserving the sample through the testing period. Reserve samples must also reflect the storage container in which the items are normally stored. For example: sealed double-polyethylene bags cannot be replaced with a cardboard box for the reserve samples. The container from which the item/material is removed must be resealed in adequately to prevent contamination when returned to the quarantine storage area.

The requirements of (c)(6) are met by attaching a label to the sampled container with "Sampled By" and initials/date of the person performing the sampling.

d. *Samples shall be examined and tested as follows:*
  1. *At least one test shall be conducted to verify the identity of each component of a drug product. Specific identity tests, if they exist, shall be used.*
  2. *Each component shall be tested for conformity with all appropriate written specifications for purity, strength, and quality. In lieu of such testing by the manufacturer, a report of analysis may be accepted from the supplier of a component, provided that at least one specific identity test is conducted on such component by the manufacturer and provided that the manufacturer establishes the reliability of the supplier's analyses through appropriate validation of the supplier's test results at appropriate intervals.*
  3. *Containers and closures shall be tested for conformance with all appropriate written procedures. In lieu of such testing by the manufacturer, a certificate of testing may be accepted from the supplier, provided that, at least, a visual identification is conducted on such containers/closures by the manufacturer and provided that the manufacturer establishes the reliability of the supplier's test results through appropriate validation of the supplier's test results at appropriate intervals.*
  4. *When appropriate, components shall be microscopically examined.*
  5. *Each lot of a component, drug product container, or closure that is liable to contamination with filth, insect infestation, or other extraneous adulterant shall be examined against established specifications for such contamination.*
  6. *Each lot of a component, drug product container, or closure that is liable to microbiological contamination that is objectionable in view of its intended use shall be subjected to microbiological tests before use.*

Components, containers, and closures used for pharmaceutical production must comply with their predefined testing specifications. Vendors/suppliers to the industry are normally familiar with the regulatory requirements and customer requirements for a vendor certification program when they have been supplying quantities for large-volume customers.

VENDOR QUALIFICATION

A vendor qualification program is not only a regulatory expectation but makes both quality and business sense for the manufacturer making the purchases. Manufacturers need to establish supplier agreements, including quality aspects, with sufficient details to include the requirement of supplying certificates of analysis and compliance to current good manufacturing practices (cGMPs) for each batch and as defined in a SOP. A risk assessment of the vendor/supplier is performed to determine if an on-site or questionnaire audit is required. The results of which include QA recommendations for use or continued use of the vendor/supplier. Vendors/suppliers can only be used if they are on an approved list, which Quality maintains, and is used by purchasing. Comparison of the vendor/supplier and customer test results form part of the initial and ongoing vendor qualification program. A new vendor/supplier or a change in the location where the items are produced will result in the requirement to perform full testing for a minimum of the first three lots of materials received or as defined in the customer SOP.

Following initial supplier qualification the approved certificates of analysis are provided with each batch containing all the individual test results and the specifications. Any differences in results between supplier and customer test results must be investigated.

After establishment of supplier's consistent ability to provide items/materials to the required specifications with supporting documentation the supplier may be considered for reduce testing with adequate justification and complete testing periodically performed according to procedure requirements. Regulatory requirements include a minimum of one identity test, which for some containers and closures may be considered as visual, depending on usage. For chemicals, the identity test should be specific, for example, infrared spectroscopy or chromatographic methods. Any parameter that could be subject to change during shipping and that could impact on the quality of the item needs to be tested and justification documented with rationale for any tests not being performed, for example, some tests may pose significant safety risks and are performed by the supplier but have limited quality impact.

A vendor qualification relies on a written agreement (business and quality) and collaboration between the supplier and customer to be successful. For essential items of components, containers, and closure, customers qualify more than one vendor in case there are supply difficulties related to quality, quantity, or timelines. A business continuity plan with risk assessments for each item and the active/excipients is a strategic business decision so that interruption of the finished product supply chain is minimized.

While not a 21 CFR 211 regulatory requirement, the FDA is interested in maintaining the supply of products to patient. A note on the FDA Web page includes "FDA responds to potential drug shortages by taking actions to address their underlying causes and to enhance product availability. FDA determines how best to address each shortage situation based on its cause and the public health risk associated with the shortage.

For manufacturing/quality problems, FDA works with the firm to address the issues. Problems may involve very low risk (e.g., wrong expiration date on package) to high risk (particulate in product or sterility issues). Regulatory discretion may be employed to address shortages to mitigate any significant risk to patients.

FDA also works with other firms making the drugs that are in shortage to help them ramp up production if they are willing to do so. Often they need new production lines approved or need new raw material sources approved to help increase supplies. FDA can and does expedite review of these to help resolve shortages of medically necessary drugs. FDA can't require the other firms to increase production."

Key steps involved in a vendor qualification and ongoing monitoring program include:

1. Establishment of the program in a SOP that outlines the steps required and responsibilities of involved personnel.
2. Vendors are aware of their participation in the program and the steps for qualification with understanding of the requirements to maintain it and process of disqualification. Initial selection of potential vendors should take into account history of quality, delivery, and support service as well as the importance of the specific item to the business. Vendor qualification has a greater chance of success with suppliers who are committed to quality and provide customer service.
3. Following a risk assessment it will be determined if an on-site audit of the supplier or a written questionnaire is warranted. Consideration of the standard (ISO/GMP) the vendor needs to produce the items under should be performed. Not all components, containers, and closures are produced under GMP-related requirements but do meet some quality standard, have quality management systems including training, and document management.
4. The purchaser/user of the item is responsible for ensuring that the components, containers, and closures are fit for their intended use. The communication of this to the supplier is through comprehensive specifications. The vendor may primarily supply the item to another industry, for example, sucrose to the food and beverage industry, and therefore the financial incentive to supply increased specification requirements to pharmaceuticals is not worth it. Another is filters that may be different if a specific type/size is only used in the beverage industry but the specifications may not meet those required by a pharmaceutical manufacturer. Major filter manufacturers provide large volumes to the pharmaceutical/biotech industry and are very familiar with the requirements and understand the need for documentation in support of their products.
5. The quality agreement between the vendor and manufacturer is essential for managing changes to the vendor's manufacturing process or specifications for the item. The agreement defines what and how proposed changes are communicated in writing. Some changes are for information but all changes can potentially impact the manufacturer's product, and they are responsible for performing and documenting the assessment in their quality management system. If the vendor's change impacts the product, the manufacturer still has to determine if the impact can be managed/accepted or an alternative vendor needs to be qualified. Some changes can result in a revision to the regulatory filing and could require approval before product is shipped.
6. Vendors are continually monitored for factors that could impact the manufacturer, for example, on-time delivery (delays impact production), completeness of delivery and any damage in transport, and items failing to meet agreed specifications. These factors are reported by the supply chain periodically and are also part of the overall vendor evaluation with the periodic audits.

   Failure to meet requirements, especially for the supplied items, can result in disqualification (purchasing cannot place orders with the vendor). The manufacturer may have an alternate supplier already qualified or be able to qualify a second vendor to ensure that there is no disruption to production.
7. Any lot of components, drug product containers, or closures that meet the appropriate written specifications of identity, strength, quality, and purity and related tests under paragraph (d) of this section may be approved and released for use. Any lot of such material that does not meet such specifications shall be rejected.

These requirements are clearly stated and understood. If an item fails to meet predefined specifications, it is rejected. Sound and substantial evidence with justification by executive management is needed for any other actions.

Refer to Chapter 9, "Contracting and Outsourcing for related information".

§211.86 USE OF APPROVED COMPONENTS, DRUG PRODUCT CONTAINERS, AND CLOSURES

Components, drug product containers, and closures approved for use shall be rotated so that the oldest approved stock is used first. Deviation from this requirement is permitted if such deviation is temporary and appropriate.

The first batch released in the warehouse is the first one allocated to production. However, if the next product requires only 10,000 containers and that batch was received after the other one, then this would be a reasonable use justification; it is appropriate and temporary. Another example would be the evaluation of a new vendor when the components are being tested against requirements in use, and this can also be justified as a deviation from this requirement.

§211.87 RETESTING OF APPROVED COMPONENTS, DRUG PRODUCT CONTAINERS, AND CLOSURES

Components, drug product containers, and closures shall be retested or reexamined, as appropriate, for identity, strength, quality, and purity and approved or rejected by the quality control unit in accordance with §211.84 as necessary, e.g., after storage for long periods or after exposure to air, heat, or other conditions that might adversely affect the component, drug product container, or closure.

The reason for this requirement is to ensure that at the time of use in production, the components, containers, and closures (items) still meet their specifications. Additionally, testing is required if there have been any adverse storage conditions that potentially could impact the item, and it is expected that a retest date is assigned with adequate data/justification. Reevaluation does not necessitate complete testing according to the specification but those requirements known or which could possibly have changed. Items that may be adversely impacted by storage conditions should be stored appropriately according to manufacturer's directions, and where these are not provided then justification and suitable testing should be performed. Conditions in a warehouse can vary depending on the location in the racking system and time of year, for example, top rack in summer of a flat-roof warehouse where temperatures are only suitable for outer shippers. Lower-level racking has been temperature mapped to provide evidence that a suitable temperature can be maintained for excipients.

§211.89 REJECTED COMPONENTS, DRUG PRODUCT CONTAINERS, AND CLOSURES

Rejected components, drug product containers, and closures shall be identified and controlled under a quarantine system designed to prevent their use in manufacturing or processing operations for which they are unsuitable.

This requirement is another example that appears to state the obvious; however, experience has seen that this is not always followed. It is noted that although a segregated reject area is not required, it is difficult to maintain adequate control and convince auditors that there is an adequate system to prevent use of rejected items even with a materials management system. Once materials/items are assigned a "Reject" status, they need to be locked in a caged area with restricted access. FDA investigators frequently visit the reject area to ensure the above is being implemented and also to compare the contents with the reject list to confirm adequate control. When rejections occur, there must be an investigation irrespective if the material, item, in-process material, or product has been completely used or processed. Additionally, rejects need to be processed promptly for disposal. Sometimes vendors do not respond very quickly, as it is a lower priority, and other times finance is negotiating reimbursement.

§211.94 DRUG PRODUCT CONTAINERS AND CLOSURES

a. *Drug product containers and closures shall not be reactive, additive, or absorptive so as to alter the safety, identity, strength, quality, or purity of the drug beyond the official or established requirements.*

b. *Container closure systems shall provide adequate protection against foreseeable external factors in storage and use that can cause deterioration or contamination of the drug product.*

c. *Drug product containers and closures shall be clean and, where indicated by the nature of the drug, sterilized, and processed to remove pyrogenic properties to assure that they are suitable for their intended use.*

d. *Standards or specifications, methods of testing, and, where indicated, methods of cleaning, sterilizing, and processing to remove pyrogenic properties shall be written and followed for drug product containers and closures.*

Assessment of the suitability of containers and closures is described in Section 21 CFR 211.166 (stability testing).

Note that on May 26, 2017, the USP issued the following notification: "In accordance with the Rules and Procedures of the 2015-2020 Council of Experts, the General Chapters—Packaging and Distribution Expert Committee has revised General Chapter <659> Packaging and Storage Requirements and Chapter <661.1> Plastic Materials of Construction. The General Chapter <661.2> Plastic Packaging Systems for Pharmaceutical Use has also been revised.

The specific revisions are as follows:

• Delay until May 1, 2020 the implementation of new requirements of General Chapters <661.1> and <661.2> as currently specified in General Chapter <659>.
• Incorporate into General Chapter <661> the requirements previously specified in the USP 38–NF 33 version of General Chapter <661>. Reference General Chapter <661> in General Chapter <659> to make these previous requirements applicable until May 1, 2020.
• Clarify in General Chapter <659> that early adoption of the requirements of <661.1> and <661.2> is permitted by USP, and that packaging systems in compliance with these requirements in advance of May 1, 2020 will no longer need to comply with the reinstated <661> requirements to be considered by USP to be in conformance with the USP–NF.
• Remove the current exemption to General Chapters <661.1> and <661.2> for plastic materials and packaging systems previously approved by a regulatory authority.
• The <661.1> Plastic Materials of Construction Revision Bulletin will supersede the monograph becoming official in USP 40–NF 35. The Revision Bulletin will be incorporated in USP 41–NF 36."

The U.S. Pharmacopeia, ⟨661⟩, also provides information on specifications and test methodology for a range of container materials.

These include:

1. Light transmission—glass and plastics containers
2. Chemical resistance—glass container
3. Physicochemical tests—plastics
4. Containers for ophthalmics
5. Biological tests—plastics and other polymers
6. Chemical tests—polyethylene containers for dry oral dosage forms
7. Polyethylene terephthalate (PET) and PET G containers
8. Polypropylene containers
9. Repackaging into single unit containers

These tests may also be modified to apply to the use of plastics other than polyethylene, polypropylene, PET, and the use of plastics with liquid dosage forms. Where other plastics are involved, any specific signal compounds may need evaluation, for example, vinyl chloride monomer levels from polyvinylchloride (PVC) containers as well as antioxidants and anti-ozonants and other additives that are susceptible to leach into liquid drug formulations.

U.S. Pharmacopeia, ⟨381⟩ Elastomeric Enclosures for Injections was revised January 1, 2018, with an opening paragraph: "Elastomeric closures for containers used in the types of preparations defined in the general test chapter Injections and Implanted Drug Products are made of materials obtained by vulcanization (cross-linking) polymerization, polyaddition, or polycondensation of macromolecular organic substances (elastomers). Closure formulations contain natural or synthetic elastomers and inorganic and organic additives to aid or control vulcanization, impart physical and chemical properties or color, or stabilize the closure formulation. This chapter applies to closures used for long-term storage of preparations defined in the general test chapter Packaging and Storage Requirements <659>, Injection Packaging. Such closures are typically used as part of a vial, bottle, or pre-fill syringe package system."

The chapter also contains information for the manufacturer (user) of the materials: "The manufacturer of the injectable product (the end user) must obtain from the closure supplier an assurance that the composition of the closure does not vary and that it is the same as that of the closure used during compatibility testing. When the supplier informs the end user of changes in the composition, compatibility testing must be repeated, totally or partly, depending on the nature of the changes. Closures must be properly stored, cleaned for removal of environmental contaminants and endotoxins, and, for aseptic processes, sterilized prior to use in packaging injectable products."

Testing includes multiple physiochemical and functionality requirements.

A summary of these requirements is:

a. Manufacturer's must provide evidence from studies that the containers/closures do not impact the safety, identity, strength, quality, or purity of the drug beyond the official or established requirements.
b. Containers and closures must protect (temperature, humidity, etc.) the drug during storage and use: storage through shelf life and use (one time or in the case of eye drops multiple times). This would be covered in the stability program.
c. Cleaning of the containers and closures is required: the extent of this, including depyrogenation as applicable needs to be assessed and proven.
d. All the specifications, testing methods, storage, cleaning, usage, etc. needs to be validated, proceduralized, evidence documented, and as with all other requirements, they must be followed.

The FDA issued Guidance for Industry: "Container Closure Systems for Packaging Human Drugs and Biologicals" in May 1999, which includes general considerations and specific dosage forms. There are other documents covering container/closures included in the Suggested Reading below.

TAMPER-RESISTANT REQUIREMENTS

The following requirements were issued and revised as result of cyanide tampering with Tylenol® capsules in 1982, which resulted in seven deaths. The Federal Anti-tampering Act (FATA) was passed in 1983 as a result of the Chicago area Tylenol® incident, which outlaws:

- Tampering with any consumer product or its labeling or container
- Tainting any consumer product or rendering its labeling or container materially false or misleading with intent to cause serious injury to the business of any person
- Knowingly communicating false information that a consumer product has been tainted, if such tainting would create a risk of death or bodily injury to another person

- Knowingly threatening to tamper with a consumer product, its labeling, or container
- Conspiring to tamper with a consumer product, its labeling, or container

Requirements of the tamper-resistant packaging (TRP) regulations covering most OTC products were published by FDA in the FEDERAL REGISTER of November 5, 1982.

The regulations require that all OTC human drug products (except dermatologics, dentifrices, insulin, and throat lozenges) (21 CFR 211.132), cosmetic liquid oral hygiene products and vaginal products (21 CFR 700.25), and contact lens solutions and tablets used to make these solutions (21 CFR 800.12) be packaged in tamper-resistant packaging.

The packaging must use an indicator or barrier to entry that is distinctive by design (such as an aerosol container), or must employ an identifying characteristic (a pattern, name, registered trademark, logo, or picture). Further, the regulations require a labeling statement on the container (except ammonia inhalant in crushable glass ampules, aerosol products, or containers of compressed medical oxygen) to alert the consumer to the specific tamper-resistant feature(s) used. The labeling statement is also required to be placed so that it will be unaffected if a TRP feature is breached or missing.

An amendment to the TRP regulations for OTC human drug products published as a final rule in the Federal Register on February 2, 1989. The new requirements (21 CFR 211.132[b][1] and [2]) are:

1. For two-piece, hard gelatin capsule products subject to this requirement, a minimum of two tamper-resistant packaging features is required, unless the capsules are sealed by a tamper-resistant technology.
2. For all other products subject to this requirement, including two-piece, hard gelatin capsules that are sealed by a tamper-resistant technology, a minimum of one tamper-resistant feature is required.

Manufacturers were given until February 2, 1990, to comply with the new requirements.

In addition, the Agency has reevaluated currently available tamper-resistant packaging technologies and concluded that some technologies as designed or applied are no longer capable of meeting the requirements of the TRP regulations.

EXAMPLES OF OBSERVATIONS FROM FDA CITATIONS

- Your firm failed to establish and follow an adequate written testing program designed to assess the stability characteristics of drug products (21 CFR 211.166[a]).
- During your stability studies of povidone-iodine drug products, which purport to be sterile, you failed to test sterility. Therefore, there is no assurance that your povidone-iodine drug products can meet their specifications for sterility through their 36-month expiration period. Products manufactured as sterile must maintain their container-closure integrity and sterility throughout the labeled expiration period.
- Specifically, your firm receives drums of (redacted) raw material from your supplier without any identifying labels. Your firm does not perform identity testing or any other analysis on incoming raw materials upon receipt or prior to use, and you have no procedure that permits you to trace the source of the (redacted) in each batch of finished products.
- During aseptic manufacturing of your sterile ophthalmic products (b)(4) (lot redacted) and (b)(4) (lot redacted), you documented numerous leaking containers and other bottle formation defects. To address these defects, you routinely adjusted your (b)(4) (redacted) equipment and resumed production. You subsequently released these lots. Following distribution, you received customer complaints of leaking containers. In addition, you found numerous critical container-closure defects, including leaking products, during media fills studies. Container integrity is imperative to ensure sterility of ophthalmic drug products. The lack of assurance that your (b)(4) equipment consistently manufactures an integral container-closure system diminishes confidence in the sterility of your marketed products.

- You failed to demonstrate that the drug product containers and closures used in the manufacture of your allergenic products are not reactive, additive, or absorptive so as to alter the safety, identity, strength, quality, or purity of the drug beyond the official or established requirements (21 CFR 211.94[a]). Specifically, extractable and leachable studies have not been conducted on the **(b)(4)** stoppers used in the manufacture of your allergenic products.
- You failed to establish the reliability of the supplier's certificate of testing through appropriate validation of the supplier's test results at appropriate intervals (21 CFR 211.84[d][3]). Specifically, you have not performed periodic endotoxin, bioburden, or particulate matter testing on your stoppers to validate the supplier's CoA. Your SOP QCG021 entitled "**(b)(4)**" only requires visual inspection and dimension verification of the stoppers used in the manufacture of your allergenic products.
- Although you state that you require vendor surveys to qualify your suppliers, your management indicated that you had only one survey available out of the ten supplier surveys the investigator requested during the inspection. In addition, you accepted some components, without a CoA and did not conduct identity testing. As a result, you lack assurance that your components meet all appropriate specifications.

REFERENCE

1. Preamble to 21CFR211 Federal Register, Vol. 43, No. 190—Friday, September 29, 1978.

SUGGESTED READINGS

- USP <1207> Sterile Product Packaging-Integrity Evaluation.
- USP <1207.1> Package Integrity and Test Method Selection.
- USP <1207.2> Package Integrity Leak Test Technologies.
- USP <1207.3> Package Seal Quality Test Methods.
- US Food and Drug Administration (FDA) Compliance Program Guidance Manual, Chapter 56 Drug Quality Assurance Program 7356. 002A-October 31, 2017.
- PDA White Paper: Container Closure Integrity Control versus Integrity Testing during Routine Manufacturing (Ewan, S. et al., 2015).
- FDA Guidance for Industry: Container Closure Systems for Packaging Human Drugs and Biologics, May 2002.
- Parenteral Drug Association. Technical Report 27, Pharmaceutical Package Integrity, July, 1998.
- FDA Guidance for Industry: Container and Closure System Integrity Testing in Lieu of Sterility Testing as a Component of the Stability Protocol for Sterile Products, 2008.
- Kumbhar, Manoj Shivaji et. al. Tamper Evident Pharmaceutical Packaging—Needs and Advances, *International Journal of Pharmaceutical Sciences Review and Research*, Vol 13, Issue 2, March–April 2012; Article-030, pages 141–153.

13 Holding and Distribution

Andrew Acker

CONTENTS

§211.142 WAREHOUSING PROCEDURES

Written procedures describing the warehousing of drug products shall be established and followed. They shall include:

(a) *Quarantine of drug products before release by the quality control unit*
(b) *Storage of drug products under appropriate conditions of temperature, humidity, and light so that the identity, strength, quality, and purity of the drug products are not affected*

Quarantine of drug products may be efficiently controlled with the use of an Enterprise Resource Planning software (ERP), which can be developed, or purchased, to track the storage location and control the release of product under quarantine. Systems such as this should be validated to prove effectiveness and adequate controls. Failure to control quarantined materials results in them being used before release by Quality, and inadequate control of product may result in unauthorized release of product to the market resulting in a formal field action, such as notification, correction, removal, or product recall. ERP software can be programmed to automatically enter product data and identification via bar coding, which can include information regarding the product's status (quarantined, restricted, or released), labeling, and expiration. ERP systems also limit who has the ability and authorization for release of quarantined product, which is only designated to the Quality Department.

Storage of drug products can also be controlled with an ERP system. Incoming product (also includes active pharmaceutical ingredients, raw materials, disposables, supplies, and components) can be immediately quarantined or segregated via bar coding (or other means of identification) at receipt and entered in the system under a hold condition. Product needs to be properly stored based on established parameters and access restricted to only authorized personnel. For temperature-controlled products, the storage areas need to be adequately temperature mapped to determine if they meet predefined limits before use and monitored continuously with alarm notification when limits are exceeded. The storage area should also be routinely cleaned, be part of a sitewide pest control program (internal/external traps and fly "zapper" lights), and precautions taken to prevent flying and crawling insects/birds from entering the premises with well-sealed access points (doors/windows). Loading and unloading areas often have fans that blow air towards the outside preventing ingress of flying pests. Periodic audits and maintenance inspections must be scheduled at established intervals to ensure compliance with requirements. Any excursions need to be reported immediately and contingency actions taken upon notification.

The introduction of a properly implemented, validated, monitored, and controlled ERP system should address FDA concerns regarding the quarantine and proper storage/release of temperature/ time sensitive materials, especially those where extreme temperatures or low relative humidity need to be maintained for product conditions. There are often time limitations for moving received product into cold/freezer storage and also retrieving it prior to shipment to minimize temperature fluctuations. The ERP systems also address FDA concerns for maintaining product status and establishing product access limits. Records need to be completed that capture environmental conditions during the transportation and storage of temperature sensitive products to ensure that product was not exposed to environmental conditions that exceed the established parameters.

Historically, containers of components, containers, closures, and drug products were labeled with the product status and only changed by authorized personnel. With the ERP system, quarantined product can be assigned a shelf location next to released materials without a physical status label attached to the container, including refrigeration and freezer units. Physical separation is required for hazardous or toxic materials and also those materials that are covered by Drug Enforcement Agency regulations. An effective paper or control system with attachment of status labels is still acceptable.

The following storage definitions are defined in the General Notices section of the United States Pharmacopeia (USP) for recommended conditions commonly specified on product labels (1).

1. **Freezer**: A place in which the temperature is maintained thermostatically between −20°C and −10°C (−4°F to 14°F).
2. **Cold**: Any temperature not exceeding 8°C (46°F). A refrigerator is a cold place in which the temperature is maintained thermostatically between 2°C and 8°C (36°C–46°C).
3. **Cool**: Any temperature between 8°C and 15°C (46°F to 59°F). An article that requires cool storage may be stored in a refrigerator, unless otherwise specified by the individual USP monograph.
4. **Room temperature**: The temperature prevailing in the workplace.
5. **Controlled room temperature**: A temperature maintained thermostatically that encompasses the usual and customary working environment of 20°C–25°C (68°F to 77°F) that allows for brief deviations between 15°C and 30°C (59°F to 86°F) that are experienced in pharmacies, hospitals, and warehouses. Articles maybe labeled for storage at "controlled room temperature" or at "up to 25°C" or other wording. An article for which storage at *Controlled room temperature* is directed, may, alternatively, be stored in a cool place unless otherwise specified in the individual monograph or on the label. (See the entire revised definition of *Controlled room temperature* in the *Ninth Supplement* to *USP XXII-NF XVII*.)
6. **Warm**: Any temperature between 30°C and 40°C (86°F to 104°F).
7. **Excessive heat**: Any temperature above 40°C (104°F).
8. **Protection from freezing**: Where, in addition to the risk of breakage of the container, freezing subjects an article to loss of strength or potency, or to destructive alteration of its characteristics, the container label must bear an appropriate instruction to protect the article from freezing.

With the exceptions of special storage conditions (refrigeration, freezer, etc.) there are typically two types of warehouse storage conditions for room temperature:

1. **Ambient room temperature conditions**: For some products, an adequate shelf life can be determined that encompasses the relatively wide range of conditions that constitute "ambient." Monitoring of temperature data in the warehouse provides the assurance that the requirements continue to be met. Humidity and light are rarely controlled—however,

humidity can be monitored—but does not normally impact packaging unless it is very high and has been known to cause mold growth on cardboard in refrigerators.

2. **Controlled room temperature**: Storage areas may be similar to the ambient conditions depending on the location and seasonal weather. These areas are typically monitored for temperature (some cases humidity) and controlled with a heating ventilation and air-conditioning system to maintain the required conditions. Monitoring locations are selected based on the mapping studies throughout the facility and different seasons, especially when these are extreme high or low temperature/humidity.

It is important to note that staging of incoming and pre-shipment materials and product requiring specific conditions cannot be left at ambient temperature for extended periods that could impact their shelf life.

§211.150 DISTRIBUTION PROCEDURES

Written procedures shall be established, and followed, describing the distribution of drug products. They shall include the following:

(a) *A procedure whereby the oldest approved stock of a drug product is distributed first. Deviation from this requirement is permitted if such deviation is temporary and appropriate.*

(b) *A system by which the distribution of each lot of drug product can be readily determined to facilitate its recall if necessary.*

As in all FDA-regulated applications, establishing and documenting data on the operating environments that are "scientifically sound" needs to be performed to maintain compliance to regulatory requirements. Product supply chain stakeholders must understand their environmental conditions and product parameters and be able to convey that understanding through objective evidence. Proper procedures and product/process documentation is key to establishing this understanding and control. Product and material distribution records must document approved product usage per a first-in, first-out (FIFO) system ensuring that the oldest approved product stock is utilized and distributed first prior to the use of newer stock. Any deviation to this established system needs to be handled and documented by a formal deviation process.

Distribution records for all products need to be completed and maintained in the event a field action or notification is required. Field actions include the removal, correction, or recall of products. A notification would be a formal letter to the customer. Product recalls may need to be facilitated if a product is found to be adulterated, contaminated, or otherwise found unfit to perform in its intended and advertised manner. If product is to be recalled, the following steps need to be taken to facilitate this according to the standard operating procedure:

- Identify product lot numbers and define how much product is affected (ERP systems contain this information).
- Identify who the recalled product has been shipped to and how much they have (including warehousing, distribution, and storage areas).
- Identify who in the customer's organization to contact if product has reached the customer beyond the distribution centers.
- Draft a letter stating a recall has been issued and include all the relevant details.
- Draft a document explaining the defect and how to distinguish good product from suspect product and what to do with it or how to return it.
- Provide a postcard-type return postage paid mailer to sign and return stating they have received your contact and confirming their action/status regarding product.
- Ensure that the information is distributed to all the required customers.

- Follow up with customers who have not responded until you have established due diligence.
- Document all communications as evidence of the process.
- Maintain statistics during the return process when the product is being returned or the confirmation of any other requested actions to verify effectiveness of the recall.
- Ensure all returned product is managed and segregated immediately with appropriate labeling/signage.

All distribution records should be maintained for a minimum three-year period after the distribution process for any control number has been completed. If expiration dating is used for a product, distribution records must be maintained at least for one year past the expiration date of the product [§211.180(b)].

COLD-CHAIN DISTRIBUTION

The cold-chain distribution process is a part of good manufacturing practice (GMP) requirements that all drugs and biological products are required to adhere to. As such, the distribution process must be qualified to ensure that there is no negative impact to the safety, efficacy or quality of the product.[1]

The manufacturer is responsible for assuring materials and product are stored as defined on the label while they are in their control and this includes during shipment from the facility. Shipping studies are performed that provide data to prove that the required conditions were met and there are no excessive fluctuations that impact the material/product. Thermocouple probes and separate temperature data loggers are used to measure temperatures within the shipment under test conditions. Replicate testing based on a qualification protocol is used to create a final qualification report that can be used to support the load configuration under the environmental conditions. After qualification, temperature monitoring devices are places in predefined locations throughout the load, and the data is reviewed and approved upon receipt before the material can be further processed. Some companies have a set time on Fridays after which shipments of specific temperature-controlled materials/product are not shipped to minimize the potential of delays in transporting impacting the product shipment. A procedure needs to be established to manage any deviations or temperature excursions outside of established parameters.

AUDITING OF DISTRIBUTORS

When auditing a distributor, the assessment of procedures and inspection of the facilities is performed. There needs to be specified procedures for the storage and distribution requirements and conditions according to an agreement and include any "special" storage conditions. A qualification audit needs to be performed prior to a distribution agreement to establish the distributor's ability to meet stated requirements and confirm compliance with current good manufacturing practices (cGMPs). A qualification audit should include but not be limited to the following:

- Security and access to authorized personnel, including restricting driver access
- Facilities and utilities suitable for intended use
- HVAC system qualification and maintenance
- Cleaning schedule and material/product spill procedure
- Store and cycle product (FIFO)
- Defining what shipping method to use
- Receipt and staging product for shipment
- Segregation to avoid mix-ups: management through inventory control system
- Protecting the product from contamination or adulteration
- Management of damaged containers, deviations of counts, and labeling

- Restrictions on the types of materials handled (high potency)
- What is the product flow, movement, pick and pack, verification of selecting materials/ product, and final checks before shipment
- Use of ERP system and review of the validation documents

COUNTERFEITING

The U.S. closely regulates the import of all life science commodities. Such commodities are regulated either by the Food and Drug Administration (FDA) or by the U.S. Department of Agriculture (USDA). Generally, the commodities covered under such regulations are items that are either ingested or applied to the human body or in some way modify or may have ill effects on the body. Shippers have various requirements for shipments of these commodities. In some instances, this is related to registration that must be carried out prior to shipping, in addition to what is required to be declared on air waybills and commercial invoices.[2,3]

The FDA website (www.FDA.gov) contains information and alerts relating to drug counterfeiting and is a useful reference for the latest incidents. The FDA website notes that "Counterfeit medicine is fake medicine. It may be contaminated or contain the wrong or no active ingredient. They could have the right active ingredient but at the wrong dose. Counterfeit drugs are illegal and may be harmful to your health."

The U.S. Federal Food, Drug, and Cosmetic Act prohibits the interstate shipment (which includes importation) of unapproved new drugs. Thus, the importation of drugs that lack FDA approval, whether for personal use or otherwise, is a violation of the above law. Unapproved new drugs are any drugs, including foreign-made versions of U.S. approved drugs, which have not been manufactured in accordance with or pursuant to an FDA approval. Under the Act, FDA may refuse importation of any drug that "appears" to be unapproved, placing the burden on the importer to prove that the drug sought to be imported is, in fact, approved by the FDA.

On September 27, 2007, the Food and Drug Administration Amendments Act of 2007 (Public Law 110-85) was signed into law. Section 913 of this legislation created Section 505D of the Federal Food, Drug, and Cosmetic Act, which requires the Secretary of Health and Human Services (the Secretary) to develop standards and identify and validate effective technologies for the purpose of securing the drug supply chain against counterfeit, diverted, subpotent, substandard, adulterated, misbranded, or expired drugs. Subsequently, the FDA issued a guidance to industry[4] in March 2010 covering this requirement.

FDA's enforcement policy with respect to the application of CGMP to Radio-Frequency Identification (RFID) technology is provided in Compliance Policy Guide (CPG) Section 400.210.[5]

Raw drugs and raw pharmaceuticals must be accompanied by a Toxic Substances Control Act statement, which must be completed and treated as an additional page to the Commercial Invoice.

The following information is required on the Commercial Invoice for drugs:

- Correct country of origin/production
- Correct manufacturer site
- Product code
- Precise description of product, including packing, form, dosage, generic name, chemical consumption, and derivation
- Intended use (for use on humans)
- Accurate statement of quantity (must be applicable to product)
- Confirmation as to whether the drugs contain any animal derivatives (if USDA regulation applies)
- Affirmation of Compliance Codes:
  - Drug Establishment Registration number for manufacture
  - Drug Listing number

- New Drug Application number
- Exemption for Investigational New Drug
- Number for investigational or clinical trial use (need name of drug; Study Number is not sufficient).

Exports may require a Shipper's Export Declaration (SED). The key to effective export controls is the collection and screening of export transaction information prior to the departure of cargo from the U.S. The Automated Export System (AES) was first deployed to collect export transaction information for statistical and enforcement purposes. AES continues to be a key tool for Customs and Border Protection. The departments of Commerce and Homeland Security have authored a Final Rule, which would revise Part 30 of Title 30 of the Code of Federal Regulations, Foreign Trade Statistics Regulations (15 CFR Part 30) to implement mandatory AES filing of SEDs.

The Prescription Drug Marketing Act (PDMA) of 1987 was signed into law by the President on April 22, 1988. The PDMA was enacted (1) to ensure that drug products purchased by consumers are safe and effective, and (2) to avoid the unacceptable risk to American consumers from counterfeit, adulterated, misbranded, subpotent, or expired drugs. The legislation was necessary to increase safeguards in the drug distribution system to prevent the introduction and retail sale of substandard, ineffective, or counterfeit drugs.

The FDA issued a guidance[6] to assist industry and state and local governments in understanding how to categorize the entities in the drug supply chain in accordance with the Drug Supply Chain Security Act (DSCSA). DSCSA establishes product tracing requirements for certain trading partners in the drug supply chain, including manufacturers, repackagers, wholesale distributors, and dispensers. DSCSA also requires that trading partners of manufacturers, wholesale distributors, dispensers, and repackagers must meet the applicable requirements for being "authorized trading partners."

FDA led a collaboration within Asia Pacific Economic Cooperation economies to create a Supply Chain Security Toolkit for Medical Products to maximize available global resources and to deliver quality trainings and best practices and for securing the global supply chain for medical products.[7]

The *Compliance Policy Guide 160.900*[8] was issued in 2006 and identifies proposed enforcement for:

1. High-value products in the U.S. market (price, volume, demand)
2. Prior indicators
3. Reasonable probability that a new drug will be counterfeited
4. Other violations of PDMA or other laws

EXAMPLES OF OBSERVATIONS FROM FDA CITATIONS

- No procedures available describing distribution of oldest stock first or any record of batch numbers entering distribution.
- Products requiring specific storage conditions, 59°F–86°F, were stored in a non-air-conditioned warehouse at 90°F.
- No defined quarantine area for incoming finished drug products to be repacked.
- Failure to have adequate written procedures for the receipt, identification, quarantine, storage, sampling, testing, handling, and approval or rejection of raw materials. For example, when our investigator asked for a list of your critical raw materials and your sampling requirements, you told our investigator that you had no written procedures for testing and sampling incoming materials. Instead, you explained, your warehouse employees accounted for incoming raw material handling, sampling, and testing "in their heads."
- Your firm failed to maintain adequate separate defined areas necessary to prevent contamination or mix-up (21 CFR 211.42[c]). "You did not utilize any quarantine markings or physical segregation of finished drug products from the lawn care and cleaning chemicals in your

warehouse. You did not designate your quarantined finished drug products with quarantined status. During the inspection, your Vice President of Operations stated that your firm does not quarantine any finished products before they are released by quality because you "thought of the product as good once it was manufactured.""

- Your firm failed to establish a written distribution procedure to include a system by which each lot of drug product can be readily determined to facilitate its recall if necessary (21 CFR 211.150[b]). "Your firm lacked any procedures describing your drug distribution system. Your distribution system was deficient in that it could not differentiate between the lot number your firm assigns and the lot number assigned by the manufacturer, and therefore there is no product traceability if a recall is required. Our investigator observed that neither your receiving or shipping records included the lot numbers of products you received and shipped."

REFERENCES

1. Bishara RH. Cold chain management—An essential component of the global pharmaceutical supply chain. *Am. Pharm. Rev.* January/February, 2006.
2. Cracking down on counterfeiting. Pharmaceutical Technology, Aug 2, 2006. http://www.pharmtech.com/pharmtech/article/articleDetail.jsp?=id361496, accessed August 25, 2006.
3. Thaul S. Pharmaceutical Supply Chain Security. Congressional Research Service. October 31, 2016.
4. FDA "Guidance for Industry Standards for Securing the Drug Supply Chain—Standardized Numerical Identification for Prescription Drug Packages." U.S. Department of Health and Human Services Food and Drug Administration Office of the Commissioner (OC), Center for Drug Evaluation and Research (CDER), Center for Biologics Evaluation and Research (CBER), Office of Regulatory Affairs (ORA) March 2010.
5. http://www.fda.gov/ICECI/ComplianceManuals/CompliancePolicyGuidanceManual/ucm074357.htm.
6. FDA Guidance for Industry: Identifying Trading Partners Under the Drug Supply Chain Security Act Guidance for Industry. Draft, March 2017.
7. https://www.fda.gov/Drugs/DrugSafety/DrugIntegrityandSupplyChainSecurity/ucm559053.htm.
8. CPG Sec. 160.900 Prescription Drug Marketing Act—Pedigree Requirements under 21 CFR Part 203.

SUGGESTED READINGS

- WHO Technical Report Series, No. 957, 2010, Annex 5, WHO good distribution practices for pharmaceutical products.
- Guidance: *Compliance Policy Guide 160.900 FDA*.
- PDA Technical Report 39, Cold Chain Guidance for Medical Products: Maintaining the Quality of Temperature Sensitive Medical Products through the Transportation Environment, 2005.
- PDA *J Pharm Sci Technol.* 2007;61(2 Suppl. TR 39):2–19. Guidance for temperature-controlled medicinal products: Maintaining the quality of temperature-sensitive medicinal products through the transportation environment.
- Guidelines of 5 November 2013 on Good Distribution Practice of medicinal products for human use (Text with EEA relevance) (2013/C 343/01).
- IBM Develops RFID System for Pharmaceutical Track and Trace. Pharmaceutical Technology August 24, 2006.

14 Returned and Salvaged Drug Products

Graham P. Bunn

CONTENTS

§211.204 RETURNED DRUG PRODUCTS

Returned drug products shall be identified as such and held. If the conditions under which returned drug products have been held, stored, or shipped before or during their return, or if the condition of the drug product, its container, carton, or labeling, as a result of storage or shipping, casts doubt on the safety, identity, strength, quality, or purity of the drug product, the returned drug product shall be destroyed unless examination, testing, or other investigations prove the drug product meets appropriate standards of safety, identity, strength, quality, or purity. A drug product may be reprocessed provided the subsequent drug product meets appropriate standards, specifications, and characteristics. Records of returned drug products shall be maintained and shall include the name and label potency of the drug product dosage form, lot number (or control number or batch number), reason for the return, quantity returned, date of disposition, and ultimate disposition of the returned drug product. If the reason for a drug product being returned implicates associated batches, an appropriate investigation shall be conducted in accordance with the requirements of §211.192. Procedures for the holding, testing, and reprocessing of returned drug products shall be in writing and shall be followed.

Products can be returned for several reasons including but not limited to: incorrectly ordered, too much ordered, or damaged in shipment. A return may actually be a customer complaint and needs to be managed according to the complaint Standard Operating Procedure requirements.

The objectives of the regulations are to manage returned products and perform an evaluation to determine if they can be used or need to be destroyed. These requirements consider:

1. Reviewing the reason(s) for returned product to determine if additional action(s) is/are required for the specific lot/batch, related lots/batches, or to the storage and distribution chain network related to the products. Some products require specific controlled temperature/ humidity shipping conditions, and there needs to be documented evidence that these were maintained to the point of delivery. Even products with room temperature shipping

conditions can be impacted by higher or lower temperatures (excessive/subzero temperatures during transportation due to adverse conditions and delays). Documentation of the shipping conditions is required throughout the distribution chain before continuing to determine acceptability of the product. Security of the product in relation to potential tampering must also be evaluated to ensure that it is still in the same condition and integrity that it was when originally released.

   Sometimes it may be appropriate, for example, essential product in short supply, to perform additional testing and evaluations to confirm that the product still meets the release specification requirements, and consideration of a product stability test regimen is typically applied. Evaluation of the results must also consider that no amount of testing will provide absolute assurance that all the units returned were subjected to the same environmental conditions while in the supply chain process.

2. Ensuring that returned product details, including quantities and dispositions, are accurately recorded. Since comprehensive distribution records (see §211.196) are maintained to account for all the batch units, it is essential that comprehensive records of any returned product are also kept. Even with distribution records maintained in a different system there needs to be procedures to ensure that accountability of the entire batch can be performed in the event of a recall.
3. Procedures covering returned product must also include the disposition approval requirements, including Quality Assurance.

Apart from the requirement to evaluate the reason(s) for the returned product, there are considerable resources required to evaluate if returned product can potentially be redistributed. Even with distribution temperature conditions documentation and test results, there can still be unknown information. Due to some of the undetermined risks associated with redistributing returned product, many companies decide not to perform the process.

§211.208 DRUG PRODUCT SALVAGING

Drug products that have been subjected to improper storage conditions, including extremes in temperature, humidity, smoke, fumes, pressure, age, or radiation due to natural disasters, fires, accidents, or equipment failures, shall not be salvaged and returned to the marketplace. Whenever there is a question whether drug products have been subjected to such conditions, salvaging operations may be conducted only if there is (a) evidence from laboratory tests and assays (including animal feeding studies where applicable) that the drug products meet all applicable standards of identity, strength, quality, and purity and (b) evidence from inspection of the premises that the drug products and their associated packaging were not subjected to improper storage conditions as a result of the disaster or accident. Organoleptic examinations shall be acceptable only as supplemental evidence that the drug products meet appropriate standards of identity, strength, quality, and purity. Records including name, lot number, and disposition shall be maintained for drug products subject to this section.

   This section very clearly states that products that have been exposed to improper storage conditions "shall not be salvaged and returned to the marketplace." This requirement needs to be equally applied to components, in-process material, and raw materials, and also containers, closures, and labeling. Caution needs to be exercised when managing these specific situations and a rigorous assessment/visual examination/testing, including risk assessment, must be performed. As with returned product mentioned above, the uncertainty or insufficient documented evidence may outweigh any possible financial savings.

   Regulatory Authorities are always interested in the management of returned product and any salvaging activities. These are exceptional events, and they are expected to be managed as such. Inadequate evaluations, unsupported conclusions, and irrational decisions will clearly suggest that the procedures and/or management are not focused on product quality; instead, they are justifying returning product to stock/available for shipping to market based on cost. An incalculable cost may result due to product not meeting all its quality attributes, and in addition Regulatory Authorities focus when product is recalled.

EXAMPLES OF OBSERVATIONS FROM FDA CITATIONS

- Records of returned drug products do not include the [name] [labeled potency] [lot, control, or batch number] [reason for return] [quantity] [date of disposition] [ultimate disposition].
- As per written procedure, returned drug products require a Return Goods Form be affixed to the product for further processing. Out of [redacted] entries, with [redacted] corresponding to xxxx tablets, only two entries documented that the required form had been issued, and those forms could not be found. Although multiple products were returned, no such forms were issued from *date to date.*
- Procedures describing the [holding] [testing] [reprocessing] of returned drug products are not [in writing] [followed].

RECOMMENDED READING

The following sections are from FDA Compliance Policy Guides relating to product reconditioning and are useful reference documents.

Sec. 160.750 Drug And Device Products (Including Biologics And Animal Drugs) Found in Violation of Good Manufacturing Practice Regulations—Reconditioning (CPG 7153.14)

Background

The question has arisen as to whether drug and device products that have been produced or held by methods or under conditions not in accordance with good manufacturing practice regulations (GMPRs), and consequently determined to be adulterated, may be reconditioned and returned to trade channels. Situations covered by this compliance policy guide (CPG) are those in which a "formal" judgment of adulteration has been rendered, e.g., drug and device products that have been seized and condemned pursuant to Section 304 of the Act due to good manufacturing practices deficiencies, drug and device products that have been recalled because they were found to be in violation of the current good manufacturing practice regulations (CGMPRs), etc. Although GMP deficiencies can be corrected in subsequent batches or lots of the involved product(s), it may be difficult or impossible to correct the effect of the deficiencies retrospectively in batches or lots already produced.

Policy

The reconditioning of drug and device products found to be adulterated as a result of having been produced, processed, or held under conditions which are deficient with regard to GMPRs may be, providing all of the following conditions are met as follows:

1. Any reconditioning proposal must be reviewed by all parties concerned (District, Center, OE,* OCC*) to determine whether the plan can reasonably be expected to bring the drug device product(s) into compliance.
2. In order to be acceptable, a proposed reconditioning plan must overcome any observed GMP deficiencies and correct any known product defects present.

3. If the lot to be reconditioned is held within the facility where the GMP violations occurred, the violative conditions must be corrected in advance of accepting a reconditioning proposal, or included as part of the reconditioning proposal.
4. If the lot is held in a facility separate from the one in which the GMP violations occurred and the separate facility is in compliance, a reconditioning proposal can be considered as provided for in paragraphs 1 and 2 earlier.

No product shall be released until all reconditioning commitments are fully met as verified by the FDA.
Material between asterisks is new or revised
Issued: 3/1/83
Revised: 3/95, 8/96

CPG Sec. 448.100 Reconditioning of New Drugs Which Do Not Have Approved NDAs/ANDAs (7132c.03)

Background

Prior policy under the drug efficacy study implementation (DESI) program permitted the marketing of new drugs evaluated as effective upon the submission of a new drug application (NDA) or abbreviated new drug application (ANDA). This policy was challenged and overturned in a decision handed down on July 29, 1975, by the U.S. District Court for the District of Columbia (*Hoffman La Roche v. Caspar Weinberger, et al.*). The Agency implemented this order, Judge Green's decision, through Compliance Program 7332.26 covering products identical or related ("me too" drugs) to DESI drugs identified in a list published 1/76 (DHEW publication No. [FDA] 76–3009).

Agency policy as set forth in the program required that such new drugs be discontinued from marketing and recalled if substantial stocks remain in trade channels. When responsible firms have failed to initiate the above actions after being warned by issuance of a *warning letter,* unapproved new drugs have been seized.

Although recall or seizure may have been necessary for uniform enforcement and protection of the public health, destruction of such recalled or seized material is not always required, provided adequate safeguards are taken.

Policy

In those instances in which an ANDA has been submitted and is currently pending, we will not insist upon destruction of recalled or seized material resulting from implementation of CPG 7132c.02 involving DESI effective drugs provided:

1. Recalled stocks are quarantined by the formulator and not held by consignees, i.e., substantial stocks in the hands of consignees must be disposed of either by return to the formulator or by destruction. Failure to do so will result in recommendation for regulatory action by the district, preferably seizure.
2. Recalled (quarantined lots at the formulator) or seized material may not be released until and unless all the following conditions are met:
   a. Approval of an NDA or ANDA is received.
   b. The firm can validate that the lots in question were manufactured in accordance with the specifications of the approved NDA/ANDA including the following:
      1. Compliance with current good manufacturing practice (CGMP).
      2. Affected lots meet all purity, potency, and labeling standards specified by the approved NDA/ANDA.

3. Where an unapproved new drug has been seized, under either Section 505 or 502, and as a result of subsequent ANDA approval, it is not in the public interest that it be condemned and destroyed under Section 304(d)(1), the Agency may consider entering into a stipulation of dismissal incorporating the following principles:

a. The claimant shall assure the Agency, by way of appropriate records, that the drug is in full compliance with the approved ANDA prior to dismissal of the complaint.

b. Where consistency with the approved ANDA requires labeling modifications, and compliance cannot be assured by a records review as in *"a"* above, the court may order the seized article be remanded to the custody of the claimant for the sole purpose of making the required modifications. If and when the agency is satisfied that the required modifications have been made, and the article is in all respects consistent with the approved ANDA, the complaint may be dismissed.

c. All activity undertaken to assure that the seized article is in compliance with the law shall be at the expense of the claimant, including investigatory and laboratory work performed by agency personnel. Current fee and mileage schedules shall apply, and payment shall be received prior to dismissal of the action and full release of the article.

Where no NDA/ANDA has been submitted, or if the district has information that quarantined or seized lots will not meet the above conditions or approval of a current pending application does not appear probable within a reasonable time frame (three months), then we will insist upon destruction of stocks. In the case of the latter, concurrence by Division of Drug Labeling Compliance (HFD-310) is required.

Except upon the specific conditions outlined above, nothing in these provisions shall be construed as altering agency policy that articles seized pursuant to Section 304 may not be reconditioned by agency consent without the entry of a decree condemning the articles and providing for reconditioning under agency supervision.

* Material between asterisks is new or revised*

Issued: 10/1/80

Revised: 3/95

Questions and Answers on Current Good Manufacturing Practices, Good Guidance Practices, Level 2 Guidance—Returned and Salvaged Drug Products

June 18, 2015

https://www.fda.gov/drugs/developmentapprovalprocess/manufacturing/ucm252324.htm

15 Active Pharmaceutical Ingredients

Joseph C. Near

CONTENTS

This chapter is intended to provide guidance on current good manufacturing practices (CGMPs) for the manufacturing of active pharmaceutical ingredients (APIs) and the current thinking by the United States Food and Drug Administration (FDA).

FOOD AND DRUG ADMINISTRATION REQUIREMENTS

An API is defined in ICH Q7[1] as "any substance of mixture of substances intended to be used in the manufacture of a drug product and that, when used in the production of a drug, becomes an active ingredient in the drug product. Such substances are intended to furnish pharmacological activity or other direct effect in the diagnosis, cure, mitigation, treatment or prevention of disease or to affect the structure and function of the body." Historically, other terms have also been used by the FDA and industry to mean an API, including Drug Substance and Bulk Pharmaceutical Chemical. FDA requirements cover APIs that are manufactured by chemical synthesis, extraction, cell culture/fermentation, and recovery from natural sources.

Historically, it has been recognized that there is a significant difference between the processes used for API manufacturing and those used for the manufacture of dosage forms. API processes are frequently diverse chemical operations. These operations often range from final purification/isolations steps to complex processes that employ multiple organic synthesis steps prior to the purification, isolation, and packaging of the final API. These chemical entities are usually better defined, thus making the task of testing and quality evaluation easier.

The quality of an API must be assured by building quality into the manufacturing process. Long gone are the days when the industry believed quality could be achieved through testing of APIs. Manufacturing processes must include systems that assure a state of control is achieved and maintained. This state of control is built into the operations by designing the CGMPs into the manufacturing processes.

APIs are subject to the adulteration provisions of Section 501(a)(2)(B) of the Food, Drug and Cosmetic Act (the "Act"), which requires all drugs to be manufactured in conformance with CGMP. No distinction is made between an API and a finished pharmaceutical in the Act, and the failure of either to comply with CGMP constitutes a violation of the Act. For years, the CGMP regulations (21 CFR 210 and 211) acted as a general guide for API manufactures since the definition of "drug" in the Food, Drug and Cosmetic Act includes both dosage forms and APIs, and Section 510 (a)(2) (B) requires that all drugs are manufactured, processed, packed, and held in accordance with the GMPs. In 1991, in an effort to establish consistency among inspectors, the FDA issued a revised version of the Guide to the Inspection of Bulk Pharmaceutical Chemicals. This was not a regulation, but this document provided guidance and support for FDA field investigators. Compliance with this guide effectively became a requirement for approval in FDA Pre-Approval inspections. With the issuance of the Guidance for Industry Q7A[1] Good Manufacturing Practice Guidance for Active Pharmaceutical Ingredients, the CGMP expectations of API manufactures became better defined.

In the introduction of the Guidance for Industry Q7A[1] Good Manufacturing Practice Guidance for Active Pharmaceutical Ingredients, the FDA states that this document is intended to provide guidance regarding good manufacturing practice (GMP) for the manufacturing of APIs under an appropriate system for managing quality. It is also intended to help ensure that APIs meet the quality and purity characteristics that they purport, or are represented, to possess. Manufacturing is defined to include operations of receipt of materials, production, packaging, repackaging, labeling, relabeling, quality control, release, storage, and distribution of APIs and associated related controls. All APIs manufactured or used in a drug product should be produced following CGMP stated in this guidance.

API starting materials are defined as raw materials, intermediates, or APIs that are used in the manufacturing process of an API. These materials typically become a significant structural fragment of the final API structure. Normally, API starting materials have well-defined structures and chemical properties.

Defining when the API process begins and associated critical process steps is crucial in assuring compliance with regulatory expectations. Companies must document their rationale on designating the point at which API manufacturing begins. In order to minimize the potential for disagreements with regulatory agencies, companies should provide a strong scientific rationale in defining the start of an API process. Critical process steps that have been determined to impact the quality of the API should be validated. At times, the company may choose to validate other steps to assure a state of control throughout the process or facility. However, it should be noted that choosing to validate a process step does not indicate that step is critical. This CGMP guidance does not apply to steps prior to the introduction of an API starting material. The following table indicates the application of the CGMP guidance to API manufactures (Table 15.1).

API GMPs

The details provided in Guidance for Industry Q7A[1] Good Manufacturing Practice Guidance for Active Pharmaceutical Ingredients are intended to provide guidance regarding GMP for the manufacturing of APIs under an appropriate quality management system.

RESPONSIBILITIES OF THE QUALITY UNIT

As with drug products, the FDA expects that the quality unit of an organization will be involved in all quality-related matters. The quality unit is expected to be an independent organization, and their main duties are not to be delegated. Key duties would include but are not limited to the following:

TABLE 15.1

Application of the CGMP Guidance to API Manufactures

Type of Manufacturing	Application of this Guidance to Steps (Shown in Italics) Used in this Type of Manufacturing				
Chemical manufacturing	Production of the API starting material	*Introduction of the API starting material into the process*	Production of intermediates	*Isolation and purification*	*Physical processing and packaging*
API derived from animal sources or extracted from plant sources	Collection processes	Cutting, mixing, and/or initial processing	*Introduction of the API starting material into process*	*Isolation and purification*	*Physical processing and packaging*
Biotechnology: fermentation/ cell culture	Establishment of master cell bank and working cell bank	*Maintenance of working cell bank*	*Cell culture and/or fermentation*	*Isolation and purification*	*Physical processing and packaging*
"Classical" fermentation to produce an API	Establishment of cell bank	Maintenance of the cell bank	*Introduction of the cells into fermentation*	*Isolation and purification*	*Physical processing and packaging*

Abbreviation: API, active pharmaceutical ingredients.

1. Releasing or rejecting raw material, purchased intermediates, packaging components, labels, and all APIs
2. Approving master batch records, standard operating procedures, and all specifications
3. Reviewing and approving batch records and laboratory records
4. Reviewing and approving validation protocols and summary reports
5. Reviewing and approving all investigations of all critical deviations and ensuring appropriate corrective actions are implemented
6. Reviewing results of the stability-monitoring program
7. Reviewing all quality-related returns, complaints, and recalls

BUILDINGS AND FACILITIES

Buildings and facilities used to manufacture intermediates and APIs should be designed and constructed to facilitate manufacturing, cleaning, and maintenance. Facilities should be designed and operated to minimize the potential for contamination. There should be adequate space for the placement and storage of equipment and materials. Defined areas to ensure control of activities such as receipt of materials, storage, sampling, cleaning, productions, and packaging should be established to prevent mix-ups or contamination.

Laboratory areas are typically separated from manufacturing areas. Laboratory areas used for in-process controls can be located in the manufacturing area, provided they do not adversely impact the accuracy of the laboratory measurements.

Critical utilities that can impact product quality (e.g., steam, gas, compressed air, heating, ventilation, and air conditioning) should be defined by the company. These utilities should be qualified, monitored, and appropriate action taken if defined limits are exceeded. HVAC systems and exhaust systems should be designed and constructed to minimize risks of contamination and cross contamination and should include temperature and humidity controls as appropriate for the stage of manufacturing being performed.

Water used in API manufacturing should be demonstrated to be suitable for its intended use.

Unless more stringent requirements are needed to ensure the quality of the API, potable water may be used, provided it meets the regulatory requirements for drinking water. Where purified water is used, the process must be validated and include microbial controls. Water used in the final isolation and purification steps should be monitored and controlled for total microbial counts, objectionable organisms, and endotoxins.

When highly sensitizing materials, such as penicillins or cephalosporins, are being produced, dedicated processing areas, including air-handling equipment, should be used.

PROCESS EQUIPMENT

The FDA places a high value on the cleanability of equipment to prevent the possibility for contamination. Written procedures should be developed and put in place for the cleaning process of equipment and utensils. Cleaning procedures must include sufficient details to enable operators to clean each type of equipment in a reproducible and effective manner. The procedures should define who performs the cleaning, cleaning frequency, cleaning agents to be used, and recording of any critical cleaning parameters. Acceptance criteria for residues and cleaning agents should be defined and justified. The cleaning activities should be documented either in the batch record, a separate worksheet, or a logbook. Dedicated equipment should be used for production when equipment is not readily cleanable. Using appropriate signage, equipment should be identified as to its contents and cleanliness status.

As with drug products, written maintenance and calibration procedures should be established. Key equipment and critical instruments should be defined by the company. Control, weighing, measuring, monitoring, and testing equipment critical for ensuring the quality of intermediates or APIs should be done following an established schedule. Deviations from approved standards of calibration on critical instruments should be investigated to determine if any impact on quality occurred.

COMPUTERIZED SYSTEMS

A focus on ensuring computerized systems employed in both manufacturing and laboratory operations are validated for their intended use has increased over the past decade. GMP-related computerized systems must be appropriately validated. The depth and scope of validation will depend on the complexity and criticality of the computerized application. Written procedures for the operation and maintenance of computerized systems must be developed and implemented. Changes to the automation must be made in adherence to established change control procedures. Records should be maintained of all changes that demonstrate the system is maintained in a validated state.

DOCUMENTATION AND RECORDS

Over the past decade, it has become the expectation that companies employ a systems approach to documentation. During regulatory inspections, the failure of companies to produce proper documentation has led to regulatory citations and action. A robust and effective documentation system is critical for the overall compliance posture of the organization. Written procedures must be established for preparing, reviewing, approving, and distributing documents associated with the manufacture of intermediates or APIs.

The documentation system should establish a retention schedule for all CGMP documents (e.g., batch records, laboratory records, validation protocols, raw material testing, and calibration records for critical instruments). The documentation system should establish norms of recording information. Training on proper documentation should be delivered to both operating and technical personnel to ensure good documentation practices are routinely followed. Entries of information or data should be made with indelible ink in the space provided at the time the activity is performed, and should identify the person making the entry. Corrections to entries should be dated and signed and leave the original entry still legible.

The company should develop and implement written procedures for the review and approval of batch production and laboratory control records, including packaging and labeling, to ensure the compliance of the intermediate or API with established specifications. The quality unit must review and approve all completed batch production and laboratory control records of critical process steps prior to release of product.

MATERIALS MANAGEMENT

In API manufacturing, deliveries of materials routinely consist of large numbers of containers. A system to identify the status of the material should be established. This system would typically be used as an acceptable alternative to a designated quarantine area. Containers of materials or group of containers should be properly identified and labeled with a distinctive code (e.g., batch number, lot number, or receipt number).

It is acknowledged that the specific batch identity will be lost with the storage of some materials and solvents in bulk. However, prior to mixing bulk deliveries with existing stocks (e.g., solvents or stocks in silos), they should be tested and released. Procedures should be available to prevent the discharging of incoming materials wrongly into the existing stock. Inventory levels and date and time of discharging of the incoming materials should be recorded to provide traceability of the material. External storage is also acceptable, provided labeling remains legible and that containers are cleaned prior to opening.

Testing to verify the identity of each lot of material should normally be conducted. A supplier's certificate of analysis can be used in place of performing additional tests. However, if a supplier's certificate of analysis is used, the company must have a system in place to evaluate its suppliers.

Release of hazardous materials with reliance on the manufacturer's certificate of analysis is also acceptable. To establish the identity of the hazardous materials a visual inspection of storage containers, labels, and recording of lot numbers is routinely included as part of the system. The company should develop and document appropriate justification for not testing these materials.

Storage of raw materials, intermediates, and APIs should be done in a manner to prevent degradation and contamination. Storage conditions should be defined and documented by the company for a period that has no adverse effect on their quality. The company should have an inventory system employed that assures the oldest stock of material is routinely used first. Appropriate space needs to be provided for the storage to allow for cleaning and inspection of storage facilities. To reduce the potential of damage and contamination, materials stored in fiber drums, bags, or boxes should be stored off the floor. The company should establish expiry periods for materials and written reevaluation procedures to determine their suitability for use.

PRODUCTION AND IN-PROCESS CONTROLS

As with drug products, the FDA expects companies to assure that materials are weighed, measured, or subdivided in a manner to assure the quality of the material and to prevent contamination. After dispensing and weighing, materials should be properly labeled (e.g., material name, item code, receiving number, weight, and reevaluation date). Critical weighing and dispensing activities require a verification step. The operation can be witnessed by a second person or should be subject to equivalent control, such as electronic confirmation of weights and activities performed.

In the API process, expected yields should be defined, and appropriate yield ranges should be established for designated steps based on previous laboratory, pilot scale, or manufacturing data. Actual yields should be compared with expected yields. Deviations in yield should be investigated to determine their impact on quality, determine root cause, and implement corrective actions, as appropriate. Where appropriate, established time limits for completion of phases of production should be established.

It is not unusual to recover additional material from mother liquors in API processes. Often the recovery is designated as a second crop isolation and is reused in subsequent production batches. Additionally, solvents are routinely recovered and reused. These materials are frequently mixed prior to further processing. Appropriate documentation and/or testing should be established to track these materials and ensure their use does not adversely impact the quality of the API produced. In-process mixing of fractions from single batches (e.g., centrifuge loads from a single crystallization batch) or combining fractions from several batches for further processing is considered to be part of the normal production process and is not considered to be blending.

Blending is the process of combining materials within the same specification to produce a homogeneous intermediate or product. As with dosage forms, blending of out-of-specification or nonconforming material with conforming material is not acceptable.

In API processes, it is acknowledged that some carryover from one batch to another may occur due to the physical inability to completely empty a process tank, centrifuge, or other processing vessel. This carry over should not include degradants or microbial contamination that could impact the quality of the API or its API impurity profile.

In order to ensure a process is maintained in a state of control, critical process steps and parameters should be defined based on the information gained during development, scale-up, or from historical data and documented. In-process controls and their acceptance criteria should be put in place to monitor and control the performance of critical processing steps. Deviations from established ranges should be investigated to ensure no impact to the quality of the product. Since many API processes are multistep, less stringent in-process controls may be appropriate during the early processing steps.

As with drug products, in-process testing by manufacturing personnel is acceptable, provided the quality unit has the final decision-making responsibility for release or rejection of product.

Many pharmaceutical manufacturers are converting their processes to adopt continuous production. Continuous production is a process by which active ingredients are produced in compact, closed units, with a higher degree of automation and fewer manual interventions. For this purpose, the production steps that are performed sequentially in a classic batch process are integrated in a continuous process. FDA has been a strong supporter of continuous processing as early as 2004 when it released *Pharmaceutical CGMPs for the 21st Century–A Risk-Based Approach*. In addition to reduced inventory, lower capital costs, a smaller ecological footprint, and more flexible operation, FDA is an advocate of the fact that continuous manufacturing reduces manual handling of products and allows for better process control. Online monitoring characteristic of continuous processing can facilitate real-time testing approaches and can support FDA's quality-by-design initiatives. While many of the regulatory expectations related to quality for continuous manufacturing are the same as those for batch processing, sampling considerations will differ from batch; deviations might need to be handled differently; variability should be controlled; manufacturing changes may need to be managed differently; and how you identify a batch of material will need to be defined.

PACKAGING AND LABELING

Labeling requirements are similar to those for drug products with respect to storage of labeling, issuance, and reconciliation. Written procedures that describe the receipt, identification, quarantine, sampling, examination and/or testing, release, handling of packaging, and labeling materials should be developed and implemented. Labels should have a defined storage area with access limited to authorized personnel. Label procedures will include reconciliation of label quantities issued, used, and returned. All discrepancies found between the numbers of containers labeled and the number of labels issued must be investigated with final approval by the quality unit.

LABORATORY CONTROLS

Laboratory controls for API manufacture have evolved to be more consistent with the expectations of drug products. Due to the diverse nature of API processes, specifications and testing requirements for different raw materials can vary significantly depending on the nature of the raw material and its criticality in the synthetic process. API specifications are expected to be more comprehensive and should include limits for solvents. Specifications should be scientifically sound and appropriate to ensure quality and purity of the material produced. Specifications and test procedures should be consistent with those presented in regulatory filings.

When an API has a specification for microbiological purity, action limits for total microbial counts and objectionable organisms should be established and met. When an API has a specification for endotoxins, appropriate action limits should be established and met. Out-of-specification result obtained for any test should be investigated and documented according to written procedures and final approval obtained from the quality unit.

Analytical methods are expected to be validated in accordance with a written protocol that has been approved by the quality unit.

STABILITY TESTING

An ongoing stability-testing program should be established to monitor the stability characteristics of APIs. Since APIs are frequently stored in commercial containers that are not practical for stability (e.g., 50 kg fiber drums, carboys, or silos), it is an accepted practice to store stability samples in containers that "simulate or approximate the market container." The container/material contact surfaces should be the same and where possible offer an equivalent amount of secondary protection. For example, polybags used in small cardboard containers may be considered equivalent to a polyliner in a 50-kilo fiberboard drum. The results should be used to confirm appropriate storage conditions and retest expiry dates.

RESERVE SAMPLES

Reserve samples for each API batch are to be retained for three years after distribution is complete or for one year after expiry date of the batch, whichever is longer. Additionally, for APIs with retest dates, reserve samples should be retained for three years after the batch has been completely distributed.

VALIDATION

API manufacturers must establish a validation policy that defines their method and approach to validation. This policy should be documented and approved by the quality unit. The policy should include but is not limited to validation of manufacturing processes, cleaning procedures, analytical methods, test procedures, computerized systems, persons responsible for design, implementation, approval, and documentation of each phase of validation.

The critical parameters and quality attributes are typically identified or defined during process development, scale-up, or from historical data. During the technology transfer or process demonstrations, expected ranges for each critical process must be identified and subsequently used by manufacturing to ensure the quality of the API produced. Operations determined to be critical to the quality and purity of the API are normally validated.

CHANGE CONTROL

A written change control system that evaluates all changes that could impact the production and control of the intermediate or API must be developed and put in place to ensure a state of control is maintained. In addition to evaluating the potential impact of a proposed change (specification, test procedures, production processes, and equipment) with respect to validation and regulatory impact, the need to notify the customer is included.

After the change is approved, there should be careful evaluation of the initial batches manufactured using the modified process. This evaluation should be built into the change control process.

EXAMPLES OF OBSERVATIONS FROM FDA CITATIONS

- *Failure to adequately validate the process for cleaning and maintenance of equipment.*

  You have not conducted cleaning validation studies to demonstrate that your cleaning procedures for non-dedicated production equipment are adequate to prevent potential cross contamination between your API (e.g., [b][4]), which include (b)(4) drugs. Your firm also processes intermediates on this equipment.

  More specifically, you failed to conduct cleaning validation for the majority of the critical non-dedicated production equipment you use to manufacture (b)(4) intermediates and API.

  Reactors (b)(4) are examples of critical multi-use equipment used by your firm.

  During the inspection, your staff also stated that it was not required to document equipment cleaning between manufacturing runs. For example, for (b)(4) batch (b)(4), your firm was able to provide a cleaning record for only one piece of equipment (a [b][4]) to demonstrate that cleaning was performed prior to batch manufacture.

- *Failure of your quality unit to exercise its responsibility to ensure the API manufactured at your facility is in compliance with GMP.*

  Your quality unit failed to perform a number of critical functions to ensure that the (b)(4) powder USP API was manufactured according to CGMP. For example, your quality unit failed to ensure that the records it reviewed included complete data derived from all tests conducted to ensure compliance with established specifications and standards prior to the distribution of an API batch. Your quality unit did not document details, such as sample weight and preparation for tests such as (b)(4) content, (b)(4), (b)(4) or (b)(4), and (b)(4) content.

  Your quality unit also failed to ensure that samples intended for stability studies are stored with controlled temperature and humidity. Your firm kept retain and stability samples of (b)(4) USP in a cabinet in the quality control laboratory without monitoring temperature and relative humidity.

  In addition, your quality unit did not ensure the cleanliness of buildings and facilities used to manufacture API. You lacked sufficient controls to prevent the presence of pests in your packaging material storage area. At least twice, our inspector observed insects and spiderwebs in and on plastic-wrapped stacked containers used for packaging API.

  Your quality unit also did not ensure that your cleaning validation records are accurate and contain appropriate documentation. For example, you did not document rinse times in your study to validate cleaning of the (b)(4) you use to manufacture API.

- *Failure to adequately investigate out-of-specification results and implement appropriate corrective actions.*

  Your firm rejected (b)(4) batch (b)(4) for assay failure on October 23, 2015. You opened an investigation the same day and subsequently closed the investigation a few months later on March 20, 2016. You determined the root cause of the failure to be (b)(4) from the (b)(4) in March, 2016, but as of our December 2017 inspection, more than two years after the failure, you had not implemented a corrective action to address the root cause you identified. In the interim, your quality unit released at least (b)(4) batches of finished (b)(4) API.

- *Failure to properly maintain equipment and to keep complete records of major equipment maintenance.*

Our investigator found damaged product-contact surfaces on your multi-product equipment. For example, the manhole gasket of (b)(4)111 was deteriorating and wrapped in peeling tape. A gasket on the (b)(4)102 was also cracked in one area and wrapped in peeling tape.

- *Failure to have adequate written procedures for the receipt, identification, quarantine, storage, sampling, testing, handling, and approval or rejection of raw materials.*

  For example, when our investigator asked for a list of your critical raw materials and your sampling requirements, you told our investigator that you had no written procedures for testing and sampling incoming materials. Instead, you explained, your warehouse employees accounted for incoming raw material handling, sampling, and testing "in their heads."

- *Failure to have laboratory control records that include complete data derived from all laboratory tests conducted to ensure compliance with established specifications and standards.*

  For example, our investigator reviewed the audit trail from your assay testing for (b)(4) lot (b)(4) and found that you tested the same sample set three times over several days without documentation or investigation. You reported only the result of the third and final test for purposes of completing your certificate of analysis and releasing this batch of API.

EXAMPLES OF DEFICIENCIES THAT SHOULD RESULT IN RECOMMENDATIONS FOR REGULATORY ACTION

The following is a list of deficiencies that if observed during inspections should result in recommendations for regulatory action (taken from the FDA Compliance Program Manual 7356.002F: *Active Pharmaceutical Ingredient (API) Process Inspection (revised October 11, 2015)*)

1. Contamination of APIs with filth, objectionable microorganisms, toxic chemicals or significant amounts of other types of chemicals, or a reasonable potential for such contamination because of a finding of a demonstrated route of contamination
2. Failure to show that API batches conform to established specifications
3. Failure to comply with commitments in drug applications
4. Distribution of an API that does not conform to established specifications
5. Deliberate blending of API batches to dilute or hide filth or other noxious contaminants, or blending to disguise a critical quality defect in an attempt to obtain a batch that meets specifications
6. Failure to demonstrate that water and any other solvents used in the final step of the API process are chemically and microbiologically suitable for their intended use and do not adversely alter the quality of the API
7. Lack of adequate validation of critical steps in the API process
8. Implementation of retrospective process validation for an existing API process when the process has changed significantly, when the firm lacks impurity profile data, or when there is evidence of repeated batch failures due to process variability
9. Failure to establish an impurity profile for each API process
10. Failure to show that a reprocessed batch complies with all established standards, specifications, and characteristics
11. Failure to test for residues of organic/inorganic solvents used during manufacturing that may carry over to the API using analytical procedures with appropriate levels of sensitivity
12. Failure to have a formal change control system in place
13. Failure to maintain batch and quality control records

14. Incomplete stability studies to establish API stability for the intended period of use, and/or failure to conduct forced degradation studies on APIs to isolate, identify, and quantify potential degradants that may arise during storage
15. Use of laboratory test methods that are inadequate or have not been validated or the use of an inadequately qualified or untraceable reference standard
16. Packaging and labeling in such a way that introduces a significant risk of mislabeling

REFERENCE

1. FDA Guidance for Industry: Q7A Good Manufacturing Practice Guidance for Active Pharmaceutical Ingredients, September 2016.

16 Pharmaceutical Excipient Good Manufacturing Practices

Irwin Silverstein

CONTENTS

BACKGROUND

As noted in Chapter 15, "Active Pharmaceutical Ingredients (APIs)," there appears to be universal agreement by regulatory agencies that there are significant differences between the processes used for the manufacture of dosage forms and those used for the manufacture of the API. There are even greater differences between excipient processes and those of either the dosage form or API. These differences include:

- Dosage form manufacture involves mixing components and forming the drug product, whereas API and bulk pharmaceutical excipient manufacturing involve chemical reactions and processing.
- Excipient manufacture ranges from minerals that are mined and purified to natural substances, often foods that are chemically modified, to chemicals synthesized from basic chemicals, such as ethane and oil via multi-step processes.
- The excipient manufacturing process like that of the API often includes purification of the component to achieve the necessary excipient quality, whereas purification of the drug product is not possible in dosage-form manufacture.
- Unlike the API, which is usually a single chemical entity, the excipient is often a complex mixture, and thus the excipient is more difficult to assay or to develop an impurity profile.
- Virtually all excipients have other non-pharmaceutical applications often representing higher volumes and sales dollars (e.g., sucrose and starch), whereas APIs are seldom used in non-pharmaceutical products.
- Often the excipient is nonhomogeneous within the lot for one or more properties of the excipient, such as moisture or particle size, unlike the API where homogeneity is often easier to achieve due to differences in scale of manufacture and facility.

The current good manufacturing practice (CGMP) regulations (21 CFR 210 and 211) were designed for drug product manufacture and can only be used only as a general guide for the manufacture of excipients. However, the definition of "drug" in the Food, Drug, and Cosmetic (FD&C) Act (Section 201[g][1][d]) includes both drug products and their components, and Section 510 (a)(2)(B) requires that all drugs be manufactured, processed, packed, and held in accordance with CGMPs. The requirement for GMP manufacture creates a problem for excipient manufacturers since implementation of the Act requires compliance, but there are no GMPs applicable to excipients. FDA has adopted ICH Q7, *Good Manufacturing Practice Guidance for Active Pharmaceutical Ingredients*, as guidance for the manufacture of APIs in conformance with GMP. In December 2014, the American National Standards Institute (ANSI) adopted NSF/IPEC/ANSI 363-2016, *Good Manufacturing Practices (GMP) for Pharmaceutical Excipients* (363 Standard[1]) to address the requirement of the FD&C Act.

As noted in the chapter on APIs, it is clearly stated that 21 CFR 210 and 211 should be applied to APIs at a point that "it is reasonable to expect GMP concepts to start to become applicable... where a starting material enters a biological or chemical synthesis or series of processing steps, where it is known that the end product will be a API." This concept of the starting point for GMP is reinforced in ICH Q7. As noted earlier, unlike the API, excipients are usually also sold for use in other industries. Excipients are generally produced using the same equipment and processing as the material designated for other industries, for example, food. Therefore, the excipient is indistinguishable, chemically and physically, from the material sold to other markets. Thus, the application of excipient GMP requirements can begin later than in the manufacturing process when product may be produced for other markets. Where there are no other markets for the material or the facility is dedicated to the production of excipient grade only, the consideration for the starting point for GMP is the same as discussed in ICH Q7 for the API. Thus,

1. Where there is no non-pharmaceutical commercial use for the excipient or its precursors, GMP begins:
   a. With that step in a chemical synthesis where a significant structural fragment is formed or
   b. When a chemical reaches a point in its isolation and purification where it is intended that it will be used in a drug product.
2. Where there are other non-pharmaceutical commercial sales of the chemical or its precursors, GMP begins:
   a. At the step in the chemical synthesis where the final molecule is formed or
   b. When the chemical undergoes its final purification.

The excipient manufacturer is expected to justify and document their selection of the point in the manufacturing process where full GMP requirements are to be applied.

Excipients are typically produced by companies whose primary business is not pharmaceutical ingredient manufacture (excipient) let alone pharmaceutical dosage-form manufacture. Seldom does the excipient manufacturer even produce APIs. The excipient manufacturer is usually a chemical manufacturer who may also be a supplier to the food and/or cosmetic industry as well as industrial markets. Excipient manufacturers are often refiners of inorganic chemicals, large-scale manufacturers of commodity chemicals, specialty chemical companies, food-additive producers, or food processors. As such, it should be recognized that their understanding of the quality system needed to produce pharmaceutical ingredients may be minimal. Likewise, it is important to note that pharmaceutical companies seldom disclose to their excipient suppliers the dosage forms in which the excipient is used or the role of the excipient in their formulation. This lack of information sharing makes it difficult for the excipient manufacturer to ensure for all customers the excipient is suitable for its intended use.

It is important for the excipient manufacturer to understand that consistent composition of the excipient is the prime concern of their pharmaceutical customers relative to the quality of the excipient, not the assay of the excipient. The pharmaceutical manufacturer desires excipients whose compositional analyses as described by its purity and impurities is unchanged from lot to lot and within the lot (batch homogeneity). By contrast, it is also important for the pharmaceutical manufacturer to appreciate that the excipient manufacturer is driven by competitive pressures from the other markets in which the material is sold, to reduce the cost of manufacture and perhaps also improve the quality of the non-pharmaceutical grades of the product. These conflicting forces can be difficult for the excipient manufacturer to reconcile where both pharmaceutical and non-pharmaceutical grades are produced using the same equipment and chemical processing.

INTERNATIONAL PHARMACEUTICAL EXCIPIENTS COUNCIL

To help address the issues identified above as well as others, the International Pharmaceutical Excipients Council (IPEC), a trade association of excipient producers, distributors, and pharmaceutical manufacturers, was formed in 1991. IPEC quickly became a global organization with associations in the United States, IPEC-Americas; Europe, IPEC Europe; China, IPEC Association (China); India, IPEC India; and Japan (JPEC). All of these associations coordinate their activities through the IPEC Federation.

An early objective was to address the lack of guidance concerning the quality system to be used in the manufacture of excipient ingredients. The IPEC-Americas GMP Committee immediately organized and began work on development of excipient GMP requirements. The GMP Committee, comprised of representatives from excipient producers as well as pharmaceutical manufacturers, issued *The IPEC Good Manufacturing Practices Guide for Bulk Pharmaceutical Requirements* in 1995. This guideline was organized according to the International Organization for Standardization (ISO) 9002:1994 guidelines since many excipient suppliers were either ISO 9002 certified or were in the process of seeking certification. Organizing the GMP requirements in this manner simplified comprehension of conformance requirements for the excipient producer. The guideline was adopted by IPEC affiliates and was updated in 2001 and 2006, the later to include provisions recommended by the Pharmaceutical Quality Group (PQG).

The focus of excipient GMP requirements is primarily to ensure that the quality of excipient ingredients is suitable to assure the safety and efficacy of the excipient in the pharmaceutical dosage form. Secondarily, the GMP requirements establish the documentation and records necessary for confirmation that these ingredients are properly produced under an appropriate quality system. Thus, the focus of excipient GMPs is somewhat different from the dosage form GMP in that the safety and efficacy of the drug formulation will have already been established through clinical trials (see Chapter 8). The drug application establishes the foundation for the manufacture of the drug product. The drug GMPs, as specified in 21 CFR 210, 211, have as their primary focus the documentation and record-keeping requirements for verification that the drug was produced in conformance with the drug application.

In 2000, the United States Pharmacopeia (USP) issued excipient GMP requirements in General Chapter <1078>. This chapter falls within the section of voluntary requirements. However, since the USP requires that all compendial articles be manufactured in conformance with appropriate GMPs, excipients listed in the *USP–NF*, would be expected to be produced in accordance with the requirements of <1078>. The USP worked with IPEC to update <1078> to the current excipient GMP requirements, now reflected in the 363 Standard.

Unlike the situation for manufacturers of dosage forms and even the API, there is a dearth of regulatory and compliance information for the excipient producer. Therefore, IPEC has been working to provide guidelines for the industry. This initiative received additional impetus with the glycerin poisoning in Haiti[*] in 1996 where over 80 children were poisoned with acetaminophen

---

[*] Malebrance R. et al., "Fatalities associated with ingestion of diethylene glycol–contaminated glycerin used to manufacture acetaminophen syrup-Haiti," November 1995–June 1996, *Morbidity and Mortality Weekly Report*, Centers for Disease Control and Prevention, August 2, 1996; 45(30). https://www.cdc.gov/mmwr/preview/mmwrhtml/00043194.htm.

syrup contaminated with diethylene glycol. The source of this poison was traced to the glycerin excipient, which was shown to contain approximately 50% diethylene glycol (DEG). As a consequence, the U.S. FDA asked IPEC to help assure the safety of excipient ingredients. More recently, in 2006 over 100 people were confirmed dead in Panama from ingesting cough syrup containing DEG misrepresented as 99.5% glycerin.* While Glycerin USP is a common and safe excipient, diethylene glycol is a component of antifreeze. When DEG is ingested, it results in renal failure and often death, especially in children. The original incident of contaminated glycerin with DEG occurred in 1938[†] in the USA and is commonly referred to as the "Sulphanilamide Tragedy" because children were taking the antibiotic were also ingesting DEG.

To support conformance to excipient GMPs, IPEC issued the following guideline documents:

- The IPEC-Americas *Good Manufacturing Practices Audit Guideline for Bulk Pharmaceutical Excipients*, 1998. The guideline provides checklists useful for auditing conformance to the IPEC excipient GMP guide. The guideline was updated in 2004 and has been updated and retitled the *Joint IPEC-PQG Good Manufacturing Practices Audit Guide for Pharmaceutical Excipients*, 2007.[2]
- The IPEC *GMP Audit Guideline for Distributors of Pharmaceutical Excipients*, 2000. This guideline provides details concerning the application of excipient GMP requirements for distributors of excipients as well as guidance concerning auditing their operation. This guideline has subsequently been replaced by the IPEC-Americas *Good Distribution Practices Audit Guide for North American Distribution of Pharmaceutical Excipients*, 2011. This updated guideline is linked to the IPEC *Good Distribution Practices Guide*, which is based on the World Health Organization (WHO) *Good Trade and Distribution Practices for Pharmaceutical Starting Materials*, 2003.
- The IPEC *Certificate of Analysis Guide for Pharmaceutical Excipients*, 2000, subsequently updated in 2013.[3] This guideline establishes the requirements for the content of an excipient Certificate of Analysis (COA). Among other items, it requires that the COA provide for traceability of the excipient back to the excipient manufacturer.
- The *IPEC-Americas Significant Change Guide for Pharmaceutical Excipients*, 2004[4] and subsequently revised for 2014.[4] This document provides a framework for the evaluation of changes in the manufacture of excipient ingredients and establishes requirements for notification of such change to the customer and regulatory authorities.

REGULATORY CHANGES

The 363 Standard is a consensus Standard developed by a committee at NSF International that included representatives from IPEC, both excipient makers and pharmaceutical users, FDA, and academia using the IPEC-PQG *Good Manufacturing Practices Guide for Pharmaceutical Excipients 2006*[5] as a foundation document.

Congress passed the National Technology Transfer and Advancement Act (NTTAA) in 1996 to codify Office of Management and Budget (OMB) directive (OMB Circular A-119), Federal Participation in the Development and Use of Voluntary Consensus Standards, and in Conformity Assessment Activities. NTTAA assigns the National Institute of Science and Technology (NIST) with responsibility to coordinate federal, state, and local standardization and conformity assessment activities. Agencies are directed to adopt private sector standards, particularly those developed by standards developing organizations, wherever possible, in lieu of creating proprietary,

* *New York Times*, "From China to Panama, A Trail of Poisoned Medicine," May 6, 2007. http://www.nytimes.com/2007/05/06/world/americas/06poison.html?pagewanted=all&_r=0.
† Geiling EMK, Cannon PR. "Pathologic effects of elixir of sulfanilamide (diethylene glycol) poisoning. A clinical and experimental correlation: Final report." *JAMA* 1938;111:919–926.

non-consensus standards. The goal is to reduce unnecessary government standards that create confusion and add expense for compliance.

While the FDA has yet to indicate how the agency will use the 363 Standard, they may choose to adopt it as guidance as they have ICH Q7, *Good Manufacturing Practice Guidance for Active Pharmaceutical Ingredients*. However, it also seems possible that the FDA will use the 363 Standard as the basis for excipient GMP regulation.

On March 19, 2015, the final version of a guideline *on the formalised risk assessment for ascertaining the appropriate good manufacturing practice for excipients of medicinal products for human use* was published in the Official Journal of the European Union under Article 46(f) of the European Falsified Medicines Directive (FMD). This guideline describes the use of risk assessment by the manufacturing authorization holder (MAH) (drug manufacturer) to ascertain the appropriate GMP required for each excipient used in their drug formulation.

This guidance consists of three main sections:

- Chapter 2, "Determination of Appropriate GMP Based on Type and Use of Excipient" provides guidance on how to assess and rank the risk presented by the excipient. The assessment should consider risks to quality, safety, and performance of the excipient arising from the raw material source used to produce the excipient and the excipients' use and function in the drug product to develop a risk profile for the excipient. The resulting assessment is used to establish the GMP elements the excipient supplier is expected to meet.
- Chapter 3, "Determination of Excipient Manufacturer's Risk Profile" requires a gap assessment by the MAH against the GMP elements identified by the risk profile. Data/evidence to support the gap assessment is to be obtained through audit or from information received from the excipient manufacturer. The MAH then assigns a control strategy that ranges from acceptance of the supplier through control measures, for example, additional incoming inspection, and finally to "unacceptable" status for the different risk profiles.
- Chapter 4, "Confirmation of Application of Appropriate GMP" presents guidance for ongoing risk review. The guideline lists several supplier performance measures that should be monitored to support the current control strategy or to indicate a change in strategy.

The guidance allows for the use of supplier certification of the quality system and/or GMP in lieu of performing the gap assessment. However, the MAH is to consider the standards against which such certification has been granted. Two standards of relevance that an excipient manufacturer may hold are ISO 9001 *Quality Management Systems-Requirements* and the 363 Standard. Since ISO 9001 establishes general quality system requirements, it would seem insufficient as a replacement for performing the gap assessment. However, certification of the supplier to the 363 Standard should meet the requirement for a gap assessment if the third-party certifying body is suitably accredited. In the U.S., ANSI provides certifying body accreditation.

There is a second excipient GMP certification scheme called EXCiPACT.* This scheme relies on conformance of the excipient manufacturer to ISO 9001 and in addition requires conformance to a GMP Annex to ISO 9001 that was developed by the scheme owners. The intention of EXCiPACT is to provide certification to excipient GMP that is comparable to that of the 363 Standard. To that end, EXCiPACT was represented on the NSF International 363 Standard writing committee.

Certification to either the 363 Standard or EXCiPACT reduces the burden of complying with the FMD by both the MAH and the excipient producer by allowing certification and certification audit reports to provide a basis for determining the risk from the excipient supplier.

As noted, the focus on excipients is increasing as regulatory authorities place more emphasis on their oversight by the drug manufacturers.

GOOD MANUFACTURING PRACTICES GUIDE
FOR PHARMACEUTICAL EXCIPIENTS

The remainder of this chapter will review the ANSI NSF/IPEC/ANSI 363-2016 Standard[1] highlighting key requirements and emphasizing expectations for excipient manufacturers not applicable to manufacturers of API or pharmaceutical drug product. The discussion follows the organization of the 363 Standard. The section and title are provided for easy reference to the 363 Standard.

GENERAL

The excipient manufacturer should establish a proper quality management system and methods, facilities, and controls including appropriate tests to assure consistent excipient quality. The manufacturer is to also retain objective evidence to demonstrate conformance to GMP requirements.

REFERENCE DOCUMENTS

References are provided for use with the 363 Standard.

DEFINITIONS

The 363 Standard provides definitions for terms that have a specific technical meaning when used in the 363 Standard.

QUALITY MANAGEMENT SYSTEM

This section establishes the requirement for the manufacturer to maintain and continually improve their quality management system and conformance to GMP.

The company is to have defined roles, responsibilities, authorities, and inter-relationships of organizational units that impact the quality management system. Outsourced activities that may impact excipient quality are to be identified and control measures implemented.

Quality risk management is to be used to justify those requirements of the 363 Standard that do not apply to the excipient produced at the site. Also, quality risk management is to be used to assess the impact of changes to the quality management system.

A Quality Manual is required for conformance to the 363 Standard. The manual should define the scope of the quality management system, for example, list the excipients or excipient processes covered by the manual. The manual also provides the identity and justification of the processing step from which point full compliance with the 363 Standard is required, the so-called starting point for excipient GMP. The Quality Manual should be written as a road map for hosting an audit and thus provides references for supporting documentation that shows either how each clause of the 363 Standard has been met or justification through risk assessment for why the provisions of a clause is not applicable.

A system should be in place for the control of documents, such as procedures, work instructions, process documentation, test methods, and specifications, including documents of external origin, such as customer specifications and quality agreements. The system should protect the documents from deterioration, facilitate their retrieval, and assure that only current copies are available for use. Documents should be periodically reviewed and updated as necessary. Revision to these documents should be made only after review and approval by qualified personnel. Obsolete documents are to be identified, if retained. An electronic documentation system is acceptable if it ensures a comparable level of assurance that only properly authorized documents are available for reference.

The same document control system should be suitable for the control, retrieval, and use of records. This includes completed checklists, forms, test data including instrument output, and so on, which must be retained as part of the production record for each lot of excipient produced. Correction to entries on records are to be made so that the original entry is legible, and the new entry is to be signed and dated. Such records are retained for at least one year past the expiry date or two years beyond the retest date of the excipient lot. If there is neither an expiry date nor retest date assigned for the excipient, records are retained for a minimum of five years from the date of manufacture.

Finally, this section requires a change control process such that all changes that can impact the quality of the excipient are evaluated using risk assessment. Changes, such as to manufacturing instructions and equipment, specifications, sampling plans, instruments, and test methods, are approved prior to use with final approval given by an independent organization such as the Quality or Regulatory function. All changes are assessed for their potential impact to the excipient in accordance with the IPEC *Significant Change Guide for Pharmaceutical Excipients* and are communicated to customers and regulatory authorities as recommended in the guide.

MANAGEMENT RESPONSIBILITY

This section stipulates management responsibility for the goals and objectives of the quality management system and provides for review of performance against management goals and objectives.

Top management is assigned the responsibility for complying with the 363 Standard. The 363 Standard defines Top Management as a person or group of people who direct and control an organization at the highest level defined by the company as either at the site or corporate. Top Management conveys to the company the importance of complying with the 363 Standard as well as to other applicable statutory and regulatory requirements. Top Management establishes a Quality Policy stating the intention to meet GMP requirements. The 363 Standard requires effective communication and escalation processes so that issues may be raised to Top Management.

Top Management is to conduct periodic reviews of the performance of the excipient quality system by demonstrating performance against Quality Objectives. Such objectives are deployed throughout the company, are measurable, and consistent with the Quality Policy.

Top Management is expected to supply adequate resources for the manufacture of excipient ingredients. This includes an independent quality unit with defined responsibilities for overseeing the proper manufacture of the excipient and compliance as defined by the 363 Standard. The 363 Standard allows the quality unit to delegate responsibility for some of their assigned activities, if justified, but the quality unit retains accountability and is expected to provide oversight.

Top Management assigns a management representative with responsibility for ensuring the requirements of the 363 Standard are implemented. The management representative is to be qualified and have appropriate experience and must have a senior position in the quality unit unless otherwise justified. There is a requirement for communication of the 363 Standard and applicable regulatory requirements through the organization that includes the effectiveness of the quality management system. The Standard requires risk assessment for events that affect excipient quality to determine if notification to Top Management is warranted.

Top Management is to conduct periodic reviews to confirm ongoing conformance to the 363 Standard. Suggested review inputs include internal and external audit findings, customer feedback, excipient quality and process performance, and changes to the quality management system. Review output leads to adjustments to the quality system to improve conformance. As noted earlier, those changes to the quality system are to be assessed.

RESOURCE MANAGEMENT

This section establishes the resources that management is to provide for complying with the 363 Standard. The resources are a combination of facilities, equipment, and personnel necessary to manufacture, package, test, store, and release each batch of excipient.

To this end, employees are to be trained in both their job responsibilities, including personal hygiene and an appropriate understanding of excipient GMPs. Records demonstrate that employees were trained to perform their tasks and were also trained in relevant excipient GMP requirements. It is important to provide employees with GMP training on a continuing basis. For this industry, ongoing training requirements can be met by providing a refresher course in appropriate excipient GMP requirements every one to two years.

The 363 Standard requires a risk assessment to identify areas where the excipient is at risk from personnel and their activities. Risk mitigation is to be employed after identifying an unacceptable level of risk. During manufacture, the excipient is often only exposed to the environment at packaging. As a consequence, unless there is exposure of the excipient to the employee during processing, no special employee garments need be specified. At packaging and other areas where there is exposure to the excipient, the employee should wear appropriate clothing, including a clean outer garment, head covering, and gloves as necessary to protect the excipient.

A risk assessment is to be performed to identify the risk to excipient quality from buildings and facilities. A major emphasis in the construction and maintenance of excipient facilities is the potential for contamination from other chemical processes or from airborne contaminants. Since much processing occurs in closed systems dedicated to the production of the excipient and lesser grades of the chemical, the risk of such contamination occurring is usually limited to raw material charging, purification, drying, and packaging. Unlike APIs, air-handling systems are seldom a concern since air-handling systems used are typically dedicated to the manufacture of the excipient. However, the risk assessment should demonstrate that operational practices do not constitute a potential for contamination, cross contamination, or mix-up.

Oftentimes, chemical plants that produce excipient ingredients also produce a range of other products, including those that are poisonous, such as herbicides and pesticides. The excipient manufacturer is expected to take appropriate precautions to ensure that harmful products produced on-site cannot contaminate the excipient. Such precautions might involve enclosing the excipient manufacturing area, redirecting air intakes, and other risk mitigating measures.

Excipient production often occurs outdoors, particularly where continuous processing is used, and is acceptable provided the processing occurs in closed equipment. Where the excipient is exposed to the environment, such as during charging of ingredients and packaging, the area is expected to be under environmental control to prevent airborne contamination. Environmental control involves protecting the excipient from precipitation, airborne contamination, and overhead accumulations of dust and dirt. Generally, operations where the excipient is exposed are conducted in a room with washable walls, floor, and ceiling. Also the area is maintained under positive pressure with air filtered through a furnace-type filter, which is generally sufficient to protect the excipient from particulate. The environmental control exercised should be demonstrated to be adequate to protect the excipient.

Production equipment is to be maintained in a good state of repair, suitable to facilitate cleaning, maintenance, and proper operation, and designed, installed, and stored when not in use to maintain clean and sanitary conditions. Change parts, utensils, and hoses are to be stored clean.

Equipment is to be commissioned prior to use. A risk assessment is to be performed where utilities and process materials may impact excipient quality. Where risk mitigation measures are insufficient to prevent contact with the excipient, materials suitable for food contact are to be used. If other materials are used, their use is to be justified.

Maintenance is important not only to the quality of the excipient but also to the safe operation of the facility. It should be recognized that where processing occurs within the equipment and the material is not exposed to the environment, the exterior equipment surface condition is merely of cosmetic importance. Even so, it is wise to remember that the appearance of the equipment creates an averse first impression to the auditor.

Computer systems used for GMP purposes are to be qualified. Computer systems are demonstrated to perform as designed. Unauthorized use of the computer system is prevented through unique user identification and secure passwords. Provisions are made for the backup and archive of copies of both the software program files and data. Finally, changes to the computer system, hardware, and software are governed by change control with review and approval of the details of the change to be made and assessment of the impact of the change to confirm the impact meets expectations.

The 363 Standard requires a risk assessment to excipient quality from utilities, such as nitrogen, compressed air, steam, and water. Control measures, such as filters, are often employed to mitigate such risk.

While it is advisable to use potable water in the preparation of excipients, it is recognized that it is not always feasible since excipient production may represent a rather small portion of the total manufacturing output of the facility. Also, potable water may not be available at the site. Finally, many chemical processes use water where the time and temperature of processing to which the water is exposed would exercise control over microorganisms introduced from the water.

Justification for not using potable water can be made by using results from a study showing processing produces a reduction in microbes to acceptable levels or that continuous microbial monitoring of the excipient shows no elevated levels of microorganism. Where processing conditions do not exercise control over microbes in non-potable water and the site wants to confirm the water meets portable standards, the manufacturer is expected to test the process water to confirm it meets the drinking water standard. Such testing includes all EPA requirements for potable water and is conducted at least once each quarter.

Where potable water is supplied from a municipality, the FDA has allowed reliance on data provided by municipal water authorities to demonstrate the water is potable. However, recent experience with FDA visits indicate it is appropriate, from time to time, to recheck the water quality at the point of use in the plant since this is often a long distance from the municipal testing point. Where purified water is used, the process must be validated to demonstrate continuing conformance to the specification for the purified water as well as for adequate control of microbes.

The excipient manufacturer needs to conduct a risk assessment to identify the controls required for contamination from air handling systems, special environments, clean and sanitary conditions, waste, and pests. Where excipient quality is at risk from air handling, the system is designed and maintained to provide air of suitable quality. This generally involves proper air handling equipment and adequate air filtration.

Where a controlled environment is necessary to protect excipient quality, environmental conditions might be monitored. If an inert atmosphere is required, the gas is to be treated as a raw material (quarantined, tested to specification before release). Also, interruptions to environmental control are to be investigated for potential impact to the excipient.

Where the risk assessment shows housekeeping is important to excipient quality, such areas are cleaned in accordance with procedures that include a description of schedules, methods, equipment, and materials (cleaning/sanitization agents) and by personnel with assigned responsibility. Waste is either promptly disposed or stored in appropriate containers.

From the processing step where full GMP requirements are applied, wherever the excipient is exposed to the environment or where the packaged excipient is stored, a pest-control program is required to be in place. Oftentimes, the principle area of excipient exposure is at packaging. Where excipient is shipped to the customer in bulk, such as tankers, no insect and rodent control measures are expected aside from routine precautions. Typically, the pest control program involves having an exterminator inspect the areas where excipient is exposed or stored in packages. The exterminator applies appropriate pest control measures using only FDA-approved materials. The exterminator is expected to leave a report of their findings concerning insect and rodent activity, this is reviewed and approved before filing. Any remediation actions or recommendations need to be are taken and documented.

Other requirements for the work environment include lighting that is adequate for employees to carry out their assigned task. Lights are protected from breakage even where packaged excipient is stored, since glass on the exterior of the excipient package may inadvertently get into the drug product during dispensing.

Proper drainage is important so there is no standing water that might contaminate the excipient, breed insects, or encourage microbial growth. Finally, employees are provided with appropriate employee washing and toilet facilities and required to follow proper hygiene procedures.

EXCIPIENT REALIZATION

The excipient manufacturer is expected to implement the actions identified through risk assessment and have plans and controls that are appropriate to the production process. These include human resources, equipment, and facilities for storage and testing; testing programs for materials and finished excipient; and environmental and hygiene controls to minimize the potential for excipient contamination. Records demonstrate that the processes and controls were followed.

Conformance to excipient GMP requirements includes good communication with the customer. Where customer requirements differ from the monograph or the excipient manufacturer's specification, there should be mutual agreement to the specification.

The excipient manufacturer ensures that quality-related documents shared with the customer are controlled. Such documents include sales specifications, marketing literature, and technical reports. Also, there is a system for responding to customer inquiries and for handling complaints from the customer. Feedback of the conclusions from complaint investigation is expected to be promptly provided to the customer. In addition, there is a procedure that describes how changes to the process are assessed, and the results communicated to the customer where the change has the potential to impact the excipient. Finally, a procedure governs the return of excipients from customers if there is a deviation in excipient quality.

Whereas GMP requirements clearly begin for the pharmaceutical manufacturer, at the very latest, at the receiving area of pharmaceutical-grade ingredients, the same expectation cannot be applied to excipient operations. As discussed earlier, the excipient manufacturer determines the production step where full excipient GMP requirements must be applied. However, it should be recognized that certain good manufacturing principles are applied beginning with the receipt of raw materials. Generally, these earlier operations are conducted in conformance with the requirements of an ISO 9001 quality system. As such, a risk assessment is used to identify key raw materials and services, and their suppliers are evaluated to confirm that the supplier quality system is sufficient to ensure delivery of materials and services that conform to mutually agreed requirements. Suppliers of raw materials are requested to provide notification of changes that have the potential to impact the material they supply to the excipient manufacturer.

Wherever possible, raw materials are accepted after Quality Control has at least confirmed their identity and verified from COA data that the lot meets specification. Justification is provided when it is not feasible to sample incoming raw material that may impact excipient quality, such as for pipeline or bulk deliveries. For these materials, conducting a site audit to affirm the validity of the COA is a suitable alternative to validating the COA through periodic sampling and testing. Where the raw material is deemed too hazardous to sample, the identity test can be confirmation that the paperwork from the supplier, such as the Bill of Lading and the placard, matches the material name on the COA material name, grade, and lot as appropriate. Primary or contact packaging is received upon review of the Certificate of Conformance to confirm the packaging was produced to the desired specification.

Unlike the situation with APIs, a physical quarantine of unapproved raw materials is often not feasible. Typically, the excipient manufacturer will assure that unapproved raw material is not released for use through the status of the raw material lot in the computerized inventory system. This practice is acceptable where the accuracy of the inventory locator system is high and there is suitable control over who can make status changes.

Oftentimes, raw materials are delivered in bulk vehicles and the excipient manufacturer is expected to ensure the material has not been contaminated by the prior load. Therefore, the delivery should be accompanied by a Certificate of Cleaning from the transporter listing the contents of the prior load.

Bulk deliveries are usually stored in tanks until consumed, which results in a loss of lot identity. This practice is acceptable as long as records are sufficient to provide an indication, via a point in time, when the lot was likely consumed in the production of the excipient. It is recognized that in the event of a problem associated with bulk raw material, the impact of not being able to trace raw materials by discrete lot to the excipient so produced results in a greater quantity of excipient whose quality is suspect.

Storage of raw materials, especially in bulk, often occurs outdoors. These raw material storage tanks are to be protected from the weather, insects, and birds. Preferred venting of the tank is to use a conservation vent where a suitable gas creates a slight positive pressure at the vent. Where a gooseneck vent is used for a tank under ambient conditions, the opening is to be screened preventing entry by birds or insects.

Outdoor storage of drummed raw materials is acceptable provided the container labels remain legible. However, it is recognized that allowing water to collect atop a drum containing liquid raw material presents a risk when a sharp drop in the temperature of the contents results in a partial vacuum, and water on top of the drum is sucked in through the bung.

Excipients are produced either via batch or continuous processing or oftentimes a combination of the two. The requirements for the content of excipient production instructions are similar to that for the drug product and API except that the production records are not verified and issued by the quality unit for each batch. The batch record is to be sufficiently detailed to identify all materials and equipment used and operations performed to manufacture the excipient lot. However, unlike the pharmaceutical dosage-form manufacturer where logs are kept for each major piece of equipment, this is seldom the case for the excipient manufacturer. The maintenance department will often keep records of equipment service and repair, whereas production maintains records of the equipment used to produce the batch and the cleaning of the equipment. Even so, the excipient manufacture is able to reconstruct from applicable records, regardless of where they are kept, the sequence of activities with the subject equipment.

These records should be reviewed as part of lot release conducted by the quality organization or their designate. Where continuous processing is conducted, this presents a problem since these records are usually either a continuously maintained log with no direct relationship to the finished lot or an electronic file containing operating settings and parameters. Even though it is difficult and inconvenient to provide the information to the quality unit for review, means should be taken to meet the intent of the requirement, such as periodic audit of those records.

The emphasis of API manufacturers for equipment construction is on cleanability and the potential for cross contamination, whereas excipient producers focus more on maintenance and reliability since equipment is usually dedicated. However, even dedicated equipment must be periodically cleaned if only after maintenance activities or prior to start-up after a scheduled shutdown. There should be justification for the cleaning instructions, outlined with sufficient detail to ensure cleaning is done repetitively, and for the frequency of equipment cleaning. Excipient equipment is almost always cleaned in place, often with restricted access to the interior surfaces not only for the purposes of cleaning but also for subsequent inspection to verify efficacy and completeness of cleaning. However, the excipient manufacturer is expected to demonstrate the efficacy of their cleaning procedures through suitable means, such as monitoring the effluent for contaminant.

Process performance may be monitored through in-process testing at the production unit. Where such testing is performed with online instruments, the instruments need to be properly calibrated and maintained and have been shown to provide suitable measurements. Where the testing is performed at the production line by the personnel, there should be an assurance that production personnel have the ability to provide measurements comparable to that produced in the Quality Control laboratory.

Packaging that comes into direct contact with the excipient (primary or contact packaging) is to be traceable to the excipient lot where used. The packaging lot number of contact packaging is included in the production record. Where the excipient is packaged directly into a container rather than into a bag in a container, it is important to evaluate the container manufacturer's quality system through an on-site audit since it is not feasible for Quality Control to inspect each container to confirm the container meets specification. In addition, packaging personnel should be instructed by quality unit personnel to look for obvious signs the container is not suitable.

Packaging and labeling operations present a risk of mix-ups between different lots and different materials. Therefore, before such operations begin, there is expected to be an inspection of the area for the presence of materials used for prior packaging activities, particularly if they contain labeling, and if any are found, they are removed from the area.

Validation is now an expectation of excipient manufacturers. The qualification of equipment is a problem for the industry since much of the equipment in use was installed before equipment qualification became an expectation. Even so, the manufacturer will need to present evidence to support the proper installation and operation of equipment that can affect excipient quality from the point at which full GMP requirements apply. Such assurance can be provided through a documented review of maintenance and production records, as long as the equipment was not changed during the time interval.

Validation activities by excipient manufacturers range from the continuous monitoring of process capability to conducting validations using approved protocols and issuing reports. Generally, it is expected that the excipient manufacturer has demonstrated the process is capable of producing excipient lots in conformance to quality requirements from the point at which full GMP requirements have been determined to begin.

Traceability requirements are similar to those for pharmaceutical dosage forms and API. However, it is recognized that raw materials are often stored in bulk tanks, which makes unique traceability to a raw material lot unfeasible. Also, excipients are often produced using continuous processing, which again makes traceability to a lot of raw materials or intermediates impractical. In either event, the excipient manufacturer is expected to be able to place boundaries around a finite amount of excipient that may have contained the raw material or intermediate lot being traced.

The excipient label identifies the manufacturer and site where the excipient is produced. It is preferred that this information be stated on the label, but it is acceptable to provide this information through codes on the label, as long as the customer is made aware of the meaning of the code.

Finished excipient is sometimes stored in bulk, typically stored outdoors. This is acceptable where the practice has been demonstrated not to adversely affect excipient quality. Where excipient storage, whether discrete or bulk, requires controlled conditions, such as temperature or inert atmosphere, records are expected to demonstrate specified conditions were met.

Excipient packaging systems are demonstrated to protect the excipient during transport to the customer and under the recommended storage. Unless the packaging system has been used for an extensive time frame, studies should demonstrate that the packaging system continues to assure the excipient meets quality requirements during its shelf life. Unless justification demonstrates it is not feasible, a tamper-evident seal is expected to be used to facilitate customer identification of any packages that have been opened.

Where delivery of the excipient to the customer final destination is under contract, the excipient manufacturer is responsible for ensuring controlled conditions in transport are maintained. Where delivery is in non-dedicated bulk trucks or railcars, the excipient manufacturer is to confirm the cleanliness of the vehicle. Also for bulk shipments, the manufacturer is to provide the transport company either with a list of restricted prior cargoes or allowed prior cargoes. Distribution records to the initial customer are expected to be adequate to identify and trace the excipient.

Excipient manufacturers are to use calibrated or verified measuring and test devices that have appropriate specificity and sensitivity. Unless otherwise justified, there are procedures for the calibration of these devices. Calibration is conducted in accordance with a schedule using traceable standards. If no standard exists, the basis for calibration or verification should be justified.

MEASUREMENT, ANALYSIS, AND IMPROVEMENT

The 363 Standard requires the planning and implementation of monitoring, measurement, and improvement activities through analysis of product and process trends. This includes assessment of customer satisfaction.

There is a requirement for an internal audit program that includes scheduled audits of the excipient quality system. The frequency of internal audit is based on findings from previous audits, performance measures, and the potential impact of the activity on excipient quality. Corrective and preventive measures are identified and the effectiveness confirmed.

The manufacturer identifies the tests and measurements needed to control the manufacture and quality of the excipient. The review of tests and measurements as well as process performance parameters and critical quality attributes are conducted to assess the need for improvements. For finished excipient, the manufacturer is to establish suitable test methods and procedures to verify the excipient meets specification. Where the excipient is to comply with a pharmacopoeia or official compendium, non-official analytical methods are demonstrated to be at least equivalent to the compendia method. Also, the excipient is to comply with applicable monographs, general chapters, and notices. Finally, responsibility for monitoring the pharmacopoeia or official compendia are assigned.

Laboratory controls include sufficient data and tests needed to verify the excipient conforms to the specification or standard claimed. The laboratory record demonstrates that sample preparation conforms to test requirements. Laboratory reagents and test solutions, whether purchased or prepared in-house, are labeled with the name, concentration, date of first use or date of preparation, and the assigned date of expiration or restandardization.

A review of all records associated with the production, packaging, labeling, and testing of the excipient prior to offering the lot for sale is performed by the quality unit. The review confirms there are records showing that the manufacturing and packaging instructions were followed, there is a retained copy of the package label, and finally all required lab testing was performed and the results meet predefined specifications.

Out-of-specification test results are investigated by the laboratory in accordance with a site procedure that assures a thorough and objective review that supports the final disposition of the lot with the discrepant result. The procedure provides criteria for retesting the original sample, criteria for resampling, and the need to perform an investigation of the manufacturing processes/documentation to determine the cause of the failure when there is no assignable cause from the laboratory investigation. The result of the investigation is either to invalidate the original test result when an assignable cause is found or accept the validity of the result and improve process control.

The stability of the excipient is demonstrated through a scientific study.[6] This usually involves setting aside the excipient in the market container under the recommended storage conditions to show that the excipient continues to meet the intended specification until the expiration or retest date. This study is often conducted as a kinetics experiment, in which the initial samples are taken frequently, with the interval between sampling increased as the duration of the study progresses. Although it is expected that stability testing of pharmaceutical drug products and APIs involve the use of stability-indicating test methods, such testing is not possible for most excipients. Excipients often do not have an assay and are very stable molecules. Excipients such as inorganic salts do not degrade due to temperature or humidity conditions, and organic excipients may produce different decomposition products when degradation is forced. Therefore, verification of excipient stability[6] is usually measured by continued compliance with the excipient specification when stored in the unopened package.

A representative-retained sample of each excipient batch is kept for a justified retention period.

The excipient manufacturer is to conduct a study of the impurities typically present in the excipient. The collection of these impurities in excipients is referred to as the composition[7] profile rather than an impurity profile since, oftentimes, an excipient impurity is important to the functionality of the excipient in some customer formulations.[7] Therefore, the pharmaceutical customer prefers the quantity of impurities present in the excipient to remain constant lest a change in impurity adversely impacts their drug formulation. Limits for known impurities in excipients are established based on safety considerations, regulatory requirements, official compendia, and customer requirements.

Nonconforming raw material, intermediate, and excipient are isolated, and the root cause for the failure to meet specification is investigated. Evaluation and disposition of such material is governed by procedure. Procedures prevent shipment of excipient that is unacceptable to certain customers when a lot fails their customer-specific requirement but may allow shipment to other customers that do not have the same requirement. There is also a procedure for the retrieval of nonconforming excipient already in distribution.

Even though the excipient manufacturer often regrades nonconforming material for use in other industries or reprocesses the excipient, an investigation into the reason for failing to meet specification should still be conducted. Likewise, returned excipient is often downgraded and sold to other industries. However, if returned excipient is offered for sale as excipient grade, there is expected to be a documented review showing the excipient was returned from the intended customer, packaging was not compromised, and the excipient was not exposed to environmental conditions in transport and storage that deviate from labeled recommendations. Excipient lots that fail specification are seldom reworked due to the risk the reworked excipient will fail to meet performance expectations in the customer formulation since there are other markets for which the quality of such material is suitable. However, if the excipient is reworked, the customer is to be notified as such.

The excipient manufacturer evaluates the effectiveness of the quality management system, excipient process capability, conformance to the ANSI Standard, and supplier nonconformance. There is a periodic review to identify opportunities for improvement, including review of corrective and preventive actions.

CONCLUDING REMARKS

The ANSI NSF/IPEC/ANSI 363-2014 Standard[1] was developed for the United States but with intent to be applicable globally. The consensus standard was written by the NSF Joint Committee on Pharmaceutical Excipients under NSF International. The committee included participants from both the United States and Europe.

As in the United States, the European Commission has adopted ICH Q7 as the standard under which the API is to be manufactured. Also, like in the United States, there is currently no European regulatory requirement that excipients for use in human medicines must comply with specified GMP requirements. The industry is waiting for comment from the U.S. FDA on the use of the 363 Standard for regulation of excipient GMPs. The expectation is the European Commission will also provide comment.

REFERENCES

1. NSF/IPEC/ANSI 363-2014 Good Manufacturing Practices (GMP) for Pharmaceutical Excipients. The following guides are available, at no cost, at www.ipecamericas.org.
2. The Joint IPEC-PQG, Good Manufacturing Practices Audit Guide for Pharmaceutical Excipients, 2007.
3. The IPEC Certificate of Analysis Guide for Pharmaceutical Excipients, 2013.
4. The IPEC Significant Change Guide for Pharmaceutical Excipients, Third Revision, 2014.
5. The Joint IPEC-PQG Good Manufacturing Practices Guide for Pharmaceutical Excipients, 2006.
6. The IPEC Excipient Stability Program Guide, 2010.
7. The IPEC Excipient Composition Guide, 2009.

17 Packaging and Labeling Control

Graham P. Bunn

CONTENTS

§211.122 MATERIALS EXAMINATION AND USAGE CRITERIA

a. *There shall be written procedures describing in sufficient the detail of the receipt, identification, storage, handling, sampling, examination, and/or testing of labeling and packaging materials; such written procedures shall be followed. Labeling and packaging materials shall be representatively sampled, and examined or tested upon receipt and before use in packaging or labeling of a drug product.*

b. *Any labeling or packaging materials meeting appropriate written specifications may be approved and released for use. Any labeling or packaging materials that do not meet such specifications shall be rejected to prevent their use in operations for which they are unsuitable.*

c. *Records shall be maintained for each shipment received of each different labeling and packaging material indicating receipt, examination or testing, and whether accepted or rejected.*

Subpart G covers labeling and packaging including preprinted cartons and corrugated shippers but excludes containers and closures, which are covered in Subpart E (Control of Components and Drug Product Containers and Closures).

The Food and Drug Administration (FDA) guidance for industry "Quality Systems Approach to Pharmaceutical CGMP Regulations"[1] notes "Packaging and labeling controls, critical stages in the pharmaceutical manufacturing process, are not specifically addressed in quality systems models. However, the Agency recommends that manufacturers always refer to the packaging and labeling control regulations at § 211 Subpart G. In addition—and this is consistent with modern quality systems—FDA recommends that, as part of the design process, before commercial production, the controls for all processes within the packaging and labeling system be planned and documented in written procedures. The procedures should outline quality control activities and the responsible positions. Specifications and controls for the packaging and labeling materials should also be determined before commercial production. Distinct labels with discriminating features for different products, such as a product marketed with different strengths, should be included to prevent mislabeling and resulting recalls."

According to Stericycle Expert Solutions,[2] recalls of pharmaceuticals from the market related to labeling errors in 2017 and 1Q 2018 average about 16% of the total recalls. The effective control of printed labeling (labels, inserts, cartons, foil) begins well before materials are ordered; as noted in the guidance[1] above, it starts at the design and approval stage. Written procedures for the inspection, documentation, and approval/rejection of incoming labels and packaging must also be in place to effectively control them. The requirements for labeling are defined in §21 CFR 201 Labeling and the corresponding subparts. It is noted in §211 CFR 201.1 Subpart A—General Labeling Provisions (k)(l) that "A drug product is misbranded under Section 502(a) of the Act if its labeling identifies a person as manufacturer, packer, or distributor, and that identification does not meet the requirements of this section." The Act is Section 502(c) of the Food Drug Cosmetic Act, 21 USC 352(c). Although the requirements in Part §21 CFR 314 Applications for FDA Approval to Market a New Drug include Subpart A 314.3 "Definitions," it does not include labeling. Further detailed requirements concerning labeling and related packaging requirements can be found at www. FDA.gov.

The USP36-NF31 defines the following: "The term *labeling* designates all labels and other written, printed, or graphic matter on an article's immediate container or on or in any package or wrapper in which it is enclosed, except any outer shipping container. The term *label* designates that part of the labeling on the immediate container. A shipping container that contains a single article, unless the container also is essentially the immediate container or the outside of the consumer package, must be labeled with a minimum of product identification (except for controlled articles), lot number, expiration date, and conditions for storage and distribution.

In addition to compendial requirements, articles in *USP–NF* also are subject to compliance with more comprehensive labeling requirements promulgated by governmental bodies."

Requirements for the receipt, identification, storage, and handling will follow incoming receiving procedures, including general physical inspection before verification of supplier, quantity, and order details then placing in a quarantine status.

Sampling from each shipment received is performed using approved sampling plans followed by visual examination, and/or testing of labeling, and packaging materials. Electronic image comparison of labeling samples with an approved master copy for the correct text, position, density, and color can be performed with validated systems, which reduces the chance of human error during examination. This is especially important for patient insert leaflets with a large amount of text, complicated text containing numbers, and also when labeling is in languages other than English. Dimensional size tests and the ability of the packaging to protect the primary container from light and also protect it during shipment are also evaluated. Additionally, testing of the bar codes incorporated in the labeling confirms identity of the item and also reduces errors. If the test results meet specifications, the labeling and packaging materials can be released by the Quality Control Unit from the quarantine status. Note that the requirements specifically cover examination/testing before use in packaging or labeling of a drug product.

The FDA guidance for industry "Container Closure Systems for Packaging Human Drugs and Biologics"[3] notes that "For most drug products, a drug product manufacturer may accept a packaging component lot based on receiving a Certificate of Analysis (COA) or Certificate of Certification (COC) from the component supplier and the performance of an appropriate identification test, provided the supplier's test data are periodically validated (21 CFR 211.84[d][3]). Acceptance of a packaging component lot based on a supplier's COA or COC may not be appropriate in all cases (e.g., some packaging components for certain inhalation drug products)." The reader is encouraged to understand this specific guidance, as it contains useful information for establishing sound inspection/testing rationales.

Initial approval and any subsequent revisions of labeling and packaging materials, including printed cartons, label content, materials, ink composition and paper/cardboard used in the packaging and also the use of new vendors/suppliers requires a pre-approved change control. Proposed changes at the vendors/suppliers to the materials must be communicated to the packager since they are ultimately responsible. A quality supplier agreement is essential in maintaining the required controls with appropriate approvals from the purchasing company, including Quality Assurance (QA). Stability studies will have generated data supporting product shelf life in the container/closure system; it is imperative that any proposed changes are also adequately controlled.

Launch of new or changes to existing labeling and packaging requires multifunctional and interrelated responsibilities, which must be coordinated to ensure adequate controls and compliance with regulatory requirements. These include approvals with defined responsibilities from the following:

- Regulatory Affairs and Legal departments: compliance with country requirements
- Medical Affairs: medical correct content
- Editorial: original content or changes are correct
- Marketing: when and how the new/changes will be introduced to the market depending on the regulatory approvals
- Production: ensures equipment is available with any re/validation and personnel training is completed

- Materials management: coordinates with production for the availability of the new/revised batches or labeling/packaging.
- Quality Control Unit: ensures that overall procedures, packaging records, and requirements are followed and any new documents (specifications) are approved prior to being needed

Requirement in §211.122(b) to reject materials that do not meet the specification are obvious and with technology available the color, text density, position/location, and dimensions can all be measured with a high degree of accuracy. Development of preapproved justifiable specification ranges prior to testing results in defendable disposition decisions by the Quality Control Unit.

Records must be retained to document the evaluation results and disposition of each delivery of material; even if the same batch is received on a consecutive day, it must still be independently examined/tested. Results and data are used to monitor supplier/vendor performance against specifications and delivery metrics with appropriate actions being taken as necessary.

    d. *Labels and other labeling materials for each different drug product, strength, dosage form, or quantity of contents shall be stored separately with suitable identification. Access to the storage shall be limited to authorized personnel.*
    e. *Obsolete and outdated labels, labeling, and other packaging materials shall be destroyed.*

    Storage of labels and labeling must be controlled to minimize the potential for mix-ups and is often performed by physical containment in segregated sections. Clear identification of the locations and maintenance of the tidiness/order of the area and storage locations, often with plastic bins, is important.

    While unprinted bulk packaging materials are stored in the warehouse, there are dedicated and restricted personnel access label storage areas/rooms with defined temperature and humidity conditions. These areas are limited to authorized personnel, and issuance/ return of labeling materials is strictly controlled. Obsolete/outdated materials can result from a revision to the content and need to be promptly segregated and destroyed with supporting documentation.

    f. *Use of gang printed labeling for different drug products or different strengths or net contents of the same drug product is prohibited unless the labeling from gang printed sheets is adequately differentiated by size, shape, or color.*
    g. *If cut labeling is used for immediate container labels, individual unit cartons, or multiunit cartons containing immediate containers that are not packaged in individual unit cartons, packaging and labeling operations shall include one of the following special control procedures:*
      1. *Dedication of labeling and packaging lines to each different strength of each different drug product;*
      2. *Use of appropriate electronic or electromechanical equipment to conduct a 100% examination for correct labeling during or after completion of finishing operations; or*
      3. *Use of visual inspection to conduct a 100% examination for correct labeling during or after completion of finishing operations for hand applied labeling. Such examination shall be performed by one person and independently verified by a second person.*
    h. *Printing devices on, or associated with, manufacturing lines used to imprint labeling upon the drug product unit label or case shall be monitored to assure that all imprinting conforms to the print specified in the batch production record.*

Gang printing consists of different labeling (strength/product) on the same sheet, which is then cut and separated into the different strength/product labels. This technique has a high risk for mix-up during the cutting and separating stages, and is rarely used today. Regulations prior to 1994 acknowledged the risks but did allow gang printing on the condition that certain safeguards were employed during these stages. Further revision of the requirements prohibited gang printing unless the individual items are sufficiently different.

Subsection (g) addresses the use of the cut labeling on the packaging lines. The individual unit carton labeling is the outermost container in which a drug product is usually marketed. Therefore, consumers will read this labeling when using the product. For multiunit cartons containing immediate containers that are not packaged in individual unit cartons (e.g., sterile vials in trays but immediate containers lack unit cartons), consumers/health-care professionals rely on the outer multiunit container labeling as the initial identification and then the immediate container label. Similar labels with multiple strengths of different products can result in confusion.

While the risks at the printing company/supplier are significantly less than for gang printing, the potential for mix-ups is still high. The regulations now require additional checking, preferably by electronic or other automated means, although visual confirmation is allowed for hand labeling operations.

Some pharmaceutical operations still include in-house printing of components either online or off-line. This include ceramic or silk-screen printing of ampoules as well as printing of tubes and plastic bottles. These printing operations must be set up, operated, and controlled the same as a supplier. Printing screens, when used, should be carefully examined for conformity to approved text, correct layout, absence of tears and holes, and absence of blocked holes or letters.

§211.125 LABELING ISSUANCE

a. *Strict control shall be exercised over labeling issued for use in drug product labeling operations.*
b. *Labeling materials issued for a batch shall be carefully examined for identity and conformity to the labeling specified in the master or batch production records.*
c. *Procedures shall be written describing in sufficient detail the control procedures employed for the issuance of labeling; such written procedures shall be followed.*

Issuance of labeling materials is a critical process that requires multiple controls with appropriate checks. Label room procedures require a written order/request for the issuance of each quantity of material for a specific packaging operation/run. This bill of material/label issuance form is part of the batch production records. Only designated personnel can request, collect with signature, and issue the materials that are locked in a container/cage in the label room before delivery to the packaging floor. The container/cage is only unlocked on the packaging floor where the contents are verified for identity and quantity against the request and issuance details. Note that the regulations stress "Strict control..." and this needs to be reflected in the procedure requirements and consistently implemented.

d. *Procedures shall be used to reconcile the quantities of labeling issued, used, and returned, and shall require evaluation of discrepancies found between the quantity of drug product finished and the quantity of labeling issued when such discrepancies are outside narrow preset limits based on historical operating data. Such discrepancies shall be investigated in accordance with §211.192. Labeling reconciliation is waived for cut or roll labeling if a 100% examination for correct labeling is performed in accordance with §211.122(g)(2).*
e. *All excess labeling bearing lot or control numbers shall be destroyed.*
f. *Returned labeling shall be maintained and stored in a manner to prevent mix-ups and provide proper identification.*

Prior to bar coding labels and high-speed readers, the reconciliation of labels was challenging to maintain. To perform the reconciliation, the issuance relies on the accuracy on the label rolls from the supplier, or every roll would have to be counted at receipt prior to use. The label use with scanners, determination of the number rejected/destroyed, and returned quantities is possible for each packaging run. Reconciliation limits are based on historical operating data and must be justifiable.

Destruction

Destruction of any labeling material (with or without lot numbers) must be controlled, as these could be diverted for other use or inadvertently attached to other containers. Destruction can be in the form of defacing (marker pen through each label) when there are smaller quantities or placed in restricted access containers the contents of which are then shredded under controlled conditions. Adequate control and documented evidence of destruction are essential.

The return of any excess labeling is permitted, provided it does not contain any lot number/ expiry dates and is undamaged, that is, meeting the same specification it did upon initial receipt. The labeling is retuned in the same way it was delivered: in a locked container/cage with supporting documentation and is verified and signed for by the label control personnel at receipt. Placement of the labeling back in the correct location and stock adjustments with traceability to the batch issued/ returned are performed according to procedures.

§211.130 PACKAGING AND LABELING OPERATIONS

There shall be written procedures designed to assure that correct labels, labeling, and packaging materials are used for drug products; such written procedures shall be followed. These procedures shall incorporate the following features:

a. *Prevention of mix-ups and cross contamination by physical or spatial separation from operations on other drug products.*
b. *Identification and handling of filled drug product containers that are set aside and held in unlabeled condition for future labeling operations to preclude mislabeling of individual containers, lots, or portions of lots. Identification needs not be applied to each individual container but shall be sufficient to determine name, strength, quantity of contents, and lot or control number of each container.*
c. *Identification of the drug product with a lot or control number that permits determination of the history of the manufacture and control of the batch.*
d. *Examination of packaging and labeling materials for suitability and correctness before packaging operations, and documentation of such examination in the batch production record.*
e. *Inspection of the packaging and labeling facilities immediately before use to assure that all drug products have been removed from previous operations. Inspection shall also be made to assure that packaging and labeling materials not suitable for subsequent operations have been removed. Results of inspection shall be documented in the batch production records.*

This section, as with several others, specifically requires written procedures for labels, labeling, and packaging and that they shall be followed. However, there is no description of a specific type of record as there is in Subpart F, Production and Process Controls, covering the overall manufacturing process. Although not specifically described in detail, Sections §211.130(d) and (e) reference the "batch production record," and it is an expectation and reflected in practice that a document (Packaging Record/ Order) is approved and issued covering the requirements and capturing the information and data for the packaging operations. Since it is the function that the document serves rather than what it is called that is important and a broader reading of "Process Controls" also include packaging/labeling. Additionally, review of the following subpart identifies other requirements relating to the packaging record:

Subpart J—Records and Reports Sec. 211.188 Batch production and control records.

Batch production and control records shall be prepared for each batch of drug product produced and shall include complete information relating to the production and control of each batch. These records shall include:

a. *An accurate reproduction of the appropriate master production or control record, checked for accuracy, dated, and signed*

b. *Documentation that each significant step in the manufacture, processing, packing, or holding of the batch was accomplished, including:*
   1. *Dates*
   2. *Identity of individual major equipment and lines used*
   3. *Specific identification of each batch of component or in-process material used*
   4. *Weights and measures of components used in the course of processing*
   5. *In-process and laboratory control results*
   6. *Inspection of the packaging and labeling area before and after use*
   7. *A statement of the actual yield and a statement of the percentage of theoretical yield at appropriate phases of processing*
   8. *Complete labeling control records, including specimens or copies of all labeling used*
   9. *Description of drug product containers and closures*
   10. *Any sampling performed*
   11. *Identification of the persons performing and directly supervising or checking each significant step in the operation, or if a significant step in the operation is performed by automated equipment under 211.68, the identification of the person checking the significant step performed by the automated equipment*
   12. *Any investigation made according to 211.192*
   13. *Results of examinations made in accordance with 211.134*

[43 FR 45077, Sept. 29, 1978, as amended at 73 FR 51933, Sept. 8, 2008]

Subsection 211.130(a) requires spatial separation to prevent mix-up and cross contamination: since filled containers, labels, and tablets cannot just "travel" across open space, but some packaging areas also have physical barriers provided that items do not get trapped under them and they can be cleaned. Potential cross contamination is also mentioned, but film-coated tables minimize this problem, and there is limited discussion of this is regulatory observations.

Subsection (b) refers to adequate control of "bright stock" (packaged but not labeled) and is still a practice seen today, the labeling of the sealed outer cartons holding the filled containers is defined, and there is supporting documentation. Reasons for doing this include: labeling not available but packaging can be performed and stock held, packaging configurations are the same for multiple markets and labeling will be performed in separate runs, or packaging is performed at one facility and stock shipped to another for labeling. Provided the standard operating procedures (SOPs) and packaging documentation support these types of situations, it can be performed after first verifying there is no impact to the stability of the product.

Subsection (c) has no different requirements than other traceability of materials and product batches. Subsection (d) requires confirmation before use that the packaging materials are suitable, since it may have been some time since they were released (still within expiration), and a general reinspection is required together with the "correctness," that is, these are the required materials (item code), quantities, and they are the correct lot numbers as designated on the bill of materials. Any discrepancies would be documented and corrected with investigations as required by SOPs.

The final Subsection (e) requires inspection of the facilities (packaging and labeling area/lines and equipment) immediately before use to ensure that all drug product from the previous run has been removed. This is commonly referred to as "line clearance" and has been a significant challenge for some companies, as their failure to consistently perform this correctly has resulted in product recalls and increasing regulatory authority attention. Clearance at the end of the run and immediately prior to starting the next ensures that there is no remaining drug product; however, they specifically note that any packaging and labeling materials not suitable for subsequent packaging activities are removed, allowing any that are to remain on the line/area. This does negate the need to account for all the material quantities.

Adequate and comprehensive line clearance performed consistently is not difficult, but it must be performed methodically, with attention to fine detail according to procedure. There is no reason to rush through the steps, other than the next batch is waiting to be packaged and that is no justification. The fact that production has performed the checks does not mean that the check by the QCU is less important, and with all second checks, the first has its own importance; otherwise, there would only need to be one check performed. Detailed procedures with pictures of the points/places that have been determined through risk assessment and sometimes through experience to trap tablets, capsules, labels, etc. need to be consistently used and supported with documented evidence. Subsection 211.188.(b)6 is clear that the check is performed before and after use to ensure previous drug product is not still on the line and also that none have been placed on the line after clearance was performed and before the new batch was brought onto the line. There may be a gap of a few hours or days between these essential checks.

The master batch packaging and labeling record for each container size and corresponding market labels contains the same type of requirements defined in Section § 211.186 Master production and control records. See also § 211.188 above for discussion relating to packaging and labeling records. For example, the following would be expected to be defined and completed with information/data as appropriate:

1. Drug product name, identification number, and strength
2. Names, identification/item number, and quantities of each packaging and labeling material:
   a. Primary container: bottle, closure and liner, foil, laminate
   b. Labels: primary and cartons
   c. Cartons
   d. Packaging insert/patient information leaflets
   e. Tamper-evident and child-resistant components
   f. Shipper, dividers, any other protective packaging
3. Complete description/identification of the equipment and corresponding settings to be used for the packaging and labeling operations
4. Specific environmental monitoring requirements (e.g., temperature/humidity)
5. Sampling requirements/quantities and frequency: testing to be performed
6. Alert and action limits/specifications for test results, for example, quantities and torque removal, with directions if any are exceeded
7. Batch numbers, quantities, reconciliation, and yields also included

Adequate and complete directions are essential so that after suitable training the packaging and labeling operators can consistently execute the requirements.

The master batch packaging and labeling records has the same management and controls as the manufacturing record and is also written and approved by appropriate personnel, including production and independently approved by validation, Regulatory Affairs, and QA/QCU. Creation and subsequent changes are managed through a change control process and documents maintained through document control.

Equipment calibration and qualification together with packaging/labeling operations validation are also required to be performed before commercial runs. Any set-up testing performed on the equipment prior to the start of each packaging run and periodically during the run are defined and the results documented.

§211.132 TAMPER-RESISTANT PACKAGING REQUIREMENTS FOR OVER-THE-COUNTER HUMAN DRUG PRODUCTS

a. *General.* The FDA has the authority under the Federal Food, Drug, and Cosmetic (FD&C) Act (the Act) to establish a uniform national requirement for tamper-resistant packaging (TRP) of over-the-counter (OTC) drug products that will improve the security of OTC drug packaging and help assure the safety and effectiveness of OTC drug products. An OTC drug product (except a dermatological, dentifrice, insulin, or throat lozenge product) for retail sale that is not packaged in a tamper-resistant package or that is not properly labeled under this section is adulterated under Section 501 of the Act, or misbranded under Section 502 of the Act, or both.

b. *Requirement for tamper-resistant package.*
   1. Each manufacturer and packer who packages an OTC drug product (except a dermatological, dentifrice, insulin, or throat lozenge product) for retail sale, shall package the product in a tamper-resistant package, if this product is accessible to the public while held for sale. A tamper-resistant package is one that has one or more indicators or barriers to entry, which, if breached or missing, can reasonably be expected to provide visible evidence to consumers indicating that tampering has occurred. To reduce the likelihood of successful tampering and to increase the likelihood that consumers would discover whether a product has been tampered with or not, the package is required to be distinctive by design (e.g., an aerosol product container), or by the use of one or more indicators or barriers to entry that employ an identifying characteristic (e.g., an aerosol product container), or by the use of an identifying characteristic (e.g., a pattern, name, registered trademark, logo, or picture). For purposes of this section, the term "distinctive by design" means the packaging cannot be duplicated with commonly available materials or through commonly available processes. For purposes of this section, the term "aerosol product" means a product that depends upon the power of a liquefied or compressed gas to expel the contents from the container. A tamper-resistant package may involve an immediate-container and closure system, or secondary-container or carton system, or any combination of systems intended to provide a visual indication of package integrity. The tamper-resistant feature shall be designed to, and shall remain intact when handled in a reasonable manner during manufacture, distribution, and retail display.
   2. In addition to the tamper-evident packaging feature described in paragraph (b) (1) of this section, any two-piece, hard gelatin capsule covered by this section must be sealed using an acceptable tamper-evident technology.

c. *Labeling.*
   1. In order to alert consumers to the specific tamper-evident feature(s) used, each retail package of an OTC drug product covered by this section (except ammonia inhalant in crushable glass ampoules, containers of compressed medical oxygen, or aerosol products, that depend upon the power of a liquefied or compressed gas to expel the contents from the container) is required to bear a statement that:
      i. Identified all tamper-evident feature(s) and any capsule sealing technologies used to comply with paragraph (b) of this section;
      ii. Is prominently placed on the package; and
      iii. Is so placed that it will be unaffected if the tamper-evident feature of the package is breached or missing.
   2. If the tamper-resistant feature chosen to meet the requirement in paragraph (b) of this section is one that uses an identifying characteristic, then that characteristic is required to be referred to in the labeling statement. For example, the labeling statement on a bottle with a shrink band could say, "For your protection, this bottle has an imprinted seal around the neck."

d. *Request for exemptions from packaging and labeling requirements.* A manufacturer or packer may request an exemption from the packaging and labeling requirements of this section. A request for an exemption is required to be submitted in the form of a citizen petition under §10.30 of this chapter and should be clearly identified on the envelope as a "Request for Exemption from Tamper-resistant Rule." The petition is required to contain the following:

1. The name of the drug product or, if the petition seeks an exemption for a drug class, the name of the drug class, and a list of products within that class.
2. The reasons that the drug product's compliance with the tamper-resistant-packaging or labeling requirements of this section is unnecessary or cannot be achieved.
3. A description of alternative steps that are available, or that the petitioner has already taken, to reduce the likelihood that the product or drug class will be the subject of malicious adulteration.
4. Other information justifying an exemption.

e. *OTC drug products subject to approved new drug applications.* Holders of approved new drug applications for OTC drug products are required under §314.70 of this chapter to provide the agency with notification of changes in packaging and labeling to comply with the requirements of this section. Changes in packaging and labeling required by this regulation may be made before FDA approval, as provided under §314.70(c) of this chapter. Manufacturing changes by which capsules are to be sealed require prior FDA approval under §314.70(b) of this chapter.

f. *Poison Prevention Packaging Act of 1970.* This section does not affect any requirements for "special packaging" as defined under §310.3(1) of this chapter and required under the Poison Prevention Packaging Act of 1970.

This section was introduced in 1982 into the current good manufacturing practice (CGMP) regulations less than a month after several deaths resulting from the malicious addition of cyanide to over the counter Tylenol® capsules.

Key elements of the regulation are:

1. It only applies to OTC products, since these tend to be on open display with ready access to the public. It was considered that prescription products are maintained under the control of the pharmacist and consequently are less vulnerable to tampering. The exemption of insulin was for the same reason. The other excluded categories—dentifrices, lozenges, and dermatological products—were considered to be less prone to potential tampering because of their inherent nature or their use.
2. No test methodology or effectiveness criteria were established. It was considered that the development of these would be difficult, time-consuming, and probably highly controversial and would delay the introduction of tamper-resistant packaging—which an apprehensive public needed in order to retain confidence in this essential form of medication (OTC). Instead, some guidance was provided on currently available forms of tamper-resistant technology (Sec. 450.500 Tamper-Resistant Packaging Requirements for Certain Over-the-Counter [OTC] Human Drug Products [CPG 7132a.17]). These included film wrappers, with certain restrictions and limitation; blister or strip packs; bubble packs; heat-shrink bands or wrappers but not wet shrink, which were considered reusable; foil, paper, or plastic pouches; bottle-mouth inner seals; tape seals; breakable caps; sealed metal tubes, or plastic blind-end heat-sealed tubes; sealed cartons but not glued seals; aerosol containers; and sealed cans. The tamper-resistant feature may apply to either the primary or the secondary packaging.

   Use of a tamper-resistant feature on the secondary package allows the consumer to examine the product for possible tampering before purchase. However, any inadvertent damage to the feature during shipping or storage can result in refusal of the purchase. Application to the primary container, or a bottle-mouth seal, will preclude this possibility.

The Compliance Guide does not suggest that any application of the features mentioned earlier will automatically assure compliance with §211.132, but the manufacturer should be able to demonstrate effective use of the technology. Conversely, other technologies are not excluded, since advancements continue to offer other means to meeting the requirements.

3. Two-piece hard gelatin capsules have been most vulnerable to tampering since once the contents have been replaced it is unlikely that the consumer will detect the differences, especially if the contents are a white powder. Use of bead formulations, especially if colored, increases security. The regulations (the sealing requirement was effective November 4, 1999, while labeling changes had to be implemented by November 6, 2000) require that such OTC capsules have two tamper-resistant features. Two-piece capsules must have the two halves sealed, and this is considered acceptable as one of the two features. Because of this inherent higher vulnerability, some manufacturers have ceased to provide this form of dosage, and some companies have introduced gelatin-coated tablets that look like capsules. These provide the consumer the ability to swallow with ease the smooth, elongated tablets and the strong medicine perception of a capsule.

4. The tamper-resistant feature is to be "distinctive by design or by use of an identifying characteristic." This is to preclude the possibility of removal of the feature and replacement by a commonly available material. An aerosol package is considered to be distinctive by design. Overwraps and seals usually require a distinctive characteristic, such as the company logo or the product name. A generic expression such as "Factory Sealed" or "Open Here" are not be sufficiently specific. A further concern relates to the possibility of taking a bottle-mouth seal from a larger size bottle and adjusting the size with gluing to fit a smaller size.

5. Labeling is to include specific reference to the tamper-resistant feature used and must be sufficiently explicit that a malicious replacement can be identified by the consumer.

The tamper-evident statement must be prominently placed on the drug product package to alert consumers about the product's tamper-evident features (21 CFR 211.132). The tamper-evident statement describes its feature of the product package and advises consumers that, if the feature is breached or missing when the product is purchased, tampering may have occurred. Tamper-evident packaging with an appropriate labeling statement will be more likely to protect consumers because the consumers will be in a better position to detect tampering when they have the knowledge that a tamper-evident feature has been incorporated into the product design. The Agency allows flexibility in the placement of this statement on the package and does not require that it be included within the Drug Facts section. However, if included in this section, the statement must appear under the heading "Other information" [21 CFR 201.66(c)(7)].

The Agency also noted in the final rule preamble for the Drug Facts regulation that many products are now marketed with "peel back" or "fold out" labels affixed to the product package and that these labels could be used to accommodate all of the FDA-required information in the Drug Facts section (64 FR 13254 at 13268; March 17, 1999). These types of labels were not in use at the time the tamper-evident requirements became effective. Recently, interested parties have inquired whether the tamper-evident statement may be included in a Drug Facts section that appears in such "peel back" or "fold out" labels.

It is important that the consumer inspects the tamper-evident statement before purchase and use of the product so that they will be more aware of the tamper-evident features and any signs of tampering. If the consumer fails to examine these features before opening, then it becomes difficult to determine if the statement was intact at the time of opening. A tamper-evident statement inside a "peel back" or "fold out" label that is not visible on the outside of the package is unlikely to be reviewed. The FDA recommended instead in these circumstances that the tamper-evident statement be provided outside the Drug Facts box in another part of the label, where the statement is clearly visible without further manipulation of that label.

6. Tamper-resistant packaging components are to be treated identically to other components (Compliance Policy Guide 7132.14). Those coming into direct contact with the drug product are subject to the container and closure provisions of the CGMP regulations (Subpart E). Other tamper-resistant components are subject to the appropriate provisions of Subpart G; in particular, any components with labeling information would need to comply with the provisions for labeling, including accountability.

At the present time, the currently available technologies do provide significant protection to the consumer, but it must be noted that products are not tamper-proof. Some seals and neck bands provide consumers with special challenges, especially when they have limited dexterity and reduced strength in their ability to grip/tear the physical tamper evident materials to access the products.

Those portions of tamper-resistant packaging that contain labeling, as defined in Section 201(m) of the FD&C Act will be considered as any other labeling and, as such, are subject to the control and accountability provisions of Subpart G of the CGMP regulations.

Those portions of tamper-resistant packaging that contact the drug product are considered part of the container closure system and, as such, are subject to the control and accountability provisions of Subpart E of the CGMP regulations.

Those portions of tamper-resistant packaging that do not fall into the categories mentioned earlier will be considered as general packaging material, subject to the general controls for packaging contained in Subpart G of the CGMP regulations.

In addition, the Agency has reevaluated the currently available tamper-resistant packaging technologies and concluded that some technologies as designed or applied are no longer capable of meeting the requirements of the tamper-resistant packaging regulations.

The FDA published "Compliance Policy Guide 7132a.17 (Sec 450.500) Tamper-Resistant Packaging Requirements for Certain OTC Human Drug Products" in 1992. This guide outlined those configurations and materials that are currently considered as not acceptable to render the OTC product tamper-resistant.

CPG Sec. 450.500 Tamper-Resistant Packaging Requirements
for Certain Over-the-Counter Human Drug Products

The regulations require that all OTC human drug products (except dermatologics, dentifrices, insulin, and throat lozenges) (21 CFR 211.132), cosmetic liquid oral hygiene products, vaginal products (21 CFR 700.25), and contact lens solutions and tablets used to make these solutions (21 CFR 800.12) be packaged in tamper-resistant packaging.

The packaging must use an indicator or barrier to entry that is distinctive by design (such as an aerosol container) or must employ an identifying characteristic (a pattern, name, registered trademark, logo, or picture). Further, the regulations require a labeling statement on the container (except ammonia inhalant in crushable glass ampules, aerosol products, or containers of compressed medical oxygen) to alert the consumer to the specific tamper-resistant feature(s) used. The labeling statement is also required to be placed so that it will be unaffected if a tamper-resistant packaging feature is breached or missing.

An amendment to the tamper-resistant packaging regulations for OTC human drug products published as a final rule in the FEDERAL REGISTER on February 2, 1989. The new requirements (21 CFR 211.132[b][1] and [2]) are:

1. For two-piece, hard gelatin capsule products subject to this requirement, a minimum of two tamper-resistant packaging features is required, unless the capsules are sealed by a tamper-resistant technology.
2. For all other products subject to this requirement, including two-piece, hard gelatin capsules that are sealed by a tamper-resistant technology, a minimum of one tamper-resistant feature is required.

Manufacturers were given until February 2, 1990, to comply with the new requirements.

In addition, the Agency has reevaluated currently available tamper-resistant packaging technologies and concluded that some technologies as designed or applied are no longer capable of meeting the requirements of the tamper-resistant packaging regulations.

Packaging Systems

Manufacturers and packagers are free to use any packaging system as long as the tamper-resistant standard in the regulations is met. The tamper-resistant packaging requirements are intended to assure that the product's packaging "can reasonably be expected to provide visible evidence to consumers that tampering has occurred."

Examples of packaging technologies capable of meeting the tamper-resistant packaging requirements are listed below. The use of one of these packaging technologies does not, by itself, constitute compliance with the requirements for a tamper-resistant package. Packaging features must be properly designed and appropriately applied to be effective tamper-resistant packaging.

1. **Film Wrappers.** A transparent film is wrapped securely around the entire product container. The film must be cut or torn to open the container and remove the product. A tight "fit" of the film around the container must be achieved, for example, by a shrink-type process. A film wrapper sealed with overlapping end flaps must not be capable of being opened and resealed without leaving visible evidence of entry.

   The use of cellophane with overlapping end flaps is not effective as a tamper-resistant feature because of the possibility that the end flaps can be opened and resealed without leaving visible evidence of entry.

   The film wrapper must employ an identifying characteristic that cannot be readily duplicated. An identifying characteristic that is proprietary and different for each product size is recommended.

   Tinted wrappers are no longer acceptable as an identifying characteristic because of the possibility that their material or a facsimile may be available to the public.

2. **Blister or Strip Packs.** Dosage units (e.g., tablets or capsules) are individually sealed in clear plastic or plastic compartments with foil or paper backing.

   The individual compartment must be torn or broken to obtain the product. The backing materials cannot be separated from the blisters or replaced without leaving visible evidence of entry.

3. **Bubble Packs.** The product and container are sealed in plastic and mounted in or on a display card. The plastic must be torn or broken to remove the product. The backing material cannot be separated from the plastic bubble or replaced without leaving visible evidence of entry.

4. **Heat-Shrink Bands or Wrappers.** A band or wrapper is securely applied to a portion of the container, usually at the juncture of the cap and container. The band or wrapper is heat shrunk to provide a tight fit. The band or wrapper must be cut or torn to open the container and remove the product and cannot be worked off and reapplied without visible damage. The use of a perforated tear strip can enhance tamper-resistance.

   Cellulose wet shrink seals are not acceptable. The knowledge to remove and reapply these seals without evidence of tampering is widespread.

   The band or wrapper must employ an identifying characteristic that cannot be readily duplicated. An identifying characteristic that is proprietary and different for each product size is recommended.

   Tinted bands or wrappers are no longer acceptable as an identifying characteristic because of the possibility that their material or a facsimile may be available to the public.

5. **Foil, Paper, or Plastic Pouches.** The product is enclosed in an individual pouch that must be torn or broken to obtain the product. The end seams of the pouches cannot be separated and resealed without showing visible evidence of entry.

6. **Container Mouth Inner Seals.** Paper, thermal plastic, plastic film, foil, or a combination thereof, is sealed to the mouth of a container (e.g., bottle) under the cap. The seal must be torn or broken to open the container and remove the product. The seal cannot be removed and reapplied without leaving visible evidence of entry. Seals applied by heat induction to plastic containers appear to offer a higher degree of tamper-resistance than those that depend on an adhesive to create the bond.

Polystyrene foam container mouth seals applied with pressure-sensitive adhesive are no longer considered effective tamper-resistant features because they can be removed and reapplied in their original state with no visible evidence of entry.

The Agency recognizes that technological innovations may produce foam seals that will adhere to a container mouth in a manner that cannot be circumvented without visible evidence of entry. Container mouth seals must employ an identifying characteristic that cannot be readily duplicated. An identifying characteristic that is proprietary and different for each product size is recommended.

7. **Tape Seals.** Tape seals relying on an adhesive to bond them to the package are not capable of meeting the tamper-resistant packaging requirements because they can be removed and reapplied with no visible evidence of entry.

However, the Agency recognizes that technological innovations may produce adhesives that do not permit the removal and reapplication of tape seals. In addition, tape seals may contain a feature that makes it readily apparent if the seals have been removed and reapplied. Tape seals must employ an identifying characteristic that cannot be readily duplicated.

8. **Breakable Caps.** The container (e.g., bottle) is sealed by a plastic or metal cap that either breaks away completely when removed from the container or leaves part of the cap attached to the container. The cap, or a portion thereof, must be broken in order to open the container and remove the product. The cap cannot be reapplied in its original state.

9. **Sealed Metal Tubes or Plastic Blind-End Heat-Sealed Tubes.** The bottom of the tube is heat sealed and the mouth or blind-end must be punctured to obtain the product. A tube with a crimped end is capable of meeting the definition of a tamper-resistant feature if the crimped end cannot be breached by unfolding and refolding without visible evidence of entry.

10. **Sealed Cartons.** Paperboard cartons sealed by gluing the end flaps are not capable of meeting the tamper-resistant packaging requirements. However, the Agency recognizes that technological advances may provide sealed paperboard packages that meet the requirements of the tamper-resistant packaging regulations.

11. **Aerosol Containers.** Aerosol containers are believed to be inherently tamper-resistant because of their design. Direct printing of the label on the container (e.g., lithographing), is preferred to using a paper label, which could be removed and substituted.

12. **Cans (Both All-Metal and Composite).** Cans may be composed of all metal or composite walls with metal tops and bottoms. The top and bottom of a composite can must be joined to the can walls in such a manner that they cannot be pulled apart and reassembled without visible evidence of entry. Rather than attaching a separate label, direct printing of the label onto the can (e.g., lithographing) is preferred.

CAPSULE SEALING TECHNOLOGIES

Technologies for sealing two-piece hard gelatin capsules are available that provide evidence if the capsules have been tampered with after filling. Such sealing technologies currently in use include sonic welding, banding, and sealing techniques employing solvents and/or low temperature heating. These examples are not intended to rule out the development and use of other capsule-sealing technologies. Manufacturers may consult with the FDA if they are considering alternative capsule-sealing processes.

Sealed capsules are not tamper-resistant packages. They are required to be contained within a package system that utilizes a minimum of one tamper-resistant packaging feature.

TAMPER-RESISTANT PACKAGING LABELING STATEMENT(S)

1. **Bottle (Container) Caps.** In the past, some manufacturers have placed the tamper-resistant packaging labeling statement on bottle caps. This practice is unacceptable in cases where it may be a simple matter to substitute another unlabeled bottle cap for the one with the tamper-resistant warning statement. Such an act could easily be accomplished without any apparent sign of tampering.

2. **Package Inserts.** The practice of placing the tamper-resistant packaging labeling statement solely on the product's inserts is not acceptable. While package inserts may be a useful supplement for consumer education purposes, they are not acceptable in lieu of label statements.

3. **Carton/Container (Outer and Inner).** If the tamper-resistant packaging feature is on an outer carton, the inner container (e.g., bottle) needs to bear a statement alerting the consumer that the bottle should be in a carton at the time of purchase. This policy applies only to situations where the inner container is so labeled that such a container might reasonably otherwise be displayed on the retail shelf without an outer carton.

4. **Identifying Characteristic.** When a tamper-resistant packaging feature is required to have an identifying characteristic, that characteristic needs to be referenced in the labeling statement (e.g., "imprinted" neck band). It is recommended that the labeling statement specifically identify the characteristic (e.g., imprinted with XYZ on the neck band).

5. **Tamper-Resistant Packaging Feature(s).** All required tamper-resistant features must be referenced in the labeling statement. When two tamper-resistant packaging features are used for unsealed two-piece hard gelatin capsules, both features must be referenced in the labeling statement. If one tamper-resistant packaging feature plus sealed capsules are used, the labeling statement must reference both the capsule seal and the tamper-resistant packaging feature.

REGULATORY ACTION GUIDANCE

The tamper-resistant packaging requirements are part of the CGMP regulations. Regulatory actions for deviations from these requirements should be handled in the same manner as any other deviation from the GMP regulations.

Material between asterisks is new or revised

Issued: 3/1/88
Revised: 5/21/92

§211.134 DRUG PRODUCT INSPECTION

a. *Packaged and labeled products shall be examined during finishing operations to provide assurance that containers and packages in the lot have the correct label.*
b. *A representative sample of units shall be collected at the completion of finishing operations and shall be visually examined for correct labeling.*
c. *Results of these examinations shall be recorded in the batch production or control records.*

The objective of these requirements is to confirm that during packaging and labeling activities the resulting packages consistently meet the requirements they are intended to in the record supported by the packaging validation. As with any process, sampling at the end to find out that the label was applied in the incorrect place on the carton or the batch number printed on the label became unreadable after half the batch was packaged would be unacceptable. The International Society for Pharmaceutical Engineering issued a paper "Overview of Packaging Validation for Drug Products,"[4] which provided details of the various guidance documents available from regulatory authorities on the approach to validation for the primary, secondary, and tertiary packaging.

In-process checks and the final sample at the end of operations are taken by a quality function, often referred to as "On the floor QA." These personnel may also perform the verification of line clearance and other quality-related activities while reporting into the Quality Control Unit organization. They are also a quality resource for production in the real-time resolution of quality issues.

REPRESENTATIVE SAMPLE OF UNITS

The World Health Organization (WHO) provided sampling guidance in the WHO guidelines for sampling of pharmaceutical products and related materials: "As for packaging materials, sampling plans for finished products should be based on defined sampling standards such as BS 6001-1, ISO 2859 or ANSI/ASQCZ 1.4-1993."[5]

The sampling and inspection procedure must be statistically designed and is usually based on the classification of the inspected items as "defective" or "non-defective." The objective is to identify the types/classification and number of defects that occur so that an objective decision to be made on the disposition of each packaged batch can be made. Additionally, appropriate action can be initiated to determine and eliminate the cause of any such defects and enable appropriate actions to eliminate them.

Defects may be classified according to significance—critical, major, and minor—and the sampling plan, inspection level, and acceptance criteria is approved by the Quality Unit.

Records will capture the number and types and details of the defects identified. Critical defects will be reported immediately to management, who will initiate additional inspection to ascertain the extent of the problem as directed in the packaging record or SOP. Involvement of Quality may result in suspension of the activity until a course of action has been agreed and documented.

Production management is expected to maintain metrics for the inspection results and report these as overall metrics to executive management. Any trends or unexpected results need to be promptly investigated to determine what has changed and describe a course of action. Out-of-limits and upward trending of unacceptable inspection results may indicate that equipment maintenance frequency needs to be reviewed because parts are wearing to unacceptable tolerances, calibration of sensors/bar code readers may have been impacted, materials may have changed but this could not be detected during incoming inspection, only when for example the cartons are being run in the packaging equipment.

§211.137 EXPIRATION DATING

   a. *To assure that a drug product meets applicable standards of identity, strength, quality, and purity at the time of use, it shall bear an expiration date determined by appropriate stability testing described in §211.166.*
   b. *Expiration dates shall be related to any storage conditions stated on the labeling, as determined by stability studies described in §211.166.*
   c. *If the drug product is to be reconstituted at the time of dispensing, its labeling shall bear expiration information for both the reconstituted and unreconstituted drug products.*
   d. *Expiration dates shall appear on labeling in accordance with the requirements of §201.17 of this chapter.*
   e. *Homeopathic drug products shall be exempted from the requirements of this section.*
   f. *Allergenic extracts that are labeled "No U.S. Standard of Potency" are exempt from the requirements of this section.*

g. *New drug products for investigational use are exempted from the requirements of this section, provided that they meet appropriate standards or specifications as demonstrated by stability studies during their use in clinical investigations. Where new drug products for investigational use are to be reconstituted at the time of dispensing, their labeling shall bear expiration information for the reconstituted drug product.*

h. *Pending consideration of a proposed exemption, published in the Federal Register of September 29, 1978, the requirements in this section shall not be enforced for human OTC drug products if their labeling does not bear dosage limitations and they are stable for at least three years as supported by appropriate stability data.*

Although a logical statement for the requirement of the expiration date, it has always been necessary for this to be defined; otherwise, the health professional/consumer will be unable to determine if the product still meets it label claims. Requirements (a) to (d) are subsequently met since this data has to be submitted for the marketing authorization approval. Exemptions to these requirements are defined in (e) to (h) with specific criteria.

See also Chapter 8, "Clinical Trial Supplies".

The exemption for homeopathic products (21 CFR 211.137[e]) is based on the inability to quantitatively evaluate the low levels of ingredients in such products and the inability to relate effectiveness to quantitative composition.

In the Federal Register of February 26, 2004 (69 FR 9120), the FDA published a final rule requiring certain human drug and biological products to have on their labels a linear bar code that contains, at a minimum, the drug's NDC number (21 CFR 201.25). The rule also requires the use of machine-readable information on blood and blood component labels (21 CFR 606.121[c][13]). The guidance[6] states: "Bar codes will allow health care professionals to use bar code scanning equipment to verify that the right drug (in the right dose and right route of administration) is being given to the right patient at the right time. This new system is intended to help reduce the number of medication errors that occur in hospitals and health care settings." The FDA issued the Guidance for Industry "Bar Code Label Requirements Questions and Answers"[6] in August 2011 and amended/incorporated previous guidances. Exemptions to the requirements are covered in the guidance.

DRUG QUALITY AND SECURITY ACT (DQSA)

The Drug Quality and Security Act (DQSA), was enacted by Congress on November 27, 2013. Title II of DQSA, the Drug Supply Chain Security Act (DSCSA), outlines steps to build an electronic, interoperable system to identify and trace certain prescription drugs as they are distributed in the United States. This will enhance the FDA's ability to help protect consumers from exposure to drugs that may be counterfeit, stolen, contaminated, or otherwise harmful. The system will also improve detection and removal of potentially dangerous drugs from the drug supply chain to protect U.S. consumers.

Additionally, the DSCSA directs the FDA to establish national licensure standards for wholesale distributors and third-party logistics providers and requires these entities to report licensure and other information to the FDA annually.

In-depth discussion of the requirements of this law are beyond this chapter, and the implementation of these requirements was delayed on June 30, 2017, until November 26, 2018. The FDA issued the draft guidance for industry "Product Identifier Requirements Under the Drug Supply Chain Security Act—Compliance Policy"[7] in June 2017.

Additional information is available on the FDA website specifically at https://www.fda.gov/Drugs/DrugSafety/DrugIntegrityandSupplyChainSecurity/DrugSupplyChainSecurityAct/ucm427033.htm and also guidance for industry "Incorporation of Physical-Chemical Identifiers into Solid Oral Dosage Form Drug Products for Anticounterfeiting," October 2011.[8] The reader is encouraged to search for the current requirements and further interpretations.

Recall Notifications for 2017 and 2018

1. The specified product lots are being recalled because of a confirmed customer complaint that some syringe units containing xxxx 1 mg/mL, 5 mg per 5 mL are incorrectly labeled as xxxx 1 mg/mL, 3 mg per 3 mL. Secondary packages are properly labeled as xxxx 1 mg/mL, 5 mg per 5 mL.
2. "A" company is voluntarily recalling xxxx Tablets, USP 75 mg, packaged in bottles of 30 tablets, to the consumer level due to mislabeling. The product is labeled as xxxx USP 75 mg but may contain xxxx 75 mg or yyyy Tablets USP 10 mg.
3. The product is labeled as xxxx Tablets USP 40 mg but contained yyyy 300 mg tablets.

Examples of Observations from FDA Warning Letters

- You released packaging and labeling materials for use in drug product manufacturing without written procedures. You also stated to our investigator that you examine only yyy units of packaging material, regardless of the batch size. You had no data to demonstrate that yyy units were a representative sample.
- For example, your firm manufactured (b)(4) batches of xxxx tablets, xxx mg, and (b)(4) batches of yyyyy tablets, xxx mg, from January to May 2014. You did not monitor or evaluate the stability of these products. Their expiration dates are not based on any supportive initial or ongoing stability studies.
- "Drug name" also is misbranded under Section 502(c) of the FD&C Act, 21 USC 352(c) because neither the outer carton nor the individual packets include a lot or control number and expiration dating, which are required under 21 CFR 201.18 and 21 CFR 211.137, respectively.
- Your firm failed to ensure drug products bear an expiration date determined by appropriate stability data to assure they meet applicable standards of identity, strength, quality, and purity at the time of use (21 CFR § 211.137[a]). Specifically: At the inspection, you indicated your firm has not performed stability studies to support the expiration dates assigned to your drug products. You indicated that your contract manufacturer assigned the two-year expiration date to your xxxx products. However, you indicated you were unaware whether your contract manufacturer had performed any stability studies. You have no data to support that your products meet applicable standards of identity, strength, quality, and purity two years from the date of manufacture.
- Your firm performs repackaging and labeling operations but did not have written procedures governing the application of packaging and labeling materials to your drug products. You incorrectly labeled a container filled with xxxx tablets xx mg as xxxx, USP yy mg (Schedule IV). In the affidavit collected during the inspection, you stated, "I have no records to show the repackaging operation."
- All drugs, including OTC drugs, must be manufactured in conformance with CGMP. FDA is aware that many drug manufacturers use independent contractors, such as production facilities, testing laboratories, packagers, and labelers. FDA regards contractors as extensions of the manufacturer. You are responsible for the quality of drugs you produce, regardless of agreements in place with your contract facilities. You are required to ensure that drugs are made in accordance with Section 501(a)(2)(B) of the FD&C Act to ensure safety, identity, strength, quality, and purity.
- Your firm failed to exercise strict control over labeling issued for use in drug product labeling operations (21 CFR 211.125[a]). Our investigators found numerous loose and uncontrolled labels for multiple products in the open office area adjacent to the packaging lines. Unused labels were not stored in a manner to prevent mix-ups or mislabeling. Your response to this observation does not include any explanation as to why your firm allowed unused labels to remain in the production area, and lacks adequate explanation of whether this deviation has affected any production lots and led to mislabeling deviations or complaints regarding in-date marketed products.

FDA COMPLIANCE POLICY GUIDES MANUAL

FDA Compliance Policy Guides (CPG) Manual provide a convenient and organized system for statements of FDA compliance policy, including those statements, which contain regulatory action guidance information. The CPG Manual is the repository for all agency compliance policy that has been agreed to by the center(s) and the Associate Commissioner for Regulatory Affairs. Sources from which CPGs are prepared include: (a) statements or correspondence by headquarters offices or centers reflecting new policy or changes in compliance policy including Office of the Commissioner memoranda, center memoranda and other informational issuances, agency correspondence with trade groups and regulated industries, and advisory opinions; (b) precedent court decisions; (c) multicenter agreements regarding jurisdiction over FDA-regulated products; (d) preambles to proposed or final regulations or other Federal Register documents; and (e) individual regulatory actions.

CPGs explains the FDA policy on regulatory issues related to the FDA laws or regulations. These include CGMP regulations and application commitments. They advise the field inspection and compliance staffs as to the Agency's standards and procedures to be applied when determining industry compliance. CPG may derive from a request for an advisory opinion, from a petition from outside the Agency, or from a perceived need for a policy clarification by FDA personnel.

These CPGs for human drugs Chapter 4 can be accessed from the FDA website at https://www.fda.gov/ICECI/ComplianceManuals/CompliancePolicyGuidanceManual/ucm119572.htm#SubChapter430.

CURRENT COMPLIANCE POLICY GUIDES

- 400.100 Drugs, Human—Failure to Register CPG 7132.07
- 400.200 Consistent Application of CGMP Determinations CPG 7132.12
- 400.210 Radiofrequency Identification Feasibility Studies and Pilot Programs
- 400.600 Drugs—Declaration of Quantity of Active CPG 7132.03
- 400.700 Drug Product Entries in Periodic Publications CPG 7132b.17
- 430.100 Unit–Dose Labeling for Solid and Liquid Oral Dosage Forms CPG 7132b.10
- 430.200 Repacking of Drug Products—Testing/Examination under CGMPs CPG 7132.13
- 430.300 Labeling Shipping Containers of Drugs CPG 7132b.13
- 480.100 Requirements for Expiration Dating and Stability Testing
- 480.200 Expiration Dating of Unit–Dose Repackaged Drugs
- 480.300 Lack of Expiration Date of Stability Data

REPACKAGING AND RELABELING

On September 11, 2015, the FDA issued CPG 7356.002B[9] Drug Repackagers and Relabelers and noted that "The repackaging and relabeling of drugs under Current Good Manufacturing Practice (CGMP) controls has been a problem of long standing. Product mix-up, loss of product identity, contamination and cross contamination, lack of stability data to support expiration dates, and the lack of adequate control systems have been frequently documented. Drug repackaging and relabeling are manufacturing processes which must be conducted in accordance with applicable CGMP requirements. The repackager/relabeler is performing the operations a formulator would handle if the formulator was packaging the product into consumer-sized containers."

The program includes, but is not limited to, the following operations:

- Repackaging of solid and liquid bulk-dosage forms into smaller packages (may include larger containers, such as pints, quarts, half gallons, or 1000-tablet bottles, etc.)
- Repackaging from conveyances (e.g., tank cars) into smaller containers such as drums
- Contract packagers who package expressly for manufacturers of dosage forms
- Repackagers or relabelers of antibiotics
- Shared services operations (shared services operations servicing HMOs and hospital groups may be extensive operations)

EXCLUSIONS

- Repackagers/relabelers of sterile products, radioactive drugs, and relabelers of compressed medical gases
- Pre-packagers operating within the practice of pharmacy and distributing (selling) drugs upon receipt of written prescriptions

The CPG also includes the requirements for inspections:

INSPECTIONAL OPERATIONS

Inspections will be conducted in accordance with CP 7356.002 Drug Process Inspections as far as applicable. These will include Unit Dose repackagers and Shared Services operations.

INSPECTIONAL OPTIONS

This program circular provides two inspectional options: Abbreviated Inspectional Option, and Full Inspectional Option *(For this program, the Full Inspectional Option provides specific policies for Unit-Dose Repackagers.)* To determine which option should be used, an evaluation of the following is appropriate.

1. *Review and Evaluation*
   a. Determine if changes have occurred by comparing current operations against the EIR for the previous full inspection. The following type of changes are typical of those that would warrant the full inspectional option:

   New potential for cross-contamination (see Part III, page 5, item 8) or mix-ups arising through changes in process or product line.

   Use of new technology requiring new expertise, significantly new equipment, or new facilities.

   A change in the personnel directly involved in the repackaging/relabeling operation.
   b. Review the firm's complaint file, Drug Quality Reporting System (DQRS), etc., and determine if the pattern of complaints (or other information available to the District) as well as the firm's records of internal rejection warrant expanding the inspection to the full inspectional option to look for weaknesses in the firm's processes, systems or controls. Review the firm's ANDA and AADA applications and confirm that requirements are being followed.
   c. If no significant changes have occurred and no violative conditions are observed, the abbreviated inspectional option may be adequate.

    d. If significant changes have occurred, or if violative or potentially violative conditions are noted, the inspection should be expanded to the full inspectional option to provide appropriate coverage.

    e. If an inspection needs to be expanded to the full inspe6tional option, it need be expanded only for the general product or process area in question.

    f. Review the firm's labeling for misbranding violations *and determine if the nature and extent of violations warrant expanding the inspection to the full inspection option in order to look for deficiencies in the firm's labeling processes, systems, or controls.*

2. *Abbreviated Inspectional Option*

This option involves a brief inspection of the repackager/relabeler to maintain surveillance over the firm's activities. An abbreviated inspection as described below is adequate for routine coverage and will satisfy the biennial inspection requirement. The use of this option is designed to save inspectional and clerical resources.

This option should not be used on an initial inspection of a facility, nor when the District's review of information such as, past history, results of sample analysis, complaints, DQRSs, recalls, etc., indicates that an abbreviated inspectional option is not appropriate for a specific firm.

    a. Perform an inspection of the firm's repackaging/relabeling facility including master records and batch records for a representative number of products repackaged/relabeled by the firm. Products with a history of previous labeling problems should be included. *Special note should be taken of the firm's repackaging and relabeling controls.*

       For products required to be packaged in tamper-resistant packaging (TRP), determine the adequacy of the firm's TRP and required labeling statement (see Part VI, References, Page 1, Items F, G, and H).

       Any observations of inadequate controls or other significant objectionable conditions will indicate that a full inspection should be performed.

    b. The minimum reporting required for an abbreviated inspection is described in IOM 593.1. Include a brief summary describing the scope of the inspection, the persons interviewed and any changes which may have occurred since the previous inspection.

3. *Full Inspectional Option*

This option may involve a complete inspection of all systems and processes or a particular product or process as noted in 1.d. and e. above. A full inspection may also be conducted on a surveillance basis at the District's discretion. It is not anticipated that full inspections will necessarily be conducted every 2 years. They may be conducted at less frequent intervals, perhaps every third or fourth inspection. Also, whenever information becomes known which would question the firm's ability to produce quality products, an appropriate in-depth inspection should be performed.

4. *Drugs for Repackaging or Relabeling*

    a. The firm should carefully examine all incoming drug products for repackaging and relabeling to ascertain that the bulk containers of finished dosage form drug products are received intact, undamaged, and completely and properly labeled as received.

    b. Evaluate the procedures employed by the firm in the receipt, handling, and storage of drug products for repackaging or relabeling.

    c. *Drugs having a high volatility, such as nitroglycerin sublingual tablets, should not be repackaged. See Compliance Policy Guide 7132b.11—Expiration Dating of Unit–Dose Repackaged Drugs.*

5. *Control Records*
Evaluate the control record-keeping system used by the firm for their repackaging/relabeling operations. Use the standards contained in 21 CFR 211.180; 211.182; 211.184; 211.186(a), (b)(1), (2), (8), (9);
   211.188(a), (b)(1–13); 211.192; 211.198.

6. *Production and Control Procedures*
Only one drug product is to be brought into a repackaging area at a time. Upon completion of the repackaging operation, all remaining unused stock and finished stock are to be removed from the area. The packaging machinery is to be completely emptied, cleaned, and inspected before setting the equipment up for the repackaging of another drug product.
   a. The following Sections of 21 CFR 211 apply in evaluating a repackager/relabeler's adherence to CGMP requirements: 211.100, 211.103, 211.105, 211.110, 211.111, 211.113, 211.122, and 211.130.
   b. Where applicable, the term "production" or "manufacturer" includes "repackaging" and "relabeling" operations as contained in 21 CFR 211.100, 211.103, 211.105.

7. *Product Containers and Their Components*
Review the firm's specifications and SOPs regarding selection and handling of containers and closure systems (21 CFR 211.84). Evaluate the suitability of containers and closure systems with regard to 21 CFR 211.94. Report and document deficiencies.

8. *Packaging and Labeling*
Evaluate the firm's adherence to the following CGMP requirements for packaging and labeling operations. The following criteria of 21 CFR 211 are applicable for the purposes of this program: 211.122, 211.125, 211.130, 211.132, and 211.134.

   For products required to be packaged in tamper-resistant packaging, determine the adequacy of the firm's tamper-resistant packaging and required labeling statement (see Part VI, References, Page 1, Items F, G, and H).

   The manufacture of penicillin must be separate from other drug products, including cephalosporin. The specific requirements for such separation are covered in Sections 211.42(d) and 211.46(d) of the CGMP regulations.

   There is no specific prohibition against the manufacture or repackaging of cephalosporin drug products in the same facility as other non-penicillin drug products. However, FDA discourages such practice since there is some clinical and laboratory evidence of partial cross-allergenicity of the penicillins and cephalosporins and the subsequent possibility that a patient could be hypersensitive to a cephalosporin received from a contaminated non-penicillin drug product. At the present time, there is no formal guidance on the separation of cephalosporin from the non-penicillin products beyond the present provisions in the CGMP regulations relating to control of cross contamination between non-penicillin drug products. However, regulations do require appropriate controls to prevent cross contamination.

9. *Stability*
Evaluate the stability testing program. Determine whether stability studies are conducted by the firm, or for the firm, and whether such documentation is, in fact, a part of the record-keeping system maintained by the repackager/relabeler. For program purposes, evaluate on the basis of 21 CFR 211.166(a), (b), (c).

   Determine if the firm uses expiration dating periods beyond those used by the manufacturer and, if so, the rationale. Carefully evaluate the basis for any extensions. They must be based on adequate stability data and necessary awareness of any changes in the formula or manufacturing procedures used by the manufacturer.

10. *Laboratory Controls*
Determine whether the firm has an established and ongoing control program. It is not necessary to perform chemical analyses on oral solid drug products in finished dosage form,

provided adequate physical identification of the drug to be repackaged is performed *(See Compliance Policy Guide 7132.13).* Determine whether accurate and meaningful test results or examinations are performed by the repackager, such as, organoleptic examinations of incoming bulk drug products, visual inspection of labeling, and, where appropriate, stability data to justify assigned expiration dates. The following 21 CFR 211 criteria are applicable: 211.194; 211.160(a), (b)(1, 3 & 4); 211.170(a), (b) and 211.176. (For purposes of this program, the term "manufacturing" includes "repackaging operations.")

11. *Distribution Records*
Evaluate the firm's distribution records systems and determine whether the criteria of 21 CFR 211.142 and 211.150 are met.

12. *Expiration Dating*
Evaluate the expiration dating system as it pertains to stability information under 21 CFR 211.137. Pertinent program criteria are listed in 21 CFR 211.137(a), (b), (c).

The expiration date on the manufacturer's original container may be assigned to a solid oral dosage form repackaged *into a "unit-of-use" or other container/closure system containing more than a single dose,* which is equal to or better than the original container/closure system, provided all labeling statements pertaining to storage conditions as specified by the original manufacturer are also used in and on the new labeling. This expiration policy does not apply to liquids, creams, ointments, and suspensions.

13. *Complaint Files*
Criteria are listed in 21 CFR 211.198. Evaluate the firm's system and policy regarding product complaints other than those of an economic nature. Determine whether meaningful investigations are made and proper dispositions are handled in accordance with 21 CFR 211.192.

*b. *Unit-Dose Repackagers*
For this program, the full inspectional option provides specific policies for Unit-Dose Repackagers.

The following practices, if completely met, are adequate to allow Unit-Dose repackagers to comply with current good manufacturing practices in the specific areas described below. For all other areas, follow guidance in 3a:

1. *Expiration Dating for Unit-Dose Containers:*
A unit–dose container is a non-reusable container designed to hold a quantity of drug intended for administration as a single dose, which is to be used promptly after the container is opened.

A firm may repackage solid oral dosage forms into unit-dose containers and utilize an expiration date of not more than six months from the date of repackaging without conducting stability studies, provided that all of the following conditions are met:
a. The unit–dose container complies with the Class A or Class B standard described in the current revision of the United States Pharmacopeia, Physical Tests, Single-Unit Containers, and Unit-Dose Containers for Capsules and Tablets.*
*b. The original bulk container has not been previously opened and the entire contents are repackaged in one operation.
c. The expiration period does not exceed 25% of the remaining time between the date of repackaging and the expiration date shown on the original manufacturer's bulk, container of the drug repackaged.
d. The repackaging and storage of the drug product is accomplished in a humidity-controlled environment and within the temperature specified in the USP monograph or the product labeling. If no temperature/humidity is specified, a controlled room temperature, as defined by the USP, with a relative humidity not exceeding 75% should be maintained. *Documentation must be on file to verify that all the conditions listed above are met.*

2. *Labeling*

In addition to the general packing and labeling requirements (see Part III, Page 5, Item 8), all unit–dose repackaged products are to be placed into larger containers and each container must be fully labeled prior to removal from the premises.*

LABELING REQUIREMENTS (SEE THE CPG ON THE FDA WEBSITE)

The FDA issued "Repackaging of Certain Human Drug Products by Pharmacies and Outsourcing Facilities"[10] Guidance for Industry in January 2017. It is noted that "This guidance sets forth the FDA's policy regarding repackaging by State-licensed pharmacies, Federal facilities, and facilities that register with FDA as outsourcing facilities under Section 503B of the Federal Food, Drug, and Cosmetic Act (FD&C Act or the Act). This guidance describes the conditions under which FDA does not intend to take action for violations of Sections 505, 502(f)(1), 582, and where specified, Section 501(a)(2)(B) of the Act, when a State-licensed pharmacy, a Federal facility, or an outsourcing facility repackages human prescription drug products.

This guidance *does **not** address* the following:

- Biological products that are subject to licensure under Section 351 of the Public Health Service (PHS) Act. The repackaging of biological products subject to licensure under Section 351 is addressed in a separate guidance document.[3]
- Repackaging drug products for use in animals
- Repackaging non-prescription drug products
- Radiopharmaceuticals"

The WHO issued definitions of Relabeling: "The process of putting a new label on the material (see also labelling)." Labeling: "The action involving the selection of the correct label, with the required information, followed by line-clearance and application of the label." Also the definition of Repackaging: "The action of changing the packaging of the material."

The Technical Report[11] also includes a section relating to Repackaging and Relabeling:

7.1 Operations, such as combining into a homogeneous batch, repackaging and/or relabeling, are manufacturing processes, and their performance should therefore follow GMP.

7.2 Special attention should be given to the following points:
- Prevention of contamination, cross contamination and mix-ups.
- Security of stocks of labels, line clearance checks, online inspections, destruction of excess batch-printed labels.
- Good sanitation and hygiene practices.
- Maintaining batch integrity (normally mixing of different batches of the same solid material should not be done).
- As part of batch records, all labels that were removed from the original container during operations, and a sample of the new label, should be kept.
- If more than one batch of labels is used in one operation, samples of each batch should be kept.
- Maintaining product identity and integrity.

7.3 When different batches of a material from the same original manufacturing site are received by a distributor and combined into a homogeneous batch, the conformity of each batch with its specification should be confirmed before it is added.

7.4 Only materials from the same manufacturing site received by a distributor and conforming to the same specifications can be mixed. If different batches of the same material are mixed to form a homogeneous batch, it should be defined as a new batch, tested, and supplied with a batch certificate of analysis. In such cases, the customer should be informed that the material supplied is a mixture of manufacturers' batches. The supplied material must have a certificate of conformity to a specification at date of supply.

7.5 In all cases, the original COA of the original manufacturer should be provided. If retesting is done, both the original and the new COA should be provided. The batch referred to on the new COA should be traceable to the original COA.

7.6 Repackaging of materials should be carried out with primary packaging materials for which the quality and suitability have been established to be equal to or better than those of the original container. The approval of the supplier is necessary for the packaging material used for the repackaging.

7.7 The reuse of containers should be discouraged unless they have been cleaned using a validated procedure. Recycled containers should not be used unless there is evidence that the quality of the material packed will not be adversely affected.

7.8 Materials should be repackaged only if efficient environmental control exists to ensure that there is no possibility of contamination, cross contamination, degradation, physicochemical changes, and/or mix-ups. The quality of air supplied to the area should be suitable for the activities performed, for example, efficient filtration.

7.9 Suitable procedures should be followed to ensure proper label control.

7.10 Containers of repackaged material and relabeled containers should bear both the name of the original manufacturing site and the name of the distributor/repacker.

7.11 Procedures should be in place to ensure maintenance of the identity and quality of the material by appropriate means, both before and after repackaging operations.

7.12 Batch release procedures should be in place in accordance with GMP.

7.13 Only official pharmacopoeial methods or validated analytical test methods should be used for the analysis.

7.14 Samples of active pharmaceutical ingredients (APIs) and excipients of appropriate quantities should be kept for at least one year after the expiry or retest date, or for one year after distribution is complete.

7.15 The repacker and relabeler should ensure that the stability of the material is not adversely affected by the repackaging or relabeling. Stability studies to justify the expiry or retest dates assigned should be conducted if the pharmaceutical starting material is repackaged in a container different from that used by the original manufacturer. It is recognized that some excipients may not need additional stability studies.

The United States Pharmacopoeia (USP) Chapter <1178> Good Repackaging Practices[12] notes that "This chapter is intended to provide guidance to those engaged in repackaging of oral solid drug products; and the chapter provides information to any person who removes drugs from their original container–closure system (new primary package) and repackages them into a different container–closure system for sale and/or for distribution.

This chapter does not apply to pharmacists engaged in dispensing prescription drugs in accordance with state practice of pharmacy."

EXAMPLES OF OBSERVATIONS FROM FDA CITATIONS

- The FDA inspected your pharmaceutical manufacturing (repackaging and relabeling) facility. During our inspection, we found your Quality Unit did not approve your written SOPs for numerous critical processes, such as Quality Unit responsibilities, expiration date extension, material quarantine, product distribution, equipment cleaning, product return, complaint handling, product recalls, supplier qualification, raw material testing, and annual product reviews. We also found your Quality Unit did not review and approve quality-related documents, batch records, COAs, and the extension of API expiration dates.

- You extended API manufacturers' expiration dates by as much as two years and listed the new expiration dates in your COAs for APIs repackaged at your facility. You tested APIs to verify that the results complied with the manufacturers' specifications. However, you did not perform stability testing to ensure that APIs met all specifications for the expiration dates you listed on your COAs. You have no scientific justification for extending the expiration dates.

- Your firm weighs and repackages bulk powder APIs including hormones, tricyclics, muscle relaxants, NSAIDS (non-steroidal anti-inflammatory drugs), antifungals, and quinolones in non-dedicated suites using non-dedicated equipment. During the inspection, the investigator found expired cleaning products that your cleaning procedure or operators identified as cleaning agents for the suite and equipment. These include (b)(4) detergent (b)(4) (expiration 10/13), (b)(4) (expiration 10/12), and (b)(4) Sterile (b)(4)(expiration 05/2010). In addition, your operators used cleaning agents that are not documented in your cleaning procedure. Specifically, **(b)(4) are** used to clean surfaces of the non-dedicated suites. Neither of these cleaning agents are listed in your cleaning procedure.

- Moreover, you have not performed cleaning validation studies to determine the effectiveness of your current cleaning agents to remove residual powders following repackaging operations in order to prevent cross contamination.

Further information:

The following CPGs are provided as reference reading and were current at the time of writing. The reader is encouraged to confirm the requirements on the FDA website with professional advice before taking any actions/decisions.

EXPIRATION DATING OF UNIT-DOSE REPACKAGED DRUGS: COMPLIANCE POLICY GUIDE 5/31/2005 SEC. 480.200 (CPG 7132B.11)

INTRODUCTION

Background

Unit–dose packaging systems are currently widespread in health care. Some unit–dose containers are available directly from manufacturers and repackagers, and some drugs are packaged into unit–dose containers by hospital/community pharmacies or shared service establishments. A shared service repackaging operation is one which exclusively serves one or more hospitals and/or related institutions, each having separate or no pharmacy services, and each having responsibility for restricting distribution of those drugs received from the shared service to the institution.

The nature of drug distribution within hospitals in particular has made such packaging useful and convenient in assuring proper administration of medication to patients. Questions have arisen, however, as to whether drugs thus repacked need expiration dates based on stability data on the drugs in the unit–dose containers. The issue gained sharper focus with the inclusion of pharmacopeial standards for Single-Unit Containers and Unit–Dose Containers for Capsules and Tablets published in the General Tests section of the Fifth Revision to the Nineteenth Edition of the United States Pharmacopeia (changes official May 1, 1979). In light of these standards, under certain conditions the Food and Drug Administration would not ordinarily deem it necessary for health protection, nor for assurance of stability of the drug, to require that stability studies be done on the drug in the unit–dose container.

The current good manufacturing practices regulations require that, with certain exceptions, drug products must bear expiration dates derived from tests conducted on samples stored in the same immediate container closure system in which the drug is marketed. This is to ensure the drugs' safety and efficacy over their intended *shelf life.* Concerning the issue of repackaging into unit–dose containers, we interpret compliance with the conditions enumerated in this guide to meet the stability requirements of the CGMP regulations.

Policy

No action will be initiated against any unit–dose repackaging firm, including shared services, or drug product in a unit–dose container meeting all other conditions of FDA's repackaging requirements solely on the basis of the failure of the repackaging firm to have stability studies supporting the expiration dates used, provided:

1. The unit–dose container complies with the Class A or Class B standard described in the twentieth edition of the United States Pharmacopeia, General Tests, Single-Unit Containers and Unit-Dose Containers for Capsules and Tablets (page 955).
2. The expiration date does not exceed six months and.
3. The six-month expiration period does not exceed 25% of the remaining time between the date of repackaging and expiration date shown on the original manufacture's bulk container of the drug repackaged, and the bulk container has not been previously opened.

This policy only applies to solid and liquid oral dosage forms in unit–dose containers. We will continue to impose all requirements on other dosage forms and other types of packages.

Exceptions

This policy does not apply to antibiotics or to nitroglycerin sublingual tablets, which are known to have stability problems that preclude them from being repackaged.
    Material between asterisks is new or revised

Issued: 2/1/84
Revised: 3/95

REPACKAGING CPG: SEC. 430.200 REPACKING OF DRUG PRODUCTS—TESTING/EXAMINATION UNDER CURRENT GOOD MANUFACTURING PRACTICES (CPG 7132.13)

BACKGROUND

Questions have periodically arisen regarding how various testing and/or examination requirements under the CGMP regulations (21 CFR Parts 210 and 211) are to be applied to repackers of finished dosage form drugs. In particular, there have been questions regarding whether it is appropriate to apply various "component" requirements in the CGMP regulations (such as those under Section 211.84 concerning identity testing and analysis or receipt of a report of analysis for purity, strength, and quality) to finished dosage form drugs that an establishment receives and repackages. It has also been questioned how the requirements under 211.165 are to be applied to repackers, insofar as the requirements for appropriate laboratory determination for identity and strength of each active ingredient prior to release are concerned.
    We have carefully considered the suitability of applying the requirements concerning "components" in the CGMP regulations to repackers of finished dosage form drugs. Due to the definitions of "component" under 210.3(b)(3) and "drug product" under 210.3(b)(4), we have concluded that the requirements for "components" under Part 211 cannot be suitably applied to finished dosage form drugs, which are received by an establishment and repackaged without alteration to the "drug product" itself.

In the preamble to the final order for the CGMP regulations, it is pointed out in regards to a manufacturer that there is no intent under 211.165(a), once the product is in its finished dosage form, to require potency testing of both the bulk and packaged drug product phases, and that manufacturers could choose to do potency assays at either phase (43 FR 45062, paragraph 389). We believe a similar principle is applicable to drug product repackers where the manufacturer of the finished dosage form in a bulk container is required to perform appropriate analytical testing for all appropriate specifications, including the identity and strength of each active ingredient; we do not consider it necessary for the repacker to repeat such testing upon such drug products he receives and repacks with label declarations consistent with those on the bulk container and without altering the properties of the finished dosage form product.

POLICY

Generally, we do not consider the CGMP regulations (21 CFR Parts 210 and 211) to require repackers of finished dosage form drugs to perform analytical testing, such as chemical identity tests or assays, or to require receipt of reports of analysis, on a batch-by-batch basis for drug products that are repacked under the following circumstances:

1. The incoming bulk containers of finished dosage form drug products are received in intact, undamaged containers, which are completely and properly labeled as received, and there is no reason to suspect they have been subjected to improper storage or transit conditions prior to receipt;
2. The repacking operations are conducted under conditions, which assure that the properties of the incoming drug product are not altered; and
3. The repackaged containers are labeled with the same substantive labeling declarations (e.g., identity, strength, and directions for use) concerning the properties and use of the drug product, which are consistent with the labeling on the incoming bulk containers.

Under such circumstances, we consider that requirements for appropriate specifications and testing/examination procedures for repacked drug products will be met by an appropriate system involving examination of the labeling and sufficient organoleptic examination of the drug product to confirm its identity in accordance with corresponding specifications established by the repacker.

The policy in this CPG applies only to the question of adequate batch-to-batch testing/examination criteria for routine acceptance and release of drug products, which are repacked. It does not alter any testing that repackers may be required to perform on drug products from other standpoints: stability test to establish appropriate expiration dates in the container–closure system used by the repacker, test to determine the suitability of the repacker's drug product containers and closures, test to establish appropriate time limits for the completion of each phase of production, or test on non-penicillin drug products for the presence of penicillin.

Issued: 7/1/81

SEC. 430.100 UNIT-DOSE LABELING FOR SOLID AND LIQUID ORAL DOSAGE FORMS (CPG 7132B.10)

BACKGROUND

In recent years, the pharmaceutical industry has responded to an increased demand for drug products that are packaged for "unit-dose" dispensing, that is, the delivery of a single dose of a drug to the patient at the time of administration for institutional use, for example, hospitals.

The drug product is dispensed in a unit-dose container—a non-reusable container designed to hold a quantity of drug intended for administration (other than the parenteral route) as a single dose, directly from the container, employed generally in a hospital unit-dose system. The advantages of unit-dose dispensing are that the drug is fully identifiable and the integrity of the dosage form is protected until the actual moment of administration. If the drug is not used and the container is intact, the drug may be retrieved and redispensed without compromising its integrity.

In view of the intended use of unit–dose packaging, each unit-dose container is regarded as a drug in package form subject to all requirements of the Act and implementing regulations. However, the pertinent labeling regulations (21 CFR 201.10[i] and 201.100) present problems in interpretation in that they are inconsistent with respect to exemptions for containers too small or otherwise unable to accommodate a label with sufficient space to bear all mandatory information. As a result of several recent regulatory actions emphasizing these inconsistencies, the regulations will be rewritten in the future to clarify the requirements.

Because of the general lack of uniformity in the labeling for unit-dose containers due to inconsistent interpretations of the regulations, or to a lack of knowledge of unit-dose labeling requirements, we are issuing this Compliance Policy Guide.

This CPG does not encompass "Unit of Use" packaging, which is defined as a method of preparing a legend medication in an original container, sealed and labeled, prelabeled by the manufacturer, and containing sufficient medication for one normal course of therapy. (Reference: Proceedings Unit of Use Packaging Conference, January 24–26, 1979).

POLICY

Until the regulations are revised, the attached document describes the labeling requirements for oral solid and liquid dosage forms packaged in unit-dose containers. The requirements apply to all firms that package drugs into unit-dose containers.

Since unit dosage forms are primarily intended for institutional use rather than sale to the general public, we will not require the warnings described in 21 CFR, Part 369 or the statements described under Item 6.b. (Section I and II) of Attachment A to be on the label; however, this information must appear elsewhere in the labeling.

Where unit-dose repacking is performed by a single facility for a closed membership or group (e.g., "shared services"), a current package insert bearing adequate directions for use, located on the premises of each member to whom the repacked goods are shipped, is regarded as satisfying this requirement. The absence of such a current package insert on the premises of a member to which a drug product is shipped will cause that drug product to be misbranded.

Solid and liquid oral dosage forms in unit-dose containers shall be deemed misbranded under Section 502 of the Act if they deviate from the attached list of requirements.

Other unit-dose forms, for example, topical ointments/creams, or ophthalmic, etc. are not included in this document. They will be considered at a future date should circumstances warrant.

ATTACHMENT A

UNIT–DOSE LABELING

    I. PRESCRIPTION DRUGS (Solid and Liquid Oral Dosage Forms, e.g., Capsules, Tablets, Solutions, Elixirs, Suspensions, etc.)
    The label of the actual unit-dose container must bear all of the following information (except item 9).

NOTE: A firm may not claim an exemption on the basis that the label is too small to accommodate all mandatory information if all available space is not utilized or the label size can readily be made larger, or if the type size on the label can readily be made smaller without affecting the legibility of the information.

1. The established name of the drug and the quantity of the active ingredient per dosage unit, if a single active ingredient product; if a combination drug, the established name and quantity of each active ingredient per dosage unit. In each case, the label must bear the established name and quantity or proportion of any ingredient named in Section 502(e) whether active or not. For solid dosage forms, a declaration of potency per tablet/capsule will suffice; for liquid dosage forms, the total volume shall be declared as well as the quantity or proportion of active ingredient contained therein, for example, Cimetadine HCL Liquid 5 mL, 300 mg/5 mL or 300 mg per 5 mL; or Septra/Bactrim Suspension 5 mL, contains Trimethoprim 40 mg and Sulfamethoxazole 200 mg per 5 mL; or each 5 mL contains…

2. The expiration date (see Attachment B). (Ref. 21 CFR 201.17, 211.137).

3. The lot or control number (Ref. 21 CFR 201.100[b], 211.130).

4. The name and place of business of the manufacturer, packer, or distributor as provided for in 21 CFR 201.1.

5. For a drug recognized in an official compendium, the subject of an approved new drug application (NDA/ANDA) or as provided by regulation:
   A. Required statements such as "Refrigerate," "Protect From Light" or "Dilute Before Using," etc. (Ref.: FD&C Act 502[f][1], 502[g], and 505)
   B. Any pertinent statement bearing on the special characteristics of the dosage form, for example, sustained release, enteric coated, chewable, suspension, etc. (Ref. FD&C Act 502[e], 502[a], 201[n]).

6. For any drug product, not subject to 5:
   A. Any pertinent statement bearing on special characteristics of the dosage form, for example, sustained release, enteric coated, sublingual, chewable, solution, elixir, or suspension (Ref. FD&C Act 502[e], 502[a], 201[n]).
   B. While not required to be on the label per se, it is strongly recommended that:
      1. Any pertinent statement bearing on the need for special storage conditions, e.g., "Refrigerate," "Do not Refrigerate," "Protect from Light," etc. (Ref. FD&C Act 502[f][1]) appear on the label, and
      2. Any information needed to alert the health professional that a procedure(s) is necessary prior to patient administration to prepare the product as a finished dosage form, for example, "Shake Before Using" (Ref: FD&C Act 502[f][1]).

7. If more than one dosage unit is contained within the unit-dose container (solid dosage form), the number of dosage units per container and the strength per dosage unit should be specified (e.g., two capsules; each capsule contains 300 mg Rifampin).

8. The statement "Warning: May Be Habit Forming" where applicable, the controlled drug substances symbol required by Drug Enforcement Administration (DEA), and the name and quantity or proportion of any substance as required by Section 502(d).

9. The National Drug Code designation is recommended, although this is not mandatory.

In addition to all of the above (except item 9), the following information must appear on the outer package from which the unit-dose container is dispensed:

10. The number of unit-dose containers in the package, for example, 100 unit doses. If more than one dosage unit is within each unit-dose container, this should also be stated (e.g., "100 packets; each packet contains two tablets," or "100 packets of two tablets each").

11. Full disclosure information, as detailed in 21 CFR 201.100. Where unit-dose repacking is performed by a single facility for a closed membership or group (e.g., "shared services"), a current package insert bearing adequate directions for use, located on the premises of each member to whom the repacked goods are shipped, is sufficient to satisfy this requirement. The absence of such a current package insert on the premises of a member to which a drug is shipped will cause that drug to be misbranded.
12. The prescription legend.

II. OVER THE COUNTER DRUGS (Solid and Liquid Oral Dosage Forms, e.g., Capsules, Tablets, Elixirs, Suspensions, etc.)
The label of the actual unit-dose container must bear all of the following information (except item 9).

NOTE: A firm may not claim an exemption on the basis that the label is too small to accommodate all mandatory information if all available space is not utilized, the label size can be made larger, or if the type size on the label can readily be made smaller without affecting the legibility of the information.

1. The established name of the drug, if it contains a single active ingredient; if a combination drug, the established name of each active ingredient. If a compendial drug, the label must express the quantity of each therapeutically active ingredient contained in each dosage unit, for example, Aspirin Tablets, 325 mg., (USP—General Notices), and the quantity or proportion of any ingredient, whether active or not, as required by Section 502(e).
2. The expiration date (see Attachment B).
3. The lot or control number.
4. The name and place of business of the manufacturer, packer, or distributor as provided for in 21 CFR 201.1.
5. For a drug recognized in an official compendium, the subject of an approved new drug application (NDA/ANDA) or as provided by regulation:
   A. Required statements such as "Refrigerate," "Protect from Light," or "Dilute before Using" (Ref. FD&C Act 502[f][1], 502[g], and 505).
   B. Any pertinent statement bearing on special characteristics of the dosage form, for example, sustained release, enteric coated, chewable, or suspension (Ref. FD&C Act 502[e], 502[a], 201[n]).
6. For any drug product not subject to 5:
   A. Any pertinent statement bearing on special characteristics of the dosage form, for example, sustained release, enteric coated, sublingual, chewable, solution, elixir, or suspension, etc.; (Ref. FD&C Act 502[e], 502[a], 201[n]).
   B. While not required to be on the label, per se, it is strongly recommended that:
      1. Any pertinent statement bearing on the need for special storage conditions, for example, "Refrigerate," "Do not Refrigerate," or "Protect from Light" (Ref. FD&C Act 502[f][1]) appear on the label, and
      2. Any information needed to alert the user that a procedure(s) is necessary prior to patient administration to prepare the product for use, for example, "Shake Well" or "Dilute Before Using" (Ref: FD&C Act 502[f][1], 21 CFR 201.5).
7. If more than one dosage unit is contained within the unit-dose container, the number of dosage units per container should be specified (e.g., two tablets aspirin; each tablet contains 325 mg).
8. The statement "Warning: May Be Habit Forming" where applicable, the controlled drug substances symbol required by DEA, and the name and quantity or proportion of any substance required by Section 502(d).

9. The National Drug Code designation is recommended, although this is not mandatory. In addition to all of the above (except item 9), the following information must appear on the outer package from which the unit-dose container is dispensed:
   1. The number of unit-dose containers in the package. If more than one dosage unit is within each unit-dose container, this should also be stated (e.g., "100 packets; each packet contains two tablets," or "100 packets of two tablets each.")
   2. The labeling, that is, the outer carton or a leaflet enclosed within the package, must bear adequate directions for use as specified in 21 CFR 201.5 and should include:
      A. Statement of all conditions, purposes, or uses for which the drug product is intended.
      B. Quantity of dose, including usual quantities for each of the uses for which it is intended and usual quantities for persons of different ages and conditions.
      C. Frequency of administration.
      D. Duration of administration.
      E. Time of administration (in relation to time of meals, time of onset of symptoms, or other time factors).

ATTACHMENT B

EXPIRATION DATING OF SOLID AND LIQUID ORAL DOSAGE FORMS IN UNIT-DOSE CONTAINERS (SEE CPG 7132B.11)

No action will be initiated against any unit-dose repackaging firm, including shared services or drug product in unit-dose containers meeting all other conditions of FDA's repackaging requirements, solely on the basis of the failure of the repacking firm to have stability studies supporting the expiration dates used provided:

1. The unit-dose container complies with the Class A or Class B standard described in the Twentieth Edition of the United States Pharmacopeia, General Tests, Single-Unit Containers and Unit-Dose Containers for Capsules and Tablets (page 955) and;
2. The expiration date does not exceed six months; and
3. The six-month expiration period does not exceed 25% of the remaining time between the date of repackaging and the expiration date shown on the original manufacturer's bulk container of the drug repackaged, and the bulk container has not been previously opened.

This policy does not apply to antibiotics or to nitroglycerin sublingual tablets, which are known to have stability problems that preclude them from being repackaged.

Issued: 2/1/84

It is suggested that the reader confirm the current CPG and regulatory requirements for packaging and labeling on the FDA web site.

REFERENCES

1. FDA Guidance for Industry: Quality Systems Approach to Pharmaceutical CGMP Regulations, 2006.
2. Stericycle Expert Solutions: https://www.stericycleexpertsolutions.com/.
3. FDA Guidance for Industry: Container Closure Systems for Packaging Human Drugs and Biologics, May 1999.
4. ISPE. Overview of Packaging Validation for Drug Products.
5. WHO Guidelines for Sampling of Pharmaceutical Products and Related Materials, Annex 4, WHO Technical Report Series, No. 929, 2005.
6. FDA Guidance for Industry: Bar Code Label Requirements Questions and Answers, August 2011.

7. FDA Guidance for Industry: Product Identifier Requirements Under the Drug Supply Chain Security Act—Compliance Policy, June 2017.
8. FDA Guidance for Industry: Incorporation of Physical-Chemical Identifiers into Solid Oral Dosage Form Drug Products for Anticounterfeiting, October 2011.
9. CPG 7356.002B Drug Repackagers and Relabelers, September 11, 2015.
10. FDA Guidance for Industry: Repackaging of Certain Human Drug Products by Pharmacies and Outsourcing Facilities, January 2017.
11. WHO Technical Report Series 38th Report WHO Expert Committee on Specifications for Pharmaceutical Preparations, 2003.
12. United States Pharmacopoeia (USP) Chapter <1178> Good Repackaging Practices, USP 40.

SUGGESTED READINGS

- WHO Technical Report Series, No. 902, 2002, Annex 9, Guidelines on Packaging for Pharmaceutical Products, World Health Organization.
- FDA Guidance for Industry: Sterile Drug Products Produced by Aseptic Processing—Current Good Manufacturing Practice, U.S. Department of Health and Human Services, Food and Drug Administration, Center for Drug Evaluation and Research (CDER), Center for Biologics Evaluation and Research (CBER), Office of Regulatory Affairs (ORA), September 2004, Pharmaceutical CGMPs.
- Technical Report. Current Practices in the Validation of Aseptic Processes—1992, 1996, and 2001, Parenteral Drug Association.
- The Global Harmonization Task Force: Quality Management Systems-Process Validation Guidance Ed. 2, 2004.
- Title II of the Drug Quality and Security Act, SEC. 202. Pharmaceutical Distribution Supply Chain, Chapter V (21 USC 351 et seq.), Subchapter H—Pharmaceutical Distribution Supply Chain, United States Food and Drug Administration.
- United States Pharmacopeia <1136> Packaging—Unit-of-Use, USP34-NF29, 1 December 2011.
- EU Guidelines for Good Manufacturing Practice for Medicinal Products for Human and Veterinary Use, EudraLex, Volume 4, October 1, 2015, European Commission Directorate-General for Health and Food Safety.
- BS EN ISO 11607-2:2006+A1:2014, Packaging for terminally sterilized medical devices. Validation requirements for forming, sealing and assembly processes, May 31, 2006, British Standards Institution.
- Compliance Policy Guide, Section 480.100, Requirements for Expiration Dating and Stability Testing, United States Food and Drug Administration, Issued 20 June 201985, Reissued 4 September 1987 and March 1995.
- Guideline of process validation for finished products—Information and data to be provided in regulatory submissions, EMA/CHMP/CVMP/QWP/BWP/70278/2012, Rev 1, Corr.1, 21 November 2016, European Medicines Agency.
- International Council for Harmonisation (ICH), ICH Harmonised Tripartite Guideline, Pharmaceutical Development—Q8(R2), August 2009, www.ich.org.
- ISPE Good Practice Guide: Applied Risk Management for Commissioning and Qualification, International Society for Pharmaceutical Engineering, First Edition, October 2011, www.ispe.org.
- USP General Chapter <1177> Good Packaging Practices.
- FDA Guidance for Industry: Labeling for Human Prescription Drug and Biological Products—Implementing the PLR Content and Format Requirements, February 2013.

18 Laboratory Controls

Alex M. Hoinowski

CONTENTS

The *Code of Federal Regulations (CFR)* for Laboratory Controls as listed in this chapter provides some general requirements on the systems and policies a laboratory needs to have in place for compliance. However, it does not necessarily define the exact details or processes a laboratory must follow to be compliant. Generally, a Quality Management System (QMS) will provide the underlying compliance framework that satisfies general regulatory requirements such as the *CFR*, as well as specific procedures and Standard Operating procedures (SOPs) to satisfy the essential details of how laboratories achieve and maintain compliance.

From the author's experience, the effective implementation of Laboratory Controls noted in the CFR subparts of this chapter should also include, as applicable, documented Quality System (QS) requirements that address:

1. **The testing environment**:
    1.1.   Adequate laboratory electrical power, lighting, working space, and temperature control, as well as provision for special conditions as required (e.g., glove boxes, laminar flow hoods).

   1.2. Proper ventilation: where necessary, the laboratory must be equipped with laminar flow hoods, fume hoods, or separate HVAC systems.

   1.3. Procedures for control of the sterility testing laboratory environment.

2. **Laboratory logistics**:

   2.1. Receipt into the laboratory, control and use of all samples, standards, reagents, animals, other laboratory materials, test methods, and instruments/equipment.

   2.2. Shipment of samples to external laboratories and the receipt/handling of those results.

   2.3. Formal approval of any external laboratories providing testing.

   2.4. Laboratory access restricted to authorized personnel.

   2.5. The appropriate labeling of instruments and equipment that are not available for use (e.g., out of service, calibration or qualification in progress).

   2.6. The training and qualification of all personnel to perform specific tasks according to a defined, documented training program.

      2.6.1. Analysts' proficiency with the test method demonstrated prior to running the method for an official test result.

3. **Method development, validation, and transfer as well as verification of Compendial methods**:

   3.1. The laboratories' role or interface clearly defined.

   3.2. The necessity for clarity of procedures and with sufficient detail for critical steps.

   3.3. Analytical procedures used for testing must be validated, qualified, and/or verified for intended use according to regulatory and compendial requirements.

   3.4. All changes to validated methods, including analytical software upgrades, must be verified and assessed prior to use through Change Control.

   3.5. All automated calculations performed using data systems and spreadsheets must be controlled and validated for intended use, unless a manual recalculation has been performed as part of the review process.

      3.5.1. Automated calculations in spreadsheets must be qualification and then locked to prevent inadvertent changes to the equations.

   3.6. Consideration should be given to demonstrating a new or revised method can generate equivalent or better results than the prior method (i.e., method comparability studies).

4. **Sampling plans and sampling processes**:

   4.1. Written procedures for creating, revising, and controlling sampling plans and sampling processes.

   4.2. Written sampling plans and sampling processes created and that conform to these written procedures.

   4.3. The use of scientifically sound practices to ensure samples are representative of the parent population and/or material.

   4.4. Compliance with regulatory and good manufacturing practice (GMP) requirements of the countries where the products are marketed.

5. **Laboratory equipment qualification, calibration, standardization, and verification of calibration**:

   5.1. The laboratories' role or interface clearly defined.

   5.2. Laboratory equipment or other measuring devices must be appropriately qualified, calibrated according to procedures that are consistent with good scientific practices, and comply with appropriate regulatory and compendial requirements.

      5.2.1. Must have the accuracy and range required for the measurements being made.

   5.3. All calibration, maintenance, and requalification frequencies defined and justified based on factors such as manufacturer's recommendations, equipment performance, usage, and criticality.

6. **Laboratory errors, deviations, and investigations associated with methods, analysts, or instruments**:
   6.1. Documentation, assessment, and handling clearly defined.
   6.2. Reagents, preparation solutions, and last sample dilution (as applicable) must be retained, if stable, until results are confirmed to facilitate a laboratory investigation if required.
7. **Test performance**:
   7.1. Processes for Laboratory Analysts to ensure the use of the current approved version of test procedures and associated forms and that instruments, equipment, and laboratory materials are appropriate for their intended use as required by the test method prior to use.
   7.2. All entries follow current good manufacturing practice (CGMP) documentation practices.
   7.3. The handling of significant figures, performing calculations, and rounding of data and test results in accordance with industry and compendia standards.
   7.4. Preparation of test samples, controls, standards, and reagents must be documented on controlled worksheets or in bound preparation logbooks, as appropriate.
   7.5. Analysts verifying and recording calibration of instruments and equipment as well as expiration dates of reagents, standards, and method controls prior to use.
   7.6. Expiry/retesting requirements for laboratory materials (including storage and disposal).
   7.7. Detailed procedures for documenting and reviewing data. For example, the data package must include items such as:
        7.7.1. A complete record of all data from each test, including all graphs, charts, and spectra from laboratory instrumentation, properly identified to show the specific material or product and lot tested.
        7.7.2. Test results, including observations, and calculations, including units of measure, conversion factors, and equivalency factors, and the review must verify items such as:
        7.7.3. The analytical data package is complete.
        7.7.4. The correct version of SOPs, test methods used.
        7.7.5. Results are within acceptance criteria and specification.
        7.7.6. Instruments and equipment used are documented.
        7.7.7. Standards, controls, and critical reagents are correct and within expiry.
        7.7.8. Injection index/sequence files for automated analytical instrumentation are correct.
   7.8. Laboratory performance metrics that measure test method performance, including error rates and method control results.
8. **Test records**:
   8.1. The archiving and storage of records that ensures they are readily retrievable, whether they are handwritten, hardcopy, microfiched, or electronic.
9. **Change control**:
   9.1. The change control system(s) used by the laboratory are clearly defined for all aspects of laboratory operations (i.e., SOPs, test procedures, sampling, sample management, lab equipment).

In April 2016, the FDA issued a Draft Guidance for Industry, *Data Integrity and Compliance with CGMP*, to clarify the role of data integrity in CGMP for drugs. The document provides the FDA's definition of data integrity (the completeness, consistency, and accuracy of data) and uses the acronym ALCOA, which stands for Attributable (A), Legible (L), Contemporaneously recorded (C), Original or a true copy (O) and Accurate (A). It defines the creation and handling of data in accordance with CGMP requirements in a structure of 18 questions with corresponding answers.

Additional guidance documents addressing data integrity have been recently written by the World Health Organization (WHO),[1] U.K. Medicines & Healthcare Products Regulatory Agency (MHRA),[2] Pharmaceutical Inspection Co-operation Scheme (PIC/S),[3] Australian Therapeutic Goods Administration (TGA)[4] and the International Society for Pharmaceutical Engineering (ISPE).[5] See also Chapter 24, "Data Integrity and Fundamental Responsibilities."

For Laboratory Controls, the documented QS requirements (noted above) include the basis for laboratory data integrity by providing the right foundation for implementation, as well as managing data across the data life cycle. Part of the foundation for data integrity is the engagement and involvement of management within the organization ensuring data integrity and data governance is set firmly in place within the context of the QS. The data integrity policies should cascade down to laboratory data integrity procedures and ensure staff have initial and ongoing data integrity training.

In the laboratory, data integrity starts with sampling, transporting the sample to the laboratory, and sample management in the laboratory. To ensure data integrity, test methods used must be appropriately validated or qualified; the analytical instruments, software that controls it, and/or computerized systems used in the laboratory must be qualified for the specified operating range and validated for their intended purpose. The records acquired and interpreted by the software must be adequately protected, especially if the records are held in directories in the operating system. This should be addressed during the computerized system validation. The electronic files created during the course of an analysis need to be identified and a determination made if they are vulnerable within the data life cycle (e.g., the storage of data electronically in temporary memory, in a manner that allows for manipulation, before creating a permanent record). If so, these electronic files must be adequately protected by implementing suitable controls, such as mitigation, transfer, or elimination.

IN-PLACE AND IN-USE FOR DATA INTEGRITY

There should be a procedure(s) covering chromatographic integration, including detailed measures for the use and control of manual integration. Chromatography data systems should clearly indicate which injections have had any manual intervention and a review of all manual integration operations should be conducted periodically and an assessment made as to whether manual intervention is being used excessively.

To ensure chromatographic samples are not being tested into compliance, procedures should require a regular search for sequences that have only one or two injections, or sequences that have had reinjections of samples, injections that have been interrupted, injections that have been aborted, or injections that have not been processed. The resulting information can then be used as a guide to where to look, in order to further investigate the history behind this data.

For instrumental analytical systems and computer systems such as Laboratory Information Management System (LIMS), attention should be paid to curbing the ability to alter data in temporary memory before it becomes permanent. For example: data that is entered into LIMS should be automatically saved if the user attempts to leave the data-entry area without explicitly saving it; if a user attempts to change a previously entered value, they should be immediately prompted to provide a reason for the change. Audit trail reviews must be performed and should include all data—both the explicitly saved data and any data left in temporary memory—and there should be evidence available to confirm that review of the relevant audit trails have taken place.

Although the above and regulatory observations have appeared to focus on data integrity issues associated with chemical analyses, especially high-performance liquid chromatography (HPLC), the challenge to ensure data integrity in the microbiology laboratory remains. A significant portion of microbiological data is typically evaluated and recorded manually by microbiologists trained in contamination detection and colony counting. Hence, its data integrity risks and actions to mitigate them are associated with items such as real-time data entry difficulties; incomplete or incorrect data entries; no second opinion for subjective interpretation of test results; performing incorrect method or sample preparation; falsification or lack of authentic data; issues with chain of custody for samples; and delays in testing and times not documented.

§211.160 GENERAL REQUIREMENTS

a. *The establishment of any specifications, standards, sampling plans, test procedures, or other laboratory control mechanisms required by this subpart, including any change in such specifications, standards, sampling plans, test procedures, or other laboratory control mechanisms, shall be drafted by the appropriate organizational unit and reviewed and approved by the Quality Control Unit (QCU). The requirements in this subpart shall be followed and shall be documented at the time of performance. Any deviation from the written specifications, standards, sampling plans, test procedures, or other laboratory control mechanisms shall be recorded and justified.*

For items listed in official compendia, such as the *United States Pharmacopeia* (USP) test methods and acceptance criteria are defined in the article's monograph, applicable General Chapters, and General Notices. Although these compendial test methods are the final arbiters for the drugs and components listed in them, a manufacturer is allowed to substitute other test methods or automated equipment, provided the results are consistent with those obtained using the official methods and method bias is demonstrated to be absent. In the event of a dispute or query, the official methods are to be applied.

Compendial products must comply with the compendial specifications (test methods and acceptance criteria) unless the noncompliant parameter is clearly stated on the label. The USP monographs provide useful guidance on the typical contents of monographs for drug substances, excipients, and dosage forms. Both the USP and FDA have emphasized the need to provide adequate details on the impurities in bulk drug substances. This includes both the expected impurities from the synthesis and degradation of the bulk drug, with the main impurities and residual solvents identified.

Where compendial specifications and methods are not available, the manufacturers must develop their own based on current scientific practices.

Material and product test methods and acceptance criteria for new products are often generated by the Research and Development (R&D) department. They must, however, ultimately be approved by the quality unit before commercial implementation. The FDA reviewing chemists may be critical of proposed and acceptance criteria that are wider than the results seen in development batches. The reason for this is obvious—if the toxicology and clinical data were generated on batches with narrower specifications, there may be no justification for wider ranges. This can create a dilemma for industry, since the earlier batches (for toxicology and clinical studies) may have been small-scale batches produced by R&D chemists. Later, full-scale production may involve different equipment, operators rather than researchers, and different sources of some materials. It may be impossible, due to time and financial constraints, to perform this early evaluation work on a commercial scale. Also, the processes are still under development. Consequently, if commercial specifications need to be wider than those seen during development, supporting data with justification for the wider specification will be required.

The International Conference on Harmonisation (ICH) has provided guidance on specifications for impurities in new drug substances (ICH Q3A[R2], October 2006) and new drug products (ICH Q3B[R2], June 2006). Impurities were classified under headings of organic, inorganic, and solvents. For these it is noted that:

1. *Organic impurities* are considered actual or potential impurities likely to arise during synthesis, purification, or storage. Sources include starting materials, reagents, by-products, intermediates, and degradants. ICH Q3A(R2) provides guidance on how results on these impurities should be presented in an application file.

2. *Inorganic impurities* may arise from reagents, catalysts, heavy metals, charcoal, and filter aids. These are usually evaluated by compendial methods and apply compendial limits.

3. *Solvents remaining from the process* tests and limits are usually those included in the compendia. For other solvents, toxicity should be taken into account in defining appropriate limits.

   The FDA has provided guidance for registration applications on the content and qualification of impurities in new drug substances produced by chemical syntheses (and not previously registered in a region or member state) in its Guidance for Industry, *Q3A Impurities in New Drug Substances June 2008 ICH Revision 2*. This document defines limits as of which impurities must be identified or qualified. Attachment 2, *Illustration of Reporting Impurity Results for Identification and Qualification in an Application*, includes clarifying information and examples.

   The QMS must address change control and must be designed into the approval process for procedures, thereby ensuring that no changes are made without quality unit review and approval. This includes any change in such specifications, standards, sampling plans, test procedures, or other laboratory control mechanisms.

   The requirement to document any act at the time of performance precludes the use of intermediate or temporary recording of data, such as during weighing and subsequently discarding after transcription of the information into the formal system. Such intermediate records are acceptable if retained. However, wherever possible, data should be recorded directly into the final format, eliminating the possibility for transcription errors.

   Procedures should establish the process and requirements for documenting and handling an unplanned event, unexplained discrepancy, or a departure from an approved instruction (e.g., procedure, batch record, test method, or specification). Determination must be made whether it will have any adverse impact on the product with justification provided. Reviews and approvals of the documentation and all actions should be defined and dependent upon the nature of the deviation (QA, suitably qualified individuals such as supervisor or manager).

b. *Laboratory Controls shall include the establishment of scientifically sound and appropriate specifications, standards, sampling plans, and test procedures designed to assure that components, drug product containers, closures, in-process materials, labeling, and drug products conform to appropriate standards of identity, strength, quality, and purity. Laboratory Controls shall include:*

1. *Determination of conformity to applicable written specifications for the acceptance of each lot within each shipment of components, drug product containers, closures, and labeling used in the manufacture, processing, packing, or holding of drug products. The specifications shall include a description of the sampling and testing procedures used. Samples shall be representative and adequately identified. Such procedures shall also require appropriate retesting of any component, drug product container, or closure that is subject to deterioration.*

2. *Determination of conformance to written specifications and a description of sampling and testing procedures for in-process materials. Such samples shall be representative and properly identified.*

3. *Determination of conformance to written descriptions of sampling procedures and appropriate specifications for drug products. Such samples shall be representative and properly identified.*

Whereas subsection (a) deals with the drafting and approval of any specifications, standards, sampling plans, and test procedures, subsection (b) applies to the application of these components, containers, closures, in-process materials, labeling, and drug products.

The procedures for the determination of conformity to applicable written specifications, sampling, and testing procedures are to be scientifically sound and appropriate. Where possible, established specifications and test methodology such as USP will be applied. Otherwise, knowledge of the composition, potential impurities (synthesis intermediates, solvent residues, heavy metals, etc.), and degradation products should be taken into account. The specifications should be designed to control any such impurities within acceptable levels and to monitor trends. As indicated previously, the application of "action levels"—that are based on historical data and are more rigorous than the specifications—is a useful and practical way of highlighting adverse trends and bringing them to the attention of Quality Control (QC) management.

A common practice is to set the action levels such that 95% of all acceptable results will fall within these levels; the exceptional 5% will then be highlighted. In-process control action levels for physical parameters such as tablet weight or fill volumes are more usually approached by way of control charts.

For a new product, with no available historic data, control levels may be calculated from the USP <905> criteria for "Uniformity of Dosage Units." In-process testing typically involves weighing a composite of 10 tablets at a determined frequency, that is, every 15 minutes.

The test methods used may vary for different applications. For example, in-process test methods performed in production areas by production personnel may need to be more robust than those performed by QC laboratory personnel; nonavailability of equipment or servicing may result in the use of different methods in different countries. Hence, in these instances the concepts of Quality by Design (QbD) described in ICH Q8, 9, 10, and 11 should be considered.

The effectiveness of test methodology is further dependent on two additional factors. First, the methods must be written in sufficient detail that no interpretation is necessary. If there is any doubt, then a query should be raised with QC management and the procedure should be rewritten. Second, only trained individuals must be allowed to perform testing.

Sampling requirements may also vary with component or product history. Comments on reduced testing and supplier validation are included in (§211.84).

The regulations also require retesting of components, closures, or containers that may be prone to deterioration. Testing should be restricted to evaluation of parameters known or expected to change during storage. This subject is addressed in (§211.87).

Confirmation of conformance to specifications usually involves two groups within the quality unit. The laboratory function—QC—is responsible for sampling (which may be formally delegated to "quality" unit or production, provided it is a clearly defined responsibility and personnel are adequately trained), testing, and test results, whereas a Quality Assurance (QA) unit reviews the resulting data and conclusions. This review by QA forms part of the overall batch review procedure.

4. *The calibration of instruments, apparatus, gauges, and recording devices at suitable intervals in accordance with an established written program containing specific directions, schedules, limits for accuracy and precision, and provisions for remedial action*

in the event accuracy and/or precision limits are not met. Instruments, apparatus, gauges, and recording devices not meeting established specifications shall not be used.

Equipment qualification and calibration are critical aspects of test methodology. Laboratory equipment and software must be qualified to demonstrate that the equipment FDA performs as expected and required. Calibration programs should define who is responsible for the calibration, the frequency, how the calibration is to be performed, and action to be taken if the equipment is found to be outside acceptable ranges. Refer to the Chapter 11, "Equipment."

In some instances, calibration programs are contracted out to third parties. The responsibility for calibration must still reside within the manufacturer's organization, including the review and approval of the third-party's data and results. The manufacturer must approve the calibration procedure, the acceptance criteria, and the frequency. Calibration results must be recorded; it is not sufficient to report that the equipment is acceptable.

Frequency is usually determined on the basis of the equipment manufacturer's recommendation, experience, and past performance. Any equipment found to be outside of acceptable operational ranges must be immediately taken out of service until it is returned to normal performance. Additionally, the potential impact of such equipment on testing performed since the previous calibration needs to be investigated, evaluated and documented in a formal system. The potential implications of this are extensive. For example, an analytical balance that is serviced and calibrated every three months that is found to be significantly inaccurate (out of calibration) might place in jeopardy some of the analytical results generated since the previous calibration. The rechecking of all analytical results would involve a significant amount of work. However, the recording of the specific pieces of equipment used during testing (§211.105) will narrow the field. To avoid or at least minimize the possibility outlined in the example above, it is usual to perform more frequent performance checks or verifications (such as daily performance checks on balances). Although less comprehensive, and not adequate as calibrations, these do provide a high degree of assurance that the equipment is performing satisfactorily. Additional calibrations should be initiated if there is reason to suspect that equipment may not be performing satisfactorily.

§211.165 TESTING AND RELEASE FOR DISTRIBUTION

a. *For each batch of drug product, there shall be appropriate laboratory determination of satisfactory conformance to final specifications for the drug product, including the identity and strength of each active ingredient, prior to release. Where sterility and/or pyrogen testing are conducted on specific batches of short-lived radiopharmaceuticals, such batches may be released prior to completion of sterility and/or pyrogen testing, provided such testing is completed as soon as possible.*

b. *There shall be appropriate laboratory testing, as necessary, of each batch of drug product required to be free of objectionable microorganisms.*

As a result of a court ruling against Barr Laboratories in 1993, FDA investigators increased their level of attention to laboratory operations. The main points relating to laboratory operations noted from the Barr case included:

1. Inadequate evaluation of the cause of out-of-specification (OOS) results.
2. Use of an outlier test to discount failing results.
3. Lack of a defined procedure to evaluate OOS results.
4. Long delays in completion of the evaluation of failures—a maximum of 30 days was proposed.
5. Frequency of failures (product history).
6. Use of different samples to reevaluate a failing result, especially for content uniformity and dissolution.

7. Averaging of results, for example, three assay values of 89, 90, and 91 cannot be averaged to allow release of a product with a 90% minimum assay specification.

8. Samples taken from blends were too large; they should not be more than three times the active ingredient dosage size.

9. Sampling blends after they have been transferred to drums is not an acceptable alternative to sampling from the blender.

The regulations require confirmation of conformance of drug products to specifications prior to release. Identity testing and assay of active ingredients by the QC laboratory is specifically required. In-process data from production personnel may be acceptable for most other parameters, provided operators have been properly trained, have adequate equipment, and performance is audited. The availability of process validation data and process control data does not eliminate the need for finished product testing. This is somewhat at variance with the acceptance of parametric release (ICH Q6A) as an alternative to sterility testing for terminally sterilized products (which must be approved by regulatory authorities—see §211.167). However, for sterility testing to be statistically valid, the sample size would be impracticable with a high probability of obtaining false-positive results.

An exception is made to the testing before release requirement for the sterility and pyrogen testing of short-lived radiopharmaceuticals. Since the test time may be a significant part of the product shelf life, release prior to completion of testing is allowed. Obviously, in such instances, the process should be thoroughly validated and controlled to minimize the chance of a sterility or pyrogen failure.

The need to test each batch of product, required to be free of objectionable microorganisms, applies to both sterile products and to those products where specific organisms are to be absent (e.g., absence of *Pseudomonas aeruginosa* and *Staphylococcus aureus* in topical products). Products covered by this requirement include terminally sterilized products and aseptically processed products, such as injections, and products produced under clean and hygienic conditions to exclude specific organisms and/or to minimize the level of microorganisms. The processing conditions for these products is described in (§211.113).

The effective microbiological control of nonsterile products, where required, will usually include evaluation of levels of total microbial content, absence of specified organisms, presence of adequate levels of any added antimicrobial agent or preservative, and review of the environmental data generated during the process. The subject of sterility testing is addressed in §211.167.

c. *Any sampling and testing plans shall be described in written procedures that shall include the method of sampling and the number of units per batch to be tested; such written procedure shall be followed.*

d. *Acceptance criteria for the sampling and testing conducted by the QC unit shall be adequate to assure that batches of drug products meet each appropriate specification and appropriate statistical QC criteria as a condition for their approval and release. The statistical QC criteria shall include appropriate acceptance levels and/or appropriate rejection levels.*

The need for written sampling and testing plans and definition of acceptance criteria is basic. Appropriate "action levels" should be built into the acceptance criteria. As emphasized elsewhere, it is important that any atypical situations are immediately brought to the attention of senior personnel (supervisors/manager) so that appropriate actions can be initiated.

Where testing is delegated to production personnel, there should be adequate supporting data to demonstrate that the personnel were adequately trained, that equipment is suitable and properly maintained and calibrated, and that the results obtained are equivalent to those obtained by QC. Audit programs should be in place to confirm these requirements.

e. *The accuracy, sensitivity, specificity, and reproducibility of test methods employed by the firm shall be established and documented. Such validation and documentation may be accomplished in accordance with §211.194(a)(2).*

The regulatory environment for pharmaceuticals mandates that analytical methods be validated or qualified. This includes chemical, biological, compendial, and microbiological assays used for product release, product stability, verification of cleaning, and in-process determinations. There are no specific regulations on method validations, but the FDA, other agencies, and industry task forces have developed guidelines for method validation. For example, ICH Q2(R1) *Validation of Analytical Procedures: Text and Methodology*, FDA Draft Guidance *Analytical Procedures and Methods Validation for Drugs and Biologics* (February 19, 2014), and current USP–NF. These cover a multitude of tests such as identification tests, quantification of impurities, limit tests for impurities, and assay of actives or other key components of drug products and microbiological tests. These also provide guidance on how to perform the testing of the validation parameters (e.g., linearity, specificity, quantitation, and detection limit).

As drug development progresses from Phase 1 to commercialization, the analytical method typically will follow a similar progression. Requirements for validation change throughout the life cycle of drug development. Method qualification is the approach used during early development. Method qualification is an acceptable level of method performance evaluation applied to analytical methods used during preclinical, Phase 1, and early Phase 2 clinical trials. No predetermined method acceptance criteria may be necessary, and only minimal method performance capabilities must be demonstrated. Full ICH validation is required for Phase 3 clinical trials and the release of finished product. Validation parameters defined in the ICH Q2 (R1) guidance document should be evaluated as applicable for each method.

The analytical method selected may be from a relevant pharmacopeia or other recognized standard reference and have been previously validated as a requirement for inclusion. Such methods may then just be verified by the laboratories implementing them for use. *(USP < 1226>).* The suitability should be verified under actual conditions of use and documented. Verification is not required for basic compendial test procedures that are routinely performed (i.e., loss on drying, pH) unless there is an indication that the compendial procedure is not appropriate for the article under test. Validation may be necessary if the method is utilized on product of different composition, etc. If critical method parameters are changed or optimize to accommodate a test article, the method must be revalidated to demonstrate acceptable performance characteristics with the modified parameters.

The company's overall policy, intentions, and approach to validation and verification of analytical methods and in-process control test procedures should be documented. When a method is validated at a site external to the testing laboratory, it must be formally transferred to or co-validated at the testing site. This should include verification of compendial methods at the testing site.

From the author's experience, a method validation protocol (in-line with guidelines on method validation) with acceptance criteria is reviewed and approved (e.g., laboratory management and quality assurance). The method validation experiments are well planned and described to ensure efficient use of time and resources during execution of the method validation. The analytical procedure is described in sufficient detail to allow a competent and trained analyst to reproduce the necessary conditions and obtain results comparable to the validation data. Aspects of the analytical procedure that require special attention are noted. Appropriate qualification and calibration of analytical equipment are undertaken and verified as such before initiating the validation. Individuals taking part in the validation work are appropriately trained. The protocol is executed, data is analyzed, and the report is written, and then the analytical method procedure is finalized. (Note: for an unacceptable result, certain aspects of the method may need to be modified and revalidated). Method Transfer Studies are conducted when applicable.

Change control then goes into effect for the validated method. A need for method change may be identified by analyst recommendation, annual review, investigation, compendial change, etc.

Revalidation, verification, or development of a new or modified method may be necessary in circumstances, such as changes in the synthesis of the drug substance, the composition of the finished product, in the manufacturing process that have the potential to change the analytical profile of the drug substance and drug product, or laboratory-related changes (i.e., specification, method, site, instrument components, reagents). The degree of revalidation required depends upon the nature of the changes. Typically, a planned change involves a team from development, QC, and, as applicable, regulatory affairs.

f. *Drug products failing to meet established standards or specifications and any other relevant QC criteria shall be rejected. Reprocessing may be performed. Prior to acceptance and use, reprocessed material must meet appropriate standards, specifications, and any other relevant criteria.*

Failure to meet specifications or noncompliance with the approved process should result immediately in quarantine of the material until the cause of the event is ascertained. Materials and products are in a quarantine status until released or rejected, but additional notations (paper and/or electronic) provide further information should the batch status be accessed. The approach to be used in evaluating an OOS result should be clearly defined in an SOP. As indicated earlier, this area was one of the main issues in the Barr Laboratories case.

In October 2006, the FDA formalized the 1998 Draft Guidance on Investigating OOS Test Results for Pharmaceutical Products and issued: *Guidance for Industry Investigating Out-of-Specification (OOS) Test Results for Pharmaceutical Products.*[6] The 2006 Final Guidance can be summarized as:

1. Scope includes:
    1.1. Finished drug testing, active pharmaceutical ingredients (APIs), raw materials, in-process materials, and stability
    1.2. Contract laboratories
2. Phases of the investigation process:
    2.1. Phase 1: Laboratory Investigation with delineation of the responsibilities of the analyst and the laboratory supervisor
    2.2. Phase 2: Full-Scale OOS Investigation with guidance on:
        2.2.1. The review of production and sampling procedures
        2.2.2. Additional laboratory testing (retesting and resampling)
3. Definition of and emphasis on the responsibilities of the QCU for full investigation and evaluation of investigation results
4. Examples for averaging of test results and resampling
5. Description of the steps of the procedure:
    5.1. The failure investigation
    5.2. Identifying root cause
    5.3. Identifying impact (severity and impact on other batches including those already distributed)

    5.4.   Evaluating the need for corrective and preventive actions
    5.5.   Implementing the corrective action(s) and preventive action(s), as appropriate
    5.6.   Verifying effectiveness of the corrective action(s) and preventive action(s)
  6. Discussions on Field Alerts for impacted marketed products

With the above in mind, for laboratory testing noncompliance situations, the following guidance is provided.

THE RECOGNITION OF AN OBVIOUS ERROR

During the testing process, an obvious, recognized error may occur that invalidates the results. Such errors could be caused by the analyst or by instrument failure and do not require the performance of a formal laboratory investigation, whether or not data have been generated. When recognized, testing should be stopped, the supervisor immediately notified, and the data invalidated and documented per QMS system procedures.

RECOGNITION OF AN OOS RESULT

Analysts detecting an OOS result must report that result promptly to the supervisor. The analyst and supervisor then immediately conduct a brief review for obvious errors. If no obvious error is revealed, the OOS result is reported to the QA unit with information on the impacted or potentially impacted batches/lots. The analyst and the supervisor then initiate and conduct Phase 1 of the laboratory investigation to determine whether or not the OOS result is assignable to the testing laboratory. Checklists of possible sources of error are typically used to aid this phase of the investigation.

LABORATORY ASSIGNABLE CAUSE DETERMINED

If the Phase 1 investigation determines a laboratory assignable cause, then the original OOS result is invalidated and the original sample is tested again as if it were a new sample. (If this repeat result is OOS, it should have its own Phase 1 investigation, because the initial test was invalidated. However, depending on the outcome it may be linked with the initial investigation.) The root cause/most probable cause for laboratory assignable cause of the OOS result is documented, and the impact of the finding on other data is determined. Corrective actions and preventive actions (CAPA) that may be applicable should be determined and taken to prevent recurrence of this source of error. The investigation then is closed, and the effectiveness of the CAPA monitored.

NO LABORATORY ASSIGNABLE CAUSE DETERMINED IN PHASE 1

If the Phase 1 investigation determines that the OOS result cannot be assigned to the testing laboratory, then a Phase 2 full-scale OOS investigation with review of production and sampling procedures by the QCU is initiated (as applicable). The QCU should be involved in determining, justifying, and documenting the need for additional laboratory testing, retesting, and resampling.[6] The documentation should include defining the retest/resample protocol, and when and how resampling/retesting is conducted and concluded.

THE FUTURE OF THE SPECIFIC BATCH IN QUESTION

The 2006 FDA CDER Guidance[6] states that the QCU is responsible for interpreting the results of the investigation. An initial OOS result does not necessarily mean the subject batch fails and must be rejected. The findings of the investigation, including retest results, should be interpreted to evaluate the batch and reach a decision regarding release or rejection (§211.165).

For confirmed OOS, when the batch does not meet established standards or specifications, it results in rejection of the batch in accordance with §211.165(f). This also indicates a batch failure, and the investigation must be extended to other batches or products that may have been associated with the specific failure (§211.192). The CDER Guidance[6] discusses actions for inconclusive investigations.

If reprocessing is viable, it must be done according to written and approved instructions. Where New Drug Application/Abbreviated New Drug Application (NDA/ANDA) products are involved, the reprocessing should be in conformance with the approved NDA/ANDA methods/procedures. The reprocessed product must meet all of the product specifications. Additional data may also be required to confirm that the product will behave in a similar manner to a typical batch. Such additional data could include accelerated stability and ingredient degradation evaluation, which might be included in a stability monograph but not in a release monograph.

OTHER LABORATORY INVESTIGATION PROCEDURES

In addition to procedures for documenting and investigating OOS results, laboratories should have similar procedures for documenting and investigating out-of-trend (OOT) and out-of-expectation (OOE) results. There should also be procedures that provide direction on in handling of known laboratory errors and invalid data/results such as System Suitability failures.

While the 2006 Final Guidance applies to chemistry-based laboratory testing of drugs regulated by CDER, QC Microbiology Laboratories should have similar investigation procedures for test failure, for example, on testing for Sterility, Microbial Limits, Preservative Efficacy, Endotoxin, and Potency Assay, as well as Growth Promotion Testing on Media for use in the laboratory. Some information specific to this testing for consideration (because microbial contamination is typically inhomogeneous) are:

1. **Sterility testing**:
    1.1. Repeat sterility testing can be performed if there is compelling documented evidence that there was a laboratory assignable cause associated with the original discrepant result.
        1.1.1. The adventitious agent cannot be correlated with any coincidental production deviation for a given batch of product.
        1.1.2. After determination of the identity of the microorganisms isolated from the test, the growth of this species (or these species) may be ascribed unequivocally to faults with respect to the material and or the technique used in conducting the sterility test procedure.
2. **Microbial limits testing**:
    2.1. Microbial limits repeat testing may only be performed if there is documented evidence that there was a laboratory assignable cause associated with the original discrepant result such as: media failure, environmental/aseptic control failure, or evidence the sample was compromised.
    2.2. Retesting may be conducted as an investigational tool but should be clearly noted as such.
3. **Bioburden testing**:
    3.1. Repeat testing may be performed if there is documented evidence that there was a laboratory assignable cause, such as the enrichment broth or test plates being accidentally contaminated during the testing or incubation phase.
    3.2. Retesting may be conducted as an investigation tool but should be clearly noted as such.
4. **Growth promotion testing**:
    4.1. Repeat testing may be performed if there is documented evidence that there was a laboratory assignable cause such as an incorrect strain being used, a subthreshold

inoculum being used, or if improper handling/incubation conditions were used during the testing process (e.g., contaminated negative controls invalidate the test).

4.2.   Retesting may be conducted as an investigational tool but should be clearly noted as such.

ANALYST TRAINING

Analyst training is not specifically referenced in §211.165. However, its importance is obvious. Training, which must be recorded, should include:

1. Basic analytical techniques
2. Specific methods where these are complex
3. Laboratory practices and relevant SOPs
4. Laboratory safety
5. New methods transferred from R&D (method transfer)
6. Retraining for analysts whose results are atypical

§211.166 STABILITY TESTING

a. *There shall be a written testing program designed to assess the stability characteristics of drug products. The results of such stability testing shall be used in determining appropriate storage conditions and expiration dates. The written program shall be followed and shall include:*
   1. *Sample size and test intervals based on statistical criteria for each attribute examined to assure valid estimates of stability*
   2. *Storage conditions for samples retained for testing*
   3. *Reliable, meaningful, and specific test methods*
   4. *Testing of the drug product in the same container–closure system as that in which the drug product is marketed*
   5. *Testing of drug products for reconstitution at the time of dispensing (as directed in the labeling) as well as after they are reconstituted*
b. *An adequate number of batches of each drug product shall be tested to determine an appropriate expiration date, and a record of such data shall be maintained. Accelerated studies, combined with basic stability information on the components, drug products, and container–closure system, may be used to support tentative expiration dates provided full shelf-life studies are not available and are being conducted. Where data from accelerated studies are used to project a tentative expiration date that is beyond a date supported by actual shelf-life studies, there must be stability studies conducted, including drug product testing at appropriate intervals, until the tentative expiration date is verified or the appropriate expiration date determined.*
c. *For homeopathic drug products, the requirements of this section are as follows:*
   1. *There shall be a written assessment of stability based at least on testing or examination of the drug product for compatibility of the ingredients, and based on marketing experience with the drug product to indicate that there is no degradation of the product for the normal or expected period of use.*
   2. *Evaluation of stability shall be based on the same container–closure system in which the drug product is being marketed.*
d. *Allergenic extracts that are labeled "No U.S. Standard of Potency" are exempted from the requirements of this section.*

The purposes of stability studies are to predict and/or confirm product shelf life under the climatic conditions expected during trade storage, shipping, house storage, and use.

Before commencement of a stability evaluation, the stability protocol must be written and approved—usually by technical services and QA. The key elements of a stability protocol typically include:

1. Study purpose
2. Responsibilities
3. Product description, including the strengths and batch sizes
4. The source, that is, manufacturing site
5. Description of the container–closure system(s) (e.g., type, size, reference, and source of primary packaging material).
6. Sample requirements, that is, number required for the study plus extras should they be needed for investigations, etc.
7. Description of the conditions of storage
8. Study duration and test intervals
9. Pull windows (time period for removing samples from specific storage conditions) and test windows (time period from sample removal to testing)
10. Relevant physical, chemical, microbiological, and functional stability-indicating tests.
11. Acceptance criteria for each test attribute
12. Justification for use of bracketing or matrixing, as applicable
13. Other applicable parameters specific to the product/material, such as position (upright/inverted) of samples during storage

ICH Harmonised Tripartite Guidelines provide a wealth of information and guidance covering a multitude of stability study parameters. The main guideline is Q1A(R2): *Stability Testing of New Drug Substances and Products*; February 2003. This guideline defines the stability data package for a new drug substance or drug product that is sufficient for a registration application within the three regions of the EC, Japan, and the United States. For drug substances and drug products, this guideline covers: selection of batches, container–closure system, specification, testing frequency, storage conditions, stability commitment, evaluation, and statements/labeling. In addition, stress testing is covered for drug substances and photostability testing for drug products.

Other applicable ICH guidelines are:

1. ICH Q1B: *Stability Testing: Photostability Testing of New Drug Substances and Products*; November 1996
2. ICH Q1C: *Stability Testing for New Dosage Forms*; November 1996
3. ICH Q1D: *Bracketing and Matrixing Designs for Stability Testing of New Drug Substances and Products*; February 7, 2002
4. ICH Q1E: *Evaluation of Stability Data*; February 2003

The ICH guidelines do not specifically address the position of samples during storage. This is especially important for liquid products where leakage and product closure interaction need to be evaluated. One approach is to store samples both upright and inverted but only to test the inverted samples. The upright samples may be used as controls in the event that problems are identified with the inverted samples. For products with closures at two ends, such as prefilled syringes and semisolids in tubes, horizontal storage is more appropriate.

Test Methodology

The stability-testing monograph need not include all of the criteria defined in the product release monograph. Only those parameters that are potentially susceptible to change during storage and that may impact quality, safety, or efficacy need to be evaluated. The characteristics evaluated will include actives, degradants, antimicrobial agents, antioxidants, and key physical characteristics such as dissolution, fragility, color, moisture, and volume. Closure integrity may also be required; however, evaporation or leakage will normally show up in other tests. Functional effectiveness should also be evaluated: child-resistant closures, tamper-evident packaging, syringability for pre-filled syringes and openability of containers. For tamper-evident packaging, there are currently no generally accepted methods of evaluation and in-house methods should be developed.

For parenteral or other sterile products, testing should include sterility assurance. This may be achieved by normal sterility testing, but because of the large number of samples evaluated during the stability protocol, there would be some chance of a "false-positive" result, which could create difficulties with interpretation. A validated closure integrity test may therefore offer a better approach and can be used with a larger number of samples if required. FDA microbiologists appear to favor this approach.

TEST FREQUENCY

This should be adequate to demonstrate any degradation and to provide enough data points for statistical evaluation. For the scale-up batches and the first three commercial batches, testing is expected initially, at three-month intervals during the first year, six-month intervals in the second year, and yearly thereafter. Some companies do not evaluate beyond 36 months. A different frequency may be more appropriate for ongoing stability evaluation.

As indicated earlier, these ICH guidelines relate only to new chemical entities and the products made from these materials. However, the FDA expects the same conditions for stability studies (with less data at the time of filing) for ANDAs and for supplements. The FDA has published several Scale-Up and Post-Approval Changes (SUPAC) guidelines[7,8] for different types of dosage forms. These guidelines provide suggested stability studies that are expected to support various levels of change to previously approved processes. An approach significantly different from that indicated in the respective SUPAC guideline should be discussed in advance with the FDA to avoid problems with ultimate NDA supplement approval.

BRACKETING AND MATRIXING

For some drug products, there can be a number of variants—different package sizes, different strengths (some with the same formulation), and different packaging/closure arrangements. In such circumstances, the extent of the stability evaluation can become enormous. To accommodate these situations, bracketing and "matrixing" approaches were introduced to reduce the amount of testing required.

Bracketing involves making conclusions about all levels of a parameter based on the evaluation of the extremes. Suggested applications include:

1. Same formulation and container–closure system involving different container sizes and/or different fill volumes
2. Different strengths of the same formulation (e.g., different capsule sizes or different tablet weights from the same granulation)

Matrixing involves a statistical experimental design that allows only a fraction of the total number of samples to be tested at each sampling point. Since fewer tests are performed, there is usually more variability in the data and a shorter predicted shelf life may result. However, this can be "corrected" when more data eventually become available. Matrix designs should be applicable:

1. For the same formulation in different strengths (same granulation)
2. For different but closely related formulations
3. For different sources of bulk drug substance

An example of a matrix design would be a tablet product produced in three strengths (same granulation, different compression weights) and packaged into three different bottle sizes. Three batches of granulation are produced, each of which is compressed into three sublots with the different compression weights. Each of these nine sublots of tablets is then packaged into the three different bottle sizes—27 sets of stability samples. Testing is to be performed at 0, 3, 6, 9, 12, 18, 24, and 36 months.

A complete evaluation would therefore involve 27 × 8 (216) sets of testing. Three alternative matrix designs could be applied. In each of these, all of the different combinations are tested at 0 and 36 months. In a complete one-third design, one-third of the samples are tested at each intermediate point, and in the complete one/two-thirds design, one-third of the samples are tested at some points and two-thirds at others.

This matrix results in the testing of 108 samples—half of the total if all combinations had been tested. The number of samples tested could be further reduced by testing only one sample of each granulation batch (three samples rather than 27) or one sample from each strength of each granulation batch (nine samples rather than 27).

A matrix approach may also be applied to the actual tests performed on the samples—each test need not be performed at each test interval.

It is recommended that bracketing and matrixing proposals should be reviewed and agreed on with the FDA prior to introduction.

Stability Studies Can Be Classified into Three Types

1. Studies, usually under accelerated conditions, to predict a tentative shelf life for a new or modified product or process. For a new drug substance, these studies usually commence with a preformulation evaluation. The effect of stress conditions, such as temperature, humidity, light, acidity, and oxygen can provide much useful information to the formulator. The potential interactive effects of the bulk drug and the anticipated dosage form excipients may also be evaluated. It should also be noted that any ingredient that interferes with the official assay of a USP product automatically makes the product noncompliant with that monograph—regardless of whether an alternate assay has been developed. Where degradation is observed, attempts should be made to identify the decomposition products, since this information could be of value later in developing analytical methodology for product stability studies.

   The accelerated studies at elevated temperatures on the dosage form should allow some extrapolation to provide a tentative shelf life. The ICH guidelines allow extrapolation of six-month data under accelerated conditions with 12 months data at 25°C/60% RH or 30°C/65% RH to predict a shelf life of up to 24 months. Shelf life in excess of 24 months should rarely be extrapolated from accelerated data. There are also some parameters such as dissolution, whose shelf-life performance cannot be predicted from accelerated study data. Consequently, any significant change in dissolution during accelerated studies should be a signal for caution until adequate real-condition data are available.

   For changes in container–closure, formulation, or material supplier, the FDA usually requires accelerated data comparing the revised product with the existing product plus a commitment to continue the stability study. The previously designated shelf life may be retained if there are no observed differences. A similar approach should be used when reprocessed material is incorporated into a batch.

   Where there is a change of manufacturing facility for the dosage form, but using the same process and similar equipment, three months accelerated data may suffice, again with the commitment to monitor the first three commercial batches.

2. Studies under conditions appropriate to the market are used to provide real-time data for confirmation of the predicted tentative shelf life. These studies are usually performed using

controlled environmental cabinets. A typical warehouse may be an acceptable alternative provided temperature and humidity are recorded. For certain physical parameters such as dissolution, tablet fragility and parenteral sterility, accelerated conditions may not provide useful data for extrapolation.

Where such studies demonstrate that the predicted tentative shelf life was too optimistic, it would be necessary to consider recall of released batches.

Real-time studies are also used to extend the defined shelf life when sufficient satisfactory real-time data have been obtained, as defined in the approved ANDA.

3. Stability studies on current production. Once the shelf life is established, it is necessary to evaluate some ongoing batches to confirm that current production is behaving in a similar manner. This is to detect the possible impact of any subtle or unknown changes to the components or process. In the event that a change is observed, it will be necessary to perform a root cause analysis.

At this stage, there should be a considerable amount of available stability data that identify the shelf-life limiting factors. This may allow elimination of some tests. The frequency of testing should also relate to the shelf life.

The FDA is prepared to recommend action, such as a warning letter or seizure, if there is inadequate evidence to support the shelf life. Specific concerns include lack of sterility assurance; lack of, or noncompliance with, a stability program; absence of an expiry date; inadequate test methodology; lack of ongoing stability; lack of assurance of preservative effectiveness; and distribution after expiration date.

The stability requirements for homeopathic products are less demanding than for other drug products. The levels of "active ingredients" are frequently so low that determination of degradation products, or even assay of the active itself, may not be practicable. The requirements allow examination for compatibility as an alternative to testing.

The immediate container and closure play an important role in the product shelf life. They may accelerate degradation reactions, be an additive to or an adsorbent of the drug substance, or be ineffective in protecting the contents from environmental conditions. Four types of containers–closures are commonly analyzed for pharmaceutical preparations: glass, plastic, rubber (natural and synthetic), and metal. Each has characteristic properties that should be recognized.

GLASS

Glass, because of its many variations and resistance to chemical and physical change, is still used as a container material. Several inherent limitations exist with glass:

1. Its alkaline surface may raise the pH of the pharmaceutical and induce chemical reaction.
2. Ionic radicals present in the drug may precipitate insoluble crystals from the glass (such as barium sulfate).
3. The clarity of the glass permits the transmission of high-energy wavelengths of light, which may accelerate physical or chemical reactions in the drug.

To overcome the first two deficiencies, alternate types of commercial glass, each possessing different reactive characteristics, are available. Borosilicate (USP type I) glass contains fewer reactive alkali ions than the other three types of USP-recognized glass. Treatment of glass with heat and/or various chemicals, as well as the use of buffers, can eliminate many ionic problems normally encountered. Amber glass transmits light only at wavelengths above 470 nm, thereby reducing light-induced reactions. When light sensitivity is a stability issue, the secondary packaging, with appropriate labeling, may provide adequate protection.

PLASTICS

These packaging materials include a wide range of polymers of varying density and molecular weight, each possessing different physical and chemical characteristics. Various additives to the polymeric material are often required to provide suitable characteristics for molding, to minimize impact damage or for color. As a result, each must be considered in relation to the pharmaceutical product that will be in contact with it to determine that no undesirable interaction occurs. Several problems are encountered with plastic:

1. Migration of the drug through the plastic into the environment
2. Transfer of environmental moisture, oxygen, and other elements into the pharmaceutical formulation
3. Leaching of container ingredients into the drug
4. Adsorption or absorption of the active drug or excipients by the plastic

Since each plastic possesses intrinsic properties, varying conditions and drug formulations must be tested to optimize stability of the final product by selecting the appropriate container. Again, chemical treatment of the material prior to use may reduce reactivity, migration characteristics, and transmitted light. It must be remembered that neither the drug nor the container should undergo physical or chemical changes that affect the safety and efficacy of the product. The use of light transmission by plastics as a measure of light protection is complicated by the fact that plastics are only semitransparent. Light that is admitted to the container is reflected and diffused back into the product so that light energy available to degradation processes is much higher than that which might be indicated by transmission characteristics. The proper test is a diffuse reflectance measurement. Appropriate testing procedures and specifications are given in the USP.

METALS

Various alloys and aluminum tubes frequently are utilized as containers for emulsions, ointments, creams, and pastes. These materials are generally inert to their contents, although instances of corrosion and precipitation have been noted with products at extreme pH values or those containing metallic ions. Coating the tubes with polymers, epoxy, or other material may reduce these tendencies but impose new stability problems on the pharmaceutical product. The availability of new, less expensive polymers has sharply reduced the use of metal packaging components during the last few years (except for metal screw cap closures).

RUBBER

The problems of extraction of drug ingredients and leaching of container ingredients described for plastics also exist with rubber components. The use of neoprene, butyl, or natural rubber, in combination with certain epoxy, Teflon®, or varnish coatings, substantially reduces drug–container interactions. The pretreatment of rubber vial stoppers and closures with water and steam removes surface blooms and also reduces potential leaching that might affect chemical analysis, toxicity, or pyrogenicity of the drug formulation. The impact of additional treatments, such as siliconization to enhance movement of elastomeric components during handling in production or for plunger action in syringes, must also be evaluated.

§211.167 SPECIAL TESTING REQUIREMENTS

a. *For each batch of drug product purporting to be sterile and/or pyrogen-free, there shall be appropriate laboratory testing to determine conformance to such requirements. The test procedures shall be in writing and shall be followed.*

b. *For each batch of ophthalmic ointment, there shall be appropriate testing to determine conformance to specifications regarding the presence of foreign particles and harsh or abrasive substances. The test procedures shall be in writing and shall be followed.*
c. *For each batch of controlled release dosage form, there shall be appropriate laboratory testing to determine conformance to the specifications for the rate of release of each active ingredient. The test procedures shall be in writing and shall be followed.*

Specific testing requirements for sterile products, ophthalmic ointments, and controlled release products are delineated in this section.

As written, §211.167(a) requires testing to confirm sterility and where appropriate pyrogen testing on each batch of sterile or pyrogen-free product. The necessity for such testing would seem superfluous for terminally sterilized products prepared by the application of validated processes. The sterility test in these circumstances is more a challenge of the technique in the microbiology laboratory than an assurance of sterility. The FDA, which in 1985 approved the replacement of the sterility test by parametric release for certain large-volume parenterals, recognized this.

Parametric Release is a sterility assurance release program where demonstrated control of the sterilization process enables a firm to use defined critical process controls, in lieu of the sterility test to fulfill the intent of 21 CFR 211.165(a) and 211.167(a). The release of each batch is based on satisfactory results from monitoring specific adequately validated terminal sterilization parameters during the terminal sterilization phase(s) of drug product manufacturing. These parameters are more reliable in predicting sterility assurance than is end-product sterility testing because they can generally be more accurately controlled and measured. ICH Q6A: *Specifications: Test Procedures and Acceptance Criteria for New Drug Substances and New Drug Products: Chemical Substances*, October 6, 1999, provides additional details.

The special requirements for ophthalmic ointments relate to the potential presence of abrasive particulate matter. This is of obvious concern in such preparations and especially since metal tubes are frequently used for their packaging. The USP <751>, *Metal Particles in Ophthalmic Ointments*, includes specifications and methodology for the presence of metal particles in ophthalmic ointments. Although metal particles are considered to be the biggest risk, especially from metal tubes, it should be noted that §211.167(b) refers more generally to "foreign particles and harsh or abrasive substances." For products packaged in other configurations, such as plastic tubes, it would seem appropriate to apply the USP metal particle limits and to establish appropriate methodology to allow visualization of other particulate matter.

Subsection (c) refers to controlled release products and is somewhat generic in nature—"there shall be appropriate laboratory testing to determine conformance to the specifications for the rate of release of each active ingredient." Products with the same active ingredients may be formulated by different manufacturers to have different release patterns. This creates no problems with respect to drug registration, but it does for the USP and for the consumer with respect to over-the-counter (OTC) products. The USP is moving toward generic-style monographs, which define ranges for release rates at three or four-time intervals: 0.125, 0.250, 0.500, and 1.00D, where D represents the dosing interval (e.g., 8 hours). Where possible, the criteria defined in the USP for Drug Release <724> will be applied. This allows for different release patterns from different products. The release pattern would be presented on the product label, which allows the knowledgeable consumer some choice.

§211.170 RESERVE SAMPLES

a. *An appropriately identified reserve sample that is representative of each lot in each shipment of each active ingredient shall be retained. The reserve sample consists of at least twice the quantity necessary for all tests required to determine whether the active ingredient meets its established specifications, except for sterility and pyrogen testing. The retention time is as follows:*

1. *For an active ingredient in a drug product other than those described in paragraphs (a) (2) and (3) of this section, the reserve sample shall be retained for 1 year after the expiration date of the last lot of the drug product containing the active ingredient.*

2. *For an active ingredient in a radioactive drug product, except for nonradioactive reagent kits, the reserve sample shall be retained for:*

   i. *Three months after the expiration date of the last lot of the drug product containing the active ingredient if the expiration dating period of the drug product is 30 days or less; or*

   ii. *Six months after the expiration date of the last lot of the drug product containing the active ingredient if the expiration dating period of the drug product is more than 30 days.*

3. *For an active ingredient in an OTC drug product that is exempt from bearing an expiration date under §211.137, the reserve sample shall be retained for 3 years after distribution of the last lot of the drug product containing the active ingredient.*

   The regulations require retention of active ingredients but not of inactive ingredients. This relaxation for inactive ingredients was in response to comments that some materials are hazardous or unstable. However, samples of hazardous or unstable active ingredients are to be retained. It should be noted, however, that European Union (EU) countries require the retention of excipient samples, with varying time periods for their retention.

   The rationale for retaining samples is to allow evaluation in the event of a complaint or query. Consequently, it is prudent to retain samples of all ingredients, active and inactive.

   If a batch of ingredient is delivered on more than one occasion, samples from each delivery are to be retained. This is in line with the evaluation of such deliveries.

b. *An appropriately identified reserve sample that is representative of each lot or batch of drug product shall be retained and stored under conditions consistent with product labeling. The reserve sample shall be stored in the same immediate container–closure system in which the drug product is marketed or in one that has essentially the same characteristics. The reserve sample consists of at least twice the quantity necessary to perform all the required tests, except those for sterility and pyrogens. Except for those drug products described in paragraph (b)(2) of this section, reserve samples from representative sample lots or batches selected by acceptable statistical procedures shall be examined visually at least once a year for evidence of deterioration unless visual examination would affect the integrity of the reserve samples. Any evidence of reserve sample deterioration shall be investigated in accordance with §211.192. The results of the examination shall be recorded and maintained with other stability data on the drug product. Reserve samples of compressed medical gases need not be retained. The retention time is as follows:*

   1. *For a drug product other than those described in paragraphs (b) (2) and (3) of this section, the reserve sample shall be retained for 1 year after the expiration date of the drug product.*

   2. *For a radioactive drug product, except for nonradioactive reagent kits, the reserve sample shall be retained for*

      i. *Three months after the expiration date of the drug product if the expiration dating period of the drug product is 30 days or less; or*

      ii. *Six months after the expiration date of the drug product if the expiration dating period of the drug product is 30 days.*

   3. *For an OTC drug product that is exempt for bearing an expiration date under §211.137, the reserve sample must be retained for 3 years after the lot or batch of drug product is distributed.*

The retention of batch samples of product allows evaluation in the event of complaints or queries. For large package sizes, where product costs and storage space could be a problem, it is acceptable to retain the samples in a smaller version of the immediate container–closure system. The actual storage conditions for retained samples are not defined. It would seem appropriate to use conditions that are reasonably related to those likely to be experienced by the commercial product. This would probably equate to warehouse conditions for products with no special storage requirements. However, this would not be appropriate for a product required to be stored in a refrigerator (see also §211.166).

The FDA acknowledged that the evaluation of all retained batches was a time-consuming exercise. As a consequence, (b) was revised in 1994 to allow evaluation of a statistically selected number of batches only.

The FDA allows the annual review to be omitted if in so doing the integrity of the sample would be affected. For example, if a product is stored in a colored or translucent container that must be kept closed, then visual examination of the dosage form may be impractical. However, examination of the exterior of the container and the label should still be performed. If any problems are noted with these aspects, the quality of the dosage form enclosed in the package may be suspect.

The results of any visual examination may be held with other stability data and need not be entered into individual batch records.

§211.173 LABORATORY ANIMALS

Animals used in testing components, in-process materials, or drug products for compliance with established specifications shall be maintained and controlled in a manner that assures their suitability for their intended use. They shall be identified and adequate records shall be maintained showing the history of their use.

Minimum standards for the care and health of research and test animals are described in the following sources:

1. Animal Welfare Act (7 USC §§2131-2156 as amended 10-20-2013)
2. Title 9, Code of Federal Regulations, §§ 1.1-11.41
3. "Good Laboratory Practice for Nonclinical Laboratory Studies," 21 CFR Part 58
4. *Guide for the Care and Use of Laboratory Animals*, The National Academies Press, 8th Edition, Washington, DC.

In addition to these requirements, current interpretation of GMP would regard animals as sources of product contamination. Considerations such as separate facilities, constructed away from manufacturing areas, with closed water, waste removal, air conditioning, and other systems would, therefore, be ideal. If these are not possible due to construction or other limitations, animal areas should be segregated as far as possible from all production activities with closed air, water, and waste systems, as well as limited personnel access. The same standards of cleanliness prescribed for other work areas are also applicable to these spaces.

Record requirements for animals are necessary to maintain control of their use in experimentation, testing, or assay procedures. Data fields for individual animals should include:

1. Identification number or letter assigned to each animal or group of animals
2. Characteristics and description of animal
3. Source of animals (breeder, vendor)
4. Date of arrival
5. Age at arrival
6. How used
7. Date used

If the animal is to be used for repeated assay procedures, that is, pyrogen testing, a time period sufficient to permit complete clearance of the drug and recovery of the test animal is required.

§211.176 PENICILLIN CONTAMINATION

If a reasonable possibility exists that a nonpenicillin drug product has been exposed to cross contamination with penicillin, the nonpenicillin drug product shall be tested for the presence of penicillin. Such drug product shall not be marketed if detectable levels are found when tested according to procedures specified in "Procedures for Detecting and Measuring Penicillin Contamination in Drugs," which is incorporated by reference. Copies are available from the Division of Research and Testing (HFD-470), Center for Drug Evaluation and Research, FDA, Washington, DC or available for inspection at the Office of the Federal Register, Washington, DC.

It is unacceptable to release a product unless all applicable CGMP requirements have been met. 21 CFR 211.42(d) requires that manufacturing operations for penicillin drug products be performed in facilities separate from those used for nonpenicillin human drug products. Similarly, 21 CFR 211.46(d) requires that air-handling systems for penicillin and nonpenicillin drug products be completely separate. Thus, if a nonpenicillin product is made in a facility that, for example, shares equipment or an air-handling system with a penicillin production area (in violation of § 211.46[d]), the nonpenicillin product cannot be made CGMP-compliant through testing alone. However, if a door is accidentally left open between a penicillin-dedicated area and other separate production areas, resulting in possible exposure of the other areas to penicillin, testing those other products for penicillin could justify their release for distribution. They must be tested using the codified method and found not to be contaminated with penicillin. As per 21 CFR 211.165, all sampling plans and acceptance criteria used for testing and release of the nonpenicillin product, including any testing for penicillin contamination, must be adequate to ensure the tested product meets all of its specifications.

EXAMPLES OF OBSERVATIONS FROM FDA CITATIONS

- There is a failure to thoroughly review any unexplained discrepancy and the failure of a batch or any of its components to meet any of its specifications whether or not the batch has been already distributed.
- Your firm's investigation attributed the results to a sampling error; however, the investigation lacked reporting detail and documentation as to how they made this determination.
- Failure to ensure that test procedures are scientifically sound and appropriate to ensure that key starting materials and intermediate(s) conform to established standards of quality and/or purity.
- Your laboratory uses nonvalidated assays for testing of key starting materials and for an intermediate used in the manufacture of (b)(4) API. Please submit method validation reports to support the scientific validity of these methods. In addition, please submit the validation status of all other noncompendial analytical methods used in your laboratory along with a timeline for completing any necessary validation activities.
- Your release of drug product for distribution did not include appropriate laboratory determination of satisfactory conformance to the identity and strength of each active ingredient prior to release as required by 21 CFR 211.165(a).
- Failure to perform stability testing to determine the appropriate expiration dating period as required by 21 CFR 211.166(b).
- Failure to follow a written stability program designed to assess the stability characteristics of drug products to support a two-year expiration dating period as required by 21 CFR 211.166(a).
- There is no written procedure that describes the visual examination of reserve samples of finished drug products for deterioration. A report titled, "2005 Annual Product Inspection (Visual/Odor)" indicates that all inspected products passed. However, there is no written procedure that describes how the examination is done or that defines the pass/fail criteria. In addition, the lot numbers and number of units examined are not documented in the report.

- Your firm failed to establish a scientifically sound and appropriate test procedure to determine conformance of the finished drug product to an established specification (21 CFR 211.160(b)).
- The accuracy, sensitivity, specificity, and reproducibility of test methods have not been established and documented. Specifically, your firm failed to perform an adequate method validation for xxx Capsules. The current approved analytical procedure for the analysis of [xxxx] for drug release (STM 696, 697, 698, 699, 700) requires the use of [xxxx] as the dissolution media.
- SOP xxxx uses a statistical outlier test to invalidate OOS results; statistical outlier tests are inappropriate for use with validated methods.
- Stability testing SOPs contained no provision for increased testing of either additional lots or additional intervals or shortened intervals after confirmed stability failures.
- There is neither statistical analysis nor graphical representation of the firm's stability data in the annual product reviews.
- There are no data to show that the methods used to analyze stability samples were validated as stability indicating with respect to acid and base hydrolysis, oxidation, thermal degradation, and photolysis.
- Failure to validate the software, which is used to collect raw data from the HPLC units, to integrate peaks and to perform analytical calculations for assaying products.
- The firm used the service of an outside microbiology laboratory for microorganism quantitation and identification. The laboratory had never been audited by the firm.
- There are no criteria established for OOS results defining at what points testing ends, product is evaluated, and rejected if results are not satisfactory.
- Stability test failures not reported to the FDA.

REFERENCES

1. MHRA, GMP *Data Integrity Definitions and Guidance for Industry*, March 2015.
2. WHO, *Guidance on Good Data and Record Management Practices*, May 2016.
3. PIC/S Guidance, *Good Practices for Data Management and Integrity in Regulated GMP/GDP Environments—Draft 2*, August 2016.
4. TGA, *Data Management and Data Integrity*, April 2017.
5. ISPE, GAMP® Guide: Records and Data Integrity, April 2017.
6. FDA Guidance for Industry: Investigating Out-of-Specification (OOS) Test Results for Pharmaceutical Production, October 2006.
7. *Immediate Release Solid Oral Dosage Forms Scale-Up and Post-approval Changes: Chemistry, Manufacturing, and Controls, In Vitro Dissolution Testing, and In Vivo Bioequivalence Documentation*, CDER November 1995.
8. FDA Guidance for Industry: Submission of Documentation in Applications for Parametric Release of Human and Veterinary Drug Products Terminally Sterilized by Moist Heat Processes Parametric Release, FDA February 2010.

SUGGESTED READINGS

- FDA Draft Guidance for Industry: Data Integrity and Compliance With CGMP, April 2016.
- FDA Draft Guidance for Industry: Product Development Under the Animal Rule, May 2014.
- FDA Guidance for Industry: Quality Systems Approach to Pharmaceutical CGMP Regulations, September 2006.
- FDA Draft Guidance for Industry: Comparability Protocols—Chemistry, Manufacturing, and Controls Information, February 2003.
- FDA Guidance for Industry: Q3A Impurities in New Drug Substances, June 2008 ICH Revision 2.

- The FDA Draft Guidance for Industry: Analytical Procedures and Methods Validation for Drugs and Biologics, 2/19/2014.
- FDA Good Laboratory Practice Regulations—Questions and Answers, June 1981.
- FDA Pyrogen and Endotoxins Testing: Questions and Answers, June 2012.
- FDA Validation of Chromatographic Methods—Reviewer's Guidance, 11/1/1994.
- Alex M. Hoinowski, Sol Motola, Richard J. Davis, and James V. McArdle, "Investigation of Out-of-Specification Results," *Pharmaceutical Technology*, January 2002.
- Hafez Abdel-Kader et al., "Analytical Method Comparability in Registration and Post-Approval Stages: A Risk-Based Approach," *Pharmaceutical Technology*, October 2014.
- Heather Bridwell et al., "Perspectives on Method Validation: Importance of Adequate Method Validation," *Pharmaceutical Formulation & Quality*, December/January 2010.
- USP38/NF33: General Notices: 6. Testing Practices and Procedures.
- USP38/NF33: General Chapters:
  - <724> Drug Release.
  - <751> Metal Particles in Ophthalmic Ointments.
  - <905> Uniformity of Dosage Units.
  - <1086> Impurities in Drug Substances and Drug Products.
  - <1097> Bulk Powder Sampling Procedures.
  - <1117> Microbiological Best Laboratory Practices.
  - <1223> Validation of Alternative Microbiological Methods.
  - <1224> Transfer of Analytical Procedures.
  - <1225> Validation of Compendial Procedures.
  - <1226> Verification of Compendial Procedures.
  - <1033> Biological Assay Validation.
  - <1086> Impurities in Drug Substances and Drug Products.
- ICH Harmonised Tripartite Guidelines:
  - Q1A(R2): Stability Testing of New Drug Substances and Products, February 6, 2003.
  - Q1B: Stability Testing: Photostability Testing of New Drug Substances and Products, November 6, 1996.
  - Q1C: Stability Testing for New Dosage Forms Annex to the ICH Harmonised Tripartite Guideline on Stability Testing for New Drugs and Products, November 6, 1996
  - Q1D: Bracketing and Matrixing Designs for Stability Testing of New Drug Substances and Products, February 7, 2002.
  - Q1E: Evaluation for Stability Data, February 6, 2003.
  - Q1F: Stability Data Package for Registration Applications in Climatic Zones III and IV, February 6, 2003.
  - Q2(R1): Validation of Analytical Procedures: Text and Methodology, November 2005.
  - Q3A(R2): Impurities in New Drug Substances, October 25, 2006.
  - Q3B(R2): Impurities in New Drug Products, June 2, 2006.
  - Q3C(R5): Impurities: Guideline for Residual Solvents, February 4, 2011.
  - Q3D: Guideline for Elemental Impurities, December 16, 2014.
  - Q3: Decision Trees (associated with Impurities).
  - Q6A: Specifications: Test Procedures and Acceptance Criteria for New Drug Substances and New Drug Products: Chemical Substances, October 6, 1999.
  - Q6B: Specifications: Test Procedures and Acceptance Criteria for Biotechnological/Biological Products, March 10, 1999.
  - Q6A: Decision Trees.
- FDA Guide to Inspection of Pharmaceutical Quality Control Laboratories, July 1993.
- United States of America v. Barr Laboratories Inc. et al. Defendants, No. CIV A 92-1744, United States District Court, D. New Jersey, February 5, 1993.

- *Animal Welfare Act* (7 USC §§2131-2156 as amended 10-20-2013).
- Good Laboratory Practice for Nonclinical Laboratory Studies, 21 CFR Part 58.
- *Guide for the Care and Use of Laboratory Animals*, The National Academies Press Eight Edition, Washington, DC.
- Immediate Release Solid Oral Dosage Forms Scale-Up and Post-approval Changes: Chemistry, Manufacturing, and Controls, In Vitro Dissolution Testing, and In Vivo Bioequivalence Documentation, CDER November 1995.
- FDA Guidance for Industry: Submission of Documentation in Applications for Parametric Release of Human and Veterinary Drug Products Terminally Sterilized by Moist Heat Processes Parametric Release, FDA February 2010.
- FDA Guidance for Industry: CMC Post-approval Manufacturing Changes to Be Documented in Annual Reports, FDA March 2014.

19 Microbiological Aspects of Pharmaceutical Aseptic Processing in the Compounding Pharmacy

Dawn McIver

CONTENTS

This chapter will discuss the microbiological aspects of aseptic processing in the compounding pharmacy. This includes microbiological aspects of facility qualification, contamination control methodologies, the disinfection program, environmental sampling, performing media fills, and product testing.

BACKGROUND

USP <797> Pharmaceutical Compounding—Sterile Preparations was published for the first time on January 1, 2004.[1] The most recent version of the chapter became effective May 1, 2016. This chapter details risk levels and responsibilities for compounding sterile preparations in hospital and health-care institutions, patient treatment clinics, pharmacies, and other locations where compounded sterile products (CSPs) are prepared, stored and transported.

On November 27, 2013, the Drug Quality and Security Act (DQSA) was signed into law. Title 1 of the new law, the Compounding Quality Act, requires compliance of compounding pharmacies with current good manufacturing practices, Section 501(a)(2)(B).

With the implementation of these documents, the auditing and responsibilities for compliance, which was previously held by the state pharmacy boards, was added to the responsibilities of the FDA. Compounders that register as 503(b) facilities for human drug compounding are now required to comply with good manufacturing practices (GMP). This chapter attempts to interpret and simplify the requirements for compounding pharmacies to facilitate compliance.

Drugs that are made in compounding facilities, including those that are produced in facilities registered for human drug compounding are not considered FDA approved.

Many of the requirements specified in USP <797>[1] depend on the risk classification of the compounding being performed. In order to discuss the requirements, first, some definitions of risk levels are needed. Low-risk CSPs are those that are compounded entirely within an ISO 5 area, using only sterile ingredients, products, components, and devices. To be considered low risk, no more than three sterile ingredients may be combined. Storage conditions must be less than 48 hours at controlled room temperature (RT), no more than 14 days at cold temperature, or no more than 45 days at −25°C to −10°C.

Medium risk CSPs include multi-dose products, either for multiple patients or for the same patient on multiple occasions. It also includes formulations that involve complex manipulations or processes that are lengthy, such as dissolution or mixing. Storage conditions must be less than 30 hours at controlled RT, no more than 9 days at cold temperature or no more than 45 days at −25°C to −10°C.

High-risk CSPs include those products that are prepared by dissolving nonsterile bulk drug and nutrient powders to make solutions that are then terminally sterilized. These also include products where sterile ingredients and components are exposed to air quality that does not meet ISO 5 for more than one hour.

FACILITY QUALIFICATION

The facility design is an integral part of the GMP compounding environment. Qualification of the facility and continued demonstration of adherence to the ISO standard are a key part of the contamination control program. Facilities should be designed to minimize airborne viable contamination and to keep contamination from reaching the designated compounding area surfaces. Sterile preparations classified as low-risk level are to be compounded in an ISO 5 environment, which is surrounded by an ISO 7 Buffer Zone. For low-level, medium-level, and high-level risk processes, an ISO 8 area surrounding the buffer zone is specified. These classifications originate with ISO 14644-1[2] and are based on the number of 0.5 μm particles. The maximum allowable levels are shown below (Table 19.1).

The most common sources of ISO 5 air quality are horizontal and vertical laminar airflow workbenches, compounding aseptic isolators (CAIs), and compounding aseptic containment isolators

TABLE 19.1

Maximum Allowable 0.5 μ Particles/m³ for the ISO Class

ISO Class Number (N)	Maximum Allowable Concentrations (0.5 μ particles/m³)
5	3,520
7	352,000
8	3,520,000

(CACIs). These are referred to as process engineering controls (PECs). These PECs include unidirectional airflow at a velocity that allows for sweeping of particles from the compounding area. Smoke studies are used to demonstrate proper airflow is maintained.

Pressure differentials are utilized between areas that are different classifications. A minimum differential pressure of −0.02 to −0.05-inch water column. For buffer areas that are not physically separated from the Ante-Areas, the principle of displacement is utilized. Using this principle requires an air velocity of 40 feet per minute. Pressure differentials need to be routinely monitored and recorded.

Media fills are performed in order to qualify the environment and the compounding process, as well as to qualify the personnel who will be performing the compounding. Media fills consist of utilizing sterile growth media to perform the most challenging compounding process that is performed in that controlled area. Trypticase soy agar (TSA) is typically utilized for this purpose. After manipulation of the media, the samples are incubated at 20°C to 25°C or 30°C to 35°C for 14 days or a combination of the two temperatures for 7 days each. Media is examined visually to determine whether contamination is present, which is evidenced by visible growth or turbidity of media. This qualification is performed initially when a new compounding area is commissioned and then annually for low- and medium-risk CSPs or twice per year for high-risk CSPs. All compounding personnel are required to qualify and requalify by performing media fills. Procedures are needed to define the media fill process. This should include rationale for what manipulations are performed, what containers and closures are utilized, and details regarding the manipulations to be performed. The duration and complexity of the media fill needs to mimic the worst-case process.

Selection of environmental sampling sites for the qualification of ISO 5 areas, buffer zones, and Ante-Rooms should be based on a number of factors. First, the minimum number of sites for particle count monitoring is determined based on Table A.1 presented in ISO 14644-1[2] and is based on the area of the room or PEC being monitored. Sites need to be selected based on risk factors, such as personnel activity, airflow, and possible sources of contamination.

For viable monitoring, ISO 14698-1[3] provides some guidance. The standard does not specify a minimum number of sampling sites but instead relies on the users of the area, along with Quality Assurance to perform a risk assessment to determine the monitoring to be performed, including the number of sites, frequency, and sampling methods. In many facilities, the number of sites that are collected for airborne viable monitoring will be established to match the number of particle counts specified in ISO 14644-1[2]. The rationale for this approach is that when monitoring is performed both airborne particle counts and airborne viable counts in the same area will provide a more complete picture of potential contamination issues in the area. These two pieces of information together provide the most complete environmental "picture." In cases where issues are detected, having this information can improve the investigation process and assist in determining the root cause of the excursion.

Performing a Hazard Analysis Critical Control Point (HACCP) risk assessment of the compounding process is an effective way to gather information, rank risks associated with the process, and document the rationale for site selection for environmental sampling. This methodology is common in food manufacturing and pharmaceutical manufacturing facilities.[4,5] It is a technique that is also applicable and useful for compounding pharmacies.

CONTAMINATION CONTROL

In order to qualify a facility and to maintain the facility in a state of control, continued efforts must be made to maintain a consistent contamination control program. This includes establishing criteria for personnel garbing (gowning), cleaning and disinfection of the controlled area, and controlling incoming materials. A breakdown in any of these controls, and contamination control can be in jeopardy.

GARBING

The level of personnel cleaning and garbing required varies with the processes to be performed as well as the classification of the area. The following table contains the minimum garbing levels that can be considered under various process situations and the personnel cleaning that is detailed in USP <797>[1] (Table 19.2).

CHOOSING CLEANERS AND DISINFECTANTS

Disinfectant choices are a critical aspect of contamination control. When selecting a disinfectant, a number of factors need to be considered. First, the types of surfaces that need to be cleaned. Second, the types or organisms that are present in the environment and criticality of the environment. Choose disinfectants from reputable vendors who have performed testing to demonstrate effectiveness. Keep in mind that disinfectants and sporicidal agents only work on surfaces that are clean. If a surface is covered with a layer of dirt, dust, product, or other residue, the disinfectant will be bound up and rendered ineffective. For the most effective disinfection, surfaces will be cleaned and then disinfected. Although isopropyl alcohol is an effective sanitizer, it does not contain a surfactant and is not suitable for cleaning. Many disinfectants are available that contain surfactants for cleaning as well as disinfectants. These types of products can eliminate the need to pre-clean the surfaces and can be good choices for routine cleaning and disinfection. Keep in mind that these disinfectants are not especially effective against spore-forming organisms and mold. In some cases, surfaces may be wiped with water to remove product residues or dust prior to disinfection.

Sporicidal agents are critical to eliminate molds and spore-forming bacteria, such as *Bacillus* sp. Sporicidal agents need to be part of the overall program for disinfecting the facility and should be

TABLE 19.2

Minimum Garbing Levels Considered Under Various Process Situations and the Personnel Cleaning: USP <797>

ISO Classification	Process Being Performed	Garbing and Personnel Cleaning (In order)
Prior to entry into the controlled area, personnel must remove personal outer garments, including coats, hats, scarves, bandanas, sweaters, and vests. All cosmetics and all visible jewelry must also be removed. Natural nails must be neat and trimmed.		
ISO 7 or ISO 8 (Ante-Area)	First layer of controlled area that separates uncontrolled area from controlled area; Support activities such as weighing and mixing for high-risk level CSPs	Dedicated shoes or shoe covers; Hair cover; Beard cover; Face mask; Fingernail cleaning, hand and forearm washing and drying; Non-shedding gown
ISO 7 (Ante-Area)	Buffer area for ISO 5 where aseptic compounding occurs	In addition to the requirements to enter the Ante-Area additional hand cleaning with a persistently active alcohol-based product with persistent activity is required; After allowing hands to dry; Sterile gloves.
ISO 5 area, laminar air flow hood/biological safety cabinet (LAFH/BSC) where compounding occurs	Compounding products	Sterile gloves are last step prior to beginning compounding activities. For added sterility assurance, consider two pairs of sterile gloves and sterile gown.
ISO 5	Closed CAIs and CACIs	Sterile gloves are last step prior to beginning compounding activities. For added sterility assurance, consider two pairs of sterile gloves.

considered for wiping down all materials that are passed into cleanrooms. No single product can meet all the cleaning and disinfection needs of a cleanroom facility. An overall program should include a cleaner, disinfectant, sanitizer, and sporicidal agent. The frequencies for cleaning and disinfection should directly relate to the criticality of the processes being performed, the frequency of operations in the area, and the environmental monitoring data that is being generated. Specific minimum frequencies are specified in USP <797>[1]. These include cleaning ISO 5 areas at the beginning of each shift and at least every 30 minutes when compounding activities are occurring, after spills, and when surface contamination is suspected. Counters and other cleanable surfaces and floors are to be disinfected daily. Walls, ceilings and storage shelving are to be disinfected a minimum of monthly.

PREPARATION OF DISINFECTANTS/SANITIZERS AND SPORICIDAL AGENTS

Once agents have been chosen, it is important that they are prepared as instructed by the manufacturer. This means measuring accurately, so the facility needs to be equipped with pipettes or graduated cylinders to measure concentrated disinfectants and water that is added. For critical cleanroom applications, the solutions need to be sterile so they need to be prepared and then filter sterilized or purchased sterile.

DISINFECTANT APPLICATION

The materials that are used to apply disinfectants are a critical consideration to get the best cleaning and disinfection. If mops are used, they should be clean and non-shedding. Mops that are specifically designed for cleanrooms are the best choice.

Once solutions have been prepared they need to be applied in a consistent manner, to ensure that all surfaces are contacted, like painting a surface. To ensure the best coverage, start in the furthest corner of the area being cleaned, work systematically across or down the surface, always consistent in the methodology. Do not go over the same surface multiple times; just wipe the disinfectant on and move over to the next area. If using a mop, a multiple bucket system can be employed to ensure cleaner application. For this method, two buckets are used so that one bucket can rinse the bulk debris from the mop and the second bucket can be used to pick up clean disinfectant. When using a wipe to clean, wipe the surface and then fold the wipe to expose a clean surface frequently. If the wipe becomes visibly soiled, discard it and replace with a new wipe. After application, ensure that the disinfectants are given adequate contact time. Disinfectants do not work on contact. After wiping or applying with a mop, allow the disinfectant the minimum contact time specified by the manufacturer before proceeding with use of the equipment or facility. Allow the surface to air dry and ensure that surfaces are maintained in a clean, dry state.

QUALIFICATION OF DISINFECTANTS

Disinfectants need to be qualified for use. USP <1072>[6] gives guidance for the methodology for qualifying disinfectants. This qualification is an extension of what the vendors perform when they put a disinfectant on the market. This qualification incorporates the materials of construction that are used in your particular cleanroom and should include testing organisms that are actually recovered from your facility. This will ensure that the disinfectants will work effectively in your cleanroom. This testing is typically done by coupons that are the same materials as the cleanroom, such as walls, floors, hoods, doors, conveyors, and isolator gloves.

For disinfectant qualification, the contact time is a critical parameter to consider. Typically, 5–10 minutes will yield the required log reduction. Ensure that the time that is qualified matches the contact time that will be routinely applied in the manufacturing area under real-time use.

DISINFECTANT HOLD TIMES

Another factor to consider is the hold time of the disinfectant after it is prepared. This should be considered when setting up your disinfectant study. If the disinfectant will be held routinely for seven days after preparation, then the disinfectant used for the study should see that same hold time prior to testing. This data will provide evidence that the practices routinely employed do not compromise the effectiveness of the solution.

MAINTENANCE OF THE DISINFECTION PROGRAM—CHANGE CONTROL

Like all validated processes, the disinfection program should be included in the change control program. No changes should be made to procedures, cleaning solutions or disinfectants, cleaning frequencies, or materials of construction of the cleanroom without consideration of the impact of the change on the qualification of the disinfection program.

TRAINING THE CLEANING STAFF

The cleaning staff is one of the most important assets in the facility. A good crew that is adequately trained can ensure that the facility is in a state of control. The crew should be trained on all aspects of cleaning, including the preparation of disinfectants, handling and preparing the tools for cleaning, the appropriate water to the used, the hold times of solution, and the proper order of application. It is important that the procedures are accessible to the cleaning crew and are written clear and concise and in a language that can be understood by those who are performing the cleaning. Clear, concise forms for documenting the cleaning steps as they are performed will ensure that the process is performed consistently and that documentation is available to verify the cleaning was performed accurately.

MATERIAL TRANSFER

Transferring materials into the cleanroom or ISO 5 area is an often-overlooked factor in contamination control. As materials are brought in, they need to be cleaned and disinfected or sterilized. Wiping down materials needs to be performed much the same way that cleanroom cleaning is done, systematic, with one-way wiping and adhering to contact times that are qualified for the disinfectants used. Materials that can be purchased double or triple bagged can be passed in by removing an outer layer of packaging.

If materials need to be transferred on carts, every effort should be made to employ a cart-to-cart transfer method. For this method, one cart is left inside the cleaner area, and the second cart is passed into the pass-through area but kept on the "dirty" side. The receiving cart is wiped down with disinfectant. Materials are then disinfected as they are transferred from the incoming cart to the cart on the clean side.

ENVIRONMENTAL SAMPLING (ES)

Environmental sampling is performed to qualify the areas where compounding will be performed to ensure that controlled areas remain in a state of control. USP <1116>[7] provides guidance on sampling. No one method for monitoring can tell a complete story, so a number of different methods are typically employed. A complete program will include particulate monitoring, active airborne viable monitoring, and surface monitoring. Surface monitoring is performed with either contact plates or swabs depending on the surface being monitored. Sampling is performed when an area is initially commissioned, following any servicing of the facility or equipment, as part of recertification (every six months), in response to problems with end products, staff technique, or products.

In addition, gloved fingertip monitoring is performed to qualify new compounders and to recertify personnel during media fills.

Particulate monitoring is performed to determine the number of total particles in a defined sample size (typically m^3). The count reflects all particles in that volume of air including dust, lint, fibers, and viable organisms. There is no way to differentiate using this method whether the count reflects non-viable or viable particles, but the biggest advantage of particulate monitoring is that data is available as soon as the sample is collected and issues can be detected in real time. A variety of manufacturers produce particle monitoring instruments. Selecting a sampler should include consideration of calibration methods, sampling time needed to collect the desired sample size, ease of use, and the ability of the sampler to print out and store retrievable results.

Active airborne viable monitoring is performed a minimum of every six months as well to determine the number of viable (live) organisms in a given volume of air. An air sampler containing microbiological growth media is used to collect the organisms that are present in the air and allow them to grow to levels that allows them to be seen. The number of colonies on a media plate after incubation is counted and reported per volume of air collected. Selecting a viable air sampler should include consideration of calibration methods, sampling time needed to collect the desired sample size, ease of use, size of sampling plates that are used in the sampler, and whether or not the sampler can be easily transported to the sampling sites selected.

Surface monitoring is another important part of the environmental sampling program. This monitoring employs either a contact plate containing microbiological media or a swab to collect organisms from the surfaces in the cleanroom. This monitoring is performed to determine the effectiveness of the cleaning program and to monitor the state of the surfaces where critical activities area occurring. Contact plates are curved so the media can be touched directly to the surface to be sampled. Organisms that are present on the surfaces cling to the media and once the plates are incubated colonies become visible and can be enumerated and identified. Swabs are used on surfaces that are not suitable for contact plates and in areas where it is not appropriate to touch the surfaces with microbiological media. Typically, the swab is wetted with a diluent, the swab is wiped across the surface to be sampled, and then placed into the diluent. The diluent is then transported to the laboratory and either added to growth media for a presence/absence test (qualitative) or filtered and enumerated for a quantitative result. Organisms from environmental sampling are identified if they exceed recommended levels. All organisms should be characterized by gram stain to determine the type of flora present in the facility.

Gloved fingertip sampling is performed using contact plates containing TSA with neutralizers. A sample is collected from the fingertips and thumb of both hands by lightly pressing on the agar surface.

Incubation of plates from active air monitoring, surface monitoring, and gloved fingertip sampling are incubated and enumerated. TSA plates, with and without neutralizers, incubate at 30°C to 35°C for 48 to 72 hours and malt extract agar (MEA) plates incubate at 26°C to 30°C for 5 to 7 days. TSA is typically utilized for detection of bacteria, and MEA is typically employed for growth of fungi. If the levels of organism detected are elevated, it can indicate that the HVAC system is not effectively filtering the air or that the actions occurring in the controlled area are generating organisms. Typically, this data is trended and used to determine whether an area is operating in a state of control. Regardless of the number of organisms detected, actions to be taken are to be based on the identification of the organisms detected. A genus-level identification is expected. Highly pathogenic organisms require remediation regardless of count. The following table is summarized from recommendations given in USP <797>[1] and is presented only as a guideline (Table 19.3).

TABLE 19.3
Microbial Limits Relative to the ISO Class Summarized from USP <797>

Classification	Air Sample (cfu/cubic meter)	Surface Sample (cfu/plate)	Gloved Fingertip (cfu/sample)
ISO Class 5	>1	>3	>3
ISO Class 7	>10	>5	N/A
ISO Class 8 or worse	>100	>100	N/A

STERILIZATION METHODS

Methods for terminal sterilization of compounded materials vary depending on the material to be sterilized. These methods include steam sterilization, dry-heat sterilization (depyrogenation), gas sterilization (frequently ethylene oxide), ionizing radiation (gamma and E-beam), and sterilization by filtration.

Compounded products that are considered high risk require terminal sterilization. USP <1211>[8] provides information regarding the details of each type of sterilization and the requirements for validating the sterilization process.

STERILITY TESTING

Sterility testing methods are described in USP <71>[9]. This testing is required for compounded products when they are stored for durations longer than specified in Chapter <797>[1] for each risk level. Sterility testing is required for all high-risk CSPs that are prepared in groups of 25 or more or in multi-dose vials for administration to multiple patients or that are exposed longer than 12 hours at 2°C to 8°C and longer than 6 hours at warmer than 8°C before they are sterilized. Membrane filtration is the preferred test method. Direct INOCULATION may be performed if membrane filtration is not feasible. Qualification of the sterility test methods is performed by determining and demonstrating the methodology that can be used to test samples that overcome any bacteriostatic or fungistatic effects that the products may exhibit. This is an important part of compliance with USP <71>[9].

ENDOTOXIN TESTING

This testing is performed according to USP <85>[10] and is required for all high-risk CSPs that are prepared in groups of 25 or more or in multi-dose vials for administration to multiple patients or that are exposed longer than 12 hours at 2°C to 8°C and longer than 6 hours at warmer than 8°C before they are sterilized. Limits for endotoxin in these products are to meet USP <85>[10] based on the route of administration or compendial limits where they are published. Qualification of the endotoxin test methods is performed by determining and demonstrating the methodology that can be used to test samples that overcome any inhibition or enhancement of the test that the products may exhibit. This is an important part of compliance with USP <85>[10].

SUMMARY

In summary, the safety and efficacy of compounded products is crucial. A comprehensive contamination control program is needed to ensure the safety of these products. This includes engineering controls, facility qualification, ongoing cleaning and disinfection, and contamination control practices that are performed consistently. Documentation of all these measures helps to ensure they are consistent, measurable, and traceable. Testing the environment and the products further documents that the controls have been effective.

EXAMPLES OF OBSERVATIONS FROM FDA CITATIONS

- Your firm failed to use adequate contact times for sporicidal agents used as part of your disinfection program for the aseptic processing area.
- Your firm failed to establish and follow appropriate written procedures that are designed to prevent microbiological contamination of drug products purporting to be sterile, and that include validation of all aseptic and sterilization processes (21 CFR 211.113[b]).
- Your firm does not have, for each batch of drug product purporting to be sterile and/or pyrogen-free, appropriate laboratory determination of satisfactory conformance to final specifications for the drug product (21 CFR 211.167[a]).

- Your firm failed to establish and follow an adequate written testing program designed to assess the stability characteristics of drug products and to use results of such stability testing to determine appropriate storage conditions and expiration dates (21 CFR 211.166[a]).
- Your firm's sole entrance to the sterile compounding room, where aseptic production occurs, is through a small unclassified vestibule, which has carpeting on the floor.
- The investigators observed that your firm used a non-sterile cleaning and disinfecting agent on the ISO 5 classified work surfaces, and that your sporicidal agent's contact time was insufficient to ensure efficacy. In addition, investigators observed a gap in the ceiling tile located above of the aseptic production area. The investigators also found that your firm did not perform post-filtration integrity testing of the filter used to sterilize drugs intended to be sterile according to the manufacturer's recommendation. Also, your firm failed to demonstrate, through appropriate studies, that your hoods are able to provide adequate protection of the ISO 5 areas where sterile products are processed.
- Your firm performed poor aseptic practices, including:
  a. An operator that (b)(4) by placing gloved hands directly over open sterile containers.
  b. An operator stoppering product vials and touching product contact surfaces of the sterile stoppers with their gauntlet gloves during sterile drug production.
- Your (b)(4) was located on a table of laminated wood with an exposed wood cutout, which may harbor contamination and is difficult to clean and disinfect.
- Your (b)(4) ceiling tiles had numerous unsealed gaps between the ceiling tiles surrounding the (b)(4) filter and above the (b)(4).
- Your (b)(4) was visibly dirty. Specifically, the main chamber had reddish-orange spots on the interior surface, crystal-like residues along the interior of the viewing windows, and a yellowish debris-like material on (b)(4).

REFERENCES

1. United States Pharmacopeia, USP 39, Chapter <797> Pharmaceutical Compounding-Sterile Preparations, In *US Pharmacopoeia* 2018.
2. ISO 14644-1:2015(E) Cleanrooms and associated controlled Environments—Part 1: Classification of air cleanliness by particle concentration.
3. ISO 14698-1 (E) Cleanrooms and associated environments—Biocontamination Control—Part 1: General principles and methods.
4. WHO Technical Report Series, No. 908, 2003, Annex 7, Application of Hazard Analysis and Critical Control Point (HACCP) Methodology to Pharmaceuticals.
5. International Conference on Harmonization of Technical Requirements for Registration of Pharmaceuticals for Human Use, ICH Harmonized Tripartite Guideline, Quality Risk Management Q9, June 2006.
6. United States Pharmacopeia, USP 39, Chapter <1072> Disinfectants and Antiseptics, In *US Pharmacopoeia* 2018.
7. United States Pharmacopeia, USP 39, Chapter <1116> Microbiological Control and Monitoring of Aseptic Processing Environments, In *US Pharmacopoeia* 2018.
8. United States Pharmacopeia, USP 39, Chapter <1211> Sterilization and Sterility Assurance of Compendial Articles, In *US Pharmacopoeia* 2018.
9. United States Pharmacopeia, USP 39, Chapter <71> Sterility Testing, In *US Pharmacopoeia* 2018.
10. United States Pharmacopeia, USP 39, Chapter <85> Bacterial Endotoxins Test, In *US Pharmacopoeia* 2018.

SUGGESTED READINGS

- Current Good Manufacturing Practice—Interim Guidance for Human Drug Compounding Outsourcing Facilities Under Section 503B of the FD&C Act, Draft Guidance for Industry, FDA July 2014.
- Facility Definition Under Section 503B of the Federal Food, Drug, and Cosmetic Act Guidance for Industry, FDA May 2018.
- Case 1:14-cr-10363-RGS *SEALED* Document 1 Filed 12/16/14 United States District Court District of Massachusetts v. New England Compounding Company.

20 CGMP Enforcement Alternatives in the United States

Daniel G. Jarcho and Cathy L. Burgess

CONTENTS

The U.S. Food and Drug Administration (FDA) has a comprehensive arsenal of remedies that it can invoke to enforce current good manufacturing practice (CGMP) requirements for drugs. These remedies range from informal demands to formal agency regulatory proceedings. To pursue an enforcement case in court, the FDA must rely upon the U.S. Department of Justice to bring the case, because the FDA has no legal authority to litigate its own enforcement lawsuits. However, in such court cases, the FDA still is a driving force behind the legal claims asserted and the strategies pursued.

RECALLS

A recall is one remedy for marketed drugs manufactured under conditions involving significant CGMP violations. By definition, a recall is "a firm's removal or correction of a marketed product that [the FDA] considers to be in violation of the laws it administers and against which the agency would initiate legal action...."[1] If a firm has manufactured marketed drugs under conditions involving more minor CGMP violations for which the FDA would not initiate legal action (or under conditions involving no violations), the removal or correction of the drugs is defined as a "market withdrawal" (and not a "recall").[2]

The FDA characterizes drug recalls as "voluntary" actions by the affected firm.[3] Many observers are surprised to learn that the FDA has no legal authority to mandate a recall of drugs to remedy regulatory violations (including CGMP violations). The agency's mandatory recall authority is

---

[1] 21 CFR § 7.3(g).

[2] *Ibid.* § 7.3(j). Removal or correction of a product that has not been marketed, or that has not left the direct control of the firm, is a "stock recovery" (and not a "recall"). *Ibid.* § 7.3(k).

[3] *Ibid.* § 7.40(a).

limited to other types of FDA-regulated products (such as medical devices and food).[4] Although drug recalls are deemed voluntary, the agency has substantial power to insist that recalls must occur. The FDA usually makes a prompt demand for a recall as soon as it is informed of a situation for which the agency believes a recall is needed. The agency backs its demand with the implicit or explicit threat of adverse publicity—through an FDA press release or public warning—if the firm does not pursue the recall. Few firms decide to suffer the risk of such publicity, and it therefore is commonplace for firms to pursue recalls demanded by the FDA. The firm also has another incentive to pursue a recall demanded by the FDA; there is a possibility that the agency could initiate a seizure of drugs that are not recalled, particularly if they present a serious public health risk. Because an informal demand for a recall is typically so effective, it is rare that the agency must pursue the procedure of a "Food and Drug Administration-requested recall," which is a formal written demand for a recall (also characterized as "voluntary" but backed by a threat of adverse publicity if the recall is not pursued).[5]

It may seem perplexing, at first, that an agency as powerful as the FDA lacks legal authority to mandate a recall of drugs. However, agency enforcement officials generally prefer the informal procedure described above instead of the more formal process that a mandatory recall would require. A formal mandatory recall process would include due process rights for the affected firm (such as the ability to contest the recall in an administrative hearing).[6] A hearing like that would be cumbersome, and delay prompt action, when the FDA believes a recall is necessary to protect the public health. The informal procedure that the FDA pursues for drugs is much nimbler, because the affected firm typically has no procedural rights through which it could object to the agency's recall demands. In addition, because of its informal character, an agency request for "voluntary" action (coupled with a threat of adverse publicity) may not provide the basis for a successful legal challenge by the affected firm.[7] Because an FDA recall demand is so potent—and typically leaves the affected firm without a realistic means of challenging it if the firm disagrees with the agency's position—it is imperative for FDA officials to use good judgment when deciding whether to demand a recall, and if so, what its scope should be.

The risk of adverse publicity noted above may be reduced, but certainly not eliminated, if the firm does pursue the recall. If there is a situation in which drugs may pose a significant health hazard and recalled product is in the hands of consumers, the FDA typically demands that the firm must issue its own press release. The FDA asks to review the press release in advance. If the firm refuses to issue the press release (or issues a press release that the agency deems inadequate), the FDA will issue its own press release.[8]

FDA guidance addresses the level or "depth" of recall that may be necessary.[9] The depth of a recall is the level to which notification is required (i.e., wholesale, retail, or consumer). In the case of a product distribution that has reached consumers, the FDA advises a "sub-recall" or instructions to retailers to initiate mini-recalls of the distributed product.[10]

The FDA publishes reports of recalls in the Enforcement Report posted on the agency's website. The Enforcement Report includes recall classifications designating the FDA's assessment of the relative hazard presented by a product. A Class I recall occurs when there is a "reasonable probability" that the violative product will result in serious adverse health risk or death. A Class II recall occurs when the violative product "may cause temporary or medically reversible" adverse health impacts, or there is a remote risk of serious health consequences. A Class III recall occurs when the violative product is unlikely to cause adverse health outcomes.[11]

---

[4] Food & Drug Admin., Guidance for Industry: Product recalls, including removals and corrections (2003), *available at* http://www.fda.gov/Safety/Recalls/IndustryGuidance/ucm129259.htm [Hereinafter Product Recalls Guidance].

[5] *See* 21 CFR § 7.45.

[6] *See, e.g.,* 21 USC § 360h(e)(1)(B) (requiring informal hearing before FDA can mandate medical device recall); *Ibid.* § 350l(c) (requiring informal hearing before FDA can mandate food recall).

[7] *See, e.g., Trudeau v. Federal Trade Comm'n,* 456 F.3d 178 (D.C. Cir. 2006) (affirming dismissal of claims alleging harm from agency press release).

[8] Product Recalls Guidance, at 6–7.

[9] *Ibid.* at 7.

[10] *Ibid.*

[11] 21 CFR § 7.3(m).

ADVISORY ACTIONS

WARNING LETTERS

Warning Letters are the FDA's principal means of achieving prompt voluntary compliance with requirements of the Federal Food, Drug, and Cosmetic Act (FDCA)—including CGMP requirements. Warning Letters notify firms of violations that have regulatory significance, (i.e., those that may lead to enforcement action by the FDA if not promptly and adequately corrected).[12] Warning Letters notify top management of the severity and scope of the identified violations, achieve voluntary compliance/corrective actions, prevent recurrence, and establish prior notice of violations. Warning Letters are advisory in that they do not commit the FDA to take any particular enforcement action. Warning Letters also are not a prerequisite for the FDA to take enforcement action.[13] If an establishment does not take corrective action, documentation that the agency provided prior notice may strengthen its position in an enforcement action.[14]

For domestic inspections, the recommendation for the issuance of a Warning Letter typically begins at a District Office, where the letter is drafted within 15 working days after the completion of the inspection, and then circulated to the applicable Center for review and concurrence.[15] The Center has 15 working days from receipt of the District's Warning Letter recommendation to review and notify the District of its position.[16]

FDA attorneys at the Office of Chief Counsel also have had a role in reviewing and approving Warning Letters, given that they assert claims of legal violations. The extent of attorney review has evolved over time. In 2001 and 2002, the FDA implemented a procedure for FDA attorneys to review all Warning Letters for legal sufficiency and consistency with agency policy. In 2009 and 2010, the FDA changed those procedures, limiting attorney review of Warning Letters to those addressing a specific list of legal issues. Under the 2009/2010 procedures, the FDA does not require attorney review and approval for Warning Letters that only address drug CGMP violations.[17]

After a Warning Letter is issued, the District or the Center may initiate follow-up action if it finds that the facility's response is inadequate, or if the facility fails to respond to the Warning Letter.[18] If a response to a Warning Letter appears adequate, the FDA will verify that commitments have been fulfilled and corrections achieved, typically through a follow-up inspection.[19] Once that verification occurs, if the follow-up does not identify other significant violations, the FDA will issue a close-out letter indicating that the Warning Letter issues have been adequately addressed.[20] The FDA publishes the date of close-out letters on its Warning Letter Web page.

Warning Letters have significant consequences. Redacted Warning Letters are posted on the FDA's Warning Letter Web page. Third parties may request copies of Warning Letters under the Freedom of Information Act.[21] Such publicity may have a negative impact on the manufacturer and public perceptions of its products. Publicity also may lead to products liability lawsuits. In addition, the FDA routinely advises other federal agencies of Warning Letters so that the other agencies may take them into account when considering the award or renewal of government contracts.

[12] Food & Drug Admin., Warning Letters, in Regulatory Procedures Manual 4-1-1 (2018), *available at* http://www.fda.gov/downloads/ICECI/ComplianceManuals/RegulatoryProceduresManual/UCM074330.pdf [hereinafter Warning Letters].
[13] *Ibid.* at 4-1-1.
[14] *See* Food & Drug Admin., Prior Notice, in Regulatory Procedures Manual 10-2-4 (2018), *available at* http://www.fda.gov/downloads/ICECI/ComplianceManuals/RegulatoryProceduresManual/UCM074292.pdf ("Warning Letters are the principal means by which the agency provides prior notice of violations and of achieving voluntary compliance." *Ibid.* 4-2-5.).
[15] Warning Letters at 4-1-7.
[16] *Ibid.*
[17] *Ibid.* Exhibit 4-1.
[18] *Ibid.* at 4-1-8.
[19] *Ibid.*
[20] *Ibid.*
[21] *See* 5 USC § 552.

UNTITLED LETTERS

As the name suggests, Untitled Letters are letters issued without the title "WARNING LETTER" in the heading. Untitled Letters cite "violations that do not meet the threshold of regulatory significance for a Warning Letter."[22] Untitled Letters do not threaten enforcement action, and a follow-up inspection is not required. The FDA also does not routinely advise other federal agencies about Untitled Letters. The recommendation for the issuance of an Untitled Letter begins at the District level, and the Center must provide concurrence before the FDA issues an Untitled Letter. The FDA's procedures do not establish any particular time frame for issuance of an Untitled Letter.

IMPORT DETENTIONS AND IMPORT ALERTS

The FDA has the responsibility to evaluate imported drugs to determine whether they should be admitted into domestic commerce. The FDA can refuse admission of drugs that were manufactured in violation of CGMP requirements.[23]

The FDA has authority to collect, and conduct an examination of, samples of imported drugs to determine whether the agency should refuse their admission into domestic commerce. If the FDA's examination indicates that the drugs should be refused, the agency detains the drugs and gives their owner or consignee notice and an opportunity for an informal hearing.[24] Following the hearing, the FDA refuses admission of drugs proven to violate CGMP requirements.

When the FDA has inspected a foreign drug manufacturing facility and found significant CGMP violations, the agency may decide to prohibit importation of drugs from that facility without even examining samples of the drugs. This process is called Detention Without Physical Examination, and the FDA implements the prohibition through an Import Alert. The Import Alert provides notice to all ports of entry that the FDA should detain imported drugs from the affected facility. In general, the FDA will only agree to lift the Import Alert if the agency has reinspected the foreign facility and determined that the CGMP issues have been satisfactorily resolved.[25]

REVOCATION OF DRUG APPROVAL

The FDA also has statutory authority to withdraw a drug approval based on CGMP violations at the facility where the drug is manufactured. To pursue this remedy, the FDA must first provide the affected firm with notice and an opportunity to cure the violations claimed. If the FDA determines that the violative conditions were not corrected within a reasonable time, the agency can seek to withdraw the approval.[26]

The withdrawal process begins with a notice of opportunity for a hearing. That notice does not guarantee that there will be a hearing. The person requesting a hearing must show specific facts establishing that there is a genuine and substantial issue of fact.[27] The Supreme Court has ruled that the FDA is entitled to withdraw a drug approval in the absence of a hearing if there is no genuine and substantial issue of fact.[28] Even if there is no such issue, the FDA may grant a hearing if it determines that a hearing would be in the public interest.[29]

---

[22] Food & Drug Admin., Untitled Letters, in Regulatory Procedures Manual 4-2-1 (2018), *available at* http://www.fda.gov/downloads/ICECI/ComplianceManuals/RegulatoryProceduresManual/UCM074330.pdf.
[23] 21 USC § 381(a)(3) (providing authority to refuse admission of adulterated drugs); *Ibid*. § 351(a)(2)(B) (drugs are adulterated if manufactured in violation of CGMP requirements).
[24] 21 USC § 381(a); 21 CFR §§ 1.90, 1.94(a).
[25] Food & Drug Admin., Import Operations and Actions, in Regulatory Procedures Manual 9-8-12, 9-8-15 (2017), *available at* https://www.fda.gov/downloads/ICECI/ComplianceManuals/RegulatoryProceduresManual/UCM074300.pdf.
[26] 21 USC § 355(e).
[27] 21 CFR § 314.200(g).
[28] *Weinberger v. Hynson, Westcott & Dunning, Inc.*, 412 U.S. 609 (1973).
[29] 21 CFR § 314.200(g)(6).

If a hearing occurs, the FDA follows its procedural regulations for a formal evidentiary public hearing.[30] Among other things, these regulations provide for discovery of certain FDA records and a trial-type evidentiary hearing before a neutral agency Presiding Officer involving testimony by, and cross-examination of, witnesses.[31]

The approval withdrawal process is a relatively cumbersome means for the FDA to address CGMP violations, because the process includes so many procedural protections for the drug manufacturer. As a result, the FDA rarely uses this process as a remedy for CGMP violations.[32]

CIVIL ENFORCEMENT ACTIONS

The FDA does not have statutory authority to litigate civil enforcement actions in court. The FDA refers recommended civil enforcement actions to the U.S. Department of Justice, which files the cases and takes the lead in the litigation, supported by the FDA. FDA enforcement personnel and attorneys review and approve cases before they are referred to the Justice Department. At that point, the Justice Department follows its own independent review and approval procedures before filing civil enforcement actions. The Justice Department declines some, but not many, of the cases that the FDA refers. Depending on the circumstances, these different decision points within the FDA and the Justice Department may make it possible for affected companies to attempt to intervene, through counsel, before there is a final decision to file the case.

The FDCA gives the Justice Department (working with the FDA) statutory authority to pursue two types of civil enforcement actions for drug CGMP violations: seizure actions and injunctive actions.[33] The unit within the Justice Department that files a seizure action is typically the U.S. Attorney's Office in the jurisdiction where the disputed drugs are held. The Justice Department's Consumer Protection Branch in Washington, DC is typically the unit that files an injunctive action.

While the FDA's inspectional and compliance resources are heavily focused on drug CGMP issues, the vast majority of drug CGMP disputes with the FDA are resolved without recourse to seizure or injunctive actions. In fiscal year 2016, for example, the FDA initiated only one seizure action and three injunctive actions addressing drug regulatory violations of any kind (not just CGMP issues).[34]

SEIZURE ACTIONS

A seizure action freezes allegedly violative drugs in the place where they are physically held, making it unlawful to move the drugs without permission from the court. The Justice Department only needs to make a minimal showing of probable cause to obtain the court authorization necessary to effectuate the seizure. The owner of the drugs will typically have no advance notice of the action and will only have the opportunity for a court hearing (to challenge the seizure) after the seizure already has occurred. A seizure action therefore gives the FDA a potent and immediate remedy that prevents distribution of drugs alleged to violate CGMP requirements.

"Open-ended" seizures cover all lots of a specific product or products. "Lot-specific" seizures cover a specific lot or batch. "Mass" seizures cover all FDA-regulated products at an establishment.[35] The FDA will consider conducting a mass seizure when all of the drugs at a facility were manufactured under conditions alleged to violate CGMP requirements. As a practical matter, an

---

[30] 21 CFR §§ 10.50(c)(16), 12.1(a).

[31] *See generally*, 21 CFR part 12.

[32] *See, e.g., John D. Copanos & Sons, Inc. v. FDA*, 854 F.2d 510, 514 (D.C. Cir. 1988) (noting that this 1988 case was the "first contested withdrawal of approval . . . . on CGMP grounds").

[33] 21 USC §§ 332, 334.

[34] 2016 FDA Enforcement Statistics, *available at* https://www.fda.gov/downloads/ICECI/EnforcementActions/UCM540606.pdf.

[35] Food & Drug Admin., Types of Seizures, in Regulatory Procedures Manual 6-13- (2018), *available at* https://www.fda.gov/downloads/ICECI/ComplianceManuals/RegulatoryProceduresManual/UCM074317.pdf.

open-ended seizure or mass seizure of a manufacturer's drugs effectively shuts down the firm's operations. Current inventory under seizure cannot be sold, and distribution of other newly manufactured inventory places the firm at risk of more seizures.

The owner of seized drugs may decide not to contest the FDA's claims. If the owner does nothing in response to the seizure, the court will enter a default judgment, and the drugs will be destroyed under FDA supervision. Alternatively, the owner may decide to settle the seizure case by entering into a consent decree. As part of the consent decree, the owner seeks to bring the drugs into compliance or have them destroyed. In a seizure action based on CGMP violations, the consent decree option may not be attractive from the owner's perspective. There is no need to enter into a consent decree to have the drugs destroyed—taking no action will have the same result. And drugs manufactured in violation of CGMP requirements typically cannot be brought into compliance at a later time, because the original conditions of manufacture cannot be changed after the fact. Furthermore, entering into a consent decree may involve significant burdens for the owner. In recent years, the FDA has sought to have provisions added to seizure consent decrees that enjoin future unlawful acts by the company and give the agency ongoing supervisory authority over various aspects of the company's operations (like the provisions of consent decrees in injunctive actions described below).

The owner's remaining option is to contest the seizure by denying some or all of the government's allegations. In order to contest a seizure, the owner must file a verified claim with the court stating its interest in the drugs. At that point, the case proceeds like an ordinary civil litigation, with discovery and an eventual trial. If the claimant prevails, the goods are released. If the government prevails, the goods are either destroyed or (if possible) reconditioned in a manner acceptable to the FDA. In order to consider this litigation option, the owner must be able to weather a prolonged period of time (likely a year or longer) in which the seized inventory cannot be sold. Companies facing an open-ended seizure or mass seizure are unlikely to be able to sustain their operations under these circumstances, because significant drug inventory cannot be distributed while the litigation is pending. Under those circumstances, the FDA may have considerable leverage in convincing the company to enter into a consent decree that will allow operations to resume under conditions acceptable to the agency.

INJUNCTIVE ACTIONS

The FDA also can address CGMP violations by requesting the Justice Department to seek an injunction from a court. An injunction is a court order requiring the affected company to take, or refrain from taking, specified actions. An injunction directed to CGMP violations requires the manufacturer to remedy past violations and prevent future violations. A manufacturer that fails to obey an injunction's requirements is subject to penalties for contempt of court.

The FDA typically pursues an injunctive action (instead of a seizure action) when the agency has concluded that a manufacturer has substantial, systemic, and persistent CGMP violations.[36] The reason is that an injunction can mandate very specific and detailed changes in a manufacturer's operations. An injunction can provide a new blueprint for a manufacturer's quality assurance program that is designed to isolate and cure the root causes of CGMP violations. For example, the FDA may seek an injunction including requirements that the manufacturer must retain an independent third-party CGMP expert, initiate product recalls, or revalidate its manufacturing processes. In an injunctive action, the FDA also may seek disgorgement of profits received from the sale of noncompliant drugs.

The FDA tends to view injunctive actions as more effective than seizure actions as mechanisms to achieve systemic reform at a manufacturer. A seizure action simply freezes inventory in place (pending a court hearing) and does not require prospective reforms (unless the manufacturer enters

---

[36] See Food & Drug Admin., Injunctions, in Regulatory Procedures Manual 6-2-4 (2018), *available at* http://www.fda. gov/downloads/ICECI/ ComplianceManuals/RegulatoryProceduresManual/UCM074317.pdf.

into a consent decree with injunctive provisions). However, an injunctive action is potentially more cumbersome than a seizure action as a means of remedying CGMP violations. In an injunctive action, the FDA must prove its case at a trial before the court will issue an injunction. During the interval between the time the case is filed and the time a trial concludes (which may be a year or longer), there is no court order prohibiting the manufacturer from continuing to produce and distribute drugs. In a seizure action, by contrast, the FDA obtains an immediate remedy (freezing the affected inventory in place) and does not need to prove its case to a court until a later time. (The FDA may never need to prove its case to a court following the seizure, because the agency will typically attempt to settle a seizure action through a consent decree).

The FDA may seek the systemic-reform benefits of an injunction yet conclude that the public health would be undermined by waiting for that remedy until after a trial. Under those circumstances, the agency and Justice Department may seek a preliminary injunction, which is an injunction entered on a preliminary basis early in the case (and which typically remains in effect until the trial concludes). In determining whether to issue a preliminary injunction, the court will usually consider the following four factors: (1) whether the government is likely to succeed on the merits of its CGMP claims at trial; (2) whether the government is likely to suffer irreparable injury if the preliminary injunction does not issue; (3) whether the balance of equities tips in the government's favor; and (4) whether the public interest favors granting the preliminary injunction.[37]

To resolve an injunctive action without the expense and uncertainty of litigation, many manufacturers will settle the case by signing a consent decree with the government. Consent decrees are injunctions agreed to by the government and the manufacturer (and usually by its top executive and regulatory compliance official), signed by the court, and enforceable through contempt penalties for noncompliance. FDA consent decrees typically contain requirements for the manufacturer to retain an outside CGMP expert; revamp CGMP procedures to address violative conditions that the expert identifies; obtain a certification from the expert that the firm is in substantial compliance with CGMP requirements; and have a satisfactory reinspection by the FDA before the conditions of concern are deemed resolved. Consent decrees may contain a provision requiring the firm to stop manufacturing some or all product lines until a reinspection satisfactory to the FDA occurs. Consent decrees also may contain a provision authorizing the FDA to prohibit manufacture of some or all product lines in the future—or recall drugs—if future violations occur. Consent decrees generally last for a minimum of five years, and manufacturers are required to petition the court in order to have the decree lifted. If the decree is not lifted, it is in place permanently, and its obligations typically pass to any successors or assigns of the company that entered into the decree.

CRIMINAL PROSECUTIONS

If the FDA concludes that a manufacturer's CGMP violations are particularly egregious, the agency may refer the matter to the Justice Department for a criminal prosecution. FDA agents have authority to investigate potential criminal violations. However, it is the Justice Department that files criminal charges and takes the lead in litigating criminal prosecutions, supported by the FDA. Depending on the case, the unit within the Justice Department with primary responsibility for the prosecution may be the U.S. Attorney's Office where the manufacturer is located or the Consumer Protection Branch in Washington, DC. In some cases, both of those Justice Department units may share equivalent responsibility to prosecute the case.

---

[37] See, e.g., Winter v. Nat. Res. Def. Council, Inc., 555 U.S. 7, 20 (2008). A temporary restraining order is a different type of pretrial injunction that can be entered (on an emergency basis) even earlier than a preliminary injunction. A temporary restraining order is only in effect for fourteen days unless the court renews it. See Fed. R. Civ. P. 65(b)(2). In order to persuade a court to issue a temporary restraining order, the government would need to satisfy the same four factors cited above with respect to preliminary injunctions. The FDA typically does not pursue temporary restraining orders in enforcement cases. If the need for a remedy is that emergent, the FDA typically relies upon a seizure action or Import Alert, which the FDA can implement immediately without first proving its case to a court.

Manufacturing drugs in violation of CGMP requirements (and distributing them in interstate commerce) is a "prohibited act" under the FDCA.[38] The statute imposes felony liability on an entity or individual that commits a prohibited act with intent to defraud or mislead. The statute also imposes felony liability on an entity or individual that commits a prohibited act following a prior FDCA criminal conviction.[39] Penalties for felony violations include imprisonment for up to three years per violation and fines up to $250,000 per violation for an individual and up to $500,000 per violation for an entity. Alternatively, the court may impose a fine of up to twice the gross gain or twice the gross loss from the violations.[40]

The statute also imposes misdemeanor liability on an individual or entity that a commits a prohibited act, even if there is no evidence of intentional wrongdoing.[41] Penalties for misdemeanor violations include imprisonment for up to one year per violation and fines up to $250,000 per violation for an individual and up to $500,000 for an entity. Alternatively, the court may impose a fine of up to twice the gross gain or twice the gross loss from the violations.[42] The FDCA is unusual in imposing misdemeanor liability without wrongful intent. To protect against unfairness, the statute shields individuals and entities from misdemeanor liability under some circumstances if they act in good faith, including when they receive a guaranty from a supplier affirming that the products at issue do not violate FDCA requirements.[43]

Because misdemeanor liability can be imposed without wrongful intent, the Justice Department could theoretically pursue a misdemeanor prosecution for the very same CGMP violations typically addressed by civil enforcement actions. Yet the consequences of a misdemeanor prosecution may be much more severe than the consequences of a civil enforcement action. Prosecutors therefore must use sound judgment in determining which violations (lacking wrongful intent) should fairly be pursued as misdemeanor prosecutions.

The Supreme Court's decision in *U.S. v. Park* governs misdemeanor liability for individuals under the FDCA. The so-called *Park* doctrine establishes that an individual can be liable for an FDCA misdemeanor without intentional wrongdoing (and even without awareness of wrongdoing) if the individual has a "responsible relationship" to or a "responsible share in a violation of the Act."[44] No misdemeanor liability may be imposed on a corporate agent that was "powerless" to prevent or correct the alleged violation.[45] Yet relying on dependable subordinates to address violative conditions may not be sufficient to insulate a corporate officer from criminal liability.[46] Misdemeanor liability attaches to an officer that has "a responsible relation to the situation and by virtue of his position … had … authority and responsibility to deal with the situation."[47] Accordingly, the *Park* doctrine also is referred to as the "responsible corporate officer" doctrine.

---

[38] 21 USC § 351(a)(2)(B) (drugs are adulterated if manufactured in violation of CGMP requirements); *Ibid.* § 331(a) (distributing adulterated drugs in interstate commerce is a prohibited act).

[39] 21 USC § 333(a)(2).

[40] *Ibid.*; 18 USC §§ 3571(b)(3), (c)(3), (d). *See, e.g., U.S. v. Vintage Pharm, Inc.*, No. 3:04-cr-00201 (W.D.N.C. June 22, 2006) (Judgment) (felony prosecution for drug expiration dating that did not comply with CGMP requirements, resulting in $4.8 million fine for the corporation); Gregory Roumeliotis, *U.S. Generic Drug Manufacturer Pleads Guilty to Felony*, June 27, 2006, *available at* https://www.in-pharmatechnologist.com/Article/2006/06/28/US-generic-drug-manufacturer-pleads-guilty-to-felony.

[41] 21 USC § 333(a)(1); *U.S. v. Dessart*, 823 F.3d 395, 403 (7th Cir. 2016) (addressing corporate liability without wrongful intent); *U.S. v. Park*, 421 U.S. 658 (1975) (addressing individual liability without wrongful intent).

[42] 21 USC § 333(a)(1); 18 USC §§ 3571(b)(4), (c)(4), (d). *See, e.g., U.S. v. McNeil-PPC, Inc.*, No. 2:15-cr-00082 (E.D. Pa. Mar. 10, 2015) (Judgment) (misdemeanor prosecution for CGMP violation involving failure to initiate corrective or preventive action for particles found in drug products, resulting in $20 million fine for the corporation); Press Release, *McNeil-PPC Inc. Pleads Guilty in Connection with Adulterated Infants' and Children's Over-the-Counter Liquid Drugs* (March 10, 2015), *available at* https://www.justice.gov/opa/pr/mcneil-ppc-inc-pleads-guilty-connection-adulterated-infants-and-childrens-over-counter-liquid.

[43] 21 USC §§ 333(c)(1), (c)(2).

[44] *Park*, 421 U.S. at 673–674.

[45] *Ibid.* at 673. It appears that to date, this defense has not been successful in any published reports.

[46] *Ibid.* at 677.

[47] *Ibid.* at 674 (internal quotations omitted).

Most criminal statutes do not impose liability in the absence of wrongful intent. The Supreme Court nonetheless justified criminal liability in *Park* on the ground that corporate officers in FDA-regulated companies have special burdens, because they have special responsibilities to protect the public health:

"The requirements of foresight and vigilance imposed on responsible corporate agents are beyond question demanding, and perhaps onerous, but they are not more stringent than the public has a right to expect of those who voluntarily assume positions of authority in business enterprises whose services and products affect the health and well-being of the public that supports them."[48]

Given that reliance on a corporate structure with "dependable subordinates" will not, standing alone, insulate corporate officers from criminal liability, they should ensure that CGMP violations are properly identified, addressed, corrected, and monitored to prevent recurrence. As the CGMP regulations confirm, manufacturers must have procedures in place to ensure that responsible corporate officers are aware of complaints, returned drug products, drug products that have been improperly stored, and other CGMP compliance issues.[49]

ENFORCEMENT ACTIONS INVOLVING BOTH CIVIL AND CRIMINAL LIABILITY

When the FDA decides to pursue CGMP violations in an enforcement action, the scope of potential liability can be extraordinarily broad. The enforcement action can sweep in both civil and criminal liability, statutory and regulatory violations unrelated to CGMPs (or even unrelated to the FDCA), substantial financial payments, and onerous consent decree obligations.

For example, in 2010, GlaxoSmithKline PLC and its subsidiary, SB Pharmco Puerto Rico Inc., settled a major drug CGMP enforcement action relating to SB Pharmco's Cidra, Puerto Rico manufacturing site. The violations claimed by the FDA and the Justice Department included failure to ensure that finished products were free from contamination by microorganisms, distribution of products with the potential to lack therapeutic effect, distribution of products with the potential to lack a controlled release mechanism, and distribution of products that did not always contain the FDA-approved mix of active ingredients.[50] SB Pharmco pleaded guilty to a felony violation of the FDCA and agreed to pay a criminal fine of $150 million, which included a $10 million asset forfeiture. GlaxoSmithKline entered into a civil settlement agreement in which it agreed to pay an additional $600 million to resolve claims that it caused false claims to be submitted to the Indian government in connection with the drugs.[51]

Another major civil and criminal enforcement matter occurred in 2012 and 2013, arising from conditions at manufacturing facilities in India owned and operated by Ranbaxy Laboratories Limited, the parent company of Ranbaxy USA, Inc. The enforcement action followed almost a decade of CGMP deficiencies documented by the FDA, three FDA Warning Letters, and an Import Alert barring importation of more than 30 drugs into the United States. The CGMP issues uncovered by the FDA included incomplete testing records; failure to investigate evidence indicating that drugs did not meet their specifications; failure to prevent cross contamination between penicillin drugs and non-penicillin drugs; failure to have adequate procedures to prevent contamination of sterile drugs; and inadequate stability testing.[52]

---

[48] *Ibid.* at 672.

[49] *See* 21 CFR § 211.180(f). ("Procedures shall be established to assure that the responsible officials of the firm, if they are not personally involved in or immediately aware of such actions, are notified in writing of any investigations conducted under §§ 211.198, 211.204, or 211.208 of these regulations, any recalls, reports of inspectional observations issued by the Food and Drug Administration, or any regulatory actions relating to good manufacturing practices brought by the Food and Drug Administration.")

[50] Maame Ewusi-Mensah Frimpong, Deputy Assistant Attorney General, Address at the 2013 CBI Pharmaceutical Compliance Congress (January 29, 2013), *available at* https://www.justice.gov/opa/speech/deputy-assistant-attorney-general-maame-ewusi-mensah-frimpong-speaks-2013-cbi.

[51] Press Release, GlaxoSmithKline to Plead Guilty & Pay $750 Million to Resolve Criminal and Civil Liability Regarding Manufacturing Deficiencies at Puerto Rico Plant (Oct. 26, 2010), *available at* https://www.justice.gov/opa/pr/glaxosmithkline-plead-guilty-pay-750-million-resolve-criminal-and-civil-liability-regarding.

[52] Press Release, U.S. Files Consent Decree for Permanent Injunction Against Pharmaceutical Ranbaxy Laboratories (January 25, 2012), *available at* https://www.justice.gov/opa/pr/us-files-consent-decree-permanent-injunction-against-pharmaceutical-ranbaxy-laboratories.

To settle the matter, Ranbaxy first entered into a consent decree that the Justice Department described as "unprecedented in its scope," among other things because it was "groundbreaking in its international reach" in requiring fundamental changes to manufacturing plants in both the United States and India.[53] Ranbaxy later reached criminal and civil settlements including what the Justice Department described as "the nation's largest financial penalty paid by a generic pharmaceutical company for FDCA violations."[54] To resolve criminal liability, the company paid $150 million and pleaded guilty to seven felony counts charging introduction of adulterated drugs, failure to file timely field alert reports, and false statements in annual reports to the FDA. To resolve civil liability, the company paid $350 million in connection with claims that Ranbaxy had caused health-care programs to submit false claims to Medicare and Medicaid.[55]

The cases described above arise from the extensive reach of FDA regulatory requirements (including CGMP requirements), the authority to impose civil and criminal remedies under the FDCA (even in the absence of wrongful intent), and the overlay of requirements under other statutes that govern the heavily regulated drug industry. The federal government has extraordinarily broad power in CGMP enforcement actions. Drug manufacturers are well advised to avoid such enforcement actions by instilling a culture that prioritizes CGMP compliance.

---

[53] *Ibid.*

[54] Press Release, Generic Drug Manufacturer Ranbaxy pleads Guilty and Agrees to Pay $500 Million to Resolve False Claims Allegations, CGMP Violations and False Statements to the FDA (May 13, 2013), *available at* https://www.justice.gov/opa/pr/generic-drug-manufacturer-ranbaxy-pleads-guilty-and-agrees-pay-500-million-resolve-false.

[55] *Ibid.*

21 FDA Inspection Process

Cathy L. Burgess and Daniel G. Jarcho[1]

CONTENTS

The Federal Food and Drug Administration's (FDA's) arrival for an inspection can create a sense of panic or determination, depending on a firm's level of preparedness. Lack of organization and delays will give the FDA the impression that the firm is out of control and could lead to greater scrutiny and a belief that the firm has something to hide. A firm that prepares for inspections on a routine basis, and has a good understanding of its compliance profile and proper inspection management, is more likely than an unprepared firm to have a successful inspection. In addition, addressing concerns that the FDA identifies during an inspection in a thorough manner, that evaluates potential product and patient impact taking a systems-based approach, helps to ensure that a firm is discharging its regulatory obligations and that FDA will be satisfied that the firm is capable of addressing its own problems, without the need for increased oversight or enforcement action by the Agency.

PRE-INSPECTION PREPARATION

UNDERSTANDING FDA'S INSPECTION AUTHORITY

In order to prepare adequately for an FDA establishment inspection, firms first must be knowledgeable about the FDA's inspection authority, which is quite broad. The FDA is authorized to conduct inspections of any "factory, warehouse, or establishment in which...drugs...are manufactured, processed, packed or held for introduction into interstate commerce or after such introduction."[2] FDA investigators are entitled to request and review "records, files, papers, processes, controls and facilities" bearing on whether drugs are adulterated, misbranded, or otherwise violative.[3] The fact that a

---

[1] The authors gratefully acknowledge the assistance of Seth Olson, an associate of Alston & Bird, LLP.
[2] Federal Food, Drug, and Cosmetic Act § 704(a)(1), 21 USC § 374(a)(1).
[3] Note that compounding pharmacies that are not registered as "outsourcing facilities" are exempt from FDA's records inspection authority. See *Ibid.* § 374(a)(2)(A). Specifically, the FDCA states that FDA's records inspection authority does not extend to "pharmacies which maintain establishments in conformance with any applicable local laws regulating the practice of pharmacy and medicine and which are regularly engaged in dispensing prescription drugs or devices, upon prescriptions of practitioners licensed to administer such drugs or devices to patients under the care of such practitioners in the course of their professional practice, and which do not, either through a subsidiary or otherwise, manufacture, prepare, propagate, compound, or process drugs or devices for sale other than in the regular course of their business of dispensing or selling drugs or devices at retail." *Ibid.* Registered outsourcing facilities are subject to FDA's records inspection authority. See 21 USC § 353b(b)(4)(A).

record or process is confidential and proprietary is irrelevant in the context of an FDA inspection, and, as discussed below, refusing to furnish information on such grounds puts the firm at risk of enforcement action. There are certain limits on FDA's inspection authority, but they are quite narrow. FDA is not authorized to inspect:

- Financial data
- Sales data other than shipment data
- Pricing data
- Personnel data other than information establishing the qualifications of technical and professional personnel
- Certain research data except to the extent such information may be required to be made available for inspection or submitted to FDA for particular products

Failure to comply with an inspection request authorized under Section 704 is considered an inspection "refusal" and is a prohibited act under Section 301(e)–(f) of the Federal Food, Drug, and Cosmetic Act (FDCA).[4] In addition, refusing an inspection renders adulterated a drug manufactured, processed, packed, or held in the facility for which the inspection was refused.[5]

On July 9, 2012, Congress granted FDA additional statutory authority related to establishment inspections, by including in the Food and Drug Administration Safety and Innovation Act (FDASIA) several provisions related to the drug supply chain.

Section 705 replaced the previous biennial inspection frequency with a risk-based schedule for inspections.[6] The risk-based model utilizes inspection criteria to prioritize facility inspections. The risk-based criteria include:

- The compliance history of the drug firm
- The record, history, and nature of recalls linked to the drug firm
- The inherent risk posed by the drug manufactured, prepared, propagated, compounded, or processed at the drug firm
- The inspection frequency and history of the drug firm, including whether the firm has been inspected within the last four years
- Whether the drug firm has been inspected by a foreign government
- Any other criteria deemed necessary and appropriate for purposes of allocating inspection resources

---

[4] *Ibid.* at §§ 331(e)–(f).
[5] 21 USC § 351(j).
[6] Section 705 provides statutory authorization for the risk-based approach that FDA had already begun to implement. Specifically, with the launch of "Pharmaceutical CGMPs for the 21st Century—A Risk-Based Approach," FDA began to prioritize the inspection of domestic pharmaceutical manufacturing sites. *See* Food & Drug Admin., Pharmaceutical CGMPs for the 21st Century—A Risk-Based Approach (September 2004), *available at* https://www.fda.gov/downloads/drugs/developmentapprovalprocess/manufacturing/questionsandanswersoncurrentgoodmanufacturingpracticescgmp-fordrugs/ucm176374.pdf. The goal of this approach has been to achieve a measure of predictability in identifying and conducting inspections that will have the greatest potential of safeguarding the public health. *Ibid.* FDA has made clear that "[a] risk-based systems audit approach is recommended in which higher risk, therapeutically significant, medically necessary and difficult to manufacture drugs are covered in greater detail during an inspection." Food & Drug Admin., Investigations Operations Manual 2018, Sec. 5.5.1.2.
    Under this risk-based approach, once a firm has developed an established record of compliance, FDA inspections are likely to occur less frequently than for those firms whose compliance history shows continuous or repeated violations of CGMPs. In 2015, FDA formalized its process for selecting firms for inspection based on a risk-based site selection model. *See* Food & Drug Admin., Compliance Program Guidance Manual (2017), Ch. 56, Sec. 7356.002 [hereinafter FDA CPGM 7356.002] at 4, *available at* https://www.fda.gov/downloads/ICECI/ComplianceManuals/ComplianceProgramManual/UCM125409.pdf.

Section 706 amended Section 704(a) of the FDCA by allowing the FDA to request records outside of an inspection context.[7] Sections 705 and 706 operate in concert, giving the FDA the ability to use information collected under its Section 706 authority to determine the risk profile of a facility for purposes of establishment inspection under the Section 705 risk-based model. Section 707 strengthened the FDA's authority regarding inspection refusals so that delaying, denying, limiting, or refusing to permit inspection causes a drug to be adulterated. 21 USC §351(j).

In addition, FDASIA granted the FDA explicit authority under Section 710 to engage with foreign counterparts with respect to drug inspections and records exchange.[8] With respect to exchanging records, the legislative history revealed that the provision was designed to help the FDA leverage its resources through cooperation with trusted foreign governments.[9] Under Section 710, the FDA has the authority to provide information to a foreign government that has been certified as having the ability to protect trade secret information. Under a written agreement with the foreign government, the FDA may disclose information related to an establishment inspection for civil regulatory purposes. The FDA is also authorized to disclose information to a foreign government for purposes of an investigation, if the FDA has reason to believe that a drug could cause serious injury or death.

Section 711 of the FDASIA amended Section 501 of the FDCA by adding the following language: "For purposes of paragraph [501](a)(2)(B), the term "current good manufacturing practice" (CMGP) includes the implementation of oversight and controls over the manufacture of drugs to ensure quality, including managing the risk of and establishing the safety of raw materials, materials used in the manufacturing of drugs, and finished drug products."[10]

Section 711 gives the FDA the authority to require finished product manufacturers to establish oversight and controls over their suppliers, including contract manufacturing organizations. Moreover, if a finished product manufacturer fails to establish oversight and controls related to raw materials, components, and contract manufactured finished products, its distributed products are in violation of CGMPs and deemed to be adulterated so that the introduction of those products in interstate commerce is a prohibited act.

How FDA Prepares for Inspections

The FDA's Investigations Operations Manual (IOM) describes an establishment inspection as "a careful, critical, official examination of a facility to determine its compliance with laws administered by FDA."[11] The IOM states that the purposes of a drug inspection are: to evaluate whether a firm is in compliance with sanitation and CGMP; to determine whether there is evidence of deficiencies that could lead to the manufacture and distribution of adulterated or misbranded products; to obtain correction of deficiencies; and to determine whether the firm is complying with all applicable postmarket reporting requirements.[12]

The IOM instructs FDA investigators to prepare for an establishment inspection by understanding the firm's compliance history. Specifically, investigators are instructed to review Establishment Inspection Reports (EIRs), which provide comprehensive discussions of prior inspections. Investigators also review applications (new drug applications [NDAs], abbreviated new drug applications [ANDAs],

---

[7] Food and Drug Administration Safety and Innovation Act (FDASIA), Pub. L. No. 112-144, § 706, 126 Stat. 993, 1067-68 (2012). Effective August 25, 2017, FDA issued Staff Manual Guide (SMG) 9004.1 to implement and align all centers that are involved in drug inspections. *See* SMG 9004.1, August 25, 2017, *available at* https://www.fda.gov/downloads/ AboutFDA/ReportsManualsForms/StaffManualGuides/UCM418261.pdf.

[8] Food and Drug Administration Safety and Innovation Act (FDASIA), Pub. L. No. 112-144, §§ 710, 712, 126 Stat. 993, 1070-72 (2012). Section 710 authorizes FDA to disclose certain information to foreign governments, and Section 712 allows recognition of foreign government inspections.

[9] HR Rep. No. 112-495, at 33 (2012).

[10] 21 USC § 351.

[11] Food & Drug Admin., Investigations Operations Manual 2018 [hereinafter IOM], Sec. 5.1.2.

[12] *See Ibid.* at Sec. 5.5.1.

biologics license applications [BLAs], and investigational new drug [IND] applications) for application products, and over-the-counter (OTC) monographs for non-application products. In order to identify potential or emerging problems with product quality, investigators review information that the FDA has received regarding complaints and product recalls, as well as Field Alert Reports and Biological Product Deviation Reports (BPDRs). Investigators are also instructed to use this information to identify drugs that violate the FDCA due to misbranding, lack of approval, fraud, or withdrawn applications or products that have been removed from the market because of safety concerns.[13] The IOM also instructs FDA investigators to focus on drug products that are difficult to manufacture, are complex dosage forms, or require special tests, processes, or equipment.[14] Firms that focus on inspection readiness take a similar approach in preparing for FDA inspections, by understanding their own compliance history and ensuring that deficiencies that have the potential to affect product quality have been addressed.

The FDA's Compliance Program Guidance Manual CP 7356.002 recommends a systems and risk-based approach to establishment inspections and identifies the following six systems for inspection: Facilities and Equipment, Materials, Laboratory Controls, Production, Packaging and Labeling, and, most importantly, Quality. The FDA will cover at least four systems in a full inspection and two systems in an abbreviated inspection. The IOM, which provides guidance to FDA's field investigators, emphasizes that "[d]uring the evaluation of the Quality System it is important to determine if top management makes science-based decisions and acts promptly to identify, investigate, correct, and prevent manufacturing problems likely to, or [that] have led to, product quality problems."[15]

As described in the IOM, the FDA investigator's authority to inspect is "predicated on specific obligations to the firm... It is [the investigator's] responsibility to conduct all inspections at reasonable times and within reasonable limits and in a reasonable manner."[16]

THE INSPECTION PROCESS

Upon arrival at the registered establishment, the investigator is required to present his or her credentials as well as a Form FDA-482, Notice of Inspection, to the firm's top management official.[17] The IOM notes that while the inspected firm is allowed to examine credentials and document the investigator's number and name, investigators should not permit the firm to photocopy the investigator's credentials, because this would be a violation of federal law under 18 USC § 701.

The firm's inspection management standard operating procedure (SOP) should contain instructions for staff to follow upon the FDA's arrival. If the firm received advance notice of the inspection, the investigator(s) should be escorted to the meeting room that the firm has already prepared for the inspection. In the event that FDA arrives unannounced, the SOP should also provide instructions for quickly and seamlessly notifying staff of FDA's arrival, and for the activation of a predetermined inspection management plan. Management should be prepared to conduct a brief presentation that provides general details about the firm. This presentation should be updated periodically, so that it is available and up to date in the event of an unannounced inspection.

The IOM instructs investigators to conduct a preliminary tour of the facility in order to establish the depth of the inspection and the inspection strategy. This visual inspection provides information about firm housekeeping, manufacturing operations, and training of staff. During the preliminary tour, investigators are instructed to look for obvious potential product problems.[18] As part of their record review, investigators typically will review complaint files, deviations, and out-of-specification investigations. This review also helps investigators to identify suspect products.[19] For sterile products,

[13] *Ibid.* at Sec. 5.5.1.1.
[14] *Ibid.*
[15] *Ibid.* at Sec. 5.5.1.2.
[16] *Ibid.* at Sec. 5.1.1.1.
[17] *See Ibid.* at 5.1.1.3; 21 USC § 374(a)(1).
[18] IOM, *supra* note 11, Sec 5.1.2.2.
[19] *Ibid.* at 5.5.1.2.

particularly products that are aseptically processed, FDA investigators are instructed to evaluate cleanroom design, process design, appropriate environmental controls required for areas at different production stages, and adequate microbial control over components and containers of sterile products.[20]

Sample collection is also an important part of the FDA's inspection process. Under the inspection provisions of Section 702(a) of the FDCA, the FDA is granted authority to conduct investigations and collect samples.[21] The IOM contains a comprehensive policy governing sampling protocols.[22] One reason the sampling protocols are so comprehensive is that collected samples may be used as evidence in enforcement actions, and the FDA wants to ensure samples are collected appropriately and in such a way that they will be admissible in court.[23] As a starting point, the IOM describes "official samples" as those subject to federal jurisdiction, specifically physical samples from a lot that was introduced, delivered, or received in interstate commerce or a lot that was manufactured in a U.S. territory or the District of Columbia.[24] If a lot becomes adulterated or misbranded after its shipment in interstate commerce, that is, when held for sale, the authority relied upon to sample is Section 301(k) of the FDCA.[25] "301(k)" sampling is distinguishable from other official samples in that this type of sampling must have documentation or other evidence of the act that caused the misbranding or adulteration.[26]

Other types of samples include "documentary" samples, such as product labels, transit paperwork, or photographs.[27] Often this type of sampling is associated with misbranding charges.[28] "Investigational" samples are collected to support regulatory actions or observations but are not necessarily collected from a product lot that has entered interstate commerce or is otherwise under federal jurisdiction.[29]

As discussed above, in evaluating whether a firm is in compliance with CGMPs, FDA investigators focus on identifying deficiencies that could lead to the manufacture or distribution of adulterated and/or misbranded products.[30] Investigators will confirm that a firm's registration and drug listing are in compliance[31] and will ensure that firms are reporting field alerts for NDA and ANDA products, as required by 21 CFR § 314.81, and BPDRs for therapeutic biologics, as required under 21 CFR § 600.14. Investigators may also inspect to determine whether the firm is in compliance with reporting requirements for adverse drug experiences.[32] The depth of an establishment inspection

---

[20] *See* Food & Drug Admin., Compliance Program Guidance Manual (2015), Ch. 56, Sec. 7356.002A, *available at* https://www.fda.gov/downloads/ICECI/ComplianceManuals/ComplianceProgramManual/UCM125409.pdf. *See also* Food & Drug Admin., Guidance for Industry: Sterile Drug Products Produced by Aseptic Processing—Current Good Manufacturing Practice (September 2004), *available at* https://www.fda.gov/downloads/Drugs/Guidances/ucm070342.pdf.

[21] IOM, *supra* note 11, Sec. 4.1.1.1.

[22] *See Ibid.* at Ch. 4.

[23] *Ibid.* at Sec. 4.1.2.

[24] *Ibid.* at Sec. 4.1.4.

[25] *Ibid.* at Sec. 4.1.4.4.

[26] *Ibid.*

[27] *Ibid.* at Sec. 4.1.4.2.

[28] *See Ibid.*

[29] *Ibid.* at Sec. 4.1.6.

[30] *See Ibid.* at 5.5.1.

[31] Any person who owns or operates an establishment that is "engaged in the manufacture, preparation, propagation, compounding, or processing of a drug or drugs" is required to register as an establishment and list drug products that the firm distributes. *See* 21 USC § 360; 21 CFR § 207.17; 21 CFR § 207.41. Registration requirements apply to firms engaged in repackaging, relabeling, or salvaging. *See Ibid.* Registration requirements apply to establishments in foreign countries if drugs are imported or offered for import into the U.S. *See Ibid.* Failure to register an establishment or list a drug is a "prohibited act," and the penalties for failure to register are fines, imprisonment, or both. See Federal Food, Drug, and Cosmetic Act §§ 301(p), 303(a); 21 USC §§ 331(p), 333(a).

[32] The reporting requirements are set forth in 21 CFR § 310.305 (for drugs without approved NDA/ANDAs); 21 CFR §§ 314.80, 314.98, and 314.540 (application drug products); 21 CFR § 600.80 (therapeutic biologics) and Section 760 of the FDCA (nonprescription products).

depends upon the reason the FDA is conducting the inspection, the type of information the FDA seeks, and whether there are suspected violations.[33]

During the inspection, an investigator may indicate his or her decision to photograph a particular location or activity. While the FDA takes the position that it is authorized to take photographs during establishment inspections, there is no explicit authority for photographs under Section 704 of the FDCA. The FDA relies on two court cases for its authority, *Dow Chemical v. United States*, 476 U.S. 227 (1986), and *U.S. v. Acri Wholesale Grocery Co.*, 409 F. Supp. 529 (S.D. Iowa 1976).[34] In 2012, the IOM was revised to provide explicit instruction to investigators in the event that a firm refuses to allow photographs. The following is the instruction that appears in the current IOM.

"[O]btain name and contact information for the firm's legal counsel and advise your program division management immediately. If the firm does not have legal counsel on retainer, collect the name and contact information for the most responsible individual. Program division management will inform their ORA [FDA's Office of Regulatory Affairs] Regional Counselor in the Office of Chief Counsel (OCC) of the situation, and OCC will then contact the firm's legal counsel or most responsible individual to discuss the FDA's legal right to take pictures during inspections. OCC will relay the results of this conversation to program division management."[35]

As discussed above, a provision of FDASIA enacted in 2012 provides that a drug is adulterated if it has been manufactured, processed, packed, or held in a facility that "delays, denies, or limits an inspection."[36] In FDA's guidance on this subject, the FDA takes the position that resisting or limiting photography by an FDA investigator may constitute an unlawful "limitation" of an inspection.[37]

The "refusal to permit entry or inspection as authorized by Section 704" has long been a prohibited act (21 USC § 331[f]). However, because a refusal now causes all drug products in that establishment to be adulterated, Congress required the Agency to elaborate on circumstances that would fall within the scope of 21 USC § 351(j). FDA's Final Guidance entitled "Circumstances that Constitute Delaying, Denying, Limiting, or Refusing a Drug Inspection," issued in October 2014, provides the FDA's current thinking regarding conduct that constitutes prohibited conduct.[38]

The Guidance provides examples of unacceptable delays related to scheduling, inspection management, and production of records. Examples of an inspection denial include (1) not allowing an FDA investigator to inspect the facility because certain staff members are not present; and (2) informing the FDA that the facility does not engage in drug manufacturing operations.

Limiting an inspection could include a refusal to permit FDA investigators access to certain areas without a reasonable explanation. Examples include:

- Ordering the discontinuation of manufacturing during the duration of the FDA inspection
- Limiting the FDA's opportunity to perform direct observation
- Unreasonably restricting entry to a particular facility or a portion of the facility.

The Guidance also states that limiting the investigator's ability to take photographs without a reasonable explanation, providing the investigator documents that have been "unreasonably redacted," or refusing to allow the FDA to collect samples constitutes a limitation of the inspection.

Finally, the Guidance provides examples of inspection refusals, which include active and passive conduct. In certain instances, the FDA may not consider conduct described in the Guidance

[33] IOM, *supra* note 11, Sec 5.1.2.1.
[34] *Ibid.* Sec. 5.3.4.1.
[35] *Ibid.*
[36] 21 USC § 351(j).
[37] Food & Drug Admin., Guidance for Industry, Circumstances That Constitute Delaying, Denying, Limiting, or Refusing a Drug Inspection (October 2014) [hereinafter DDLR Guidance] at 7, available at https://www.fda.gov/downloads/regulatoryinformation/guidances/ucm360484.pdf.
[38] The Final Guidance also raises the question whether the FDA could consider these types of conduct to be prohibited acts in inspections related to other types of FDA-regulated products.

to be a prohibited act if the facility provides a "reasonable explanation" and the issue is resolved within a reasonable period of time.[39] Examples of reasonable conduct, as described in the Guidance, include requiring an investigator to comply with safety requirements or gowning procedures prior to inspection of a particular area.[40] In addition, if a facility's manufacturing schedule does not include production of a particular drug during the FDA's requested time period,[41] or if key personnel are not initially available for an unannounced inspection, the FDA could consider these limitations to be reasonable.[42] In terms of an inability to provide immediate access to records, a potentially reasonable explanation might be that the records are currently in use for a manufacturing process or that the records need to be translated to meet the investigator's request for English translations.[43] While there is no bright line test for what is "reasonable," if a delay occurs during the course of an FDA inspection, the manufacturer must provide a factual, truthful explanation for the delay and must ensure that the delay is resolved within a reasonable amount of time.

The Final Guidance highlights the need for proper inspection management training prior to an inspection. Companies need to understand the scope of the FDA's inspection authority and the legal significance of an inspection refusal. In addition, companies need to establish well-defined procedures for the FDA's entry and notice of inspection and need to understand what to do if those procedures are not followed. For example, law enforcement personnel who are conducting a criminal investigation will not provide a Form FDA-482, Notice of Inspection. It is important for outside counsel to be involved in order to ensure that the client manages these investigations appropriately.

Outside counsel should assist the company in preparing employees for interactions with FDA investigators. For example, counsel often advise employees of the need to be truthful in all cases, and the legal risks of not doing so. Similarly, counsel often advise not to alter or hide documents, and the legal consequences of not providing requested information.

Outside counsel should also assist the company in preparing employees whom the FDA may ask to sign affidavits. Section 704 of the FDCA does not provide explicit authority for affidavits, but the IOM informs the investigator that an affidavit can be used in court "either to establish federal jurisdiction or fix the responsibility for a violation."[44] The IOM instructs the investigator to have the individual whom FDA proposes as an affiant review the affidavit and make edits, if necessary, before signing. "Mistakes, corrected and initialed by the affiant are an indication [that] he/she has read and understood the statement."[45] The IOM also encourages investigators to obtain handwritten statements that the individual understood the affidavit.

If it appears that the individual will not sign the affidavit, the IOM instructs the investigator to be persistent, asking the individual to read and edit the affidavit, and to add the following handwritten notation at the bottom of the affidavit: "I have read this statement and it is true, but I am not signing it because…"[46]

---

[39] DDLR Guidance, *supra* note 37, at 5 ("In instances where the facility provides a reasonable explanation for delaying production of records, the facility should also ensure that the resulting delay is of a reasonable duration.").

[40] *See Ibid.* at 7 ("Training specified by the Occupational Safety and Health Administration is required before an individual may enter a particular area of the facility, and the FDA investigator has not completed such training."); *Ibid.* at 5 ("A facility does not provide the FDA investigator access to aseptic processing areas until the investigator accommodates the facility's documented gowning procedures.").

[41] *Ibid.* at 4 ("Manufacturing at the facility is not on-going, for example running only one manufacturing campaign per month…").

[42] *Ibid.* at 6 ("At the beginning of an unannounced inspection, appropriate personnel are not immediately available to accurately answer the FDA investigator's questions."). Comparatively, preventing an inspection from occurring due to the absence of certain personnel may be considered a denial of the inspection. *Ibid.* ("A facility does not allow the FDA investigator to inspect the facility because certain staff members are not present, without a reasonable explanation.").

[43] *Ibid.* at 5.

[44] IOM, *supra* note 11, Sec. 4.4.8.

[45] *Ibid.* at Sec. 4.4.8.1.

[46] *Ibid.* at Sec. 4.4.8.2.

While the facts of individual situations might differ, legal counsel often advise company representatives not to sign or otherwise acknowledge FDA affidavits, which can be found to be admissions against the interests of the company. A manufacturer should consider incorporating requirements related to affidavits into its inspection management procedures. Such procedures might instruct personnel not to read, edit, acknowledge, or listen to the contents of an affidavit. The IOM anticipates the possibility that individuals will refuse to sign "upon advice of corporate counsel" or "per corporate policy" and instructs the investigator to document such a reason for refusal on the affidavit.[47]

The FDA typically utilizes affidavits when the inspection has uncovered significant findings. For example, the FDA has sought to use affidavits in inspections that have uncovered issues related to data integrity. Since 2014, the FDA has issued a number of Warning Letters with data integrity observations. These Warning Letters have identified conduct such as audit trail functions that were disabled at time of inspection; "unofficial" testing of samples, discarded results, and results from additional tests reported as results of record; discarded hard-copy records found during inspection; testing into compliance; failing results not included in official lab control records, and not reported or investigated; batch records signed by individuals who did not perform the review; and activities that were not performed but were recorded in batch records.[48]

These types of findings prompted the FDA to issue the Data Integrity (DI) Draft Guidance in April 2016, to clarify the role of data integrity in the drug manufacturing environment.[49] The DI Draft Guidance applies to finished pharmaceuticals, regulated under 21 CFR Parts 210 and 211, and to positron emission tomography (PET) drugs, regulated under Part 212.

The DI Draft Guidance highlights certain regulatory requirements for data integrity, such as requirements for data security[50] and preservation;[51] concurrent documentation;[52] control of

---

[47] *Ibid.*

[48] Based on a search of the FDA's Warning Letter Database, the number of CGMP-related FDA Warning Letters that include data integrity findings has continued to increase since 2014: 5 issued in 2014, 7 issued in 2015, 13 issued in 2016, and 14 issued in 2017. *See generally* Food & Drug Admin., *Inspections, Compliance, Enforcement, and Criminal Investigations: Warning Letters*, https://www.fda.gov/ICECI/EnforcementActions/WarningLetters/default.htm (Last Updated March 8, 2018). The inspections causing the Warning Letters continue to identify particularly concerning issues. *See, e.g.*, Food & Drug Admin., *Warning Letter # 320-18-02 to Kim Chemicals Private Ltd.* (October 16, 2017) ("Your quality system does not adequately ensure the accuracy and integrity of data to support the safety, effectiveness, and quality of the drugs you manufacture. We strongly recommend that you retain a qualified consultant to assist in your remediation."); Food & Drug Admin., *Warning Letter # 320-17-17 to FACTA Farmaceutici S.p.A* (January 13, 2017) ("You stored original data in an 'unofficial' and uncontrolled electronic spreadsheet on a shared computer network drive. Your analyst stated that original data was first recorded in this 'unofficial' spreadsheet and transcribed later to an 'official' form.'"); Food & Drug Admin., *Warning Letter # 320-16-29 to Pan Drugs Limited* (August 25, 2016) ("[Y]our quality unit failed to identify data integrity issues in 11 batch production records reviewed by our investigator. Your production manager admitted that he falsified the signatures of other employees in the 'Prepared By,' 'Reviewed By,' 'Approved By,' and 'Authorized By' sections."); Food & Drug Admin., *Warning Letter # 320-16-19 to Chongqing Lummy Pharmaceutical Co., Ltd.* (June 21, 2016) ("[O] n March 4, 2016, your analyst set the GC personal computer (PC) clock back to make it appear as if testing had been done seven months earlier—on August 3, 2015."); Food & Drug Admin, *Warning Letter # 320-16-10 to Polydrug Laboratories Pvt. Ltd.* (April 14, 2016) ("During the inspection our investigator found a torn sheet of paper titled 'Product Quality Complaints' on the floor of your warehouse. We compared it to your firm's official complaint log and discovered that only 2 of the 17 customer complaints on the torn sheet were recorded in your firm's official complaint log."); Food & Drug Admin., *Warning Letter # 320-15-12 to Mahendra Chemicals* (July 13, 2015) ("[O]ur investigators found backdated batch production records dated February 10 to February 25, 2014, signed by your Production Manager and Technical Director in the 'Batch Manufacturing Record Reviwed [sic] by' section. The Technical Director stated that he was not in the facility on these dates and was 'countersigning' for another person who allegedly performed these review activities. However, these records did not contain signatures (contemporaneous or otherwise) of the alternate reviewer who purportedly conducted the review.").

[49] Food & Drug Admin., Draft Guidance for Industry, Data Integrity and Compliance with CGMP (April 2016) [hereinafter DI Draft Guidance], *available at* https://www.fda.gov/downloads/drugs/guidances/ucm495891.pdf.

[50] 21 CFR § 211.68(b) ("Appropriate controls shall be exercised over computer or related systems to assure that changes in master production and control records or other records are instituted only by authorized personnel.").

[51] 21 CFR § 212.110(b).

[52] 21 CFR § 211.100(b) ("Written production and process control procedures shall be followed in the execution of the various production and process control functions and shall be documented at the time of performance.").

laboratory records;[53] retention of originals, "true copies," "accurate reproductions" of records;[54] and requirements to preserve complete records of all data and tests performed.[55]

The DI Draft Guidance is structured as a series of questions and answers and defines "data integrity" as "the completeness, consistency, and accuracy of data. Complete, consistent, and accurate data should be attributable, legible, contemporaneously recorded, original or true copy, and accurate (ALCOA)."[56] The DI Draft Guidance is, for the most part, focused on electronic data, and provides the FDA's current thinking regarding minimum requirements for audit trails, computer system validation, and access controls, such as restricting rights to alter files or settings to personnel who are independent from those responsible for content of the records, and restrictions on the use of credentials. The DI Draft Guidance also provides recommendations consistent with those outlined in the Application Integrity Policy for addressing data integrity problems. Specifically, the DI Draft Guidance recommends hiring an independent auditor, determining the scope of data integrity lapses, and developing and implementing a global plan to correct data integrity problems, and removing personnel who have engaged in objectionable conduct with respect to data integrity from regulated manufacturing activities.

Section 5.2.3 of the IOM states that investigators make "every reasonable effort" to discuss observations as they occur or on a daily basis "to minimize surprises, errors and misunderstandings when the FDA 483 is issued."[57] The IOM also informs investigators that firm management may ask questions about observations, request clarification, and inform the investigators about corrections that have been made or will be made during the inspection.

During the inspection close-out meeting, management should take the opportunity to ask additional questions if an observation is not clear. If the firm believes that there are factual mistakes or that an observation is based on a misunderstanding, it is appropriate to respectfully bring this to the attention of the investigator or inspection team.

POST-INSPECTION RESPONSE

While there is no formal requirement to respond to a Form FDA-483, establishments that do not respond risk possible administrative or enforcement action. If the FDA determines that responses to Form FDA-483 observations and the corrective actions taken by the establishment are not satisfactory, the FDA may issue a Warning Letter or take other administrative action, such as placing the company on import alert. Preparing a response to a Form FDA-483 can be a time-consuming and stressful process. It diverts resources from other activities and, if not managed properly, the process can be overwhelming. However, if a Form FDA-483 response is well-written, factually correct,

---

[53] 21 CFR § 211.160(a) ("The requirements in this subpart shall be followed and shall be documented at the time of performance. Any deviation from the written specifications, standards, sampling plans, test procedures, or other laboratory control mechanisms shall be recorded and justified.").

[54] 21 CFR § 211.180(d) ("Records required under this part may be retained either as original records or as true copies such as photocopies, microfilm, microfiche, or other accurate reproductions of the original records.").

[55] 21 CFR § 211.188 ("Batch production and control records shall be prepared for each batch of drug product produced and shall include complete information relating to the production and control of each batch"), § 211.194(a) ("Laboratory records shall include complete data derived from all tests necessary to assure compliance with established specifications and standards . . . ") and § 212.60(g) ("Each laboratory performing tests related to the production of a PET drug must keep complete records of all tests performed to ensure compliance with established specifications and standards . . . ").

[56] DI Draft Guidance, *supra* note 49, at 2.

[57] IOM, *supra* note 11, at Sec. 5.2.3.

and complete, it will demonstrate that the firm has taken or is in the process of taking appropriate corrective and preventive action. This can allay the FDA's concerns about the firm's compliance and reflect positively on the firm. If the response is poorly written, contains errors, or omits critical information, the FDA will not be able to determine that adequate corrective actions have been implemented, which may in turn potentially trigger additional inspections or a Warning Letter. If the firm submits inadequate responses to a Warning Letter, the firm is at risk for seizures, suspension of product approvals, injunctive action, or possibly criminal prosecution.

A common mistake is to use blanket admissions, that is, acknowledging or agreeing with a Form FDA-483 observation. An admission could be used against the firm in an FDA enforcement action, or in a product liability or securities lawsuit brought by a private plaintiff. Another common mistake is the use of template responses, with boilerplate language for certain types of observations. This is a missed opportunity. Crafting an acceptable response requires thoughtful analysis and precision, and is an opportunity to communicate to the Agency an understanding of the firm's compliance obligations. It is also an opportunity to demonstrate that the firm has corrected, or will correct, any deficiencies identified in the response and will ensure that the problems do not recur.[58] In drafting the response, the manufacturer should be careful to address the FDA's concerns and demonstrate an understanding of the scope of the problem. For example, the manufacturer should determine whether the observation describes an isolated incident or a systemic problem, and whether the problem is limited to a single lot or extends to other lots of the same product or other products. The manufacturer should also determine whether the problem is contained within a particular department or extends to other departments or other facilities.

The firm also should conduct a thorough investigation and take appropriate corrective action. Far too often, manufacturers respond to Form FDA-483s by simply defending their actions or relating the history of a problem. The quality unit should thoroughly investigate the FDA's concerns and describe the investigation, investigation results, and corrective actions in the response. Responses should be factual, complete, and easy to read. They should include reasonable timelines, address issues item by item, and demonstrate an understanding of regulatory requirements. Each response should be accompanied by supporting documentation, as evidence of the firm's investigation, and its actions to correct the observation and prevent it from recurring. A poorly written or defensive response suggests that the firm does not pay attention to detail and does not understand the significance of the observations.

During the inspection close-out meeting, firms often promise to submit responses as quickly as possible. The FDA requires responses to be submitted within 15 working days, but some manufacturers attempt to respond sooner in order to demonstrate quick action. A better approach is to use the time allowed. A lengthy Form FDA-483 or one involving complicated issues could require more investigation than anticipated. If the manufacturer is unable to complete all corrective actions within 15 working days, the FDA expects the manufacturer to explain the reason for the delay and when the corrective actions will be completed. In this circumstance, the manufacturer should commit to provide periodic updates to the FDA until its corrective actions are substantially complete.[59]

A firm should set timetables for corrective and preventive actions that demonstrate an appropriate sense of urgency. Commitments should be realistic, and firms must meet their commitments. Failure to take appropriate corrective action to address objectionable conditions will result in repeat observations (often the basis for a Warning Letter or other enforcement action).

---

[58] Note that in its subsequent inspection, the FDA will ensure that the manufacturer has taken the corrective actions described in the Form FDA-483 response and will verify the adequacy of those corrective actions.

[59] Depending on the significance of the FDA's observations, manufacturers generally submit updates on a monthly or quarterly basis.

RECENT DEVELOPMENTS RELATED TO DRUG INSPECTIONS

On June 6, 2017, the FDA published its "concept of operations" white paper to describe how Center for Drug Evaluation and Research (CDER) and ORA will work in a "vertically-integrated, programmatically-aligned environment" regarding drug inspections.[60] Among other things, when communicating the findings of an inspection to a firm, the FDA will issue a Field Management Directive (FMD)-145/decision letter within 90 days following the closing of an inspection.[61] An FMD-145/decision letter is an ORA-wide procedure for releasing a copy of an EIR to an establishment subject to an FDA inspection.[62]

On August 31, 2017, as discussed above, the FDA made changes to the FDA Staff Manual Guide (SMG) 9004.1 regarding policies and procedures for requesting records in advance of or in lieu of a drug inspection.[63] The purpose of this change to the SMG was to implement the authority granted the FDA in Section 704(a) of the FDCA to request records or other information from a firm "engaged in the manufacture, preparation, propagation, compounding, or processing of a drug."[64] The FDA may use the records received through a Section 704(a) request to inform its inspection planning and its preparation for an inspection. The FDA can also use the records obtained from a Section 704(a) request in lieu of certain inspections or to adjust the interval time between facility inspections.[65]

CONCLUSION

The FDA conducts establishment inspections in order to assess the ability of a drug manufacturer to produce safe and effective products, and to ensure the integrity of data. FDA investigators seek to determine whether manufacturers understand their regulatory obligations and take prompt action to address problems so they are corrected and do not recur. Firms that do not appreciate the significance of establishment inspections or FDA inspectional observations often pay the price, in terms of Warning Letters, negative publicity, and escalating enforcement. Firms that are rigorous in terms of self-evaluation, oversight, and problem solving are far more likely to have successful inspections than firms that are focused exclusively on financial gain. Moreover, thorough preparation, disciplined inspection management, and well-developed inspection responses will give the FDA the assurance that the firm is operating in a state of compliance.

---

[60] Food & Drug Admin., Integration of FDA Facility Evaluation and Inspection Program for Human Drugs: A Concept of Operations, June 6, 2017, *available at* https://www.fda.gov/downloads/AboutFDA/CentersOffices/OfficeofGlobalRegulatoryOperationsandPolicy/ORA/UCM574362.pdf.

[61] *Ibid.* at 4.3.

[62] Food & Drug Admin., Release of Establishment Inspection Reports (FMD#-145), March 1, 2012, *available at* https://www.fda.gov/downloads/ICECI/Inspections/FieldManagementDirectives/UCM295101.doc.

[63] *See* SMG 9004.1, *supra* note 7.

[64] *Ibid.*

[65] *Ibid.*

22 FDA Pre-approval Inspections

Cathy L. Burgess, Justin Mann, and Seth Olson

CONTENTS

INTRODUCTION

In this chapter, we discuss establishment inspections that the Food and Drug Administration (FDA) conducts in order to verify manufacturing data associated with a new drug application (NDA) or abbreviated new drug application (ANDA), and to determine whether the manufacturer of the product is in compliance with current good manufacturing practice (CGMP) requirements. As part of a pre-approval inspection (PAI), the FDA also conducts a general CGMP inspection. For general information concerning establishment inspections, please see Chapter 21, "FDA Inspection Process."

BACKGROUND

The current PAI program is described in FDA's Compliance Policy Guide Manual, CPGM 7346.832. In 2002, under the FDA's Pharmaceutical CGMPs for the twenty first century initiative, the agency developed "scientific, risk-based approaches that incorporate inspection of the level of the firm's process and product understanding, an evaluation of the firm's manufacturing readiness, and verification of authenticity of submitted data."

The program is tied to the user-fee programs authorized by Congress under the Prescription Drug User Fee Act and the Generic Drug User Fee Act. In order to comply with a Congressional mandate that "user-fee" due dates are met, it requires the coordination of all offices involved in the pre-approval program—Center for Drug Evaluation and Research (CDER) Office of Pharmaceutical Science; CDER Office of Compliance; Office of Regulatory Affairs (ORA) district offices; and FDA analyzing laboratories.

Certain aspects of the program predated the passage of drug user-fee acts. For example, under the Generic Drug Enforcement Act of 1989, the PAI program was significantly expanded to include a greater emphasis on data integrity (DI).

Under the PAI program, the FDA considers whether to conduct on-site inspections of manufacturers named in the Chemistry, Manufacturing, and Controls (CMC) section of an NDA, ANDA, or Biological Licensing Application (BLA).

The program extends to domestic and foreign manufacturers and may cover the manufacture of active pharmaceutical ingredients (APIs), finished drug product manufacturing, and control testing laboratories.

In some cases, the FDA may determine that an on-site inspection is not necessary because the FDA has sufficient information without the need for a PAI. For example, the FDA may have establishment inspection reports (EIRs) from recent FDA inspections, or reports from foreign regulatory authorities that provide sufficient information upon which to make a determination regarding site acceptability. CPGM 7346.832 states that the PAI program's "risk-based decision criteria for performing an on-site inspection for an application ensure that inspection resources are directed to the greatest possible protection of public health. This program also provides risk-based strategies for the scope of inspectional coverage and clarifies roles in order to establish more efficient communication."

BEFORE THE INSPECTION

TWO TYPES OF PAIs: PRIORITY AND DISCRETIONARY

As will be described in more detail later, for every establishment named in the CMC section of a marketing authorization application, the FDA assesses whether an inspection of that establishment is required prior to approving that application. The FDA divides pre-approval inspections into two main categories: Priority Inspections and non-Priority Inspections (i.e., Discretionary).[1] To be considered a Priority Inspection, one or more of the following criteria must be met:

1. First time that the facility has been named in an application.
2. First time that the facility has submitted an application.
3. First ANDA filed for a previously approved drug.
4. Finished product application with a New Molecular Entity.
5. Finished product proposed label indicates the need for dosing to be titrated.
6. Finished product is a narrow therapeutic index drug (e.g., with an assay specification of 95%–105%).
7. Finished product is expected to require titrated dosing (does not apply to supplements).
8. Finished product or API is a substantially different dosage form, or is manufactured using a substantially different process from other products manufactured at the facility.

---

[1] FDA's Compliance Policy Guide Manual, CPGM 7346.832 § 2.2.1 [hereafter PAI CPGM].

9. The process by which API is derived is considered high risk (e.g., API is derived from animal tissues).

10. Proposed use of the API is significantly different from currently approved versions of API (e.g., API previously used in non-sterile product is now intended for a sterile drug product).

11. The establishment has submitted a number of applications and/or experienced a significant number of recent changes, such that there is a question as to whether the establishment can handle the change while remaining within a "state of control."

12. The drug in the application has an "unacceptable" profile class.

13. For original applications or significant pre-approval CMC supplements, the profile class status of the drug associated with the application has not been updated via a site inspection within the past two years (three years for control laboratories and four years for packaging and labeling).[2]

A Discretionary Inspection is an inspection that the district chooses to perform, despite that the inspection does not qualify for a Priority Inspection. While the FDA has not established specific criteria for determining when to schedule a Discretionary Inspection, the FDA has indicated that an applicant filing multiple applications, or being named in multiple applications, in a relatively short amount of time may trigger a Discretionary Inspection. Also, a Discretionary Inspection may be warranted if the establishment has a negative inspection history (e.g., "significant deficiencies" during the last pre-approval inspection) or some other indicator that might call into question the establishment's compliance capabilities (e.g., numerous recalls or a recent change in leadership).

Process for Determining whether a PAI is to Be Scheduled

Three main divisions of the FDA are involved in determining whether a PAI drug establishment inspection is to be scheduled: CDER Office of Pharmaceutical Science (OPS), CBER Division of Manufacturing and Product Quality (DMPQ),[3] and ORA. OPS reviews all applications to identify each establishment listed in an application.[4] OPS then creates an Establishment Evaluation Request (EER) and sends the EER to DMPQ. DMPQ is responsible for determining whether the inspection qualifies as a Priority Inspection, based on the criteria outlined above.[5] Once DMPQ has completed its assessment, it sends the results of that assessment to ORA. For domestic establishments, the DMPQ assessment goes to the district office. For foreign establishment, the assessment goes to Division of Field Investigations, which is also part of ORA.

When DMPQ has determined that an inspection meets the Priority Pre-Approval Inspection (PAI) criteria, ORA (either the district office or the International Compliance Branch) has 10 calendar days to decide whether to schedule the inspection.[6] If ORA decides not to conduct a Priority PAI, it must provide a recommendation as to whether CDER should approve an application. There are a number of reasons why ORA might decline a Priority PAI, but this is an indication that FDA

---

[2] *Ibid.*

[3] PAI CPGM § 2.3.3. For Biological Licensing Application (BLA) inspection assignments DMPQ determines whether a pre-license inspection should be performed.

[4] PAI CPGM § 2.3.1.1. Regarding Investigational New Drug (IND) Applications, district offices will typically not inspect a clinical trial manufacturer unless directed to do so by CDER. However, for Treatment INDs, based on the fact that patients typically can be those with more serious or life-threatening disease or conditions, and typically no alternative drugs or treatments exist, an establishment inspection can be a high priority for CDER. If CDER determines to perform an inspection, the district office is instructed to complete the inspection within 10 calendar days from receiving the inspection request. PAI CPGM § 2.3.2.

[5] PAI CPGM § 2.3.1.2.1.

[6] *Ibid.*

already has enough information to make a recommendation without the need for an inspection (e.g., positive inspection history with more complex products; negative inspection history with unresolved issues; results from a recent inspection by a recognized foreign health authority). Whether ORA would be able to meet the application's user-fee date is also a consideration.

FDA Preparing for Inspection

The FDA's preparations for a PAI include scheduling the inspection, choosing the inspection team, and conducting a pre-inspection review of available information.

To schedule an inspection, a number of factors will be considered, including the user-fee date, importance of the inspection to application approval decision, and other inspections that are planned or due at the facility.[7] As an important consideration for establishments preparing for a PAI, if the FDA has already begun inspection planning, the establishment can make a written submission to the FDA indicating that it is not ready for the inspection, but in these cases the FDA policy is to enter a Withhold Approval recommendation for that establishment.

The PAI inspection team will generally consist of one investigator and one analyst.[8] Sometimes the inspection team members may include personnel from CDER. ORA can make a request to CDER for support (e.g., from Office of Pharmaceutical Science or the Office of Compliance), which is especially encouraged in the case novel product attributes, manufacturing processes, or analytical methods. CDER, through DMPQ, can also request to be included on an inspection team.

Since launching its *Pharmaceutical CGMP for the 21st Century—A Risk-Based Approach* initiative in 2002, a focus in the last 15 years has been improving the effectiveness and efficiency of the FDA's inspection programs.[9] Inspection preparation is one area in particular where the FDA has emphasized collaboration and information sharing between CDER and ORA as a means of ensuring a robust inspection. The CPGM for PAIs has general evidence throughout encouraging CDER and ORA to collaborate both prior to an inspection and in the course of an inspection.[10] A more formal manifestation of this collaborative approach is FDA's Knowledge Transfer Program.[11] Through their review of an application, CDER gains significant insight into the application drug and the establishments associated with that application. The purpose of the Knowledge Transfer Program is to systematically communicate that information to ORA, which often includes CDER issuing a formal Knowledge Transfer Memorandum (KTM). The goal is for ORA to receive the PAI prior to the inspection.

In addition to reviewing the KTM, below are a few other inspection preparation activities CPGM encourages:

- Review of the CMC sections of related Drug Master Files (DMFs) for the establishment to be inspected and development report.
- Communicate with the CDER reviewers for the application to gain their insights into the application, including any recommendations they might have for particular areas to focus on during the inspection.

---

[7] PAI CPGM § 3.1.

[8] PAI CPGM § 3.2.

[9] PAI CPGM Part VII.

[10] *See, e.g.*, PAI CPGM § 3.4.2, "Following the principles of ICH guidelines Q8, Q9, and Q10, the agency is implementing a more integrated approach towards preparing for and conducting inspections. CDER and ORA will collaborate in order to provide an efficient and effective use of inspectional resources. Questions that arise during an inspection should normally be directed to the DMPQ/MAPCB contact, who will coordinate a response within CDER, and the PAM." Attachment A of the PAI CPGM states the following: "Roles of Investigator and CDER Product Reviewers by Specific Area of CMC Review and Assessment" to the CPGM for formerly outlines the roles of ORA versus CDER during the life cycle of the inspection.

[11] PAI CPGM § 2.5.

- Where the inspection team has questions about the content of the application or the intricacies of a particular CGMP requirement, they are encouraged to reach out to experts within FDA.
- Develop a strategy for the inspection.

DURING THE INSPECTION

For information concerning the general conduct of the establishment inspection, please refer to Chapter 21, "FDA Inspection Process".

PAI PROGRAM OBJECTIVES

There are three primary inspectional objectives of this PAI program: (1) readiness for commercial manufacturing of the product under review, (2) conformance to the application, and (3) DI.

Priority Inspections should cover at least one of the three objectives highlighted above. Which objectives are chosen is generally dependent on the processes at the establishment for the application and how those activities are different than previous activities at the establishment (e.g., the establishment had historically manufactured only non-sterile APIs, but application relates to sterile APIs).[12] For example, if an establishment has never been inspected before or it has a negative inspection history (e.g., previous Voluntary Action Indicated (VAI) status), FDA guidance is to cover all three objectives.[13] Conversely, if the establishment has a recent, positive inspection history, including for related products, then FDA guidance indicates that covering only two objectives may only be required.

OBJECTIVE 1: READINESS FOR COMMERCIAL MANUFACTURING

The FDA will evaluate whether an establishment's quality system is sufficiently robust to achieve sufficient control over the facility and commercial manufacturing operations. The FDA will review the following information:[14]

1. Manufacturing and laboratory changes, investigations, and trends relating to the development of new drug substance and product manufacturing demonstrate that the establishment has appropriately assessed related issues.
2. A sound and appropriate program for sampling, testing, and evaluation of components (including APIs), in-process materials, finished products, containers, and closures for purposes of releasing materials or products has been established.
3. The establishment has sufficient facility and equipment controls in place to prevent contamination of and by the application product (or API).
4. Adequate procedures exist for change control; investigating failures, deviations, complaints, and adverse events; conducting recalls; and for reporting this information to the FDA.
5. The feasibility of the proposed commercial process and manufacturing batch record, including instructions, processing parameters, and process control measures are scientifically and objectively justified. This objective is linked to the firm's process validation program.

---

[12] PAI CPGM § 3.4.1.
[13] *Ibid.*
[14] *Ibid.*

Objective 1(a): Manufacturing and Laboratory Changes, Investigations, and Trends Relating to the Development of New Drug Substance and Product Manufacturing Demonstrate that the Establishment Has Appropriately Assessed Related Issues.[15]

A common area of FDA concern in general CGMP inspections is a manufacturer's ability to properly document, investigate, and address issues that might arise in the course of the manufacturing process.[16]

For the laboratory, the inspection covers out-of-specification (OOS) results, out-of-trend results, and lab incidents for issues affecting raw materials, in-process materials, and finished products.[17] The FDA is also concerned with method validation, in terms of issues that might have arisen during the validation process, as well as any changes that have been made to the analytical method since validation.[18]

Deviation investigations are a primary focus in the manufacturing operations area.[19] The FDA will look not only at deviations and trending for the application product, but also for any other marketed products that might have a similar manufacturing process. Equipment and equipment maintenance is also an important aspect of Objective 1(a), particularly if the firm is already utilizing commercial equipment that it plans to continue using post-approval.[20]

Ultimately, the FDA reviews investigations prior to approval to determine the manufacturer's ability to handle issues that will arise in commercial production.

Objective 1(b): A Sound and Appropriate Program for Sampling, Testing, and Evaluation of Components (Including APIs), In-Process Materials, Finished Products, Containers, and Closures for Purposes of Releasing Materials or Products Has Been Established[21]

A "sound and appropriate program for sampling" includes a scientific justification for the sampling program[22] and results in representative samples.[23] A robust sampling plan also covers not only finished products but also in-process materials, intermediates, raw materials, labeling, and stability batches.[24]

Factors that should be considered in forming a scientific justification for a plan would include:

- Acceptable quality limits
- Experience with the material
- Variability in the material
- Critical control points
- Points where the process is particularly vulnerable

---

[15] PAI CPGM § 3.4.1.

[16] FDA Warning Letter to Celltron Inc., January 26, 2018 (FDA cited that firm "failed to thoroughly investigate any unexplained discrepancy or failure of a batch or any of its components to meet any of its specifications, whether or not the batch has already been distributed").

[17] PAI CPGM § 3.4.1.

[18] For more information pertaining to the validation/verification of analytical methods, see 21 CFR § 211.160–167, and 211.194. For additional information regarding the validation of analytical methods for APIs, see FDA Guidance, "Q7 Good Manufacturing Practice Guidance for Active Pharmaceutical Ingredients," April 2018, available at, https://www.fda.gov/ucm/groups/fdagov-public/@fdagov-drugs-gen/documents/document/ucm605076.pdf.

[19] For more information related to product deviations and investigations, see 21 CFR § 211.100, 211.192, and 211.198. For additional information related to APIs, see FDA Guidance, "Q7 Good Manufacturing Practice Guidance for Active Pharmaceutical Ingredients," April 2018, available at, https://www.fda.gov/ucm/groups/fdagov-public/@fdagov-drugs-gen/documents/document/ucm605076.pdf.

[20] PAI CPGM § 3.4.1. For additional information related to equipment maintenance, cleaning, and sanitation, see 21 CFR § 211.67(a).

[21] PAI CPGM § 3.4.1.

[22] PAI CPGM § 3.4.1. See also 21 CFR § 211.160.

[23] Sampling plans for finished products are required to be in writing and meet statistically sound quality control criteria. See 21 CFR § 211.165. For additional information related to sampling of APIs, see FDA Guidance, "Q7 Good Manufacturing Practice Guidance for Active Pharmaceutical Ingredients," April 2018, available at, https://www.fda.gov/ucm/groups/fdagov-public/@fdagov-drugs-gen/documents/document/ucm605076.pdf.

[24] For more information see 21 CFR §§ 211.110, 211.134, and 211.166.

The FDA defines a "representative sample" as "a sample that consists of a number of units that are drawn based on rational criteria such as random sampling and intended to assure that the sample accurately portrays the material being sampled."[25] The variables that the FDA considers when assessing whether a sample is representative include:

- The methodology for sample selection
- How samples are collected (e.g., one sample per batch or one sample from the top, middle, and bottom of a batch)
- Sample size and numbers statistical rationale

Objective 1(c): The Establishment Has Sufficient Facility and Equipment Controls in Place to Prevent Contamination of and by the Application Product (or API).[26]

The focus of this objective is to ensure that there are adequate controls to protect against cross contamination from other products being manufactured in the same facility. In the case of application products that are highly potent, the FDA focuses on controls to prevent cross contamination of other products being manufactured in the same facility. This objective covers all components of the facility, including buildings, equipment, and utilities. In particular, the FDA focuses on new components (e.g., new construction) or newly constructed buildings/areas.

Objective 1(d): Adequate Procedures Exist for Change Control; Investigating Failures, Deviations, Complaints, and Adverse Events; Conducting Recalls; and for Reporting This Information to the FDA.[27]

For new companies, the FDA reviews the design of the quality system, including the change control process, along with any objective evidence that is required prior to having an approved application. For companies that have marketed products, the FDA is likely to take a sampling of various pieces of documentation (e.g., failures, deviations, change controls, complaint investigations, recalls, outputs from the AE reporting system[28]) to confirm that the quality system is functioning as designed.

Objective 1(e): The Feasibility of the Proposed Commercial Process and Manufacturing Batch Record, Including Instructions, Processing Parameters, and Process Control Measures, Are Scientifically and Objectively Justified. This Objective is Linked to the Firm's Process Validation Program.[29]

Under this objective, the FDA assesses whether it believes that the proposed commercial process is able to reliably produce drug products that have the identity, strength, quality, and purity that is described in the marketing application.[30] While a large part of this assessment will be to review process validation, the FDA looks more granularly, with a particular focus on the studies conducted to justify the proposed process. The FDA reviews development studies, studies to establish key controls, and scale-up studies. When the FDA is reviewing a study, it not only looks at the results, it reviews the protocol, how the study was executed, and how reliable the data are.

Note that the FDA is aware that, depending on the timing of the PAI, not all studies may be completed, or that the manufacturer may need to make changes to the process submitted in the marketing application. The FDA may also review process validation studies for marketed products as a general means of assessing the manufacturer's ability to perform process validation. It is also

[25] 21 CFR § 210.3(b)(21).
[26] PAI CPGM § 3.4.1.
[27] *Ibid.*
[28] The CPGM instructs the investigator to recommend a standalone inspection of the AE reporting system if they have concerns, under CP7353.001A.
[29] PAI CPGM § 3.4.1.
[30] *Ibid.*

possible that the investigator will have reviewed process validation information prior to arriving on-site, if CDER has shared such information with ORA.[31]

In terms of the output, the FDA will be asking questions such as the following:

- What did the studies tell the manufacturer about potential variability or vulnerability in manufacturing process?
- What are the critical quality attributes (CQAs)?
- What are the parameters, instructions, and controls established for those attributes, and how are they captured in the master production record?
- And how did the studies justify setting those controls?
- How does the firm plan to monitor process once it begins commercial operations?

The FDA may consider certain issues to warrant further review, including situations where a drug product or API has not been demonstrated to meet its critical quality attributes and/or a root cause determination has not been made. Other examples include records that show for unclear reasons an unexpected highly variable process; inconsistent execution of batch record or manufacturing instructions; control measures do not appear to align with the critical quality attribute; sampling and monitoring plans are not properly sufficient or justified; or there is a lack of objective scientific data to justify critical process parameters such that material impact is unknown.

OBJECTIVE 2: CONFORMANCE TO APPLICATION

The purpose of Objective 2 is to confirm that the actual operations of the manufacturer, as well as the raw data that were not submitted with the application, are consistent (i.e., in "conformance") with the information listed in the CMC section of the application for the biobatch, APIs, and proposed commercial batch. This will likely include a physical observation and examination of the manufacturing operations and analytical testing, as well as reviewing additional information.

For manufacturing operations, the investigator reviews everything from the equipment to processing lines. This also includes observing the manufacturing operations in action. The investigator compares the batch production records to ensure the steps and operations match the manufacturing process described in the application.

Similarly for the analytical testing, the investigator will confirm that the analyses being carried out at the facility follow the analytical methods and processes described in the application. The investigator reviews records, including lab notebooks, to identify differences from the filed method, especially in terms of specifications. This review includes observing the analytical method being performed to identify deviations from filed method. If an investigator is unable to observe the performance of all analyses, they will likely prioritize any observations of analyses that are complicated, unique to the application, or related to a CQA.

The review of manufacturing and analytical records also includes comparing documents between the biobatch and commercial batch. For example:

- Are the same manufacturing steps used for the biobatch being used for the commercial scale batch?
- Do the specifications for assay differ between the two?

This review is likely to include comparison objective evidence of the commercial batch (e.g., inventory and shipping records) to the similar records submitted for the biobatch. One of the reasons for

---

[31] *Ibid.*

focusing on comparability between the biobatch and commercial batch is to ensure stability data that are generated can be relied upon to determine expiration.[32]

This review of manufacturing and analytical records is not limited to finished products. The investigator will also be reviewing components (e.g., raw materials), in-process materials, and APIs.[33] For example, is the API manufacturer listed in inventory records the same as the one listed in the application? If the application includes a secondary API manufacturer, is there evidence to show that the supply from the secondary supplier is equivalent to the primary supplier? Are the raw materials being examined or tested in the same manner for the commercial scale batch as they were for the biobatch?

The CPGM describes this review in terms of documents that provide "factual integrity" (e.g., raw data that confirms a reported value in the application) and those that provide "contextual integrity" (i.e., records like analytical data and manufacturing records that support but do not directly prove the factual integrity of the document). Factual integrity is essential, but it is important to note that when data or documents are missing that should provide contextual integrity, this could cause the FDA to question the overall integrity of the application.

OBJECTIVE 3: DATA INTEGRITY

In April 2016, the FDA issued the draft guidance "Data Integrity and Compliance with CGMP."[34] The DI Draft Guidance clarifies the role of DI in CGMPs for drugs. This guidance specifically applies to the requirements set out under 21 CFR Parts 210, 211, and 212.

The DI audit conducted as part of the PAI will include an audit of raw data in order to verify that all of the relevant data submitted in the CMC section is complete and accurate.[35] The DI audit may include a review of specification of components and finished product and possibly the data contained in the development report.

The DI audit should include a review of the accuracy and completeness of data in the CMC section for the quality and specifications of components and finished product, and if submitted, data in the development report. The DI audit may take an in-depth review of raw data files to support the data/information contained in the application as being complete and accurate. This allows FDA reviewers to perform an objective analysis.

If DI integrity discrepancies are observed during the audit, the FDA investigator is instructed to identify the personnel responsible for the application submissions and who are responsible for deciding to include or exclude the data involved in the discrepancies. The FDA investigatory will look at what actions or inactions, if any, may have contributed to the DI discrepancy and if any corrective actions were taken or are to be taken to resolve the discrepancies. If discrepancies are observed, the investigator will also look to determine whether omitted data is present that should have been submitted to the application. For example:

- Was there any "passing" data submitted to the application that was substituted in place of "failing" data (i.e., OOS or unfavorable) without a sufficient investigation and resolution of the discrepancy?
- Did the firm improperly invalidate OOS results, which were therefore not submitted in the application?

---

[32] For more information regarding the submission of biobatches and stability batch information and finished product testing results, see 21 CFR §§ 211.165, 211.166, 211.188, and 314.50(d)(1)(ii)(b).

[33] For additional information related to API GMPs, see FDA Guidance, "Q7 Good Manufacturing Practice Guidance for Active Pharmaceutical Ingredients," April 2018, available at, https://www.fda.gov/ucm/groups/fdagov-public/@fdagov-drugs-gen/documents/document/ucm605076.pdf.

[34] FDA Draft Guidance for Industry, Data Integrity and Compliance with CGMP [hereinafter DI Draft Guidance], April 2016, available at https://www.fda.gov/downloads/drugs/guidances/ucm495891.pdf.

[35] Inspection team should determine if the operations appears beyond the capability of the firm and review various production records to determine if batches were truly produced at the site, or are being produced at a subcontracted "shadow factory" without FDA knowledge.

If discrepancies are found, the district office is instructed to follow the agency's Application Integrity Policy (AIP) and consider submitting an AIP recommendation to CDER/DMPQ.

INSPECTION PROCESS FOR PAIs

For more general information regarding the Inspection Process, please refer to Chapter 21, "FDA Inspection Process".

SAMPLE COLLECTION OR SAMPLE SUBMISSION REQUESTS

The following types of samples are associated with the drug application review process; however, FDA investigators are instructed to not routinely collect method validation/verification samples, profile–innovator and applicant drug samples, and biobatch facility samples during the PAI.[36] These various types of samples may be requested at other steps in the application review process or based on a for-cause determination.[37]

AFTER THE INSPECTION

At the conclusion of a PAI, the investigator will report any reportable inspection observations through an FDA-483.[38] Additionally, the investigator will provide a more detailed finding through an EIR. If the district office recommends approval at the conclusion of the PAI, a streamlined EIR may be submitted. Details about what is in a streamlined EIR are found in CPGM 7346.832. Note that if any corrective actions are promised by an establishment during the PAI, the investigator will record those in the EIR.

If the PAI is classified as Official Action Indicated (OAI) for objectionable conditions, the application will not be approved.[39] For example, if the district office observes significant DI problems because of significant differences between the information contained in the application and what the investigator covered at the inspection, the district will likely recommend to withhold approval. For additional details regarding other types of deficiencies that would result in the district office recommending to withhold approval, see CPGM 7346.832. If the PAI classification is OAI, the agency will likely consider issuing a Warning Letter.[40]

---

[36] PAI CPGM § 3.5.
[37] Ibid.
[38] PAI CPGM § 3.5. For more general information related to the inspection process, refer to Chapter 21, "FDA Inspection Process".
[39] See FMD 86: Establishment Inspection Report Conclusions and Decisions, Version 6, December 28, 2014, https://www.fda.gov/downloads/ICECI/Inspections/FieldManagementDirectives/UCM382035.pdf.
[40] See FDA Regulatory Manual 4–1: Warning Letters https://www.fda.gov/downloads/ICECI/ComplianceManuals/RegulatoryProceduresManual/UCM074330.pdf.

23 Worldwide Good Manufacturing Practices

Dominic Parry

CONTENTS

There are various different types of good manufacturing practice (GMP) across the world. All aim to do essentially the same thing: to protect the end user from poor quality of medicines. This chapter provides an overview of some of the main GMP standards outside of the United States. As such, we will cover the following:

1. GMP in the European Union
2. GMP in Japan
3. The Pharmaceutical Inspection Co-operation Scheme GMP (PIC/S GMP)
4. World Health Organization GMP (WHO GMP)
5. GMP for Active Pharmaceutical Ingredients

GMP IN THE EUROPEAN UNION

The European Union (EU) is an economic and political partnership between 28 European countries that together cover much of the continent of Europe. The EU was created in the aftermath of the Second World War. The first steps were to foster economic cooperation: the idea being that countries who trade with one another become economically interdependent and so more likely to avoid conflict. The result was the European Economic Community (EEC), created in 1958, by its six founding countries: Belgium, Germany, France, Italy, Luxembourg, and the Netherlands. Further expansion happened in the 1970s when the United Kingdom (UK), Ireland, and Denmark joined the group, and also in the 1980s when other countries such as Greece, Portugal, and Spain also joined. The union has expanded since and now includes 28 European countries, or Member States, as they are sometimes referred to. Today it is called the European Union, or EU. The current members of the EU are: Austria, Belgium, Bulgaria, Croatia, Cyprus, Czech Republic, Denmark, Estonia, Finland, France, Germany, Greece, Hungary, Ireland, Italy, Latvia, Lithuania, Luxembourg, Malta, Netherlands, Poland, Portugal, Romania, Slovakia, Slovenia, Spain, Sweden, and the United Kingdom. However, in 2016, following a referendum, the UK voted to leave the European Union, the first country ever to do so. The process of the UK leaving the EU (referred to as BREXIT) is still underway at the time of writing (June 2018), so the ramifications of this are not currently fully known.

Over time, the EU has worked to promote the ease of trade between its members, aiming for consistent rules and harmonization of standards. As a result, a product made in one EU country should meet the requirements all of the others. For example, a car made in Germany should meet the standards required by all the other Member States.

Before the early 1990s, there were different GMP standards for the manufacture of pharmaceuticals/drugs across Europe. There was British GMP, German GMP, French GMP, and so on. Manufacturing sites in these countries would not only be inspected by their own national Regulatory Authority, but they would also be inspected by neighboring country's Regulatory Authorities. In the mid-1980s, work began to harmonize a large number of rules across Europe, and included in this was GMP. As a result, European Union GMP (EU GMP) was born in 1991. From this point onward, individual GMPs for each Member State disappeared to be replaced by a single EU GMP to be adopted across the whole of the EU. Plus, Member States were no longer inspected by Regulatory Authority inspectors from other EU countries. Now you would be inspected by your own Regulatory Authority on behalf of the whole of Europe. To this day, this is still the largest mutual recognition agreement in place for GMP across the whole world. One GMP across the whole of the EU, with all of the EU's Regulatory Authorities working together to get consistent inspections.

European law works by Directives being issued from the EU. These Directives must then be incorporated into national law by each Member State of the EU. There is normally a few years allowed for this to occur. In 1991, two "GMP Directives" were issued, one for human medicinal products and one for animal medicinal products. The requirements were very similar, and the standard expected for animal GMP is very similar to human GMP. These two Directives were Directive 91/356/EEC (for human medicinal products) and Directive 91/412/EEC (for veterinary medicinal products). Note that the prefix is the year in which the Directive was issued (1991); the middle number is the sequential number for the Directives issued in that year (i.e., these were the 356th and 412th Directives of 1991); and the suffix ends with EEC—what the EU was known as at the time. At the same time, the *European Guide to GMP* was also issued, and the connection between the European GMP Directives and the Guide to GMP is explained shortly.

These European GMP Directives contain the high-level legal framework and requirements for European GMP, with each Directive consisting of a series of articles, all of which are European law. The human Directive was updated in 2003, mainly due to the additional requirements for clinical trial materials (also referred to as Investigational Medicinal Products [IMPs]), which also need to be made to GMP requirements. The new human GMP Directive from this time was therefore 2003/94/EC, issued on October 8, 2003. Note that the suffix is now EC, which stands for the European Commission, the executive branch of the EU that now issues its laws.

In summary, there are two GMP Directives, one for humans and one for animals. The human one is Directive 2003/94/EC and the animal one is Directive 91/412/EEC. They both have the same structure, and the requirements are still quite similar; it is just that the human Directive has some additional requirements concerning the packaging and labeling of clinical trial materials, that is, IMPs, and the need to unblind and stop a clinical trial if anything should go wrong.

It is a legal requirement that sites in Europe making human or animal medicinal products work to the relevant Directive. In order to get the right to make medicines, the site must have a Manufacturing Authorization—a licence to make medicines that is granted by the national Regulatory Authority.

From this point, we will focus just on the human GMP Directive. The human GMP Directive (2003/94/EC) has a series of articles within it. Each article is EU law. The first two cover the scope of the Directive and some definitions. Their titles are listed below:

GMP Directive (2003/94/EC)

Article 1.   Scope
Article 2.   Definitions

The next three articles form a very important part of the whole GMP framework and the inspection of GMP by the EU Regulatory Authorities. Article 3 gives the Regulatory Authority the right to inspect sites with a Manufacturing Authorization (in other words, those making pharmaceutical/ drug products). This inspection can be at any time. Article 4 makes it a legal requirement that sites making medicines make them according to EU GMP. Article 5 also makes it a legal requirement that sites making medicines make then according to the conditions described in their Marketing Authorization. The Marketing Authorization is the approval (or licence) for the product itself. As such, Articles 4 and 5 make it a legal requirement that manufacturing sites make product to EU GMP and the conditions described in its Marketing Authorization. These next three articles are listed below:

GMP Directive (2003/94/EC)

    Article 3.   Inspections
    Article 4.   Conformity with Good Manufacturing Practice
    Article 5.   Compliance with Marketing Authorisation

The next 10 articles of the GMP Directive are also very significant. These provide the legal framework for GMP itself. They are listed below:

GMP Directive (2003/94/EC)

    Article 6.   Quality Assurance system
    Article 7.   Personnel
    Article 8.   Premises & Equipment
    Article 9.   Documentation
    Article 10. Production
    Article 11. Quality Control
    Article 12. Work Contracted Out
    Article 13. Complaints, Product Recall, and Emergency Unblinding
    Article 14. Self-inspection
    Article 15. Labelling (of IMPs)

They provide a high-level legal requirement that manufacturing sites must work to. They are normally a few sentences long, or sometimes a short paragraph or two. An example using Article 6 is stated below:

Article 6: The manufacturer shall establish and implement an effective pharmaceutical quality assurance system, involving the active participation of the management and personnel of the different departments.

This makes it a legal requirement that manufacturing sites have a Quality Assurance (QA) system that involves everyone. Note that it gives no detail on how to establish a QA system though!

The articles continue to Article 15. Article 15 is not in the equivalent animal GMP Directive (91/412/EEC), and the wording of Article 13 in the animal Directive is also different. Then there are four more articles covering how and when the whole Directive became law, but these will not be discussed in this chapter.

In 2017, the Directive for making human medicines (2003/94/EC) was updated again. This time separating out the manufacture of conventional medicines and medicines used for clinical trials (IMPs). As a result, two Directives were issued; Commission Directive (EU) 2017/1572 to cover the manufacture of conventional medicines and (EU) 2017/1569 to cover the manufacture of IMPs.

The new directive for conventional medicines (EU) 2017/1572 follows a similar structure and wording for the previous Directive (2003/94/EC) that it replaced, without reference to the manufacture of IMPs.

So far we have highlighted the high-level legal requirements of the GMP Directive. As a reminder, in Article 5 it stated that manufacturing sites must work to EU GMP, and so we need to bring the *EU Guide to GMP* into the equation.

The *EU Guide to GMP* was published at approximate the same time as the first GMP Directives in 1991. It consists of an introduction followed by nine chapters. The content of EU GMP is listed below:

THE *EU GUIDE TO GMP*—CHAPTERS

Introduction

    Chapter 1. Pharmaceutical Quality System
    Chapter 2. Personnel
    Chapter 3. Premises & Equipment
    Chapter 4. Documentation
    Chapter 5. Production
    Chapter 6. Quality Control
    Chapter 7. Outsourced activities
    Chapter 8. Complaints, Quality Defects, and Product Recalls
    Chapter 9. Self-inspection (internal auditing)

Note the similarity in titles of Chapters 1 through 9 of the *EU Guide to GMP* and Articles 6 to 14 of the GMP Directive. They are practically the same. Here we can now see how EU GMP starts to work. The chapters of the *EU Guide to GMP* provide guidance on how each corresponding article can be met. So if you need to know how to *"establish and implement an effective pharmaceutical quality assurance system, involving the active participation of the management and personnel of the different departments" (Article 6 of the GMP Directive)* then the corresponding Chapter 1—Pharmaceutical Quality System provides pages of guidance on how you could achieve this goal. The same can be said for the following eight chapters and articles of the *Guide to GMP* and GMP *Directive* respectively.

In addition to the nine chapters, there are also around 20 annexes in the *EU Guide to GMP*. These cover additional GMP requirements for certain situations, and about half of these are relevant to different types of dosage forms of the medicinal product. The annexes are listed below (note Annex 13 covering IMP):

The EU Guide to GMP—Annexes

    Annex 1.   Sterile manufacturing
    Annex 2.   Biological products
    Annex 3.   Radiopharmaceuticals
    Annex 4.   Veterinary medicinal products
    Annex 5.   Immunological veterinary products
    Annex 6.   Medicinal gases
    Annex 7.   Herbal medicinal products
    Annex 8.   Sampling of starting materials
    Annex 9.   Liquids, creams & ointments
    Annex 10. Metered dose inhalers
    Annex 11. Computerised systems
    Annex 12. Use of ionizing radiation

Annex 13. Investigational medicinal products

Annex 14. Products derived from human blood

Annex 15. Qualification & validation

Annex 16. Certification by a qualified person

Annex 17. Parametric release

~~Annex 18. GMP for Active Pharmaceutical Ingredients~~*

Annex 19. Reference samples

* Annex 18 has been crossed out for a reason that will be explained shortly.

A site working to EU GMP must work to the nine chapters of GMP **plus** any annexes that are relevant to the products and activities involved. So if you are making a sterile pharmaceutical product (free from microorganisms), you work to the nine chapters of GMP **plus** Annex 1.

Historically, GMP in the EU has evolved using the annexes. New annexes have been added or updated over the past 20 years. It is rare to update the nine chapters. However, between 2012 and 2015 all of the chapters of EU GMP have been updated, except Chapter 9. The new Chapters 1–8 contain new GMP requirements. These mainly include additional requirements for controlling cross contamination (in Chapters 3 and 5), more detailed coverage of supplier approval and the whole supply chain (Chapter 5), more detailed analysis and investigations required following problems (Chapter 8), the increasing use of computer systems (Chapter 4), a greater role for Senior Management (Chapters 1 and 2), and more contemporary ideas with regard to Quality Assurance, Quality Management, and continual improvement (Chapter 1). Plus, there are more detailed requirements for making decisions based on the risks involved in all of the new chapters.

All of these chapters and annexes, as well as the GMP Directives, can be downloaded for free from the EU's main GMP website—Eudralex. See Volume 4 of Eudralex, which covers all of the guidelines for GMPs for medicinal products for human and veterinary use.

It is also worth pointing out that the *EU Guide to GMP* is a guide. The legal side of things are covered by the GMP Directive, and within this it is a legal requirement to work to GMP (Article 4 of 2003/94/EC). But GMP is a guide, and in any sort of guidance, there is normally some form of flexibility. This final paragraph of the introduction chapter to the *EU Guide to GMP* is important. It states:

> It is recognised that there are acceptable methods, other than those described in the Guide, which are capable of achieving the principles of Quality Assurance. The guide is not intended to place any restraint upon the development of any new concepts or technologies which have been validated and which provide a level of Quality Assurance at least equivalent to those set out in this guide (*EU Guide to GMP—Introduction*).

In other words, organizations working to EU GMP can do things differently. It is a guide after all. But you can only do things differently to what is described in the guide (the chapters and annexes) as long as you can prove that your way is at least equivalent. For example, you could scan your finished batch records and store them electronically instead of keeping the original paper document. There is, however, no such scope for maneuver against the GMP Directive and its articles—as these are law.

PARTS 1, 2, AND 3 OF EU GMP

There is an anomaly with regard to Annex 18 of EU GMP. Annex 18 used to cover GMP for Active Pharmaceutical Ingredients (API GMP). This separate GMP standard for making the active ingredient will be covered later in this chapter. However, when first adopted in the EU, this guide was put at Annex 18, which was a mistake. It was later move to a newly created Part 2 of GMP at around 2006. This resulted in EU GMP having a new structure. There was Part 1 of GMP and Part 2.

Part 1 contains the nine chapters of GMP and is used for the manufacture of the finished pharmaceutical/drug. Part 2 contains GMP for APIs. The annexes of GMP mentioned earlier are relevant to both Parts 1 and 2.

More recently, a newly created Part 3 of EU GMP has been created. This contains additional guidance that can be used by sites to improve what they do and are used to clarify regulatory expectations. Part 3 is now the home (within EU GMP) for some internationally agreed GMP practice that have come from the International Conference on Harmonization (ICH). In Part 3 of the EU GMP, you will find ICH Q9 on Quality Risk Management and ICH Q10 on Quality Management Systems. Organizations working to GMP can use these if they like. As chapters and annexes of EU GMP are updated, many of the requirements of ICH Q9 and Q10 (especially Q10) work their way into the main chapters and annexes of GMP itself.

Pharmaceutical manufacturing sites are routinely inspected by their national Regulatory Authority to ensure that they are meeting the requirements of EU GMP. Any non-conformities seen during audits (or inspections) will be highlighted against the relevant clause of the *EU Guide to GMP*. Should the problem be serious enough, then the site may be taken to court and prosecuted against the GMP Directive.

Beyond the European Union

European Union GMP is used within the EU and also beyond. There are some countries of the continent of Europe that are not in the EU. These include countries such as Iceland, Liechtenstein, and Norway. They are in Europe but not in the EU. These three countries plus the countries of the EU form the European Economic Area (EEA). The three countries have trade agreements with the EU, and pharmaceutical manufacturing sites in these countries work to EU GMP in order to help the general trade and movement of pharmaceuticals. Likewise, Turkey and Switzerland are not in the EU or the EEA, yet these two countries use EU GMP as its standard for making medicines, as it makes life easier for selling these medicines into the EU.

Following BREXIT, the UK is likely to try and negotiate a deal with the EU to stay as closely aligned with the EU pharmaceutical regulatory mechanism as possible. It is likely, but not certain, that the UK will continue to work to EU GMP, even though it is no longer a member of the EU. The arrangements of the ongoing relationship between the UK and the EU are, at the time of writing (June 2018), currently being negotiated.

EU GMP and the Qualified Person (QP)

Probably the main aspect of EU GMP that differs from all other GMPs is the requirement for a Qualified Person (QP). The definition of a QP is in Article 48 of Directive 2001/83/EC, as amended, and Article 52 of Directive 2001/82/EC. A QP normally works for a pharmaceutical company, although they can be, under certain circumstances, a consultant. To become a QP, you need to be approved to be in that position by your national Regulatory Authority. You must also be subject to a Code of Practice by your professional body that you will be a member of. The role of the QP is to ensure that only product that is suitable for release onto the market is released. In addition to an undergraduate degree in a science subject (e.g., microbiology, pharmacy, chemistry) training of the QP involves attending core residential courses at registered teaching establishments, remote work, and final exam/viva.

The courses include theoretical and practical study bearing upon at least the following basic subjects:

- Applied physics
- General and inorganic chemistry
- Organic chemistry
- Analytical chemistry

- Pharmaceutical chemistry
- Analysis of medicinal products
- General and applied biochemistry (medical)
- Physiology
- Microbiology
- Pharmacology
- Pharmaceutical technology
- Toxicology
- Pharmacognosy

This is in addition to the QP having acquired practical experience over at least two years, in one or more undertakings that are authorized to manufacture medicinal products, in the activities of qualitative analysis of medicinal products, of quantitative analysis of active substances, and of the testing and checking necessary to ensure the quality of medicinal products. The duration of practical experience may be reduced by one year where a university course lasts for at least five years and by a year and a half where the course lasts for at least six years. Passing the requirements can take several years part time before being registered. The QP is also registered by the company with the Regulatory Authorities for the release of the specific products.

At the end of the manufacture and testing of a batch, a QP needs to be assured that the batch was made and tested according to EU GMP, that the batch meets the conditions described in its Marketing Authorization, and that the active ingredient has been made according to API GMP. If they are satisfied, they can sign a register (or equivalent) that these provisions have been met. This is called QP Certification and must be performed before a batch is released to the market. The QP is taking personnel responsibility for each batch, and they can be removed from their position and even prosecuted if they are ever found to be negligent. The QP, therefore, needs to have good oversight of everything involved in the manufacture and testing of each batch as well as the whole Quality Management System.

Once a batch has been QP certified in one EU country, then it does not need to be recertified again within the EU, unless the batch is unpackaged or altered in some way. It is a requirement of EU GMP to have a QP. However, QP certification is also needed for batches made outside of the EU. If a batch is made in a non-EU country, then a QP must certify on importation that the main provisions have been met. In other words, they need to certify that the batch was made and tested according to EU GMP (or an equivalent standard), that the batch meets the conditions described in its Marketing Authorization, and that the active ingredient has been made according to API GMP. Therefore, it is likely that a QP will want to regularly audit and review key documents from any manufacturing site making products that they are then certifying into the EU.

QP certification is also needed for batches made for export from the EU, that is, will not be sold in the EU. This is because the rules for EU GMP and the QP cover not only where the product is to be sold but also where it is made. Products made in the EU must be made to EU GMP and QP certified even if they are not going to be used within the EU. Further guidance on the role of the QP can be found in Annex 16 of EU GMP.

GMP IN JAPAN

In Japan, GMP is regulated and inspected by the Ministry of Health, Labor, and Welfare (MHLW). The Pharmaceutical Affairs Law (PAL) in Japan sets the legal framework for GMP. The MHLW have, over time, issued three Ministerial Ordinances that cover the legal requirements for Japanese GMP. As well as medicines, these Ministerial Ordinances also cover requirements for cosmetics and medical devices.

Ministerial Ordinance No. 2 (1961) is a very dated document that covers the basic requirements for having suitable facilities. It covers general facilities and facilities for biological and sterile products. Due to the age of document (over 50 years old) and its ambiguity, it is rarely referred to in Japan any more.

Ministerial Ordinance No. 179 (2004) is more widely used and referred to. It covers standards for Manufacturing Control and the Quality Control of drug products. Within it are the requirements for Quality Control, controlling production and avoidance of cross contamination, validation, change control, and control of deviations.

Ministerial Ordinance No. 136 (2004) is also widely used and referred to. It covers "Good Quality Practices" (GQP rather than GMP). It is the nearest equivalent to GMP in Japan. Within it are requirements for the General Manager (site head), personnel, documentation and records, storage, QA, internal audits, batch release, and recall.

These three Ministerial Ordinances collectively make up the requirements for GMP in Japan. Getting hold of well-translated copies for use outside of Japan can be difficult too! Now that Japan is a member of PIC/S, PIC/S GMP is becoming more relevant.

THE PHARMACEUTICAL INSPECTION CO-OPERATION SCHEME GMP (PIC/S GMP)

PIC/S is the abbreviation used to describe both the Pharmaceutical Inspection Convention (PIC) and the Pharmaceutical Inspection Co-operation Scheme (PIC Scheme). PIC has been in operation since the early 1970s, and PIC/S came into being in 1995. The terms PIC/S is generally used all of the time to describe both. The aim of PIC/S is to provide harmonization and agreement with regard to GMP and the inspection of GMP across the world. The EU is a member of PIC/S. This helps pharmaceutical manufacturers in the EU import and export pharmaceutical products in and out of Europe. If a country is a member of PIC/S, then the standard of GMP in that country and the inspection of GMP facilities by the country's Regulatory Authority is seen as meeting a standard equivalent to what occurs in Europe. PIC/S has its own GMP guide. This is almost exactly the same as EU GMP; however, there is no QP required. If you look at PIC/S GMP, it has the same chapters and nearly the same annexes as EU GMP. It is also split into two parts like EU GMP (Part 1 for the finished product and Part 2 for the API). The structure and content of PIC/S GMP is therefore almost exactly the same as EU GMP, but the chapters and annexes may not be updated at the same rate. PIC/S GMP chapters and annexes do normally get updated following a corresponding update in EU GMP, but there is often a few year's lag before this occurs. Examples of countries in PIC/S include Member States of the European Union, Japan, Australia, New Zealand, and Canada.

WORLD HEALTH ORGANIZATION GMP (WHO GMP)

The World Health Organization (WHO) also produces a Guide to GMP. This again is very similar to the structure and content of EU GMP, again without the need for a QP. WHO GMP is generally used in countries of Africa, Asia, and South America that are not in PIC/S. It is a minimum GMP standard, but, unlike PIC/S, does not include an agreement that the inspection of manufacturing sites is equivalent to that in the EU. With PIC/S, the idea is that the GMP standard and the inspection of that standard is equivalent. WHO GMP simply is a standard, with no link to the equivalence of inspection by the pertinent Regulatory Authorities in the counties where WHO GMP is used. The WHO does employ GMP inspectors, many of whom used to work for national Regulatory Authorities. They inspect sites working to WHO GMP more on a voluntary basis to assess compliance to WHO GMP and promote an understanding of WHO's GMP requirements.

GMP FOR ACTIVE PHARMACEUTICAL INGREDIENTS

At the turn of the century, a new GMP guide was produced for manufacturing sites making the Active Pharmaceutical Ingredients (APIs), sometimes referred to as the "Active" or "Active Substance." API GMP was created following international concern over the quality of the APIs used in the finished medicinal product. At the time, no standard existed, and conventional GMPs were not always appropriate for making a bulk chemical. API GMP was produced by the ICH. The ICH is a collection of the world's leading Regulatory Authorities and includes representation from the United States, the EU, and Japan. API GMP had the reference number ICH Q7A. The "Q" was due to it belonging in the "Quality" series of guidelines produced by the ICH. This name has stuck, and API GMP, ICH Q7A, and Part 2 of EU GMP are all exactly the same document. API GMP provides 19 chapters of guidelines for manufactures of the active ingredient. Its legal status across the world varies, but it is the only recognized standard for the manufacture of APIs.

SUGGESTED READINGS

- EudraLex—the rules for pharmaceutical manufacture in the European Union. http://ec.europa.eu/health/documents/eudralex/vol-4/index_en.htm.
- Japan GMP http://www.pmda.go.jp/files/000153399.pdf, http://apps.who.int/medicinedocs/documents/s18576en/s18576en.pdf.
- PIC/S GMP http://www.picscheme.org/publication.php.
- WHO GMP http://www.who.int/medicines/areas/quality_safety/quality_assurance/production/en/.
- FDA Guidance for Industry: Q7 Good Manufacturing Practice Guidance for Active Pharmaceutical Ingredients, Questions and Answers, April 2018.
- FDA Guidance for Industry: ICH Q7 Good Manufacturing Practice Guide for Active Pharmaceutical Ingredients, September 2016. http://www.ich.org/products/guidelines/quality/article/quality-guidelines.html.
- Annex 16 of EU GMP.
- FDA Guidance for Industry: ICH Q9 Quality Risk Management, June 2006. http://www.ich.org/products/guidelines/quality/article/quality-guidelines.html.
- FDA Guidance for Industry: ICH Q10 Quality Management Systems, April 2009. http://www.ich.org/products/guidelines/quality/article/quality-guidelines.html.
- Qualified Person Association, "Good Practice Guide No 2: Duties and Responsibilities for Qualified Persons in the EU," (Heidelberg, Germany, 2009).
- The Role of the Qualified Person in European Pharmaceutical Regulations October 02, 2010, by Pharmaceutical Technology Editors, Pharmaceutical Technology, Volume 34, Issue 10.

24 Data Integrity and Fundamental Responsibilities

Randy Hightower and Michele Pruett

CONTENTS

INSIGHT TO DATA INTEGRITY AND FUNDAMENTAL RESPONSIBILITIES

Randy Hightower

Current Good manufacturing practices (CGMPs), which are the applicable regulations that must be followed when producing a pharmaceutical product, first came into being in the 1970s published in the CFR. These regulations established the "minimum" requirements for all manufacturers of pharmaceutical drug products commercially produced and distributed in the U.S. The Food and Drug Administration (FDA) is the federal agency authorized by the U.S. Congress to enforce these regulations, and over time, the regulations evolved to provide flexibility, clarity, and guidance to the industry as a whole. While the FDA has no legal enforcement authority within countries other than the United States, they have been empowered to prevent adulterated goods from entering the United States by imposing Import Alerts, which effectively prevent adulterated or misbranded goods such as traditional drugs, biologics, medical devices, and dietary supplements from entering the United States.

Organizationally, the FDA is comprised of two primary functional areas (1) Office of Regulatory Affairs (ORA) and (2) Office of Criminal Investigation (OCI). Routine facility inspections and other technical aspects associated with production of the drug products are handled through ORA, and observations are issued to manufacturing sites on forms referred to as a 483s. The 483 observations represent a "snapshot" by the FDA inspectors in terms of a general compliance with GMP requirements at that point in time. However, a company's response and remediation activities definitely create a compliance history and reputation that the FDA can and will use to justify other, more stringent, enforcement actions to achieve a positive outcome with respect to the regulations. In general, a firm that continues to receive repeated citations for non-compliance with GMPs is likely to receive an FDA Warning Letter, which represents a clear escalation of enforcement action by the Agency in order to resolve the situation and bring the offending company into compliance with the applicable regulations.

For at least the last 12 years, the FDA has been actively involved in a number of enforcement actions with Pharma manufacturers in particular. It is worth noting that such enforcement activities have not been confined only to the United States but have also become common-place in other countries as well, due to the rapid shift of generic manufacturing to locations where U.S. regulations and FDA compliance inspections have not kept pace with industry growth. Countries such as India and China stand out as the two most heavily populated countries in the world today and which affords huge labor pools and low labor costs. As a result of the FDA's increased focus on GMPs and data integrity compliance, there has recently been a corresponding increase in enforcement actions that are taking place in India and China. While enforcement actions come typically from GMP non-compliance, the focus of late is on the integrity of data that is being transmitted to the FDA. Today, it is not uncommon to hear the phrase "Data Integrity" when used to describe lack of documentation or lack of traceability for underlying raw data supporting submission applications and commercial batches.

It is interesting to note, however, that the seemingly recent flurry of activity concentrating on data-integrity issues actually has roots with the generic scandal of the 1980s. In order to better understand the basis for FDA questioning a company's data integrity, one only needs to gain insight into the evolution of both the FDA and the generic pharmaceutical industry in general. Generic pharmaceuticals have been around for well over 30 years, but they did not have an official application pathway to approval with the FDA until the Hatch–Waxman Act was passed in 1984.[1] The new pathway required generic firms to produce three exhibit batches and perform clinical bioequivalence studies as a means of demonstrating equivalency with the branded drug already approved by the Agency. At this point in time, generic companies were also incentivized with six months of exclusivity by virtue of being the first company to file for a generic drug equivalent. Within a few short years, many companies were competing for the coveted "first" to file application, which quickly overwhelmed the FDA with applications. Some companies even began submitting fraudulent applications and resorting to bribery of FDA officials to receive approval of their generic drug equivalents. In the more egregious cases, companies resorted to submitting branded drugs as substitutes for their own generic versions rather than manufacturing the prerequisite three exhibit batches to show equivalence. As a result of these increasing instances of fraudulent applications, the FDA began to focus attention on strengthening the applicable regulations.

In 1991, the OCI was created to investigate criminal cases that the ORA brought to them for persistent non-compliance, legal handling, and final disposition within the U.S. Judicial system.[2] It is at this point that enforcement actions began to be escalated to the level of a legal consent decree between the United States government and the offending company. A consent decree may appear to be simply a legal and mutual agreement, but heavy fines are almost always imposed on the offending firms, and they nearly always include additional agreements to retain and utilize third-party experts, at their own expense, to assess and resolve the compliance issues to the FDA's satisfaction. Around the same time that the OCI was formed, the Agency also began to issue public notices and issue guidance documents to the industry as a way to clarify and put forth the Agency's current policies and approach about resolving various documentation and data integrity concerns.

In September 1991, the FDA published "Fraud, Untrue Statements of Material Fact, Bribery, and Illegal Gratuities; Final Policy"[3] and a related document titled "Points to Consider for Internal Reviews and Corrective Action Operating Plans,"[4] which are collectively referred to as the FDA's Application Integrity Policy (AIP).[5] As a result of the FDA invoking AIP on a company, the underlying message was that there is not only a "cloud of suspicion" hanging over the company, but there is also strong objective evidence that the company has generated data, which brings into question the identity, strength, quality, and purity of its products. In conjunction with such serious integrity concerns, the FDA immediately ceases technical review of any pending applications and does not resume reviews until AIP has been revoked. In 1997, as electronic data systems became more commonplace, 21 CFR Part 11 relating to "Electronic Records and Electronic Signatures" was issued. As companies became more familiar with the regulation, it later became necessary to issue "Guidance to Industry for Part 11 compliance priorities" in 2003.[6]

Since the time that FDA started to enhance and clarify documentation requirements and improve overall data integrity, there have been several other notable instances of data integrity infractions occurring: Schien Pharmaceuticals—2000; Able Laboratories—2005; Ranbaxy Laboratories—2006; Activis Totowa—2007. From September 2013 to January 2015, Indian companies such as Apotex Pharmachem India PVT Ltd., Sun Pharmaceuticals, USV Limited, Wockhardt, and Agila Specialties PVT Ltd. have also been cited by the FDA for a variety of data integrity concerns as the trend appears to be continuing. In response to the increasing data integrity observations, the FDA issued a Draft Guidance for industry in April 2016: "Data Integrity and Compliance with CGMP,"[7] with the goal of presenting the current thinking of the FDA on the topic. To summarize, the FDA expects documentation of batch data to follow ALCOA. The guidance is also presented in a Question and Answer format to address key issues that the industry is most concerned with as related to data integrity citations. Interestingly, the last question-answer presented in the draft guidance details the FDA's recommendations for data integrity problems that have been identified during inspections, Warning Letters, and other regulatory actions. The response is identical to the AIP and "Points to Consider for Internal Reviews and Corrective Action Operating Plans" documents that were issued in 1991.

Data integrity concerns have fast become a worldwide phenomenon impacting other regulatory agencies as well. The European Medicines Agency, for example, provides similar guidance for documentation and data governance within the European Union to address recent data integrity trends observed in the industry.[8] A new Data Integrity Guidance section was added in August 2016, just four months after the FDA Draft Guidance document was issued and includes a series of questions and answers.

Independent organizations such as the Health Research Institute have recently published studies suggesting a major shift in the way that the FDA will oversee drug quality in the future.[9] Historically, the FDA has conducted facility inspections every two years, but the compliance history of a company may soon become the driving force with respect to inspection frequency, as data integrity citations have increased tenfold since 2012. Moreover, the shift and concerns by the FDA relate to the potential that products with substandard quality may cause harm or even death to consumers.

Over a 35-year career in an FDA-regulated industry, two things are abundantly clear: (1) FDA's primary objective is that companies follow the regulations and (2) that companies are expected to reference the applicable FDA guidance documents for clarification. To do otherwise puts companies at a very high risk of being cited for non-compliance and potential enforcement actions. Companies under consent decree related to data integrity issues would be well served to follow the tried and tested model that has been used in India over the past five years. The most common and successful approach that has been taken to resolve data integrity issues with the FDA has involved periodic face-to-face meetings to clarify expectations for deliverables, submission of investigational protocols for review before execution, interim progress updates, and final conclusion reports to satisfactorily resolve ALL data integrity concerns of the Agency.

Most companies incorrectly perceive the FDA's citations of data integrity as being a one-dimensional issue. In other words, once faulty Quality Systems have been significantly improved or enhanced, companies believe that the problems should disappear once the Agency reinspects the sites. In fact, that is only the tip of the iceberg since the FDA has not only collected evidence and examples that the Quality System is deficient but that unreliable data has also been generated. The sobering reality is that while data may be correctly handled and processed after system remediation, the FDA still has concerns about the safety, quality, purity, and strength of batches that have made their way into commercial distribution via the deficient system. Therein lies the challenge for companies that are under the "cloud of suspicion," especially since evidence suggests that questionable or even falsified data may have been used to process and release batches into the hands of the consumer. In such cases, the data integrity problem becomes highly magnified and must be addressed using forensic investigation tools and qualified third-party experts.

There are two key components designed to address the FDA's data integrity concerns: (1) internal review and (2) validity assessment. The internal review component will, by far, require the greatest commitment in terms of time and resources. The Agency frequently describes their expectations for the conduct of a "credible" internal review, which suggests that the review must be comprehensive in scope and fully address the integrity issues at the very foundation. As already mentioned, the FDA has cited numerous instances of objectionable findings or wrongful acts that exist on Form 483s and in Warning Letters, so they view the internal review as a supplement to their own findings. Companies should logically view the internal review as an extension of the FDA's investigation rather than simply an additional opportunity to rationalize their findings. With respect to the credible internal review, the FDA wants to know the historical period in which the wrongful acts occurred, the names and tenure of management and personnel directly involved in or responsible for the functional areas where wrongful acts occurred, and the complete list of wrongful acts that have occurred, not only at the primary site of the FDA inspections but at every site of the company. When one clearly understands the outputs that are expected through the internal review process, the commitment of time and resources comes into much better focus.

The internal review process begins with a preapproved protocol that is developed by the third-party expert and the client company in order to characterize both the current and external working environments across all sites. The most effective mechanism to describe what the working conditions are like is to conduct formal interviews with a cross section of functional area management and first-line personnel. From a historical perspective, interviews should also include ex-employees to gain insight into the corporate cultures of the past and help establish a historical period that the wrongful acts occurred. Often the interviews will provide clues about adverse conditions, weak management, wrongful acts that were occurring, and even names of individuals who were directly involved in the wrongful acts. By analyzing the verbatim of all interviews, one is able to accurately characterize the site's working conditions and corporate cultures that existed over a specified period of time. While initial interviews generally provide preliminary background information about a company and its cultures, additional targeted interviews that are based on detailed data reviews of batch records, testing records, and other relevant control documents will be necessary to identify and categorize specific instances of wrongful acts that were occurring at the site. During the targeted interview phase, direct-line employees, such as manufacturing operators, laboratory analysts, and Quality associates, are questioned about specific observations previously flagged by the FDA and any new data irregularities identified by the qualified third party within submission batches and commercial production batches, as available. Upon compilation of a preliminary historical period and list of wrongful acts, it will be necessary to evaluate organizational charts during the preliminary historical period to identify individuals in positions of authority for areas where the wrongful acts occurred. At the conclusion of the internal review process, the third party prepares and submits a final report of its findings, which presents the historical period that wrongful acts occurred, a list of all wrongful acts (including those identified by the FDA), and a listing of any current employees directly involved or in positions of authority over areas where wrongful acts occurred and might continue in the future. The Internal Review Report is typically transmitted simultaneously to the FDA and the client in order to allow the client an opportunity to take immediate corrective actions regarding personnel, as appropriate. Once the FDA has reviewed the content of the internal review, they will communicate with the client as to acceptability of the report and any additional follow-up questions, if necessary.

With respect to the internal review, there are certain indicators that may indicate that a discrepancy exists. For example, when assessing direct-line employees who are documented in the testing records or batch records, it is a good idea to request attendance and timesheets for the employees as a way of authenticating their presence. The key component for conducting a credible review is to authenticate all primary evidence with a reliable secondary source and to assure total traceability for all reported data. It is not uncommon to identify errors that have occurred, but the difference between inadvertent errors and intentional errors may be very subtle and must be evaluated in terms of patterns and practices with the intent to conceal an unfavorable situation. In other words, intent is very difficult to prove and requires a great deal of forensic investigation.

The final element required to fully address FDA's data integrity concerns is the validity assessment, which must also be conducted in accordance with a preapproved protocol to assess all elements of a given submission that has been reviewed and approved by the Agency. The learnings from the completed internal review, that is, wrongful acts, involved personnel, and historical period, are then incorporated into the comprehensive review of all abbreviated new drug application (ANDA) submission documentation. For the most part, the validity assessment report includes comprehensive verification and assessment of the underlying raw data for the manufacture of exhibit batches, stability storage and testing, annual updates, and bioequivalence studies. The third-party experts must make a final determination as to the validity of the submission data and present all findings of the data in the report to the FDA. A final decision is rendered by the Agency regarding whether or not the ANDA is considered valid and if the client may resume marketing or obtain approval.

As stipulated in Regulations and Guidance documents, there are minimum requirements that must be met in terms of documentation and submission of the same to Regulatory Agencies for review and approval. The importance of the reliability and traceability of the underlying documentation (ALCOA) cannot be overstated, as it relates to authenticating the manufacturing and testing of a batch. In some cultures, however, documentation is not thought of as a primary activity, but rather it is an afterthought and as such, represents a significant risk to the manufacturer in terms of loss of revenue, punitive actions and product liability, and overall reputation.

Nevertheless, as advocates for the consumers, the FDA and other Regulatory Agencies expect regulations to be followed to the letter, and the Agency has been intently focused on matters of data integrity since 1991, which does not appear to be tapering off. In fact, the FDA has been continually increasing their focus and even implementing internal programs aimed at providing specialized data integrity training to field inspectors. Based on the emphasis being placed on data integrity inspections today, the foreseeable future seems to be headed for more regulatory and enforcement actions.

MANAGEMENT RESPONSIBILITY AND DATA INTEGRITY

Michele Pruett

Data integrity is fundamental in current good manufacturing practice (CGMP) compliance and should be included in periodic GMP training for all employees. To support that a firm is meeting the GMPs, the minimum requirements for compliance, all data needs to be complete, consistent, and accurate across all departments and systems. Management has the overall responsibility to ensure that all areas are producing and maintaining data that is original, legible, contemporaneous, and accurate.

The concept of data integrity is not a new one to the world of pharmaceutics; rather, it is embedded in how we ensure that our product is consistently safe, effective, and pure. Although technology has changed with regard to how we document our actions, the recording of these actions, the requirements for what we record, and why we are recording it, has remained a constant. The regulations in place are applicable no matter what tools we use to collect, interpret, and maintain the data. It is required that critical activities be documented at the time of performance and that laboratory controls be scientifically sound.[10,11] The regulations require that records are complete and contain all information, all tests performed, and all data derived from those tests.[12,13] They outline that we must retain records and that they may be maintained as original records or true copies that are accurate reproductions of the original records.[14] There are requirements for the storage,[1] backup, and protection of data.[15]

In order to meet these regulations, we create structure around what data we collect and requirements for ensuring that data creates a picture that is well constructed, whole, and allows consistent interpretation. It is understood that data integrity is applicable to GMP records, the data, documents, and results, which will be used to make a quality decision. Going back to basics the GMP record is simply the consistent application of the scientific method; where the question we ask is "Have I produced a quality product?" through systemic observation, measurement, and experimentation. This process is not limited to the laboratory; it appears everywhere in our manufacturing and development process. Information is collected, evaluated, a standard is applied, and the question "Is this product safe, effective, and pure?" is posed. If the information being input into the process is incomplete, incorrect, or inaccurate, then we cannot have confidence in our answer.

When viewed from the lens of the laboratory the burden is clear. The laboratory scientists must know where the sample came from, how the sample should be tested, how to evaluate, and report the results in relation to the standard or specification. All this information must be maintained and preserved, as how the question is posed and answered is just as important as what answer was arrived at. The laboratory ensures through documentation so that any other scientist, with the same skill set, can review what was done and come to the same conclusion. Once, this preservation was completed by keeping a written, legible record in a bound laboratory notebook. Today, we record our information electronically. The data itself and its required properties has changed little; however, how we ensure those properties, evaluate, and maintain data has dramatically shifted with the advent of Information Technology.

Technology has provided us with not just a place to record data but an aid in the testing and evaluation of the data we collect. With this new tool, we need to outline new conventions and vocabulary for how we observe, measure, evaluate, and document, while still ensuring that data is Attributable, Legible, Contemporaneous, Original, and Accurate (ALCOA). Concepts of source, record and data type, traceability, security, and preservation/protection become key to our discussions. For example, we discuss metadata as the contextual information required to understand data—organized information that aids in the explanation, retrieval, use, and management of data. However, the metadata cannot stand alone, as it requires support of the other elements. "Metadata is structured information that describes, explains, or otherwise makes it easier to retrieve, use, or manage data. For example, the number '23' is meaningless without metadata, such as an indication of the unit 'mg.' Among other things, metadata for a particular piece of data could include a date/time stamp for when the data were acquired, a user ID of the person who conducted the test or analysis that generated the data, the instrument ID used to acquire the data, audit trails, etc."[7]

Using the metadata and the audit trail, we can evaluate that the information collected is attributable and contemporaneous. Metadata in combination with the data type (static or dynamic), supports how we read the data. Is it legible? Does the static record have the view that will allow another scientist to review and come to the same conclusion? Does the dynamic record have the necessary elements present so that the original interpretation is evident at a later time? It is a critical role of Information Technology to ensure that not just the data and their metadata are preserved but the relationship between them is also preserved. As with a paper record, we also need to capture who is making changes to the record and why; we replace the cross-out, date, and initials with the audit trail. It is the responsibility of Information Technology to back up, maintain, and secure the data so that the original information we used to reach the conclusion that our product is of acceptable quality is preserved and protected.

There is a great deal of recent focus on the laboratory in relation to data integrity; however, it is key to understand that not all data is generated and evaluated in the laboratory. We also collect, record, and evaluate data in the manufacturing areas. Whether we use paper master batch records or electronic records, data is being collected and evaluated. The importance of having attributable, legible, timely, original, and accurate documentation of equipment, critical parameters, and output is as important to the quality of the product as in-process or release testing is. This is the metadata, contextual information required to understand the data, of the batch. Without this information, the quality of the batch cannot be assured even if the results meet the specification.

Those involved in the collection of data for the determination of what equipment should be used, critical parameters, and specifications are responsible to ensure that the information they document is comprehensible, complete, correct, accurate, and contemporaneous. Ensuring the integrity of the documentation assembled during validation, qualification, and calibration is key to the development of limits, parameters, and specifications by which we assess the quality of our products. The soundness of the measurement and testing processes can only be as complete, correct, and accurate as the data that was used to create them.

Whose responsibility is it to ensure that all the data that being input for evaluation is complete, correct, and accurate? The simple answer is everyone involved. Anyone involved in the handling of data is responsible to ensure that the data is attributable, legible, contemporaneous, original, and accurate. When we view this holistically, what person or group is ultimately responsible for all areas of the company and therefore the integrity of all data that is generated at a site? Management. It is the responsibility of management to ensure that everyone with responsibilities working in a GMP environment has the knowledge, experience, and training to collect and interpret data consistently, correctly, and accurately. We must maintain guidelines derived from systemic observation, measurement, and experimentation with the goal of ensuring the validity and credibility of scientific data to guarantee our consumers consistently safe, efficacious, and quality drug products. The Code of Federal Regulations (CFR) clearly delineates that there must be procedures in place that ensure that the responsible officials of the firm (management) be notified in writing of any investigations, recalls, or inspectional observations.[14]

Management must ensure that all the data is being created and handled in a manner that meets the regulations. The company's quality control unit (QCU) and the responsibilities assigned to it are key factors in this process. The CFR requires that a firm have a QCU that reviews and approves all written procedures, has responsibility and authority to approve or reject all materials, and review all records.[16,17]

These written procedures are a key element to making certain that data is appropriately collected and maintained. Establishing procedures, master records, and specifications that outline what data is collected and how that data is recorded and handled ensures that the data is consistently accurate, legible, contemporaneous, and original. Both blank documents for the collection of data, such as master production or packaging records, laboratory notebooks and worksheets, and the completed documents, must be controlled. Blank documents should be version controlled, be issued for use, and reconciled during review. All issued documents, including those that may be incomplete or incorrect, must be maintained as part of the record. If replacement is required, due to erroneous entries or illegibility, then a written justification must be documented and maintained as part of the original record.

There also needs to be procedures in place defining who has access and authority over the data records, be they paper or electronic. The QCU is assigned the authority to review records to assure that no errors have occurred or, if errors have occurred, that they have been fully investigated.[16] In a paper environment, the QCU identifies changes visually and is responsible for the physical maintenance and security of those documents. When working in an electronic environment, records are reviewed and secured using tools such as audit trails and system access controls. The U.S. regulations require that computer or related systems, such as computer hardware, software, peripheral devices, networks, and cloud infrastructure,[7] have appropriate controls in place, input and outputs to the system are checked for accuracy, and backup files are maintained.[15]

The FDA has defined audit trail to mean a secure, computer-generated time-stamped electronic record that allows for reconstruction of the course of events relating to the creation, modification, or deletion of an electronic record. An audit trail is a chronology of the "who, what, when, and why" of a record. Electronic audit trails include those that track creation, modification, or deletion of data (e.g., deleting processing parameters and results) and those that track actions at the record or system level.[7] It is expected that the QCU will review the audit trails of systems that are used to capture critical data as a part of the record review prior to the approval of that record. This review would include a check of critical process parameters, identification of materials or samples, run sequences, and any changes made to these. It should be clear from the audit trail who performed the test or action, when the test was performed, how the test file was collected (e.g., processing parameters and filenames), how the results were interpreted (e.g., integration parameters or factors used), and if changes were made who made them and justification for the change. It is essential to understand that audit trails be active, and the information they contain must be complete.

Access controls are required to assure that changes in master production and control records or other records (e.g., process parameters, test methods and calculations, specifications and test results) are instituted only by authorized personnel.[15] Computerized systems should have sufficient controls to prevent unauthorized access or changes to data. There should be controls to prevent omissions in data (e.g., system turned off and data not captured). There should be a record of any data change made, the previous entry, who made the change, and when the change was made (ICH Harmonized Tripartite Guideline Q7 Good Manufacturing Practice Guide for Active Pharmaceutical Ingredients). It is expected that systems collecting or maintaining GMP data be 21 CFR 11 compliant and that all authorized users understand the meaning of their electronic signature. The practice of sharing user identification/password must be clearly and strictly prohibited. Access should be granted to individuals (unique user identification), not groups, in a manner that actions are attributable to the individual.

Different levels of access should be based on job function/role and responsibility. Access should only be granted after training or other demonstration qualification has been completed. The rights to alter files, method settings, turn off the audit trail, or other critical or security setting (i.e., system administrator access) should be limited to personnel independent from the generation of the data. If personnel change responsibilities or leave the environment, then their access should be modified accordingly upon effectivity of that change. Periodic review of administrator/user access and their corresponding permissions needs to be performed and any discrepancies investigated, corrected, and documented.

Not only must data be maintained safely and securely but a backup file of all that data entered into the computer or related system must also be maintained.[15] The FDA uses the term *backup* to refer to a true copy of the original data that is maintained securely throughout the records retention period. The backup file should contain the data, including related metadata, and should be in the original format or in a format compatible with the original format. This should not be confused with backup copies that may be created during normal computer use and temporarily maintained for disaster recovery (e.g., in case of a computer crash or other interruption). Such temporary backup copies do not satisfy the requirement to maintain a backup file of data.[7] All GMP data, any data supporting a quality decision, should be periodically reviewed to ensure that it is complete, correct, and accurate and is being maintained according to the requirements.

If a data integrity failure is detected, management must be promptly notified so that the breach can be immediately addressed. Management is responsible for determining the scope, completing an impact evaluation, assessing the risk, and developing a remediation plan. In the recent instances in which the FDA has identified a data integrity concern, they have required a third party to assess the firm's comprehensive evaluation of the extent of inaccuracies in recorded and reported data and the risk assessment of the potential effects of observed failures on the quality of their drug products, including the effects of the firm's deficient practices on the quality of drug substances or products released for distribution. Additionally, the firm must determine whether submissions to the FDA may have been impacted, and the firm's management strategy that includes the details of their global corrective action and preventive action plan.

As part of the investigation into these types of incidents, a protocol should be developed to determine the nature and root cause of the inaccuracies. The protocol should comprehensively cover all areas of your GMP operation and should not be limited to only the area where it was identified. This protocol defines the areas/departments, any computer or related systems those areas use, the personnel of the department, and the nature of deficiencies under investigation. An evaluation of procedures and practices, the data itself, and the personnel is conducted to determine the extent of the data integrity lapse and its time frame. Individuals determined to be responsible for the data integrity failure should be removed from GMP activities until corrective measures (e.g., training, procedural update, or revision of job responsibilities) have taken place.

Next, a risk assessment is conducted to outline the potential impact of identified data integrity failures on the quality of your drug substances and/or products. This assessment must determine what products were affected, their status, impact to current operations (i.e., should operations be halted, mitigation strategies put in place, or can production continue with the actions completed), and where they are located (e.g., warehouse, distribution center, or with the consumer). If any drug is with the consumer or has been consumed by patients, an analysis of the risk to the patient must be conducted and documented.

The final component is the management strategy or remediation plan. This document details the immediate, interim, and long-term corrective and preventive actions that have been determined to address the identified root causes and impacts, and assigns responsibilities. These actions vary and may include training, conducting additional testing, halting a process, revising a procedure, the design and implementation of new controls, amending a submission, and product recall. If the FDA or other regulatory body identified the data integrity lapse, then expect them to evaluate whether the scope of the lapse has been identified, evaluate the risk has been adequately assessed, and evaluate the appropriateness, implementation, and effectivity of your remediation activities. Expect that this follow-up audit will not be limited to the area, process, personnel, or systems where the data integrity lapse occurred.

Data integrity is not a new concept; it is the basis for all GxP (Good Laboratory Practices, Good Manufacturing Practices, Good Clinical Practices) compliance. A data integrity breach can negatively impact product quality, patient safety, and regulatory agencies' confidence in a firm. Management has the overall responsibility to ensure that personnel across all departments and systems have the training and expertise to properly and appropriately collect, interpret, and maintain the GMP data. Data must be original, legible, contemporaneous, and accurate regardless of whether data is collected and maintained on paper or electronically it. Data integrity must the foundation of a firm's documentation in order to demonstrate control and compliance.

Data integrity is not only a concern of U.S. regulatory bodies. The 2016 WHO, *Guidance on Good Data and Record Management Practices* was created to highlight and clarify the application of data management procedures.[18] This WHO annex, like the FDA guidance, stresses that data integrity principles are implicit in the existing guidelines and that if not robustly implemented can impact on data reliability and completeness, which can undermine the robustness of decision-making based upon those data.[18] Annex 5 sets the expectation that good documentation and data management practices are key elements of a pharmaceutical Quality System and applicable throughout the product life cycle. We are also introduced to ALCOA-plus, a commonly used acronym for "attributable, legible, contemporaneous, original, and accurate," which puts additional emphasis on the attributes of being complete, consistent, enduring, and available—implicit basic ALCOA principles.[18] The guidance identifies management responsibility, quality culture, and risk management as key principles of data management. This document also asserts that contract givers are ultimately responsible for the robustness of all decisions made on the basis of GxP data, including those made on the basis of data provided to them by contract acceptors. It goes further to require that contract givers perform risk-based due diligence to assure themselves that contract acceptors have in place appropriate programs to ensure the veracity, completeness, and reliability of the data provided.[18] It also contains specific guidance on how to design systems and processes to comply with the outlined principles.

The Medicines and Healthcare products Regulatory Agency (MHRA) introduced *GMP Data Integrity Definitions and Guidance for Industry* in 2015 and updated the document in March of 2018.[19] The MHRA guidance also stresses that it is critical to apply the principles of data integrity across the regulated good practices or GxP. This new document reflects not only the regulators thinking but also includes the collected stakeholder inputs.

The guidance goes beyond simply providing definitions by describing the expectations for the industry and outlining specific organizational responsibilities. It contains specific actionable direction that includes the establishment of risk, based on the criticality of data collected and its potential to be deleted, as well as design of the data collection environment.

Australia's Therapeutic Goods Administration (TGA) outlined their expectations regarding data management and integrity in April of 2017.[20] Like the FDA, the TGA stressed that the requirements for data management and integrity are not new thinking but rather have been embedded in GMP requirements.

The gravity of data integrity issues is underscored in the TGA definition of a "critical" deficiency:

A deficiency in a practice or process that has produced, or may result in, a significant risk of producing a product that is harmful to the user. Also occurs when it is observed that the manufacturer has engaged in fraud, misrepresentation or falsification of products or data.

As a Pharmaceutical Inspection Convention and Pharmaceutical Inspection Co-operation Scheme (PIC/S) member, the TGA references the PIC/S Good Practices for Data Management and Integrity in Regulated GMP/GDP Environments[20] in its inspectional observations and in the review of submissions in support of clearance applications.

The 2016 PIC/S Guidance, "Good Practices for Data Management and Integrity in Regulated GMP/GDP Environments" also focuses on the expectations and application of data integrity, defined as "the extent to which all data are complete, consistent and accurate, throughout the data life cycle." The intent of this document is to provide inspection guidance both on-site and remote (desktop) inspections of those sites performing manufacturing (GMP) and distribution (GDP) activities by providing an overview of key principles regarding data management and integrity.[21] We again see the ALCOA plus or ALCOA+5 approach to good documentation (Attributable, Legible, Contemporaneous, Original, Accurate + Complete, Consistent, Enduring, and Available). The PIC/S guidance aligns with the WHO guidance[18] with a focus on key data integrity principles and data governance, defining data governance as the sum total of arrangements irrespective of the process, format, or technology, which provides assurance of data integrity. This document provides specific directions for administrating both paper and computer-based data management systems. Considerations for computerized systems include qualification/validation, security, audit trails, data capture, review, and storage. In paper-based systems, there is a clear requirement for procedures outlining the good documentation practices and arrangements for document control within the quality management system (QMS). Expected procedures include:

- Creation, approval, and maintenance of master documents and procedures
- The distribution and control of collection tools used to record data
- Direction for the data collection and review of collected data
- A strategy for the filing, retrieval, retention, archival, and disposal of records
- The retrieval and disaster recovery processes regarding records

We are also introduced to the periodic assessment of the effectiveness of the data integrity control measures to ensure that controls over the data management life cycle are operating as intended. This expectation extends beyond routine data verification checks and self-inspection activities to a wider review of control measures, which include the evaluation of personnel understanding of data integrity, ensuring that the working environment is focused on quality in the context of protecting of the patient, and ensuring the maintenance of a quality-focused working environment as well as reviewing reported data/outcomes against raw data entries.[21] The PIC/S standard also discusses outsourced activities and the importance of a firm's understanding of the data integrity procedures and limitations of information obtained from the supply chain and the challenges of virtual supervision. An important component of this is comprehending the difference between "true copy" and "summary report" data and the risks associated with each when making contractor and supply-chain qualification decisions.

In March 2017, ISPE issued a GAMP® Guide: Records and Data Integrity,[22] which provides principles and practical guidance on meeting current expectations for the management of GxP-regulated records and data, ensuring that they are complete, consistent, secure, accurate, and available throughout their life cycle.

REFERENCES

1. Margaret A. Hamburg, M.D., FDA Voice blog, (2014 September 24), Celebrating 30 years of easier access to cost-saving generic drugs; Retrieved from FDA Voice @blogs.fda.gov
2. About the Office of Regulatory Affairs (ORA) and About the OCI; Retrieved from fda.gov website.
3. Fraud, Untrue Statements of Material Facts, Bribery, and Illegal Gratuities; Final Policy (1991 September 10); Retrieved from fda.gov website
4. Points to Consider for Internal Reviews and Corrective Action Operating Plans; (1991 June); Retrieved from fda.gov website
5. Application Integrity Policy (AIP); Retrieved from fda.gov website

6. FDA Guidance for Industry: Use of Electronic Records and Electronic Signatures in Clinical Investigations Under 21 CFR Part 11 (2017 June).
7. FDA Guidance for Industry: Data Integrity and Compliance with CGMP, FDA (2016 April).
8. Guidance for Data Integrity: Key to Public Health Protection (2016 August 11); Retrieved from ema.europa.eu
9. Major shift ahead in how FDA regulates drug quality (2016 February), Health Research Institute.
10. Code of Federal Regulations: 21 CFR 211.110.
11. Code of Federal Regulations: 21 CFR 211.160.
12. Code of Federal Regulations: 21 CFR 211.188.
13. Code of Federal Regulations: 21 CFR 211.194.
14. Code of Federal Regulations: 21 CFR 211.180.
15. Code of Federal Regulations: 21 CFR 211.68.
16. Code of Federal Regulations: 21 CFR 211.22.
17. Code of Federal Regulations: 21 CFR 211.100.
18. 2016 WHO, Guidance on Good Data and Record Management Practices.
19. 2018 MHRA, GMP Data Integrity Definitions and Guidance for Industry.
20. 2017 TGA, Data Management and Data Integrity.
21. 2016 PIC/S Guidance, Good Practices for Data Management and Integrity in Regulated GMP/GDP Environments—Draft 2.
22. 2017 ISPE, GAMP® Guide: Records and Data Integrity.

EXAMPLES OF OBSERVATIONS FROM FDA CITATIONS

- For example, a supervisor said he photocopied a blank out-of-specification (OOS) form and transcribed the information because he had made mistakes in the original document. Although your procedures required correcting mistakes on the original form, he made a new copy of a blank OOS form and rewrote the data.
- Our investigator documented that your employees used paper shredders to destroy critical laboratory and production records without the appropriate controls and procedures. Shredded documents included high-performance liquid chromatography chromatograms and a partially completed OOS form.
- Your quality unit is responsible for reviewing and approving these critical production records to ensure that, if an error occurred, a comprehensive investigation is conducted. Uncontrolled destruction of CGMP records also raises concerns, because retention of CGMP records must follow established procedures approved by your quality unit.
- These findings raise questions about the effectiveness of your quality unit and the integrity and accuracy of your CGMP records.
- Furthermore, you acknowledged serious gaps "especially with respect to the suspected data integrity and falsification" in data generated in your environmental monitoring program.

SUGGESTED READINGS

- "An Analysis of 2017 FDA Warning Letters on Data Integrity" Unger Barbara, Unger Consulting Inc. Pharmaceutical Online, May 18, 2017.
- FDA Guidance for Industry: Data Integrity and Compliance With Drug CGMP Questions and Answers, December 2018.

Index

Note: Page numbers in bold and italics refer to tables and figures, respectively.